MSDE Developer's Guide

MSDE Developer's Guide

Dan Rahmel

M&T Books
An imprint of IDG Books Worldwide, Inc.

Foster City, CA • Chicago, IL • Indianapolis, IN • New York, NY

MSDE Developer's Guide
Published by
M&T Books
An imprint of IDG Books Worldwide, Inc.
919 E. Hillsdale Blvd., Suite 400
Foster City, CA 94404
www.idgbooks.com (IDG Books Worldwide Web site)

Copyright © 2000 IDG Books Worldwide, Inc. All rights reserved. No part of this book, including interior design, cover design, and icons, may be reproduced or transmitted in any form, by any means (electronic, photocopying, recording, or otherwise) without the prior written permission of the publisher.

ISBN: 0-7645-4698-8

Printed in the United States of America

10 9 8 7 6 5 4 3 2 1

1B/QZ/QY/QQ/FC

Distributed in the United States by IDG Books Worldwide, Inc.

Distributed by CDG Books Canada Inc. for Canada; by Transworld Publishers Limited in the United Kingdom; by IDG Norge Books for Norway; by IDG Sweden Books for Sweden; by IDG Books Australia Publishing Corporation Pty. Ltd. for Australia and New Zealand; by TransQuest Publishers Pte Ltd. for Singapore, Malaysia, Thailand, Indonesia, and Hong Kong; by Gotop Information Inc. for Taiwan; by ICG Muse, Inc. for Japan; by Intersoft for South Africa; by Eyrolles for France; by International Thomson Publishing for Germany, Austria, and Switzerland; by Distribuidora Cuspide for Argentina; by LR International for Brazil; by Galileo Libros for Chile; by Ediciones ZETA S.C.R. Ltda. for Peru; by WS Computer Publishing Corporation, Inc., for the Philippines; by Contemporanea de Ediciones for Venezuela; by Express Computer Distributors for the Caribbean and West Indies; by Micronesia Media Distributor, Inc. for Micronesia; by Chips Computadoras S.A. de C.V. for Mexico; by Editorial Norma de Panama S.A. for Panama; by American Bookshops for Finland.

For general information on IDG Books Worldwide's books in the U.S., please call our Consumer Customer Service department at 800-762-2974. For reseller information, including discounts and premium sales, please call our Reseller Customer Service department at 800-434-3422.

For information on where to purchase IDG Books Worldwide's books outside the U.S., please contact our International Sales department at 317-596-5530 or fax 317-572-4002.

For consumer information on foreign language translations, please contact our Customer Service department at 800-434-3422, fax 317-572-4002, or e-mail rights@idgbooks.com.

For information on licensing foreign or domestic rights, please phone +1-650-653-7098.

For sales inquiries and special prices for bulk quantities, please contact our Order Services department at 800-434-3422 or write to the address above.

For information on using IDG Books Worldwide's books in the classroom or for ordering examination copies, please contact our Educational Sales department at 800-434-2086 or fax 317-572-4005.

For press review copies, author interviews, or other publicity information, please contact our Public Relations department at 650-653-7000 or fax 650-653-7500.

For authorization to photocopy items for corporate, personal, or educational use, please contact Copyright Clearance Center, 222 Rosewood Drive, Danvers, MA 01923, or fax 978-750-4470.

Library of Congress Cataloging-in-Publication Data
Rahmel, Dan.
    MSDE developers guide / Dan Rahmel.
        p. cm.
    ISBN 0-7645-4698-8 (alk. paper)
    1. Database design. 2. SQL server. I. Title.
QA76.9.D26 R335   2000
005.75'85--dc21   00-040988

LIMIT OF LIABILITY/DISCLAIMER OF WARRANTY: THE PUBLISHER AND AUTHOR HAVE USED THEIR BEST EFFORTS IN PREPARING THIS BOOK. THE PUBLISHER AND AUTHOR MAKE NO REPRESENTATIONS OR WARRANTIES WITH RESPECT TO THE ACCURACY OR COMPLETENESS OF THE CONTENTS OF THIS BOOK AND SPECIFICALLY DISCLAIM ANY IMPLIED WARRANTIES OF MERCHANTABILITY OR FITNESS FOR A PARTICULAR PURPOSE. THERE ARE NO WARRANTIES WHICH EXTEND BEYOND THE DESCRIPTIONS CONTAINED IN THIS PARAGRAPH. NO WARRANTY MAY BE CREATED OR EXTENDED BY SALES REPRESENTATIVES OR WRITTEN SALES MATERIALS. THE ACCURACY AND COMPLETENESS OF THE INFORMATION PROVIDED HEREIN AND THE OPINIONS STATED HEREIN ARE NOT GUARANTEED OR WARRANTED TO PRODUCE ANY PARTICULAR RESULTS, AND THE ADVICE AND STRATEGIES CONTAINED HEREIN MAY NOT BE SUITABLE FOR EVERY INDIVIDUAL. NEITHER THE PUBLISHER NOR AUTHOR SHALL BE LIABLE FOR ANY LOSS OF PROFIT OR ANY OTHER COMMERCIAL DAMAGES, INCLUDING BUT NOT LIMITED TO SPECIAL, INCIDENTAL, CONSEQUENTIAL, OR OTHER DAMAGES.

Trademarks: All brand names and product names used in this book are trade names, service marks, trademarks, or registered trademarks of their respective owners. IDG Books Worldwide is not associated with any product or vendor mentioned in this book.

IDG BOOKS WORLDWIDE® is a registered trademark or trademark under exclusive license to IDG Books Worldwide, Inc. from International Data Group, Inc. in the United States and/or countries.

M&T Books™ is a trademark of IDG Books Worldwide, Inc.

ABOUT IDG BOOKS WORLDWIDE

Welcome to the world of IDG Books Worldwide.

IDG Books Worldwide, Inc., is a subsidiary of International Data Group, the world's largest publisher of computer-related information and the leading global provider of information services on information technology. IDG was founded more than 30 years ago by Patrick J. McGovern and now employs more than 9,000 people worldwide. IDG publishes more than 290 computer publications in over 75 countries. More than 90 million people read one or more IDG publications each month.

Launched in 1990, IDG Books Worldwide is today the #1 publisher of best-selling computer books in the United States. We are proud to have received eight awards from the Computer Press Association in recognition of editorial excellence and three from Computer Currents' First Annual Readers' Choice Awards. Our best-selling ...*For Dummies*® series has more than 50 million copies in print with translations in 31 languages. IDG Books Worldwide, through a joint venture with IDG's Hi-Tech Beijing, became the first U.S. publisher to publish a computer book in the People's Republic of China. In record time, IDG Books Worldwide has become the first choice for millions of readers around the world who want to learn how to better manage their businesses.

Our mission is simple: Every one of our books is designed to bring extra value and skill-building instructions to the reader. Our books are written by experts who understand and care about our readers. The knowledge base of our editorial staff comes from years of experience in publishing, education, and journalism — experience we use to produce books to carry us into the new millennium. In short, we care about books, so we attract the best people. We devote special attention to details such as audience, interior design, use of icons, and illustrations. And because we use an efficient process of authoring, editing, and desktop publishing our books electronically, we can spend more time ensuring superior content and less time on the technicalities of making books.

You can count on our commitment to deliver high-quality books at competitive prices on topics you want to read about. At IDG Books Worldwide, we continue in the IDG tradition of delivering quality for more than 30 years. You'll find no better book on a subject than one from IDG Books Worldwide.

John Kilcullen
Chairman and CEO
IDG Books Worldwide, Inc.

Eighth Annual Computer Press Awards ≥1992

Ninth Annual Computer Press Awards ≥1993

Tenth Annual Computer Press Awards ≥1994

Eleventh Annual Computer Press Awards ≥1995

IDG is the world's leading IT media, research and exposition company. Founded in 1964, IDG had 1997 revenues of $2.05 billion and has more than 9,000 employees worldwide. IDG offers the widest range of media options that reach IT buyers in 75 countries representing 95% of worldwide IT spending. IDG's diverse product and services portfolio spans six key areas including print publishing, online publishing, expositions and conferences, market research, education and training, and global marketing services. More than 90 million people read one or more of IDG's 290 magazines and newspapers, including IDG's leading global brands — Computerworld, PC World, Network World, Macworld and the Channel World family of publications. IDG Books Worldwide is one of the fastest-growing computer book publishers in the world, with more than 700 titles in 36 languages. The "...For Dummies®" series alone has more than 50 million copies in print. IDG offers online users the largest network of technology-specific Web sites around the world through IDG.net (http://www.idg.net), which comprises more than 225 targeted Web sites in 55 countries worldwide. International Data Corporation (IDC) is the world's largest provider of information technology data, analysis and consulting, with research centers in over 41 countries and more than 400 research analysts worldwide. IDG World Expo is a leading producer of more than 168 globally branded conferences and expositions in 35 countries including E3 (Electronic Entertainment Expo), Macworld Expo, ComNet, Windows World Expo, ICE (Internet Commerce Expo), Agenda, DEMO, and Spotlight. IDG's training subsidiary, ExecuTrain, is the world's largest computer training company, with more than 230 locations worldwide and 785 training courses. IDG Marketing Services helps industry-leading IT companies build international brand recognition by developing global integrated marketing programs via IDG's print, online and exposition products worldwide. Further information about the company can be found at www.idg.com.   1/26/00

Credits

ACQUISITIONS EDITORS
Ann Lush
Grace Buechlein

PROJECT EDITORS
Brian MacDonald
Alex Miloradovich

TECHNICAL EDITOR
Charles J. Urwiler

COPY EDITORS
Mildred Sanchez
Bill McManus
Robert Campbell

PROOF EDITOR
Neil Romanosky

PROJECT COORDINATORS
Joe Shines
Danette Nurse

QUALITY CONTROL TECHNICIAN
Dina F Quan

MEDIA DEVELOPMENT SPECIALIST
Megan Decraene

MEDIA DEVELOPMENT ASSISTANT
Marisa Pearman

PERMISSIONS EDITOR
Carmen Krikorian

MEDIA DEVELOPMENT MANAGER
Stephen Noetzel

GRAPHICS AND PRODUCTION SPECIALISTS
Robert Bilhmayer
Jude Levinson
Victor Pérez-Varela
Ramses Ramirez

BOOK DESIGNER
Jim Donohue

DESIGN SPECIALISTS
Kurt Krames
Kippy Thomsen

ILLUSTRATORS
Mary Jo Weis
Gabriele McCann

PROOFREADING AND INDEXING
York Production Services

COVER ILLUSTRATION
©Noma/Images.com

About the Author

Dan Rahmel is a partner and co-founder of Coherent Data, an independent consulting company specializing in information systems and Internet marketing. Dan has spent over 13 years designing and implementing client systems. He has created information systems for numerous clients, and is an expert at deploying mid-sized client/server systems with client front-ends built using Visual Basic and Visual FoxPro. His database expertise includes significant work with Microsoft SQL Server, Oracle, and AS/400. Dan is a regular contributor to magazines such as *DBMS*, *Internet Advisor*, *American Programmer*, *ComputorEdge*, *Sales Doctors*, and others.

This book is dedicated to the spirit of Henry Ford. He pioneered the concept that by constantly reducing the price of a product, more people could make it their own. If done right, everyone benefits. Since MSDE embodies this idea, it is only appropriate to honor the genius who showed the way by creating the original Model T.

Preface

THE FACT THAT YOU'RE reading this book probably means that you know about the tremendous bonus that you received for free on the Office 2000 CD-ROM. The Microsoft Data Engine (MSDE) is a feature-complete version of Microsoft's database server product: SQL Server. The MSDE implementation of the SQL Server engine is limited only in terms of how many users may access it productively (about five at any one time), how many processors it can use in the server machine (only one), and how large the database can grow (a maximum of 2GB).

Although SQL Server doesn't have these limitations, most medium size applications easily fit within MSDE's constraints. MSDE gives you an opportunity to use the SQL Server engine in a real-world application without spending over $3,000 to gain the advantages of such a system. For almost two decades now, Microsoft has embraced the software development community by making great programming tools and providing inexpensive support (relative to other vendors) for complex products. They have taken enterprise software out of the hands of the few and provided it at levels accessible to everyone from home developers to large corporate IT staff members.

I think that shipping MSDE with every copy of Office 2000 Professional may be the most dramatic developer offering yet. The resources necessary to learn to use an enterprise-level database server were not readily available to most general developers. The chasm between the annual salaries of a Microsoft Access database developer and a SQL Server programmer attests to the difficulty in gaining the development training on a database server. MSDE bridges this gap.

In this Developer's Guide, I will help you learn how to use MSDE (and as a result, you will also know SQL Server). You can follow the book on a guided tour that will take you through database design and construction, creating server-based functions, programming the database server, and more. You will learn real-world solutions to database problems from the simple to the complex.

Scattered throughout the book are Notes and Tips that will provide extra information for particular areas and topics. These annotations will come in handy not only while you're reading the book, but also for quick reference later. They will help simplify some of the complexity involved in learning all of the little details of a complete database server.

You might find the MSDE server a challenge at first, especially when compared with the simplicity of Microsoft Access or other desktop database. Please hang in there. The power the SQL Server engine brings to an MSDE project can mean a world of difference to both you and your project. The skills that you develop while learning this new system will reward you again and again, both practically and monetarily.

Acknowledgments

I WOULD LIKE TO THANK Ann Lush, the IDG Books Acquisition Editor who worked with me from the start to develop the idea that became this book. Without her, there would be no book at all.

Thanks to the IDG Books staff who often made the difficult seem easy. I'd like to thank the people on the IDG Books staff with whom I often interacted (Judy Brief, Grace Buechlein, Brian MacDonald, Mildred Sanchez, Ann Lush), and all the others who had to work tirelessly in production and editing to produce this book. The artists who created the beautiful graphics from my simple diagrams are truly exceptional.

I'd like to specially thank both of the primary editors on this book: Chuck Urwiler and William McManus. Mr. Urwiler provided superb technical knowledge and excellent suggestions for greatly enhancing the technical content of the book. Mr. McManus did a first-class job clarifying much that was difficult to understand. I felt blessed having these two excellent editors on a single project. They contributed greatly to excellence of this book and any mistakes found between the covers are strictly my own.

I'd also like to thank my parents (Ron and Marie), siblings (David and Darlene), and friends (David Rahmel, Don Murphy, John Taylor (and Bailey), Greg Mickey, William Muckelberg, Bernard Arroyo, Lorinda Pate, Ted Ehr, Juan Leonffu, Ed Gildred, Weld O'Connor, Joel Harris, WTC, and Thomas Rommel) for their unconditional support.

Most of all, I'd like to thank you – the reader. I feel privileged to be able to share the world of database servers. I remember the first time I got to use one of the "big iron" database servers that were so expensive back in the day. In amazes me that MSDE, several times more powerful than that old database system, can be run on a desktop computer. I hope this book helps you take advantage of the opportunities presented by this breakthrough server.

Contents at a Glance

Preface ix

Acknowledgments xi

Part 1	Access and MSDE
Chapter 1	Concepts and Basics 3
Chapter 2	Access 2000 and MSDE 23
Chapter 3	The Access Wizards 41
Chapter 4	Architectural Overview 63
Chapter 5	The Basics of the SQL Language 79
Chapter 6	Advanced SQL 97
Chapter 7	Stored Procedures 115
Chapter 8	Access Data Project (ADP) 141
Chapter 9	ADO Overview 151
Chapter 10	VBA, MSDE, and Advanced ADO 173

Part II	Using MSDE
Chapter 11	Using the Enterprise Manager 189
Chapter 12	Using the Database Designer 207
Chapter 13	Using Data Transformation Services and Packages 237
Chapter 14	Working with Views 263
Chapter 15	Replicating Data 283
Chapter 16	Using SQL-DMO 327
Chapter 17	Creating User-Defined Data Types 361

Part III	Advanced MSDE
Chapter 18	Monitoring MSDE 373
Chapter 19	Working with SQL Server Agent.............. 391
Chapter 20	Accessing the Web with Remote Data Services ... 415
Chapter 21	Tuning for Optimum Performance 429
Chapter 22	Working with MSDE Logs 453
Chapter 23	Moving Data Into and Out of MSDE........... 467
Chapter 24	Using Stored Procedures in MSDE 489
Chapter 25	Implementing Security...................... 507
	Appendix: What's on the CD-ROM............ 533
	Index................................... 541
	End-User License Agreement 572
	CD-ROM Installation Instructions............. 576

Contents

Preface ix

Acknowledgments xi

Part 1   **Access and MSDE**

Chapter 1   **Concepts and Basics** 3
- Basic Structural Concepts 3
  - Rows and Columns 3
  - SQL Language 4
  - Indexes 4
  - Relational Tables 6
  - Database Schema 9
- Installing MSDE 9
  - Installing the MSDE Engine 9
  - Installing the Microsoft Query Tool 12
  - Staging Server Versus Deployment Server 13
- Creating a Database 13
  - Using the SQL create database Command 13
  - Using the SQL create table Command 14
  - Understanding Null Values 14
  - Creating the Database 15
  - Creating the Table 17
  - Entering Basic Data 17
  - Displaying the Data 18

Chapter 2   **Access 2000 and MSDE** 23
- Origins of MSDE and Access/JET 23
- Evaluating MSDE and the JET Engine 24
  - Client-Based Databases and Database Servers 26
  - Network Access 28
  - Storage Capabilities 29
  - Transactions 29
  - Backup 30
  - Scalability and SQL Server Compatibility 31
  - Coding: VBA and Transact-SQL 32
  - Ease of Use 33
  - Deployment and Configuration 33
  - Established Reputation 34
- Command-Line Installation of MSDE 35
- MSDE Installation Files 37
- Migrating from MSDE to SQL Server 38

Contents

Chapter 3   **The Access Wizards** 41
    How the Upsizing Wizard Works 42
        Moving from JET to MSDE............................ 42
        Choosing Upsizing Elements 43
        The ADP Database Project File...................... 43
    Exploring Some Conversion Issues................... 44
        Triggers 44
        Validation Rules................................... 45
        Default Values 45
        Upsized Table Relationships........................ 45
        Changes That Will Occur 46
        Timestamp Columns............................... 47
    Examining Your Database for Problems 47
    Upsizing the Northwind Database.................... 49
        Upsizing the Database 50
        The Upsizing Wizard Report........................ 54
        Examining the Upsized Database 55
    Other Access/MSDE Capabilities..................... 56
        Creating a Database in Access 2000.................. 56
        Configuring ODBC................................. 58
        Linking Tables in Access 59
        Shrinking a Database.............................. 61

Chapter 4   **Architectural Overview** 63
    Basic Design Concepts 63
        Column Definition 64
        Column Data Types 65
        Using the Identity Setting on a Column............... 68
        Illegal Nulls and Default Values..................... 68
        Database Creators and Owners...................... 69
        Data Cleaning 69
        Data Concurrency and Consistency 71
    Normalization..................................... 72
        First Normal Form 74
        Second Normal Form.............................. 75
        Third Normal Form 75
        Denormalization................................... 76

Chapter 5   **The Basics of the SQL Language** 79
    SQL Queries and Select Statements................... 80
        Using Microsoft Query............................. 80
        Select Clause 83
        Mathematical Operators............................ 85
        Where Clause..................................... 87
        Order By Clause 91
    Insert Into Statements.............................. 92
    Update Statements 92

	Delete Statements 93
	Beyond the Basics. 94
Chapter 6	**Advanced SQL 97**
	Mastering SQL 97
	Aggregate Functions. 99
	The Group By Command. 101
	The Having Clause 103
	The Compute Clauses 103
	The In Keyword Function. 104
	The Union Keyword 105
	Multiquery Select Statements 107
	Comparison for a Subquery 109
	Using the Exists Keyword for a Correlated Subquery 109
	The Select Into Statement 111
	Advanced Joins 111
	Nested Loop Joins. 112
	Merge Joins 112
	Hash Joins 112
	Commenting SQL Code 112
Chapter 7	**Stored Procedures. 115**
	The Transact-SQL Language 115
	Working with Stored Procedures. 116
	Creating a Stored Procedure. 117
	Executing a Stored Procedure 120
	Using Variables and Arguments 121
	Applying Transact-SQL. 126
	Control-of-Flow in Stored Procedures 126
	The If...Then...Else Structure. 126
	Iteration Control in Stored Procedures 127
	Labels and the Goto Command. 128
	Error Handling in Stored Procedures 128
	Stored Procedure Specifics 129
	Nesting Stored Procedures 130
	Deferred Name Resolution 130
	Altering Procedures 131
	Renaming and Deleting Procedures 131
	Transaction Control in a Stored Procedure 132
	The MSDE Environment 134
	System Functions and Variables. 134
	User-Defined System Procedures 135
	Temporary Stored Procedures. 135
	Procedure Information 136
	Extended Stored Procedures. 137
	The WaitFor Command. 137
	Using the Go Command 138

Contents

Chapter 8 Access Data Project (ADP) 141
  ADP Versus MDB 141
    Data Storage. 141
    Data Communication 142
  Creating an ADP Project 143
    Using the New Dialog Box 143
    Using the Upsizing Wizard 144
  Tables 145
    The Table Designer Window 145
    Changing Table Triggers 145
  Views 146
  Stored Procedures 147
  Database Diagrams 147
  Connection Properties 149

Chapter 9 ADO Overview 151
  Understanding ADO 151
    The OLE DB Interface Layer 152
    The ADO Interface 153
    ADO and MSDE 153
    The ADO Object Model 154
  ADO Quickstart 155
  Making a Connection: The Connection Object ... 157
    Connection Object Properties 158
    Opening a Connection 158
    Programming a Connection Object 159
    Action Queries 160
    The Error Object 160
  Executing a Query: The Recordset Object 161
    The Field Object 164
    Hierarchical Recordsets 165
  Asynchronous Background Execution 166
  Using Stored Procedures: The Command Object .. 167
    The Create Proc Command 167
    Using the Command Object 169
    The Parameter Object 170
  The Property Object 171

Chapter 10 VBA, MSDE, and Advanced ADO 173
  Working with Advanced ADO 173
    Asynchronous Queries 174
    Hierarchical Queries 175
    Programming Hierarchical Recordsets 177
    Programming Hierarchical Aggregates 179
  VBA to Transact-SQL Conversion 180
    Handling Embedded VBA Code 180
    Common VBA Functions 180

Contents

	Using Triggers.	183
	Distributed Queries Procedures	185
	E-Mailing with SQL Server	185
Part II	**Using MSDE**	
Chapter 11	**Using the Enterprise Manager**	**189**
	Accessing the Enterprise Manager	189
	Enterprise Manager Overview	190
	Server Registration	190
	Database Server Configuration	191
	The Databases Folder	191
	The Data Transformation Services Folder	194
	The Management Folder	196
	The Security Folder	201
	The Support Services Folder	203
	Using the Tools Menu	204
	Replication	204
	Full-Text Indexing	204
	SQL Server Profiler	205
Chapter 12	**Using the Database Designer**	**207**
	Before You Begin	207
	Creating a Database with the Database Designer	208
	Creating the Visual InterDev Project	209
	Modifying the Database	213
	Filling the Tables with Data	215
	Creating a Database Diagram	218
	Working with ASP Reporting Pages	221
	Adding the Report Pages	221
	New Response Submissions	228
	Visual Modeling	232
Chapter 13	**Using Data Transformation Services and Packages**	**237**
	Discovering DTS	237
	How DTS Works	239
	Understanding Package Objects	240
	The Connection Object	242
	The Task Object	242
	The Step Object	243
	Quick-Starting DTS	243
	Scheduling DTS Execution	252
	Programming DTS	254
	Using Scripts in a Process	254
	DTS Programming from VBA	255
	Using the DTS Designer	257
	The dtsrun Utility Application	259

Contents

Chapter 14   Working with Views 263
    How Views Work 263
    Creating a View 264
        Creating Views in SQL 265
        Limitations on Using a View 266
        Creating Views in Access 268
        How a View Is Stored 272
        View Properties 272
    Modifying a View 273
    Encrypting a View 273
    Using Server Functions in a View 274
    Using Variables to Customize a View 275
        Creating the userReference Table 275
        Creating the View 277
    Obtaining Information about the View 279
    Accessing Views from Object Models 281

Chapter 15   Replicating Data 283
    Replication Overview 284
        The MSDE Replication System 285
        Configuring the MSDE System 286
        Choosing a Replication Type 288
        Structuring Replication 291
    Creating and Configuring a Replication Process 291
        Creating an Account for the SQL Server Agent 292
        Configuring the Publisher 293
        Configuring a Subscriber 299
        Partitioning 301
        Replication Agents 302
        Planning for Replication 303
        Managing Replication through Access 306
        Conflict Management 307
        Using the Enterprise Manager Replication Wizards .. 310
        Working with the Replication Monitor 311
    System Stored Procedures 312
        Creating a Publication through Stored Procedures ... 312
        Creating a Subscription through Stored Procedures .. 316
        Subscription Procedures 317
        Publisher Procedures 318
        Article Procedures 319
        Distribution Procedures 319
        Agent Procedures 320
        Miscellaneous Procedures 320
    Replication across Other Data Sources 321
    Replication Security 322
        Role Requirements 323
        Agent Login Security 323

Contents   xxi

	Using the Access Replication Manager 323
	SQL Distribution and Merge ActiveX Controls 324
Chapter 16	**Using SQL-DMO........................... 327**
	Understanding SQL-DMO Objects..................... 327
	Testing the SQL-DMO System........................ 329
	SQL-DMO Overview 332
	The SQLServer Object................................ 332
	The Database Object................................. 333
	Other DMO Objects.................................. 334
	Creating DBDoc 335
	Creating the Access Database.......................... 336
	Databases Table 336
	Tables Table 337
	StoredProcs Table................................... 338
	Create the Relationships between the Tables 339
	Making the Object Selection Form 340
	Coding SQL-DMO and ADO Routines..................... 343
	Retrieving Schema Information 344
	Making a MakeDB Utility 351
	Creating a New Table................................ 354
	Adding a Column to an Existing Table..................... 355
	Creating an Index................................... 356
	SQL-DMO Events 357
	Possible SQL-DMO Applications..................... 359
Chapter 17	**Creating User-Defined Data Types 361**
	Understanding UDTs............................... 361
	Creating a New Type in Transact-SQL 362
	Using the New Type 364
	Binding a Default to a UDT......................... 364
	Binding a Rule to a UDT........................... 365
Part III	**Advanced MSDE**
Chapter 18	**Monitoring MSDE 373**
	Monitoring with Transact-SQL...................... 373
	Monitoring General Performance: sp_monitor............... 374
	Using sp_who for User Information 376
	Monitoring with SQL-DMO and VBA 377
	Using the Current Activity Window in Enterprise Manager.. 380
	Working with Windows NT Performance Monitor........ 381
	Monitoring Disk Access 384
	Processor Queue Length.............................. 385
	Monitoring Replication............................. 386
	Monitoring Through the Log Files 386
	Using SQL Server Profiler........................... 387

Contents

Chapter 19   **Working with SQL Server Agent** **391**
    How SQL Server Agent Works 391
        Starting the SQL Server Agent 392
        Working with Replication Agents 394
        How the Snapshot Agent Works 394
        Using Agent Utilities 395
        Configuring the SQL Server Agent 397
        Defining Operators 398
    Programming the Agent 399
        Creating a job on the Agent 399
        Transact-SQL Implementation 400
        Using the SQL-DMO Objects 406
    Using the Enterprise Manager 407
    Examining the Agent Log 408
        Execution Steps 409
        The Alerts Event System for Agents 410
    Grouping Objects in Categories 411
    Scheduling 413

Chapter 20   **Accessing the Web with Remote Data Services** ... **415**
    An Overview of RDS 416
        RDS System Requirements 420
        RDS Execution Process 420
        RDS Programming 420
    Scripting in the Browser 421
        Choosing VB Script over JavaScript 421
        Constants in VB Script 422
        Object Creation in VB Script 423
    ADO Access to RDS 423
        Server Activation 425
        Client Activation 426
    ADO Recordset Classes 426
    Secure Access Through RDS 428

Chapter 21   **Tuning for Optimum Performance** **429**
    MSDE Solution Optimization 430
    Actual Performance Versus Perceived Performance 430
    Database Organization 431
        Denormalization 432
        Rebuilding the Master Database 432
    Client Optimization 433
        ADO Versus ODBC 433
        Using SQL Batch Statements 433
        Using the Application Performance Explorer (APE) 434
    Stored Procedure Optimization 435
        Query Caching 435
        Using the Show Plan Feature to Examine a Query Process 435

Index Optimization................................ 436
    Complex or Compound Indexes............................ 436
    Clustering Indexes....................................... 437
    Index Tuning Wizard..................................... 439
Query Optimization................................. 443
    Checking the Execution Plan............................. 444
    Flattening Nested Queries................................ 447
    Merge Joins... 447
    Hash Joins.. 447
Database Server Optimization....................... 447
    Server Machine.. 447
    Using the Tracing Capabilities........................... 448
Working with tempdb Space......................... 448
    Using Transact-SQL Commands........................... 449
    Using the Enterprise Manager............................ 449

Chapter 22 Working with MSDE Logs 453
MSDE Activity Logs................................ 453
    Error Logs.. 454
    Agent Logs.. 456
Transaction Logs................................... 457
    ACID Properties of a Transaction......................... 458
    Truncating the Log...................................... 459
    Managing Transaction Logs.............................. 461
    SQL-DMO Transaction Log Access........................ 463
Long-Running Query Logs.......................... 464

Chapter 23 Moving Data Into and Out of MSDE 467
Choosing an Approach.............................. 467
Using the Import and Export Data Wizard............. 468
    Exporting the Northwind Database........................ 469
    Importing the Customers Table........................... 473
Copying in Bulk.................................... 474
    BCP Program Utility..................................... 474
    Bulk Insert SQL Command............................... 478
Using the Data Transformation Services (DTS).......... 480
    Creating a DTS Package in VBA........................... 480
    Handling DTS Package Events in VBA..................... 484
Using the NT Mirroring Capabilities.................. 486
Replication.. 486
Losing Information................................. 486

Chapter 24 Using Stored Procedures in MSDE 489
The SP Configure Routine........................... 489
Replication Stored Procedures....................... 490
Sending Mail...................................... 494
Agent Stored Procedures............................ 495

	Security Procedures 499
	User Commands 499
	Role and Group Commands 500
	Distributed Queries Procedures 502
	Miscellaneous Useful Stored Procedures 503
	The SQL-DMO Model 503
Chapter 25	**Implementing Security 507**
	Security Planning 507
	MSDE Security 510
	Configuring the Security Authentication Mode 510
	Standard SQL Server Security 511
	Windows NT Trusted Security 513
	Mixed Security Model 515
	Default Login 515
	Windows 95/98 Security 516
	OS and Browser Integration 516
	Network Protocol Options 516
	Database Roles 517
	Roles versus Groups 518
	Guest Account 520
	Database Owners 520
	Security Management through SQL Code 520
	Primary Security Commands 520
	System Stored Procedures 523
	Security for Linked MSDE Servers 526
	Executing Some Security Code 527
	Replication Security 528
	Package Security 529
	Active Directory and Windows 2000 529
	General Tips for Security Planning 530
	Appendix: What's on the CD-ROM 533
	Index 541
	End-User License Agreement 572
	CD-ROM Installation Instructions 576

Part I

Access and MSDE

CHAPTER 1
Concepts and Basics

CHAPTER 2
Access 2000 and MSDE

CHAPTER 3
The Access Wizards

CHAPTER 4
Architectural Overview

CHAPTER 5
The Basics of the SQL Language

CHAPTER 6
Advanced SQL

CHAPTER 7
Stored Procedures

CHAPTER 8
Access Data Project

CHAPTER 9
ADO Overview

CHAPTER 10
VBA, MSDE, and Advanced ADO

Chapter 1

Concepts and Basics

IN THIS CHAPTER

- ◆ Basic structural concepts
- ◆ Installing MSDE
- ◆ Creating a database

YOU MAY ALREADY HAVE extensive experience with database construction. If you are an advanced database developer, you may want to skim the current chapter. On the other hand, if you are at the beginner or intermediate level relative to database work, this chapter contains crucial information for designing and populating the database structure. Overall design, field selection, field typing, installation, and construction will all be covered.

This chapter will also demonstrate how commands in the core database language, known as the Structured Query Language (SQL), can be used to create the structure of the database. To execute these commands, you will use the Microsoft Query application that is included with Microsoft Office 2000. In later chapters, you will use more advanced tools, such as Access (Chapter 2), the Enterprise Manager (Chapter 11), and the Database Designer (Chapter 12) for this task. It is very useful, however, to know how to set up a database using only raw SQL statements, because, in the end, you will probably find some tasks that can be done most effectively from SQL.

Basic Structural Concepts

The core concepts of database construction are fairly easy to understand. They involve the logistics of how databases are put together. You'll begin by covering rows and columns — terms used to describe how data is stored within each database table. You will then learn about the SQL language, indexes, and how relations are created between multiple tables to create a database system.

Rows and Columns

From previous Access databases you may have used, you are probably already familiar with the terminology of fields and records. Each record stores information in several fields (such as FirstName, LastName, and so on). In SQL-based systems, the terminology is slightly different. Each table is divided into rows and columns, much like a spreadsheet representation of a table.

The following table shows an example of a simple contact table. This table has four columns (the leftmost column shows the record number) and four rows (the top row shows the column names).

	LastName	FirstName	Phone	ZIP
1	Smith	John	555-1212	93112
2	Doe	John	555-1313	90233
3	Bond	Fred	555-1333	91122
4	Jackson	Joe	555-1444	97223

The terms for a field and column or a record and row can be used interchangeably. This book often uses the common terms of "field" and "record," simply because using them usually makes the text clearer and avoids some of the confusion that can be created when using the SQL terms.

SQL Language

The SQL language is one of the core elements of the MSDE database engine. It is a language that was written specifically to allow for database management with a few simple lines of code. Later in the chapter, you will use SQL code to create a database, create a table, insert some data into the table, and request the database to return and display that information.

Because SQL is so crucial to advanced operation of the MSDE server, this book covers the language in detail. By the time you finish reading the book, you will have an advanced understanding of the language and how to accomplish most database tasks from SQL code.

Indexes

In early computer development, the designers of database systems recognized how slow it was to sort a set of data. A vast amount of work was put into optimizing and inventing new ways of sorting information, but sorting was still very expensive in terms of processor power and time. Further, every time a different sort on the same data was needed (for example, sort by last name rather than by ZIP code), the data had to be reshuffled.

To solve this problem, designers invented the database *index,* a sorted list of references to all of the records in the table. The records in the table never have to be moved or rearranged. Instead, the index holds a reference to each of the rows (much like the index of a book), and the order of the references in the index is sorted.

Figure 1-1 shows an example of a table that stores the last names of various people. The actual storage order shows that the names of these people are not alphabetical. By creating an index of the LastName field, the database server creates a reference list to hold the sorted order of the names through the original order number of the records. When the sorted list is required, the database server simply retrieves the index and returns the records in the order it lists.

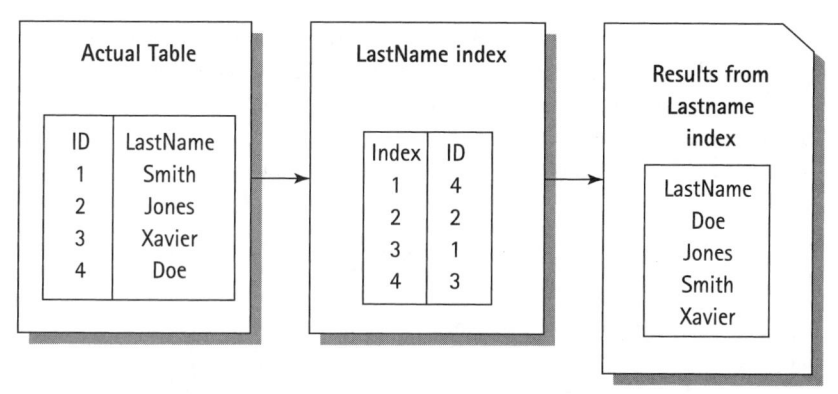

Actual Table			LastName index			Results from Lastname index
ID	LastName		Index	ID		LastName
1	Smith		1	4		Doe
2	Jones		2	2		Jones
3	Xavier		3	1		Smith
4	Doe		4	3		Xavier

Figure 1-1: An index for the LastName column allows the last name to be sorted without changing the table.

In addition to providing fast sorting access, indexes prevent the requirement of re-sorting the records for each time the data needs to be viewed from a different perspective. An index can exist for multiple fields of the table, so one index might provide a sort based on the last names found in the table, and another index might provide a sort based on the ZIP code.

When multiple columns are always sorted together, such as first name and last name columns, an index can be defined that coordinates both of these fields together as a *composite index*. Using composite indexes can dramatically speed the processing of certain types of complex queries. Composite indexes are usually created at a late stage in the development of an application, after lengthy queries have been created that need to be optimized.

Indexes make locating records in a database so much faster that they are critical to an effectively functioning relational database system. Tables in a relational system hold values that are used to connect records in one table to records in another. This connection data must use indexes to ensure that the location of related records can be accomplished quickly.

Relational Tables

In a relational database, two or more tables can be connected to provide an additional dimension to data storage and processing. Relations between tables cut down on duplication of information. For example, you might have business with other companies that have multiple contact people. Doing business with a large company, such as Xerox or IBM, might require dozens of contact entries. If each entry were to contain all the general company information (such as mailing address, URL, and so forth), the database would be large and unwieldy. Further, if the headquarters of that company were to move, each contact record would have to be adjusted to reflect the new address.

Instead of storing all the company information in each record, however, each contact might simply hold a reference to a single company record in a different table (see Figure 1-2). To allow tables to be related, each related table must hold a field that makes the connection between records possible. In this example, the field CompanyID is used to hold the reference between the two tables.

Original Table

Columns
ContactID
LastName
FirstName
Company
CompanyAddress
CompanyState
CompanyZip
CompanyPhone

Related Tables

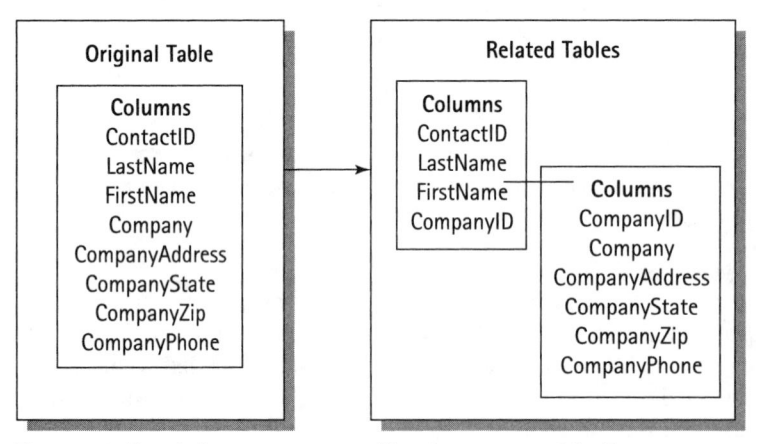

Columns
ContactID
LastName
FirstName
CompanyID

Columns
CompanyID
Company
CompanyAddress
CompanyState
CompanyZip
CompanyPhone

Figure 1-2: By relating two or more tables, the amount of duplicate information can be greatly reduced.

KEY FIELDS: PRIMARY AND FOREIGN

Each table in a related database must contain some type of field to make the relation possible. The fields that allow the relation to exist are known as *key fields*. Any column type (int, char, varchar, and so on) may be used as a key field, although numeric fields are the most common form of key field.

The following are the two types of key fields:

- **Primary key field:** Exists as a unique identifier of each record in that table. For example, in an employee table, the social security number of each person might be the primary key to identify each person.

Chapter 1: Concepts and Basics

- ◆ **Foreign key field:** Exists in the other table to hold a reference to a primary key record. In the employee example, a quarterly personnel evaluation table might contain a field for each record to store a foreign key. This foreign key would hold the primary key value of the employee record to which the evaluation table was related.

JOINS

The process of joining two or more related tables together in a query using key fields is called a *join*. A join is not an actual database structure; it is a part of the SQL code that is sent with each query. When a request for a query is made, part of the statement requests that the key fields within the tables match each other for a returned data set that is related.

The following are the two primary types of joins:

- ◆ **Inner join:** Selects all of the records for which the fields in both tables match (see Figure 1-3). Records that do not match (in other words, are not related in one or the other table) are not included in the recordset that is returned.

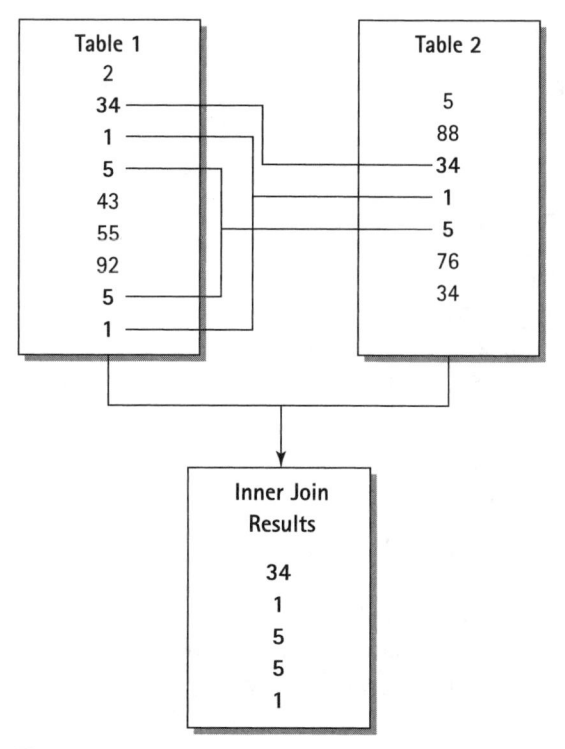

Figure 1-3: An inner join selects only the records for which the fields in both tables match.

- **Outer join:** Includes records for which the relations do not match. For example, in an advertisement-tracking database, one table might contain all of the advertisement records, and the other table might contain the leads generated by each ad. You may need a query for this database that returns a list of all the ads in your database and any leads they might have generated. Some ads may have returned no leads, but you would still want them listed.

By using an outer join, you can specify that all of the advertisement records will be included in the result set, and the total leads generated by the ad, if any (see Figure 1-4). The ad rows that don't have any corresponding lead records will simply contain a null value in the column of the non-matching rows.

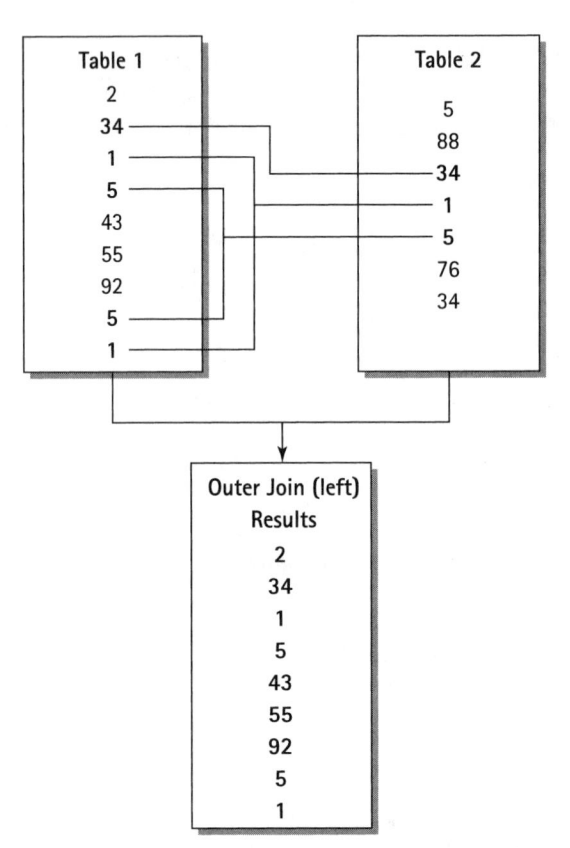

Figure 1-4: The outer join includes all of the items from one table, and all the items that match from the other table.

Actually, outer joins are categorized into two specific types: a left join and a right join. The direction of the join is used to specify the direction the join will take place. In the outer join figure (refer to Figure 1-4), a left join was used to include all of the records from the left table and all of the records that had a matching ID from the right table. If a right join had been used, instead, all of the right table's records would have been included in the result set, whereas only the matching records of the left table would have been returned. The direction of the join is far more apparent when viewed in a database diagram such as those available in the Database Designer or the Relationships window in Microsoft Access.

MSDE supports joins through both SQL code and advanced relationships in the database that enable you to codify the relations for insertion and deletion. You'll learn more about using joins from within SQL queries as the book progresses.

Database Schema

The *database schema* defines all of the items within a database, including the tables, indexes, stored procedures, triggers, and other database structures. The schema is the server configuration that is modified when a new table is placed into the database. As you learn about MSDE, you will see how you can directly access the database schema to gain access about the structure holding the data as well as the data it contains. A database schema can include tables, indexes, stored procedures, views, users, roles, triggers, rules, defaults, and so on. All of these items, taken together, can be stored within an MSDE database.

Installing MSDE

If you already have MSDE or SQL Server 7 installed, you can skip this section completely. MSDE is the actual database engine that you can use and ship with your applications, but it does not include many of the configuration or access tools necessary for database management. Microsoft suggests that you use the SQL Server 7 tools for complete MSDE development. In these opening chapters, however, you will only need to have Microsoft Query and Microsoft Access installed. You will use these two applications, both included with Office 2000, to configure the objects inside the MSDE data source.

Installing the MSDE Engine

The complete MSDE engine ships with Office 2000 (also available through the Visual Studio Web site and with an MSDN subscription), but it does not install by default. Instead, a separate MSDE installer needs to be executed. The installer places the MSDE engine on the local machine and activates the basic database management utilities. About 60MB of drive space is required, and a minimum of 64MB of RAM is recommended. MSDE can be installed on Windows NT, Windows 2000, Windows 95, or Windows 98.

If you already have SQL Server 7 installed, you do not actually need to install MSDE on your development machine. MSDE and SQL Server are 100-percent feature-compatible, so you can do all of your development on SQL Server and simply load the final database into MSDE. Because SQL Server 7 and MSDE use essentially the same settings and configuration, you cannot have both installed on a single machine simultaneously.

On the Office 2000 CD-ROM, the installer executable is normally located in the following path (if your CD-ROM drive is located at E):

`E:\SQL\x86\Setup\SetupSQL.exe`

The latest version of the MSDE engine is also available for download on the Microsoft site at `http://officeupdate.microsoft.com/`.

This executable will install the MSDE engine and requires approximately 54MB of space for installation of the program files, system, and sample data files. To install MSDE, follow these steps:

1. Execute the SetupSQL.exe application, and you will be presented with the opening wizard window. On Windows NT, this window may appear similar to the one shown in Figure 1-5.

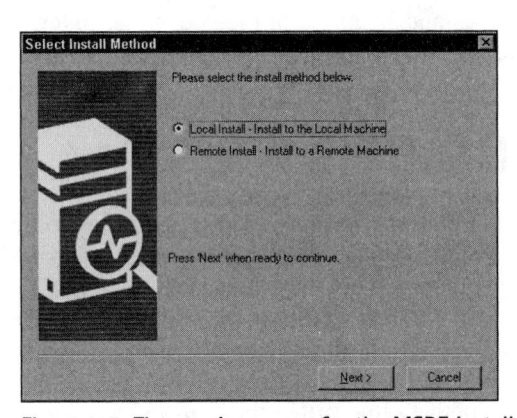

Figure 1-5: The opening screen for the MSDE installer should be displayed.

2. Leave Local Install selected and click the Next button.

3. Click the Next button to accept the default options until you reach the screen titled Services Accounts.

4. In the Service Settings, select the Use the Local System Account option. On Windows NT, this setting lets the autostart service execute on the local account. If you are installing MSDE to a Windows 95/98 machine, ignore this step, because the Service Settings don't apply.

5. Click the Next button to accept the Service Setting.

6. Click the Next button to begin copying files to your system. If you left the default location, most of the files will be copied into the c:\mssql7 directory, which will be the location of all the binary, data, and settings files for the current MSDE installation.

7. After all of the files are copied and the registration has completed, click the Finish button to complete the setup.

After the MSDE installation is complete, the service will be ready to start the MSDE engine for execution in the background. You will have a new program folder in your Start menu that contains the following applications:

- **Import and Export Data:** Provides the Data Transformation Services Wizard so that data can be imported and exported to text files, spreadsheets, and any ODBC data source
- **Client Network Utility:** Configuration utility for the protocols and identity of a remote MSDE/SQL Server
- **Server Network Utility:** Configuration utility for the protocols and identity of the MSDE/SQL Server
- **Service Manager:** Enables the MSDE service to be started, stopped, or paused
- **Uninstall MSDE:** Uninstalls the MSDE engine, but leaves any database files on the drive

To start the MSDE engine, you execute the Service Manager utility; you should see a window similar to the one shown in Figure 1-6. Click the green Start/Continue button. After the engine executes all of its beginning processes, the Start/Continue button should appear on the picture of the server. If you leave the Auto-start setting at the bottom of the window checked, the engine will automatically start each time the system is booted.

Figure 1-6: The Service Manager enables you to start, stop, and pause the MSDE engine.

You can close the Service Manager application after you've started the service, and it will continue to run in the background. In the Windows tray, located in the bottom-right corner of the screen, you should now see a small icon that indicates the server is running. Double-clicking this tray icon automatically executes the Service Manager, in case you ever need quick access to it.

With the MSDE installation, you will have several tools and sample databases automatically installed that can be used for testing.

Installing the Microsoft Query Tool

By default, the Microsoft Query tool is not installed with Office. If you want to see whether it is present on your system, you can do a search for the filename:

```
MSQRY32.EXE
```

The default installation folder for MS Query has this path:

```
D:\Program Files\Microsoft Office\Office\MSQRY32.EXE
```

If you don't have MS Query currently installed on your machine, insert your Office 2000 CD-ROM and execute the Setup application. Select the Add/Remove Components option. The tree for all of the available applications will be displayed. You need to expand the Office Tools item to see all of the available tools.

The Microsoft Query item should be right below the Microsoft Photo Editor selection (see Figure 1-7). Click the location icon for Microsoft Query and set the menu option to Run From My Computer. Click the Update Now button to perform the installation.

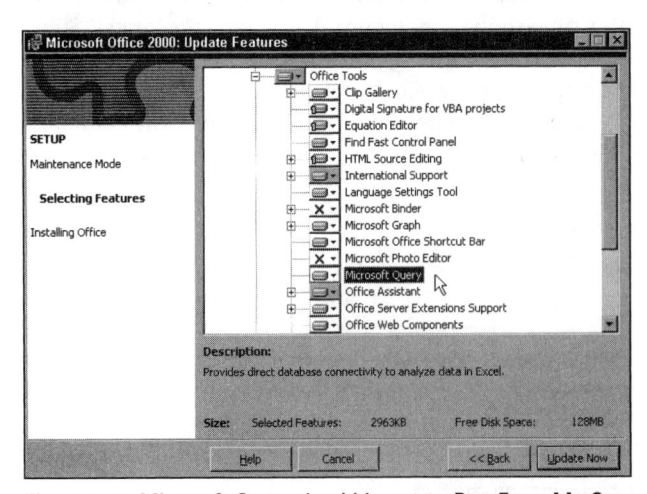

Figure 1-7: Microsoft Query should be set to Run From My Computer.

Staging Server Versus Deployment Server

Developing, as a rule, should be done on a different machine from the one that will eventually be used for deployment. This prevents errors, reboots, or system reconfigurations from affecting users who need mission-critical access to the server. For this reason, it is a good idea to have both a staging server and a deployment server.

The staging server, often called the *test server,* is the server on which the test application will execute until it is ready to actually be accessed by real users. The staging server should mirror the hardware configuration of the deployment server as closely as possible. That will prevent surprises when the application needs to "go live."

The deployment server, often called the *production server,* is the server on which the application will finally reside for daily interaction with users. By separating this server from the testing (staging) server, the application being tested will not affect any existing applications currently running on the deployment server.

Creating a Database

To round out your understanding of table definition, it is useful to actually create a database in MSDE. By defining a new database, your conceptual understanding of design will be linked with hands-on experience. Although Microsoft Access databases typically are created by using only the Microsoft Access system, numerous ways exist to define a database on the MSDE server.

Within the MS Query tool, you can enter SQL commands and execute them directly against MSDE. In this section, you'll use this capability to define a new database, add a table to it, insert some sample data, and query that data. Don't worry if you don't understand the exact functioning of the commands that you enter. This example is meant to provide a quick start with MSDE, so you can see some of its execution in action.

Using the SQL create database Command

The schema of a database can be created manually through the use of the SQL command `create database`. The simplified syntax of this SQL command appears like this:

```
create database dbName [ON DEFAULT = size]
```

A database in MSDE is similar to a database file that you've already used in Microsoft Access (files with the .mdb extension). In this case, however, MSDE handles all of the file maintenance, so you don't need to specify a path or set up a new file. Databases are added to the MSDE server before they can be addressed.

Using the SQL create table Command

The `create table` command enables you to define columns, column types, and default values; specify whether nulls are allowed; and identity column seed values, column sizes, and any other table properties available on that data source.

For example, a simple three-column table could be created with a command like this:

```
create table addressbook
   ( uniqueid int identity,
      lastName varchar(30),
      firstName varchar(20) )
```

This command creates a table named addressbook and defines it to include three columns: uniqueid, lastName, and firstName. The uniqueid column will be set to the identity type, which is a field that will be automatically set when a new record is inserted to provide a unique identifying number for that row. The lastName and firstName columns will both hold variable-length text strings with lengths of 30 characters and 20 characters, respectively.

Understanding Null Values

An important concept to understand when defining tables is the use of *nulls*. A null value indicates that no data is stored in the field, so no disk space is taken to accommodate it. For example, suppose that a table has a column called streetaddress that is a char data type defined to hold 255 characters. In each record, if the column contains an empty string (""), the 255 characters would still be allocated on the disk. With 10,000 rows containing an empty string in that column, almost 2,550,000 bytes would be allocated to these empty columns and would have to remain unused on the drive. In addition to the waste of drive space, the database server would be required to manage all of this empty storage.

Storing a null value in the column, in contrast, indicates that the column is unfilled with any valid data, which means that the space for the field is not allocated until a value is placed within it. In the previous example, if the fields were set to a null value instead of an empty string, almost none of the 2,550,000 bytes would have to be used. The only storage allocated will be the space that holds the null-value indicator. Only when valid data is inserted into that column in a row will the field space be taken on the storage device. Within a table, individual columns may be set to accept or reject null values.

In the addressbook table that was defined with the `create table` command, the definition did not specify whether or not nulls would be allowed for any of the columns. Because the setting was not specified, each column defaulted to a configuration appropriate to it. The identity field, which provides a unique identifier for each row, cannot be empty. Therefore, it was set to reject any null values. The other two columns, having the data type of variable-length character strings, are enabled to accept nulls as values.

Creating the Database

For this example, you'll create a database called adTrack. This example database can be used to track the responses to magazine and direct mail advertisements for an advertising campaign.

You can begin by defining a database called adTrack that is 5MB in size. To execute the SQL commands necessary to create the database, create the associated tables, and enter data, you need to execute the MS Query tool, as follows:

1. Execute the Microsoft Query tool by double-clicking the EXE file in the Office folder or the shortcut you created when you installed it earlier.

2. Under the File menu, select the Execute SQL option. The Execute SQL dialog box will appear (see Figure 1-8). By default, when you installed the server, an account called sa (system administrator) was created as the default administrator account. It was assigned a blank or empty password, so no password is required for logon. The display window has a large, empty text box titled SQL statement, which is where you enter the SQL commands.

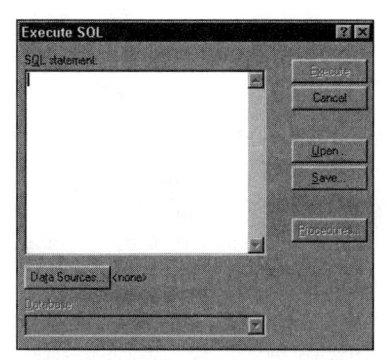

Figure 1-8: The Execute SQL dialog box enables you to execute a SQL statement against the MSDE server.

3. Enter the following code into the SQL statement text box:

```
create database adTrack ON DEFAULT = 5
```

4. Click the Data Sources button below the SQL text box. You need to create a connection to the MSDE server.

5. Double-click the <New Data Source> option in the databases list.

6. Enter the name of the data source as **dsnMSDE**.

7. Select the driver as SQL Server.

8. Click the Connect button.

9. Select the (local) option for the server combo box, set the Login ID to sa, leave the password entry blank, and then click OK to accept these settings. The application will attempt to make a connection to the MSDE server. If all goes well, your data source configuration should look similar to the one shown in Figure 1-9.

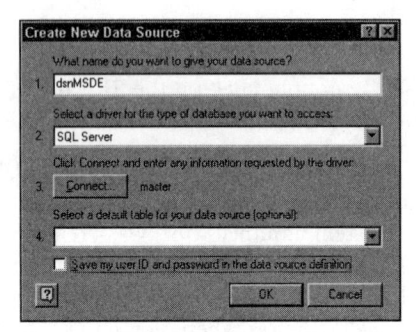

Figure 1-9: The new data source configuration to connect to MSDE is complete.

10. Click the OK button to accept the data source settings.

11. The dsnMSDE source should now appear in the Databases list. Make sure it is selected, and click the OK button in the Choose Data Source window.

12. In the Execute SQL window, click the Execute button. The MSDE server will create the database and present you with a confirmation dialog box. The confirmation dialog window tells you the size of the created database and its log file.

13. Click the OK button to dismiss the confirmation dialog box, and click the Cancel button to dismiss the Execute SQL window.

After the command completes its execution, your MSDE system will have a 5MB database called adTrack created on it. You'll find the file containing the database located in the following path (if MSDE is installed to the standard root):

```
c:\MSSQL7\DATA
```

The database is much like an empty container. You have a container, but now you need to create a table in it that will actually hold data.

Creating the Table

Within a database, one or more tables can be defined. In this case, you can use SQL code to define a new table. Many graphical tools are available for defining tables (such as Microsoft Access, the Database Designer, and so on), but introducing you early to the SQL code will help you to understand that the MSDE server can always be directly accessed on a core level. SQL code definition of tables can even be executed from a non-Windows machine with datasource access (such as ODBC) to the MSDE server.

To create the table within the database using SQL code, the `create table` command is used. Follow these steps to create a table to hold advertisement entries:

1. Under the File menu, select the Execute SQL option.

2. Click the Data Sources button.

3. From the list, select the dsnMSDE and click the OK button.

4. Enter the following code in the SQL window:

   ```
   use adTrack
   create table advertisements
       ( uniqueid int identity(1,1) not null,
         adName varchar(30),
         locationPlaced varchar(30),
         datePlaced datetime,
         dateAppearing datetime,
         adType int,
         adCode char(10) )
   ```

5. Click the Execute button. The MSDE Server will notify you that you are now using the adTrack database.

6. Click the OK button to dismiss the notification box.

You've now taken another step forward. The database and the table are both defined on the MSDE database server. The Database combo box at the bottom of the screen should now read adTrack, which means that the adTrack database is the one to be used by further SQL statements. You can use another SQL command to actually enter data into the table.

[handwritten margin note: only after closing and reopening MSQuery]

Entering Basic Data

The table is now ready to access values. You can use the SQL `Insert` command to create a new row that holds some basic sample data:

1. Delete the current text in the SQL statement text box.

2. Make sure adTrack is selected in the Database combo box at the bottom of the window (see Figure 1-10).

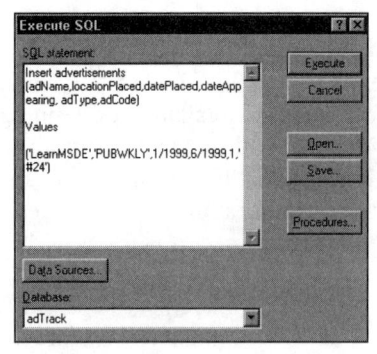

Figure 1-10: The adTrack data source should be selected in the Database combo box.

3. Enter the following code:

```
Insert advertisements
    (adName,locationPlaced,datePlaced,dateAppearing,
     adType,adCode)
    Values
    ('LearnMSDE','PUBWKLY',1/1/1999,6/1/1999,1,'#24')
```

4. Click the Execute button to execute the SQL code.

When the code executes, the Results tab should return the following statement:

```
Execute SQL statement successfully
```

This message notifies you that a row was inserted into the table. Repeat steps 2 and 3, except change the information that will be inserted. That way, when you retrieve the information from this sample database, more than one row will be displayed. When you're finished, close the Execute SQL window.

Displaying the Data

The Microsoft Query application was actually created to enable you to query any data source available through the Microsoft database driver system. MS Query has a wizard that can take you step by step through the creation of a query and a connection to a data source. After you construct the query, the data entered into the adTrack table can be displayed in the MS Query window.

To begin creating the necessary query, follow these steps:

1. Under the File menu, select the New option. This displays the data sources list. You actually need to define a new data source that addresses the adTrack database specifically.

2. Double-click the <New Data Source> item. You will be presented with the window to name and form the new data source.

3. Set the name to **dsnAdTrack** and select the SQL Server driver from the combo box.

4. Click the Connection button to open the dialog that enables you to configure the settings for the connection source.

5. Set the Connection to the (local) MSDE server and enter the Login ID as **sa**. After these settings are complete, click the Options button to expand the window for additional settings. For this data source, the adTrack database needs to be set to the default database.

6. Click the Options >> button, which extends the window to display additional settings available for the data source.

7. Select the adTrack database in the Database combo box. Your login dialog box should look similar to the one shown in Figure 1-11.

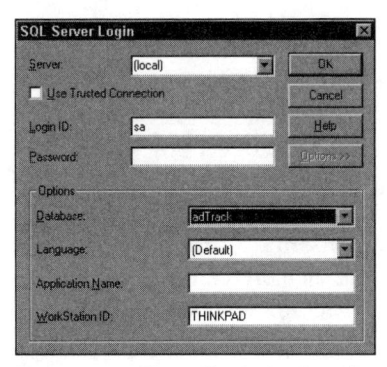

Figure 1-11: The adTrack database is selected as the default database.

8. Click the OK button to accept these settings.

9. Click the OK button to accept the new datasource creation.

10. Make sure the dsnAdTrack source is selected in the Choose Data Source window and click the OK button. You will be presented with the Query Wizard window (see Figure 1-12). The advertisements table should already be selected in the Available tables and columns list box. You need to transfer this table to the Columns in your query list box.

11. Click the right-arrow (>) button to move the advertisements table into the Columns in your query list box. All of the columns for that table should now appear in the list box.

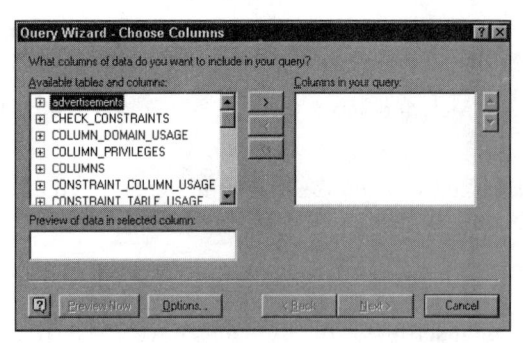

Figure 1-12: The Query Wizard enables you to select the columns to be included in the query.

12. Click the Next button. The Filter Data step is unnecessary at this point because so little information is stored in the table.
13. Click the Next button. The Sort Order step is also unimportant.
14. Click the Finish button to create the query.

The query will return all the records contained in that table. You should see the data that you entered earlier using the `Insert` commands. The Microsoft Query tool can be used to add explicit queries constructed from direct SQL statements as easily as you used the wizard to create a new query. In fact, if you select the SQL option under the View menu, you can examine and even edit the underlying SQL `Select` query statement that was generated by your wizard selections.

With a SQL query statement, you can do far more complex results generation, including sorting and grouping of records. The SQL language is explored in much more detail in Chapters 5 and 6, in which you learn how to use the entire language for every type of task solution.

Summary

You now have MSDE installed and have learned how to create a simple database and table. Learning the terminology and concepts, such as rows and columns, join types, and data normalization, will help you as you use MSDE for more advanced applications. In this chapter, you covered the following:

◆ **Database schema:** The schema defines the structure of the database, including the table structures and the elements of the tables themselves, such as the columns of each table.

◆ **Multiple indexes:** When a particular multicolumn search is commonly used against a table, you can define an index that spans multiple fields.

- **Joins:** Using a SQL equivalence operator to coordinate two or more tables is called a join. The two primary types of joins are inner joins and outer (left and right) joins.

- **Left and right joins:** Which records are returned for the join depends on the direction of the join. The left outer join returns all of the records from the table on the left side of the join and the records that match in the right table. The right outer join does exactly the opposite.

- **Creating databases and tables:** When using SQL commands, you created a sample database and a table within that database.

- **Inserting and viewing data:** By executing SQL code, you were able to insert data into the table and retrieve all of the entered data for viewing.

Chapter 2

Access 2000 and MSDE

IN THIS CHAPTER

- Origins of MSDE and Access/JET
- Evaluating MSDE and the JET engine
- Command-line installation of MSDE
- MSDE installation files
- Migrating from MSDE to SQL Server

WHEN A DATABASE developer begins designing a new application, choosing which database engine to use has become dramatically more difficult than it was in the past. Before MSDE, the SQL Server engine was too expensive in both licensing fees and resources to be considered for use on anything but the bigger applications. The release of MSDE has changed the dynamics of database system development.

The availability of powerful and inexpensive desktop computers, along with tremendous increases in hard drive capacity, has made it possible to run an entire database server on a desktop machine. Also, because MSDE can be installed from any Office 2000 CD-ROM and Microsoft has provided a free license for MSDE database server deployment, it can be used in many situations where a desktop database used to be the only alternative. Inexpensive hardware coupled with Microsoft's decision to release MSDE with Microsoft Office makes using MSDE as your key database engine an attractive option.

However, just because MSDE is widely available does not make it perfect for every solution. The original Microsoft Access database engine is often more effective for desktop and server use. To understand how to choose a database engine for your particular application, it is helpful to see the limitations of each engine. The easiest place to begin is to study the vastly different history of each engine.

Origins of MSDE and Access/JET

The two different database engines included with Microsoft Access 2000 are the JET engine and MSDE. The JET engine is the database engine that has been shared between Microsoft Access (since version 2) and Visual Basic (since version 3). Microsoft Access began as a powerful desktop database and started to really gain enterprise momentum when people began deploying local area networks (LANs).

The ability to provide multiuser access was added to the Access database system to allow a LAN-based database file to be employed by multiple users.

The JET engine began as a method of enabling a development system to share core database functionality. JET databases were stored as a single file with an .mdb extension. The MDB file contains all of the tables, views, queries, forms, and reports of a Microsoft Access application. Programs remotely accessing a JET/MDB file could execute the queries, access the tables, and reference the views, but could not execute the forms or view the reports without the Microsoft Access run-time file.

In contrast to the Access database engine, which originated as a desktop database, SQL Server was initially created to support industrial-strength enterprise applications. The creation of SQL Server enabled Microsoft to compete with the mainframe and UNIX-based database server market as it promoted its new enterprise operating system — Windows NT.

MSDE is an evolution of the SQL Server engine family. SQL Server began as a co-development project between Microsoft and Sybase (a large enterprise database developer) to provide a UNIX-level database server for Windows NT. The first few versions enabled Microsoft and Sybase to share source code and experience, so that Microsoft could move toward enterprise applications, and Sybase could begin to move into the desktop PC market.

When Microsoft and Sybase decided to end their business partnership, the SQL Server engine was at version 4.21 and nearly 100-percent compatible with the equivalent Sybase database server. Since then, the features and implementation of the two servers have diverged, although many of the language constructs between the two systems remain compatible because of their common origin.

Because the Access/JET database engine began as a desktop database, that's the platform it has been optimized to use. MSDE/SQL Server began as a multiuser database server meant for large-scale enterprise solutions. The inexpensive power of today's desktop machines has made it possible for the full SQL Server engine to run on even the current low-end machines.

MSDE forces a database developer to answer the following question: "Why should I use an advanced desktop database engine when I can run a full-featured database server for the same price?" This chapter will try to help you to answer this question and to evaluate when it is most appropriate to stay with the Access database engine.

Evaluating MSDE and the JET Engine

To begin the comparison of MSDE and Access, you should already be familiar with the basic operations of Microsoft Access. With that understanding as a foundation, you can begin to examine the technology that makes up the MSDE server. MSDE is a full-featured database server and provides most of the database functionality you will need for any solution.

Some of the key features of MSDE are listed here:

- **Use of a transaction log:** Features a transaction log, so even in a complete system fault, most database changes are recoverable and the database itself is almost impossible to corrupt
- **Availability to portable or remote users:** MSDE supports access through the TCP/IP protocol, allowing direct Internet addressing of the database server
- **Integrated with NT security:** MSDE uses either custom SQL Server security or can be integrated with the NT login and Windows 2000 Active Directory
- **Future scalability:** Allows upgrade to SQL Server without any changes to the application, which will enable the server to handle over 2,500 simultaneous users
- **Point-in-time recovery:** Through the transaction log, the recovery can be specified to any time before the time of failure
- **Provides a desktop database server:** MSDE acts as a desktop version of SQL Server, so a full SQL Server application can be executed without any modifications

A full description of the MSDE system is available on the MSDE Web page at `http://msdn.microsoft.com/vstudio/msde`.

MSDE is not a one-size-fits-all solution. Many application designers will still want to use the older Microsoft Access database engine. Comparing MSDE and Access in the following key areas and then prioritizing the importance of each area to your application will help you to decide which database engine to use:

- Database processing: Client-based versus server-based
- Ease of network access
- Storage capabilities
- Transactions
- Backup
- Scalability and SQL Server compatibility
- Coding: VBA and Transact-SQL
- Ease of use
- Established reputation

Comparing each of the database engines in these key areas and prioritizing the importance of each area to your application will help you to decide which database engine to use.

Client-Based Databases and Database Servers

At their core, a key difference exists between the engines of Access and MSDE in the way they handle their processing. Microsoft Access, built as a desktop database, handles all the processing of database requests within the Access run-time file. In contrast, MSDE was built to execute as a service under the operating system so that it is always available.

With the JET engine, no matter where the database is located, all database processing occurs on the client machine. As a file-based database engine, Access executes on the client machine even if the database file is located on a remote file server (see Figure 2-1). The Access JET engine loads into the execution space of the application that is accessing it.

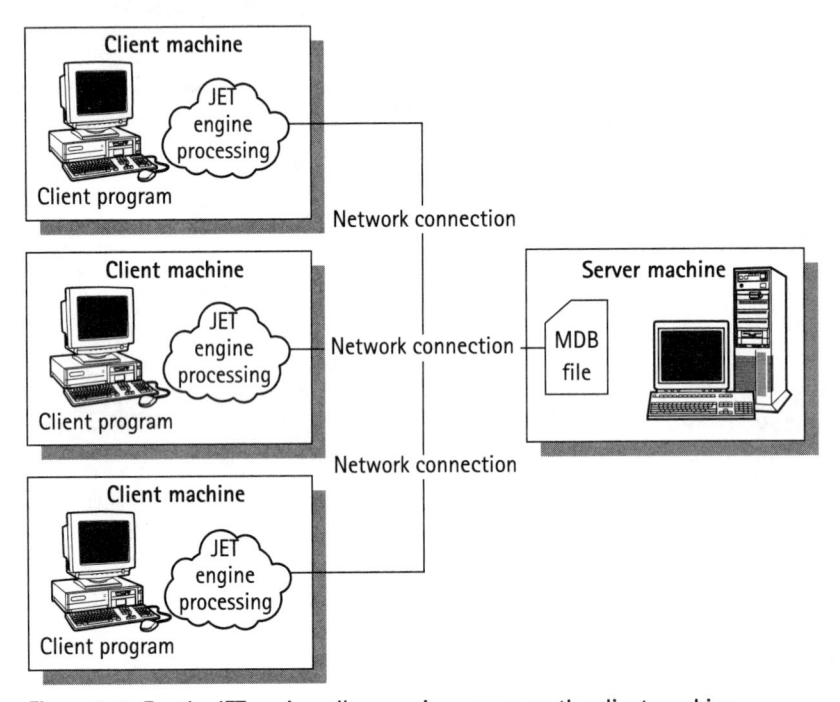

Figure 2-1: For the JET engine, all processing occurs on the client machine.

MSDE, in contrast, executes as a service that may be run on a remote machine (see Figure 2-2). MSDE runs as a service in the background. In contrast to the JET engine that loads with the application, MSDE is always running in the background, waiting for a database command or request. These database requests can come from any machine on the network, and the processing is still done only on the machine that hosts the MSDE engine.

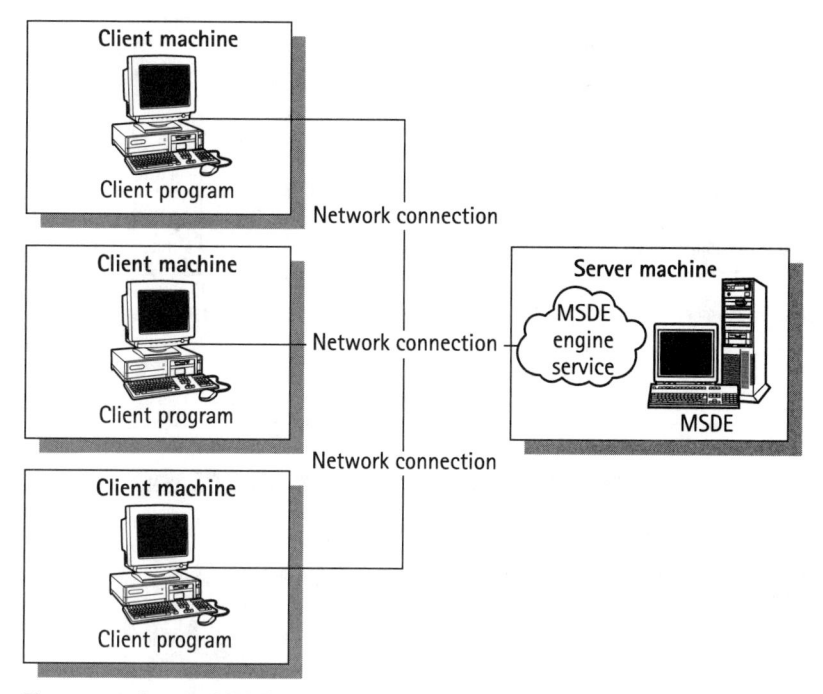

Figure 2-2: For the MSDE engine, requests from one or more client machines are answered by the server.

File-based systems (such as Microsoft Access) encounter a bottleneck when many concurrent users seek to read and write different parts of the database simultaneously. Because the processing is actually occurring on the client machine, large portions of the database file must be pulled across the network to complete the requested query. This creates a tremendous amount of network traffic, even on a LAN.

In contrast, MSDE does all of the processing on the server machine where it is located. When a client application executes a query, it merely sends a small request in the SQL language to the MSDE engine. Instead of transporting large chunks of the database over the network, MSDE searches the database on the machine where it is located (see Figure 2-3). When the result set is ready, the database server merely transfers the results, dramatically reducing the amount of network traffic required to complete the operation.

Additionally, because MSDE does not have numerous clients all attempting complete file access simultaneously, it can queue requests. Resources can then be managed by the database server to most effectively respond to requests and commands. The multithreaded implementation of MSDE enables it to handle many simultaneous requests easily.

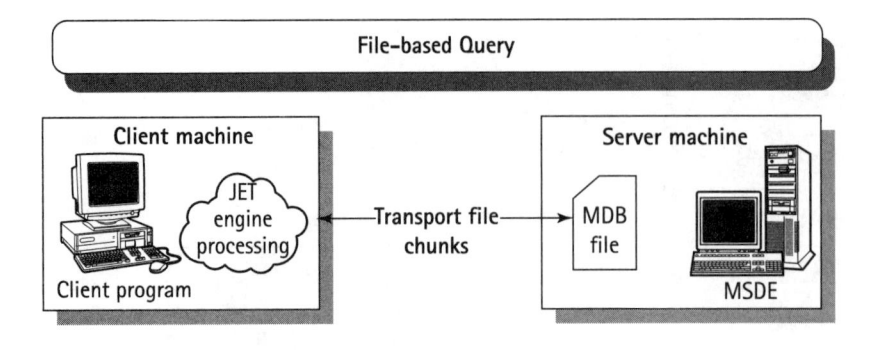

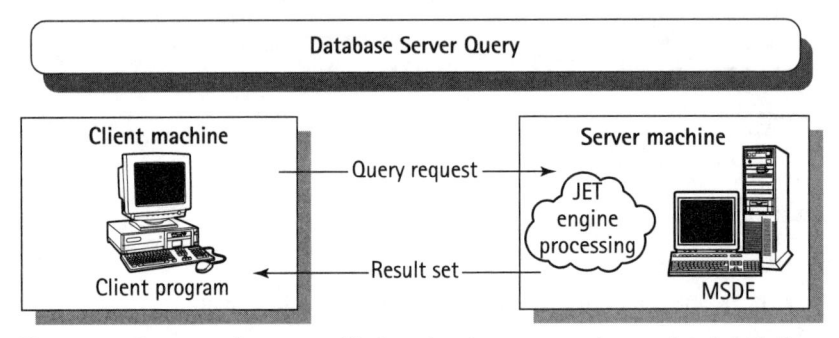

Figure 2-3: For network access, a file-based system uses much more bandwidth for queries than does a database server.

Network Access

Because MSDE executes as a service (which means that it is always running in the background of the server machine), it can be remotely accessed through the Internet. The MSDE engine can be addressed primarily using the TCP/IP protocol, although it also supports various other protocols, including IPX/SPX, NetBIOS, and AppleTalk. A remote client simply needs to know the network name, URL, or IP address of the MSDE server and have logon permission to access it.

To allow remote connections to a Microsoft Access database, you need to implement some form of file sharing. On a LAN, the file sharing can occur through the use of a network drive. On a WAN or the Internet, access becomes significantly more complicated. One of the best methods would include the implementation of a *virtual private network (VPN)*, which makes the computer believe it is actually located on the physical network. With a file-based database engine, however, the data transfer of a remote connection may make this option prohibitively slow.

Storage Capabilities

The amount of data that MSDE and JET can store is actually identical: 2GB. However, the ease of transition from MSDE to SQL Server makes its realistic limitations much higher. Because SQL Server can store over 2 terabytes and no conversion is required to move an MSDE database to SQL Server, the storage limitations are all but nonexistent for all but the largest database solutions.

More importantly, because the MSDE engine is designed to handle large amounts of data, as the database approaches a substantial percentage of the limit, it can continue to function very well. Conversely, with the Access engine, a database over 100MB quickly begins to affect the performance of most sorting and searching operations.

Transactions

As databases became more advanced, and extremely reliable data storage became critical for most database systems, the technology of transactions was invented. A *transaction* is a database process in which multiple operations (such as inserts, updates, or deletes) are treated as a single operation. If one of the operations in a transaction fails, the transaction fails. If all the operations succeed, the transaction succeeds. This type of all-or-nothing operation is important to keep all of the information in a database valid.

In the simple example of a bank transfer, the bank needs to transfer $1,000 from John's bank account to the one held by Phil. This transfer actually involves two separate operations: subtract $1,000 from John's account and add $1,000 to Phil's account. If the first operation completes but the database faults before the second one is run (see Figure 2-4), the accounting database will show a $1,000 discrepancy. In this diagram, step 2 is never executed, because the fault occurs before it is reached.

In a transaction system, both of these database operations are encapsulated within the process of a transaction. If anything happens during the transaction (disk error, record lock rejection, and so on), all the operations in the transaction are revoked. In the previous example, the system fault would cause the entire process to be aborted, so the initial transfer would not be recorded. Transactions ensure that a database will not be corrupted by partially complete operations.

For databases such as Microsoft Access, the programmer must specify when a transaction begins and when it ends. Although this is true for MSDE, as well, at the solution level, MSDE has various levels of transactions. At the lowest level of transactions on the MSDE server, even the simplest alteration to the database is held within a transaction. This transaction feature enables MSDE to recover from nearly any type of failure and preserve the integrity of the database.

All of the information related to data or structure modifications is contained in the transaction logs of MSDE. If a power failure or other catastrophic failure occurs to the database server system, the current state of the database is recovered by examining the transaction log and bringing the database into the last known valid state.

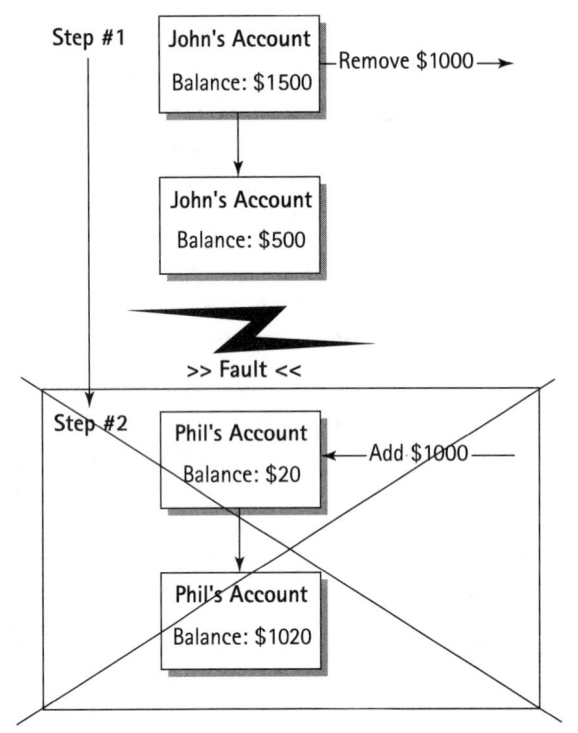

Figure 2-4: A fault of the database that occurs before the second operation completes could leave the database corrupted.

A transaction log implementation is not without its problems. The transaction log needs to be watched by the system administrator and configured so that it will not run out of room on the hard drive or exceed the maximum size limitation set for it. Such problems do not exist on an Access-based database.

Backup

MSDE and Microsoft Access databases must be backed up in very different ways. If you have ever tried to make a backup of an Access data file while a user was addressing it, you know that if an edit is in progress, the file cannot be copied. However, if a user is not actively involved in an update or delete operation, the file can be copied to a backup.

While the backup is occurring, however, the database is locked from any users executing update or delete operations. If many users are currently addressing the system, these users have to suspend executing any modifications to the database until the backup is completed.

Because the MSDE database is a service, it is always running with exclusive access to the database files. For this reason, a file that holds an MSDE database cannot be backed up or copied while the service is executing by the traditional file copy or backup methods. However, through SQL Server, MSDE has its own backup program and can actually create a backup of a database while it is operating, with only minimal performance degradation noticeable to the users who are addressing it.

The live backup functionality of the MSDE engine can be a tremendous advantage in a system such as a Web database application, for which access can occur at any time of the day or night. The live backup relieves the administrator from having to suspend user operations until the backup is complete. It also ensures that the backup is a copy with complete integrity of the database from the moment the backup begins.

Scalability and SQL Server Compatibility

One of the key advantages of using MSDE is the long-term support for a larger system. Because an MSDE database transfers seamlessly to SQL Server, the capabilities of SQL Server are really the limits imposed on your solution. Unless you are creating a colossal solution, those limits are pretty hard to strain.

Although all of the expenses (licensing fees, servers costs, and so forth) that you avoided with MSDE will be imposed when you upgrade to SQL Server, you will probably be running a mission-critical application by the time you outstrip the capabilities of MSDE. At that point, it will probably be an appropriate time for your organization to make the commitment to SQL Server.

The SQL Server has been tested to do the following:

- Handle more than 2,500 simultaneous users
- Provide access to over 2 terabytes (2,000GB) of data
- Support multiple machine clustering and failover for server deployment
- Scale up to 16 processors in a single server

Although MSDE is fully compatible with SQL Server, Microsoft has removed some of the higher-end processing muscle that enables SQL Server to be effectively used in large-scale solutions. MSDE has the following two limitations not present in SQL Server: each database is limited to 2GB of data, and only five simultaneous users can practically access the database server. Although no absolute restriction exists on the number of simultaneous users, the MSDE engine does not scale well as more than five users access the system.

> **CAUTION:** MSDE and SQL Server cannot be installed simultaneously on a single machine. Each server uses the same Registry entry locations. When the SQL Server installation is run after MSDE is installed, it will simply detect and upgrade the MSDE engine.

MSDE has a minimum recommended memory requirement of 64MB of RAM, which relates to the fact that the execution size of MSDE is twice that of the Microsoft JET Engine. The MSDE engine allocates around 7MB of memory for minimum execution. The JET engine requires only 3MB.

> **NOTE:** An MSDE solution can be upsized to SQL Server without a single change. When MSDE is run on Windows 95/98, certain features are not supported (such as the NT security support). For a complete list of the MSDE limitations on the Windows 95/98 platform, see the FAQ at http://msdn.microsoft.com/vstudio/msde/techfaq.asp.

Coding: VBA and Transact-SQL

With Access, you may be accustomed to using Visual Basic for Applications (VBA) code, which can be used even in queries or default values in an Access application. For example, you could set the default value of a field called createDate to the following VBA code:

```
=Now()
```

This code places the current date into the field when a new record is created.

In the same fashion, your queries can contain formatting commands and VBA logic. In a query that returns a currency value that is formatted in a custom style, you could simply place the FormatCurrency function directly into the query. When the query is executed, the VBA engine will interpret the command and display the value as specified.

Because MSDE is actually a database server to which many requests are made remotely, you must only use the language that exists on the server. MSDE does not include an implementation of VBA, so the same VBA commands sent to Access would generate an error if sent to the MSDE server.

In MSDE, all programming is done in the Structured Query Language (SQL). A straight version of SQL that complies with the entry-level SQL-92 international standard is not very powerful, so vendors have extended the language with proprietary additions. For MSDE, the entire SQL language and the Microsoft vendor-specific extensions are known as *Transact-SQL*.

Transact-SQL provides the capability to store compiled code on the server, introduce execution logic into a query, and define advanced database features such as automated integrity and triggers. Throughout this book, you will learn how to use Transact-SQL to execute almost any operation that you need to occur on the database server.

However, if you are already familiar with VBA, realize that you need to learn this new language to take maximum advantage of the MSDE system. For some developers, learning how to use Transact-SQL may initially be a barrier to implementing an existing Access solution on the MSDE server.

Ease of Use

The primary advantage of an Access-based engine over an MSDE one is the ease of use in areas such as user interface creation, field formatting, replication, and installation. Because Access was created from the start to provide a complete database package, all pieces that go into a final solution are well integrated and maintained in the same environment.

Unlike Microsoft Access, MSDE has no direct user interface-creation tools included with the engine — only management tools. In Access, you can create forms and reports for the users to interact with. These are stored in the database file (MDB) itself, along with the tables, indexes, and queries. Because everything is contained within a single file, it is easier to create, manage, and deploy a JET engine-based solution.

With the MSDE engine installation, no user interface structures are stored in the database. To provide an MSDE application to an end user, you have to write the front end in another program, such as Microsoft Access, Visual Basic, Active Server Pages, or Visual J++. In contrast, most JET-based systems, such as Microsoft Access and Visual Basic, integrate the client presentation with the development system.

For display and reporting, it is often much easier to use a JET-based database because field formatting can be stored directly in the database itself. MSDE doesn't have that capability. Any formatting must be done on the client side or through an explicit stored procedure to modify the input before it is written into the database.

Microsoft Access makes replication fairly easy and straightforward. Replication on MSDE is much more powerful, so implementation and configuration is substantially more complicated. Additionally, Access provides replication for free, whereas an MSDE solution requires a client access license (CAL) for each replication copy of the database.

Deployment and Configuration

MSDE is included with many other products besides Microsoft Access. MSDE ships with the Microsoft Office 2000 Professional and Premium editions. It is also available for free download to licensed users of Visual Studio or owners of any of the Professional or Enterprise development tools (Visual Basic, Visual C++, Visual InterDev, Visual J++, and Visual FoxPro). The subscribers to the Microsoft Developer's Network (MSDN) Universal and Select levels also receive it.

Although the interface construction and other features are not automatically included with MSDE, the database server can be managed with the following:

- Microsoft Query (provided with Microsoft Office 2000)
- Microsoft Access

- SQL Server 7: Developer Edition management tools
- Database Designer (included in several of the Visual Studio products)

The tools included with SQL Server are far more powerful than the few utilities included with MSDE. Because some tasks are difficult to accomplish without the SQL Server tools, starting in Chapter 11, you will learn how to use them with MSDE. Until Chapter 11, however, you will only need the tools included with Office 2000.

Moving a database in MSDE is much more difficult than copying an MDB file, such as is required when using the JET engine. An Access database can be copied like any other file. In MSDE, the entire database must be saved from the MSDE system to a separate file or the main database must be disconnected from active use in the MSDE system before backup. The database file is then used to reload into another SQL Server or MSDE installation.

The ease of use of Microsoft Access extends to the deployment of your final application. For applications that use the JET engine, particularly VB applications, the Application Package and Deployment Wizard included with the development system will create installation images. These images are stored as cabinet files (with the .cab extension), and then the wizard creates an installation application.

If MSDE needs to be installed on each of your client machines, installation becomes more complicated. Typically your application and the MSDE engine must be installed separately. That means that the MSDE installer (approximately 35MB) must be transferred to the server machine for installation.

MSDE installation is complex only in cases in which your application requires a copy of the MSDE database server on each machine. If you are using a centralized MSDE server with multiclient access, the installation process will be nearly the same as for an Access-based solution. The MSDE engine needs to be placed on only one machine, which the other machines will reference. This situation creates a client/server system.

In the case of a client/server system, you need to install and configure ODBC on each client machine to enable it to access the server. With the Microsoft Access Developer Edition, Visual Basic, and other development environments, the client software automatically handles the necessary components for the application to address the remote server.

Established Reputation

Another factor for consideration in the choice between MSDE and Access is one of established reputation. You may think that the MSDE/SQL Server, because it is running many high-level professional applications, is the front runner in terms of acceptance and reputation. MSDE/SQL Server is really established only when it is used for large, multiuser solutions.

The JET engine has been deployed successfully tens of thousands of times on all different systems and configurations. It has been used in literally millions of different applications in all shapes and sizes. MSDE is very new to the arena of widespread deployment. In the past, SQL Server was installed only on substantial NT-based server machines. Placing it on desktop systems may require more testing and support than a simpler JET installation.

Access has been used successfully on single-user and low simultaneous-user solutions (under five users) since it was first created. Creating an application using the JET engine at the core has become one of the most popular forms of database applications on the PC. Many third-party vendors ship professional solutions with this engine included.

By comparison, very few applications have ever shipped with the full SQL Server engine, because of its size, complexity, and expense. Although many client applications have been shipped that can access a SQL Server, shipping the database server itself with MSDE introduces a new set of parameters including client sophistication if the server has a problem.

Under Access, most problems could be handled simply by reinstalling the middleware access layer (ADO or DAO) or replacing the database file. With installation of an actual server on a client machine, small problems could be far more complicated to solve.

Describing these possibilities is not meant to frighten you away from deploying an MSDE solution, especially given the extra power and capabilities that it affords. Rather, it is meant to make you aware that potential pitfalls exist that you might encounter with this new database engine deployment strategy. To aid you in handling the installation of MSDE, Microsoft has included a command-line installer so that the process can be automated.

Command-Line Installation of MSDE

To deploy your MSDE solutions, Microsoft has included a command-line installation program that can be controlled by your program installer. This installer is named `msdex86.exe`.

The installer may accept scripts that tell it where installation will occur and which default settings to use. The script files have the `.iss` extension. A default unattended install script is included with MSDE and is named `unattend.iss`. You can use this script as the basis for a custom install file if you need to make modifications to the default.

Primarily, the command-line installer can be executed to set the paths for two of the primary directories:

- **szDir:** The root directory for SQL Server (default: `C:\MSSQL7`)
- **szDataDir:** The root directory for SQL Server data (default: `C:\MSSQL7`)

The following are the installation command-line switches:

- **-a:** Appends any arguments following this switch to the internal command-line argument.

- **-f1**: Accepts the string that follows this switch as the path and filename of the execution instructions.
- **-s**: Executes in silent mode so that no text is returned to the console, and the user is not prompted for any errors that occur.
- **-SMS**: Prevents network connections from closing before installation is complete (required parameter for network installations). This switch is case-sensitive and must be provided in all uppercase letters.

You can test an installation from the command line by using this command:

```
MSDEx86.exe -a -s -f1 "unattend.iss"
```

This command installs the MSDE engine in silent mode, using the file `unattend.iss` to provide the appropriate instructions.

During the installation, errors can occur. The installer will return the error code of any installation problems. Table 2-1 provides a list of the possible result codes for errors that may occur during installation.

TABLE 2-1 ERROR CODES FOR THE MSDE COMMAND-LINE INSTALLER

Error code	Description
0	No error
-1	Undefined error
-2	Invalid mode
-3	Missing required data in setup file (`setup.iss`)
-4	Not enough memory is available
-5	File not found
-6	Unable to write to response file
-7	Unable to write to log file
-8	Invalid path for response file
-9	Invalid list type (string or number)
-10	Invalid data type
-11	Undefined error during setup
-12	Dialogs out of order

Error code	Description
-51	Unable to create specified folder
-52	Unable to access specified folder
-53	Invalid option selection

These errors are displayed to the command-line console as they occur. Note that if the installation is successful, but a reboot of the machine is required, the Undefined error code (-1) will be returned.

MSDE Installation Files

After the MSDE engine is installed, it runs as a service in the background. The installation size of MSDE is about 55MB on the destination drive (34MB on the installation disk). This makes a floppy installation for an MSDE solution impractical. With the decline in price of CD-ROM writing drives, however, even most small developers have access to CD creation facilities.

When MSDE is placed on a system, the following help files are included:

- **SQL Server Enterprise Manager Help (entmgr.chm):** Information related to the Enterprise Manager used to create and modify databases, tables, users, and so forth.

- **Replication Wizard Help (replwiz.chm):** Documentation to guide you through setting up a replication chain.

> **NOTE:** In Windows 95/98, the MSDE engine is not set to automatically activate on startup. You can double-click the MSDE icon in the tray to begin the service, or use the Service Manager to set the Autostart on Boot feature.

Four databases are automatically installed with the MSDE engine:

- **Master:** Stores all the information that defines the configuration of the current databases, the server itself, and database devices that are registered in the system

- **Model:** Stores user-defined data types, rules, default values, and triggers that are globally available to the database objects in the system

- **Tempdb:** Scratch database used by SQL Server to execute joins, sorting, and other database system processes
- **Msdb:** Repository for the SQL Server Agent services

The Master and Model database always need to exist on a SQL Server system. They keep information regarding the current state of the databases registered with MSDE. When you remove a database from the database server by using the administrative tools, the entries are automatically removed from these necessary system databases.

For the full SQL Server 7 system installation, two sample databases are also included:

- **Pubs:** The traditional SQL Server equivalent of the Northwind database. Pubs contains sample data from a fictional publishing company, such as author, book title, and other data.
- **Northwind:** You are undoubtedly already familiar with the Northwind database that contains customer and ordering information related to a fictional Northwind Trading Company.

In Chapter 3, you will use the wizards in Microsoft Access to upsize the Northwind database included with Access 2000. That way, you will always have a rudimentary database that you can alter or execute sample queries on without fear of corrupting important data.

> **NOTE** The Northwind database was added in version 7 of SQL Server. If you use an older version, the database will not be available unless you use the Upsizing Wizard.

Migrating from MSDE to SQL Server

The easiest method of moving from MSDE to SQL Server is simply to install SQL Server over MSDE. SQL Server will automatically recognize all of the MSDE databases and make them available to the SQL Server enterprise system.

If you need to transport your data from a system running MSDE to the SQL Server machine, you need to save the database for transport. The easiest way to accomplish this task is by using the same methods that are used for backup and restoration of a database.

Simply back up the necessary database file in a backup file, using the backup operation in the MSDE snap-in in the Microsoft Management Console (MMC). Transport the file to the SQL Server machine and use the restore procedure to insert it into the database.

> **Note:** If you know how to execute stored procedures for addressing the MSDE server, the `sp_detach_db` routine can be used to detach the MDF file of the database from the current MSDE system. The file can then be copied to another MSDE setup or SQL Server, and the `sp_attach_db` command can be used to activate it there.

Summary

The Microsoft Access/JET database engine and the MSDE database engine each has its own niche in which its deployment is most appropriate. On small desktop solutions, the ease of use and installation of the JET engine is difficult to beat. For multiuser applications, the full feature set and scalability of MSDE make it the most attractive option. In this chapter, you covered:

- **JET engine:** A powerful file-based database used by Microsoft Access and Visual Basic.

- **MSDE:** A desktop version of the SQL Server database that is fully feature-compatible with the complete SQL Server. It is limited in file size to 2GB and has a practical limitation of five simultaneous users.

- **Transaction log:** The MSDE engine uses a complete transaction log that prevents the database from becoming corrupted even in a catastrophic failure situation. In contrast, the Microsoft Access database can be corrupted by an improper system shutdown.

- **MSDE client installation:** Installing MSDE on the client machines can be done through the command line or through the standard MSDE setup. Because the MSDE engine is available on every Microsoft Office 2000 CD-ROM, availability of the installer is rarely a problem.

- **Migrating MSDE to SQL Server:** Because MSDE uses the same file format and database format of SQL Server, scaling to SQL Server uses the same process as transferring a database from one SQL Server to another.

Chapter 3

The Access Wizards

IN THIS CHAPTER

- Introducing the Northwind sample database
- Discovering how the Upsizing Wizard works
- Exploring some conversion issues
- Examining your database for problems
- Upsizing the Northwind database
- Exploring other Access/MSDE capabilities

IN CHAPTER 1, YOU used SQL commands to create a database and a table and to enter some information into the table. If you previously have used Microsoft Access for database construction and entry, you probably think that the direct SQL method of database creation is harder and more laborious. You're right! Most advanced developers use friendly database construction tools to design and implement the initial structure, and later use direct SQL code to fine-tune the final application. Microsoft Access is a fantastic tool to create a foundation in the MSDE database.

In addition to using Access as a new-database creation environment, most developers have a large amount of legacy data stored in Microsoft Access that may need to be moved onto the MSDE server. The conversion of a database from Access to MSDE can be handled easily by the wizard included with Access (called the Upsizing Wizard), which is used to reconstruct the database schema and move all of the data to the database server. To demonstrate the how the Upsizing Wizard functions, in this chapter, you'll use the wizard to move the Northwind sample database to the MSDE server.

> Most of the examples of using Microsoft Access use the Northwind sample database, which runs the fictional company called Northwind Traders. The Northwind sample database, which is used by most of the Microsoft Access examples, contains data for Northwind orders, customers, suppliers, and other information related to tracking the Northwind business. Although SQL Server includes the Northwind database preinstalled, MSDE does not, because the

MSDE installer is made for final deployment installation. Therefore, extra space would be wasted if the sample databases were included. The absence of the Northwind database on the MSDE server works to your advantage, because it enables you to upsize a database that you are probably familiar with using.

How the Upsizing Wizard Works

Converting a database from the Access engine into an MSDE database is a simple process, thanks to the Upsizing Wizard, which makes all the necessary data type and rule conversions. The wizard not only re-creates and converts the database into MSDE, it also automatically creates attached table references in Access to the new data source.

An attached table in Access simulates that the table actually remains in the Access file. In reality, the database simply holds a reference pointer to the database located on the MSDE server. For reports, forms, database access code, and queries, the attached table can be used in the same manner as if it were still contained in the database file.

Moving from JET to MSDE

By comparing the features available to an MSDE database to those of an Access MDB file, as done in Chapter 2, you probably have a good idea of in which situations using the MSDE engine is more appropriate than using a JET database. The following is a list of factors to consider when determining whether it is time to move a database from JET to MSDE:

- **Security requirements:** The NT-based security features are significantly more robust in MSDE than any of the security features available through Microsoft Access. When executed from the Windows NT platform, MSDE uses and augments the security features made available through the operating system.

- **Backups:** The live backup features available to MSDE and SQL Server enable you to back up the database without having to close all database access to users before the backup begins. Backups can also be scheduled as tasks, so that they may be performed automatically at a preset time.

- **Fault recovery:** The transaction log provides the nearly flawless ability to restore a database to the same information state that existed prior to the failure. Any operations that modify the database (such as inserts, deletes, and so forth) are stored in the transaction log so that after a system failure, the data can be exactly reconstructed for data integrity. This means that the chances of data loss or corruption are much lower than with an Access-based system.

- **Network traffic reduction:** The file-based database access of a network-shared Access database can put great strains on the bandwidth of a network. MSDE can substantially cut down this traffic, because only the requests and result data sets need to be transferred over the network.

- **Scalability:** An MSDE database can be easily moved to SQL Server, which can effectively use up to 16 microprocessors on a single database server. This scalability provides an easy upgrade path for many more transactions to be accomplished effectively.

The database, after being placed on the MSDE server, can also be accessed over the Internet, which enables a client program to directly log in and address the MSDE server. For Access files, the only way to provide Internet access is through file services with complicated and expensive WAN software, such as a virtual private network (VPN).

Choosing Upsizing Elements

When using the Upsizing Wizard, you can choose to upsize any of the following elements:

- Tables
- Data
- Indexes
- Validation rules
- Default values
- Table relationships

In the upsizing process, you can choose to include all or only some of these elements from your existing database. The Upsizing Wizard handles all of the key functions for you – from creating the new database and tables to writing the appropriate Transact-SQL stored procedure code to duplicate the functionality provided natively in Microsoft Access.

The ADP Database Project File

The wizard will also create a new project file that contains links to the new tables located on the server, and will redirect any forms, reports, and other user interface items to address the MSDE-based database. All primary keys in tables are converted to nonclustered, unique indexes and marked as primary keys on the MSDE server.

> **NOTE** You cannot select specific indexes that will be upsized. If you ask the wizard to upsize the indexes, all indexes for any upsized tables will be transferred. Therefore, if you have any indexes that you do not want on the MSDE version of the database, make sure to remove them from the Access database before you begin the upsizing process.

While in Access, indexes are merely specified in the table definition. On the MSDE server, however, all indexes are stored as separate objects, and each index is given a unique name that may be used to address it for modification or deletion. The index used for the primary key of the table is given the prefix "aaaaa" and then is titled the same as the name of the table.

Unlike Access, MSDE does not support ascending or descending indexes. Because the optimization of MSDE/SQL Server is so effective, a single index can be used to provide fast queries in either sort direction. Therefore, specifying the ascending or descending direction in the query code itself will properly activate the index.

Exploring Some Conversion Issues

Although the Upsizing Wizard takes care of the details of the upsizing for you, that does not mean that the process of upsizing is simple. In fact, a large number of the conversions executed by the wizard are ones that you should know about. Items such as triggers, validation rules, default values, table relationships, and other general changes occur when the upsizing takes place.

Triggers

On the MSDE server, code can be set to execute when a new event occurs. If you have used VBA before, you know that a command button supports an event called Click. When a user clicks the button, the Click event activates, and any code contained in the event is executed. A trigger works in much the same manner, except that code for a trigger is executed when an event such as a new record insertion occurs.

Three triggers are available for execution when a table is modified through an update, insert, or delete. Triggers are actually stored procedures written in the Transact-SQL language. Therefore, although a trigger may be located in a particular table, it can reference other tables and retrieve data from them.

One of the triggers created when the Northwind database is upsized looks like this:

```
Alter TRIGGER "Customers_UTrig" ON Customers FOR UPDATE AS
SET NOCOUNT ON
/* * CASCADE UPDATES TO 'Orders' */
IF UPDATE(CustomerID)
```

```
BEGIN
  UPDATE Orders
  SET Orders.CustomerID = inserted.CustomerID
  FROM Orders, deleted, inserted
  WHERE deleted.CustomerID = Orders.CustomerID
END
```

You do not need to understand the meaning of this code, which is a trigger used to enforce referential integrity, because the Upsizing Wizard takes care of it for you. Most of the Access features that are not supported by MSDE are implemented as code in trigger events. When an event occurs, the trigger code executes and interprets the event to mimic the operations provided by Access features. The Upsizing Wizard already has pre-created trigger code for all the key functions that can be set in Access.

Validation Rules

The MSDE/SQL Server engine has no such thing as field validation rules. Therefore, any validation rules that appear in the Access database are converted to check constraints when they are upsized.

In addition to validation rules for fields, the option to require fields in a table is not an explicit feature included in the SQL Server engine. The flag for setting *required fields* in Microsoft Access are also not available in MSDE. Instead, the field is marked so that null values are not accepted, and a small checking code is placed in the new record insert trigger to prevent required fields from remaining empty.

Default Values

MSDE also treats defaults differently than the way in which they are treated in Microsoft Access. Default values on the MSDE server act very much like triggers insofar as they are activated by the server to place values in a new field. A default value is actually called a *default definition* in the terminology of SQL Server.

A default definition cannot be created for a field that has a data type of timestamp or that has the *identity* or *rowguidcol* property set. Also, the default value must match the type in the column, so a varchar should have a value that is a string.

When adding a new column to an existing table, you can actually have MSDE insert the default value into all records that have a null in the column for which the default definition is created. However, the Upsizing Wizard doesn't support this method directly, so you need to use a search-and-replace action to gain the same effect.

Upsized Table Relationships

The relationships created in a Microsoft Access database that are available in the Relationships window have a parallel in MSDE. In MSDE, these structures are called *Declared Referential Integrity (DRI)* relationships and enforce one side of the relationships that are established in MSDE database diagrams. The DRI relationships must all be created at the same time, so if you upsize the database gradually (separating tables), the relationship enforcement will not work properly.

> **NOTE:** DRI is a new feature to SQL Server 6.5 and later versions. If you use an older version of SQL Server (6.0 and earlier), this feature is not available. Instead, triggers and stored procedures are used to enforce referential integrity. If you happen to be using a database in MSDE and wonder why the DRI features are not being used by it, the database may have been initially created in an earlier version of SQL Server.

The DRI features enforce the referential integrity for new record insertion. However, it does not automatically provide cascading updates and cascading deletes. Instead, these features are implemented in triggers that are automatically created when your database is being upsized. Because you may not want the cascading features included with the database that is being moved to MSDE, you may optionally turn off this feature and include only the referential integrity. You can select either DRI or triggers, but not both. If you need the cascading features and the referential integrity, the triggers will supply the functionality of both in the trigger code.

JET supports cascading updates and deletes that can ensure that related tables retain their integrity. MSDE and SQL Server do not have such a capability built into the engine. Instead, triggers and stored procedures can be created to maintain the integrity of the database.

Changes That Will Occur

As the Upsizing Wizard converts your database from an MDB into an MSDE database, a variety of specific changes take place. In tables and queries, the following modifications are made:

- Duplicate columns are given an alias.
- Date delimiters are converted to SQL-compatible delimiters.
- Boolean data types are converted to bit data fields.
- Wildcard characters in the WHERE clause of a SQL statement are converted from the Access asterisk (*) to the SQL percentage sign (%).
- Although JET supports zero-length strings, in SQL Server, an undefined string is stored as a null. If null values are not allowed for a particular field, an error will be generated if the field value has not been set (such as when a new record has been added).

- The `WITH TIES` command is added to all `TOP` queries that have an `ORDER BY` clause, because all Access queries include ties.

In Access, individual queries are stored within a VBA structure known as a QueryDef. Because MSDE does not support VBA within the database server itself, and the queries will be relocated onto the server, queries are converted into *views*. Views offer a way to look at a table by using a specific query in a similar manner to Access queries.

> **NOTE:** If you have queries that retrieve parameters from controls on a form, the wizard will not upsize them into MSDE. Because you need to pass parameters to the query, it is very likely you will need to use the Parameter objects in ADO. See Chapter 9 for more information on the ADO system.

Timestamp Columns

The Upsizing Wizard enables you to add a timestamp column to tables automatically as the upsizing occurs. Adding a timestamp column in your tables can improve performance on row updates and deletions. The timestamp field is changed every time a value in the row is modified.

Therefore, for updates, MSDE only has to check the timestamp to determine whether fields need to be changed in the record on the data store. Without the timestamp, each field needs to be checked independently for changes. The more fields in a table, the more optimization the timestamp field provides.

By checking a series of parameters, the wizard can intelligently decide whether a table will benefit from a timestamp. You can leave this selection (the default) for the upsizing process, or specify that all tables or no tables will have a timestamp added.

Examining Your Database for Problems

Upsizing a database to MSDE may take a fair amount of time, especially if a substantial amount of data is involved. Because the conversion by the wizard may have problems with some implementations of your database, it is a good idea to review the database before attempting conversion. Errors may halt an object from upsizing. If such a fault occurs, you have to correct the problem in your Access database, erase the newly created MSDE database, and start again. You probably can spot many of the problem areas by a cursory examination and resolve them before you waste time beginning a conversion that will fail.

The following is a simple checklist of things to examine:

- **Queries for VBA code:** If your queries contain any code that uses VBA functions or commands, the upsizing of those queries will not work. Using VBA statements (including formatting and date-manipulation routines) is not allowed in MSDE. You must convert the VBA code to Transact-SQL.

- **Default values with code:** Access allows code to be added in many places, including the default values, where expressions can be placed. This code cannot be placed on the MSDE server, so any code in the default value expression has to be removed.

- **Deeply nested queries:** Deeply nested queries cause an error at upsizing, because the nesting can conflict with indexes and create extended query times. If you have complicated queries in your database, you might want to upsize everything *but* the queries on the first execution of the wizard. On the second execution, upsize only the queries, so if an error occurs, the query can be fixed and a new wizard conversion can easily be applied.

If you locate any instances of these problems, you can try removing them and possibly upsizing a single table or query. The Upsizing Wizard can selectively upsize database objects, so you can test individual changes.

> **NOTE** For the time being, it is best if you simply remove certain problem areas that you encounter, such as the use of VBA code. As you progress through the book, you will learn how to use Transact-SQL to accomplish many of the same functions as those facilitated by VBA. Until that time, either the database has to do without that functionality, or you need to include that logic in the client program.

Several SQL commands included in Access SQL are not supported by MSDE. These include DROP INDEX, DISTINCTROW, OWNERACCESS, ORDER BY in unions, TRANSFORM, and PARAMETERS. Although these commands are not available, the functionality they provide can be gained through other Transact-SQL methods.

> **NOTE** Microsoft's Web site has a white paper to help you convert Access items to use on MSDE. See *Using the Microsoft Access 2000 Upsizing Tools with SQL Server or MSDE* for more information. Currently, it is available at http://msdn.microsoft.com/library/techart/upsize00.htm.

Upsizing the Northwind Database

When you execute Microsoft Access, after you've installed MSDE, an option is available to automatically add the Northwind database to MSDE or SQL Server (see Figure 3-1). However, because you are learning how the Upsizing Wizard is being used, it is better to do the upsizing yourself. That way, you can try the wizard on a database that is already familiar to you.

Figure 3-1: The selection to automatically install the Northwind database to MSDE is available.

If you do not already have the Northwind database on your drive, execute the Office 2000 installer and add the database to your system. You can also retrieve it from the Office 2000 CD-ROM. If your CD-ROM drive is located at F, the path to the database is as follows:

F:\PFiles\MSOffice\Office\Samples\NWind.mdb

If you copy this file onto your drive, make sure to uncheck the read-only attribute in the file properties using the Windows Explorer. You cannot upsize the database from the CD-ROM because the Upsizing Wizard requires read/write permissions to save changes to the database file. If the read and write privileges for the database are not available, an error is generated.

> **TIP** Before you begin upsizing any Access database, you should back up your database. If something goes awry during the upsizing, a remote — but real — possibility exists that your database could be corrupted. To ensure that you don't risk valuable data, backing up your database is recommended, before you begin the upsizing process.

Before you begin the Upsizing Wizard, make sure to define a default printer to use for formatting when the upsizing report is generated. Because the report is generated automatically when the upsizing is complete, you need to configure it before the process has begun. Although the report doesn't automatically print at the completion of the upsizing process, the displayed preview window will be formatted using the currently selected printer.

You can upsize just the database schema elements, just the data, or both into the MSDE server. The wizard also enables you to upsize individual pieces of the database (such as tables or data) separately so that you can export parts of the database into MSDE.

> **TIP**
> Make sure you have enough free space on your hard drive before you begin upsizing the database. Access needs to create a temporary file to handle the information conversion, so it is a good idea to have twice the size of your current database in free space on the drive being used.

If an error occurs during the upsizing process, all of the partial database objects created, up to the point that the fault occurred, are left in the MSDE database. That means any databases, tables, indexes, or stored procedures that were already created on the server will remain there. You can use the SQL code, the Enterprise Manager, or the SQL-DMO objects to delete these objects. Be sure to delete them before you attempt another upsize, so that no conflict occurs when the wizard tries to create these objects again.

> **NOTE**
> The easiest method of removing all the objects related to the database is to use the `Drop Database` command. You can use the `Execute SQL Script` command available in Microsoft Query (shown in Chapter 1) to remove a database and all of its related objects. If your database name is *myDB*, the command `Drop Database myDB` would remove it from the MSDE server.

Upsizing the Database

After you locate the Northwind file on your drive, upsize the database by following these steps:

1. Execute Microsoft Access 2000.
2. Open the Northwind database (Northwind.mdb).
3. Select the wizard via Tools → Database Utilities → Upsizing Wizard.

> **Note:** If you have not previously installed the Upsizing Wizard, at this point you are prompted for the Office 2000 CD-ROM, after which you are led through the installation process. After the installation is complete, the window shown in Figure 3-2 is displayed.

4. You will see the window shown in Figure 3-2. Leave the selection set to Create new database and click the Next button. The wizard automatically creates a new database on the database server that you select.

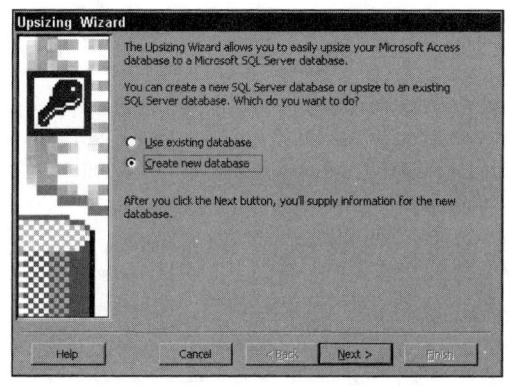

Figure 3-2: The first screen of the wizard enables you to choose to create a new database or use an existing one.

5. From the combo box, select the (local) option. If you are testing MSDE on a remote machine, you can enter the UNC or WINS path name (i.e., *myMSDEserver*) or you can use the domain name or IP address for a TCP/IP-based connection.

> **Note:** In some cases, the (local) option will not work, even though the MSDE server is installed locally and the (local) selection works in other windows. The wizard may generate the error: "Invalid use of NULL." To get it to work, use the machine name instead.

6. For the login account, type **sa**, for system administrator. Unless you have placed security on MSDE, the password for the sa account is empty, so you can leave the password text box blank (see Figure 3-3).

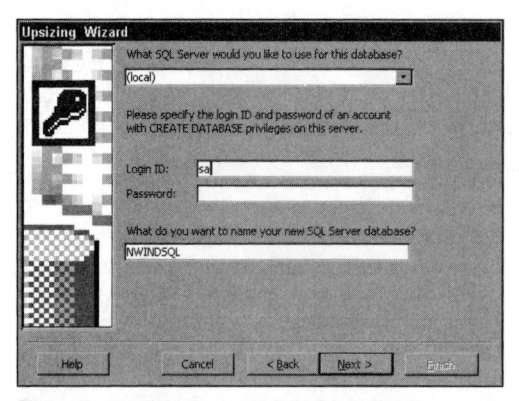

Figure 3-3: With the login and server name properly set, the wizard will access the MSDE server.

7. Click the Next button to advanced to the Table Selection page. On this page, you can choose which of the tables in the database will be transferred to the new MSDE database.

8. Click the double-arrow button (>>) to upsize all the tables included in the Northwind database (see Figure 3-4). If you only want to move individual tables, use the single-arrow button (>) to move them one at a time. Realize that if you move a table that has a relation to another table that isn't included in the upsizing, yet you check the relational integrity item, the upsizing process will generate an error.

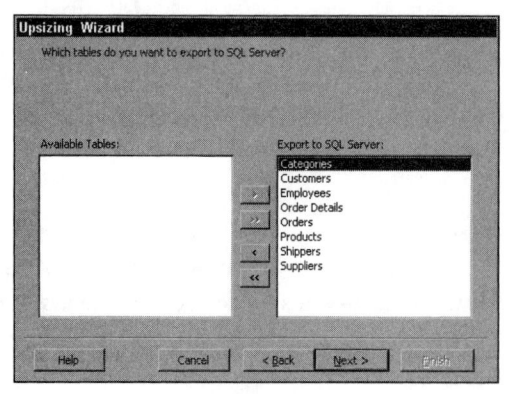

Figure 3-4: Select all of the tables to move to the MSDE database.

9. Click the Next button to advance to the options page, on which you can choose what parts of the database – including indexes, default values, and other items – will be upsized. For the Northwind database, you want to include all parts of the database in the MSDE version that is being created.

10. Leave all the options at their default settings and click the Next button (see Figure 3-5).

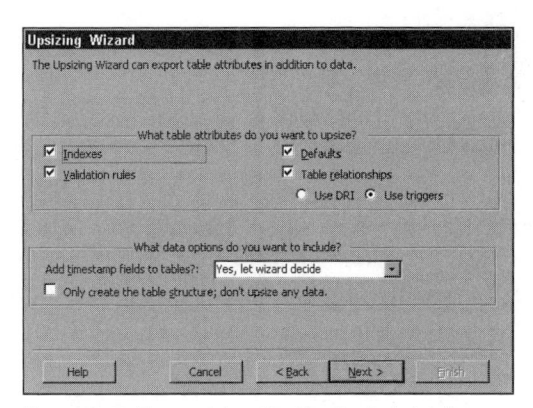

Figure 3-5: For upsizing the Northwind database, include all of the available items — indexes, default values, and so forth.

11. Click the Create a new Access client/server application option (see Figure 3-6). You can leave the default name of NWINDCS.adp.

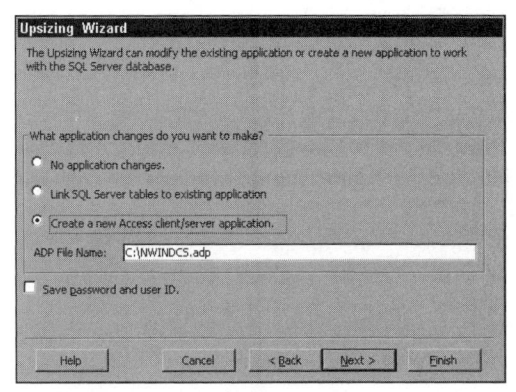

Figure 3-6: Create a new application to address the MSDE Northwind database.

12. Click the Next button. The wizard will inform you that the configuration is complete.
13. Click the Finish button to begin upsizing the database.

You will be informed of the progress of the upsizing task through the progress window (see Figure 3-7).

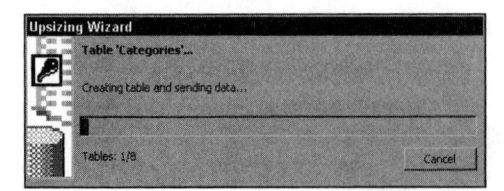

Figure 3-7: The progress window informs you as the tables are upsized, indexes are created, and data is transferred.

All of the tables and queries from the Northwind database will be transferred into the MSDE database. The new client/server project version (ADP file) connected to the database is automatically modified to reflect the new connections to the MSDE-based tables. After the upsizing process is complete, the upsizing report is automatically displayed.

The Upsizing Wizard Report

The Upsizing Wizard creates a detailed report that describes what actually occurred during the upsizing process. The report is automatically displayed in the preview mode and is stored as a snapshot file (with an .snp extension) in the folder of the database that is being upsized to MSDE.

The report contains information about the database that was created to hold the Access information. Included in the report is information about the size of the database and the log used for the destination database. Also included is all the table information, including the columns that were created, indexes, validation rules, default values, triggers, and timestamps.

A few errors should be listed on the first page. If the upsizing didn't encounter any critical errors, and your printer is set to standard 8.5 × 11-inch formatting, the report should be 26 pages in length. The report should contain the following items:

- **Database:** The name of the original database and the new database on the MSDE server.

- **Errors:** A few errors with validation rules for the Order Details table, and a hyperlink in the Suppliers table.

- **Upsizing Parameters:** Includes the options checked in the Upsizing Wizard to include or exclude from the original tables. Also shows what modifications were made to the existing database.

- **Tables:** Details each table that was upsized and all of the individual field details, including both the original field names and types and the new MSDE-based names. Indexes, triggers, and delete triggers are also listed.

- **Queries:** All of the queries contained in the database with the original query code and the upsized code. If the query code could not be upsized, it is noted, as well.

- **Relationships:** Displays a diagram of all of the relationships between the tables, as well as listing the fields involved in the relation, the enforcing triggers, and the attributes of the relation.

When you close the report, the new client/server version of the Northwind database is automatically opened. At first glance, you might not notice many differences in the project, but it has numerous significant departures from the initial database (see Figure 3-8).

Figure 3-8: The new database objects listed include Views, Database Diagrams, and Stored Procedures.

Examining the Upsized Database

Although the Queries object is no longer available, three other options now are offered: Views, Database Diagrams, and Stored Procedures. These new options are made to directly reference MSDE features on the database server.

To see how the transfer of the database affects the appearance of the tables in Access, follow these steps:

1. Select the Customers table and click the Open toolbar icon to open the table in the Data View. The way in which the table appears is identical to the way that you are used to with the Access-based table. However, the data is really being retrieved from the MSDE server.

2. Close the Data View window.

3. Select the Customers table and click the Design toolbar icon to open the table in the Design View. You can see that the Design View is completely different from the traditional Access designer (see Figure 3-9).

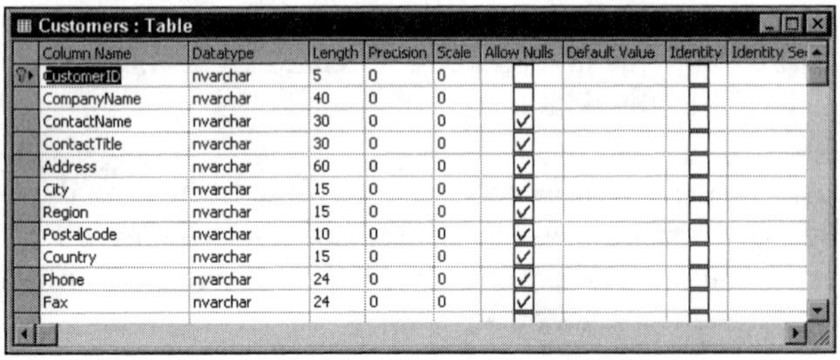

Figure 3-9: The Design View for an MSDE table is much different from the view used for an MDB file.

Other Access/MSDE Capabilities

Although the Upsizing Wizard does an effective job at creating the necessary structures on the MSDE server, you'll often want more control over the process, which you can achieve by directly creating the database in which the database objects will be placed.

For other projects, you may also want to link to the upsized database from within a normal Access MDB database file. To establish this connection, you need to define an ODBC data source that Access can use to address the MSDE database. By directly creating the database constructs on the MSDE server and properly configuring an Access project, you can construct almost any type of client/server database project.

Creating a Database in Access 2000

When you use the Upsizing Wizard, it automatically creates a new database on the MSDE server. You can use Access 2000 to manually create a database in MSDE. Then, Access can upsize the tables to the database structure on the MSDE server.

To accomplish this, you probably want to begin by creating an Access Data Project (ADP) file. An ADP file acts much like an MDB file, but it also has significant capabilities for a project based on a SQL Server engine, including the following:

◆ Direct access to stored procedures

◆ Ability to modify the design of an MSDE database

◆ Construction functionality for database diagrams

◆ Ability to create SQL views

◆ Editing capability for triggers connected to a table

In Access 2000, this new type of file was created for optimized use with MSDE and SQL Server. Any file with an .adp extension contains all the user interface information of an MDB file as well as advanced reference objects for the database objects located on a MSDE server or a SQL Server.

To create an ADP file, you can automatically activate a wizard by selecting the ADP project type. For a new ADP file, follow these steps:

1. Execute Microsoft Access 2000.

2. Select File → New to create a new database.

3. From the General tab, select Project (New Database) icon.

4. Enter the filename as **TestADP.adp** and click the Create button. The login screen is displayed (see Figure 3-10) that enables you to set the name of the new database, enter the login account and password, and select the server on which the database will be created.

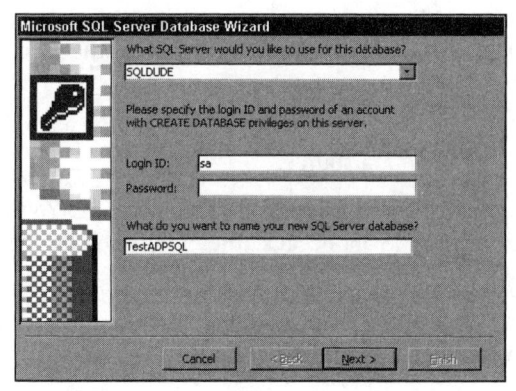

Figure 3-10: Select the MSDE server, set the login information, and enter the name of the new database.

5. Click the Next button to test the data connection. After the wizard has verified that the connection can be made, it presents a screen that enables you to finish the database creation.

6. Click the Finish button. The progress bar displays the process of creating the new database. After it is complete, you will have a new database and an ADP access file through which you can create new tables in the database.

Alternately, you can select the Project (Existing Database) item, which enables you to create a project based on an existing MSDE database. Access can address the MSDE server and retrieve the necessary information about the database to present it in nearly the same fashion as a traditional MDB file.

A database project provides native-mode access to an MSDE server through the ADO/OLE DB architecture (see Chapter 9). In the ADP file, all the user interface elements (such as forms, reports, pages, macros, and modules) are stored, whereas the database schema elements are located on the database server. A project does not contain any data or database schema objects (such as tables or relationships).

Configuring ODBC

To address MSDE databases linked in an MDB file, Access needs a way to communicate with the server. The easiest way to allow this communication is through the ODBC middleware. To use ODBC, you have to configure a connection Access can use.

To create an ODBC data source, follow these steps:

1. Under the Start menu, select the Settings → Control Panel folder.

2. Double-click the ODBC Data Sources icon to open the ODBC window.

3. Select the tab of the type of data source you want to create. You should see several tabs, including User DSN, System DSN, and File DSN. If you are constructing a client application (in Access or Visual Basic), you can use the User DSN type of data source. For a Web solution that accesses the MSDE database through a Web page, it is best to use a System DSN or File DSN type of data source.

4. Click the Add button to add a data source.

5. For the driver type, select the SQL Server item in the list box. You need to use the SQL Server driver for MSDE, because they are based on the same engine.

6. Click the Finish button. After the driver is loaded, you are prompted to enter the properties of the data source (see Figure 3-11).

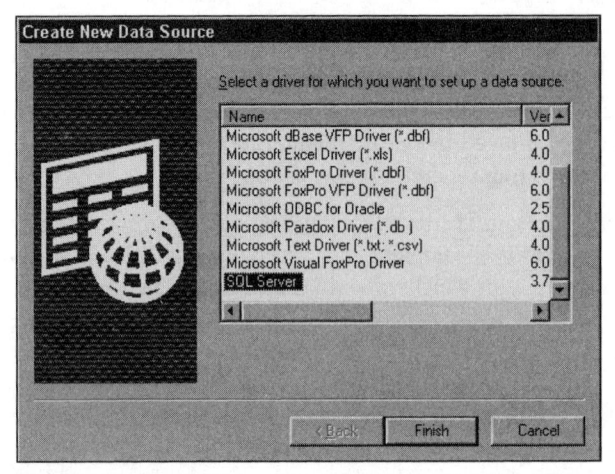

Figure 3-11: Here's where you set the properties of the data source when setting up the ODBC driver.

7. Enter **NWindMSDE** as the DSN Name and select the (local) option for the server (see Figure 3-12).

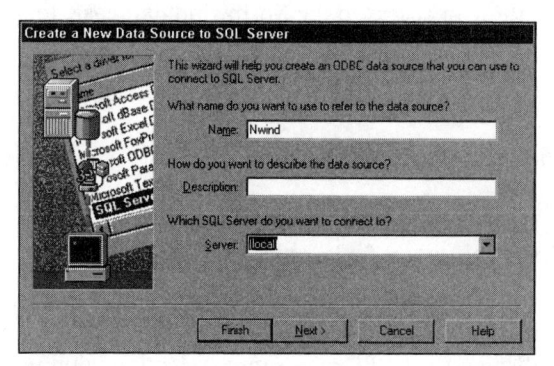

Figure 3-12: Select the (local) option for the server if you are creating the data source on the same machine as MSDE.

8. Click the Next button to advance to the login options screen. You can usually leave these settings to their defaults and allow Windows NT authentication.
9. Check the Change default database box and select the Northwind database. When a connection is made with the data source, the program will automatically select the Northwind database.
10. Click the Next button to accept the rest of the defaults.
11. Click the Finish button to create the new data source.

You will be presented with a window that details all the settings you have selected. Click the Test Data Source button to attempt a connection to the MSDE server. If everything works properly, the test will tell you it was successful. If any problems have occurred, you will be notified, and you can return and change parameters to get the source to work properly.

After the test has completed successfully, click the OK button, and you should now see the data source in the listing of all the current DSNs available. Because almost any development environment can address a data source through an ODBC DSN, you can use this source for testing.

Linking Tables in Access

The primary method of using Access with the MSDE server is through the ADP project. However, it is possible to provide the table links you created within a standard Access MDB database. The link to the database will not be as comprehensive as the one supplied through an ADP project.

A table link is not designed to provide a comprehensive design linkage to a table on the database server. It is meant to allow remote tables to appear in a database and coexist with actual database objects stored in the MDB file.

To create a sample MDB file with access to the Northwind database, follow these steps:

1. Execute Microsoft Access 2000.

2. Select File → New to create a new database.

3. Name the database as **ODBCTest.mdb**.

4. Select File → Get External Data → Link Tables.

5. Under the File of Type combo box at the bottom of the Link window, select the ODBC Databases option. Selecting this option in the combo box will automatically display the ODBC data source selection window.

6. Select the NWindMSDE DSN from the list and click OK. Access will attempt to make a connection to the data source and, if successful, display a list of the available tables that may be linked (see Figure 3-13).

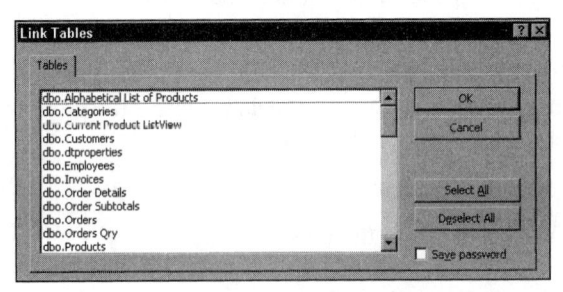

Figure 3-13: The list of available tables on the data source will be displayed.

7. Click the Select All button to link to all of the available tables. Leave out the INFORMATION_SCHEMA views from the selected list, because the link asks for a key for each view, which is unnecessary to the application.

8. Click the OK button to accept these links. Access will link to these tables and add the references to the current MDB file. If the linking mechanism cannot determine which field in the table is the Unique Record Identifier, you will be prompted to select one.

When the linking of all the tables is complete, your ODBCTest.mdb database should contain a number of links, such as those shown in Figure 3-14. You can use this method in any MDB database to link to a remote data source.

Figure 3-14: All the Northwind tables have a link through the ODBC data source to the MSDE database.

Shrinking a Database

You may already be familiar with compacting a database in Microsoft Access. Compacting must be done manually to shrink the size of the database file by removing space that is marked as unused. MSDE/SQL Server features the ability to shrink (parallel in function to compacting) a database, as well, although it is done automatically when more than 25 percent of the database file is free space. For review, this section explains how the database compaction works.

In an Access database, when a record is "deleted," it isn't actually deleted from the database. Instead, it is marked as deleted and is left in the database. Leaving the record in the database is done for reasons of performance (so the entire database doesn't have to be reordered with each deletion) and order (indexes do not have to be redone from scratch because the location of records has shifted).

You may have noticed that when you have 1,000 records in an MDB file, for example, and you delete them all, the size of the database doesn't shrink. That is because all of the records continue to exist within the database. It isn't until after you compact the database that the records are actually removed and the table is reformatted to reflect their absence. In Microsoft Access, compacting a database file requires that you create a new file from the existing one.

In MSDE, file management operations are executed by the server, and a database may be shrunk without any new files being generated. The database shrinking is done automatically, but if you have just deleted a large number of records and wish to reduce the file size of the database manually, you can right-click a database item in the MSDE Enterprise Manager and select All Tasks → Shrink Database from the menu.

Summary

By using the Upsizing Wizard to move the Northwind database onto the MSDE server, you observed how the process occurs. While the wizard handles all of the details of the upsizing, many changes take place to allow the database to function in MSDE. Most of the features of Access that are not directly supported on the MSDE server are duplicated through trigger code. In this chapter, you covered the following:

- **Upsizing Wizard:** Microsoft Access includes a wizard that converts the schema of a database and all the data it contains to MSDE or SQL Server.

- **Validation rules:** The validation rules used in Access must be converted to check constraints settings to be used on MSDE. The Upsizing Wizard automatically generates the proper structures in the MSDE database.

- **Declared Referential Integrity (DRI):** Can be used to enforce referential integrity on an MSDE database, but will not handle cascading updates and deletes. A trigger must be placed on the MSDE server to handle the cascading operations.

- **Upsizing Wizard report:** After the wizard has completed execution, a report snapshot is generated that holds information about the upsizing process. The database objects created on the MSDE server, as well as errors that occurred and relations that were created, are listed in the report.

Chapter 4

Architectural Overview

IN THIS CHAPTER

- Reviewing basic design concepts
- Understanding normalization

THE TECHNICAL DETAILS of choosing the proper database engine for your application (covered in Chapter 2) is very important to deployment considerations. After you make this choice, learning the specifics of the database system you will use, as well as understanding proper design guidelines, can help you to achieve the most effective implementation of your application. With proper design of the table architecture within each database, you can avoid many later problems.

The reasons for good database design are many. Perhaps the most obvious problem with retrofitting a poorly designed system is the entry of existing data. After data is placed in a database system, converting it into a new schema format is usually labor-intensive. Every time data transfer is required for a format change, you need to either write conversion macros or transfer the data manually through a transfer utility or SQL command.

Further complicating any core database redesign are the client application user interfaces, which typically are built around the existing database structure. These may need to be reformatted to reflect the new design choices. Minimizing database problems by using good design in the beginning is your best prospect for avoiding later repairs.

Basic Design Concepts

The structural elements of a database server, such as columns, tables, default values, and so forth, are the pieces from which a database is constructed. Depending on how you define these structural elements and the processes (such as data cleaning) that are applied to database maintenance, you can maximize durability and usability of each database.

One of the key elements of design is deciding on the content, type, and location of the columns that will be used within the database. Column definition determines how the data that needs to be input and stored for the application will be classified and available for later access and manipulation.

Column Definition

One of the first tasks when beginning any new database, even before deciding on the tables to use, is selecting what columns are needed to hold the data. Columns are often relocated among the tables during the design process, so proper column creation is initially more important than column location. Defining how each column of a table is implemented may seem rudimentary, but careful selection of the available options can dramatically increase the manageability of each table.

To make sure your table column definitions are most useful, you may find these guidelines helpful:

- **Minimize column name size:** Make sure that the column name is explicit so that its function can be readily discerned, but do not make it so long that it cannot be easily read in a diagram or takes a great deal of typing. Designers often develop a standard shorthand (for example, fNameCorpRep, lNameCorpRep, and so on) for lengthy, but common, words used in naming.

- **Like columns should be uniform:** When a column records the ZIP code, it should not be named Zip in one table and ZipCode in another. Inconsistent naming makes a database difficult to manage and confusing to people attempting to query the database.

- **Avoid character column types for key columns:** Unless the text stored in the column will be a short abbreviation, try to avoid using alphabetic characters to store as a primary key. Problems such as slow searches, case-sensitive errors, and larger indexes are all caused by character-based key fields.

- **Add extra columns to avoid redundant tables:** Often, when beginners design a database, many tables with only the slightest variation between them are generated. If three nearly identical tables exist (where only one or two fields differ between them), consider merging the tables and adding a column that holds a type value. The single type column could specify the type of each row, instead of placing that row of data in one of three nearly identical tables. Although some database design purists find this practice objectionable, rarely does this implementation cause more problems than it solves.

When the columns are properly configured, queries can be constructed much more easily and the maintenance required on the database is minimized. If the columns are properly defined, queries become more straightforward and simpler to implement. A poor choice of column definitions can produce poor query performance and create difficult debugging conditions. Choosing the appropriate data type for each column is just as important as column selection to proper database design. Initially choosing the proper type can save later table redefinition.

Column Data Types

All data stored in a database has to be assigned a specific data type, which enables the database server to provide sorting, searching, and manipulation capabilities. When the data is not stored as a data type that the database server can interpret (such as a text field), the information in that field cannot be indexed from MSDE.

The MSDE engine provides all of the standard data types that you likely have already worked with in Microsoft Access, although some of the types are named slightly differently. Additionally, the MSDE engine provides more complex data types (such as the timestamp) and the ability to add new data types (user-defined data types).

SYSTEM DATA TYPES

The MSDE/SQL Server engine supports 24 native data types. These column types, shown in Table 4-1, can be used to define how the data will be stored in a table. Unicode is now supported for three character types (nchar, nvarchar, and ntext) to provide international character storage.

TABLE 4-1 MSDE COLUMN TYPE NAMES USED WITH THE CREATE TABLE COMMAND

Column type	Description
Int	Integer with values between -2,147,483,648 and 2,147,483,647. In VBA and Visual Basic, the equivalent numeric type is Long.
smallint	Integer with values between 32,767 and -32,767. In VBA and Visual Basic, the equivalent numeric type is Integer.
tinyint	Positive integer with values between 0 and 255. In VBA and Visual Basic, the equivalent numeric type is Byte.
Float	Floating-point number that has a range from $-1.79E + 308$ through $1.79E + 308$.
Char	Character string of fixed length with a maximum size of 8,000 characters. Any time this field is non-null, the entire defined character length is used.
varchar	Character string of variable length with a maximum size of 8,000 characters. Any time this field is non-null, only the length of the current string is used.
binary	Binary storage for data up to 8,000 bytes in length.

Continued

TABLE 4-1 MSDE COLUMN TYPE NAMES USED WITH THE CREATE TABLE COMMAND *(Continued)*

Column type	Description
varbinary	Variable binary storage for data with a maximum of 8,000 bytes in length.
smalldatetime	Data and time can store a date from January 1, 1900 to June 6, 2079 with time accuracy to one minute.
bit	Binary digit, either 0 or 1.
money	Currency storage with a precision of four digits. Currency values are rounded after the fourth decimal place, as opposed to normal decimal types that simply truncate a number after the available digits have been exceeded. Can store values between -922,337,203,685,477.5808 and 922,337,203,685,477.5807.
datetime	Data and time can store a date from January 1, 1753 to December 31, 9999 with time accuracy to 3.33 milliseconds.
text	Extended text or memo field that can hold up to 2GB worth of characters.
Image	Large image or binary data that may be up to 2GB in size.
timestamp	Timestamp for the row for such things as replication and speeding record updates.
decimal	Fixes precision numeric value from $-10^{38}-1$ through $10^{38}-1$.
numeric	Same as decimal.
smallmoney	Currency storage with a precision of four digits. Currency values are rounded after the fourth decimal place, as opposed to normal decimal types that simply truncate a number after the available digits have been exceeded. Can store values between -214,748.3648 and 214,748.3647.
real	Floating-point number that can store values between $-3.4 E + 38$ and $3.4 E + 38$.
cursor	Can hold a reference to an existing cursor.
uniqueidentifier	Holds a globally unique identifier (GUID) similar to the class ID used by ActiveX components.
nchar	A fixed-length Unicode column with a length up to 4,000 characters.

Column type	Description
nvarchar	A variable-length Unicode column with a length up to 4,000 characters.
ntext	Extended Unicode text or memo field that can hold up to 2GB worth of characters.

Data types such as image, text, ntext, binary, and varbinary hold data that is difficult to index or search directly by the database engine. Because the data held in these fields is undifferentiated, the MSDE engine has no effective means of sorting this information. MSDE limits any single index to 900 characters, which means only the first 900 characters.

Each data type has characteristics that are unique to it (such as byte length, range, and so forth). The tools that you will learn to use throughout this book will provide these details when you are creating a database, so you need to know them only in specific instances. See the manual on SQL Server for this detailed information.

> **NOTE:** Of all the data types, only the bit field type cannot be altered after the table is created. During table creation, the database combines all the available bit fields into a byte field that is transparent to the user. Because all of the bit fields are stored together, you cannot alter them after initial definition.

USER-DEFINED DATA TYPES

In addition to the system data types available in MSDE, it is possible to create your own data types, known as *user-defined types*. A user-defined type is created by using an available system data type to define a new type. After you create the new type, you can place rules and constraints on the type that are automatically enabled when the type is used within a table definition.

One of the most common reasons to define a user-defined type is to place certain limits on the data that can be entered into a column. For example, a limit may be placed on a date field so that the user-defined type will only accept invoice dates past the year 1957, when the company was founded. Or, a currency field could be limited to $2,000, the legal limit of certain political campaign contributions.

Setting up a custom data type to accept the data ensures that no improper data can be entered into a field. Although rules and triggers can be disabled or damaged, the only way that a user-defined type can be overridden is by redefining the table itself to exclude or change the data type of that field to a system type.

Using the Identity Setting on a Column

Placing an identity setting on a column was covered briefly in Chapter 1 when you created the advertisements table and explicitly defined such a column. In Microsoft Access, the equivalent data type is known as an *AutoNumber column*.

The identity column is not an actual type, but rather an attribute of a data type column. Because an identity field is automatically incremented by the database engine, it must be a numeric type of field. For example, an identity column could be defined as a decimal data type, and the MSDE system would automatically maintain unique values for each new row that was inserted.

The identity field, when first created, has two attributes: the base number and increment. The *base number* (or *seed*) defines what number will be assigned to the identity column of the first row inserted into the table. The *increment* sets the increment between the numbers as each new row is inserted. After an identity has been created, you cannot change either of these properties.

Keep in mind that the MSDE/SQL Server engine began supporting the identity type after version 6. If you use another database server type or an older version of SQL Server, this type will not be available. Instead, you must place a trigger to a stored procedure to increment the field number when a new record insertion occurs.

Older versions of the Access Upsizing Wizard created the incremental trigger automatically to place Autonumber fields on the SQL Server. Therefore, you may see these types of triggers in older database implementations.

Illegal Nulls and Default Values

In Chapter 1, you learned that null values can be used to minimize the amount of drive space used by records that have empty columns. Allowing nulls will cause an error when you are creating a new record, if you do not explicitly set a value to that column. Additionally, fields such as foreign keys and integrity-based columns can cause an error when null values are placed within them.

One of the best methods of testing a new table is to insert two completely blank records. In Chapter 1, you created a table called advertisements. For that table, a blank record would be inserted with this command:

```
insert advertisements default values
```

Executing an `insert` blank command like this twice can indicate several things:

- **Required fields:** Any columns that are required to have a value will cause an error if no value is inserted. For required fields, you can bind a default value to it to prevent a possible error. If an custom entry for this field is critical for a valid row, allowing an error to be generated when no value is supplied may be justified.

- **Invalid default values:** You may place a default value in a parameter that is invalid for other rules or triggers that have been placed in the database.

- **Unique fields that aren't unique:** The possibility that two blank records will violate a unique attribute of a field is the reason to execute the blank record test twice. If the unique field is not properly configured (as an identity or other self-maintaining field), the two blank records will generate an error.

- **Field dependencies:** A record may require a foreign key to be present to ensure integrity of a relational database. A blank value in the foreign key field will generate an error for this integrity check.

After you have tested with blank inserts, you can modify the table to correct any problems that were revealed. To delete the blank records, you can delete all records that have a null value in a particular field. For the advertisements table, you can use this command:

```
delete advertisements where adName = null
```

The blank record test prevents many headaches if you are designing an application that uses bound controls. When a solution is being tested, the proper data is usually entered for the bound fields. However, when actual deployment occurs, critical fields may be left blank and the record insertion may generate an error. The blank record test will provide you with an idea of what to expect in advance.

Database Creators and Owners

Whenever a new database is created, the user who is logged into the SQL Server is denoted as the creator of it. The user who initially created the database object is recorded on the database server as the database owner, or *dbo*, of that object. Being the creator provides some special privileges. The owner has control to make modifications to the database structure and provide security access.

The designation of the owner of a database is not critical to the everyday operation of the database until you begin implementing security in Chapter 25. However, you will notice that many database objects are referenced with the prefix dbo. Database Owner (dbo) designation refers to who has ownership privileges to the individual objects.

Data Cleaning

One of the most critical and difficult steps when creating a database solution is *data cleaning,* the process of making sure that the data stored in the database is not faulty because of errors in it. Errors in data can range from simple entry errors to real-world problems reflected in the data.

You always begin the data cleaning process by examining the data and locating existing problems. Problems may involve either simple data errors that can be corrected using the search-and-replace function of a program such as Microsoft Access, or much more complex errors, requiring a custom batch process.

KEY ENTRY ERRORS

The most common problem of this type is capitalization error in character-based key fields. For example, you might have a key field called mytype that has three values allowed: small, medium, and large. If one of the records has a mistyped value of smalL, the equivalent operator (=) for the join will not detect a match with this field.

The best method of avoiding key entry errors is to use numeric values that are substantially faster than character equivalents. To the computer, each character is represented by a number. Therefore, to find a matching key, if the key column is 25 characters long, the searching algorithm may have to do 25 comparisons for each row to determine whether two keys match. With a single numeric key, only one number comparison is required.

If character-based keys are required, you can set up a relational rule that requires a matching primary to exist in the related table before the insertion is allowed. You will learn more about setting up this relation in Chapter 12 when you study column integrity methods.

REAL-WORLD PRACTICES CAUSING DATA PROBLEMS

Sometimes, clean data is difficult to obtain because of practices in the real world. For example, in an application I worked on in the past, employees were supposed to log their activities into several categories. When an activity began, they would start the logging, and when it ended, they were supposed to log out. They seemed to be very conscientious about this practice, so we assumed that the data was clean.

When we finally began running data summary reports, we found that the data was almost useless. Although employees were very good about logging off a task when they began another, events such as going to lunch did not make it into the log book. Because tasks lasted on average under 45 minutes, some of the log records would show inaccurately that the task actually lasted several hours.

Although the company was able to change this practice and the new data was mostly accurate, the past data was inaccurate at best.

To solve this problem, here are a few suggestions:

- ◆ **Change the practices causing the bad data:** Changing the behavior of a real-world practice is the most difficult and, at the same time, the most effective to most bad data problems. If the data being fed into the computer is inaccurate, the reporting can be wrong or, perhaps worse, misleading.

- ◆ **Compare data against valid data:** If you can retrieve valid data from some location (such as another supplier), it can help you reinterpret the inaccurate data. For example, a customer mailing list could be cross-checked against a city street and address database to determine invalid addresses.

- **Use historical data to modify and verify bad data:** Sometimes, no alternative exists to using the bad data that is supplied. In the logging example cited earlier, after the practices were changed, I had several months of accurate data. By eliminating an hour from calls that extended through midnight, the modified data matched the patterns set by the current accurate data that was available. Historical data can be used in many cases to understand a baseline pattern from which bad data can be interpreted.

The best way to catch data problems such as these is to run extensive summary tests on existing data. Most of the time, summary information makes bad data stand out and acts as a red flag to warn you of problems in the data set.

SOLUTIONS TO DATA CLEANING PROBLEMS

Unfortunately, all solutions to data cleaning problems are time-consuming. No magic wand or simple batch process is available that will quickly resolve existing problems. However, here are a few suggestions that have proven useful to me in the past to minimize the time required to solve these problems:

- **Query each table and record the number of records:** By knowing the number of records for each table, you can test the joins that you make and calculate the probable totals of some of the queries. When an error occurs, it will be much more noticeable.

- **Use the Select Into command:** In Chapter 6, you will be introduced to the `Select Into` command, which enables you to select records by a query and store them in another table. When you're trying to find problems with a join, it is often much easier to work with the result set than executing a complicated query each time.

- **Sort by nulls or extreme values:** Viewing a table sorted by values can often immediately make visible problem values, such as a time value set to 0:00, a date set to 01/01/1901, empty columns, or values dramatically different than the normal values (such as a shoe size value listed as 42).

- **Check data queries against existing reports:** By examining the information generated by the database system against preexisting reports, such as manual compilations, you can often spot problems and locate the source of the problem in order to find a remedy.

Data Concurrency and Consistency

In nearly every database application, users will be addressing a data source simultaneously. Preventing data corruption when this occurs is something that must be considered during the design phase of the database. By making certain that the concurrency problems are handled, you can ensure that the data remains consistent. MSDE was created to effectively handle these multiple-user situations.

Part 1: Access and MSDE

The MSDE/SQL Server engine can handle high-speed locking functionality to ensure that multiple users accessing the system at the same time are isolated so that users don't experience data loss, corruption, or inaccurate results.

MSDE features three types of locks that are automatically enacted by the system:

- **Shared lock:** Read-only lock that ensures that at the same time one user is reading a record, fields in the record cannot be updated. This type of lock prevents retrieval of a record that is only half updated. The shared lock on a typical server is placed on a record only for a fraction of a second.

- **Exclusive lock:** Activated when a modification is being attempted. It is the most intrusive lock, because no other locking operations can be set until the SQL `Update`, `Insert`, or `Delete` has occurred.

- **Update lock:** Reserves the update rights to a record by an operation and prevents multiple records from attempting an update simultaneously. If the update is kept open for longer than the lock timeout set on the database server (on MSDE, the default is set to -1, which represents no timeout), the update lock will be removed.

All of these locking modes are automatic and occur in the background for MSDE. In Chapter 9, you will use the Microsoft ActiveX Data Objects (ADO) to address a data source. You will notice that the Edit method must be enacted before fields may be changed in a record. Edit mode is automatically started when a new record is inserted. The Edit method enables an update lock on MSDE. The exclusive lock is used when the Update method is called to write the data into the database.

Concurrency settings may be changed on MSDE manually by executing system-stored procedures, but this is not recommended. MSDE/SQL Server has been optimized for multiple users, so the default settings are configured for optimal performance. Locking behavior is negotiated between the database server (MSDE) and the accessing middleware (ADO), so changes to the MSDE system will complicate this interaction. It is best to change the locking setting for individual client access through ADO.

As you become more familiar with database locking, you will see that proper design around locking is critical to an effective database solution. How simultaneous changes will occur and how data collisions will be handled need to be considered early if the application will be used by many people.

Normalization

Database normalization is the process of optimizing where the columns holding data are located among the various tables of a database. This means that each table consists of only the fields that are related to that table. The process of normalization seeks to minimize duplication of data. After a database has been normalized, a set of tables will have been organized to enable the most effective searching and collating of the stored data.

As a guide to proper normalization, the database community has created three normal forms:

- **First normal form:** Eliminates repeating columns and moves columns holding the same type of information to their own table
- **Second normal form:** All columns must be dependent on the primary key
- **Third normal form:** Removes all columns dependent on another key

Each form is progressively more stringent and builds on the one before it. Therefore, a database compliant with the third normal form is also compliant with the first and second forms. Normalization usually is not a one-shot process. The integration of tables must be examined several times in light of the final solution. Figure 4-1 shows the typical cycle of performing the normalization process.

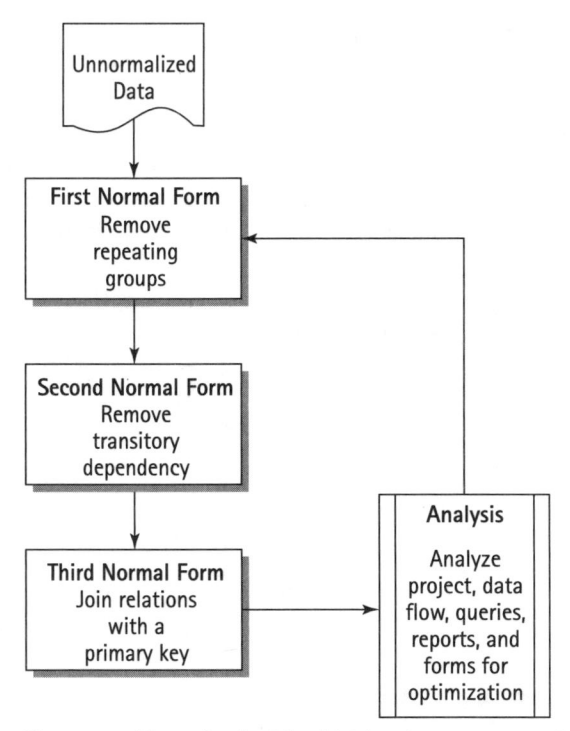

Figure 4-1: Normalization should take place over several cycles as deployment decisions are made.

Part I: Access and MSDE

When designing a database from scratch, it is usually a good idea to list all of the fields that you think will be needed for the application. After the list is complete, you can decide how the tables can be organized based on the three normal forms.

First Normal Form

The first normal form is meant to eliminate duplication within each table so that the data remains cleaner. For example, if a table for contact information has four columns to hold four different addresses (for example, address1, address2, address3, and address4), the same type of information is duplicated across four different fields. If a fifth address is needed for a contact, another column has to be added to the whole table.

To comply with the first normal form, another table should be created to specifically hold addresses. Rows in the Addresses table could contain a foreign key that relates them to individual records in the Contacts table. Having the related Addresses table enables the application to accept as many or as few addresses for each contact as necessary.

The following are the rules for database compliance with the first normal form:

- Eliminate repeating columns from each table
- Create a separate table for related data
- Create a unique key for each table

Figure 4-2 shows a table with several duplicate columns, and how it is separated into two related tables when the table is normalized to remove the field duplication.

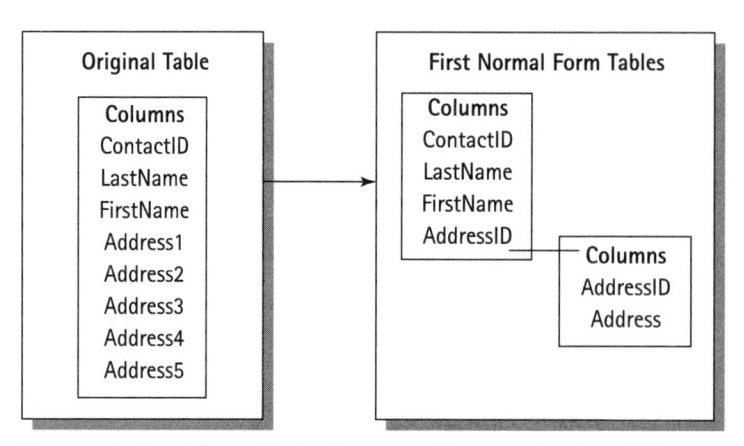

```
Original Table                    First Normal Form Tables
  Columns                            Columns
  ContactID                          ContactID
  LastName                           LastName
  FirstName             ───▶         FirstName
  Address1                           AddressID
  Address2                                          Columns
  Address3                                          AddressID
  Address4                                          Address
  Address5
```

Figure 4-2: Complying with the first normal form may involve shifting fields to a related table.

Second Normal Form

The second normal form assures that all of the columns within the table are dependent on the key field. This normal form eliminates extraneous information from a table where it does not belong.

For example, a Contacts table might have a column that holds a credit rating for the employee of the contact. Although this may affect how the contact is handled, it does not belong in the contact table because it is not dependent on the primary key of that table. Instead, this type of information would be placed in a table related to suppliers.

The following are the rules for database compliance with the second normal form:

- Create separate tables for values that apply to multiple records
- Place a foreign key in the table for relation to the table that holds the primary key

Third Normal Form

The third normal form attempts to make certain that data from related tables is not placed in the primary table. The following is the rule for the third normal form:

- Eliminate all fields that do not depend on the primary key of the table

This form is perhaps the most challenging to adopt in many database solutions. In an invoice table, you might place a column that holds the shipping address of the customer. This same address information may already be in a table holding all of the customer information.

Because the invoice will already have a foreign key referencing the complete customer record, placing the address in the invoice table will place a column whose information is dependent not on the primary key or information in the invoice, but rather on the foreign key specifying the customer. A change to the customer address would render the address stored in the invoice table invalid.

In most cases, the only reason to violate the third normal form is to preserve historical information. In an invoice system, it is common to store the invoice total rather than to simply rely on the prices of individual items to properly total to match the actual amount paid. If the prices on items change, the invoice will have the historically valid data for the amounts actually used in the transaction.

A well-designed database typically satisfies the requirements for all three normal forms. Normalization promotes a greater number of tables with each table having an explicit functional focus.

> **TIP:** When normalizing a database, try to consider how the tables will be used for data insertion, querying, and so on. Sometimes, the normalization rules indicate that a related table should be created, even though creating the related table may substantially complicate the solution and the queries that are needed, without providing any apparent benefits. Keep in mind that you don't necessarily have to follow the normalization rules explicitly. The normal forms are merely guidelines to help you build a better solution; they aren't dogma that must be followed no matter what the real-world situation may be.

Denormalization

When creating a database from scratch, you can decide how the table will be normalized. Modifying an existing system, however, may require you to rework the existing database schema. This process may involve merging a related table into a central table to optimize design and performance. The process of reversing the normalization breakdown is called *denormalization*.

The process of denormalization usually occurs for one of the following reasons:

- **Greater than four-way joins:** When more than four joins are required for a query, you should reexamine your data model. If common joins can be minimized by reorganization, it may help performance.

- **Data summarization speeds queries:** Time-intensive operations, such as aggregate queries (averages and sums, for example), should be examined in light of static tables. Some data tables seldom change, and a denormalized field holding common aggregate summaries can minimize query times.

- **Separate high- and low-access data:** In some applications, only one column value needs to be retrieved from a related table causing an extra join. Placing the value (or a duplicate of the value) in a table further up the join path can significantly increase performance.

If you do undertake the process of denormalization, be sure to run some initial tests on the intended new design. Sometimes, a query that seemingly would be much faster after denormalization is in fact slower because the old design takes advantage of structural optimization inherent in the MSDE engine. Denormalization can also increase speeds in some areas and slow down speeds in other areas. For example, to keep a denormalized summary table, you need triggers or some other update mechanism to keep the data up to date. The queries are faster, but the data entry just got slower. Therefore, testing after denormalization is critical to understanding the effects of the new implementation.

Summary

The design of the database is critical to building an effective system. After data is entered into tables, modification of the structure can be very difficult. Therefore, time spent up front examining structures and validating data can provide substantial long-term benefits. In this chapter you covered the following:

- **Testing table definitions:** Inserting two blank records into a new table can help you to test for proper default value settings, foreign key requirements, and invalid default values. Using the SQL `Delete` command with a `Where` clause that checks for null values can be used to eliminate blank rows.

- **System data types:** The common data types for a database are defined by the system. For MSDE, system data types include integer, char, varchar, text, binary, image, and others.

- **User-defined data types:** By setting up a user-defined data type, you can limit the data that can be entered into a table without having to provide rules and triggers to do the data checking.

- **Database concurrency:** Locking methods of the MSDE/SQL Server engine can ensure that multiple simultaneous users can address a single data source without corrupting the database.

- **Normalization:** The process of structuring the database schema to minimize duplication of information and maximize proper column organization is called normalization. Proper normalization is used to effectively define and organize related tables.

Chapter 5

The Basics of the SQL Language

IN THIS CHAPTER

- SQL queries and `Select` statements
- `Insert Into` statements
- `Update` statements
- `Delete` statements
- Beyond the basics

THE STRUCTURED QUERY LANGUAGE (SQL) was invented by IBM in the 1970s to provide a standard method of interacting with a database. Since its inception, SQL has grown to be the industry standard for every major database vendor and is now included in nearly every desktop database and mainframe database server.

The power of SQL comes from the flexibility it achieves with only a handful of commands. The version of SQL included with MSDE is far more robust than the one available through Microsoft Access.

SQL is a results language rather than a procedural language (such as Visual Basic or C++). In SQL, a request is issued to the database engine. The engine itself determines how best to answer the request. This process contrasts to a procedural language, in which each step-by-step instruction must direct the computer how to complete a task.

By using this method of requesting a result set, when a database or the database engine itself is optimized, the queries will automatically execute faster. Additionally, the results language implementation enables the SQL language to be much more broadly implemented on various platforms, lessening the traditional cross-platform compatibility issues encountered with procedural languages.

The core command of the SQL language is the `Select` statement. It allows a query to be issued to the engine that can return a result data set.

SQL Queries and Select Statements

The SQL `Select` statement is used to execute a query on a database engine. A straightforward command such as the SQL `Select` statement can accomplish a tremendous number of tasks, including the following:

- Execute a query and return a resultant recordset
- Match records between two or more tables and return the set
- Combine two or more data sets
- Perform calculations on column data
- Sort or group data

The simplest SQL statement would return all the columns of all of the rows in a table. For the Northwind database, it would look like this:

```
select * from customers
```

Beyond this simple query, tremendously complex queries can return almost any perspective and presentation of the data being queried.

Using Microsoft Query

All of the example queries in this chapter can be sent for data retrieval against any MSDE server that contains the Northwind database. In Chapter 1, you first used Microsoft Query to create a simple table, insert a record or two, and query that table. In this chapter, you can execute many of the queries by creating a data source that points to the Northwind database.

To use Microsoft Query to return all the rows in the customers table, follow these steps.

1. Execute the Microsoft Query application.
2. Select New from the File menu.
3. Double-click the <New Data Source> option in the Databases list. The new data source will use the Northwind database as the default database to be accessed.
4. Set the Name of the data source to **dsnNorthwind** and select the driver type as SQL Server in the driver combo box.
5. Click the Connect button to get to the window where the connection settings of the data source are configured.

6. Select the (local) option in the Server combo box. If your MSDE server is located on a remote machine, you may enter the IP address or the machine name to enable MS Query to address the intended database server.

7. Type sa in the Login ID, and leave the password blank. If you have configured the sa password, enter it into the Password text box.

8. Click the Options button to expand the window to show the Default Database selection. It is within the extra options that the database will be specified that the connection will use upon first opening a session.

9. Select the NorthwindSQL database from the combo box (see Figure 5-1).

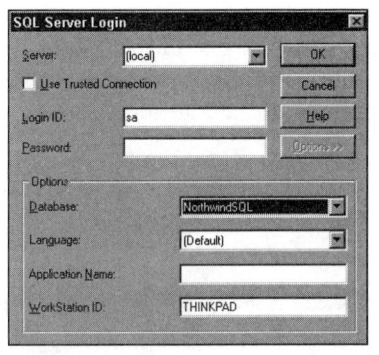

Figure 5-1: Configure the MSDE login for the sa account and the Northwind SQL data source.

10. Click OK to accept these settings. The MSDE login account settings should be complete.

11. Click OK in the Create New Data Source window. The system will create the new data source, and the listing of the dsnNorthwind item should now appear in the Databases list box.

12. Select the dsnNorthwind item and click OK. The Query Wizard window now is displayed that enables you to first configure the query to be used. After the initial query is created, you can freely modify the SQL code for that query to alter what data will be returned. First, however, you need to create a simple query that will be the foundation of later tests.

13. From the list of available columns and tables, select the customers table in the list and click the right arrow (>) to transfer the columns of the table for use by the query. All the columns of the customers table should transfer to the list of columns for the current query (see Figure 5-2).

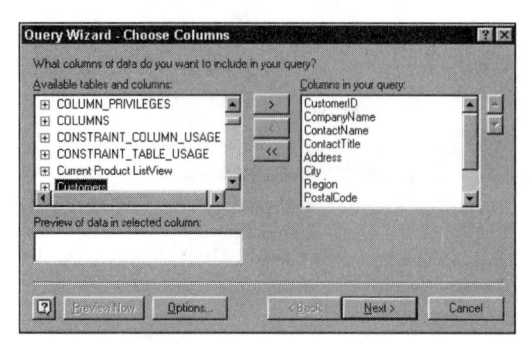

Figure 5-2: Clicking the right arrow adds all the columns of the customers table to be included in your current query.

14. Click the Next button twice to advance to the end of the wizard. You don't need to alter any settings, such as the sort order, because all modification you make in this chapter will be directly to the SQL code.

15. Click the Finish button. The query will be displayed in the Query from dsnNorthwind window (see Figure 5-3). All of the records available in the customers table will be displayed in row-and-column format.

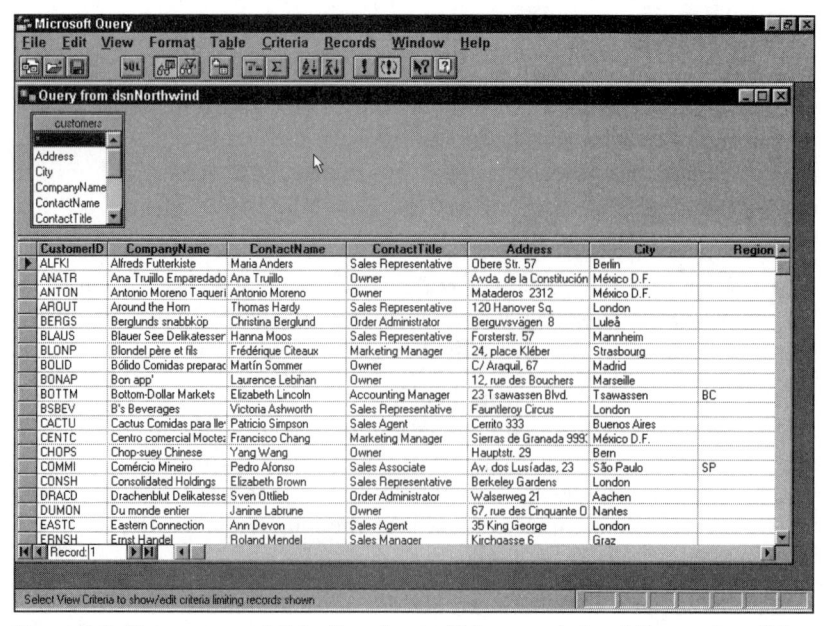

Figure 5-3: The query created by the wizard will be executed and the results will be displayed in the MS Query window.

16. Under the View menu, select the SQL option. This option displays the text box that contains the actual query code used to return the data for the query window, which should look like this:

    ```
    SELECT Customers.CustomerID, Customers.CompanyName,
    Customers.ContactName, Customers.ContactTitle,
    Customers.Address, Customers.City, Customers.Region,
    Customers.PostalCode, Customers.Country, Customers.Phone,
    Customers.Fax
    FROM NorthwindSQL.dbo.Customers Customers
    ```

17. Enter the following code in the SQL statement text box:

    ```
    select * from customers
    ```

18. Click OK to accept the code changes. The SQL code will be instantly executed against the MSDE server, and the new results of the query will be displayed in the data grid in the window.

You can see that nothing has changed in the data grid after you modified the SQL code. The new query you entered is essentially the same query generated by the wizard, only simplified. Therefore, no changes occurred in the data set that was returned. For the other query examples in this chapter, you can use the SQL window to alter the query that is executed against the Northwind database.

Select Clause

The primary keyword in the SQL language is the `Select` keyword. This keyword defines the `Select` clause, which is used to specify that a query operation is to be executed by the SQL code, as opposed to table creation, record insertion, or other available SQL operations.

The basic syntax of the `Select` keyword looks like this:

```
Select [column names] From [source tables] Where [criteria]
```

The column names can be specified in a list, each separated by a comma, or all the columns of the table may be requested by using an asterisk. The `From` keyword enables you to select the tables from which the data will be loaded. The `Where` keyword is optional and enables you to specify criteria that must be met for each row to be included in the returned recordset. If the `Where` clause of the `Select` keyword is not included, all rows from the source tables are returned.

When SQL code is sent to the MSDE engine, spaces are used to separate commands, much like normal language coding. For database objects (such as table names or column names) that have one or more spaces in the name itself (for example, the Order Details table), square brackets, [], may be used to enclose the name. Passing the name of the details table, for example, only requires including the [Order Details] text in your code.

To select columns from multiple tables, you can specify a list of tables separated by commas, such as this query that requests all the columns from two tables:

```
Select * From customers, employees
```

Using the asterisk will return the columns listed in the order that they were created in each table. To specify the order of the columns returned in the result set, you need to design the query to include the column list in the desired order.

When a `Where` clause isn't included for a query that references multiple tables, the result set returned is known as a *Cartesian product*. The number of rows returned by this type of a query, such as the preceding one that references both the customers and employees tables, is the number of rows in one table multiplied by the number of tables in the second.

> **TIP** In a Cartesian product result set, you might have a result set with many columns, with most of the columns containing null values. For example, if you were to request a query with all of the columns of the customers table (11 columns and 91 rows) and another table with 4 columns and 10 rows, the returned data set would have the product of the available rows. That would mean that the resultant data set would have 910 rows with 15 columns. In the returned set, the columns for the first records would contain nulls values.

To query the customers table of the Northwind database to retrieve the column contactname and the column companyname, in that order, a query such as this example may be used:

```
Select contactname, companyname From customers
```

To change the presentation of the returned data set, an alias may be assigned for each named column. The *alias* of a column sets the name used to address the column, and also determines how the column appears in the results presentation. For example,

```
Select contactname As [Contact Name] From customers
```

This query will display the contactname field with proper spacing and capitalization for the viewer of the set. The `As` keyword is optional, and the query will operate in the same manner if this keyword is omitted.

> **Note:** The `As` keyword is incorporated in new (SQL Server 6.5 or greater) versions of the SQL Server engine to provide compatibility with Access. If you use a data source that has an older version of the engine, simply omit the `As` keyword, and the alias will work properly. The equal (=) operator was supported in these versions instead of the `As` keyword (for example, Select contactname = [Contact Name] From customers), but it is no longer available in current MSDE/SQL Server versions. Therefore, if you see older code using this convention, eliminate the equal operator, and the code will function on newer versions.

With multiple tables, if you don't want all the columns to appear, you can specify particular fields with the dot (.) keyword. For example:

```
Select customers.contactname, employees.eid From customers, employees
```

If the two tables have a column that shares the same name, the query requires you to choose the table from which to retrieve the data. The query generates an error if the reference is ambiguous. Ideally, if two tables contain the same field name, the value contained in the column will be identical for a particular row if the tables are related.

Each table in the `From` clause may also be given an alias, much like the alias for a column name. For example:

```
Select * From customers as a, employees as b
```

The aliases can be used in the `Select` clause (as well as in other clauses, such as the `Order By`) to specify columns. For example:

```
Select a.lastname, b.employeeid From customers as a, employees as b
```

Aliases are also useful when two tables have a column with the same name, but the values contained in the column are different. For example:

```
Select a.address as [Home Address], b.address as [Work Address] From customers as a, employees as b
```

Mathematical Operators

All of the common mathematical operators are available and may be used within the column selection and even within the criteria selection clause (known as the `Where` clause). Table 5-1 contains the operators supported by the MSDE engine.

TABLE 5-1 OPERATORS SUPPORTED BY MSDE

Operator	Description
+	Addition
-	Subtraction
*	Multiplication
/	Division
%	Modulo (returns the integer remainder of a division)
&	Bitwise And
|	Bitwise Or
^	Bitwise Exclusive Or
~	Bitwise Not

For example, the multiplication operator can be used in the Northwind order details table like this:

```
Select orderid, quantity * unitprice As [Total Price]
   From [Order Details]
```

The result set will contain the general total (not including tax, shipping, and so forth) of each order item in the table. The precedence in MSDE for the mathematical operators is as follows:

multiplication, then division, then modulo, then addition and subtraction

> **NOTE** A multiplication expression — as well as other math operations, such as addition and subtraction — that includes a null value will always return a null value as the result. Therefore, 2 * null = null. The best way to work around this limitation if one of your numeric columns accepts nulls is to use the Transact-SQL `IsNull` statement. On a field that may have a null value, such as quantity, this function can provide a replacement value. For example, the code `IsNull(quantity, 0)` will return the quantity value if it is non-null. If a null value is found in the column, the number zero (0) will be returned instead.

To eliminate duplicate rows in the returned recordset, you can use the `Distinct` keyword. This keyword is used in the list of columns, so returning only a single record for each distinct region could be accomplished like this:

```
Select companyname, contactname, Distinct region From customer
```

The query will return only the first record it encounters with each distinct region.

The `From` clause in the examples so far has only specified tables to access. The `Select` statement can use the `From` clause to address tables in a different database or view. With the database name qualifier, a `From` clause would appear like this:

```
Select * From NorthwindSQL..customers
```

The statement could just as easily be used in multiple tables in multiple databases, like this:

```
Select * From NorthwindSQL..customers, master.sysconfigures
```

Although this ability exists, you should try to avoid using it except in special circumstances where the tables cannot coexist in the same database. Cross-database queries cannot use index optimization, and they put a greater strain on the database engine.

Where Clause

The `Where` clause enables you to specify criteria that determines the records to be returned in the result set. It can be used to compare column values to constants, execute mathematical operations, or provide join relations among one or more tables. The `Where` clause used by the `Select` statement is used with the same conventions for the `Update` and `Delete` commands.

The simplest form of the `Where` clause does a comparison between the data stored in a column value and a constant value. For example,

```
Select * From customers Where customerid = 'ALFKI'
```

This query returns a single row for the customer record that has a customerid that is equal to ALFKI. Other comparison operators could have been used instead of the equivalence (=) operator.

COMPARISON OPERATORS

The `Where` clause, to return a subset of the complete data set that is available, needs to isolate certain data based on criteria. The comparison operators can compare a column value either against a constant or to a different field. In Table 5-2, you can see a list of the comparison operators supported on the MSDE database server. The mathematical operators can perform basic math functions to constants, column values, and Transact-SQL variables.

TABLE 5-2 COMPARISON OPERATORS SUPPORTED ON THE MSDE DATABASE SERVER

Operator	Description
=	Equivalent
>	Greater than
<	Less than
>=	Greater than or equal to
<=	Less than or equal to
!=	Not equal
!>	Not greater than
!<	Not less than

You can use the equivalent (=) operator and the not equal (!=) operator on strings as well as on numeric values.

In addition to the comparison symbols, the Between keyword tests a value between a minimum and maximum value. The Between operator is *inclusive,* which means that it includes the minimum and maximum values for the comparison. The keyword Between may be used for numeric comparisons, like this:

```
Select * From [Order Details] Where quantity Between 1 And 10
```

In this comparison, the quantity column value is tested to be both greater than or equal to 1 and less than or equal to 10. Using symbol operators, this comparison would look like this:

```
quantity >= 1 And quantity <= 10
```

Each of the comparison operators returns either a true or false value depending on the result of the comparison. With the Boolean operators, the true/false results of several comparisons can be used together.

BOOLEAN OPERATORS

You can combine comparisons within a Select statement by using the Boolean operators. Commonly used Boolean operators (such as And, Or, and so on — as shown in Table 5-3) can provide logical integration of multiple Boolean values (True/False, Yes/No, 1/0) generated as a result of other comparisons.

TABLE 5-3 BOOLEAN OPERATORS

Operator	Description
And	For a true result, both a and b must be true: a < 5 And b > 10
Or	For a true result, either a or b must be true: a < 5 Or b > 10
Not	For a true result, a must be false: Not a = 5

These operators are used to combine two or more different comparisons. The And operator can specify that the only records returned must meet two or more specified conditions, such as a city and state search in the Northwind customers table:

```
Select * From customers Where region = 'OR' And city = 'Eugene'
```

The Boolean operators, like mathematical expressions, can be used with parentheses to give certain comparisons precedence. To require that returned rows are customers in the state of Oregon, but may be either of two cities, a query like this can be used:

```
Select * From customers Where region = 'OR' And (city = 'Eugene' Or city = 'Portland')
```

This query will return more records than the one that includes only customers from Eugene.

The In keyword can be used as a shortcut to doing numerous equivalence checks. By using the In keyword, you can create a list of values that the column value will be checked against. If it matches any of the values supplied in the In list, a true Boolean value is returned. To check against a list of possible cities, you could use a query like this:

```
Select * From customers Where region = 'OR' And city In
{'Eugene','Portland'}
```

You will use the In keyword for many types of comparisons, as well as for more complicated operations, such as nested queries.

LIKE OPERATOR

So far, you've seen only the mathematical comparison operators (such as =, <, and >) that are used for column evaluation. SQL also includes a powerful operator called Like that is used for text comparisons. In contrast to using the equivalence (=) operator for text comparisons, the Like operator allows evaluations to ignore the case of the values (making the search case-insensitive), and also provides wildcard characters for pattern matching.

For example, if the column customerid held the value ALFKI, the following query would return no records:

```
Select * From customers Where customerid = 'alfki'
```

Because the text value specified in the Where clause is sent to the query in lowercase, and the equivalence operator looks for an exact value match, the record would not be found. Using the Like statement, the same query would return the single record with the ALFKI customerid:

```
Select * From customers Where customerid Like 'alfki'
```

Because the Like command must perform more processing than the equivalence operator, it may be slower to execute your query. In exchange for the speed penalties, the Like command is much more powerful. Wildcard characters can be used in the search value passed to the Like operator. One wildcard character is the percent (%) sign, which may be used in a text expression like this:

```
Select * From customers Where contactname Like 'S%'
```

This query returns all the records where the contactname column value begins with the letter S, regardless of whether the letter S is upper- or lowercase.

> **NOTE** If you have been using Access, you might notice that the string wildcard symbol on MSDE is different from the one used on normal Access queries. Access uses the asterisk (*) character to provide wildcards in a string query. On MSDE and SQL Server, the percent (%) sign is used. On other database servers (such as Oracle), the asterisk is used like the one in Access. This implementation detail is but one of the simple inconsistencies you will find if you have to convert from one SQL implementation to another.

Wildcard characters may also be used to fill in the blanks when more than a single character of the desired text is known. A wildcard character may be placed anywhere within a string to provide general character filtering, like this:

```
Select * From customers Where contactname Like 'S%R'
```

This query returns a data set similar to the one with the S wildcard, but it also requires that the column value end with the letter R. For the Northwind database, only a single row, the contact named Simon Crowther, should fit this criteria. Therefore, the recordset returned by this query should contain a single name.

Another type of wildcard character is the underscore (_), which provides a single-character wildcard. This type of wildcard is useful when searching for a few values within a known pattern (such as a partial license plate number) or data that might contain entry errors. For example, to use it to locate customers likely named Dan, Manuel, or something similar, you could use a query like this:

`Select * From customers Where contactname Like '_AN___ %'`

This query returns any records in which the second and third letters are *A* and *N*, respectively, followed by three other letters and a space. This letter combination specifies a first name that is five characters long, where two letters are known. The space followed by the percent sign specifies the length of the first name, while accepting any available last name. The two wildcards can be combined more closely in a query statement such as this:

`Select * From customers Where contactname Like '_AN%'`

Such a query might be particularly useful in a table where data entries might only partially follow a particular pattern. The addition of the percent sign could be used to catch a last-name entry when searching for the name *Smith*, and would return entries such as *Smith, Jr.*

Order By Clause

To make the query return the results in a sorted order, you need to use the `Order By` clause. With this clause, you can specify the field or fields that should be used for the sort, as well as the direction (ascending or descending) that you want the data returned in:

`Select * From customers Order By companyname`

You can use multiple columns to sort by, and the order in which they appear in the `Order By` clause is the precedence each column will take in the final sort. In this query, the titles of the contact will be the primary sort column:

`Select * From customers Order By ContactTitle, contactname, zip`

The order of the rows may also be explicitly specified to occur in ascending (A to Z) or descending (Z to A) order. The keywords for ascending (`Asc`) and descending (`Desc`) are present after the column name, such as this:

`Select * From customers Order By ContactTitle Desc, contactname Asc`

The recordset returned by this query will have all of the contact titles listed in descending order, with the contacts within the companies listed in ascending order.

Insert Into Statements

The `Insert Into` command instructs MSDE to create a new record. Values to be stored in the record columns for that row can be passed in the `Insert`. All of the values that are not included insert a null value unless a default for the column is set.

```
Insert Into customers (customerid, companyname) Values
   ('MYCO1', 'My Company, Inc.')
```

When you execute this SQL code, if the insert occurred properly, you will be notified that one record was affected. The affected row is the new record that was just inserted into the table. The `Into` keyword is optional on the MSDE server and can be excluded like this:

```
Insert customers (customerid, companyname) Values
   ('MYCO2', 'My Company Again, Inc.')
```

If you know the ordinal (numbered) order of the columns in the table, you can exclude the column list for the `Insert` command, as follows:

```
Insert customers Values ('MYCO3', 'My Real Company, Inc.')
```

> **NOTE:** If you have created any relations in the Database Diagram, the referential integrity of these relations will be enforced. The existing relation will require that the foreign key columns specified in the `Insert` statement be filled with valid references to records in the related table. If the foreign key columns are empty or the values do not relate to an existing record, an error will be generated and the insert will not take place.

Update Statements

Updating records is handled quite a bit differently from inserting records. Instead of passing a list of values followed by a list of columns, the `Update` statement uses the equal (=) operator to directly set each column value:

```
Update customers Set contactname = 'Jon Smith'
```

This seemingly simple command actually changes all of the records in the table to have a contactname column value of the name 'Jon Smith'. To specify exactly which record or records should be altered, you need to add a `Where` clause to the update. For example,

```
Update customers Set lastname = 'Jon Smith' Where
    CustomerID = 'AKLIU'
```

This SQL code would change the row that had a column value of AKLIU to reflect the new contact name setting. The `Where` command can specify the primary key field to make sure that only a single record in the table is altered.

> **Note:** As with many SQL statements, more than one method of using the `Update` command is available to accomplish the same end result. The `Update` command can use the `From` clause to specify the table. The first example could be accomplished with the following statement: `Update contactname = 'Jon Smith' From customers`. This syntax more nearly resembles the familiar syntax used for the `Select` statement.

Delete Statements

The `Delete` statement, like the `Update` statement, provides a method of quickly changing numerous rows. This process can be very dangerous, and an erroneous `Delete` execution can quickly eliminate large quantities of data. *Do not execute any of these commands* unless you have a convenient backup. The records will be removed, and you will have to restore the tables to use further examples.

To delete all the records in a table, you could use a command like this:

```
Delete customers
```

To make it more specific, you would need to add a `Where` clause, like this:

```
Delete customers Where fax Is Null
```

The `Is` keyword ensures that the column holds a null value and deletes only those rows that meet this criteria (in the Northwind table, 23 rows have a null value for a fax). If you use the equivalent (=) operator for the null value testing, no rows will be deleted, because the `Is` operator must identify nulls.

Although the `Insert`, `Update`, and `Delete` commands can be useful in certain instances (such as testing a new table from the SQL Query Analyzer), you usually will use another method, such as ADO for database management. In contrast to the `Select` statement that is used extensively even through ADO, these statements are more cumbersome than object methods and are rarely used directly through ADO, ODBC, or other data access middleware.

The Update and Delete commands are primarily useful for bulk operations. When numerous records with specific criteria need to be altered or deleted, these commands can be much more useful and provide faster execution on MSDE than is possible by using individual record modification. A single command can be executed against the database server, instead of sending a command for each record that needs to be changed.

Beyond the Basics

In addition to the standard operators and statements defined by the SQL-92 standard, Microsoft has dramatically extended the power and flexibility of SQL by adding several custom commands. These commands include some formatting statements, the ability to use triggers and stored procedures, and a great number of built-in stored procedures available to the system.

In Chapter 6, you will learn more comprehensive options that are available through SQL for the Select statement, including grouping, data transfer, and more. Although almost all the SQL code appearing in this chapter can be used directly on the Microsoft Access JET engine, by the time you begin building stored procedures in Chapter 7, the code will apply almost exclusively to the capabilities available to the MSDE engine.

Summary

A full implementation of the SQL language is built into MSDE and used for most database interaction. Through SQL commands, a program can add new records, update or delete existing records, and query the available data. In this chapter, you covered the following:

- ♦ **Structured Query Language (SQL):** Originally invented by IBM, SQL has become the de facto standard method of addressing a relational database. The version of SQL included in MSDE together with the Microsoft custom extensions make up the implementation known as Transact-SQL.

- ♦ **Select command:** Returns a recordset based on the criteria specified in the statement; can be used to select particular columns, draw data from multiple tables, specify recordset criteria, assign aliases to table and column names, and more.

- **Insert command:** Adds a new row to the specified table and inserts any values passed to it into that row. Any column values not explicitly specified are placed with a null value or a default value (if one has been specified).

- **Update command:** Updates one or more records, depending on the criteria specified in the Where clause of the update.

- **Delete command:** Used to eliminate records; can be used for batch deletions of all records in a table or records that match a certain criteria that's specified through a Where clause.

Chapter 6

Advanced SQL

IN THIS CHAPTER

- Mastering SQL
- Using aggregate functions
- Querying with the `Union` keyword
- Using multiquery `Select` statements
- Transfering data with the `Select Into` statement
- Implementing advanced joins
- Commenting SQL code

You've learned the basics of using the SQL language with the MSDE database server. The language features you've used so far can also be used to directly code your queries for Microsoft Access. Refining your query skills and taking advantage of the advanced SQL language features is where your next challenges begin. Learning to use all of the features of the SQL language is key to professionally developing applications with MSDE.

Although many of the necessary results in an application can be returned by a simple query, addressing related tables and generating complex result sets are very common tasks that often require advanced use of SQL to properly address the problem. Understanding how complex SQL functions are used will help you regardless of whether you generate SQL code by hand or through a variety of graphical interface tools available for use with MSDE.

Mastering SQL

A common difference between an advanced SQL developer and someone new to the art of SQL programming is demonstrated by the amount of postprocessing that must be done after the results of the query have been returned. Beginners often create applications that do a great deal of postprocessing to the recordset on the client. An accomplished developer can precisely code the SQL query to return the result set in almost any form needed, without requiring additional operations, such as formatting, aggregation, and data grouping, to be performed on the client. By making the server handle most of the query processing, the level of adjustment required to the returned results is minimized.

The reason for favoring server-side code is clear: the more comprehensive the processing on the server is, the more scalable the final application will be. To increase the productivity of the application, you can perform a server upgrade, which will dramatically increase the efficiency for all the client machines addressing it. Because you are developing with the MSDE engine, scalability is likely to be an important concern in your current or future projects. An optimized and refined use of the SQL capabilities of MSDE will maximize the degree and effectiveness of scaling any database solution.

As you learn how to construct an advanced SQL-based solution, you will begin to understand how much more powerful the MSDE engine is than a database engine such as the Access JET engine. An MSDE server can be used to create and implement user-defined data types, compile and store procedures, respond to trigger events, and handle other comprehensive database functions that are foreign to the Access engine.

Although stored procedures, one of the key benefits of using a database server, are covered extensively in Chapter 7, a great many other functions in SQL are critical to your understanding. The additional clauses to the Select statement alone are important to enabling database server functionality.

Advanced SQL commands augment the SQL language to allow for more than a simple query. These commands may be used for such operations as these:

- Providing aggregate functions, such as Sum and Average, that are executed on the database server to return summary information

- Querying a table and inserting the results into another table

- Executing a subquery that supplies values to the primary query

- Grouping records based on column values

- Allowing the Union command to be used to combine two or more result sets that are returned as a single recordset

- Creating advanced joins for a variety of relations

- Commenting the SQL code for views and stored procedures, to provide explanations to yourself and other developers

You will most likely need to use all of these advanced functions over the course of several database projects. Take the time to review them closely. Understanding what each function is capable of doing is extremely useful when you encounter a problem. Like knowing what tools you have available in a tool chest, one of these SQL capabilities will come to mind as the right one to solve the database problems you encounter.

Aggregate Functions

Through the use of SQL, you have been able to create queries that request data rows to be returned in the form of a recordset. The rows held in the recordset have exactly reflected the information contained in individual records, even if the Where statement was used to select specifically which records would be included. In other words, information for a single record was returned as a single row.

Often, however, the application you are creating will need summary information from the recordset rather than individual record information. Common desired results include averages of column data, sums of numeric columns, or a simple count of the number of records that fit the criteria described in the Where clause.

Summary functions, when done on the client as a postprocessing operation, have many disadvantages. The processing tends to be slower, all of the data must be transmitted over the network when only the summary information is desired, and the post-processing can entail complicated client-side code. For these reasons, it would be much better if the summary processing could occur on the server, with only the final results transmitted to the client.

Several functions are provided in the SQL language to combine the results of many rows for summary and grouping purposes. The most common functions enable you to create a sum or average or find the minimum or maximum of the values in a numeric column. These functions in the SQL language are known as *aggregate functions*.

The simplest example of an aggregate function is the Count function. Count will not check the values of the specified column, but will instead total the number of rows in the returned recordset and place it in the column value. For example, to obtain the number of total rows in the customers table, you could execute a query like this:

```
Select Count(*) As RecCount From customers
```

The result set will appear as follows:

<u>RecCount</u>
91

In this case, counting of all the columns is specified. A much more common practice – because the count for all columns is the same – is to request a single column with the count using a query such as this:

```
Select Count(contactname) As [Total Records] From customers
```

> **NOTE:** In this case, the Count value returned by this single column aggregate is the same as the number returned by an aggregate of all columns (for example, the previous * query). However, if one of the rows were to contain a null value in the contactName column, that row would not be counted in the contactName aggregate query. Aggregate functions ignore the rows that contain null values.

The Count function is the simplest aggregate, because it does not actually interact with any of the actual column values of the table. To retrieve an average of all of the values in a particular column, you could use a query like this:

```
Select Avg(UnitPrice) As [Average Cost] From [Order Details]
```

The result set will appear as follows:

Average Cost
$26.22

Most of the other aggregate functions operate in exactly the same manner. Table 6-1 displays a list of each of the aggregate functions and describes the use of each.

TABLE 6-1 THE SQL AGGREGATE FUNCTIONS AND A DESCRIPTION OF EACH

Function Name	Description
Sum	Sums all the values in the designated columns
Avg	Averages all the data based on the current grouping
Count	Returns the count of the number of rows in the selection
Min	Returns the minimum column value of the designated columns
Max	Returns the maximum column value of the designated columns
STDev	Returns a statistical standard deviation of the column values contained in the specified expression
STDevP	Returns a statistical standard deviation of the column values of a population sample
Grouping	Used for Cube and Rollup operations to distinguish these special uses of the null value (which means all in the context of those two operators)

Function Name	Description
Var	Returns statistical variance for the designated column values
VarP	Returns statistical population variance for the designated column values

All of these functions are part of the SQL standard and do not require the MSDE SQL language extensions (hence, the same code can be used in a Microsoft Access query). The aggregate functions provide a way of generating summary information, such as an average, from a series of column values. Executing an aggregate function often causes a returned recordset to contain only a single row if the aggregate summarizes all of the available rows in the table.

All aggregate functions except Count ignore null values. Therefore, unlike traditional mathematical operators, for which a sum of column values added to a null value would return a null, aggregate functions can ignore a null value for purposes of calculation.

> Although almost all numeric data types can be used with the aggregate functions, the Bit data type is an exception. The MSDE server will generate an error if you attempt to use an aggregate function on a Bit column.

These aggregate functions are most commonly needed to summarize a group of rows, not the entire range of rows returned by the query, as was shown in the previous examples. To group the rows, the aggregate functions are often found in the same query as a Group By clause.

The Group By Command

With aggregate functions, obtaining aggregate values on groups of items rather than on the whole data set can be extremely useful. The Group By command will group one or more rows into a single row when the values of a specified column list are identical.

Using the grouping capabilities in SQL, a query could return summary rows of an organization database that might include the following information:

- Number of customers grouped by state
- Average dollar order for each order item type

- Sum of sales on taxable and nontaxable items
- Minimum number of inventory items in each distribution location

All of these aggregates would be broken down by groups of matching column values. For example, in the Northwind database, you could construct a query like this:

```
Select ProductID, Count(ProductID) As CountOfProductID
From [Order Details] Group By ProductID
```

When executed, this query will display the number of orders that include each product type. The recordset returned will look something like this:

ProductID	CountOfProductID
1	38
2	44
3	12
4	20

The queries that are used with the Group By command can be much more complicated than the one just shown. You can use the Group By command with a Where clause, and only those results that qualify for the Where specifications will be displayed. For example, the preceding query could use a join to the Products table to display the product names instead of their identifying numbers.

A developer may also want to return all of the row groups, even if no records meet the Where criteria. The Group By All command is provided to return this summarized data. It can be used in a query like this:

```
SELECT ProductID, COUNT(ProductID) AS CountOfProductID
FROM [Order Details]
WHERE (ProductID = 1)
GROUP BY ALL ProductID
```

This query will return a row for each column that has a null value. For example, the result set would look like this:

ProductID	CountOfProductID
1	38
2	0
3	0
4	0

If any null values are found in the column list for grouping (in this case, ProductID), a null group will be included in the result set. Grouping can be done on almost any column type except text, ntext, and binary type columns.

Grouping can be processor-intensive and is best accomplished when used on fields that are already indexed within the table. Because it is used in conjunction with aggregate functions, be sure to perform speed tests in the early stages of development to make sure your queries can execute in a reasonable time.

The Having Clause

The `Having` clause is used in conjunction with aggregate functions to allow for specification much like the specification possible with the `Where` clause, only in relation to aggregate values. For example, the `Having` clause could be use to make the query return only groups of records that have more than one row available. Likewise, the `Having` clause could specify that only averages that have a value over 10 be returned. These types of specifications in relation to aggregate figures cannot be made in the `Where` clause.

By add a `Having` clause to the earlier product query, the query would display only the aggregates of those products that have occurred in over 30 orders. Such a query would look like this:

```
SELECT ProductID, Count(ProductID) AS CountOfProductID
FROM [Order Details]
GROUP BY ProductID
HAVING Count(ProductID)>30
```

The `Having` clause may be used with most data types but, like the `Where` clause, cannot be used with the text, image, and ntext data types.

> **Note:** When the `Having` clause appears in a query with the `Group All` clause, the `Having` statement overrides the `All` portion of the grouping clause.

The Compute Clauses

In addition to the aggregate functions being used to create a summary query, you can use another command to add the aggregate information to the returned results of a standard query. The `Compute` clauses are available to add summary information, such as subtotals and totals, to the result set returned by a query. These clauses are most often used to facilitate report generation. Within each clause, a standard mathematical aggregate function (such as `Sum`) can be used to return the summary data.

Two different `Compute` clauses are available:

- **Compute:** Enables you to create summary columns that can be added to a result set

- **Compute By:** Adds additional rows that contain the summary information

These two clauses may be used together in the same query statement.

All of the standard aggregate functions (Avg, Sum, Min, Max, and so forth), except the Count function, may be used with the Compute clauses. The Count function may be used with the Compute clause, but not with the Compute By clause. The Distinct keyword cannot be used with the Compute By row functions. Like the aggregate functions, null values are ignored when using the Compute and Compute By clauses.

The Compute statement can be used in a query like this:

```
SELECT ProductID, quantity
FROM [Order Details]
WHERE ProductID = 1
COMPUTE SUM(quantity)
```

This query will return the results formatted like this:

```
ProductID    quantity
1            45
1            18

1            10
1            25
1            40

             sum
             ===
             828
```

> **NOTE** The Compute and Compute By clauses can be displayed only by query tools specifically built to allow for these types of query returns. Microsoft Access views and Microsoft Query cannot display the results of these clauses. To show these results, you need to use a more advanced tool, such as SQL Query Analyzer, which is introduced in Chapter 11. The two clauses can also be configured graphically for use in Access reports. See the Compute section in the Access online help.

The In Keyword Function

For the Where clause, you can use the In keyword function to compare values in a list, which saves you from lengthy And Boolean comparisons. For example, to locate a set of order items with particular ProductIDs, a query like this can use the In keyword:

```
SELECT ProductID, quantity
FROM [Order Details]
WHERE ProductID In (1, 28,29,32)
```

This query returns all of the rows with a ProductID of 1, 28, 29, or 32. You can see how useful such a command would be for items such as lists of state or significant category codes. The In keyword can also be used to compare column values to the values returned in a subquery, which is how it's used in a later section.

The Union Keyword

Although a simple query can fill almost any individual request of conditions through the Where clause, there are often times when a single query cannot be made to return all of the desired data in a result set. The Union keyword enables you to combine multiple query result sets into a single returned recordset (see Figure 6-1).

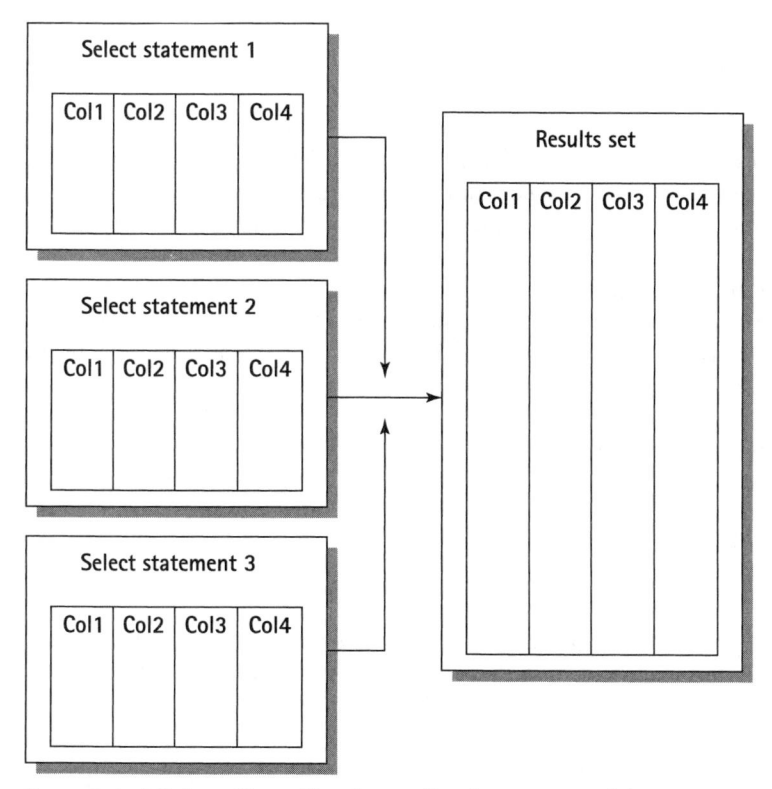

Figure 6-1: A Union will combine the results of two or more Select statements into a single returned set.

Creating SQL code that uses a union is simply a matter of creating two or more `Select` clauses and placing them in the same query, separated by the `Union` keyword. A simple union of two queries might look like this:

```
Select CompanyName, 'C' As [Relation] From customers
Union
Select CompanyName, 'S' From suppliers
```

The result set of the query would look like this:

CompanyName	Relation
Aux joyeux eccl♪siastiques	S
Bigfoot Breweries	S
Cooperativa de Quesos 'Las Cabras'	S
...	
Svensk Sj‼f‼da AB	S
Tokyo Traders	S
Zaanse Snoepfabriek	S
Rancho grande	C
Consolidated Holdings	C
Galerka del gastr%nomo	C

All the queries in the union must return the same number of columns, although the column names do not need to appear in the same order or have the same names. If the columns returned by the queries are not identical, dummy fields will have to be added.

The columns are titled with the column names specified in the first query of the `Union` group. Because the number of columns for all the unions must match, you can substitute a constant value for a column if it is not available in one of the result sets. For example,

```
SELECT CompanyName, ContactName
FROM Customers
UNION
SELECT '-',FirstName + ' ' + LastName
FROM Employees
```

This example uses a string constant to fill the missing column from the second query. The data type used by the primary column should be matched by the dummy column, so use a numeric constant for numeric column types.

> **NOTE** In Microsoft Access, when a query is created in the SQL view that implements a `Union`, editing of the query is no longer available through the graphic Query Builder window. Union queries may be edited only directly in SQL.

Within a union, the sort order of all the rows in the union is determined by the order specified (through the `Order By` statement) in the first query of the union set. If no order is set in the primary `Select` statement, the rows will be returned in the default order, usually an ascending sort of the first column value.

Except for their shared column names and sort order, the `Select` statements of a `Union` query are completely separate. They can address different tables and even different databases as long as their final results are returned in the proper number of columns and column types.

Multiquery Select Statements

Although a `Union` is used to combine two or more queries, it is possible to actually have SQL statements nested within other SQL statements. This nesting enables a primary query to use the results from another query to determine what results will be retrieved by the primary query (see Figure 6-2). The primary or outer query can have the subquery or inner query retrieve data using a completely separate `Select` statement.

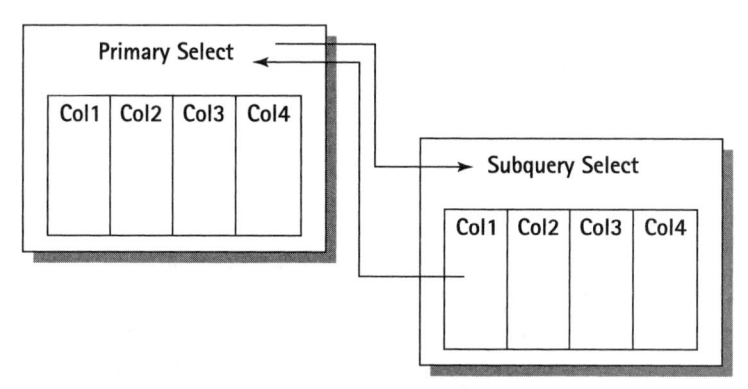

Figure 6-2: A subquery enables the subquery or inner query to supply information to the outer or primary query.

A subquery is useful for the following:

- Selecting the rows to be placed in the return data set based on information provided by the subquery
- Comparing column values of each row with the data supplied from a secondary table
- Nesting multiple queries to make category selections across many different related tables

For example, you could execute a query that returns all invoices for only those customers located in British Columbia. Because the information for the customers and the orders is located in different tables, the results of a query to select all the BC customers could be used to select order invoices from the orders table.

To use the subquery, you can add the In keyword to the Where clause, like this:

```
Select * from [Orders]
    Where CustomerID In (Select customerid From customers
        Where region = 'BC')
```

Your result set would look something like this:

OrderID	CustomerID	EmployeeID	OrderDate	RequiredDate
10389	BOTTM	4	1996-12-20 00:00:00.000	1997-01-17
10410	BOTTM	3	1997-01-10 00:00:00.000	1997-02-07
10411	BOTTM	9	1997-01-10 00:00:00.000	1997-02-07
10431	BOTTM	4	1997-01-30 00:00:00.000	1997-02-13

This subquery uses the In keyword in almost the same way it was used with the ProductID list earlier. However, this time, the list that is used by the In keyword consists of table values returned by a query.

A subquery can also be placed inside an Insert, Update, or Delete command, although it is most often used as an inner query for a primary Select outer query. The rows returned by the primary query are determined by the records returned by the inner query.

> **NOTE** In the interest of clarity, most of the examples in this section have only one nested query. The outer query will be referred to as the primary query, whereas the inner one will be identified as the subquery. In actual implementation, many nested levels of queries can be used. With these more complicated types of subqueries, an outer query and an inner query will exist at each level. In this scenario, the inner query of one level may be the outer query of the level below it. The "primary query" and "subquery" terminology is used to prevent unnecessary confusion.

Three different ways to execute a subquery are available: the In keyword, the comparison operators, and the Exists keyword. Each of these implementations can be used to generate the identical results. For many solutions, any of the subquery methods can be used if properly coded. The same query can often be created using a comparison operator with the Any, All, or Exists keyword.

Comparison for a Subquery

The easiest way to implement a subquery is the method used in the previous example. In the Where clause, one of the comparison operators (such as the equivalence (=) operator) can be used with either of the query modifiers Any or All to specify the type of comparison to be used for the subquery recordset.

The query used in the preceding section could be modified to use the Any modifier, and it would generate the same results:

```
Select * from [Orders]
   Where CustomerID = ANY (Select customerid From customers
      Where region = 'BC')
```

The All operator would be useful in this context only if the subquery would return only a single value. You would need the query to return a single comparable value in the subquery to be used effectively in this context.

The equivalence (=) operator is only one of the comparison operators that can be used in this situation. You can also use other comparisons (>, <, <=, and so forth) as well as Boolean operators to determine the qualifications of the primary rows. Using the = operator without the All or Any command means the nested subquery can return only one value, whereas the In clause allows a list of values.

Using the Exists Keyword for a Correlated Subquery

In the previous subquery examples, the database server can execute the subquery in its entirety, cache the result set, and use that for comparison with the primary query. Such a process would speed the execution of the overall query greatly and eliminate the excess work required if the subquery had to be executed for each individual row.

However, what if one of the query criteria in the subquery used a value from the current row? If the subquery referenced data from the current row of the primary query, then the subquery code would have to be executed for each row. This type of query is known as a *correlated subquery*.

A correlated subquery can be used to base the subquery on the column values of the primary query, rather than vice versa. A correlated subquery cannot be executed separately, because it needs a value provided by the rows of the primary query. The subquery is executed once per row of the primary query.

When used with the Exists keyword, the query can generate the same type of result set that has previously used the In keyword or the comparison operator. A query can reference the primary column value of the current row by specifying the named reference to the table, like this:

```
Select * from [Orders]
   Where Exists (Select * from customers where
      Orders.customerid = customerid AND region = 'BC')
```

The `Exists` subquery returns a True or False Boolean value, depending on the existence state of the subquery row. If a row exists in the subquery set, then the current row for the primary query is accepted for inclusion into the final result set to be returned to the calling program or user. Because the existence of a record is being tested, no reason really exists to specify columns in the subquery, so the asterisk (*) is typically used.

A correlated subquery (also known as a *repeating subquery*) can be used either for general query or in the `Having` clause of the primary query.

> Be aware that adding a subquery can increase the processing time required before a result set is returned. It can take far more time for a correlated query (because a search must be done on each row) than for a noncorrelated (also called *nested*) subquery that doesn't need to reference the current row data. Be sure to do testing and optimization of all of the nested queries separately before you deploy the final subquery.

Using correlated multiquery `Select` statements can simplify the amount of processing required on the client, but can also dramatically increase the processing time spent on the server. Because each row of the primary query will activate a secondary query, be careful to optimize the secondary query as much as possible. The subquery is executed once for each row of the primary query.

The `In` keyword can be used in many of the same situations as the `Exists` keyword is used. However, the `Exists` keyword usually executes more quickly, because it only needs to check for the presence of the result set.

You can also use the `Not` modifier with the `Exists` keyword to ensure that no existing records are returned by the subquery. The `Exists` keyword may not be used in a `Select` query that uses the `Into` keyword or the `Compute/Compute By` clauses.

One of the most powerful uses of the `Exists` keyword is to compare two recordsets for intersection and difference between the two result sets. The `Exists` keyword may be used to create a returned recordset that has all of the rows contained in both of two different tables or the recordset that has the rows that are different between the two tables.

Although you could generate the same results by using a certain type of join, generating a recordset containing those regions that are different from those of the suppliers would be far more difficult without the `Exists` keyword. To retrieve the recordset containing the rows that differ between the two recordsets, you could use a query like this:

```
SELECT DISTINCT region FROM customers
WHERE NOT EXISTS
    (SELECT * FROM suppliers
    WHERE customers.region = customers.region)
```

The subquery that uses the `Exists` keyword can also be processed quickly, because it isn't retrieving any data from the subquery – it merely retrieves the status of the existence of values matching the query.

The Select Into Statement

The `Select` statement can also be used to select a batch of records, create a duplicate table, and then insert the records into this table. The `Into` statement appears directly after the column list and determines the destination of the query values. For example,

```
Select * Into customersDup From customers
```

This example creates a new table called customersDup that is a complete duplicate of the customers table and all of its rows. To select specific columns and rows to be inserted, you simply modify the request of the query just like a standard query through the column list, `Where` clause, and so forth. You can simply set the `Where` clause to false if you want to duplicate the structure of the table but do not want any of the records entered into it.

You can also do mapping and calculations during the creation of the new table. For example, you could change the name of the contactname column, like this:

```
Select contactName as MyContactName,* Into customers2 From customers
```

The column contactName will now be renamed MyContactName in the new recordset, but the data contained in that row will remain the same. You can use this method to create new columns, do calculations on existing column values, and perform other manipulation during the transfer.

The `Select Into` statement is particularly useful when you are making modifications to the schema of the database itself. If you are adding tables or rearranging relations, `Select Into` can transport data from one table to the new one in order to reflect the new organization.

Advanced Joins

In Chapter 1, you were introduced to the primary types of joins used in a query. The execution plan created by the SQL Server engine to process the join may use one of three join processes (nested loop joins, merge joins, and hash joins) to return the desired results. The database server itself decides which type of join will be used, based on the criteria specified in the `Select` statement. Reviewing the various processes used by the engine can help you to consider which implementation of a join will probably execute most quickly when choosing among several alternative queries that accomplish the same results.

Nested Loop Joins

These joins, also known as *nested iteration,* loop through every row in the outer query and attempt to match that row with a value from the inner query. The nested loop join is most effective when the outer loop is small and the inner loop is large. In small transactions, the nested loop join is far superior in performance to merge or hash joins.

Merge Joins

To use the merge join, at least one Where clause with a regular equality (=) join must exist. A merge join may process either a standard join or a many-to-many relationship. The merge join is fast but requires all of the columns in the join to be indexed. It is one of the most commonly used joins when handling large data sets.

Hash Joins

In Chapter 21, you will see how some denormalization can increase the performance of a database by putting data in closer logical proximity (minimizing the number of relations to reach key data). Hash joins have been created to attempt to remedy, or at least minimize, the amount of denormalization that must take place for optimal performance.

To use the hash join, at least one Where clause must exist. The set of columns used for the join is called the *hash key,* because it is used to create the hash value used for quick sorting. The columns in a hash key can include calculation fields, as long as all the column values are available in each row.

The MSDE server will select from three different types of hash joins (in-memory, Grace, and Recursive) to provide the fastest join. The two inputs supplied to the join are used to determine how the join will be approached. Immediately, the database server attempts to determine which is smaller. The smaller input is assigned as the *build* input. The larger is set to be the *probe* input. You will study these join types more extensively in Chapter 21 when you see how to optimize an execution plan.

Commenting SQL Code

If you have ever done any amount of traditional programming, you have probably used the comment or remark command to include an English description of the purpose of a particular line of code or routine. If you've ever tried to include comments in your SQL code, you know that the Microsoft Access engine does not accept comments in the code.

MSDE, however, contains the complete functionality to add comments to your script code. You can use the brackets (/* and */) that are traditional to the C language for multiple-line comments. Commenting a simple query could look like this:

```
Select * /*        return all of the available fields
                   In the returned recordset */
From customers /* get the values from the customers table */
```

For single-line comments, you can use the double dashes (--). This type of comment keyword ignores any text that occurs after it until the end of the line. For example:

```
Select *          -- return all of the available fields
                  -- In the returned recordset
From customers    -- get the values from the customers table
```

SQL queries, much more so than procedural code, can make it difficult for you to remember the approach or purpose of choices made in implementation when examined later. For this reason, I strongly recommend providing a comment to your MSDE queries any time you make a complex decision about a query.

> **Note:** Unfortunately, you cannot include either type of comments in a Microsoft Access query. The comments (--, /*, and */), however, can be used in stored procedures and views in an Access ADP project. When you place comments in either a view or a stored procedure, they are also kept on the database server and may be examined there if they have not been encrypted. That enables you to include some documentation right on the database server to aid the understanding of other developers.

Summary

The SQL language provides enough robust commands to enable a developer to request in query code almost any form of result set that is desired. Some of the functions that are included in the language, such as aggregate functions (for example, Average, Sum, and so on), can dramatically reduce the amount of processing required for postquery recordset manipulation on the client machine. In this chapter, you covered the following:

♦ **Aggregate functions:** Functions such as Average, Sum, and Count return aggregate values that summarize a series of data values in a query. They provide server-side mathematical summary functions.

- **Group By:** This command groups and categorizes rows that are returned in the recordset, most often by grouping rows around the distinct values in a particular column.

- **Having clause:** Used much like a Where clause in a standard query, the Having clause can include or exclude groups or records based on the values returned by aggregate functions. This clause allows the use of evaluation expressions on aggregate values.

- **Compute clauses:** The Compute and Compute By clauses can enable you to add column and row aggregate summary information to a standard recordset. These clauses can allow the return of a recordset that looks like a complete report (in other words, including subtotals, totals, and so forth).

- **Union command:** The Union command enables you to combine two or more Select queries so that they are returned together in a single resultant data set.

- **Subqueries:** Select statements may be nested one within another to return values from one query that may be used in the Where clause of another. Multiple Select statements can be nested to provide the ability to execute a subquery that supplies values to the primary query.

- **Select Into:** To move data from one table to another, the Select Into command can insert data into another table based on criteria specified in the Where clause.

Chapter 7

Stored Procedures

IN THIS CHAPTER

- Introducing the Transact-SQL Language
- Working with stored procedures
- Applying Transact-SQL
- Understanding stored procedure specifics
- Using transaction control in a stored procedure
- Configuring the MSDE environment

EVEN THE MOST ADVANCED `Select` statement has limitations when compared with a traditional procedural program. A `Select` query cannot control the flow of execution for a step-by-step procedure or change the direction of flow through the use of a command such as an `If...Then` statement. These limitations would restrict the amount and types of logic that could be stored on the MSDE server, if stored procedures were not available.

The Transact-SQL language contains a complete set of language commands and functions. By learning to use the stored procedure functionality provided by the MSDE server, you can create more powerful server-based database application. You can also create library routines that, once stored on the server, can be used by several different applications for common functions.

The Transact-SQL Language

The Transact-SQL language contains Microsoft language extensions to the standard SQL language. Although Transact-SQL includes some query and database definition extensions to SQL, the bulk of capability available in Transact-SQL is provided to enable definition of compiled functions and procedures that are stored on the database server. Transact-SQL contains several programming keywords and system functions to provide these important operations.

Some of these features include:

- Creation and modification of stored procedures

- Extensions to the SQL language through functions for use within a query (such as date formatting)
- Execution logic including If...Then structures

The MSDE implementation makes few explicit distinctions between commands native to Transact-SQL and those included in the SQL-92 standard, which will be available in Microsoft Access or on a wide variety of database servers (Oracle, Informix, Sybase, and so on). Because (as I presume) you are upsizing from Access to MSDE, it will usually be unimportant which commands are backward-compatible with the Microsoft Access SQL engine. However, you can be fairly assured that any function calls (beyond the core aggregate function) or conditional execution statements are not included in the basic SQL-92 standard.

Working with Stored Procedures

So far, most of the functionality of MSDE you have examined has been similar to features that are available through the Microsoft Access JET database engine. Stored procedures are the major point of departure that separate an implementation of an application on a self-contained database engine (such as JET) from one on a true database server. Stored procedures enable you to introduce complete program logic typical of a procedural language into your database solution.

You may already be accustomed to using queries in Microsoft Access. Stored procedures can actually be used in place of many queries but are far more powerful and flexible. Although a query can only contain a single SQL statement, a procedure can contain many types of program logic. A stored procedure may include:

- **Flow control:** Evaluation of a variable setting or value through a statement, such as the If...Then structure, may change which operations are executed in the procedure.

- **Local variables:** A stored procedure may define and use variables for calculation, passing to other routines, formatting, and type conversion.

- **Arguments passed to and from procedures:** Variables and values may be sent to a routine, which, after performing its task, can also return values and even a cursor.

- **Automatic execution based on triggers and events:** A procedure can be activated by an operation performed on the database or an event and receive information as to the status of the calling routine through passed arguments.

- **System variables and functions:** Calling system functions and accessing values supplied by the server gives access to the database server resources and environment.

- **Manipulation of the database:** Within a procedure, the executing code can do everything from modifying data to creating a new database or modifying an existing database or view.

- **Shared access:** Many users and developers can all address the same logic that is stored on the database server.

To define a stored procedure, you need to choose a database where it will be located. All stored procedures are located in a particular database, not allocated in the database server itself. However, through referencing, a stored procedure in one database can call a procedure in another database by using a complete explicit reference.

Creating a Stored Procedure

Creating a stored procedure is quite a bit different from simply submitting a query for processing, because the compiled procedure is stored for later execution. Each procedure must be given a name so that it can be called by SQL code. The general syntax for the `Create Procedure` statement looks like this:

```
Create Proc[edure] procedurename
    [@parameter datatype] [= value] [Output]
```

The general syntax of a stored procedure definition includes the `Create Procedure` keyword, the name of the procedure, any variable definitions, and finally the code or `Select` statement. Defining a simple stored procedure that mimics a query is done with code like this:

```
Create Procedure myProc As Select * From customers
```

Microsoft Access provides a useful environment for creating these procedures. It enables you to switch between writing the code for the stored procedure and executing that procedure much as you do when designing a query. The Access environment also provides complete syntax checking and color highlighting for SQL keywords and commands. You can create and execute this simple procedure in Access by following these steps:

1. Execute Microsoft Access and open the NorthwindCS project.

2. Click the Stored Procedures item in the Objects column. All of the stored procedures available in the project will be listed in the details pane on the right (see Figure 7-1). You will see several procedures already in the Northwind database created by its makers.

3. Click New to create a new procedure. When you start a new procedure, Access conveniently provides a general definition template to use as a starting point for building your routine.

Part I: Access and MSDE

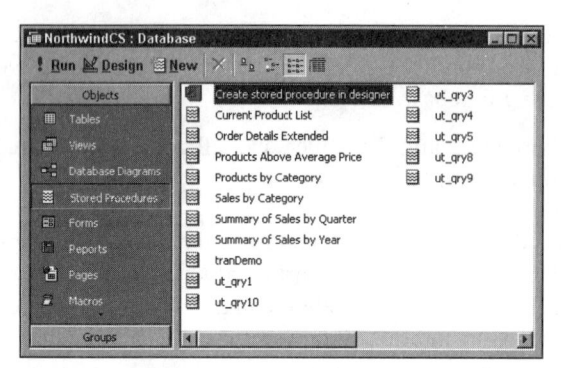

Figure 7-1: All of the stored procedures in the Northwind database are shown in the details pane.

4. Replace the dummy text provided by Access with the following code:

```
Create Procedure myProc
As
Select * From customers
```

5. To execute the procedure, click the View button on the toolbar.

6. When you are notified that you must first save the procedure before it can be executed, click the Yes button, name the routine **myProc**, and click the OK button to save it to the MSDE server. The procedure you just created simply executes a query, the results of which should now be displayed in the query grid.

> **NOTE:** With only a few more lines, the procedure can become much more powerful. The routine can include more than one query and can accept parameters that govern whether one query or another is used for the return data set.

7. Click the View button on the toolbar to return to design mode. You'll notice immediately that the text of the procedure has automatically changed to read "Alter Procedure" rather than "Create Procedure." The `Alter Procedure` command is needed to make changes once a procedure of that name exists on the database server.

8. Change the procedure code in the window to match this code:

```
Alter Procedure myProc
@myCity  int
As
If @myCity = 1
    Select * From customers Where city like 'Buenos Aires'
```

```
Else
    Select * From customers
```

9. Click the View button on the toolbar and approve the saving of changes to the procedure. When the procedure executes this time, you will be prompted for a value to be entered into the @myCity variable (see Figure 7-2). You might notice that the @myCity variable declaration comes before the As keyword and includes the *int* variable type. The location of this declaration makes the variable a parameter accepted from the calling routine rather than simply a variable used within the procedure.

> If you have ever included values in a query for an Access MDB file, you are already familiar with this interface. In a normal situation for executing a stored procedure, the procedure would be called directly and supplied the parameter. In this case, you can enter an appropriate value.

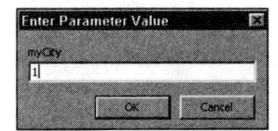

Figure 7-2: The dialog box will prompt you for a value to enter into the @myCity variable.

10. Enter the number 1 into the box and click the OK button.

The query grid should display the results generated by the stored procedure. Because the value you entered only displayed the customers located in Buenos Aires, the result set should match the one shown in Figure 7-3.

Figure 7-3: The result set adjusted to the @myCity parameter that was supplied.

If you change the Design mode and change back one more time, this time setting the @myCity parameter to a different value, you will see the change in the data that is returned. This demonstration of creating a stored procedure demonstrates the very basics of using logic in a procedure. It used the value stored in @myCity to determine which of the two queries should be executed in the recordset. The use of parameters in a procedure is one of the powerful aspects of using stored procedures.

> **Note:** Although the MSDE server can use the truncated Create Proc version of the Create Procedure command, Microsoft Access returns the error "You cannot change the object type in a script" when this command is used. Therefore, for stored procedures created in Access, use the full Create Procedure command.

When you create a new procedure name, its name must be 128 characters or less. When you are creating a procedure directly using SQL commands, the stored procedure will be created in the currently selected database. The stored procedure that you've just created is now active on the MSDE server. You can execute it from any SQL environment, including Microsoft Query, SQL Query Analyzer, or ADO.

Executing a Stored Procedure

The Execute keyword can be used to activate a stored procedure. The name of the stored procedure alone can also be entered for execution because it will implicitly understand that the Execute command is wanted. You can invoke a procedure's name with code like this:

```
myProc 'B'
```

The Execute keyword is only optional when the stored procedure name is the first and only command issued in this SQL code batch. A stored procedure can be activated simply by passing its name to the MSDE server. The Execute command can also be used to call a procedure. You can use the Execute command like this:

```
Execute myProc 'B'
```

If you know the names of the arguments that are required by the procedure, you can name them directly rather than passing them in order:

```
Execute myProc @myCity = 'B'
```

> **Note:** If a result set is returned by the procedure, you should use the `Open` command instead of `Execute` to activate the routine. It is used in the same manner as the `Execute` function. For example, this code would open the recordset opened with the `myProc` routine:
>
> `Open myProc @myCity`

When a stored procedure is compiled on the server, an execution plan for the procedure is created. Certain procedures can benefit from being recompiled every time the routine is executed. For performance reasons, the database server caches many objects used for a recent stored procedure execution in order to speed subsequent calls to that procedure.

This caching may negatively affect performance if a procedure completely changes its plan of attack given different parameter entries. The original execution plan impedes the execution of the next call. For this reason, the `With Recompile` clause is included in the Transact-SQL language. The command is placed in the procedure code before the `As` keyword. For example, to create the `myProc` routine with this setting, you can use code like this:

```
Create Proc myProc
With Recompile
As Select * From customers
```

With this option set, each time `myProc` is executed, the MSDE server will create a new execution plan and flush the currently cached objects associated with the stored procedure. This option is used primarily with large, time consuming queries and is only needed when vastly different query times are encountered for essentially the same data retrieval.

Using Variables and Arguments

Variables may be defined to be used within a stored procedure, passed to another function, or returned to the calling function. Only predefined variables maintained by the database server system are defined globally for access to all procedures on the server. All other variables must be directly associated with a stored procedure.

DEFINING VARIABLES

Within a stored procedure, variables may be defined for local use. Any variables that you define are discarded once execution of that procedure is complete. Variables used by a stored procedure must begin with the @ symbol.

Variables are defined in the create procedure code before the `As` keyword that begins the declaration of `Select` code. To create a local variable that is not to be accepted as an argument, you need to use the `Declare` keyword:

```
DECLARE @sys_usr char(30)
```

The local variable requires that a data type be specified. The type is defined directly after the variable is named. Unlike in Visual Basic, which provides the Variant data type that automatically alters itself to store any data, all variables in a procedure must have explicit types. These variable types match the types that are used to define columns.

> **NOTE:** Unlike when programming in Visual Basic, you cannot omit an optional parameter like this: `Execute myProc 'John',,'Smith'`. The only way you can omit a parameter in the middle of a list is by specifically naming each parameter value for individual setting.

RECEIVING ARGUMENTS

When creating any stored procedure, you can create a series of variables that can receive arguments passed by the calling routine or user. The values passed to the stored procedure can be used to supply information to a query used in the code, as flags to indicate a desired operation, or to designate another function that is necessary for the routine.

Arguments can be passed to a stored procedure by simply defining them at the beginning of the procedure. Any data type of argument can be passed except a cursor. A simple example of a procedure that receives a single text string would look like this:

```
Create Proc myProc
   @lastName varchar(40)
As
Select * From customers
```

The variables or parameters that are received from the calling routine may also be defined as optional. To set a parameter to be optional, you merely have to include a default value setting for that variable. For example, these three variables are all optional:

```
Create Proc myProc
   @lastName varchar(40) = 'Doe',
   @firstName varchar(20) = 'Jane',
   @title varchar(20) = null
```

```
As
Select * From customers
```

Default values are required for all parameters that will be optional, because a system error would result if the procedure finishes executing and no value is assigned to the variable either by the calling routine or the default value setting.

```
Execute myProc @lastname = 'Smith', @firstName = 'John',
   middleName = 'W.'
Execute myProc 'John','W','Smith'
```

Each parameter specified in the procedure definition must be passed to the procedure when the procedure is activated by the user or a trigger. Each parameter name must begin with the @ symbol and will be available for access only within the procedure where it is defined. A maximum of 1,024 parameters may be created for each stored procedure.

RETURNING ARGUMENTS

Many stored procedures, in addition to accepting values from the calling routines, will return values in addition to a recordset. A common returned value may be an error or status code that indicates how execution of the procedure went.

Arguments to be returned to the calling routine need to be marked as Output during the procedure creation:

```
Create Proc myProc
   @lastName varchar(40) = 'Doe',
   @firstName varchar(20) = 'Jane',
   @title varchar(20) = null OUTPUT
As
Select * From customers
```

If a result set is returned, it will be in the same manner that would occur if a Select statement was used. A cursor may be returned for the recordset. The data type of the parameter may be of any type (including text and image) except the cursor data type. The cursor data type can only be used as an Output parameter.

The Return command is another method of returning data to the calling procedure. This command can be used by the procedure that is called to return any error code that might have been encountered during procedure execution. The calling routine can check this returned value and take appropriate action if an error has occurred. The Return command passes a return code that uses the data type Integer.

Default values may be set for any of the parameters by using the equal (=) operator. A parameter can be defined and set to a default value like this:

```
@lastName varchar(40) = 'Smith'
```

The `Output` keyword following a parameter definition indicates that this variable will be returned by the stored procedure. The most common type of output parameter is a data set. If the stored procedure generates a query, the recordset returned by that query is automatically returned to the calling procedure as the output recordset.

At the time a stored procedure is created, the compilation only does a syntax check. It does not check whether the database objects (such as tables or indexes) referenced by the procedure actually exist. Instead, it binds these objects to the procedure during execution. Therefore, a procedure may compile correctly but generate an error when executed if the specified objects referenced by the routine are not found. A stored procedure can be used to create other database objects including defining new databases, tables, or database devices.

When a stored procedure calls another stored procedure, all of the objects created by the calling procedure may be accessed by the subprocedure, including any temporary tables created by the primary routine.

> A stored procedure may be encrypted so that although it may be executed by any authorized user, the code for the procedure can no longer be viewed. The encryption is one way. It may not be removed even by the user that placed the encryption on the routine. Therefore, make sure that you have a backup of the procedure code before you encrypt it.

RETURN KEYWORD

The `Return` keyword can be used to terminate a stored procedure, query, or batch at any place within the procedural code. Usually, the `Return` is used when an error or unacceptable value has been encountered. When used in a stored procedure, an integer can be passed by the keyword back to the calling routine, usually indicating the error type generated. If no integer value is supplied by your routine, MSDE automatically returns a zero (0) in the parameter.

For a variation on the code to test for the type of city, you could use a procedure like this:

```
Create Procedure myReturnTest
@myCity   int
As
If @myCity > 5
    Return 99
If @myCity = 1
    Select * From customers Where city like 'Buenos Aires'
Else
    Select * From customers
```

In this example, if any value greater than 5 is passed in the `@myCity` parameter, the `Return 99` line is executed. This will abort executing the statements that follow it in the code.

This command can be used very effectively with the `@@Error` system variable. Because this variable contains the error number of any encountered problem, you can set your procedure to return the error code if any problem occurs.

CURSOR OUTPUT

When the stored procedure has completed execution, it may pass a recordset back to the source of the execution. Any queries that are activated within the stored procedure will be designated as the result set. For this reason, to execute a query within the stored procedure that will return a data set needed by the stored procedure logic but will not be included with the result set, place it in a separate proc that is called by the primary routine.

Certain data sources can have a cursor that only advances forward through the records supplied by a query. For this type of cursor, known as a forward-only cursor, the rows returned in the output data set are only those at the current cursor location and after. Any records before the current position will not be returned. This means that if the cursor is at the end of the data set, no records will be returned.

When the cursor returned is any type besides a forward-only cursor, the entire recordset will be returned, regardless of cursor position. The recordset returned will have the cursor set to the same location last referenced within the stored procedure.

CREATING MULTIPLE PROCEDURES WITH THE SAME NAME

You can create multiple procedures that have the same name so that they may be dropped as a group. Creation of these procedures is done by following the procedure name with a semicolon (;) followed by an index number for each procedure. For example, these commands will create two different procedures that share the same name:

```
Create Proc myProc;1
Create Proc myProc;2
```

To execute these procedures, you need to use the semicolon (;) separator and specify the procedure number like this:

```
Execute myProc;2
```

When the `Drop` command is executed, simply specifying the `myProc` name drops both procedures.

Applying Transact-SQL

Up until this point, you have seen stored procedures that can be used essentially to take the place of queries. However, Transact-SQL has many more features. Within a stored procedure, the language can be used for complete procedural-style programming. Control-of-flow, iteration, and error handling are just a few of the aspects of the language that distinguish it from common SQL code for a query.

Control-of-Flow in Stored Procedures

Unlike a standard SQL statement, a stored procedure can change the sequence of execution. The following control-of-flow commands are available:

- `If...Then...Else`
- `Goto <label>`
- `While` (with `Break` and `Continue`)
- `Return`

Each of these statements will change the execution path of the procedure either by making conditional checks (`If...Then`) or by simply making a statement execute. You've already used some of these commands and learned a bit about the capabilities of the `Return` keyword. Many of these commands are used together for execution control.

The If...Then...Else Structure

Evaluating a condition and determining whether one set of code or another should be executed is critical to all procedural languages. Transact-SQL includes the `If...Then...Else` structure to provide the conditional control-of-flow. For this structure, a single line of code can be executed if the condition is True. If more than one line is required for execution, the `Begin...End` structure is used to encapsulate this extra code.

The `If...Then` construct can appear in a stored procedure like this:

```
Create Procedure ContactNameTest
    @contactName varchar(40)
As
If @contactName Is null
   Begin
      Print "You must supply a contact name to locate."
      Return 1
   End
Else
   Select * From customers Where contactname = @contactname
```

This simple procedure will accept a contact name and return a recordset containing all of the columns for a row that matches that value. The function of this procedure may seem redundant when the same query could be executed directly, but remember that stored procedures can be good for abstraction from the base tables.

If the format of the underlying customers table ever changed, this stored procedure could be easily altered and all routines that access it could remain the same. Changing the underlying table, however, would affect every operation that addressed it directly.

The `If...Then` construct in the procedure contains a single evaluation that determines whether the string passed to the routine contains a null value. You can use the Boolean operators on the test in the same manner they are used in queries or general programming languages.

> **NOTE:** If you have previously worked in Visual Basic or another high-level procedural language, you are probably accustomed to having a `Select Case` statement to evaluate a series of potential values against a single parameter. There is no direct equivalent of the `Select Case` statement in Transact-SQL. However, to accomplish essentially the same results, Transact-SQL enables `Else If` statements to be chained on a single `If` command. Therefore, you can construct code that uses a structure like this: `If...Else If...Else If...Else If`.

Iteration Control in Stored Procedures

Creating a program loop, not possible in a normal query, is simple to implement in a stored procedure. In Transact-SQL, the `While` command can repeat a series of commands within a loop until the value for the loop is evaluated to false. A simple `While` loop looks like this:

```
Declare @myCount Int
While @myCount < 10
    @myCount = @myCount + 1
```

Multiple instructions for the `While` loop can be encapsulated with the `Begin` and `End` commands. A multiple line loop would look like this:

```
Declare @myCount Int
While @myCount < 10
    Begin
      Print 'Current count: ' + @myCount
       @myCount = @myCount + 1
    End
```

The `Break` exits a `While` loop, whereas the `Continue` keyword restarts a `While` loop. Any code after a `Continue` loop is ignored once it is activated. The `Break` and `Continue` commands are usually used with an `If...Then` statement for conditional looping.

Labels and the Goto Command

Older languages used a command called `Goto` to just go to another place in the execution code. Because structural procedural programming has caught on, the `Goto` command has been deemphasized and phased out in most modern languages.

> **CAUTION:** The unstructured way the jump can occur makes code that uses a `Goto` command difficult to optimize, debug, and document. Therefore, I recommend that you favor other means such as `While` loops combined with `If...Then` statements over using the `Goto` command.

To use the `Goto` command, give a label to a specific location in the procedural code. A label should be given a name much like a procedure (no spaces in the name, and so on), and placed within the code followed by a colon (:) character. For example:

```
Declare @mycount = 1
MyGotoLoop:
     Print "I'm here"
     @mycount = @mycount + 1
     If (@mycount < 11) Goto MyGotoLoop
Print "I'm done."
```

This code will execute until it encounters the `If...Then` statement. The evaluation of the `@mycount` variable will determine whether it jumps back to the `MyGotoLoop` label. If the value in the `@mycount` variable has risen above 10, the `Goto` command is not executed and the final line is executed. A `Goto` command can jump to a label that exists either before or after it in the stored procedure code.

Error Handling in Stored Procedures

In the development of applications, error handling procedures are often critically important to provide an effective user experience and minimize the loss of data caused by a program fault. Most stored procedures are kept so simple, their functions so extensively tested, and the logic so clear that once the procedure is ready for deployment, error checking will add a layer of unneeded protection.

However, Transact-SQL does include commands to address error problems. The primary function useful for writing error checking routines is the `@@Error` function. It returns the error number (if any) of the last statement that was executed. If no error occurred, a zero value will be returned.

The sysmessages table may be used to take the error code returned by the `@@Error` function and obtain additional information about the error, such as an English description of it. The information stored in the sysmessages table looks like this:

error	severity	dlevel	description	msglangid
1	10	0	Version date of last upgrade: 10/11/90.	1033
21	10	0	Warning: Fatal error %d occurred at %S_DATE.	1033
102	15	0	Incorrect syntax near '%.*ls'.	1033
103	15	0	The %S_MSG is too long.	1033

The `RaiseError` function enables you to generate an error, whether that error matches an existing system error or is a custom error generated by your program. With this function, you can specify an error number and the text to be returned to the user. If the error to be generated is a system error, you can use the sysmessages table to retrieve the text explanation of the error.

Through the ArithAbort and ArithIgnore properties, you can also determine how the MSDE system handles some types of errors. Use `Set ArithAbort` to instruct the system whether to abort a query for overflow or divide-by-zero errors that occur during a query. To instruct the server to abort when one of these errors occurs, use the command like this:

```
Set ArithAbort On
```

Until this value is set to `Off`, all errors of this type will abort queries if they are encountered. `Set ArithIgnore` can be set to an `On` or `Off` value and determines whether the overflow or divide-by-zero errors are reported back to the user.

The `@@Total_Errors` function returns the number of disk read and write errors that have occurred since the MSDE server was booted. This number is included in the system report generated when the `sp_monitor` procedure is executed.

Stored Procedure Specifics

Because the stored procedure will be executing on the MSDE server, a routine can be coded to address many of the resources available on the server. For example, it can call other stored procedures created within the same or other databases. Managing stored procedures also requires special care for alteration and deletion. Because of the vendor-specific nature of the SQL language, learning how to maintain a set of stored procedures depends on examining the system on which the procedures are deployed.

Nesting Stored Procedures

A stored procedure calling chain can be nested up to 32 levels deep. Each time a stored procedure calls another within its execution code, a level is added. When the execution of the subprocedure is completed, a level is subtracted. Therefore, one procedure can call an unlimited number of procedures within the body of its code. It is only when one procedure calls another that calls another and so on, that the nested level is incurred.

You can detect whether you are about to exceed the system limit. To retrieve the current nesting level, you can use the `@@NestLevel` system function. Using an `If...Then` statement with this value can abort another level call.

> A recursive function is a function that calls itself. Usually used in programming to allow navigation of a tree hierarchy (such as a directory structure), a function repeatedly calls itself to create a nest of calls. Because nesting in Transact-SQL is available to only 32 levels, many recursive routines have a high likelihood of overloading the system. If you need to do extensive recursion on the server, create that part of the programming in C++ or another compiled language (see the "Extended Stored Procedures" section later in this chapter). Doing so will prevent a great many possible errors.

Deferred Name Resolution

When a stored procedure is compiled, the syntax of the procedure is checked to make sure that all keywords and commands are correct. In the case of references to database objects (such as tables, indexes, and other stored procedures) that are called within the compiling routine, the existence of these objects is not verified. When the procedure is actually executed, the names of the objects are resolved. This process is known as *deferred name resolution*.

> Because procedures don't resolve objects that they use until execution, if you delete a stored procedure used by other stored procedures, no error will be generated at the time of deletion. Only when the existing procedure attempts to call the deleted procedure will an error occur. Therefore, be sure to test execution of key procedures after you've deleted an object to prevent later faults.

For this reason, be sure to test all of the aspects of object access in your stored procedure before you deploy it. This testing includes trying all of the execution combinations made possible with If...Then statements. It also means checking for errors that may have been caused if a typo for the name was made or the object doesn't exist.

Altering Procedures

The `Alter Procedure` command is used to redefine an existing procedure. This command will replace any code currently stored under that procedure name. Although the procedure itself is replaced, any security access settings that have been configured for the routine remain in place.

`Alter Procedure` works identically to the `Create Procedure` command except that it redefines an existing procedure rather than creating a new one. Earlier in the chapter, you saw how Microsoft Access automatically introduced the `Alter Procedure` command to the stored procedure after you initially created and saved it. Changes to views and stored procedures are automatically updated in the system tables that hold references to them.

Renaming and Deleting Procedures

The `sp_rename` function can be used to change the name of an existing stored procedure or other user-created object, such as a table, column, or user-defined type. This routine should be executed with the current procedure name as the first parameter followed by the new name to be assigned to it. For example, this system function is used like this:

```
sp_rename myProc, myNewProc
```

The names of user-defined objects and procedures can be changed only in the database that is currently selected. Note that although some objects contained in the system tables can be renamed, most cannot be changed at all. An error will be returned if a change is attempted on a read-only object, but the integrity of the system will remain intact.

To delete a procedure, use the `Drop Procedure` command, which eliminates a procedure from the current database. You can drop the procedure that you created earlier in this chapter with this code:

```
Drop Procedure myProc
```

Transaction Control in a Stored Procedure

In Chapter 4, you learned how transactions are used to ensure that all operations encapsulated within a transaction succeed or all of them are revoked. Several Transact-SQL commands are used to invoke, commit, or revoke a transaction. These commands will enable you to manage a transaction from within a stored procedure.

The primary or outermost transaction that is opened can be given a name. Further transactions can be nested and opened within the primary transaction.

The following SQL commands are used for handling transactions:

- **Begin Transaction:** Opens a transaction that all further Insert, Update, and Delete commands will be encapsulated within until the transaction is closed. For the primary or outermost transaction, the Begin Transaction command may be followed by a name string or variable (of char, varchar, nchar, or nvarchar type) that contains a name for the transaction that is up to 32 characters long. The command may be abbreviated to Begin Tran in the SQL code.

- **Rollback Transaction:** Revokes all of the operations contained in the transaction. For the primary transaction, may be passed the transaction name to revoke the primary transaction and all transactions nested in it. Passing any other name will generate an error.

- **Commit Transaction:** Commits all of the operations contained in the transaction. Passing a name to this procedure is possible (in compliance with the SQL standard), but MSDE ignores the name sent to it. Instead, it always commits the transaction at the current nesting level.

- **Rollback [Work]:** Performs the same function as Rollback Transaction except that it does not accept a name parameter for nested operations.

- **Commit [Work]:** Performs the same function as Commit Transaction except that it does not accept a name parameter for nested operations.

- **Begin Distributed Transaction:** Activates the Distributed Transaction Controller (DTC) to handle the transaction. This will automatically occur if an Update, Insert, or Delete command is issued to a remote machine inside of a current transaction.

- **Save Transaction:** Accepts a name parameter to set a bookmark in the current transaction. A Rollback command after the point in the code where the Save Transaction command is located will revoke only the operations to the point of the save. This command is not supported with distributed transactions.

Create a new stored procedure in the NorthwindCS database in Microsoft Access by entering the following code:

```
Create Procedure tranDemo
     @commitFlag int
As
/* Make a duplicate of the customers table so primary
   Northwind tables remain intact. */
Select * Into customersDup From customers
Begin Tran
/* Make a change to all the rows of the table */
Update customersDup Set contactName = Upper(contactName)

If @commitFlag = 1
   Commit Tran
Else
   Rollback Tran
```

The `tranDemo` procedure will make a copy of the customers table called `customersDup`. All of the contact names in this new table will be set to uppercase. When you execute the procedure, you will be prompted to set the `@commitFlag` variable to a value. If this value is the number 1, when the procedure executes, all of the changes made will be committed. Any other value will cause the changes to be revoked.

To name a transaction, simply include a character string after the `Begin Transaction` or `Begin Tran` command like this:

```
Begin Transaction 'MyTransaction'
Update customersDup Set contactName = Upper(contactName)
Commit Transaction 'MyTransaction'
```

Remember that the named transaction only counts when no other transactions are active for that session. If you name a transaction after another transaction has already been opened, the supplied name parameter will simply be ignored.

For routines that may be called within by other routines, you might use the `@@TranCount` system function. It returns the number of transactions currently open. Your routine can check if this value is greater than zero, and if so, the routine can change the execution or abort the routine.

> **CAUTION:** If a stored procedure calls a procedure on another database server, any database changes made by the remote procedure are not contained within any transaction currently open. Therefore, the remote procedure changes cannot be rolled back.

The MSDE Environment

Stored procedures executing on the MSDE server have access to several server resources such as system functions, system procedures, and extended stored procedures. By using the existing resources of the database server, you can accomplish many tasks that are necessary for properly implementing stored procedures and that would be difficult or impossible to accomplish on a traditional database like Microsoft Access.

System Functions and Variables

System functions and variables are available for a variety of parameters. You have already used a number of these functions for operations such as checking the level of nesting for procedure calls or determining the number of transactions that are currently open. There are many more that are used for everything from security to database maintenance. Here are some of the common ones that you will probably find most useful when creating an MSDE solution:

- **@@Rowcount:** The `@@RowCount` variable enables a procedure or query to return the total row number in relation to the current recordset or the rows affected by the last SQL command. For example, a query of all of the employees in the Northwind database would return this value as 9.

- **sp_recompile:** You can explicitly recompile a stored procedure by using the `sp_recompile` function.

- **sp_helptext:** You can use the `sp_helptext` function to display the source code of a procedure as long as that procedure has not been encrypted. Information supplied by this function includes: objects used by the procedure, owner, creation date, parameters, and the names of other procedures that it addresses.

- **Set ShowPlan On:** Returns the execution plan when a stored procedure is executed.

- **Set StatisticsTime On:** Displays the time taken to parse, compile, and execute each statement for the stored procedure.

- **RowCount(num):** The `RowCount(num)` command sets the number of rows that will be returned on the query. Setting `Rowcount` to zero (0) will turn off the setting. The `Set` keyword must be used with this command, so the actual SQL code appears like this: `Set Rowcount 4`.

- **Print:** The `Print` command can be used by a procedure to send a message to the user screen or console. This command is truly useful only if you are using a utility such as the SQL Query Analyzer. If you are using a grid-based recordset display such as the ones provided in Microsoft Access or Microsoft Query, the results of the `Print` command do not appear.

All of these functions and variables may be addressed within any stored procedure with the proper security authorization. They can also be executed directly with a tool such as Microsoft Query or SQL Query Analyzer.

User-Defined System Procedures

In this chapter, you have defined stored procedures within a particular database. However, it is possible to create a stored procedure that can be executed from any database. These procedures — system stored procedures — provide general functions that serve as global procedures.

These procedures must be created in the master database and must have the procedure name prefix of `sp_`. Therefore, creating `myProc` as a system procedure would look like this:

```
Use master
Go
Create Procedure sp_myProc
As
Select 10 As Quantity
```

A stored procedure in the master database can be marked for automatic execution, which means that the procedure will be activated every time the MSDE server is first started. This can be useful for procedures that perform some type of maintenance operation. To create such a procedure, you must be logged in to the server as a sysadmin.

The `sp_procoption` procedure is used to set the procedure to execute on startup. The startup option determines whether the procedure is automatically executed. It is set like this:

```
sp_procoption sp_myProc, startup=true
```

Temporary Stored Procedures

Stored procedures of a type called *temporary stored procedures* automatically purge themselves from the database server. They are actually of two kinds: private temporary procedures and global temporary procedures.

Each *private temporary procedure* must have a single pound (#) character preceding its name. These procedures are eliminated as soon as the current connection is closed. Private temporary procedures are only available for execution from the connection that created them.

Global temporary procedures are available to all users on the database system. The double pound sign (##) precedes the name of each. When these procedures are created, they exist only as long as the MSDE server remains active. When the database server is shut down, all of the temporary stored procedures are automatically purged from the database.

Temporary procedures are created in the tempdb database. This database along with everything in it is recreated each time the MSDE server is started.

Creating a global temporary stored procedure can be done with code like this:

```
Create Procedure ##myTempProc
As
Select 10 As Quantity
```

> **NOTE** Temporary stored procedures can take up precious server resources. Unless you need to repeatedly access the procedure for a task, it is recommended that you use the `sp_executesql` function. This function accepts a string that can contain a series of SQL statements, and it will execute this code as if it were contained within a stored procedure.

Procedure Information

As in views, all of the information and definition text of a stored procedure is available for retrieval. The source code is stored in the system table syscomments. You can retrieve the text of a stored procedure by executing the system procedure `sp_helptext` followed by the name of your procedure (for example, `sp_helptext myProc`) will display the text used to create the procedure. Any user-created procedures except those created with the `ENCRYPTION` keyword can be viewed this way.

The text of a query may also be retrieved directly from the syscomments table with a query like this:

```
SELECT c.id, c.text FROM syscomments c, sysobjects o WHERE c.id = o.id and o.name = 'myProc'
```

In the case of any procedure created in a database on the database server, the procedure's name will be stored in the sysobjects table of the master database. The text of the procedure is stored in the syscomments table.

> **NOTE** Microsoft recommends that you use built-in routines, such as `sp_help`, to return information about database objects. Because the format of the system tables on the database server may change in the future, you are not assured that queries such as those in this section will continue to function.

Extended Stored Procedures

You can create functions in C++ that can be called from within the MSDE environment. These calls are constructed in MSDE as extended stored procedure. These extended stored procedures can be called like any normal stored procedure.

New extended stored procedures are compiled within DLL files and placed in the Binn directory. The individual functions of the DLL must be registered with the MSDE server using the `sp_addextendedproc` routine. You will need to know the name of the DLL and the name of the function to register to use code like this:

```
sp_addextendedproc 'myDLLFunction', 'myDLL.DLL'
```

or

```
sp_addextendedproc @functname = 'myDLLFunction', @dllname = 'myDLL.DLL'
```

This code will register with the MSDE server a function called `myDLLFunction` located in the DLL file myDLL.dll. The arguments passed to and from the functions will automatically be retrieved by the registration function and included in the definition of the routine. Extended procedures should only be added to the master database.

> **NOTE:** The complete SQL Server installation includes C++ examples of creating an extended stored procedure. Check the `DevTools` option with the installation to include samples such as `xp_hello`.

The WaitFor Command

The `WaitFor` command is a delay statement that pauses before the continued execution of the procedure. This command suspends all operations of the current connection or session until the delay specified has expired.

Two different value types may be used with this keyword: `Delay` and `Time`. `Delay` specifies the exact interval of how long the system will wait in minutes and seconds up to 24 hours. The `Time` keyword specifies an exact time when execution will be allowed to continue. The value for the `Time` keyword may be specified either as a datetime constant or a variable of the `datetime` type that contains an appropriate value. Only the time value of the `datetime` data type will be used, so do not pass a date value.

You can use the `Delay` keyword to pause execution for 20 seconds, like this:

```
WaitFor Delay '0:0:20'
```

You can use the `Time` keyword to pause execution until 1:30 P.M., like this:

```
WaitFor Time '13:20'
```

Using the Go Command

In a SQL execution tool such as the SQL Query Analyzer or the command line–based OSQL utility, the `Go` command can be used to force execution of all code up to the current point. For example, code such as this could be entered to create a stored procedure and subsequently execute it:

```
Create Proc myProc
As
Select * From customers
Go
Execute myProc
```

> **NOTE** The `Go` keyword is required after certain commands, because it denotes a batch. With certain keywords, the statements must be the sole command within a single batch.

Summary

Stored procedures enable you to code program logic for storage and execution on the database server. By favoring logic on the server, your application becomes much more scalable for multiuser solutions. Logic in stored procedures can also allow dynamic execution of queries, inserts, and event handling that is not available through other means. In this chapter you covered:

- **Creating stored procedures:** A stored procedure is procedural code on the MSDE server that is named and compiled for execution within a specific database. The primary advantages to using a stored procedure include performance, the capability to receive and return parameters, and means for storing important execution code on the server for shared access.

- **Control-of-flow in stored procedures:** Conditional commands (such as `If...Then`) and execution modifiers (such as `Goto`, `Break`, `Continue`, and `Return`) can be used to change the sequence of execution within a stored procedure.

- **While loops** : Using the `While` command, you can create a loop within a stored procedure.

- **User-defined system procedures:** Procedures can be defined that can be addressed from any database.

- **Extended stored procedures:** The MSDE server can use external functions stored in a DLL that are written in compiled languages such as Visual C++. Each extended stored procedure must be registered with the server and placed in the Binn directory to be available for execution.

Chapter 8

Access Data Project (ADP)

IN THIS CHAPTER

- Examining ADP versus MDB
- Creating an ADP project
- Using Tables, Views, Stored procedures, and Database diagrams in ADP
- Setting Connection properties

IN MICROSOFT ACCESS 2000, a new project type known as the *Access Data Project (ADP)* has been added. This project type is an Access-based project type that can effectively create and manage a database on MSDE/SQL Server. Previous versions of Access could make connections (known as *attached tables*) only to existing tables on a database server. The new project type is custom-made to interface with Microsoft database servers.

ADP Versus MDB

The way in which Access developers use the ADP file is very similar to the way in which they use a traditional MDB file. Likewise, all the wizards for Access (such as the Form Wizard and Report Wizard) can be used in an ADP file in the same manner they are used with a full MDB database. The appearance of the objects within the file (such as reports and forms) parallels the appearance of the MDB types, as well.

The primary difference between an MDB database and the new Access Data Project is the storage location of the objects listed in the file. In an MDB file, all objects and data are held in the MDB file itself. For an ADP file, the locations of various database objects are split between the database server and the file.

Data Storage

In an Access Data Project, objects that directly interact with the data, as well as the data itself, are stored on the database server. For these objects, the ADP file contains only references to the objects stored on the server. These references enable an Access developer to treat the database structures as if they were located in the ADP file, for design, programming, and data entry purposes. The objects that are located on the database server but appear in the ADP object list (see Figure 8-1) are Tables, Views, Stored Procedures, and Database Diagrams.

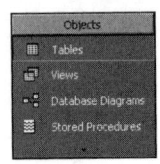

Figure 8-1: Server-based objects are stored on the MSDE server and referenced in the ADP file.

Whereas the data and database structures are located on the MSDE server, all of the user interface elements are stored in the ADP file just like they are in an MDB file. In fact, no functional difference exists between ADP-based user interface items and their MDB counterparts. The ADP file contains Forms, Reports, Pages, Macros, and Modules (see Figure 8-2).

Figure 8-2: User interface elements are stored in the ADP file.

Data Communication

To provide the communication that links the ADP project file to the MSDE data source, the SQL Server data provider is used through the connection interface of the OLE DB middleware (known as the OLE DB Data Provider for SQL Server). Most of the management functions, such as creating a new procedure or modifying a view, occur through the OLE DB driver using standard Transact-SQL commands.

> **NOTE** An Access Data Project can be used only with SQL Server version 6.5 and later (which includes all versions of MSDE). To create Access projects that reference earlier versions of SQL Server, use the attached tables in a standard MDB file.

You will want to use the ADP project for all MSDE-centric applications that do not address the SQL Server engine through ODBC. ODBC has the advantage of enabling independent configuration on each client even if the Access project has been installed to only include the run-time file (so that it cannot be reconfigured from within the Access environment on that machine). The disadvantage is the same as the advantage: each machine must be properly configured for the ODBC data source to point to the proper database server.

Creating an ADP Project

Microsoft Access provides several methods through which an ADP project can be created, including the Access automation object model. Most developers, however, use the direct methods of wizards and graphic interfaces to construct a new file. The three direct methods of creation are as follows:

- **Attach to an existing database:** A database located on the MSDE or SQL Server may be used to form the foundation of the project.

- **Create a new database:** A wizard can be used to construct a new database, and the project will be created with it. On the database server, a new database is created with a start size and primary file path location.

- **Upsize an Access database:** The Upsizing Wizard can create a new database on the database server and generate an ADP file containing connections to the newly upsized database object.

Using the New Dialog Box

To create a new project or attach an existing one, the New dialog box (see Figure 8-3) has several selections that display a wizard to create or attach them. The two selections to create an ADP file are Project (Existing Database) and Project (New Database). Each selection offers a wizard to obtain information on the intended MSDE-based database. After a developer has followed the steps of the wizard and specified the location of the database server, and an ADP file has been created, the project itself will hold a connection reference to the database to which it is attached.

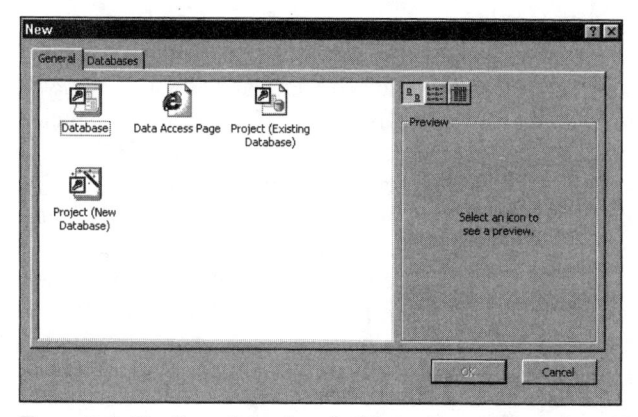

Figure 8-3: The New dialog box facilitates the creation of an ADP file through an existing database or the creation of a new one.

After the ADP file has been created, Access can use the specified connection to make addressing the structures on the database server transparent to the developer. In the same manner that is used with a traditional MDB file, VBA code can address the tables and other objects from forms, reports, data pages, and so forth.

> **NOTE** When the New dialog window is used, the Databases tab contains several sample databases to use as prototypes for your own applications. Unfortunately, none of the wizards for these sample databases will construct the database on the MSDE server. To use the databases in an ADP file, you can create these databases as MDB files and then use the Upsizing Wizard to move them to the database server.

When a new ADP file is created through the New dialog box, no information is automatically stored on the MSDE server to reference the client project. All references between the ADP file and the database that it represents are held on the client in the ADP file. This means that the server-based database does not become a slave to the ADP file and can be accessed and modified by other utilities (Enterprise Manager, Microsoft Query, and so forth) and programs (custom VB applications, database designers, and so forth).

The lack of server information about the project also means that a change to the server name, location, or communication route will not automatically alter the connection information in the ADP file. Therefore, if the database server is relocated, the developer has to reconfigure the connections for all applications that address it.

Using the Upsizing Wizard

For conversion of an Access MDB file to the MSDE server, the Upsizing Wizard will transform the data and then create the appropriate references to the new database on the database server. The Upsizing Wizard converts all of the primary database objects, such as the tables and queries, into their equivalents on the MSDE server. The forms, reports, and other user interface elements are simply copied intact from the MDB file to the ADP file. Upsizing will not convert existing VBA code if some of the objects will have their names altered in the upsizing process.

The objects stored on the MSDE that would be stored in the MDB file of a traditional database all are accessible from the main database window. Although they may appear much like the parallel objects found in an MDB, each new object has special implementation details that must be taken into account when designing an ADP-based solution.

Tables

Tables that are listed in the Objects column of a database project are actually stored on the database server. No part of the data or table structure is contained in the ADP file — it contains only references to the object on the server.

If no connection is available to the MSDE server referenced by the ADP file (for example, if the MSDE server is shut down), the project will load and show no available tables. This applies to views, database diagrams, and stored procedures as well. These items will not appear in the object list, even though the ADP file will load. Only the user interface objects will be available for modification and execution. If the location of the database server has changed, you can redirect the project to the new location.

> **Note:** If the location or address of the MSDE server changes, you can alter the ADP project file to reference the new location. This is done through the Connection selection under the File menu.

The Table Designer Window

All the tables stored on the server can be structurally modified by the table designer window. A new table can be created by clicking the New button on the window toolbar while the Tables item is selected in the Objects column. The new table, once saved, will be created on the database server. A table can also be selected in the details pane of the window, and clicking the Design icon will display the designer window.

Changes can be made to these tables regardless of whether or not they were initially constructed through the ADP file. The designer works nearly the same as that of an MDB table, except that the column properties (such as identity) and data types reflect the fact that a SQL Server–based table is being created or modified.

Changing Table Triggers

In addition to creation or modification of the tables themselves, an ADP file can be used to change the triggers that are used for tables. Right-click on the table in the main database window and select the Triggers option. The Triggers window will be displayed (see Figure 8-4), which lists all the current triggers in a combo box list.

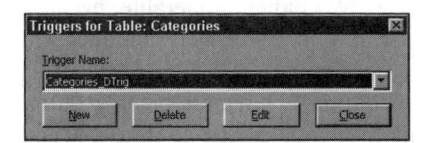

Figure 8-4: The Triggers window enables you to create, delete, and edit triggers.

Click the New or Edit button to display the SQL editing window with the code associated with the selected trigger. The Northwind database that you upsized in Chapter 3 has two triggers that are used for the Categories table. Upon examination of the code for these triggers, you will see that they provide the referential integrity for the connection with the Products table.

Views

Like the query object in an MDB file, a view can be used as a "virtual table" that is generated by a query that can contain columns from one or more logic tables. A view may also use columns from other views. A view may be constructed either through the GUI or by entering direct SQL code.

If you create a new view by selecting the Views item in the Objects column of the project and then clicking the New button, you will be presented with a window very similar to the traditional Query window used for an MDB file. The View design window (see Figure 8-5) is divided into three panes: Diagram pane, Grid pane, and SQL pane. Only the Diagram and Grid panes are shown by default, but the toolbar icons for each of these panes may be used to show or hide any of them.

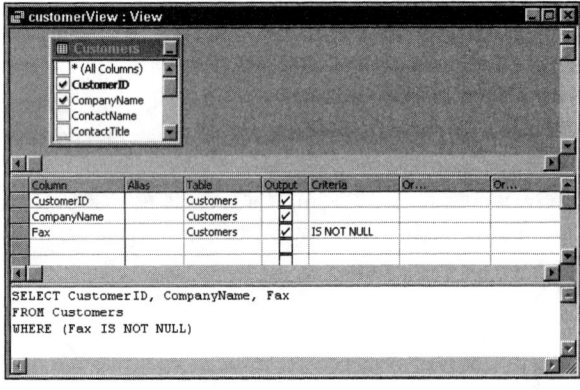

Figure 8-5: The View design window can hold the tables that are referenced in the view as well as column selections and criteria settings.

Changes made to any one pane are automatically reflected in the other panes as soon as the focus on the modified pane is moved. Changes in the SQL pane (such as adding a SQL `Union` keyword) can make the other two panes inoperable, because they are limited in their ability to handle complex queries. If the Diagram and Grid panes are disabled, they appear dimmed with a gray tint.

Views created in this window can be used to optimize interaction between an application and the data that it addresses on the MSDE server. In Chapter 14, you will learn how to use the View window extensively as you create different ways of examining data.

Stored Procedures

Through direct SQL code and MS Query, you've already created some stored procedures and accessed others. The Access Data Project provides an environment to design routines that is more robust than the functions available through the Microsoft Query tool. Syntax checking, color keyword presentation, and fast execution testing are included to enable you to quickly refine your stored procedures.

The stored procedure window will also change to reflect how the stored procedure needs to be modified. If no current stored procedure exists, the SQL command `Create Procedure` will be placed in the window. As soon as the procedure is saved, the window automatically changes to show the SQL command `Alter Procedure`, to allow any further changes to be saved to the server.

You have already seen in the last chapter how the stored procedures are edited in this window. With features such as syntax checking, the Access ADP environment provides one of the best ways to create and modify a stored procedure.

Database Diagrams

A database diagram can show one or more tables and how they are interconnected with relationships, relationship names, key locations, and other information. Diagrams are stored on the server and can create a relationship that ensures referential integrity.

> **NOTE:** If you load an ADP file into Access and the data source is not available, all of the referenced objects will not be accessible and will be labeled Disconnected. You can still edit all of the GUI elements, because they are stored in the project file.

In an ADP project, even if you are currently logged in to the system, you are asked for another login to ensure that you have administrative access for login.

To create a database diagram in the Northwind database, follow these steps:

1. In the main database window, click the Database Diagrams item in the Objects column. In the details pane, you should now see all of the currently available diagrams. Because no pre-created diagrams are included in the Northwind database, the only item shown is the Create database diagram in designer item, which can be used to create a new diagram.

2. Click either the New button in the toolbar of the database window or the creation item in the details pane of the window to create a new diagram.

3. Click the Show Table button, which floats the Show Table window over the diagram window. The Show Table window lists all the tables available. These can be dragged into the diagram window for relation construction.

4. Drag the Customers table onto the diagram. A representation of the Customers table will appear on the diagram canvas.

5. Drag the Orders table onto the diagram. The relationship that exists through the CustomerID column between these two tables will be shown by a drawn link (see Figure 8-6). On the Orders side of the relation, a small link icon indicates that the foreign key is stored in this table. On the Customers side, the key icon designates that the primary key for the relation is located in this table.

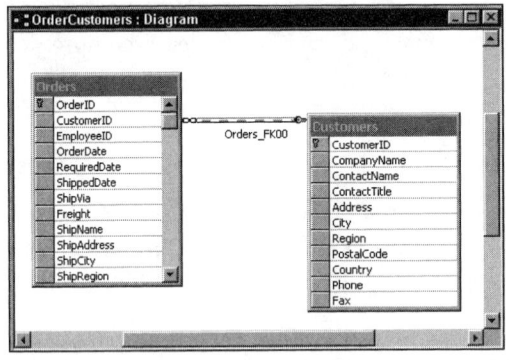

Figure 8-6: The relationship shown between two tables is displayed as a wide, linked gray line.

6. Right-click the link and select the Properties option. The Properties dialog box will be displayed showing three tabs (Tables, Relationships, and Indexes/Keys) that contain settings for the relationship. The Tables tab shows that the primary table of the relation is the Order table. On the Relationships tab, the CustomerID key is one of the relationships present in the table. The Selected Relationship combo box enables you to select from any of the relations present in the database. On the Indexes/Keys tab, the index that is used to optimize the relation is displayed. If you find that another index would optimize the relation better than the existing one, you can select it from the combo box list.

7. Right-click a blank area of the diagram and select Show Relationship Labels. On the diagram, the name of the relation appears centered under the relation.

8. Right-click a blank area and select Layout Diagram. The tables displayed in the diagram will automatically be reordered for an effective and concise layout.

In this diagram, you saw the connection between the Customers and Orders tables that demonstrated the relationship enforcement to ensure referential integrity. The connection already existed on the MSDE server, so creating the diagram simply made the connection visible within the project.

Connection Properties

Under the File menu, the Connection option allows the data link properties (see Figure 8-7) of the project to be examined and modified. In the Properties window, the server to which the ADP is connected, the login name, and the database selected for the project are presented. Clicking the Test Connection button prompts an attempt to make a connection to the configured database server.

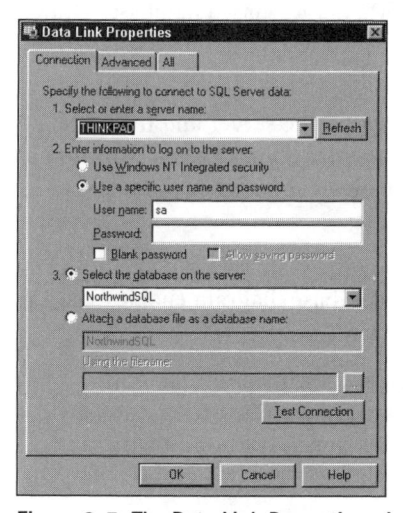

Figure 8-7: The Data Link Properties window shows the connection properties related to the connection of an ADP file.

On the Advanced tab, network security settings such as Impersonation or Protection levels may be set. Note that these security settings are enabled only when DCOM is installed, enabled, and used for secure communication for the connection. The connection timeout and various access permissions may be available for modification, depending on the driver and the database selections.

For more specific configuration values related to the OLE DB driver, the All tab provides a list of editable values. Some of the values that can be changed include: Application Name, Auto Translate, Connect Timeout, Current Language, Data Source, Extended Properties, Initial Catalog, Initial File Name, Integrated Security, Locale Identifier, Network Address, Network Library, Packet Size, Password, Persist Security Info, Use Procedure for Prepare, User ID, and Workstation ID.

Changing any of the values in the Data Link Properties dialog box affects the entire project, because the connection is used for each individual database object.

Summary

Microsoft Access 2000 offers an alternative to the MDB file. The Access Data Project (ADP) enables an MSDE data source to be treated much like an Access database, while the actual database schema remains on the database server and only the interface components are stored in the Access file. A complete development environment for editing server-based objects (such as stored procedures, databases, views, and so forth) is available through the ADP file. In this chapter, you covered the following:

- **Access Data Project (ADP):** New to Microsoft Access 2000, an ADP project type is used to provide robust access to SQL Server-based databases while allowing the user interface programming (such as reports, forms, and Web pages) to remain in a client development file.

- **Tables:** Tables in an ADP project are stored on the server and therefore use the SQL Server data types instead of the data types normally available in Access. The table construction also enables you to set such factors as the identity seed and overall table properties.

- **Database diagrams:** Roughly equivalent to the features available in the Relationships diagram in an MDB file, a database diagram enables you to construct relations for referential integrity.

- **Views:** Like a query in an MDB file, a view presents a virtual table generated by one or more query statements. In Access, a view can be constructed with the GUI standard interface for queries or directly through SQL code.

- **Stored procedures:** A stored procedures is code written in the Transact-SQL language that executes on the database server. Full syntax checking and keyword colorization is available through the Access editing window for procedures.

Chapter 9

ADO Overview

IN THIS CHAPTER

- Understanding ADO
- Learning through an ADO Quickstart tutorial
- Making a connection: the Connection object
- Executing a query: the Recordset object
- Examining asynchronous background execution
- Using stored procedures: the Command object
- Understanding the Property object

MICROSOFT HAS CREATED a set of COM objects, called the ActiveX Data Objects (ADO), that provides programming access to almost any type of data source. ADO can be used to connect to MSDE to execute queries, access stored procedures, create and manage database schema, and exploit other advanced database features. Using the objects of ADO is the most common way of addressing an MSDE data source from program code.

ADO is included with most of the Microsoft development systems, including the Microsoft Office 2000 suite, all the Visual Studio applications (Visual Basic, Visual C++, Visual J++, Visual InterDev, and Visual FoxPro), and the Microsoft Web server through Active Server Pages. The widespread implementation of the ADO data model makes it the perfect method for controlling MSDE when used for enterprise solution development.

This chapter shows you how MSDE can be addressed through the objects that make up the ADO model. Access 2000 has ADO built in, so it will be used to demonstrate the ADO features. You need to have Access 2000 installed to execute the examples, although the code can be run from Visual Basic or any VBA-capable environment as long as the ADO object model is added to the References dialog box of the project.

Understanding ADO

ADO is an evolution of an earlier database object model, known as Data Access Objects (DAO), that has been included with Visual Basic and Microsoft Access for years. When Microsoft created ADO, it simplified the object model and added several features to make it more powerful than its predecessor, DAO.

Microsoft has stated that the framework of ADO will become the standard for all database access in its high-level programming products. Because ADO includes features to address all different types of data, it can be used to replace all of the other methods (such as ODBC, DB Library, DAO, and so forth) that Microsoft products have included in the past.

The OLE DB Interface Layer

Although the high-level objects of ADO evolved from DAO, the underlying technology that makes ADO possible — known as OLE DB — is entirely new. OLE DB is a low-level database interface that enables you to use different data providers to address various types of data sources. An OLE DB data provider (see Figure 9-1) acts much like an ODBC driver insofar as it provides access to heterogeneous data sources. However, unlike an ODBC driver, which requires a SQL-based engine to facilitate data access, an OLE DB Data Provider can be constructed to bridge to any data type. It can access odd data types, such as geographic or spatial data, as easily as it can address traditional SQL-based sources.

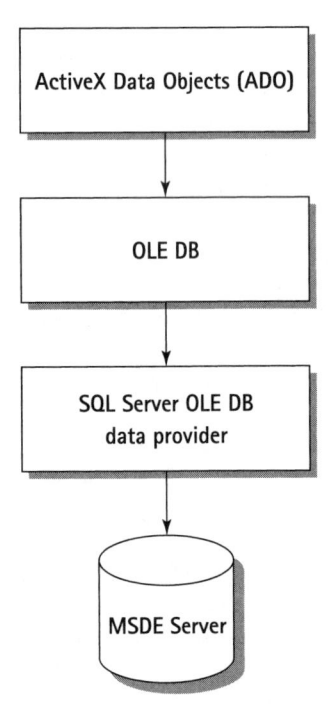

Figure 9-1: The ADO framework sits atop the OLE DB interface layer, which in turn accesses an OLE DB data provider.

The ADO Interface

The ADO interface is a high-level object model that gives most languages access to the OLE DB foundation technology. Because OLE DB is made to be addressed by a system-level language, such as C++, ADO is a developer-friendly interface that sits atop OLE DB and hides the complexity of the low-level interface while granting access to all of its features.

Because of the broad availability of ADO, the majority of new client/server and database applications on the Windows platform are written using ADO. ADO can be easily accessed by ASP, VB Script, VBA, Visual Basic, and any other OLE Automation-compatible language. The developer only needs to add a reference to the object model to the project and instantiate the required objects.

> **NOTE:** In Active Server Pages (ASP) used for Web server execution, the ADO library is available by default. To use these pages, you simply need to create the objects using the `Server.CreateObject()` method.

ADO and MSDE

Accessing MSDE from the programming interface of ADO simplifies database access by providing the following:

- **Connection abilities:** Through the OLE DB Data Provider drivers, a program can use ADO to connect to any MSDE server on the network for which a valid login account exists.

- **Recordsets and database cursors:** ADO can manage a recordset to allow for caching of records and cursor manipulation to move through a large data set.

- **Hierarchical recordsets:** Multiple queries that return related recordsets can be incorporated into the hierarchical recordset definition, allowing navigation of several levels of data query.

- **Parameterized command execution:** Entire SQL statements may be executed to do anything from sending Transact-SQL commands, to configuring server security, to creating stored procedures. Stored procedures may also be executed and may pass and receive parameters.

Any standard ADO installation includes numerous OLE DB Data Providers that give access abilities to ADO. The SQL Server 7 Data Provider and the ODBC Data Provider are both included with the default installation of ADO, so MSDE can be addressed easily through ADO.

The ADO Object Model

When programming the object model of ADO, you primarily use the three principal objects: Connection, Recordset, and Command. Figure 9-2 shows a diagram of the available objects in the ADO framework. Most development projects use at least two of these three objects.

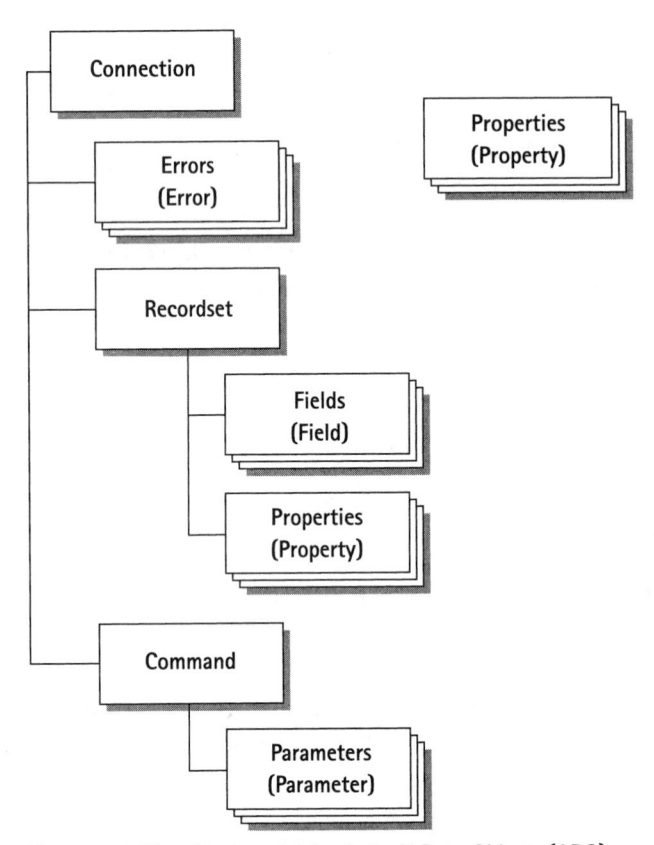

Figure 9-2: The object model for ActiveX Data Objects (ADO)

> **NOTE:** Because all of the example code in this chapter is written in Visual Basic for Applications (VBA), you can also execute this same code in Visual Basic 6 or higher without modification. Simply make certain that the ADO library is checked in the References dialog box of the project so that the objects are available for the code to instantiate.

Each of these three primary objects can be created independently of each other. Although they can be created separately, both the Recordset and Command objects must be eventually connected to a Connection object, unless they are being used for offline data access. Offline access is used primarily for a client-side data set, such as displaying grid data in a browser. Therefore, almost all instances of these two objects include a reference to a Connection object.

An independent Connection object is not required for every object. Through the reference properties of the Recordset and Command objects, multiple instances of these objects can be connected to a single Connection object. In fact, Microsoft recommends that an application should use a single connection for its data source access. Each additional connection that is created to a server expends important resources (memory, connection allocation, processor time, and so forth) on both the server and the client.

> **NOTE:** ADO can be accessed from Visual J++, as well. For Visual J++, you need to import the `msado.dll`. This DLL provides the functional definitions to instantiate and control all of the ADO objects.

ADO Quickstart

You will find that using Microsoft Access to manage ADO objects is straightforward. ADO is already a part of the installation of Access 2000 and is active in the Access environment. In this section, VBA coding is used to address the Northwind sample database on MSDE. This simple ADO code introduction provides a starting point you can refer to in the future for the most bare-bones implementation of ADO.

To create the quickstart solution, follow these steps:

1. Execute Microsoft Access 2000.

2. Select the *Blank Access database* option from the startup window. An Access ADP project could be used instead of an MDB file to hold the ADO project forms, but an ADP project attempts to connect directly to the MSDE server that the project is configured to use. By placing the ADO code in an MDB file, no connection needs to be made until it is selected by the user.

3. Create a new database file named **ADOTest.mdb**.

4. Select the Forms item in the Objects column and double-click the *Create form in Design view* item to start a new form.

5. From the toolbox palette (see Figure 9-3), select the command button icon and draw the button on the form. When the application is complete, this button will be used to activate the opening of the connection and recordset.

Figure 9-3: The toolbox palette has the command button control.

6. Cancel the Command Button Wizard window when it appears. The wizard is available for various preset functions, but the ADO coding for this example must be entered by hand.

7. Right-click the command button and select the Properties option to show the Properties window. You need to add the ADO activation code to the Click event of the button.

8. In the Properties window, select the Event tab.

9. Click in the On Click row and click the command button with the ellipses (...) on the right side of that property. This enables you to open the code window for the button.

10. Select the Code Builder option from the window and click OK. You are presented with a code window like the one shown in Figure 9-4. At the top of the window are two combo boxes. The left combo box shows the control that is currently selected for modification. The right box lists all of the events available for that control. Because you selected the Click option from the Properties window, the Command0 object should already be selected as well as the appropriate event.

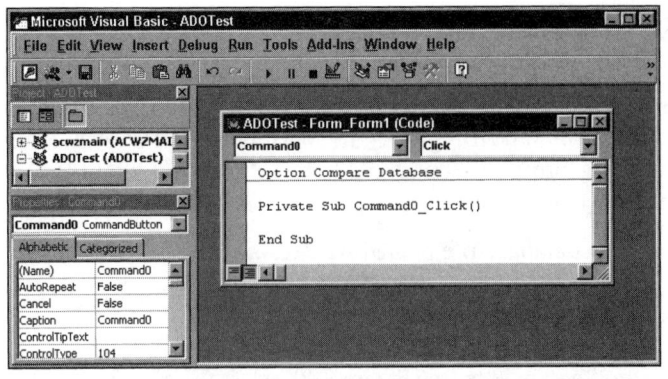

Figure 9-4: The code window that displays all the VBA code that can be associated with the form, controls, and events for the controls.

Chapter 9: ADO Overview

11. Enter the following code within the `Command0_Click` procedure:

    ```
    Dim myConn As New ADODB.Connection
    Dim myRS As New ADODB.Recordset

    ' Open a new connection
    myConn.Open "Provider=sqloledb;DataSource=srv;" & _
        "Database=NorthwindSQL;uid=sa;pwd=;"
    ' Set the recordset object to access the data source
    ' through the connection object
    Set myRS.ActiveConnection = myConn
    ' Open the recordset with a SQL query
    myRS.Open "select * from employees"
    ' Display a couple of the fields of the first record
    MsgBox "Employee Name: " & myRS.Fields("firstName") & _
        " " & myRS.Fields("lastName")
    ' Close the recordset and connection
    myRS.Close
    myConn.Close
    ' Flush the memory used by these two objects
    Set myRS = Nothing
    Set myConn = Nothing
    ```

12. Select the Close and Return to Microsoft Access option under the File menu to return to the Access environment.

13. Click the View icon on the leftmost toolbar to allow the form to execute.

14. Click the command button to execute the ADO code and open the recordset.

After you click the command button, the message box displays the employee name of the first row in the Employees table. After you click the OK button on the message box, the recordset and connection are closed. If you click the button again, new objects will be created and the connection process will repeat.

You have just had your first experience using ADO. Most of this code is probably slightly foreign to you at this point. You can examine the comments in the code to obtain a general idea of the process that is occurring. As you learn about the objects available for ADO, the actions of the code will become very clear.

Making a Connection: The Connection Object

To allow ADO to interact with the MSDE data source at all, you need to make a connection to the database server. The Connection object provides the actual link for the programming interface to the data source. The Connection object doesn't hold any data (as the Recordset object does) or address parameterized stored procedures (as the Command object does), but simply provides the conduit through which these other two objects may address the database.

When the connection is being established, parameters such as the database name, the default database, and other properties are set in the Connection object to facilitate communication. The connection for an application often involves some type of user interface, to enable the user to select which server will be accessed or at least enter the username and password of the login.

Connection Object Properties

In ADO, all operations related to the connection to a data source occur through the Connection object. Properties of the Connection object determine how and where the connection is made. Each connection must have the following information:

- **Server address:** The location of the server, indicated by an IP address, domain name, ODBC DSN name, or WINS machine name.

- **Type of cursor:** A *cursor* is a memory structure that points to which record within the recordset is currently being accessed. Cursors come in a variety of types, some of which are determined by the capabilities of the data source. For MSDE, all four cursor types available in ADO can be used: Static, Keyset, Dynamic, and Forward-only.

- **Location of cursor:** The cursor may be located on either the client (if the client supports it) or the server. To execute on the client, the user must be running Internet Explorer and have the client-side data objects installed.

- **Login security:** The password and username for the connection can be entered as parameters, properties, or may be entered at runtime by the user.

- **Locking method:** If the cursor has write access, the type of locking may be set to a variety of options for the connection. The types of locking available for an ADO connection include Optimistic, Pessimistic, Batch Optimistic, and Read Only.

Most of these properties for the Connection object default to predefined values if not explicitly set. To open a lowest-common-denominator connection to a data source, most of the default settings will work just fine, as you saw in the earlier Access example. For the connection string in that code, only a few parameters were used.

Opening a Connection

To open a connection, you need at a minimum only two parameters: the server location and the data source type or driver. The location typically is specified by a network address or network machine name. The primary driver you'll be using is the SQL Server OLE DB data provider, because MSDE is fully compatible with SQL Server.

To open a simple connection, you could use code like this:

```
Dim myConn
Set myConn = CreateObject("ADODB.connection")
myConn.Open "Provider=sqloledb;DataSource=srv"
```

This code would execute in Active Server Pages (ASP), VBA, or Visual Basic to create an active connection called myConn. The newly created connection could then be used by Recordset and Command objects to interact with the data source. In this example, the specifications, such as the provider and the data source, are passed to the Open method. For many operations in ADO, several ways to perform an operation exist. The parameters in the example could have been specified using properties of the Connection object, and then the Open method could have been called without passing any arguments.

Programming a Connection Object

To program the Connection object, you need to use the methods and properties available for it. The primary methods of a Connection object are the following:

- **Open:** Initiates the connection with the data source. If the connection cannot be created, the Open method either returns the error message to indicate whether ADO itself is having difficulty addressing the drivers for the data source, or displays the error returned by the driver.

- **OpenSchema:** Returns a recordset that contains information about the schema (structure) of the database itself. Attributes returned in the recordset can include field types, table ownership, relationships, and so forth.

- **Close:** Ends the session with the data source. Any changes entered into attached Recordset objects but not completed (using the Update method) will be lost when the connection is closed.

- **Execute:** Executes a SQL command and returns a recordset with the results. The recordset that is returned is always read-only, so this method is not a comprehensive alternative to explicitly creating a Recordset object (that provides read/write support).

- **BeginTrans:** Starts a database transaction that will encapsulate database modification operations until the transaction is committed or rolled back. Transactions may be nested.

- **CommitTrans:** Writes the operations held within the transaction into the database.

- **RollbackTrans:** Revokes all operations held within the transaction.

Either of the `Open` methods (`Open` or `OpenSchema`) must be executed with the proper configuration before you may execute SQL statements or open transactions. The `Open` method accepts various parameters required to open a session with the data source. Some of the parameters used by the `Open` method must be set as properties. The primary properties include the following:

- **Attributes:** Can be used to specify the action of a transaction, such as automatically starting a new transaction after one is committed (`adXaxtCommitRetaining`) or after one is aborted (`adXactAbortRetaining`).

- **Mode:** Indicates the current modes available for modifying data, such as `adModeRead` (read-only), `adModeWrite`, `adModeReadWrite`, `adModeShareDenyRead`, `adModeShareDenyWrite`, `adModeShareExclusive`, and `adModeShareDenyNone`.

The Connection object can also respond to events generated by the data provider. The primary Connection events include `BeginTransComplete` (completed opening of transaction), `CommitTransComplete` (committed transaction), `RollbackTransComplete` (completed transaction revocation), `ConnectComplete`, `Disconnect`, `ExecuteComplete` (completed `Execute` statement), `WillConnect`, and `WillExecute`.

Action Queries

The Connection object can also execute something called an *action query*. An action query is not a query in the traditional sense, because it may or may not return a recordset. Instead, an action query is used to execute a SQL command, such as `Insert`, `Update`, or `Delete`. You use the `Execute` method on a Connection object to activate an action query.

To insert a new contact into the Northwind database, for example, you could use an action query like this:

```
myConn.Execute "Insert customers (companyname,contactname) Values ('Duke Industries','John Doe')"
```

This method can return a Recordset object, and you can use the `Set` keyword in VBA to accept the result set. Unlike a Recordset object that you open yourself, however, all recordsets returned by the `Execute` method of the Connection object will be read-only.

The Error Object

The Error object works in the same manner as the Error object included in Visual Basic, ASP, and similar Microsoft programming environments. The Error object is stored in the Errors collection of the Connection object. Regardless of whether the error occurred in the Command, Connection, or Recordset object, the Error object is stored as a collection in the Connection object.

The type of error is stored in the Number property of the object. If the error value stored in this property is positive, then it is just a warning and does not halt the execution of the current program.

Executing a Query: The Recordset Object

Although a connection is necessary to retrieve data from MSDE, you do not need to explicitly create and instantiate a Connection object. A Recordset object, used to execute queries and hold the data information, either can be attached to a Connection object, or the recordset will be dynamically created when the primary query for the recordset is executed.

ADO supports advanced features, such as sequential data sets and hierarchical recordsets. Sequential data sets enable you to enter multiple queries in the same query request string, separated by a semicolon (;). Calling the NextRecordset method advances the Recordset object to contain the results of the query held in the string after the initial query. When the last query is reached, ADO automatically cycles back to the first query.

Hierarchical recordsets enable multiple related queries to be created from the initial query, usually to address related tables. For example, the Northwind database has a table (called Orders) that holds the information for each order invoice. The details of each order are held in a different table, called Order Details. You could create a hierarchical recordset in which the primary query returns all of the Orders information, and the two subqueries generate two different views of the order details for each individual invoice.

To configure a recordset to use an existing connection, you need to set the ActiveConnection property to the desired Connection object:

```
Set myRS = CreateObject("ADODB.recordset")
myRS.CursorType = 3 ' adOpenDynamic
myRS.CursorLocation = 2 ' Server-side
myRS.LockType = 3 ' Optimistic locking
Set myRS.ActiveConnection = myConn

' Select the general table for insertion
strQuery = "Select * from employees"
' Open the recordset
myRS.Open strQuery
```

After the Recordset object is active and connected to an MSDE data source, you can use the `AddNew` and `Update` methods to create a new record. After the code to open the connection, you might use code like this:

```
' Add a new record
myRS.AddNew
' Set the values of the two fields
myRS.Fields("lastname").Value = "Jacobs"
myRS.Fields("firstname").Value = "Joe"
' Write the information into the database
myRS.Update
```

This example uses the Fields collection of the recordset to set the values for each field. The `AddNew` method automatically places the cursor on the new record so that any changes to the fields or columns of the data set are placed in the new row. When the changes are complete, the `Update` method is called to write the changes into the data source. After this occurs, you can close the data source or continue using the recordset for other operations.

The following are the primary methods of the Recordset object:

- **Open:** Opens the Recordset object, attempts to access the data source through a Connection object, and submits a query for execution. If a Connection object is not explicitly defined in the `ActiveConnection` property, one will automatically be generated by ADO if the proper connection parameters are supplied.

- **Close:** Closes the recordset, making all the recordset constructs inaccessible, except the database schema, which can still be accessed and modified. Closing the recordset releases the connection if one was dynamically generated when the Recordset object was opened.

- **Find:** Used to locate information within the recordset returned by the initial query. The `Find` method is primarily client-side, because it doesn't attempt to requery the database server with a refined query, but instead searches the existing resultant set.

- **Filter:** Provides a method of filtering data available in the recordset by specific criteria. Affects all the record-movement methods (`MoveNext`, `MoveLast`, and so forth).

- **MoveFirst:** Moves the cursor in the recordset to the first record in the set.

- **MoveLast:** Moves the cursor in the recordset to the last record in the set.

- **MoveNext:** Moves the cursor in the recordset to the next record.

- **MovePrevious:** Moves the cursor in the recordset to the previous record.

- **NextRecordset:** Executes the next query in a multiple-recordset query. If the query string has multiple queries separated by semicolons, this command moves to the next available query and fills the recordset with records retrieved using this new query.

- **Requery:** Reexecutes the query stored in the Source property. If any new records have been added or any existing records have been updated on the data source, the changes will be reflected in the newly acquired recordset.

- **Resync:** Synchronizes changes between the data source and the records in the current recordset. Newly added records that would meet the query criteria are not added to the existing recordset when this method is called.

- **Supports:** Returns a value containing the cursor features supported by the current ADO driver. This method can be used to check whether the data source can support dynamic cursors, read/write access, deletion, bookmarking, and so forth.

The primary properties of each Recordset object include these:

- **Cachesize:** Determines the number of cached records to be held in the recordset before the server must be reaccessed.

- **EditMode:** Indicates whether the current record has been placed in edit mode. In edit mode, the lock type indicated by the configuration of the Connection object will be used.

- **Bookmark:** Inserts a placeholder in the recordset for a particular record so that the record may be quickly readdressed. Note that although bookmarks are available to MSDE data sources, not all drivers provide bookmark functionality. Therefore, be sure to use the Supports method in your code to determine whether this feature is available, before using it.

- **State:** Indicates the current state of the recordset, such as connected (adStateOpen), not connected (adStateClosed), connecting (adStateConnecting), executing (adStateExecuting), or fetching (adStateFetching).

- **Source:** Contains the text for the query or queries used to open the recordset. If SQL code was sent to generate the recordset, the code text will be stored here.

Like the Connection object, the Recordset object can respond to numerous events that occur during data access. These events include EndOfRecordset, FetchComplete, FetchProgress, FieldChangeComplete, MoveComplete, RecordChangeComplete, RecordsetChangeComplete, WillChangeField, WillChangeRecord, WillChangeRecordset, and WillMove.

Some of these events, such as `WillChangeField`, are called prior to the operation, such as the field change actually taking place. By setting the return code within the event code you create, the change may be aborted. This enables a developer to conduct a series of custom tests on the change, if necessary, to make certain it is appropriate.

To create sequential recordsets (such as the ones used by the `NextRecordset` method), two or more query commands must be passed in the string used to open a recordset. For example, you may have more than a single query for the pubs database. To show all the authors with last names that begin with *S* in the first set and *R* in the second set, you could use a command such as this:

```
myRS.Open "select * from authors where lastname like 'S%';
    select * from authors where lastname like 'R%'
```

When initially opened, the myRS recordset will contain all the records that are selected with the first query. Activating the second recordset is accomplished simply by calling the `NextRecordset` method.

The Field Object

The Field object (and Fields collection) is used by the Recordset object to store information about the fields or columns of a database. Field values can be referenced like other objects in a collection, using either the name of the item,

```
myRS.Fields("lastname").Value = "Smith"
```

or its ordinal reference,

```
myRS.Fields(3).Value = "Smith"
```

> **NOTE:** Fields can be added to a Recordset object by hand before the recordset has made any connections. This feature supports data sets that are decoupled from any data source. Such recordset creation is useful if you want to create the table structure before the connection is made to data, or for offline recordset access.

The Field object has only two methods:

- **GetChunk:** Reads binary data from a general field type. Used to retrieve data for a Binary Large Object (BLOB), such as image data, object information, or multimedia content.
- **AppendChunk:** Writes binary data into the selected field.

Both of these methods are used to access binary data stored in a database. In MSDE, BLOB data is stored in a binary or varBinary datatype field. In Access 2000, the field type used to store a BLOB can be either the Memo or OLE Object type.

Hierarchical Recordsets

One of the greatest additions to ADO is the ability to create hierarchical recordsets (see Figure 9-5). Within a Recordset object, you can store multiple related queries that provide increasing levels of detail for individual records. In many ways, hierarchical recordsets resemble drill-down reports insofar as each subsequent hierarchical level provides more detailed information.

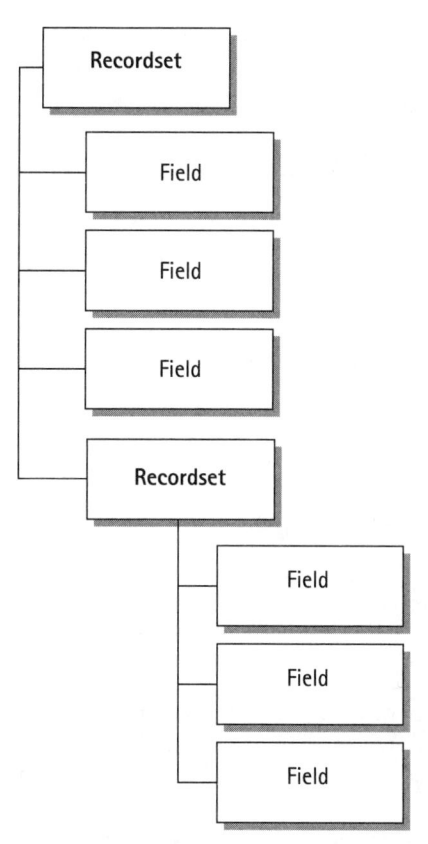

Figure 9-5: Hierarchical recordsets can contain records related to a subquery.

Asynchronous Background Execution

There are many occasions when a database operation can take a lot of time to execute. When this happens, it is often unpleasant for the user to wait for the task to complete before control returns to the application. ADO makes it possible to execute a command in the background so that the user can continue application use. When the operation is finished, the application can respond to an event is activated by the ADO object.

Usually, these ADO background tasks are implemented for asynchronous queries. Because they return control to the calling program, an abort function can be implemented that allows the process to be aborted by the user or the program for any reason.

All asynchronous operations occur on Connection and Recordset objects. The operations for a Connection object include connecting to the database, using the Execute method, and processing transactions. The Recordset object can enact asynchronous queries and updates.

To start an asynchronous operation, you need to add a flag to the Options parameter. This can be done when you call the Open method. If you have a connection ready, you can issue the following statement:

```
myConn.Open , , , adAsyncConnect
```

For a Command or Connection object, you can asynchronously call the Execute method, like this:

```
myConn.Execute "select * from authors", , adAsyncExecute
```

You can then check the state of the open operation through the State property:

```
If myConn.State = adStateConnecting Then
    ' Still in the process of connecting
End If
```

The State property is useful in a development environment that does not support ADO events. A loop could be created to watch for a change of state, at which time the program could alert the user that it has completed, or progress to the next operation.

To create event code to be activated when an operation completes, you can simply name a method in the development environment to reflect the name of the ADO object and the event procedures you want. To receive notification that a connection has completed executing a call that was made, you can use code like this:

```
Sub myConn_ExecuteComplete (ByVal RecordsAffected As Long, ByVal
pError As ADODB.Error, adStatus As ADODB.EventStatusEnum, ByVal
```

```
pCommand As ADODB.Command, ByVal pRecordset As ADODB.Recordset,
ByVal pConnection As ADODB.Connection)
    ' Finished executing command
End Sub
```

If you use an environment that supports ADO events such as Visual Basic 6, the prototypes for the event procedures can be generated automatically.

> **NOTE:** Asynchronous queries are implemented only when client-side cursors are used. Be sure to set the location of the cursor before you open the connection. The cursor location cannot be changed while the connection is active.

Using Stored Procedures: The Command Object

One of the most powerful advantages of using a complete database server such as MSDE over a database engine such as JET is the capability to store optimized and compiled stored procedures on the server itself. Whereas an Access file can keep basic queries in a database, a stored procedure can include advanced logic including `If...Then` statements. Stored procedures can be called and activated by any users who have the proper security clearances. The procedures can execute logic on the database server and may return a recordset.

The Create Proc Command

In MSDE, a stored procedure is initially created by using the `Create Procedure` (or `Create Proc`) command. This command accepts the name of the procedure and any parameters that need to be passed to it. You can create a simple stored procedure in the Northwind database to return all the names of the customers in the database.

To use the Command object to execute a simple query, you would use a `Select` statement like this:

```
Dim myCommand As New ADODB.Command
Dim myRS As New ADODB.Recordset
myCommand.CommandText = "select * from authors"
myCommand.CommandType = adCmdText
Set myRS = myCommand.Execute()
```

To have this query as a stored procedure, you could execute code like this through Microsoft Query or another SQL code application:

```
create procedure authorQuery as
select * from authors
```

The `Create Proc` command begins the definition of the procedure. To execute the `authorQuery` routine, you simply enter the name of the procedure, like this:

```
Dim myCommand As New ADODB.Command
Dim myRS As New ADODB.Recordset
myCommand.CommandText = "authorQuery"
myCommand.CommandType = adCmdStoredProc
Set myRS = myCommand.Execute()
```

The result set that is returned will be the same one that would be generated if the query were entered by hand. You can use this Command object type (set by the `CommandType` property) to execute any stored procedure available in the current database.

> **CAUTION:** Be very careful to specify a database where the stored procedure will be created. When you first create an ODBC data source, the default database selected will be the Master database. Unless you change this default in either your connection string or the ODBC default database selection, it will be selected when you open the connection. Any stored procedure you make will be stored in the currently selected database, so make sure you've selected the location you want.

The Northwind database has numerous stored procedures included. To test one of these routines, open the Microsoft Query application so that you can try executing an existing stored procedure. Select the File menu option to Execute a SQL statement, select the NorthwindSQL data source, and enter the following code in the text box:

```
[Ten Most Expensive Products]
```

You can see the recordset returned by this stored procedure. A query tool known as *SQL Query Analyzer* (which you learn to use in later chapters) displays the returned recordset, as shown in Figure 9-6. If you enter the same text into the `CommandText` property of the Command object and execute it, the recordset will contain the same records you are currently viewing in Microsoft Query.

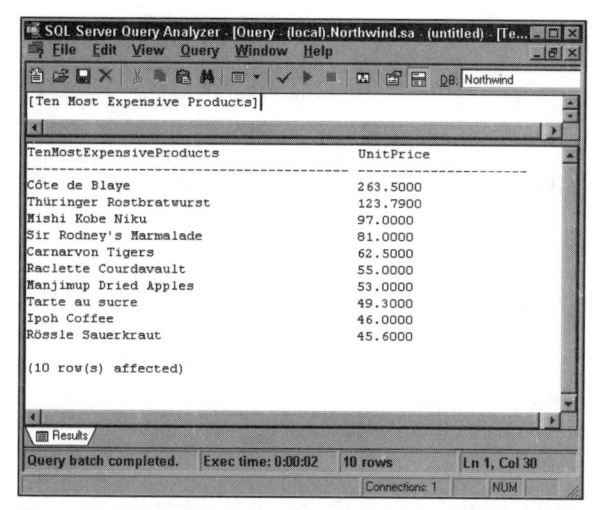

Figure 9-6: The stored procedure called [Ten Most Expensive Products] returns a recordset from the Northwind database.

Using the Command Object

To use the Command object, you can execute the following primary methods available to that object:

- **Execute:** Retrieves the data in the `CommandText` property, interprets it using the setting of the `CommandType` property, and executes the operation against the data source. Both the `CommandText` and the `CommandType` properties may be passed directly to the `Execute` method, where they take precedence over the property settings of the object. If the unknown `CommandType` property is selected, the data provider will attempt to interpret what is stored in the `CommandText` property. The `Execute` method will return a static recordset with the results of the operation.

- **CreateParameter:** Adds a Parameter object to the Parameters collection. Even though the object exists within the collection, it cannot be used until the `Append` method is used to add it to the list of parameters that will be passed to the procedure.

- **Cancel:** Cancels the current execute operation. The `Execute` method must be running in asynchronous mode in order to attain access to this method. Otherwise, this method won't be called until after the current operation has completed.

The `CreateParameter` method is used to add any parameters that are necessary to pass to a stored procedure that accepts them. The Parameters collection will contain all the arguments to be passed until the `Execute` method is called. After the stored procedure is executed, the Parameters collection can also include the values that are returned by the process.

The following are the primary properties of the Command object:

- **CommandText:** Holds the text for the query, execution parameter, stored procedure calls, or any other command operation that will be issued to the Command object.

- **CommandType:** Determines how the text in the `CommandText` property will be interpreted. The command types available include `adCmdFile`, `adCmdStoredProc`, `adCmdTable`, `adCmdTableDirect`, `adCmdText`, and `adCmdUnknown`. The `adCmdUnknown` type is used as the default if no other type is specified. The default slows execution of the command, so best performance is achieved by specifying exactly the type of Command object that is needed.

- **ActiveConnection:** Holds a reference to the Connection object that is being used to access the data source. This property can be set to hold a reference to a shared Connection that is available for the application.

- **Prepared:** Indicates to the server that the settings for the Command object are complete, so any necessary precompilation can be done. You can set this property to activate the server to do precompilation, for optimal performance.

The Parameter Object

The Parameter object, which contains the values to be passed to a stored procedure, is stored in the Parameters collection of the Command object. A separate Parameter object exists for each argument that must be passed to the procedure.

To pass parameters to a Command object, you need to add a Parameter object to the collection and set the appropriate properties. For example, you can execute the stored procedure included in the Northwind database that returns the order history of a particular customer. The `CustomerID` parameter must be supplied to the Parameters collection to be passed to the stored procedure. You could use code like this:

```
Dim myCommand As New ADODB.Command
Dim myConn As New ADODB.Connection
Dim myRS As New ADODB.Recordset
Dim myParam As New ADODB.Parameter


With myCommand
    ' Open a new connection
    myConn.Open "Provider=sqloledb;DataSource=srv;" & _
        "Database=NorthwindSQL;uid=sa;pwd=;"
```

```
    ' Set the Recordset object to access the data source
    ' through the connection object
    Set.ActiveConnection = myConn
    ' Create the CustomerID parameter in the collection
    Set myParam = .CreateParameter("@CustomerID", _
        adVarChar, adParamInput, 5, Null)
    ' Append the parameter to the collection
    .Parameters.Append myParam
    ' Set the value to be passed in the new parameter
    .Parameters("@CustomerID") = "ANATR"
    .CommandText = "CustOrderHist"
    ' Set the command type to a stored procedure
    .CommandType = adCmdStoredProc
    ' Execute the command and place the returned
    ' recordset in the myRS object
    Set myRS = .Execute
End With
```

You can see from the code that creating a Parameter object does not make it accessible to the Command object. The Parameter object must be added to the collection by using the Append method. This code will return the order history in the Recordset object supplied by the Execute method.

The Parameters collection will also contain the values that are returned by a stored procedure after it has finished executing. The name of the parameter can be used to retrieve the returned Parameter object, or you can use the For Each command to examine all the objects in the collection.

The Property Object

The Property object holds information about the settings for every other ADO object. This object is stored in the Properties collection of these objects: Connection, Command, Recordset, and Field. The type of property stored in the collection will vary based on the parent object. For example, in a Connection object, the property ConnectionTimeout will hold the value for that parameter. In a Command object, the property CommandTimeout will hold the timeout for a Command object.

Summary

The ActiveX Data Objects (ADO) library is the primary method of programming access to a data source through VBA. ADO uses three primary objects (Connection, Recordset, and Command) to make addressing most data sources possible. Through these ADO objects, you can open a connection, execute queries, call stored procedures, and perform many other database functions. In this chapter, you covered the following:

- **ActiveX Data Objects:** ADO provides the most effective way to address an MSDE data source from Visual Basic or VBA. The ADO objects provide a high-level interface to the OLE DB data access framework. An OLE DB Data Provider can be used through ADO for data source interaction.

- **Connection object:** Used for creating a connection to a data source. From a Connection object, queries may be executed to return a read-only recordset. Multiple Recordset objects may be attached to a single connection.

- **Recordset object:** Object that stores the data that is returned by a query or database server command execution. The Recordset object supports a variety of cursors, locking methods, and data retrieval methods.

- **Command object:** Primarily used to manage and execute stored procedures on the database server. This object can be used to pass parameters to a stored procedure, as well as to generate a returned Recordset object holding the results of a command execution.

- **Asynchronous queries:** Enables a program to issue a SQL command, such as a query, but execution control is returned to the calling program, allowing continued use of the application while the SQL is being handled by the server. When the operation is complete, ADO activates an event in the calling program to indicate that the results are complete.

Chapter 10

VBA, MSDE, and Advanced ADO

IN THIS CHAPTER

- Working with advanced ADO
- Converting VBA to Transact-SQL
- Using triggers
- Creating distributed queries procedures
- E-mailing with SQL Server

WITH THE MSDE APPLICATIONS you've examined so far, the implementation has been fairly straightforward. Taking advantage of the advanced features of ADO or converting a complex Access application requires special care. ADO, with its three primary objects, appears to be a very simple middleware system, but it includes very advanced capabilities, such as support for asynchronous operation and multi-level queries.

These additional ADO capabilities probably are more advanced than many of the features you are accustomed to using in Microsoft Access. The Access architecture encourages some practices that make conversion of an Access project to a real client/server architecture problematic. Usually, these practices involve blurring the line between client and server code. In Access, where the query engine can handle VBA, this causes few problems. In MSDE, where only the Transact-SQL language can be used, implemented features may need to be rethought and rewritten.

Working with Advanced ADO

After you determine the foundation details for an application, optimizing the structure and function of the code on the client can dramatically increase the effectiveness of the solution. Some of the enhancements to the application can be made by using some of the more advanced capabilities of the ADO middleware.

By adding asynchronous and hierarchical queries to your application, the responsiveness of the client-side interface can be increased. These two features can also minimize the complexity of the client code for some commonly needed operations.

Asynchronous Queries

An asynchronous query can execute the query while returning control to the calling program. It requires the ability to accept event calls from the ADO objects. That enables the completed query to activate custom routines (created by you) to signal the completion of the search.

To create an asynchronous query situation, using the events of ADO, you need to use the With Events command to active the event options. After the With Events command activates the event model, each of the primary objects in the ADO framework will include subroutines that can be activated by the occurrences of transactions completing, execution activation, and so forth.

For the Connection object, the following events are available:

- **BeginTransComplete:** A transaction has been opened. Because nested transactions are possible, this event may occur one or more times before a commit or revoke event may be activated.

- **CommitTransComplete:** Commitment of changes has been made for the current transaction.

- **ConnectComplete:** The connection requested of the Connection object has been completed successfully.

- **Disconnect:** This event is activated after the connection has been severed.

- **ExecuteComplete:** The Execute method requested has completed execution successfully.

- **InfoMessage:** An informational message event has been activated to show that error information has been added from the ODBC Driver Manager (even if the process was successful). This event also activates if an rdoError object has been added to the rdoErrors collection by the system.

- **RollbackTransComplete:** The rollback of the current transaction is complete.

- **WillConnect:** Activated when a connection has been requested through the Open method of the object.

- **WillExecute:** The Execute command has been activated for the object, and execution will progress after this event code has finished.

The Recordset object is the primary object used when implementing asynchronous operations. It has the following events:

- **EndOfRecordset:** The cursor position has reached the end of the current recordset. This event is often used to reset the cursor position to the first record so that it appears as a loop or to automatically insert a blank record at the end of the recordset, for data entry.

- **FetchComplete:** Activated when the execution of a fetch process is complete.
- **FetchProgress:** Returns the progress of the current fetch operation as a percentage.
- **FieldChangeComplete:** An `Update` method call to the recordset has completed successfully.
- **MoveComplete:** The cursor was moved to another record in the recordset and now points to the requested row.
- **RecordChangeComplete:** Alterations to the selected row are complete.
- **RecordsetChangeComplete:** An update to the current recordset has finished executing.
- **WillChangeField:** An update to the current column will be attempted after the code in this event has finished executing.
- **WillChangeRecord:** An update to the current row will be attempted after the code in this event has finished executing.
- **WillChangeRecordset:** An update to the current recordset will be attempted after the code in this event has finished executing.
- **WillMove:** A request has been made to move the cursor to a new row location.

In addition to asynchronous queries, placing code in the completion events of the various objects can enable a program to react to changes and navigation movement made to the Recordset and Connection objects.

Hierarchical Queries

A multilevel hierarchical query can provide drill-down access to data from an MSDE data source. Each level of the hierarchy automatically retrieves data as necessary, so no manual requeries to retrieve hierarchical data are required. The recordsets within the hierarchy can be addressed as if they belong to a single data set. Each child recordset is retrieved based on values found in columns on the parent set.

The simplest example of retrieving a sample recordset is through the orders information stored in the Northwind database (see Figure 10-1). The parent recordset contains all the actual order rows, while the child recordsets have the details of each order. Hierarchical recordsets enable you to return all of these records in a single structure, which you can easily address. The primary factor in making this data easy to access is the hierarchical cursor.

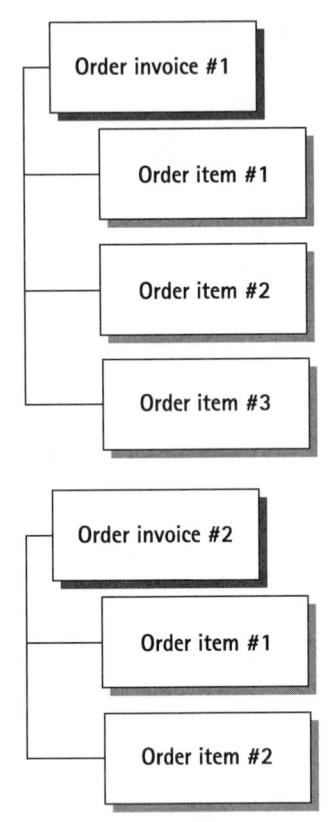

Figure 10-1: A hierarchical recordset can hold rows from multiple queries.

Hierarchical queries are accomplished through connected Command objects. Hierarchical recordsets are built with a process known as *data shaping,* which enables you to build a recordset that can use grouping hierarchies and aggregate calculations.

Data shaping uses special commands called *shape language* in an ADO query, rather than using traditional Transact-SQL code. Child recordsets can either supply records for access to the hierarchical cursor or perform aggregate functions that can be returned to the parent recordset for inclusion. The number of child recordsets (nesting) is limited only by the available system resources, although each extra level can potentially impede performance.

> **NOTE** In VB solutions, the Hierarchical FlexGrid control can directly interface to a hierarchical recordset. It can display the returned data as a series of bands that are grouped by their hierarchy. The simplest method of populating the FlexGrid control is to bind the control to hierarchical Recordset objects.

Data shaping changes the connection string that is passed to the Command object in ADO. Instead of simply specifying a data provider (such as the SQL Server driver), a Shape Provider must be passed for the connection. A Shape Provider is an OLE DB Data Provider that can pass data to another data provider. Because the SQL Server driver used by MSDE application has this capability, the connection string must be changed only slightly to specify that the provider is for a shape data source, like this:

```
MyConn.Open "Shape Provider=MSDASQL; DSN=dsnNorthwind; uid=sa; pwd=;
    database=NorthwindSQL
```

A connection string specifying a Shape Provider will execute properly only if the OLE DB driver has the capability to provide this functionality.

Programming Hierarchical Recordsets

The syntax for a Shape command appears like this:

```
Shape {parentSQL} [As aliasName]
    Append {childSQL}
    Relate(parentColumn To childColumn)
```

Both the parentSQL and childSQL arguments should hold a Transact-SQL statement that returns a recordset. The parentColumn and the childColumn arguments specify the relation column in the same way a traditional SQL join correlates two tables. The aliasName argument may be used to set the name of the returned "table" that can be referenced through the ADO recordset.

The Shape command must be used only with Recordset objects. For example, in the Northwind database, the Shape command to return the orders with all of their details would look like this:

```
Shape {Select * From [orders]}
    Append {Select * From [order details]}
    Relate(orderID To orderID)
```

The hierarchical recordset will contain each order from the Orders table with all of the details of each order available for access through the hierarchical cursor. When this code executes, a single table is returned, but a column is appended that contains the id values of the related columns. This enables the hierarchical cursor to know which rows are parents and which are children as it moves through the data.

You can use code like this in VBA to access the NorthwindSQL database and step through all of the rows to write the orders into a text file. The parent records will be left-justified, whereas all the child records for each parent will be indented

Part 1: Access and MSDE

with a single tab. Simply enter code like this into the `Click` event of a button on an Access form:

```
Private Sub myButton_Click()
    Dim myConn As New ADODB.Connection
    Dim myRS As New ADODB.Recordset

    ' Set the Shape Provider
    myConn.Open "Shape Provider=MSDASQL; DSN=dsnNorthwind;" & _
        "uid=sa; pwd=; database = NorthwindSQL"
    Set myRS.ActiveConnection = myConn

    ' Open a simple text file for the dump information
    Open "c:\OrderDump.txt" For Output As #1
    ' This property, in a hierarchical recordset, will allow the
    ' parent row position to change and not affect the current child
    ' cursor
    myRS.StayInSync = False

    ' Open the recordset with the Shape language commands
    myRS.Open "Shape {Select * From [orders]} as orders " & _
      "Append ({Select * From [order details]} as orderdetails " & _
      "Relate(orderID To orderID)) as orderdetails"

    ' Loop through the parent rows
    Do While Not myRS.EOF
        ' Write the order information into the file
        Print #1, myRS!OrderID
        Print #1, myRS!Customer
        ' Create a recordset reference to the hierarchical cursor
        Set myRSDetails = myRS(myRS.Fields.Count-1)
        ' Loop through the children rows
        Do While Not myRSDetails
            ' Add a tab character and print the child
            ' entries into the file
            Print #1, Chr(7) & myRSDetails!Product
            myRSDetails.MoveNext
        Loop
        myRS.MoveNext
    Loop
    Close #1
    MsgBox "Completed orders output!", vbInformation, _
        "Completed output"
End Sub
```

When activated, the code will output to the OrderDump.txt file on the C:\ root directory a tabbed file. This file will contain all of the orders and the individual details of each order.

Programming Hierarchical Aggregates

The children in a hierarchical relation may also be used to supply an aggregate number such as a sum or an average based on the rows returned through the child query.

The syntax for an aggregate Shape command appears like this:

```
Shape {childSQL} [As aliasName]
   Compute {aggregateColumnList}
   [By groupColumnList]
```

The aggregate functions supported by the shape language include: Sum(), Avg(), Max(), Min(), Count(), StDev(), Any(), Calc(), and New(). The Calc(expr) function allows an arbitrary mathematical expression to be passed (such as 2+2+4) to provide the computed value. New(colType [, width | scale [,precision]]) simply places a blank column of the column type specified in the returned recordset. All of the other aggregates should be familiar to you from Chapter 6.

The By clause on the aggregate command will allow more than one result of the aggregate to be returned. The list of columns specified in the By clause also indicates the column order in which these columns will appear in the parent result set.

In the earlier example, all of the items of each order were listed in the child recordset. Using the aggregate capabilities, the total quantity of each order could be supplied by using the Sum() function on all the individual Order Details items for each order. Such a query would appear like this:

```
Shape {Select * From [orders]} as orders
   Append ({Shape {Select * From [order details]} as orderdetails
      Compute (Sum(quantity)) }
   Relate(orderID To orderID)) as orderdetails
```

Executing this query will return a recordset in which the parents contain the order information, and the children have the summed values of all of the details for that order.

> **NOTE:** The complexity of using the Shape language can be overcome by using one of the Visual Studio development environments. For example, Visual Basic provides a visual construction environment and will create the necessary Shape language code for you.

VBA to Transact-SQL Conversion

In an Access application, VBA code can exist in various places. VBA can be used in queries, default values, modules, and forms. When an Access application needs to be converted to an MSDE application or when a skilled Access programmer first approaches MSDE, several changes in approach must be undertaken.

Handling Embedded VBA Code

One of the problems of approaching an existing Access solution is the presence of VBA code in objects that won't be located on the client in an MSDE solution. In Microsoft Access, you are allowed to use VBA coding in everything from SQL queries to default value settings. As you move your application to MSDE, the problems caused by this feature will become apparent. Because MSDE cannot interpret VBA code, any query that uses VBA will not transfer smoothly and will generate an error when the upsizing wizards are used. Any VBA code has to be removed and rewritten in equivalent Transact-SQL code.

Most of the MSDE coding you do will focus on placing execution code on the server. By focusing on the server-side code, you can take advantage of the power provided by the MSDE server. For existing VBA code, you need to convert much of the VBA logic into Transact-SQL code. Because the languages are very different, this may not be a straightforward task. However, much of the code that is used within queries or default values is basic in structure and minimal in length. The simplicity of the existing code will make the process much easier than cross-language translation for a full program.

Common VBA Functions

To help you convert common VBA functions to functions that are available in Transact-SQL, Table 10-1 offers a list of equivalent routines. Most of these routines generally are equivalent in function, although the syntax may be much different. Because formatting and datatype conversion are the most commonly needed functionality within queries, most of the focus of code conversion occurs in this area.

TABLE 10-1 VBA TO TRANSACT-SQL EQUIVALENT FUNCTION ROUTINES

VBA	Transact-SQL	Description
+	+	String concatenation
&	N/A	String concatenation with automatic type conversion
CStr, Format	Cast	Conversion to string data type
Cint, Format	Cast	Conversion to integer data type

Like VBA, Transact-SQL does numerous automatic or implicit data conversions between data types. In fact, most of the data types support implicit conversions in Transact-SQL. Explicit or manual datatype conversions can be executed either on conversions for which implicit conversion is not possible or in cases where you want to indicate the fact that a conversion is taking place in your code.

To make an explicit conversion, the `Cast` and `Convert` functions can be used to transform a field, value, or variable to a different data type. The `Cast` function performs a simple conversion, whereas the `Convert` function enables other parameters, such as `length` and `style`, to refine the datatype transformation.

- **Cast(expression As datatype):** Changes the passed expression into the specified data type.

- **Convert(datatype[(length)],expression [,style]):** Exactly specifies the parameters of a datatype conversion held in the `expression` argument.

You can use the `Cast` function in a stored procedure, like this:

```
Select "$" + Cast(10 as char(2)) + ".00" As myCast
```

The returned recordset will contain a single row and a single column. The name of the column will be myCast and the row value will be a character field that looks like this:

<u>myCast</u>
$10.00

Without the `Cast` function, a syntax error will occur when the MSDE server attempts to add an integer to two strings. You can use the `Convert` function for the same operation, like this:

```
Select "$" + Convert(char(2), 10)  + ".00" As myConvert
```

> **Note:** Neither of the functions (`Cast` nor `Convert`) supports the ability to convert to a user-defined data type. Data stored in such a data type must occur in the database itself.

The `length` parameter of the `Convert` function is ignored for most data types. Only the char, varchar, binary, varbinary, nchar, and nvarchar data types require the `length` parameter to be specified.

The `style` argument is used when converting a datetime/smalldatetime or a numeric field type to a string. For a date or time value, Table 10-2 summarizes the constant values that may be passed to the routine and what those style numbers will return with the conversion.

TABLE 10-2 DATE AND TIME CONSTANT VALUES AND CONVERSION RETURNS

With Century	Without Century	Format
N/A	0 or 100	mon dd yyyy hh:mi AM (or PM)
1	101	(USA) mm/dd/yy
2	102	(ANSI) yy.mm.dd
3	103	(Brit/French) dd/mm/yy
4	104	(German) dd.mm.yy
5	105	(Italian) dd-mm-yy
6	106	dd mon yy
7	107	mon dd, yy
8	108	hh:mm:s
N/A	9 or 109	mon dd yyyy hh:mi:ss:mmmAM (or PM)
10	110	(USA) mm-dd-yy
11	111	(Japan) yy/mm/dd
12	112	(ISO) yymmdd
N/A	13 or 113	(Europe format) dd mon yyyy hh:mm:ss:mmm(24h)
14	114	hh:mi:ss:mmm(24h)
N/A	20 or 120	(ODBC format) yyyy-mm-dd hh:mi:ss(24h)
N/A	21 or 121	(ODBC format) yyyy-mm-dd hh:mi:ss.mmm(24h)

Numeric conversion has far fewer possibilities. Three values are possible when converting a real or float data type to a string:

- ◆ 0: Returns a string for 6 digits maximum. This is the default setting, and the returned string will be in scientific notation if necessary.
- ◆ 1: Returns a string that is 8 digits long, in scientific notation.
- ◆ 2: Returns a string that is 16 digits long, in scientific notation.

Chapter 10: VBA, MSDE, and Advanced ADO   183

For money and small money, the following three values are possible:

- **0**: The returned string will not have commas and will have two digits to the right of the decimal point. For example: 2141265.17
- **1**: The returned string will have commas every three digits and two digits to the right of the decimal point. For example: 2,141,265.17
- **2**: The returned string will not have commas and will have four digits to the right of the decimal point. For example: 2141265.1695

Some aspects of the `Convert` function operate like the `Format` functions that are available from Visual Basic. The `FormatCurrency` and `FormatDate` functions provide similar output options for those data types.

> **NOTE**: The image data type can be converted only to binary, varbinary, or timestamp data types. Conversions to these types are implicit. Attempts to convert the image type to any other type will generate an error. If conversion to another type is required, it has to be done in multiple steps: first from the image type to a binary type, and then to the destination type.

Using Triggers

MSDE has the ability to create a special type of stored procedure called a *trigger*. A trigger is a Transact-SQL code routine that activates when a specific event occurs. Triggers can be created to activate when any of the following occurs:

- A new record is inserted
- A record in a table is updated
- A delete is attempted on a record

Triggers are defined using the same basic methods of stored procedures. In fact, a trigger appears no different than a stored procedure in coding except for limitations on the commands that can be used within the code. Each trigger can be set to activate for a SQL command, such an `Insert`, `Update`, or `Delete`.

> **NOTE**: Most of the Transact-SQL commands that create or delete objects (`Create Index`, `Drop Table`, and so forth) cannot be used within a trigger.

The syntax for creating triggers through the Transact-SQL function `Create Trigger` appears like this:

```
CREATE TRIGGER trigger_name
ON table
[WITH ENCRYPTION]
{
    {FOR { [DELETE] [,] [INSERT] [,] [UPDATE] }
        [WITH APPEND]
        [NOT FOR REPLICATION]
        AS
            sql_statement [...n]
    }
    |
    {FOR { [INSERT] [,] [UPDATE] }
        [WITH APPEND]
        [NOT FOR REPLICATION]
        AS
        {   IF UPDATE (column)
           [{AND | OR} UPDATE (column)]
                [...n]
         | IF (COLUMNS_UPDATED() {bitwise_operator} updated_bitmask)
                { comparison_operator} column_bitmask [...n]
        }
            sql_statement [ ...n]
    }
}
```

The `Create Trigger` procedure can be used, with the NorthwindSQL database selected, with source code like this:

```
Create Trigger myTrigger
On Customers
For Insert
As
IF Update(ContactTitle)
    PRINT 'New record with Contact info was added.'
```

This code creates a trigger that executes code when a new record is inserted into the table. The trigger sends a simple status statement to the progress window when viewed in ISQL, OSQL, or any other tool that understands print formatting.

Like other structures available on the MSDE server, triggers can be addressed through programming the SQL-DMO framework (see Chapter 16 for a complete SQL-DMO explanation). Each trigger is stored as a separate Trigger object. The

Trigger objects are located in the Triggers collection of each Table object in the database.

Distributed Queries Procedures

Distributed transactions that exist across multiple servers generally are automatically taken care of by the Microsoft Distributed Transaction Controller (MS DTC). For distributed queries, you need to specify how the queries must be handled. Through stored procedures, however, you can take control of this process.

You can configure and control the distribution process with the following procedures: sp_addlinkedserver, sp_addlinkedsrvlogin, sp_catalogs, sp_columns_ex, sp_column_privileges_ex, sp_droplinkedsrvlogin, sp_foreignkeys, sp_indexes, sp_linkedservers, sp_primarykeys, sp_serveroption, sp_tables_ex, and sp_table_privileges_ex.

The sp_addlinkedserver routine requires you to specify the name that will be used to reference the server, the required driver, and the connection string. You can use the routine to add a remote server, like this:

```
EXEC sp_addlinkedserver
    'RemoteSvr', '', 'MSDASQL',Null, Null,
    'Driver={SQL Server};Server=ServerName;uid=sa;pwd=;'
```

After a server has been added to the linked list by using the sp_addlinkedserver procedure, you can use either the OpenQuery or OpenRowset functions to activate a distributed query. For the OpenQuery routine, the Northwind database can be queried as follows:

```
Select * From OpenQuery(RemoteSvr,
    'Select employeeid,lastname , From NorthwindSQL..employees')
```

If all of the servers linked into the distribution list are SQL Server–based, implementing a distributed process is not very complicated. After the linked server network is specified, and objects include specifications down to the location of database objects (including which server contains them), a distributed process can be executed like any other query or update.

E-Mailing with SQL Server

The following stored procedures enable e-mail to be sent through the SQL Server. However, the SMTP server included as a standard installation with SQL Server is not included with MSDE. Therefore, although these procedures are available to the MSDE server, without the SMTP server installed, these commands will not execute properly.

- **xp_deletemail:** Deletes mail stored on the mail server
- **xp_startmail:** Opens a connection to the configured mail server
- **xp_readmail:** Processes received mail individually
- **xp_stopmail:** Stops the mail server
- **xp_sendmail:** Sends a current mail message
- **xp_findnextmsg:** Finds the next mail for processing
- **xp_processmail:** Uses the other three mail-processing routines (`xp_readmail`, `xp_findnextmsg`, and `xp_deletemail`) to process the incoming mail stored in the folders on the mail server

If properly configured, however, MSDE can use the mail services available on a Microsoft Exchange server. Therefore, if you have configuration access to an Exchange server, you can enable MSDE to send mail from within the database through either automatic execution, such as a trigger, or manual activation.

Summary

In a project that addresses MSDE, VBA code cannot be present in a view, default value, or trigger, unlike a query in an MDB file. By substituting Transact-SQL procedures, the functionality will not be lost. Also, by optimizing client-side VBA code to take advantage of some of the advanced ADO features, an Access/MSDE solution can be streamlined. In this chapter, you covered the following:

- **VBA in queries:** In Microsoft Access, VBA code can appear in queries, as well as default values and rules. When programming for the MSDE server, VBA code is not allowed. Instead, any logic stored in the database itself needs to use Transact-SQL code.
- **Distributed queries:** Through the Microsoft DTC and the features of ADO, a transaction can be distributed across several data sources, such as multiple MSDE servers.
- **Asynchronous queries:** Queries that execute in the background through the ADO asynchronous query functions can enable a program to continue processing while the query executes on the server. The autonomous nature of such queries also enables them to be manually aborted by the user if they are requiring too much time.
- **Hierarchical queries:** A hierarchical query allows multiple levels of data to be addressed without creating numerous subqueries to allow for drill-down data access.

Part II

Using MSDE

CHAPTER 11
Using the Enterprise Manager

CHAPTER 12
Using the Database Designer

CHAPTER 13
Using Data Transformation Services and Packages

CHAPTER 14
Working with Views

CHAPTER 15
Replicating Data

CHAPTER 16
Using SQL-DMO

CHAPTER 17
Creating User-Defined Data Types

Chapter 11

Using the Enterprise Manager

IN THIS CHAPTER

- Accessing the Enterprise Manager
- Examining the Enterprise Manager functionality
- Registering the server in Enterprise Manager
- Configuring the database server
- Using the Tools menu

THE NUMBER OF AVAILABLE ways to control and manage an MSDE server is vast. So far in this book, three important methods have already been covered: Microsoft Query, Microsoft Access, and ActiveX Data Objects (ADO). Through a combination of these tools and direct SQL code, you have been able to control many aspects of the server. In some cases, making modifications to the server may have seemed tedious or restrictive.

Included with the complete SQL Server installation (as well as with the Personal and Developer versions) is a tool known as the Enterprise Manager. The Enterprise Manager is the key application that you can use to set up and maintain your MSDE databases. Configuration of the entire MSDE server is simple and quick through the graphic interface of the Enterprise Manager.

Accessing the Enterprise Manager

The Enterprise Manager does not ship with MSDE. Instead, it is included with the complete version of SQL Server, in Developer editions of SQL Server (which are included with most Visual Studio development tools), and the 60-day trial editions of SQL Server available through the Web.

If you don't have access to one of these versions to obtain the Enterprise Manager, the following chapter will still be useful to you. All the functions of this application can be duplicated either through direct SQL code or through the SQL-DMO object model (covered in Chapter 16). Therefore, you can read the information related to the Enterprise Manager and learn the general concepts to apply to your creation. However, I highly recommend obtaining a licensed copy of the Enterprise Manager, for its robust MSDE management capabilities.

Enterprise Manager Overview

The Enterprise Manager is actually a snap-in to the Microsoft Management Console (MMC), an enterprise-wide configuration application that supports extensions for the management of servers ranging from SQL Server to Internet Information Server (IIS). Each database server must be registered with the Enterprise Manager before it can be manipulated. The Enterprise Manager can configure any MSDE/SQL Server anywhere that network access is possible, including addressing a server through the Internet.

The Enterprise Manager can be used to do the following:

- Start, pause, or stop any registered database servers
- Create new databases and modify existing ones
- Monitor current server activity for processes and locks
- Back up and restore databases to the server
- Schedule action items such as backups, Web publishing, and so forth
- Configure database replication
- Manage security
- Generate SQL database creation scripts
- Manage databases, tables, views, stored procedures, triggers, indexes, rules, defaults, and user-defined data types

The MSDE installer is intended for use on a deployment machine, so the Enterprise Manager is not included in the installation. However, for the most effective management of your MSDE server, the Enterprise Manager provides a powerful tool that can be used to manage many MSDE servers over a network. Any MSDE or SQL Server registered to a copy of the Enterprise Manager can be controlled over a network.

Server Registration

Management of a database server within the Enterprise Manager begins with registration of the server. When the application is first launched inside the MMC, it will request that you register a server. You can register the local server with the Enterprise

Manager by selecting the (local) option from the list or by entering its network location through the NetBIOS machine name (for example, *MyComputer*) or through its IP address (for example, 209.57.122.110). It is also possible at any time to add an additional server by right-clicking the SQL Server item and selecting the New SQL Server Registration option.

You can also add a new group to hold the managed servers with the New SQL Server Group option. A server group enables you to organize servers within the Enterprise Manager. The organization into groups is primarily useful for the administrator, for ease of organizing the servers that need to be managed.

Database Server Configuration

For each database server, the Enterprise Manager enables you to define execution settings for that server. All the servers registered with the Enterprise Manager can be configured for these options: memory allocation, multiprocessor thread settings, security authentication type, user connection limitations, mail profiles, index settings, and more. Each of these settings will have an effect on how MSDE treats the particular database in relation to the server machine that it is executing on.

If you right-click a server in the group folder and select the Properties option, you can set the configurations for the group. For example, on the Processor tab of the database server Properties dialog box, you can modify the threshold used for parallelism to a value between 0 and 32,627. This threshold helps symmetric multiprocessor (SMP) machines running Windows NT to determine when processor threads can be allocated for SQL processes. On the Processor tab, you can also set the number of processors that can be used to execute a query. The default setting uses all available processors.

Although the server configuration occurs in this Properties dialog box, most of the settings for the server appear in the individual folders that are present for each server. Five basic folders contain all the objects used by the server: Databases, Data Transformation Services, Management, Security, and Support Services. The Databases folder is the one you will most commonly access, because it allows direct access to the databases that exist on the server.

The Databases Folder

The Databases folder contains all the databases available on the MSDE server. Databases can be added to the server through various different means, including SQL construction code execution, the Database Designer, Microsoft Access, and restoration of a backup of an existing database. After becoming available on the MSDE database server, each database can be addressed by client programs, modified, or deleted. From within the Enterprise Manager, all the possible operations associated with the database can be completed (including data entry).

Each database contains numerous objects that define it. The following folders are available for each database:

- **Database Diagram:** Holds database diagram such as the ones you will construct in Chapter 12.

- **Table:** Contains all of the table definitions available in that database. The Enterprise Manager enables you to browse and change design details for each table.

- **View:** Holds all of the views of the database. Usually, views are created using a SQL command, although the Database Designer can be used in the Enterprise Manager to construct a view query graphically.

- **Stored Procedures:** Stores the stored procedures of a database. The text of the code for the procedures is stored within many of the system tables (such as syscomments) in the master database.

- **Extended Stored Procedures:** Holds all of the references to the DLLs that contain *extended stored procedures,* which are functions contained in external DLL files written in a language such as Visual C++ and registered with MSDE so that they may be activated from within stored procedures. This folder only appears in the master database.

- **Rule:** Holds the definitions for the rules of the database. In the Enterprise Manager, you can bind a rule to a column of a table or to a user-defined type.

- **Default:** Contains the default objects that are bound to columns in the tables. Unlike Microsoft Access, which stores the default values in the table with the column, default objects are created and located in the Default folder of each database and are bound to individual columns.

- **User-Defined Data Type:** Holds all of the definitions for the user-defined data types.

If you right-click any database item in the Databases folder, you can access the All Tasks submenu, which provides options to import and export data, create a maintenance plan, generate SQL scripts, back up or restore a database, and perform maintenance on a database. Most of these options are also available to objects on the primary MMC menus for the Enterprise Manager.

The Import Data task on the menu opens the Import Data Wizard, which guides you through the steps for retrieving data from various data sources, including any registered ODBC sources or ADO/OLE DB data providers. Data from text files can be imported using the text file ADO/OLE data provider. This wizard can be used to generate a package that may be used for later imports of the same type. (Packages are covered extensively in Chapter 13.)

The Export Data option displays the Export Data Wizard, which acts much like the Import Data Wizard in selecting the data source for use. Your output options for exporting include MSDE/SQL Server, dBase 5, dBase III, dBase IV, Microsoft Access, ADO/OLE DB, ODBC, Microsoft Data Link, Excel 3-8, Microsoft FoxPro, Oracle, Paradox 3-5, and text file format. The export capability available through DTS can be used to copy tables, execute a query to transfer specific data, or transfer entire database objects (if the destination is another MSDE or SQL Server database server).

The Maintenance Plan option creates a maintenance plan specifically tailored to the selected database. Tasks such as rebuilding indexes, compressing data files, updating indexes, running consistency checks, and activating backups can all occur within the context of the plan. See the section on database maintenance plans under the "Management Folder" heading, later in this chapter, for more information on the capabilities of a plan.

> **Note:** Within the Enterprise Manager, you can drag and drop various objects (such as tables, stored procedures, and so forth) from one database onto another. This capability provides substantial savings in effort, because a database and all of its data does not have to be reconstructed to be moved to a new database location.

The Generate SQL Scripts option provides the ability to generate SQL code that can be used in the re-creation of an entire database schema. In the past, when the MSDE/SQL Server interface wasn't as robust, this feature was critical. Although it's no longer as essential as it used to be, it is still extremely useful.

The database creation SQL code generated can be used to do the following:

- **Quickly create a similar database:** With only a slight modification to the code (such as changing the database name), the script can be run to create an identical database. Additional modifications can adapt the existing database structure to new requirements.

- **Re-create an empty database:** When you need to begin with a database that contains no data, it is often easier to render the SQL script, delete the entire database, and begin again, instead of emptying each existing table of information.

- **Share the structure:** With the schema held in a small ASCII text file, it is easy to e-mail the structure or share it with your peers.

- **Examine SQL construction code:** If you need to write SQL database creation code, almost no better way exists than to use the graphical interface tools in the Enterprise Manager or Access to construct the database. When the basic database design is complete, generating the creation scripts provides you with an excellent example.

- **Reconstruct the database in a different database server type:** After the SQL script has been created, it is very easy to modify it to be compatible with another database vendors product (Oracle, DB2, Informix, and so forth).
- **Documentation:** A completed project usually is associated with some form of developer documentation that explains the workings of the system. Generating the SQL scripts provides an opportunity to include the database schema in printed explanations of the entire system.

The code generated will be placed into a text file with the extension .sql. The SQL file can be reloaded into the SQL Query Analyzer for execution, or sent through an ADO Command object (refer to Chapter 6).

> **NOTE** By default, the SQL file written to the hard drive is written in Unicode format. *Unicode* is a new international standard that allocates 2 bytes for each character (versus 1 byte for ASCII-based files), enabling all the international languages to be represented. MSDE does offer an option to allow the system to output files in ANSI or DOS text file format.

The Backup and Restore Database options activate the Backup system for the SQL Server database. The Truncate Log option enables you to manually truncate the log file, rather than waiting for the log to be automatically managed or truncated when a checkpoint is reached (if that option is selected). The Shrink Database option can be used to reduce the amount of disk space currently used by a database, if deleted records or indexes have not yet been eliminated by autoshrinking. Finally, the View Replication Conflicts option enables you to examine conflicts among the replication processes that may have been constructed for individual databases.

The Data Transformation Services Folder

The Data Transformation Services (DTS) are used to import and export data from the MSDE server. Moving data from one format to another can occur through a combination of COM, ADO/OLE DB, and VB Script/JavaScript. A transformation process setup within the DTS can also be executed by a scheduled task, so the entire data import and export process can be automated if needed.

The DTS technology is also integrated with the SQL Server OLAP services. Connectivity in DTS is also provided for Access, Excel, FoxPro, SQL Server, Oracle, DB2, AS/400, and other OLE DB data providers. (See Chapter 13 for more information on using DTS.)

DTS is provided primarily to accommodate workflow operations that need data access from the SQL Server engine. DTS can be used to provide automated exchange

Chapter 11: Using the Enterprise Manager

between a variety of heterogeneous data sources. DTS is also an attempt to provide an industry-standard format for metadata and data lineage information that is supported in Microsoft Repository.

Each of the processes created in DTS are stored in a structure called a *package*. Storing information in packages, the Enterprise Manager can be used to schedule the execution of a package by the SQL Server Agent.

> **Note:** The package structure in DTS has nothing to do with the package structures used by Microsoft Transaction Server (MTS). Whereas the DTS package holds sequential instructions on how to process data, an MTS package holds an organized set of components.

Creation of a package occurs through the DTS Designer application. Both the Import and Export Data Wizards can be used to create a package that can be edited in the DTS Designer application. The DTS Designer provides a graphical interface for the creation, management, and organization of packages. You can use the DTS Designer (see Figure 11-1), to add scripts, tasks, data sources, and other executables to the design canvas.

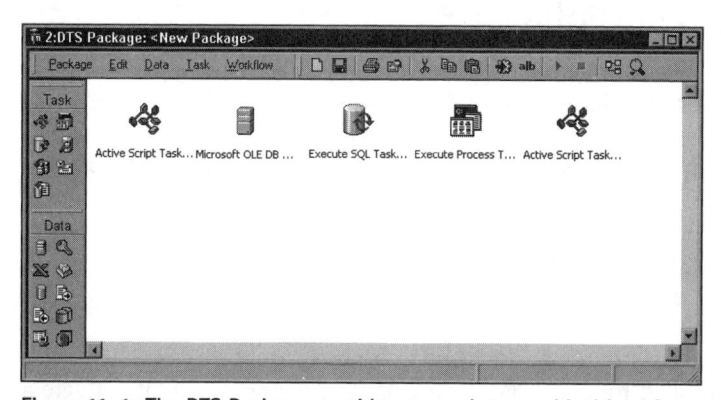

Figure 11-1: The DTS Designer provides a complete graphical interface to create a DTS process.

Packages comprise all the logic needed to accomplish a data transformation. The definitions within a package detail a number of sequential steps that executes a particular task. That task may involve executing a SQL statement against an ADO data source, calling an ActiveX DLL method, sending e-mail, or performing some other operation.

> **Note:** In addition to modification and activation through the DTS Designer, the transformation services can be programmed through the DTS object model. By extending the objects in the framework, you can even create custom tasks that are integrated with the DTS Designer user interface. These are known as *DTS custom tasks*.

The DTS folder in the Enterprise Manager contains three folders: Local Packages, Repository Packages, and Metadata. Local packages are those stored on the current MSDE/SQL Server. Repository Packages contains references to packages stored on a Microsoft Repository Server. The Metadata folder contains the information about the data transformations, the data types used, and the groupings of the data. Metadata information is used to describe the schema of the database so that a transformation may be extended in the future without foundation restructuring.

DTS may become a critical part of your MSDE solution, because most organizations have data located in various data store types. The ability to leave the data in the heterogeneous data sources and have automated import and export occur is one of the features that places MSDE/SQL Server above other brands of database servers. In Chapter 23, you will study these services in depth.

The Management Folder

The Management folder contains tools that can be used to manipulate, configure, and monitor individual database servers. Six items are held in the Management folder: SQL Server Agent, Backup, Current Activity monitor, Database Maintenance, SQL Server Logs, and Web Publishing. The SQL Server Agent is key to all automation tasks on the server, because it can be used to schedule jobs based on time events. Agent services may be used to activate Database Maintenance, SQL Server Logs, Web Publishing, or Backup for execution.

SQL SERVER AGENT

The SQL Server Agent runs in the background as a process that can execute operations based on a specified time and date. For example, the agent might activate a data transformation operation at 12:01 a.m. Monday morning to convert a week's worth of data into a format that can be examined when the work week begins.

You can use the automation features of the SQL Server Agent to define a set of jobs and alerts. Jobs and alerts can react to events on the database server and execute the specified script event code. Automation provides a way to minimize manual handling of common tasks by executing event script code to handle these tasks.

You need to create a user account on the MSDE that will be used by the agent to facilitate the login. The agent will then use this account to execute automation tasks that have been programmed. If the resources required by the agent are all local resources located on the current server, you can set MSDE to use the system account for these tasks. If resources are required from across the network, you need to create a special account with the appropriate permissions. You must stop and restart the SQL Server Agent before the changes that you made to the account will take effect.

You also need a mail profile that enables the agent to send mail. It can use Microsoft Exchange or Outlook to provide e-mail, but the client must not be configured to be password-protected. If it is password-protected, MSDE will not be able to begin the mail session.

To schedule a DTS package to be executed by the SQL Server Agent, right-click the SQL Server Agent item. First, make sure that the SQL Server Agent is running, which should display a green "play" arrow on the icon. If agent isn't executing, you can use the right-click context menu to select the Start option to activate the service. If you are scheduling jobs to run automatically, the SQL Server Agent must be set to start automatically whenever the computer boots. It will run in the background, waiting for a time to launch a scheduled event or until an alert triggers an action.

From the context menu, select New → Job. You are presented with the Job properties window that enables you to set the location of the task, the steps involved, the schedule, and the notifications when the task is complete. After you finish constructing a job in the configuration dialog box, you can click the OK button, and the execution task will be created. Accessing the Jobs item in the SQL Server Agent folder shows all scheduled tasks as well as their current status.

BACKUP FOLDER

The Backup folder holds the device that can be used to back up and restore databases from the current MSDE system. To transfer data from one MSDE server to another without replication, the backup system of MSDE usually is used, to encapsulate all of the necessary objects that relate to a database so that they may be loaded into another database server.

CURRENT ACTIVITY FOLDER

Although you can examine some of the statistics that occur on the server in the Windows NT Event Manager application, under the Current Activity folder, you can examine the following figures that show exactly what's happening on the server:

- **Process Info:** Shows the status of all the current users and the database process that is being used by them

- **Locks/ProcessID:** Shows the lock status of the database objects, categorized by the individual process ID numbers

- **Locks/Object:** Shows the lock status of the database process IDs, categorized by the database objects

This information presented in the Current Activity folder provides one general method of examining activity. For more specific information, you can use the SQL Server Profiler application that is available under the Tools menu.

DATABASE MAINTENANCE PLANS

A database maintenance plan is used to check the integrity of the database, update database statistics, and perform necessary database backups. A Database Maintenance Plan Wizard is included with MSDE to step you through the process of creating a plan.

A plan may include any of the databases currently on the system, including systems databases (master, model, and msdb) and user databases. For the databases included in the schedule, the plan can do the following tasks:

- Check database integrity
- Back up and verify data
- Back up the transaction log
- Reorganize data and index pages for optimization
- Update the statistics that are used by the query optimizer
- Remove unused space from database files
- E-mail or write a text file report of performed maintenance actions
- Write the maintenance history into a database for examination

After you decide whether or not each of these operations will be performed, you can set a frequency for how often the plan will be executed. By default, the maintenance plan is set to execute once a week on Sunday at 1 a.m. This recurring scheduled event can be changed to almost any combination of time, day, and date sequence.

SQL SERVER LOGS FOLDER

Unlike the transaction log that keeps track of the various database modification operations, the logs in this folder contain information about the user interaction with the database server, including logins, access attempts, and so forth. The SQL Server logs are the MSDE equivalent of the Event Viewer for normal Windows NT operating system events.

Events such as startup, launch progress, operation failure, file opening, and so forth are all stored in this log. You can examine the log simply by clicking either the current activity folder or one of the archive folders. All of the logged items will be displayed, as well as the source of the log entry.

WEB PUBLISHING

MSDE provides a tool called the Web Assistant Wizard that generates static HTML pages from data stored in the server. These pages should not be confused with dynamic pages that are created on-the-fly through Active Server Pages (ASP) code.

However, because Web publishing in MSDE can be assigned for job activation by the SQL Server Agent, the pages can be generated regularly to keep them up to date.

Using static pages has several advantages over dynamically running the queries with each access:

- **Saves processor time on popular reports:** Reports that are accessed often by many users require a great deal of processing power. In contrast, generating the report once allows all the server resources to be devoted to the Web server returning the HTML pages.

- **Instant user retrieval:** The visitor doesn't have to wait for the query to execute, because they can retrieve the static HTML page instantly.

- **Search engine listing:** Static pages can be catalogued much more easily by search engines than can dynamic pages that rely on input parameters.

- **Ease of distribution:** A static page, after it's generated, has no need to be hooked to a data source. Therefore, the static page can be written to a network drive of a remote Web server or copied to any machine, unlike a dynamic ASP page that requires the ASP execution engine and the MSDE server to function.

The static pages can be generated one time, scheduled for timed updates, or regenerated because of an event (through a trigger). After the pages have been manually generated, they may also be conveniently edited in an HTML editor (such as Microsoft FrontPage). Of course, any changes to the documents will not be included when the next batch is run unless the coding template is altered.

> **TIP** Whenever you generate a static report, make sure to place the date prominently on the report so that the user knows when it was generated. Otherwise, the page may seem current even if it's out-of-date.

To use the Web Assistant Wizard to create a sample page from the Northwind database (the one you upsized in Chapter 3), follow these steps:

1. Execute the Enterprise Manager.

2. Expand the Management folder on your MSDE server.

3. Right-click the Web Publishing folder.

4. Select the New Web Assistant Job option.

5. Specify the database to be used for the page data by selecting the Northwind database, and then click the Next button.

6. Set the name of the job (or leave it as the default) and set the wizard to retrieve the data from the tables and columns that you select (see Figure 11-2). Note that you can also use stored procedures or a Transact-SQL statement (which could be a simple SQL query) to return the data for the Web page.

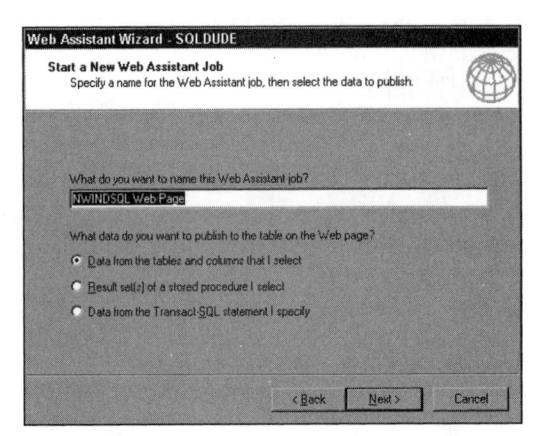

Figure 11-2: Set the name of the job and select the data source.

7. Click the Next button.
8. In the Available Tables combo box, select the Employees table.
9. Click the Add All >> button to place all of the columns in the Selected Columns list box. The upsizing process added to this table a column called upsize_ts that contains the timestamp for each record. This column won't provide any information for the Web report, so it should be removed.
10. Scroll to the bottom of the Selected Columns list, select the upsize_ts field, and click the << Remove button.
11. Click the Next button to advance to the display criteria screen, in which you can select which rows to place in the Web page. To demonstrate the full features of this wizard, you will add some criteria to return a subset of the total employee list.
12. Select the option to enter a Transact-SQL clause, and enter the following code. (This WHERE clause will return the names of all the employees who have a last name that begins with the letter *S*. Your wizard screen should appear like the one shown in Figure 11-3.)

    ```
    WHERE [Employees].LastName like 'S%'
    ```

13. Click the Next button.

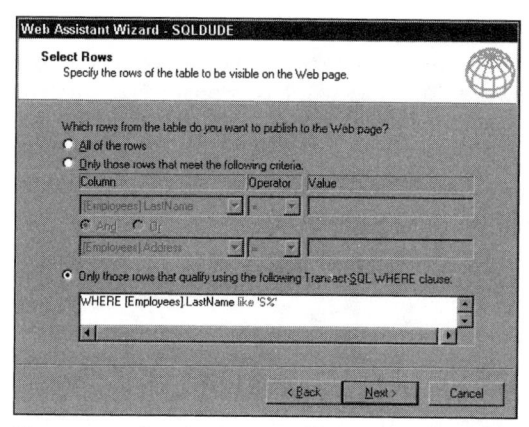

Figure 11-3: Set the Transact-SQL code to return the names of only those employees with a last name that begins with the letter S.

14. For the time interval, select the option On Demand and then click the Next button. This option will automatically check the option for automatic generation when the wizard is complete. It will also enable you to generate this report in the future.

15. This wizard screen asks you for a path to write the file. If you have IIS on the same machine, you might consider setting the path so that the page is published to your Web server for the test (for example, the path to your web server might have a path like this: `c:\inetpub\wwwroot\MSDEreport.htm`).

16. Set a path and click Next until you have completed the publishing process.

The Web Assistant should now execute the Web publication and generate the Web page at the location you specified. The Web Assistant can also be called from within a stored procedure or trigger through the system stored procedure named `sp_makewebtask`.

The Security Folder

Security will be discussed in depth in Chapter 25, but this review of the basic security interfaces in the Enterprise Manager will be helpful as you begin to configure your database system. With the increasing integration of security settings within the enterprise-wide Active Directory system included with Windows 2000, security will be integrated into a global setting. Meanwhile, MSDE/SQL Server contains a complete security framework offering user and group security that may be used to limit access (login), functions (read, write, browse, and so forth), and schema modification down to the column level.

FIRST THINGS FIRST

For ease of testing, all the logins in this book use the sa (system administrator) account with an empty password. This password is probably the first thing that should be changed when you install your MSDE server. Because this default enables anyone to interface to your server and control it at an administrative level, it is dangerous to your databases to leave it unchanged.

To change the sa account, follow these steps:

1. Open the Enterprise Manager.

2. Expand the MSDE database server.

3. Expand the Security folder.

4. Click the Logins item to select all the available login accounts. You will see at least the Administrators group and the sa user in the Details pane. If you have added any additional users and groups to the server, they will also be displayed in the Logins container.

5. Right-click the sa account and select the Properties option. The Properties dialog box will be displayed for the account (see Figure 11-4).

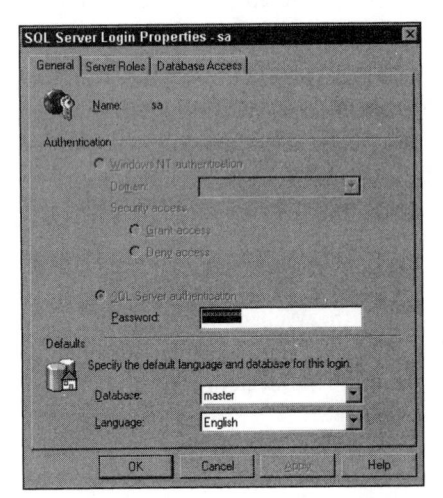

Figure 11-4: The Properties dialog box of the sa account enables you to set a new password.

6. Enter a new password and click the OK button.

You've now taken care of one of the most critical security holes in the SQL Server system. Often, beginning developers leave this password unchanged because they are only doing development work and therefore believe the system isn't in jeopardy. However, with the growth of corporate networks being hooked to the

SERVER ROLES

Internet, if someone knows of the existence of the server, they can reach right through the corporate routing and have full access to your server.

Server roles act somewhat like a group in the security framework, but have their own definition outside of the Windows NT integrated security. When Windows NT integrated security is used, groups are held in the NT security framework. In contrast, roles are available for definition only in MSDE/SQL Server and are restricted to a single database.

Although permissions are cumulative for multiple roles that a user is granted, restrictions take precedence over granted privileges. For example, if the GroupLeader role provides write access, but GroupMember denies write access, a user that includes both roles will be denied write access.

LINKED SERVERS FOLDER

The Linked Servers folder enables other database servers to be linked for distributed processing across multiple servers. This distribution can enable two or more database servers to handle updates, inserts, and queries. The SQL Server engine can break down a command sent to the server and distribute it among the linked servers.

Servers can be linked through an ADO/OLE DB data provider, DTS packages, ODBC, Internet Publishing Services, or Microsoft Directory Services. Security for communication can be handled through impersonation or mapped user accounts.

MSDE also supports remote servers, which are available solely for legacy compatibility. While linked servers can exchange any data between them, a remote server is simply a method of extending the reached of users that are logged into the current database server for executing stored procedures.

Through the remote server configuration, an authorized user connected to one MSDE or SQL Server can execute a stored procedure on another server without having to log into the second server. The functionality of remote servers has been superceded by the linked servers technology.

The Support Services Folder

The support services are those services not intimately concerned with database operations (such as e-mail) or services (such as DTC) that coordinate other technologies with the database server. Although these services are external to the server itself, they are integral to some important functions, such as transactions.

DISTRIBUTED TRANSACTION COORDINATOR (DTC)

The Distributed Transaction Coordinator (DTC), in general, is available to allow transactions across different execution processes. The DTC service for MSDE enables you to integrate transactions that span multiple databases with the general MS DTC service (available through the Control Panel → Settings folder) that allows a transaction to span multiple components (such as several ActiveX DLLs) and retain atomic transactions. To the user, transactions that use the DTC and span multiple servers are transparent. The MSDE server handles all of the necessary operations.

SQL MAIL

The SQL Mail connector allows a stored procedure or trigger to send mail from the server. It uses the SMTP service that is installed with the Windows NT Option Pack (or comes standard with Windows 2000) to provide bulk mailing services.

The SQL procedures of xp_sendmail can be used to mail from a stored procedure. With a single line of Transact-SQL code, you can send mail like this:

```
xp_sendmail 'myName@widgetco.com', 'Thanks for signing up!'
```

Using the Tools Menu

The Tools menu is a catch-all of all of the utilities that can broadly apply to many of the individual database objects. Systems such as replication, full-text indexing operation, and the SQL Profiler tool are available through this menu.

Replication

Replication is one of the most complicated aspects of MSDE. *Replication* is the process of creating multiple copies of a database that will later be synchronized so that any changes in one copy will be combined into the other copies. Replication is extremely useful in decentralized systems in which servers are geographically distant and constant communication is expensive, difficult, or unreliable. The replication automation can coordinate the synchronization late at night, enabling machines to compare and combine data in a low-traffic or inexpensive time period.

Replication is also very useful for portable applications in which the computer will be unattached and unavailable to the primary system. The growing use of portable systems has made replication a primary technology in database implementations. To accommodate the "road warrior" user, MSDE can even support replication to an Access database, allowing for broader possible data reach.

Because a database can be split among various servers that can be automatically or manually synchronized, the setup process is complex. Learning how to configure the topology of a replicated system is covered extensively in Chapter 15.

Full-Text Indexing

Full-text indexing is a feature that is new to MSDE and SQL Server 7. It allows data that is stored in char, varchar, text, ntext, nchar, or nvarchar column types to be queried from within the MSDE server. The full-text indexing allows special search forms, such as pattern matching and English language requests, to locate the desired information within the data stored in these column types.

Only a single full-text index is allowed per table. All the indexes of this type are grouped within the database in a structure known as a *catalog*. A full-text catalog is not stored within the database itself, but instead is stored as a separate file and maintained by the Microsoft Search service. The index information that is held within a catalog is known as a *population*.

Updates to the full-text indexes must be activated by an explicit rebuild command, because they are not automatically updated with the regular indexes. Data additions and updates to the index information (population) must be requested by a command or a scheduled update. Much like the static Web publishing described earlier in the chapter, full-text indexing creates a series of static files for the information present at the time of the index construction.

SQL Server Profiler

The SQL Server Profiler is a tool that enables you to examine events that are occurring to the SQL Server. It provides a graphical method of watching server connects and disconnects, Transact-SQL batches, execution of stored procedures, deadlocks, and the SQL Server error log. It receives event notification for the duration of Transact-SQL events and all the types of events being traced.

The Profiler can be used to debug stored procedures, because individual execution statements within the procedure can be monitored and any errors that occur can be examined. The individual monitoring made possible by the Profiler can be used to identify slow queries.

The Profiler may be used by a single user, or multiple Profilers may be run against the same database server, depending on the configuration. Share types include Private, to disallow other users from using the trace, and Shared, where other users may trace as well.

Summary

The primary interaction of the administrator of MSDE occurs through the SQL Enterprise Manager program supplied with SQL Server. The Enterprise Manager can be used to create, modify, and delete databases, but it can also be used for more advanced functions, such as creating DTS packages and monitoring process and locking activity. In this chapter, you covered the following:

- ◆ **Basic security:** Configuring MSDE for basic security includes changing the default empty password that is used for the system administrator (sa) account.

- ◆ **Activity monitoring:** More comprehensive than the Performance Monitor, the statistics available through the Enterprise Manager enable you to examine the processes, database objects, and locks on database objects of the executing MSDE server.

- **Data Transformation Services (DTS):** Provides automated data import and export through the COM and ADO interfaces. DTS also creates an object model through which custom transformation tasks can be added by augmenting the current object framework.

- **Web publishing:** MSDE can generate static Web pages from a SQL query or stored procedure. The generation can be activated by hand, through a scheduled event, or through a system-stored procedure.

Chapter 12

Using the Database Designer

IN THIS CHAPTER

- Preparing the Database Designer before you begin
- Creating a database with the Database Designer
- Working with ASP reporting pages
- Examining visual modeling

THE DATABASE DESIGNER is a shared program that is included with several of the Visual Studio products (Visual InterDev, Visual Basic, and Visual J++) as well as the Enterprise Manager application. The Database Designer is a tool that enables you to create a database diagram used to represent database tables and the relationships between them. A database diagram also helps you to create documentation for the database system, by allowing text annotations and graphic art (lines, arrows, and so forth) to be placed on the diagram. These graphics placed on the diagram can help clarify the relationships and functions of the schema.

The Database Designer is very similar in function and appearance to the various database and table builders, including the one in Microsoft Access. However, several differences make the Database Designer more powerful than the other tools. Because the Database Designer is used for professional development, it has been created specifically for construction, refinement, and documentation of the database objects on MSDE or SQL Server.

Before You Begin

In this chapter, the Designer will be used from the Visual InterDev (VI) application. Many developers, regardless of their primary development environment, are embracing InterDev for their Web page development needs. Because the Database Designer is shared across the development environments of Visual Studio, the appearance and functionality is almost identical in all of its forms. For the specifics of implementation of the data environment for other development products, see the program's user's manual.

> **Note:** The Database Designer will only address SQL Server–based data sources. If you set up a Visual Studio application connected to a different source, such as an Access database, the Designer appears disabled. Except for the disabled menu options, the development system gives no indication of the reason for your inability to access the tool.

The Database Designer appears on the surface much like the Relationships diagram view in Microsoft Access, which you may be familiar with. The key aspect of the Designer that is not available in Microsoft Access is the ability to add notations and draw lines, which can help you to document the database relations.

A Web solution provides an excellent example of creating a database server-based solution. To maximize the capabilities of the application and minimize the amount of processing and error checking that must take place in the Web application code, you can put a great deal of the logic on the MSDE server.

> **Note:** The legal license for the MSDE server does not allow you to connect the Web server to the MSDE data source for Internet access. Therefore, you are only licensed to use the ADO interface to connect to the database server on the local intranet for personal use, although no technical restriction stops full Web access.

Creating a Database with the Database Designer

The Database Designer is not available for independent execution. Therefore, you need to create a project (such as VB Data Project) that can encompass the database system to address the Database Designer. Because the Database Designer is a tool within another tool (such as Visual InterDev), this chapter shows you how to create a database and implement an application to address the database at the same time within the programming environment.

For Windows NT, you need to have the Internet Information Server (IIS) installed. IIS is free and built into the Windows NT Option Pack (available for download at www.microsoft.com). On Windows 95 or 98, the Personal Web Server (PWS) can be used, which is also available for download in the Windows NT Option Pack (despite the fact that the name implies it is only for NT). PWS is included on the CD-ROM of FrontPage, for ease of installation.

You need to have available the adTrack database that you created in Chapter 1. With the Database Designer, you are going to augment this database to include additional tables and relationships.

Creating the Visual InterDev Project

Several programming structures have to be put in place before you can begin the database construction. You must create a new Visual InterDev project, configure a data source connection to address the database, and add this connection to the new project. The sample application that you create in this chapter will display a list of all of the advertisements (sorted by campaign), accept responses to each advertisement, and list the responses to each advertisement.

Within the Database Designer, four different items can be created: Database Diagrams, Tables, Stored Procedures, and Views. This project uses three of these objects (tables, diagrams, and stored procedures) to implement the project.

> **NOTE:** If some of the dialog boxes appear different than those listed here, you are probably using a different version of Visual InterDev. This example uses Visual InterDev with Visual Studio Service Pack 3. Regardless of the version, you will be able to follow the same process even if the steps and dialog boxes don't match exactly.

To configure the project and the data source, follow these steps:

1. Execute Visual InterDev. The New Project window (see Figure 12-1) should be displayed. If you have the automatic New Project window disabled, select the New Project option under the File menu.

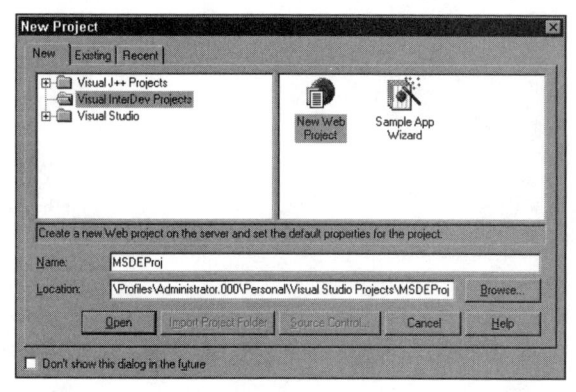

Figure 12-1: The New Project window is displayed when ou first execute Visual InterDev.

2. Enter the Project name of **MSDEProj** and click the Open button.

3. When the Web Project Wizard is displayed, select your Web server and click the Next button. The Web server must be Internet Information Server (IIS) on the Windows NT platform or Personal Web Server (PWS) on Windows 9.x. Also, the Web server must have the FrontPage extensions installed or it will not be able to connect for project creation.

> **NOTE** These FrontPage extensions are now standard installation options for most Web servers. If the wizard cannot connect to your Web server, however, make sure these extensions have been installed.

4. Create a new connection to the MSDE server. The location of this diagram is different for each of the Visual Studio applications. In Visual InterDev, you first must create a new database project on the Web server. For Visual Basic, the data project adds a data environment, and the Database Designer can be accessed through the Data View window for the environment.

5. Enter the filename as **MSDEProj** and click the Open button. The project then displays the settings page to name the new project that will be uploaded to the Web server.

6. Leave the Create a new Web application option selected (see Figure 12-2) and click the Next button.

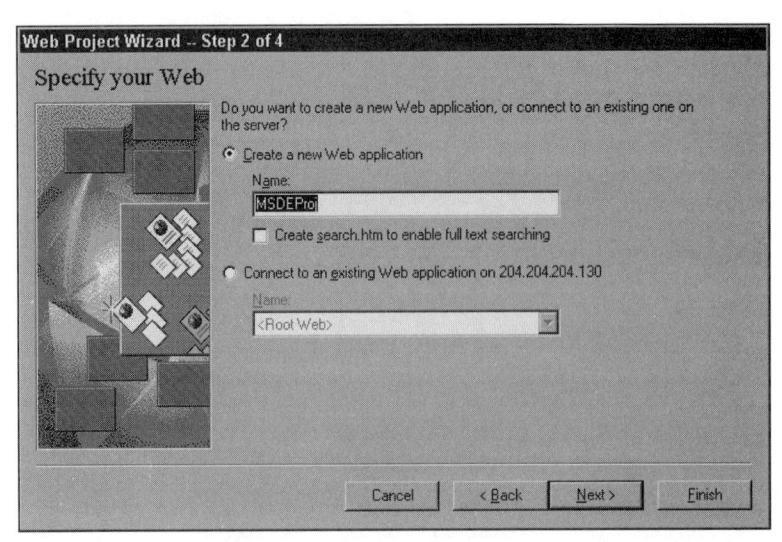

Figure 12-2: Make sure the new application selection is made, and the project name will automatically be placed in the Name text box.

Chapter 12: Using the Database Designer   211

7. For the layout step, leave the default <none> selection and click the Next button.

8. For the theme step, leave the default <none> selection and click the Finish button. The wizard will create the necessary files and folders on the Web server as well as on the selected system. The progress window will display the steps that are being executed as the project is created. After the project is complete, the Project Explorer window (see Figure 12-3) is displayed.

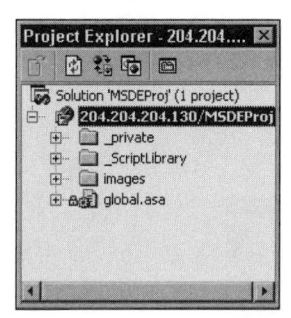

Figure 12-3: The Project Explorer displays the default items for the project.

9. From the Project menu, select the Add Data Connection option. The window used to select a data source is displayed. Because a data source connection to the adTrack database was never created, you need to make a connection that can be used by the project.

10. Leave the File Data Source tab selected and click the New button.

11. From the list of drivers, select the SQL Server driver option (see Figure 12-4) and click the Next button.

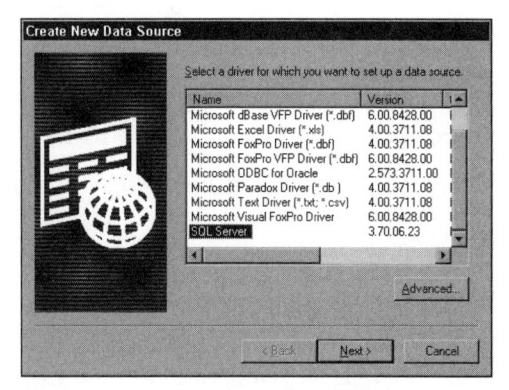

Figure 12-4: Select the SQL Server driver to create a connection to the MSDE data source.

12. Set the name of the file source to **dsnAdTrack** and click the Next button.
13. Click the Finish button to create the data source file. The configuration window for the data source is displayed.
14. From the Server combo box, select the local MSDE server and click the Next button.
15. Select the SQL Server authentication option on the login security screen.
16. Enter the Login ID and Password that you want to use.
17. Click the Next button to advance to the database settings screen.
18. Click the Change default database option and select the adTrack database from the combo box list (see Figure 12-5).

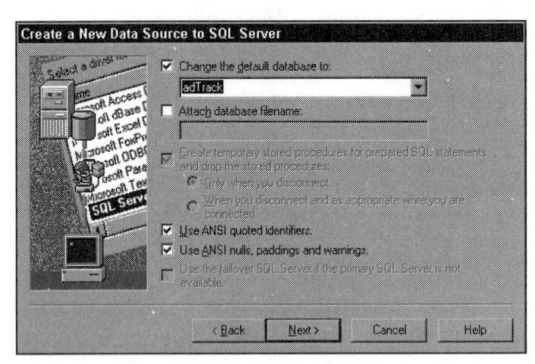

Figure 12-5: Select the adTrack database from the list of available default databases.

19. Click the Next button to advance to the MSDE server specifications screen.
20. All the default settings are fine for this solution, so click the Finish button to go to the final summary screen.
21. Click the Test Data Source button to make sure that the MSDE server is being properly addressed. If the test completes successfully, you know that the connection is properly configured.
22. Click the OK button to accept the data source settings, and you will be returned to the data source selection window. The new dsnAdTrack source will appear in the Available Sources list box.
23. Select the dsnAdTrack option in the list box and click the OK button.
24. You will be prompted for the login, so enter the proper password and click OK. After the connection has been made, you need to begin the configuration of the Connection object that will be stored in the Web project itself.

The connection will be used by the Visual InterDev wizards and controls to provide Web display of the data retrieved from the MSDE server.

25. Set the Connection Name to **connAdTrack**.

26. Select the Miscellaneous tab and change the cursor location to 2 – Use server-side cursors.

27. Click the OK button to save all of the connection settings. At this point, you are returned to the project, where you can begin working with the database itself.

Modifying the Database

Now that you have created the infrastructure for the project, you can begin the table construction, database diagramming, and data addressing. The Visual InterDev window should contain the Data View that you saw earlier in the chapter. The Data View is the window that you use to actually modify the MSDE data source. If this window is not displayed, under the View window, select the Other Windows → Data View option to display it.

To create the campaign database for the application, follow these steps:

1. In the Data View window, click the plus sign to the left of the adTrack item and expand the folder to show the available types of objects. You should see the four object types available through the Designer: Database Diagrams, Tables, Views, and Stored Procedures. This application uses only three of these four object types, because views won't be necessary for execution.

2. Expand the Tables item, and you will see the table that was created in Chapter 1. This table will form the basis of the application, with other tables that are created and relations to each ad listed in the table. You can expand the advertisements table if you want to display all of the columns that are available to it (see Figure 12-6).

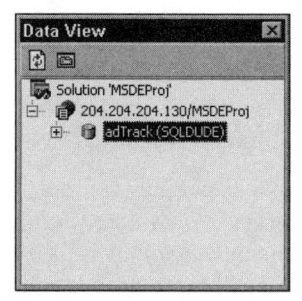

Figure 12-6: All of the tables in a database and all of the columns for each table are available in the Data View window.

3. Right-click the Tables folder and select the New Table option. You will be prompted for the name of the new table.

> **NOTE:** If you right-click the Tables folder and only a single option, Refresh, is available, then you are probably using an older version of Visual InterDev. To follow these steps, you must have installed at least Visual Studio Service Pack 3.

4. Enter **Campaigns** for the name of the new table and click the OK button. You will now see the table creation window that is nearly identical to the one you used to create a table in Microsoft Access. In this window, you can set up all of the columns of the new table.

5. Create the following columns in the table grid:

Name	Type	Length	Nulls?	Identity?	Seed	Increment
campaignID	int	4	N	Y	1	1
campaignName	varchar	30	N	N		
campaignStartDate	datetime	8	N	N		
campaignEndDate	datetime	8	N	N		
campaignOwner	varchar	50	Y	N		
comments	text	16	Y	N		

6. Select the campaignID field and click the key icon in the small table window (or the key icon located in your toolbar) to make that field the primary key.

7. Close the Designer window and save changes to the table. You will be returned to the main Visual InterDev environment.

8. Right-click the advertisements table in the Data View window and select the Design option to display the Database Designer window.

9. Modify the advertisements table to accept a campaignID column. Add the column with a type of int and allow it to accept null values. Because a single campaign may have many advertisements, it would violate normalization rules to duplicate the campaign data and have an individual campaign record for each ad.

Instead, in the solution that you are creating, an ad can belong to only one campaign, so the reference to the campaign should be stored with the advertisement record.

10. Close the Designer window and save the changes to the table.

11. Right-click the Tables folder, select the New Table option, and name the table **adResponse**. This table will track who sold each ad. Because more than a single salesperson may exist for each ad, a relation is created whereby a single advertisement row (one) may be referenced by several different (many) sales records, for a one-to-many database relation.

12. Create the following columns in the Database Designer:

Name	Type	Length	Nulls?	Identity?	Seed	Increment
responseID	int	4	N	Y	1	1
adID	int	4	N	N		
responseType	int	4	N	N		
itemDate	datetime	8	N	N		
attitude	int	4	N	N		
respondentName	varchar	50	Y	N		
respondentEmail	varchar	50	Y	N		
respondentPhone	varchar	20	Y	N		
comments	text	16	Y	N		

After you create the two new tables and modify the original advertisements table to accept the new value, you can create the relationships between the tables as a database diagram.

Filling the Tables with Data

To provide a baseline set of data, it is useful to enter values into the tables before the relations are created. After the relations have been added, individual entries are linked, so a consistent row set must be created for each record. This makes it difficult to enter data wholesale, because of generated errors.

To enter data, you can simply right-click the desired table and select the Open option. This displays the data grid for entry of new rows. The following information is provided for all three tables that you created in the last section.

Enter the following information in the adResponse table:

responseID	adID	responseType	itemDate	attitude	respondentName	respondentEmail	respondentPhone
1	3	1	5/20/00	1	Joe Armini	joe@frontgunner.com	555-3422
2	3	2	5/18/00	0	Phil Nortman	phil@backgunner.com	555-5621
3	5	2	5/18/00	2	Joe Armini	joe@frontgunner.com	555-3422
4	5	2	5/15/00	1	Bruno Maliz	bruno@bruno.com	555-6572
5	6	2	6/20/00	1	Minton Mercsnerd	minton@peopler.com	555-3462
6	1	2	5/5/00	1	Steve Bilbellow	steve@benzig.net	555-0303
7	2	2	6/29/00	2	Marc Proven	marc@racing.com	
8	8	3	5/9/00	2	Gloria Hedge	gloria@scrorelock.com	555-2923

Chapter 12: Using the Database Designer 217

For the advertisements, use this data:

uniqueid	adName	locationPlaced	datePlaced	dateAppearing	adType	adCode	campaignID
1	LearnMSDE	PUBWKLY	3/1/00	5/1/00	1	24	1
2	LearnMSDE	PUBWKLY	4/1/00	6/1/00	1	25	1
3	MSDEDev	SQLMAG	3/1/00	5/1/00	2	26	3
4	MSDEDev	SQLMAG	5/1/00	7/1/00	2	27	4
5	MSDEDev	NTMAG	3/1/00	5/1/00	1	28	3
6	MSDEDev	NTMAG	4/1/00	6/1/00	1	29	4
7	MSDEBible	SQLMAG	7/1/00	9/1/00	2	30	2
8	MSDEBible	PCWEEK	3/1/00	5/1/00	3	31	2

For the campaigns table, enter the following data:

campaignID	campaignName	campaignStartDate	campaignEndDate	campaignOwner
1	LearnMSDE	5/1/00	6/1/00	John Brown
2	MSDEBible	5/1/00	9/1/00	Ed Blue
3	MSDEDev	5/1/00	5/1/00	John Brown
4	DatabaseBooks	6/1/00	7/1/00	Mary Purple

This data is example data and can be altered as you wish. However, make sure that the relations are matched across the various tables. If you'd like to ensure the relations are proper, you can first create the database diagram for the multitable relations.

Creating a Database Diagram

The tables that you have created so far are all separate insofar as they have no logic that can ensure referential integrity. The relations between the tables are enacted only for future inserts. When creating relationships for existing tables, you may want to delete the rows of the table, to ensure that no problems occur for the future inserts. In the case of the advertisements table, you already entered the proper data that conforms to the relationship that you will be creating.

The Database Diagram in the Database Designer is different from the database diagrams stored in Microsoft Access. Although both programs display the structures from the same source, the Designer enables you to add documentation to the diagram in the form of annotations and visual cues.

When you create a diagram in the Designer, a toolbox palette will appear floating over the current window. The toolbox provides the functions for annotation, new table creation, relationship documenting, and other diagram functions.

Follow these steps to create the Database Diagram:

1. Right-click the Database Diagrams folder and select the New Diagram option. The blank diagram canvas is displayed.

2. From the Data View window, drag each of the tables (adResponse, advertisements, and campaigns) onto the canvas. Dropping the table into the canvas will add it to the display (see Figure 12-7).

3. Draw a connection from the uniqueID column in the advertisements table to the adID column in the adResponse table.

Chapter 12: Using the Database Designer 219

The Create Relationship dialog box appears, as it does whenever you draw the connection between tables, enabling you to set parameters to govern the relation enforcement.

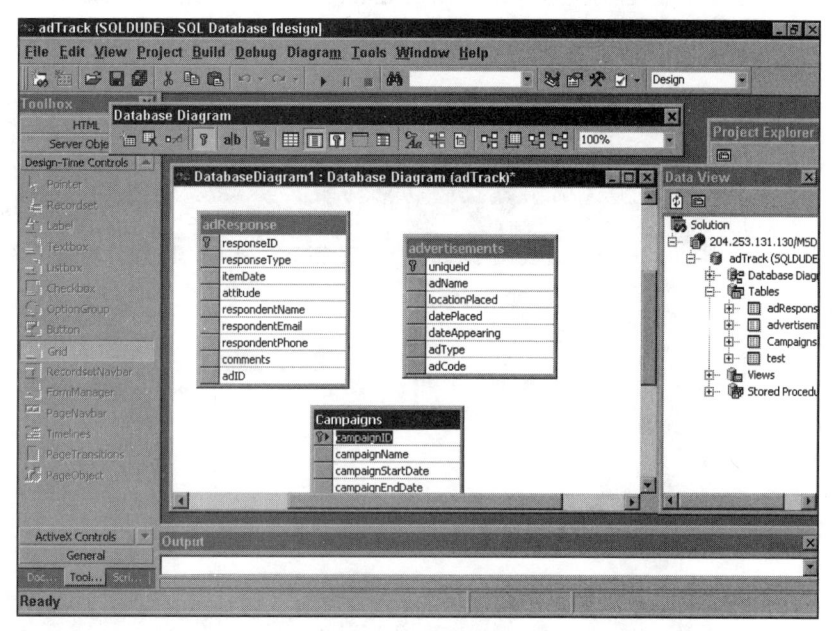

Figure 12-7: Drag the three tables from the database onto the database diagram canvas.

4. Click the Enable relationship for INSERT and UPDATE item to uncheck it (see Figure 12-8). Because a new ad may be created without any responses yet being received, the relationship integrity check shouldn't be performed at this point.

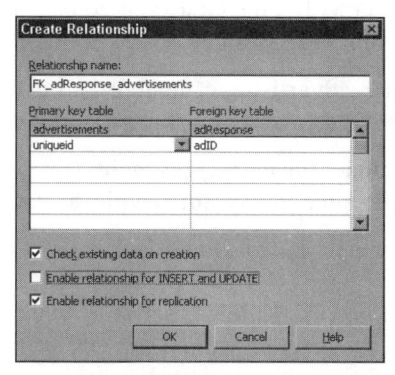

Figure 12-8: Turn off the relationship enforcement for insertions and updates.

5. Click OK to accept the relationship options.

6. Follow the same procedure to create a connection between the campaignID column in the campaigns table and the campaignID column in the advertisements table. The diagram should contain links between the three tables (see Figure 12-9).

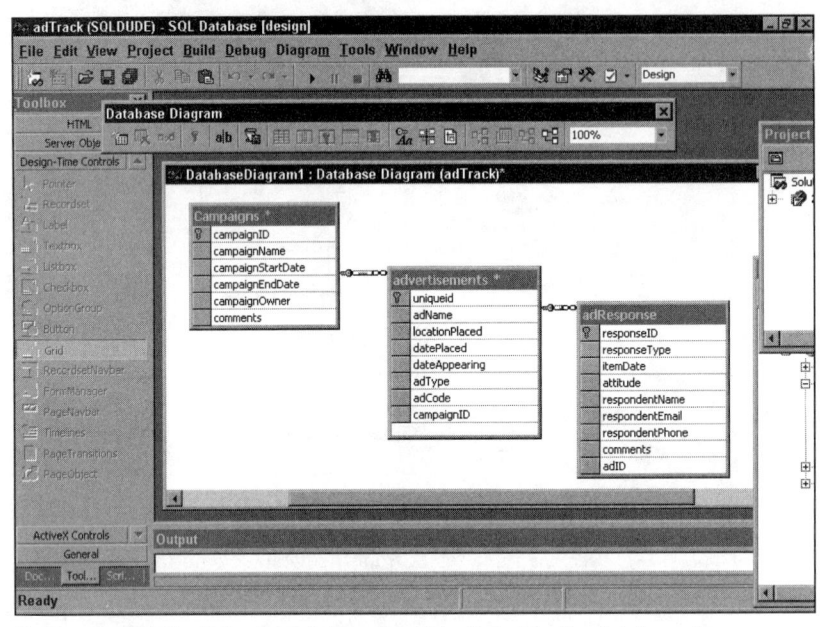

Figure 12-9: Each of the three tables should be linked in the database diagram.

7. Click the New Text Annotation tool in the palette. This option automatically inserts a text box into the diagram and enables you to create a text annotation.

8. Enter some text into the box that describes the table, and you should have a diagram. You can use the following text as an example:

    The campaign table tracks each advertising campaign and is linked to the individual ads that are used to accomplish that campaign.

9. Drag the box so that it is placed under the campaigns table. This provides some useful documentation for the table that is stored with the database.

10. Close the database diagram and save it as **TrackingModel**.

The diagram that you just created is stored on the MSDE server. If you open the Northwind database in Microsoft Access, the diagram will be present in the list of available diagrams. When you display the diagram, the relationships are shown in Access, but the annotations are not displayed. Any changes that are made to the diagram, after it is saved to the database server, will not eliminate the existing notations, although changes in position of the elements may misplace the annotations.

The database diagrams are available for multiuser access. You may break any of the relationships of these diagrams by right-clicking the link in the diagram and selecting the Delete relationship from database option. You can also use the Data View window to examine all the individual objects contained in each diagram.

The entire adTrack database has been structurally completed, but you now need some type of user interface front end. Because you are using the Database Designer in the Visual InterDev application, it is convenient to create a simple Web interface to display some of the table functionality.

Working with ASP Reporting Pages

With all of the database objects in place, you can create a simple HTML interface to examine the data as well as enter new responses to a particular advertisement. In this solution, four different ASP pages are used:

- **campainList.asp:** Generates an HTML table of all of the current campaigns and the advertisements that have been placed for each campaign. The HTML table uses color to differentiate the bands for particular rows.

- **responseList.asp:** Displays a list of all the responses, broken down by ad, from customers. Same format as the campaignList page.

- **responseForm.asp:** Presents an input form that accepts data in relation to a new response to a particular advertisement.

- **writeResponse.asp:** Writes the information supplied by the responseForm page into the adResponse table.

Adding the Report Pages

This solution has two reports: Campaign List and Response List. The Campaign List report (see Figure 12-10) shows each campaign that is stored in the campaigns table.

The primary recordset, myRS, is used to query the adTrack database for the campaigns table. When each row of the campaigns table is addressed, a second recordset is created. This second recordset, myRS2, queries the advertisements table to list all of the ads related to the current campaign.

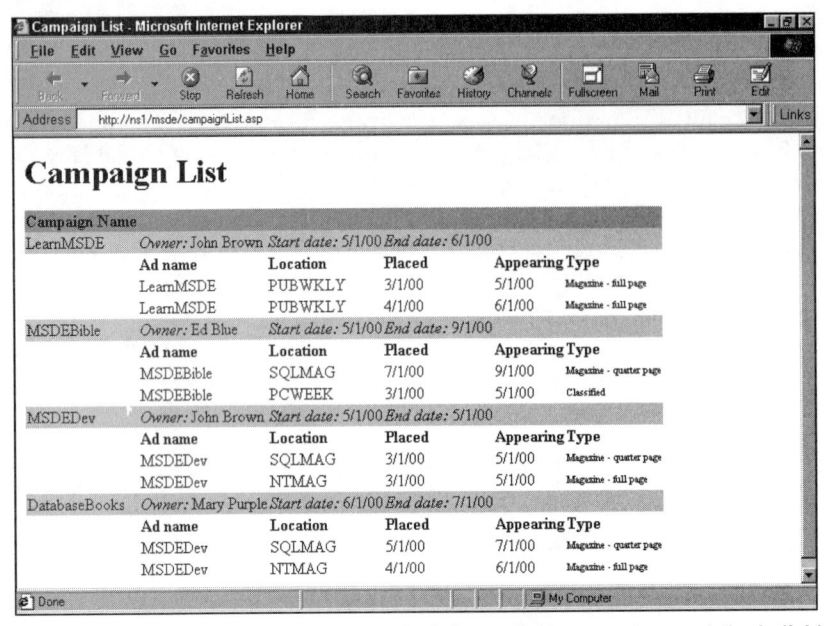

Figure 12-10: The campaign list shows all of the available campaigns and the individual advertisements that belong to each.

Add a Web page to the Visual InterDev project (using Project → Add Web Item → Active Server Page) as **campaignList.asp** and enter the following code:

```
<html>
<head>
<title>List of campaigns with ad details</title>
</head>
<body>
<H1> List of campaigns with ad details </H1>

<%
   Dim myConn
   Dim myRS, myRS2

   Set myConn = CreateObject("ADODB.Connection")

   myConn.Open _
"driver={SQL Server};SERVER=Thinkpad;Database=adTrack;UID=sa;pwd="

   If myConn.State = 1 Then
      ' Connection opened successfully
      Set myRS = CreateObject("ADODB.Recordset")
      Set myRS.ActiveConnection = myConn
```

```
myRS.CursorType = 2 ' adOpenDynamic
myRS.CursorLocation = 2 ' adUseServer
Set myRS2 = CreateObject("ADODB.Recordset")
Set myRS2.ActiveConnection = myConn
myRS2.CursorType = 2 ' adOpenDynamic
myRS2.CursorLocation = 2 ' adUseServer
Response.Write("<H1>Campaign List</H1><P>")
myParam = ""

myRS.Open "select * from campaigns"
If myRS.State = 1 Then
   Response.Write("<TABLE BORDER=0 CELLSPACING=0>")
   Response.Write("<TR bgcolor=#FFA000>")
   Response.Write( _
     "<TD><FONT SIZE=3><B>Campaign Name</B></FONT></TD>")
   Response.Write("<TD></TD><TD></TD><TD></TD>")
   Response.Write("<TD></TD><TD></TD>")
   Response.Write("</TR>")
   Do Until myRS.EOF
      Response.Write("<TR bgcolor=#FFFF00>")
      Response.Write("<TD>" & myRS.Fields("campaignName") & _
         "</TD>")
      Response.Write("<TD><I>Owner:</I> " & _
         myRS.Fields("campaignOwner") & "</TD>")
      Response.Write("<TD><I>Start date:</I> " & _
         myRS.Fields("campaignStartDate") & "</TD>")
      Response.Write("<TD><I>End date:</I> " & _
         myRS.Fields("campaignEndDate") & "</TD>")
      Response.Write("<TD> </TD>")
      Response.Write("<TD> </TD>")
      Response.Write("</TR>")

      ' Show the items in each campaign
      myRS2.Open _
         "select * from advertisements where campaignID=" _
         & myRS.Fields("campaignID")
      Response.Write("<TR>")
      Response.Write("<TD></TD>")
      Response.Write("<TD><B>Ad name</B></TD>")
      Response.Write("<TD><B>Location</B></TD>")
      Response.Write("<TD><B>Placed</B></TD>")
      Response.Write("<TD><B>Appearing</B></TD>")
      Response.Write("<TD><B>Type</B></TD>")
      Response.Write("</TR>")
      Do Until myRS2.EOF
         Response.Write("<TR>")
```

```
                    Response.Write("<TD></TD>")
                    Response.Write("<TD>" & myRS2.Fields("adName") _
                       & "</TD>")
                    Response.Write("<TD>" & _
                      myRS2.Fields("locationPlaced") & "</TD>")
                    Response.Write("<TD>" & myRS2.Fields("datePlaced") _
                       & "</TD>")
                    Response.Write("<TD>" & _
                      myRS2.Fields("dateAppearing") & "</TD>")
                    Select Case myRS2.Fields("adType")
                       Case 1
                          Response.Write( _
                 "<TD><FONT SIZE=1>Magazine - full page</TD></FONT>")
                       Case 2
                          Response.Write( _
                 "<TD><FONT SIZE=1>Magazine - quarter page</TD></FONT>")
                       Case 3
                          Response.Write( _
                 "<TD><FONT SIZE=1>Classified</TD></FONT>")
                    End Select
                    Response.Write("</TR>")
                    myRS2.MoveNext
                 Loop
                 myRS2.Close
                 myRS.MoveNext
              Loop
            Response.Write("</TABLE>")
         Else
            Response.Write("Error. Could not create recordset.<P>")
         End If
      Else
         Response.Write("Error. Connection could not be opened.<P>")
      End If
      MyRS.Close
      myConn.Close
      Set myConn = Nothing
%>
</body>
</html>
```

The Campaign List report shows one aspect of the data stored in adTrack. But, this sample application can also be used to track the responses, such as calls, letters, and e-mail that are generated by the advertisements in the campaign. The Response List report (see Figure 12-11) displays all the responses to advertisements in each campaign.

Chapter 12: Using the Database Designer 225

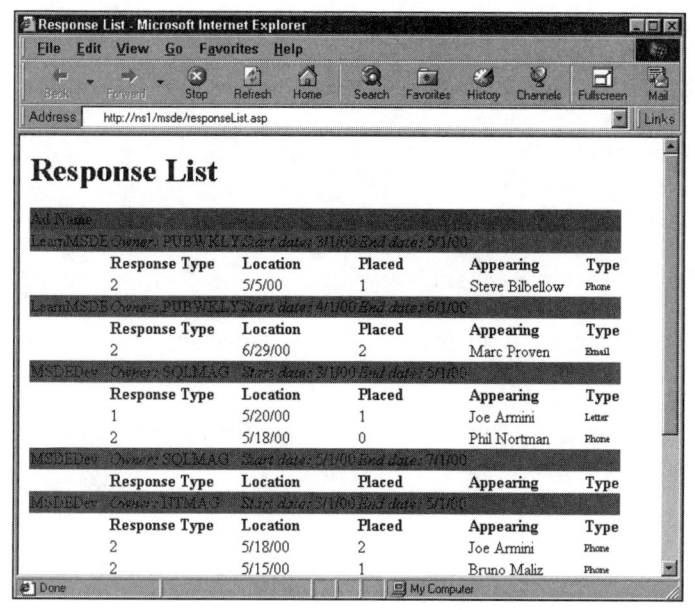

Figure 12-11: The Response List report displays all the responses to advertisements in each campaign.

Enter the following code into a new Web page titled **responseList.asp**:

```
<html>
<head>
<title>List of responses by ad</title>
</head>
<body>
<H1> List of responses by ad</H1>

<%
   Dim myConn
   Dim myRS, myRS2

   Set myConn = CreateObject("ADODB.Connection")

   myConn.Open _
"driver={SQL Server};SERVER=Thinkpad;Database=adTrack;UID=sa;pwd="

   If myConn.State = 1 Then
      ' Connection opened successfully
      Set myRS = CreateObject("ADODB.Recordset")
      Set myRS.ActiveConnection = myConn
      myRS.CursorType = 2 ' adOpenDynamic
```

Part II: Using MSDE

```
            myRS.CursorLocation = 2 ' adUseServer
            Set myRS2 = CreateObject("ADODB.Recordset")
            Set myRS2.ActiveConnection = myConn
            myRS2.CursorType = 2 ' adOpenDynamic
            myRS2.CursorLocation = 2 ' adUseServer
            Response.Write("<H1>Response List</H1><P>")
            myParam = ""

            myRS.Open "select * from advertisements"
            If myRS.State = 1 Then
               Response.Write("<TABLE BORDER=0 CELLSPACING=0>")
               Response.Write("<TR bgcolor=#A000FF>")
               Response.Write( _
                 "<TD><FONT SIZE=3><B>Ad Name</B></FONT></TD>")
               Response.Write("<TD></TD><TD></TD>")
               Response.Write("<TD></TD><TD></TD><TD></TD>")
               Response.Write("</TR>")
               Do Until myRS.EOF
                  Response.Write("<TR bgcolor=#FF00FF>")
                  Response.Write("<TD>" & myRS.Fields("adName") & "</TD>")
                  Response.Write("<TD><I>Owner:</I> " & _
                     myRS.Fields("locationPlaced") & "</TD>")
                  Response.Write("<TD><I>Start date:</I> " & _
                     myRS.Fields("datePlaced") & "</TD>")
                  Response.Write("<TD><I>End date:</I> " & _
                     myRS.Fields("dateAppearing") & "</TD>")
                  Response.Write("<TD> </TD>")
                  Response.Write("<TD> </TD>")
                  Response.Write("</TR>")

                  ' Display all of the responses to that ad
                  myRS2.Open "select * from adresponse where adID=" & _
                     myRS.Fields("uniqueID")
                  Response.Write("<TR>")
                  Response.Write("<TD></TD>")
                  Response.Write("<TD><B>Response Type</B></TD>")
                  Response.Write("<TD><B>Location</B></TD>")
                  Response.Write("<TD><B>Placed</B></TD>")
                  Response.Write("<TD><B>Appearing</B></TD>")
                  Response.Write("<TD><B>Type</B></TD>")
                  Response.Write("</TR>")
                  Do Until myRS2.EOF
                     Response.Write("<TR>")
                     Response.Write("<TD></TD>")
                     Response.Write("<TD>" & _
```

```
                myRS2.Fields("responseType") & "</TD>")
            Response.Write("<TD>" & myRS2.Fields("itemDate") _
                & "</TD>")
            Response.Write("<TD>" & myRS2.Fields("attitude") _
                & "</TD>")
            Response.Write("<TD>" & _
                myRS2.Fields("respondentName") & "</TD>"
            Select Case myRS2.Fields("responseType")
                Case 1
                    Response.Write( _
                        "<TD><FONT SIZE=1>Phone</TD></FONT>")
                Case 2
                    Response.Write( _
                        "<TD><FONT SIZE=1>Letter</TD></FONT>")
                Case 3
                    Response.Write( _
                        "<TD><FONT SIZE=1>Email</TD></FONT>")
                Case 4
                    Response.Write( _
                        "<TD><FONT SIZE=1>Fax</TD></FONT>")
            End Select
            Response.Write("</TR>")
            myRS2.MoveNext
        Loop
        myRS2.Close
        myRS.MoveNext
      Loop
      Response.Write("</TABLE>")
    Else
        Response.Write("Error. Could not create recordset.<P>")
    End If
  Else
    Response.Write("Error. Connection could not be opened.<P>")
  End If
  myRS.Close
  myConn.Close
  Set myConn = Nothing
%>
</body>
</html>
```

When either of these pages is executed, the adTrack database is queried and the results of the report are displayed in the returned Web page. To enter new data, you need to create a series of Web pages that accept the information and write it into the tables. These data input pages will use the same concepts whether each page accepts response data, a new advertisement, or a new campaign. Therefore, only one page type, a new response page, will be provided as an example, which you can then adapt for use with the other areas of the application.

New Response Submissions

Because you have created the reporting portion of the application, you need another page to accept new responses. This page will accept user input (see Figure 12-12) and then submit it to another Web page for recording in the MSDE database.

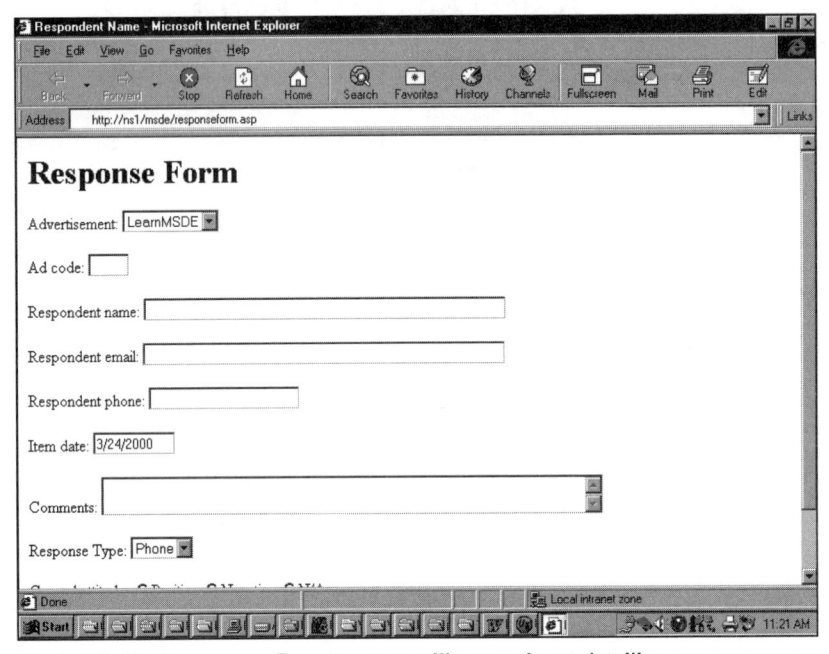

Figure 12-12: The responseForm.asp page will accept input detailing a new response.

In an HTML or ASP solution, a *form* is an HTML structure that is used to encapsulate all the input controls (such as text boxes, list boxes, and so forth) for submission to the server. When the Submit button for the form is clicked, all of this information is sent to a second Web page that actually accepts and records it to the database.

In this example, the page responseForm displays the form and accepts the input of the parameters related to the response, such as the ad that elicited the response, the name of the respondent, and so forth. After the user clicks the submission button, all the data contained in the form is sent to the writeResponse page (as configured by the ACTION parameter of the <FORM> tag).

The information is provided to the receiving page (writeResponse) in the *Request* object. In the Request object, individual parameters are available through the name that they were given in the NAME parameter of the controls on the form.

Notice in the source code that a connection and recordset is created to read each row of the advertisements table. The uniqueID of the advertisements and the adName are written into an option/combo box. That enables the person creating the response to select the ad that originated the contact.

To create the responseForm.asp page, add a new page to the Visual InterDev project, and enter the code in this listing:

```
<html>
<head>
<title>Respondent Name</title>
</head>
<body>
<H1>Response Form</H1>
<form method="POST" action="writeResponse.asp" name="frmContent">

<%
    Response.Write("<p>Advertisement: <select name=AdID size=1>")
    Dim myConn
    Dim myRS

    Set myConn = CreateObject("ADODB.Connection")

    myConn.Open _
"driver={SQL Server};SERVER=Thinkpad;Database=adTrack;UID=sa;pwd="

    If myConn.State = 1 Then
        ' Connection opened successfully
        Set myRS = CreateObject("ADODB.Recordset")
        Set myRS.ActiveConnection = myConn
        myRS.CursorType = 2 ' adOpenDynamic
        myRS.CursorLocation = 2 ' adUseServer
        myRS.LockType = 3 ' adLockOptimistic

        myRS.Open "select * from advertisements"
        Do Until myRS.EOF
            Response.Write("<option selected value=" &
myRS.fields("uniqueID") _
            & ">" & myRS.fields("adName") & "</option>")
            myRS.MoveNext
        Loop
        Response.Write("</select></p>")
        myRS.close
```

```
%>
    <p>Ad code: <input type="text" name="txtAdCode"
size="4"></p>

    <p>Respondent name: <input type="text" name="txtRespondentName"
size="50"></p>
    <p>Respondent email: <input type="text" name="txtRespondentEmail"
size="50"></p>
    <p>Respondent phone: <input type="text" name="txtRespondentPhone"
size="20"></p>
    <p>Item date: <input type="text" name="txtItemDate" value=<%=Date
%>
  size="10"></p>
    <p>Comments: <textarea rows="2" name="txtComments"
cols="60"></textarea></p>

    <p>Response Type: <select name="ResponseType" size="1">
      <option selected value="1">Phone</option>
      <option value="2">Letter</option>
      <option value="3">Email</option>
      <option value="4">Fax</option>
    </select></p>
    <p>General attitude: <input type="radio" value=1
name="radAttitude">Positive <input
  type="radio" name="radAttitude" value=2>Negative <input
type="radio" checked name="radAttitude" value=3>N/A</p>
    <p><input type="submit" value="Save Response" name="B1"></p>
</form>
</body>
</html>
```

Make sure the page is saved as **responseForm.asp**. In the <FORM> tag, you set the action to execute the writeResponse.asp page. This page will address the adTrack database and store the information in the adResponse table.

Enter the following code into a new page called **writeResponse.asp** that you created in the InterDev project:

```
<HTML>
<BODY>
<H1>Response Write</H1>
<%
    Dim myConn
    Dim myRS
```

```
    Set myConn = CreateObject("ADODB.Connection")

    myConn.Open
"driver={SQL Server};SERVER=Thinkpad;Database=adTrack;UID=sa;pwd="

    If myConn.State = 1 Then
        ' Connection opened successfully
        Set myRS = CreateObject("ADODB.Recordset")
        Set myRS.ActiveConnection = myConn
        myRS.CursorType = 2 ' adOpenDynamic
        myRS.CursorLocation = 2 ' adUseServer
        myRS.LockType = 3 ' adLockOptimistic
        myRS.Open("select * from adResponse)

        myRS.AddNew
        myRS.Fields("adID") = request.Form("AdID")
        myRS.Fields("itemDate") = request.Form("txtAdCode")
        myRS.Fields("attitude") = request.Form("radAttitude")
        myRS.Fields("responseType") = request.Form("ResponseType")
        myRS.Fields("itemDate") = request.Form("txtItemDate")
        myRS.Fields("respondentName") = _
            request.Form("txtRespondentName")
        myRS.Fields("respondentEmail") = _
            request.Form("txtRespondentEmail")
        myRS.Fields("respondentPhone") = _
            request.Form("txtRespondentPhone")
        myRS.Fields("comments") = request.Form("txtComments")
        myRS.Update
        myRS.Close
        myConn.Close
    Else
        Response.Write("Error opening MSDE data source.<P>")
    End If
%>
Response recorded.
</BODY></HTML>
```

When you access either of the report pages, the information will be displayed in an HTML table from the adTrack database. The responseForm.asp page will accept new responses, while the writeResponse.asp will store in the database the information entered into the response page.

Visual Modeling

Although the topic of modeling is beyond the scope of this book, modeling a database is one of the important skills of a midlevel database designer. As you may have seen, altering a database model after data has been entered can be difficult and time-consuming. Even the modifications you just made didn't affect client applications, which is something you will have to handle in a real-world implementation. To attempt to prevent as many after-implementation changes as possible, the process of *database modeling* was created.

All the solutions that you have created using MSDE are essentially two-tier solutions: the client software is one tier and the database server is another (see Figure 12-13). Many professional database solutions use more tiers to provide abstractions between the client machines and the actual data sources.

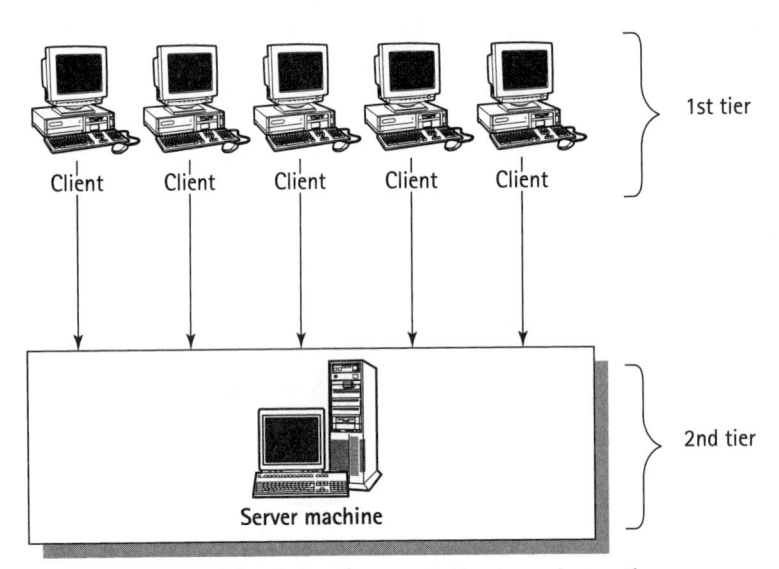

Figure 12-13: A traditional client/server solution has only two tiers: one for the client and another for the server.

By creating a custom object layer between the client and the server (see Figure 12-14), any modifications to the data source can be transparent to the client. Simply altering the objects to address the new database schema will automatically allow the same client applications to execute without modification. The objects also provide the additional feature of being able to balance the load requests effectively between two or more database server machines.

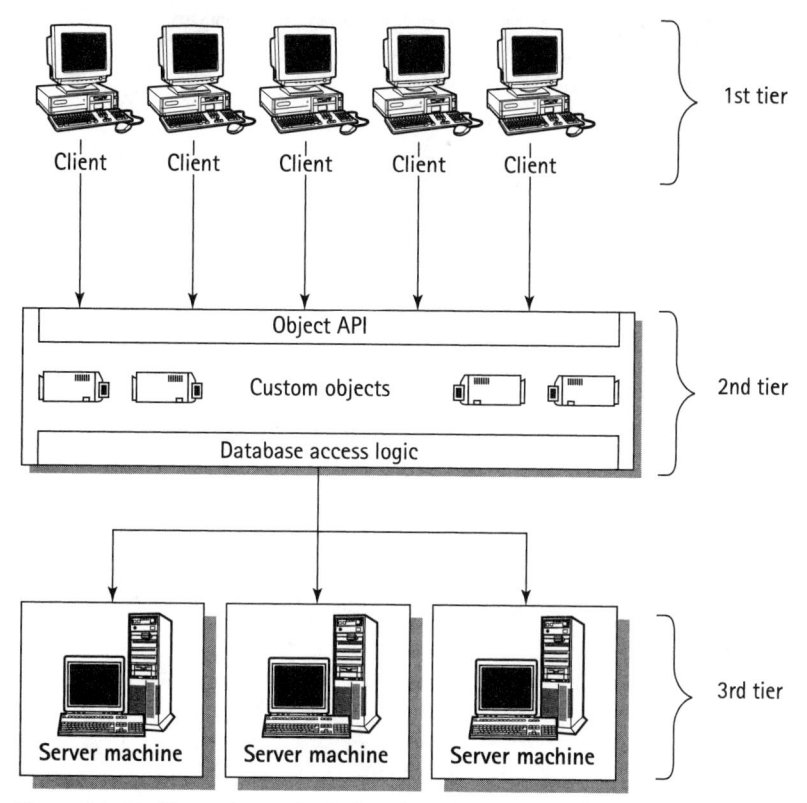

Figure 12-14: More advanced solutions introduce additional tiers of abstraction between the client machines and the servers.

Modeling enables a single person or a group of people to create a database object model with all of the components needed for an advanced multitier application. The model can be easily modified and documented and will even create prototype ActiveX components for database access. Figure 12-15 shows an example of a component diagram for a simple database system. Additionally, a modeling program can also read an existing component project and create a diagram from it.

The Visual Studio Enterprise Edition includes an application called Visual Modeler that is a lite version of the highly regarded Rational Rose modeling tool. Visual Modeler can interact with Visual Basic or Visual C++ to model and prototype a component-based project. If you advance to designing component-based database applications, consider using some of the available modeling tools to streamline the design.

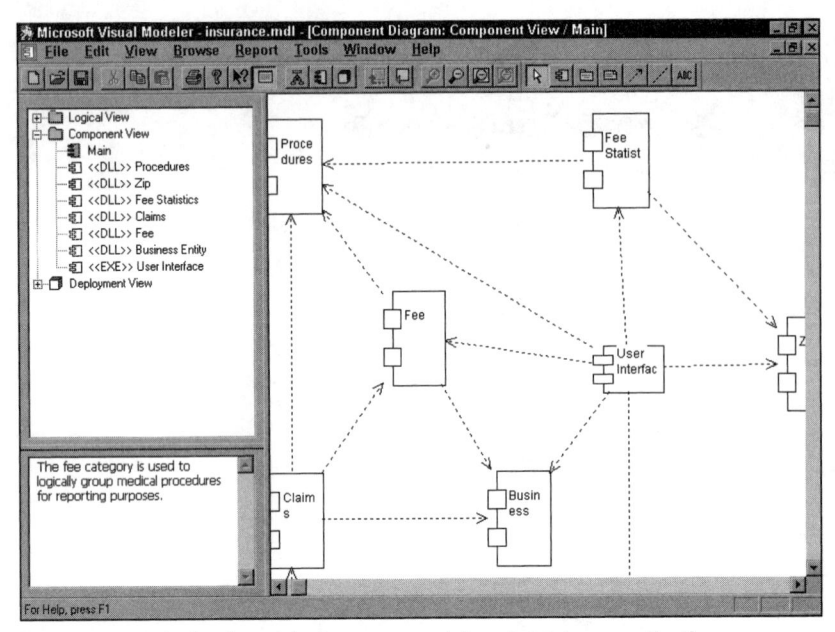

Figure 12-15: A visual model of a component-based database application can maximize planning before implementation.

Summary

The Database Designer is an effective tool for creating and documenting individual databases. By using it to create new tables, database diagrams, and stored procedures, you can integrate the design of an application with the creation of the database that it addresses. In this chapter, you covered the following:

- **Database Designer:** The Database Designer, included with Visual Studio, enables you to create database diagrams that are stored on the MSDE server. These diagrams are compatible with the database diagrams available through the Access ADP projects.

- **Table creation:** Through the table construction window, you can define the columns of a table in much the same way as you define them in the Microsoft Access table window in an ADP project.

- **Database Diagrams:** The Database Diagrams can contain text, annotations, and other documentation features. The documentation created in this diagram is stored on the database server with the database itself.

- **Referential integrity:** Creating entity relationships between the primary and foreign keys of related tables helps enforce that no orphaned rows exist that have no connection in the corresponding table.
- **ASP pages:** IIS allows execution of Web page logic to accept data or return it in the form of a Web page. The sample ASP pages in this chapter report information from the MSDE database and allow entry of new records.

Chapter 13

Using Data Transformation Services and Packages

IN THIS CHAPTER

- Discovering DTS
- Understanding How DTS works
- Understanding package objects
- Quickstarting DTS
- Scheduling DTS execution
- Programming DTS
- Using the DTS Designer
- Using the dtsrun utility application

AT THIS POINT IN examining database development, you should understand the general structure and layout of many aspects of the MSDE server. As you immerse yourself in the details of the system, it is easy to forget that understanding the capabilities of a database server are only a means to an end, that end being: make data access effective and efficient. One of the key aspects of making data useful is the ability to get data in and out of a data source. It is the acquisition and organization of the data, no matter the source, that will determine the success or failure of a new application.

Discovering DTS

MSDE provides unmatched capabilities in data import and export for a database server at its price level. MSDE features the Data Transformation Services (DTS) that automates the process of putting data into MSDE and taking it out. In a database like Access, each time data must be transferred, several manual steps must be undertaken. If automation is required, it must be laboriously coded in VBA. With MSDE, an automated process can be quickly created through one of the stored procedures or wizards available. The process itself can then be stored so that it may be reexecuted later using the same parameters or modified for a different data source. The stored process may also be executed automatically according to a time schedule or in reaction to a server-based event.

To accomplish the storage of a data transform process, DTS uses an object known as a *package* to contain the logic and structures used to import, export, validate, and transform data from any number of sources. DTS uses the database middleware of ODBC and OLE DB to allow connections, data access, and translation from numerous heterogeneous data sources.

DTS can be used for much more than simple import or export functions. Because it can actually transform data as it is moved from one medium to another, it has far broader possible applications. Some of the solutions that DTS can be used for include:

- **Data warehousing:** When a data warehouse is constructed, it holds summary data from the overall central data cache. The process of creating the data warehouse store of summary information can be automated through DTS.

- **Replication-like systems:** Many times, a complete replication system does not have the flexibility to address the broad range of vertical market data sources. Through DTS, a custom import can be used to allow almost any data types to be translated into usable information on a primary database server.

- **Flexible export:** Data stored in a format required by a third-party product can be supported by developing a custom DTS package. A possible example of this application might be the Symantec ACT database, in which a single field stores both the first and last name values together. A DTS package could be created specifically to export corporate information to this ACT format.

- **Database transfer:** DTS can be used to transport an entire database from one SQL Server–based database server to another. Rather than using a manual backup and restore, DTS can create a package that can be executed on a given schedule or activated manually.

These applications and others are possible with DTS because each package created can be completely modified and reused. Even packages created using one of the available wizards can be refined through manual coding to perform exactly as desired. To use the packages to the full extent of their capabilities, you will need to understand how the overall DTS system uses them for execution.

How DTS Works

In DTS, the wizards allow the transformation services and the packages that are used for the process to be created and configured with ease. The wizards help you circumvent the manual creation process usually required for other automation features such as an operating system batch (.bat) file. Learning about what is actually stored in a package and how the DTS relates to the information stored there can enable you to understand the bounds of what is possible using this technology.

The import and export capabilities of a package include the capability to define a data transfer process that may use entire tables or specified queries to retrieve the data and transformation rules to modify this data in the transfer process. Some of the operations that can be performed inside a package include:

- Changing the column type when transferring the data
- Executing code written in Transact-SQL or a script written in VB Script or JavaScript to modify the data as the transfer takes place
- Evaluating the data and changing the execution process based on the results of those evaluations
- Scheduling a job for later execution
- Notifying a user of a particular condition through e-mail

Any DTS process that executes requires at least one source and at least one destination for the data. DTS can address numerous data sources types, including these:

- ASCII-delimited or random access (fixed-field length) text files
- Unicode-delimited or random access (fixed-field length) text files
- ODBC data sources
- OLE DB data providers
- SQL Server databases
- Excel spreadsheets
- Access databases
- FoxPro databases
- dBase databases
- Paradox databases

These data sources types can be used for both the import and export of data. Because DTS is fully configurable and can actively transform the data that is being sent or received by the system, formatting issues that normally limit data source translation can be overcome.

The transformations in the packages can occur through the following:

- **Transact-SQL code:** A custom Transact-SQL script can be executed by the DTS system to manage the data translation.

- **Scripting:** Through VB Script, JavaScript, or another ActiveX scripting language, a transformation can be managed by script code.

- **COM objects:** The DTS objects are exposed, so they can be controlled through OLE Automation such as a program written in Visual Basic or Visual C++. Two object libraries provide access to all of the DTS functionality.

- **External EXE:** An executable can be created that can be called from the DTS system for handling of the data. The executable can then be called from the package to make modifications to the transforming data if necessary.

Both the COM interface and the External EXE are executed outside of the MSDE structure. Scripting, however, is embedded directly in the package objects and is executed by the SQL Server Agent technology.

Understanding Package Objects

A *package* is a self-contained structure that holds all of the process instructions on how the data transfer and transformation will take place for a specific DTS task. All local DTS packages are stored in the msdb database.

Within each package, several other objects contain the information and scripting that are used when the package is executed. A package object is made up of several collections that define the process of transfer and transformation of data. The objects contained in each package are linked under the primary Package object (see Figure 13-1).

The objects held in the collections of a package are:

- **Connection objects:** There is a Connection object for each data source that is used for either a source or a destination in the DTS process. The Connection object contains all of the connection information, including the driver to be used, the location and path of the data source, settings for the accessing driver, and any user names and passwords used for proper login.

- **Task objects:** Each task object defines a step in the transformation process. A task can be one of eight available predefined task types or a custom task may be designed.

Chapter 13: Using Data Transformation Services and Packages 241

- **Step objects:** Defines the sequence in which the Task objects are executed. These objects also contain the conditional execution logic that may select a task depending on the results of the task that was just completed. The step objects form the core of a multiple operation package execution.

All instances of these objects are held in the Connections, Tasks, and Steps collections, respectively. New instances of each object of the three types can be added to each collection.

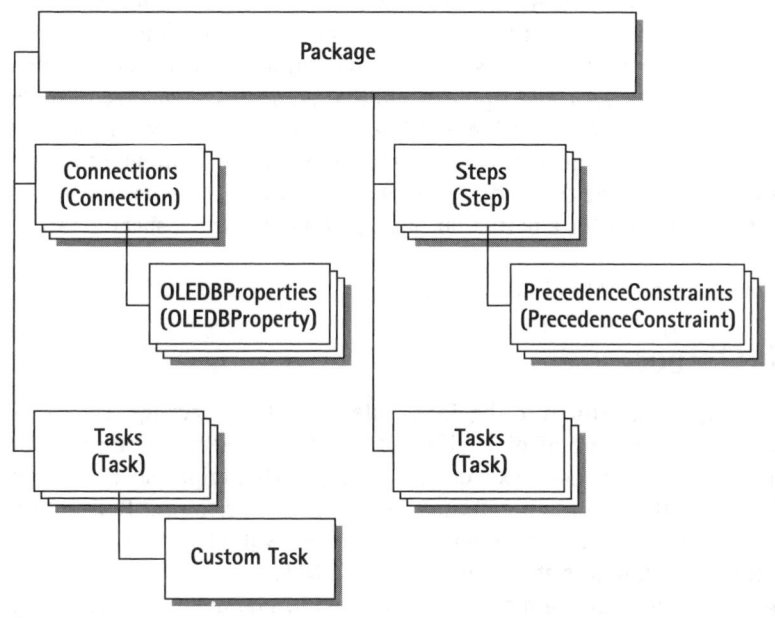

Figure 13-1: The Package object contains object collections for three object types.

> **NOTE:** You can use the Object Browser in the VBA environment of Access, Excel, or another product to examine the objects used by the DTS system. In the References dialog box, you will need to add the item Microsoft DTSPackage Object Library to a project to address the DTS framework.

The Connection Object

Only one Connection object is needed for the source DTS process and one for the destination. The system of keeping a single Connection for each side of the transfer process allows multiple steps of a DTS operation to use the same open connection.

The contents of a Connection object will vary depending on the type of the source that is represented. There are three source types depending on the connection provided: a network address, a data file path, or a data link file. A network address is the type you will use for the MSDE server. A file path would be used for a data source such as a Microsoft Access database (.mdb) to specify its location. The Connection object can use data link files (files with the .udl extension).

The execution of the package takes care of activating the connection when needed. In a program (such as a VBA application) that addresses a package through the automation objects, the AcquireConnection method can be used to preemptively activate a connection. The AcquireConnection method will attempt to make a connection for the taskname that is passed to it. In VBA, you could use this statement to execute the method for a particular package (myPkg) and a specific task:

```
myPkg.AcquireConnection("myTaskName")
```

The Task Object

Individual Task objects are stored in the Task collection of the package. Each task can be defined to execute one of nine different functions: execute Transact-SQL code, activate a Data Pump task, execute a script (in VB Script, JavaScript, or another ActiveX script), execute an external EXE program, perform a Bulk Insert, use SQL Mail to send mail, perform a query task, transfer SQL objects, or execute a user-defined custom task that is stored in an ActiveX DLL.

For a Task object, the Execute method can be used to manually execute it. The properties available to each task object include: CustomTask, CustomTaskID, Description, Name, Parent, and Properties.

A custom task executes external code in a DLL created in Visual Basic, Visual C++, or other development environments capable of creating an ActiveX DLL. All of the eight predefined tasks are created as ActiveX DLLs that address the CustomTask object.

There is a task object for each of the eight predefined task types that may be associated with the CustomTask property: ExecuteSQLTask, DataPumpTask, DataDriven QueryTask, CreateProcessTask, BulkInsertTask, ActiveScriptTask, SendMailTask, or a TransferObjectsTask. Each of these objects holds the specific properties used for creation and configuration of the task for which they were named.

In the Task object, the CustomTask property holds a reference to an instance of one of these object types depending on the type of task that has been created. The DataPumpTask is used as an OLE DB data provider to import, export, or transform data between heterogeneous data sources.

If the task object is an ExecuteSQLTask, DataPumpTask, or DataDrivenQuery Task, it must have a valid Connection object referenced in the SourceConnectionID property. When the task executes, it will use this connection object to link to the data source.

> Custom tasks can be programmed in Visual Basic. They can use the `Implements` keyword to inherit from the CustomTask object. Each new CustomTask must support the Properties collection, a Name property, a Description property, and an `Execute` method. A custom user interface may also be created by implementing the DTSCustomTaskUI object.

The Step Object

The Step object controls the sequence of execution for the Task objects. The ScriptLanguage property must be set for the script to execute correctly. By default, this property is set to a string that contains `"VB Script"`.

This object can change the course of the execution in accordance with three types of results from the Task object: Completion, Success, or Failure. With the Completion setting, the Task will be executed whether the process succeeds or fails.

Multiple constraints may be placed at each step, and all of the multiple constraints must be satisfied before the next step is executed. The ActiveXScript property holds the script that the step will execute. The FunctionName property is used to specify the function entry point.

Quick-Starting DTS

In this Quick-Start example, a DTS process will be created to export all of the orders from the Northwind database to an Access table. Because the order information is located in several tables including the Orders, Order Details, and Customers tables, a query will be used to denormalize this information for output as a single table. The DTS process will execute this query to generate the results and output them to the text file.

The query will return a data set like this:

CustomerID	OrderID	CompanyName	ContactName	ProductID	ProductName	Quantity	UnitPrice	Discount
VINET	10248	Vins et alcools Chevalier	Paul Henriot	11	Queso Cabrales	12	14.0000	0.0
VINET	10248	Vins et alcools Chevalier	Paul Henriot	42	Singaporean Hokkien Frie	10	9.8000	0.0
VINET	10248	Vins et alcools Chevalier	Paul Henriot	72	Mozzarella di Giovanni	5	34.8000	0.0
TOMSP	10249	Toms Spezialitäten	Karin Josephs	14	Tofu	9	18.6000	0.0
TOMSP	10249	Toms Spezialitäten	Karin Josephs	51	Manjimup Dried Apples	40	42.4000	0.0
HANAR	10250	Hanari Carnes	Mario Pontes	41	Jack's New England Clam	10	7.7000	0.0
HANAR	10250	Hanari Carnes	Mario Pontes	51	Manjimup Dried Apples	35	42.4000	0.1500000
1VICTE	10251	Victuailles en stock	Mary Saveley	22	Gustaf's Knäckebröd	6	16.8000	5.0000001E-2
VICTE	10251	Victuailles en stock	Mary Saveley	57	Ravioli Angelo	15	15.6000	5.0000001E-2

Chapter 13: Using Data Transformation Services and Packages

To export the orders from MSDE to an Access data file, follow these steps:

1. Execute Microsoft Access 2000.

2. At the startup screen, select the Blank access database option and click OK to create a new MDB file.

3. Name the new file **OrdersData.mdb** and click the Create button.

4. Close and exit Access 2000. The table structure creation and data entry will all be handled by the DTS Wizard.

5. Execute the Import and Export Data program under the MSDE menu (see Figure 13-2). This program encapsulates the functions of other DTS wizards and has been created as a stand-alone program.

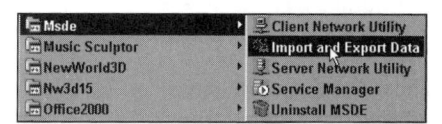

Figure 13-2: The Import and Export Data program is really one of the DTS wizards made into a stand-alone application.

6. Click Next to advance to the first options screen. In this wizard, you need to select a data source and a data destination for the transfer. This first screen enables you to specify the source of the data.

7. Set the default Source to the Microsoft OLE DB Provider for SQL Server. From the combo box, you will need to select the server addressing.

8. Set the server address to the default selection of (local) to match the screen shown in Figure 13-3. If you are not transferring the data from the machine that the MSDE server is executing, select the source server from the combo box.

9. Enter the user name and password for the account that will be used for the data transfer. If you haven't changed the default for MSDE, you can enter **sa** for the user name and leave the password blank. With the user name and password entered, the wizard can now address the source server to retrieve all of the databases that are available on it.

10. Click Refresh to the right of the databases combo box to load the available database names using the user name and password you just entered. Where the combo box was previously filled only with a single option, the default database, there will now be a list of all of the databases available on the selected server.

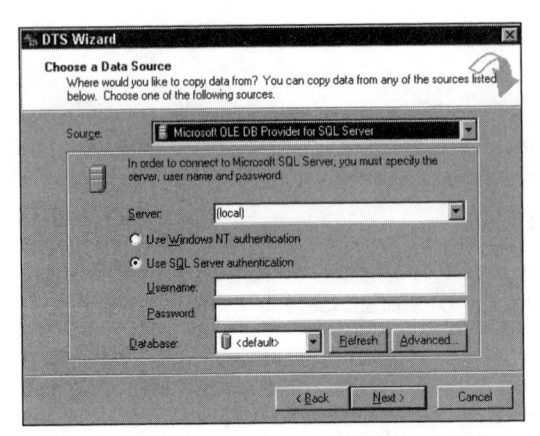

Figure 13-3: Set the source to OLE DB Provider for SQL Server and the server address to (local).

11. Select the NorthwindSQL database from the Database combo box. The Advanced tab contains settings that are particular to the driver selected, such as connection timeout, language, and auto translation settings. Unless you need to change something that is part of the default configuration, there is no need to modify anything in the Advanced Properties window.

12. Click Next to advance to the screen used to set up the destination data source.

13. In the Destination combo box, select the Microsoft Access option. You will see the frame below the combo box changes to reflect the parameters that must be set for an Access data source instead of a SQL Server-based source.

14. Click the button to the right of the text file box with the three dots (. . .) to show a standard Open file dialog box.

15. Select the OrdersData.mdb file and click Save to accept it. The destination screen should match the one shown in Figure 13-4. Because no user name or password was set for this file, those text boxes may remain blank.

16. Click Next to advance to the transfer method screen.

17. Select the Use a query to specify the data to transfer option (see Figure 13-5) and click Next. The alternate option for the transfer method enables a SQL query to select specific parts of the data. When the Copy tables option is selected, the next screen enables you to specify the destination format.

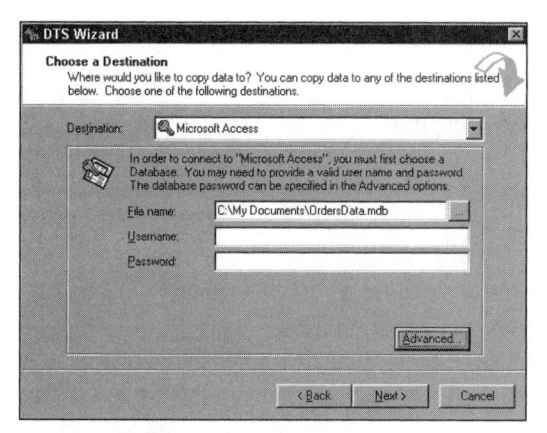

Chapter 13: Using Data Transformation Services and Packages 247

Figure 13-4: The destination screen should have the path of the Access file that was just created.

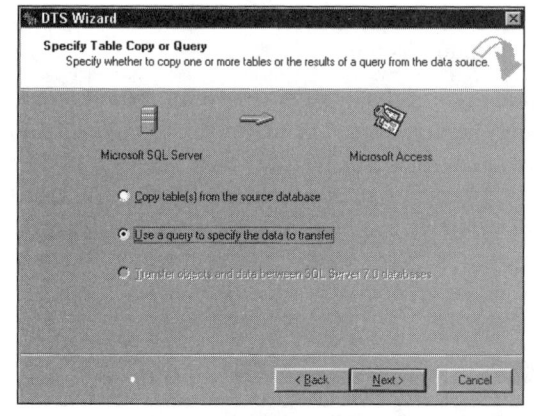

Figure 13-5: Set the transfer method to accept a SQL query that will be used to specify the rows to be inserted.

18. In the Query statement text box, type the following SQL code:

    ```
    SELECT Orders.CustomerID, Orders.OrderID,
    Customers.CompanyName,
       Customers.ContactName, [Order Details].ProductID,
    Products.ProductName,
       [Order Details].Quantity, [Order Details].UnitPrice,
    [Order Details].Discount
    ```

```
FROM Products
INNER JOIN
    (Customers INNER JOIN
        (Orders INNER JOIN [Order Details] ON Orders.OrderID =
[Order Details].OrderID)
        ON Customers.CustomerID = Orders.CustomerID)
        ON Products.ProductID = [Order Details].ProductID;
```

> **TIP** For other queries, you can easily use the Query Builder button to create a query graphically. Because this query uses a number of joins, it is easier to provide the SQL code than to lead you through the process of creating it using the builder.

19. Click Parse to make sure that no errors are found in the query text. If no errors are found, the results box for the parse function will tell you that the code in the query window is valid.

20. Click Next to continue to the source tables screen. In the column labeled Source Table, the Query option should be selected (see Figure 13-6). For the Destination table, the term Results is present to indicate that the results of the query will generate the destination. Finally, the Transform column contains a three dot (. . .) button that is used to configure the transformation. You will need to use the Transform window to properly set how the data will be accepted.

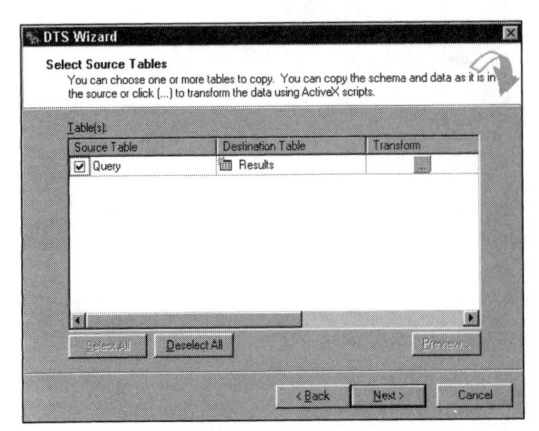

Figure 13-6: The Tables grid displays the source and destination of all of the data to be moved.

Chapter 13: Using Data Transformation Services and Packages 249

21. Click the button in the Transform column to display the Column Mappings and Transformations dialog (see Figure 13-7). You can see that the first setting on the Column Mappings tab, Create destination table, is checked. A new table will be created in the destination to match the selection made in this window.

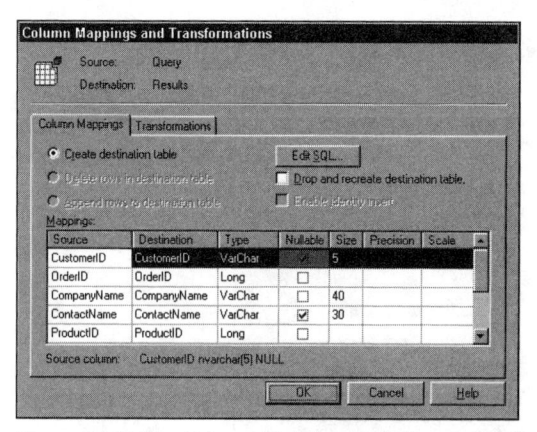

Figure 13-7: The Column Mappings and Transformations dialog box enables configuration of transformation that may take place as the data is being copied.

22. Check the Drop and recreate destination table option. Because this package will be saved for later execution, setting this option will ensure that the table is removed before the process begins.

23. Click OK to accept these changes to the transformation.

24. Click Next to advance to the screen that enables you to schedule when the export will occur. There are two option sets for configuration: the When settings and the Save settings. The When settings enable you to schedule whether the process executes immediately or will be scheduled for execution. The Save options enable you to store the package so that you can examine or modify it for later execution.

25. Click the Save DTS Package option in the Save settings. The default SQL Server option will be selected for the destination of the saved package. By saving this package, you can examine it later and possibly use it for a prototype of a custom package.

26. To run the process immediately, leave this default option and click Next. Because you have chosen to save the package, the next screen will present the options needed to save the package to the SQL server. The package will be stored in the msdb database for later modification or execution.

27. Set the Name of the package to **DTS_NorthwindOrders** and type a brief description of the package.

28. Set the password for the Owner to **owner** and the User password to **user** (see Figure 13-8). These passwords will be convenient to remember when you access the package later.

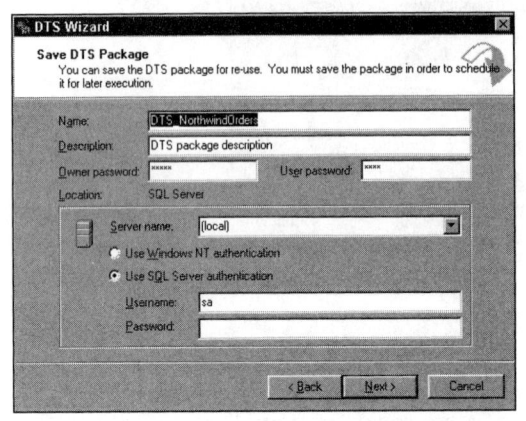

Figure 13-8: The options for saving a package include setting passwords for both the user and the owner of the package.

29. Click Next. You have now completed the wizard configuration options.

30. If all of the listed options are correct, click Finish to begin the process.

31. The transformation will occur, and you will be presented with a status box as the export progresses. When the process is finished, a success dialog box will be displayed to indicate that one table was transferred to a flat-file database (the text file).

32. Click OK on the information dialog to return to the status window.

With the export complete, you have a sample table that was created by the DTS system and a package that can be used again or modified for a custom execution. The final window on the wizard displays a progress report of the transformation process (see Figure 13-9). The table named Results is stored in the OrdersData database. When the process was begun, because the table had yet to be created, it couldn't be dropped and therefore an error occurred at that step. In the next section, you will use the package that you just created as a job to be scheduled.

You can view all of the available packages registered in the MSDE server by querying the msdb database. If you set the source to msdb, this query will display all of the current packages:

```
select * from sysdtspackages
```

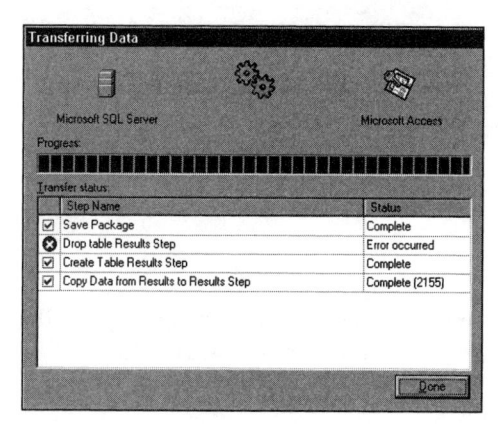

Chapter 13: Using Data Transformation Services and Packages

Figure 13-9: The progress window shows each step that occurred as the package was executed.

For the package that you just created, the data in the returned result set should look like this:

<u>Name</u>
DTS_NorthwindOrders

<u>id</u>   <u>versionid</u>
2327AF40-E3B7-11D3-BF13-444553540000   2327AF41-E3B7-11D3-BF13-444553540000

<u>description</u>   <u>categoryid</u>
DTS package description   B8C30002-A282-11D1-B7D9-00C04FB6EFD5

<u>createdate</u>   <u>owner</u>
2000-02-15   -

<u>packagedata</u>
14:49:46.4330xD0CF11E0A1B11AE1000000000000000000000000000000003E000300FEFF090006
00000000000000000000000200000002000000000000001000000500000001000000FEFFFFFF00
000000030000000800000FFFFFFFFFFFFFFFFFFFFFFFFFFFFFFFFFFFFFFFFFFFFFFFFFFFFFFFFF
FFFFFFFFFFFFFFFFFFFFFFFFFFFF

<u>owner sid</u>
0x01

It is through this package registration that any available package can be scheduled for timed execution.

Under the full SQL Server install, the wizard application you used is broken into two parts. The DTS Import Wizard provides a multistep process used to set up a package for a data import. The DTS Export Wizard, a separate but nearly identical application, is used to move data from the MSDE server. The process of using the Import or Export Wizards in Enterprise Manager is identical to the process you followed with the MSDE program Import and Export Data earlier in the chapter.

In addition to the step-by-step process that you can follow, the wizards can also be addressed through the command line as `dtswiz`. You could execute a wizard using a command like this:

```
dtswiz /i
```

Executing this wizard from the command prompt can activate any of the processes that are available through the graphic interface of the wizard. Help for all of the switches available for this utility can be displayed by passing the /? option like this:

```
dtswiz /?
```

The command-line version of the wizard can create a package like the graphical version for storage to the msdb database, a file stored in the COM Structured Storage file, or into the Microsoft Repository.

Scheduling DTS Execution

Packages or individual steps in a DTS process can be executed through the SQL Server Agent. DTS packages may be executed either manually or through some type of scheduled event. Scheduling can be configured in several ways including:

- **Exact time:** An exact time is specified, such as 1:00 a.m. This time executes based on the system clock of the MSDE server.

- **Relative time:** The process can execute at specific intervals such as every 10 minutes.

- **Calendar date:** Scheduling may occur on an exact date such as December 30, 2000.

- **Day:** The event may execute on a particular day such as the second Monday of the month.

- **Non-absolute date:** A date may be specified such as the last day of the month, which will change depending on the particular month.

Most of these formats can be mixed and matched. For example, a package could be executed on the first Thursday of every March at 10:00 a.m. This scheduling provides enough flexibility to allow the automated process to execute regularly at almost any combination of day, date, and time.

The DTS_NorthwindOrders package that you created earlier can be scheduled to be automatically activated on a time event. Scheduling a job can be accessed through Transact-SQL code.

To schedule the package for execution, follow these steps:

1. Execute Microsoft Access 2000.

2. Open the NorthwindCS ADP project. You will be creating a stored procedure to schedule the job. Alternatively, you could use Microsoft Query to immediately execute the scheduling code. A stored procedure is used in this case to demonstrate that the package scheduling sequence can be stored in the database, allowing a simple procedure call to DTS_NorthwindOrders the package.

3. Click the Stored Procedures item in the Object column.

4. Click New to create a new procedure.

5. Enter the following SQL statements in the code window:

    ```
    Create Procedure ScheduleOrdersExport
    As
    EXECUTE msdb.dbo.sp_add_job @job_name = 'ordersJob1'
    EXECUTE msdb.dbo.sp_add_jobschedule @name='ordersSched2',
    @job_name = 'ordersJob1',
    @freq_type=0x1,
    @freq_interval=0x1,
    @freq_subday_type=0x4,
    @freq_subday_interval=5,
    @active_start_time = '130000'
    ```

6. Set the variable `@active_start_time` in the stored procedure code to the current time plus five in the format of HHMMSS. The scheduling will then execute five minutes after the specified start time.

7. Click the View icon on the toolbar to write the stored procedure (set the name to **ScheduleOrdersExport**) into the NorthwindSQL database and subsequently execute it. If scheduling executes properly, the result set should contain the value 1.

If you wait six minutes and then examine the OrdersData.mdb file, you will see that the table and data that you deleted in the last section have been restored. Any time you want to execute the process again, you can simply execute the stored procedure. For example, if you loaded Microsoft Query and configured it to address the NorthwindSQL database, you could execute this statement to activate the schedule:

```
Execute ScheduleOrdersExport
```

Even if a job is scheduled for a time event, that does not preclude the job from being executed manually. A data backup, for example, might regularly occur at 1:00 a.m., but a scheduled power outage warrants executing it at 5:00 p.m. The job can be executed manually at 5:00 p.m. without affecting the scheduling of that job, which can then execute again at its scheduled time if the power has been reactivated. If the necessary network resources are available, a job can also be configured to execute across more than one server.

If a job is already executing, however, you cannot activate the same job until the current execution has completed. A current job, however, can be sent a `stop` command to abort it. If the executing job is complex, it may not halt immediately after the `stop` command is issued. The job can also delete itself if it will no longer be needed.

> **NOTE** Under Windows NT, you can use the `net send` command to notify another system or the administrator each time a package has been executed. Alternatively, an event message may also be written into the operating system event log. These two methods are provided to allow automatic notification of job progress and execution.

Programming DTS

There are several ways to control the DTS system both from within the MSDE environment itself as well as outside. A package itself can accept ActiveX scripts for execution or address most available DTS functions that can be activated through Transact-SQL code. The DTS system can also be controlled through its object model from a programming language such as Visual Basic or VBA outside of the actual MSDE environment. The object models can be used to control the DTS system in much the same way that the SQL-DMO framework can control overall processes of the MSDE server.

Using Scripts in a Process

The DTS system can accept scripts that use any features of the ActiveX scripting language. The default languages that are available include VB Script and JScript (compatible with JavaScript). Other languages such as Perlscript (compatible with Perl) are available through this language plug-in system.

Within the scripting environment supported by DTS, global variables may be used that are held in common for routines that execute within a process. A global variable can be used for individual values or may contain references to particular objects so that they may be addressed across several scripts.

You can use a script such as this one:

```
'**************************************************************
'   Visual Basic Transformation Script
'   Copy each source column to the
'   destination column
'**************************************************************

Function Main()
    DTSDestination("CustomerID") = DTSSource("CustomerID")
    DTSDestination("OrderID") = DTSSource("OrderID")
    DTSDestination("CompanyName") = DTSSource("CompanyName")
    DTSDestination("ContactName") = DTSSource("ContactName")
    DTSDestination("ProductID") = DTSSource("ProductID")
    DTSDestination("ProductName") = DTSSource("ProductName")
    DTSDestination("Quantity") = DTSSource("Quantity")
    DTSDestination("UnitPrice") = DTSSource("UnitPrice")
    DTSDestination("Discount") = DTSSource("Discount")
    Main = DTSTransformStat_OK
End Function
```

Programming the scripts provides access to all of the VB Script features, including formatting and mathematical changes. You can use operators such as the concatenation operator (represented by the ampersand [&] symbol) to combine or supplement string values.

DTS Programming from VBA

Addressing DTS is possible through VBA with programming objects. The Package object is the central object used to transform data and move data. The `Execute` method of the Package object will activate the package.

1. Execute Microsoft Access 2000.
2. Create a new project and name it **DTSAccess.mdb**.
3. Create a new form and place a command button on it.
4. Through the Properties window for the command button, open the On Click event.
5. Under the Tools menu, select the References option, find the Microsoft SQLDMO Object Library item in the list, check the box to its left, and click OK to add the SQL-DMO class definitions to the project.
6. Select the Code Builder option to allow editing in the VBA environment.

7. Enter the following code into the click event for the command button:

```
Private Sub Command0_Click()
    Dim myTable As SQLDMO.Table
    Dim myMSDE As SQLDMO.SQLServer
    Dim myJob As SQLDMO.Job, myJobStep As SQLDMO.JobStep

    Dim i As Integer

    ' Create access to the MSDE server and open a connection
    Set myMSDE = CreateObject("SQLDMO.SQLServer")
    myMSDE.Connect "MSDEservername", "sa", ""

    Set myJob = CreateObject("SQLDMO.Job")
    myJob.Name = "DTS_NorthwindInsert"
    myMSDE.JobServer.Jobs.Add myJob

    myJob.BeginAlter
    i = 0
    For Each myTable In _
       myMSDE.Databases("NorthwindSQL").Tables
        ' Only update statistics on non-system tables.
        If myTable.Attributes <> _
           SQLDMOTabAtt_SystemObject Then
            ' Increment job counter
            i = i + 1
            ' Create new job step
            Set myJobStep = CreateObject("SQLDMO.JobStep")
            ' Name the step
            myJobStep.Name = "NorthwindInsert_Step_" & i
            myJobStep.DatabaseName = "NorthwindSQL"
            myJobStep.StepID = i
            myJobStep.SubSystem = "TSQL"

            ' Issue SQL command to insert a new record
            myJobStep.Command = "Insert Into [" & _
               myTable.Name & "] Default Values"
            ' Setup event action for success and failure
            myJobStep.OnFailAction = _
               SQLDMOJobStepAction_QuitWithFailure
            myJobStep.OnSuccessAction = _
               SQLDMOJobStepAction_GotoNextStep
            ' Add step to JobSteps collection
            myJob.JobSteps.Add myJobStep
        End If
    Next
```

```
' Processing completed, indicate success
myJob.JobSteps.ItemByID(i).OnSuccessAction = _
    SQLDMOJobStepAction_QuitWithSuccess
' Reset to first step
myJob.StartStepID = 1
myJob.DoAlter
myMSDE.Disconnect

End Sub
```

8. Click on the Design button to enter execution mode.

9. Click the command button to execute the job creation.

This code can be executed within a VBA project that has the Microsoft DTSPackages object library added to the program References. It will create a new job for the agent to execute manually, because the code doesn't include creating the scheduling objects.

DTS DATA PUMP INTERFACES

The Data Pump interfaces address external COM objects to allow custom procedures to be used during the transformation process. The Data Pump is an OLE DB service provider that can be addressed either through the OLE DB framework or through ADO. The DTS Data Pump is also available as a separate object library from VBA, so it may be addressed, activated, and configured from an external program.

DTS OBJECT TRANSFER

This object is used to transfer entire database objects from one SQL Server-based system to another. This object can be used for transfer of tables, views, stored procedures, databases, defaults, rules, user-defined types, logins, users, groups, roles, indexes, and constraints. It can be used to transfer an entire object or a subset of that object and the objects that are dependent on it. For tables, transfer of only the table structure or both the structure and the data is possible.

This object, through the `ScriptTransfer` and `Transfer` methods, enacts the transfer. The transfer process occurs through the ODBC system instead of the OLE DB middleware.

Using the DTS Designer

The Enterprise Manager that is included with a full SQL Server installation includes a graphical design environment for DTS packages. If you open the Data Transformation Services folder in the Enterprise Manager, you will see all of the packages currently installed on that system. Opening one of the packages will display the DTS Designer, which will show a graphical interface used to configure DTS tasks (see Figure 13-10). The packages created in the designer can be stored on an MSDE server, a SQL server, a Microsoft Repository, or a separate COM-based file.

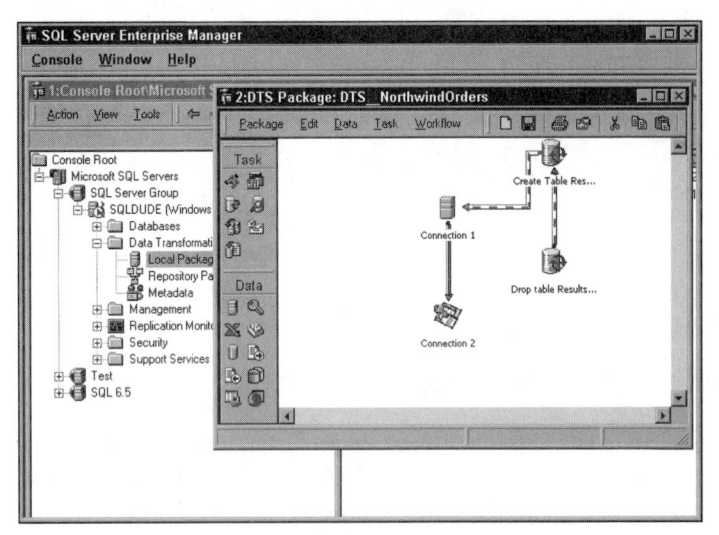

Figure 13-10: The DTS Designer provides a graphic representation of a package.

To examine the process that is occurring in the Create Table step of the process, you can right-click the item and select the Properties option. The specific dialog box will appear that relates to the particular step (see Figure 13-11). In the Properties of the Create Table item, the SQL code used to create the Results table is described, as is the connection that will be used to allow this SQL command to execute.

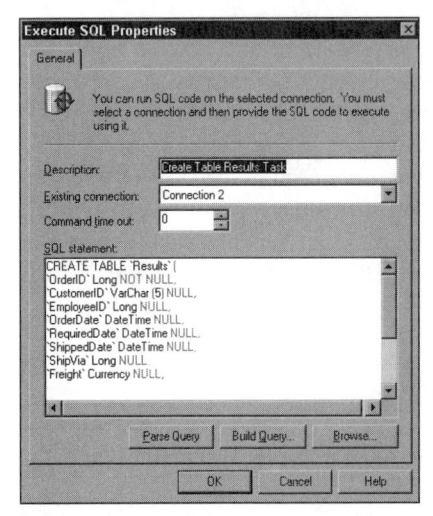

Figure 13-11: Each step of a package process can be examined through the Properties window.

Chapter 13: Using Data Transformation Services and Packages

You can even examine or modify any of the arrow lines that indicate the progress through the packages. If you right-click the line leading from the Create Table item to the step that follows it, you will see the precedence constraints that are made in this step (see Figure 13-12).

This visual design environment will allow you to quickly and easily modify the packages that have been created on an MSDE server. Rarely, however, will you use this interface from scratch. It is much more common to use the wizards to create the foundation package that you can then modify.

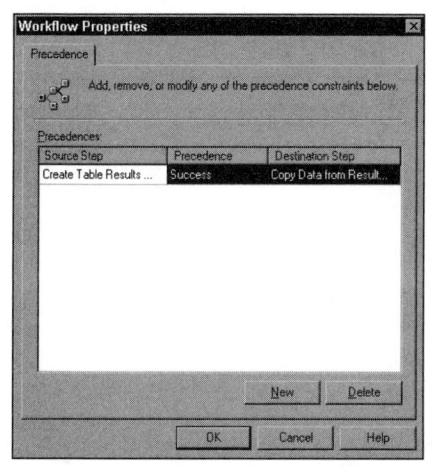

Figure 13-12: The Properties window for a connection between two steps shows the workflow logic for the progression.

> **TIP** The SQL code for modification of the package is still available through Transact-SQL even after it has been altered in the DTS Designer. I find that for a complex DTS transformation, it is often simpler to create the overall process through a wizard or the DTS Designer and then refine it using the direct SQL construction code.

The dtsrun Utility Application

A command-line utility known as dtsrun can be used to activate a DTS process external to the MSDE server. This utility can generally be found in the following path on your MSDE server:

```
C:\MSSQL7\BINN
```

It can be used to execute a DTS package from the command line by passing it the package name. The general syntax for executing a package with the dtsrun utility appears like this:

```
dtsrun /Sserver /Uuser name /Ppwd /NpkgName /MpkgPassword
```

To run the dtsrun utility, you could use code like this:

```
dtsrun /Sthinkpad /Usa /P /NmyPackage /Mpackageopen
```

This command line will execute the myPackage package on the MSDE server. For passing the individual flags and arguments, spaces may be omitted between switches and the utility will interpret the switches properly.

> **NOTE** The commands sent to the dtsrun utility are case-sensitive. Be sure to enter the switches (such as /M) exactly as they appear.

You may notice that this command line sends a password to the executable. When a package is created, it can be configured to use a package password. Because data is being moved into a potentially insecure environment, it is important to have effective security beyond the traditional login security. For this reason, each package can have its own security password to aid in controlling wholesale data export.

This command may also use the /E switch to set the utility to use a trusted connection so that the user name and password arguments do not need to be supplied. However, if the MSDE server is installed on a Windows 95/98 machine, the trusted connection option is not available.

Summary

The Data Transformation Services (DTS) allow automation of data import and export from the MSDE server. The package structure is a format to encapsulate a specific transformation process so that it may be executed at a particular time or activated by an event. In this chapter, you covered:

- ◆ **Data Transformation Services (DTS):** The DTS system allows automated import and export. DTS is one of the key services that sets it apart from a standard database engine, because DTS tasks may be stored for manual or scheduled execution.

- **Package:** A package is a structure stored on the database server that contains the process of the data transformation to used when the DTS system is activated. Packages may be created by several wizards, through system stored procedures, or using the DTS object model.

- **DTS Import and Export wizard:** The wizards, included with SQL Server, can be used to set up packages for importing and exporting. The Import and Export Data program included with the MSDE server performs the same operations and will store the transformation created in the wizard into a package.

- **ActiveX scripting:** A transformation may be guided and modified in its execution through a script in a language such as VB Script or JavaScript that is contained within the package. Because scripting may be embedded in the transformation process itself, almost any type of formatting and constraint checking is possible.

- **DTS object model:** The availability of the DTS object model allows a COM-capable development environment such as Visual Basic or Delphi to control the DTS system and even create or modify packages.

Chapter 14

Working with Views

IN THIS CHAPTER

- Understanding how views work
- Creating a view
- Modifying a view
- Encrypting a view
- Using server functions in a view
- Using variables to customize a view
- Obtaining information about the view
- Accessing views from object models

TO PROVIDE DIFFERENT SORT orders for a database, indexes are created so that alternate orders are available for queries without having to change the physical location of the various rows. To simplify the creation of queries or functional access to tables, a SQL engine enables you to create a database object known as a *view*. A view is a simulated or virtual table. It provides a logical abstraction for a table presentation, similar to the way in which an index provides an abstraction for sort presentation.

How Views Work

A view can consist of selected columns from many different tables, yet it will appear to the user that only a single table is being addressed. The view is maintained on the database server and updated dynamically. Because the view exists on the database server, any client application with the proper permissions can access it as if it were a standard table.

A view can be used to do the following:

- **Present a focused data set of interest:** The customized presentation of the data enables you to show only a specific set of data in a particular view. It also enables you to offer a custom presentation that enables different users to look at the same data in a different way, specialized to their training and understanding.

- **Simplify multitable data access:** Frequently accessed data sets with joins, subqueries, unions, and special column selections can be stored as a view for easy access.

- **Provide logical organization:** A series of views can be used to add organization that may be lacking in the underlying structure of the database. The presentation of the information through various views can also provide several different organizations of the same tables.

- **Limit access for security:** By placing only the necessary columns in a view, the access to specific data can be limited more easily than by defining individual column privileges.

- **Add a level of abstraction:** The views place a level of abstraction between the user and the actual tables. Changes to underlying tables will be unnoticed by applications accessing views as long as the views are updated.

- **Simplify data export:** Creating views with all the columns needed for data export or transfer to another data source can reduce the effort involved in either constructing a Data Transformation Services (DTS) package or using `Select Into` statements to specify the individual column and table sources of the intended export data.

- **Provide standard calculation columns:** By coding the formatting or calculation of columns into the view, you can create a standard presentation of the data.

Views are structures on the database server that, much like an index, do not contain any actual data. Instead, they access the data stored in tables that are referenced in the definition query of each view. A view may contain references to many different tables or even to other views. Each view is defined with a normal SQL `Select` statement used to determine what tables are included and the criteria used to determine the rows that will be present in the view.

Permissions on a view are inherited from the source tables. Therefore, if the user has permission to read from Table A and write to Table B, the same privileges will apply to columns from these tables included in the view definition.

However, even if the user has write permission to all five columns of Table A, if only three are included in the view, then those are all that are available through the view. Changes made to a view that allows write access are made to the underlying tables that make up the columns of the view.

Creating a View

To create a view on the MSDE server, you can use SQL statements, or construct a new view through the visual interface of a Microsoft Access ADP project. After you are more accustomed to SQL programming, using direct SQL code for view construction is very convenient and can be accomplished in any SQL query tool, including Microsoft Query.

Microsoft Access, however, provides an excellent graphical interface for view creation, as well as the ability to directly modify the Select statement that forms the basis of the view. You can use both the SQL tools and the Access project interchangeably because the Access ADP file, when opened, queries the database server for all the database objects present for the database. New views, or modifications to existing views, are reflected in the project when it is opened.

The simplified syntax of a view looks like this:

```
Create View viewname [ column1, column2, etc.]
    As [ Select statement ]
```

This definition sets the name of a view followed by the columns to be returned by that view. If no column names are specified, the column names will be assigned to match the columns returned in the Select statement. The column list acts as an alternative to using an alias for each field of the Select statement.

The As clause is used to specify the Select statement that will be used to define the data contained in the view. The Select statement may reference one or more tables and may even retrieve data from other views. It can even use the Union keyword to combine one or more data sets.

Creating Views in SQL

To begin understanding views, it is a good idea to see the actual SQL code used to create a new view on the database server. In SQL, the Create View command is sent to the server to generate a new view. Load the Microsoft Query tool or the SQL Query Analyzer with a connection to the NorthwindSQL data source so that you can execute the following SQL commands.

To create a very simple view for the Northwind database, you can use a command such as this:

```
Create View customerView As Select * From customers
```

This view simply returns all the rows and columns of the customers table when it is queried. To access the data from this view, you can treat it as a table, like this:

```
Select * From customerView
```

When the query executes, all ten columns of the customers table and the data for each row of the table will be returned.

The current view is very rudimentary. Although an existing query can be modified (which you will learn later in this chapter), you can replace the current view on the server only by dropping it and creating a new view in its place. If you execute the `customerView` creation code again, MSDE will return an error such as this:

```
Server: Msg 2714, Level 16, State 5, Procedure customerView, Line 1
There is already an object named 'customerView' in the database.
```

To drop the view so that a new one may be created using the same name, you would use this command:

```
Drop View customerView
```

Note that because `Drop View` just deletes the view structure on the server, no data is eliminated. The view is a virtual table and won't affect the underlying tables that are referenced by it. After the view has been eliminated, you can create a new view with the same name. In this case, you can create a slightly more complicated query that uses the `Where` clause to make the view a subset of the complete customers table:

```
Create View customerView As Select customerid, companyname, fax
    From customers Where fax Is Not null
```

This view uses the `Where` clause to include only the rows that do not have a null value stored in the fax column. Notice that the view has also been changed to include just three columns: customerid, companyname, and fax. When this view is addressed in a query, only these three columns will be available.

> **TIP** To a query, no essential difference exists between a view and the actual table. In complex projects, this can lead to confusion among developers who address many different data sources. For this reason, I always try to include the word *view* in the name of each view, to ensure that the person examining a query or constructing a new one will know exactly what type of database structure is being addressed.

When a view is created, it is stored in the currently selected database. It can be addressed by other database objects through an explicit path declaration, just like a table.

Limitations on Using a View

Some limitations exist to the `Select` statement that defines a view: the `Select` cannot contain the `Order By`, `Compute`, `Compute By`, or `Into` statements. It also cannot reference any temporary tables.

Each view can have a maximum of 1,024 columns. Views can reference other views, with the only restriction being that the nesting of views is limited to 32 levels. This large number of nested levels should be no limitation at all for most projects.

Inserts, updates, or deletes attempted on calculated columns in a view will generate an error, just as they do if attempted on calculated columns in a query. Modifications to any view that includes a `Group By` clause will generate an error.

You can define primary and foreign keys in a view, even if the column designated a primary key is not the same column as the one used in the source table. Make sure, however, that for updates you have the keys set properly for the virtual columns that are shown in the view.

> Before the MSDE/SQL Server 7 engine was available, earlier versions of the engine would allow updates to a view only if the view referenced only a single table. If you address other database servers that are running an older version of the SQL Server engine, where multitable views were read-only, be aware of this limitation.

Because the view is defined by a query, records are changed so they no longer meet the criteria of the `Where` clause of the query will drop out of the view data set. When creating a view, you can include the `With Check Option`, which does not allow any modification to the rows that would make them invalidate the set criteria for the view and make them drop from the set.

Views have other limitations, most relating to the capabilities of making updates. Rules and triggers cannot be associated directly with views limiting the amount of customization for inserts, deletes, and updates that may be created for the views. However, rules and triggers remain in effect for the tables that underlie the view.

A view can do much more than simply present a subset of a single table. It can also be used to include columns from several different tables through a union and present the data as if it were stored in a single table. In this example, you will create a view that combines data from the employees table and the suppliers table to provide a single list of all the companies and contacts that are connected with the company in one way or another.

The view creation code for multiple tables would look like this:

```
Create View integrateView As
Select companyname, contactname from suppliers
Union Select companyname, contactname from customers
```

If you query this view, you will see a result set that includes rows for both tables, like this:

companyname	contactname
Alfreds Futterkiste	Maria Anders
Ana Trujillo Emparedados y helados	Ana Trujillo

```
Antonio Moreno Taquerka          Antonio Moreno
Around the Horn                  Thomas Hardy
...
Forets d'erables                 Chantal Goulet
Refrescos Americanas LTDA        Carlos Diaz
Heli Sußwaren GmbH & Co. KG      Petra Winkler
```

You can see how powerful using views can be to unify the presentation of complex data. Through Microsoft Access, you can easily create additional views and also modify existing ones, such as the view you just created.

Creating Views in Access

Microsoft Access provides the View Designer, a tool that makes creating views easy. The View Designer has a graphical interface (similar to the Query window for a normal Access MDB file) that enables you to set up a query that will be the foundation of the view. In Figure 14-1, you can see that the View Designer provides a Show Table window that can be used to select any of the tables currently available on the data source.

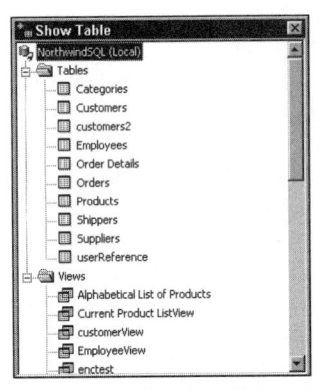

Figure 14-1: The Show Table window shows all of the tables that are available on the data source.

In this example, you will create a new view using the Access View Designer. After you define a view in the Designer, it is placed on the MSDE server as if you had defined it through standard SQL coding. Unlike a query that is stored in a traditional MDB file, the view is created on the server, so it can be addressed by any tool that can connect to the MSDE source.

To create a view from Access, follow these steps:

1. Execute Microsoft Access 2000.

2. Open the NorthwindCS ADP project you created in Chapter 3. You can create a new view in this project that will be stored on the MSDE Northwind database.

3. Click the Views tab to display the views of this project.

> **Note:** Notice that numerous views already are listed for the database (see Figure 14-2). When you used the Upsizing Wizard to convert the Northwind database to the MSDE server, all the queries contained in that database were converted to views.

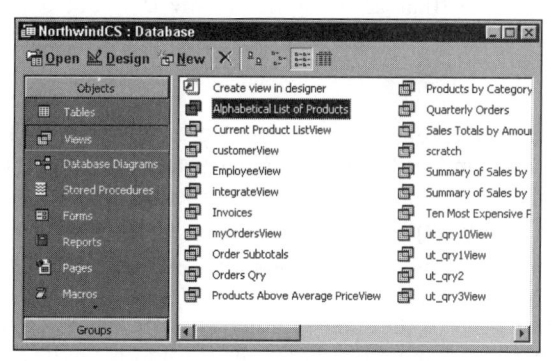

Figure 14-2: The views listed in the NorthwindCS database are the queries that were originally upsized.

4. Click the New button to begin a new view. Access automatically displays the blank View window divided into two panes: the Diagram pane and the Column Grid pane. To construct a view, the tables that make up the view need to be added.

5. Right-click the mouse in the tables area (the gray area at the top of the window) and select the Show Table option. This option displays the Add Tables window.

6. Add the employees table by dragging the employees table item from the Show Table window onto the top pane of the window that appears gray. You should see a representation of the table appear in this area.

7. Click in the asterisk (*) checkbox of the table to select all of the columns into the view.

8. Execute the view by clicking the Run button on the toolbar.

9. When prompted to name the view, enter the name employeesView.

You now have a view that displays all the employee records contained in the database. By using the panes available along the bottom of the window, you can refine the query that provides this view to include or exclude data.

The View Designer can display one or all three panes used for query design. The three window panes used for constructing a view are the Diagram pane, the Column grid pane, and the SQL pane. They all work together to create the view on the MSDE server.

DIAGRAM PANE

From the Show Table window, you can drag and drop tables for use in the view onto the table area. The tables placed in the Diagram pane have each column listed (in addition to an All Columns item) with a checkbox to the left of each column entry. Checking the box to the left of an entry places that column in the Column Grid pane as well as in the SQL pane.

Only the columns of the tables that are available in the Diagram pane of the window can be used for inclusion in the view through the Column Grid pane.

COLUMN GRID PANE

The Column Grid pane is like the column grid that you've used before in Microsoft Access to construct a query for an MDB file. It provides a grid that enables you to configure each column that will be available in the final view.

The grid column titled Column displays whichever field is selected for the view. By selecting a column name in this slot, you can assign criteria, an alias, and output settings to be used with it.

The alias creates a column alias in the same manner as using the `As` keyword in a SQL `Select` statement. In fact, when you enter an alias, if you have the SQL pane showing, you will see the `As` entry appear in the query.

In the grid, the Table column displays the source table for the field being specified in that row. The table name can actually include a fully qualified table name, to address a table contained in a different database. For example, to include the text column from the syscomments table of the master database for a view located in the NorthwindSQL database, you could enter a table name like this:

```
master.dbo.syscomments
```

Be aware that it is not a good idea to introduce columns from other tables unless either:

- ◆ The view only includes columns from a table in another database.
- ◆ The table in the other database is joined to the primary table defined in the view.

If one of these two conditions doesn't exist, the returned recordset will include many unnecessary records when merging the rows of both tables. The number of records returned is the product of the two recordsets (for example, 20 records in table 1 times 10 records in table 2 = 200 records). Therefore, be sure to test any complicated view with several different conditions before you deploy it, to avoid excessive record processing.

In the Column Grid pane, the Output checkbox simply indicates whether the current row definition will be returned in the view recordset. The conditions and criteria will not, by default, be included in the result set.

The Criteria column enables you to place one or more conditional settings on the column. This column is fairly freeform and enables you to place as many conditions as you like with SQL criteria text (such as comparisons and Boolean evaluation). The Or column is a Criteria column that adds a logical Or between the previous Criteria or Or column.

After you have configured the entire row, you will have added one of three types of definition to the view: a setting to display all columns of a table, a listing of an individual column, or the criteria for a column inclusion.

SQL PANE

The SQL pane can be displayed by either clicking the SQL button on the toolbar or selecting View → Show Panes → SQL. The SQL pane displays the SQL code for the current `Select` statement that will define the view. The SQL code shown in this window is automatically constructed and augmented by any changes made to the other two panes of the window.

Likewise, modifications to the code in the SQL pane are added to the settings in the other panes. If you've added any tables to the `From` clause, they will be displayed in the Diagram pane. Any modifications to the column list or `Where` clause are reflected in the Column Grid pane. Changes to the SQL code are not displayed in the other panes until the focus shifts away from the SQL pane.

SQL unions cannot be displayed by the Diagram pane or Column Grid pane. Therefore, if you add the `Union` keyword to the SQL view query, a dialog box similar to the one shown in Figure 14-3 is displayed. If you want to continue with the union change that you added, and thus click the Yes button, the other two panes dim and become inaccessible. Choosing the No button reverts to the last version of the view query that was moved to the other views when the SQL pane lost the focus.

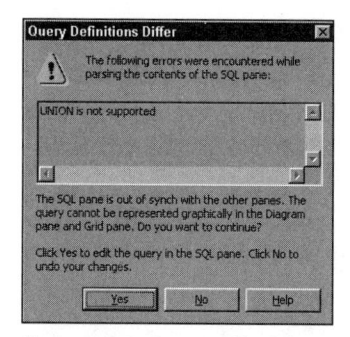

Figure 14-3: Because the Diagram and Column Grid panes don't support unions, you will be asked whether you want to continue with the union.

How a View Is Stored

A view, when it is created on the MSDE server, is not a structure that is simply stored with the tables it references. Several tables exist within the database to hold the view information. The view is stored in the following system objects:

- The name of each view is stored in the sysobjects table.
- The column information is stored in the syscolumns table.
- The column dependencies sre stored in the sysdepends table.
- The text of the view code is stored in the syscomments table.

All of these items stored in the various sys tables contain a reference to determine the database to which a view belongs. You can use the `sp_depends` system procedure to show the table and database references used by the view with the current database.

> **Note:** Although a view is compiled, the execution plan for a view is recompiled each time a view is accessed. A stored procedure, in contrast, uses the stored execution plan, making a stored procedure faster than a view with the same query statement.

View Properties

In addition to changing the columns and tables that make up the view, you can change some of the global properties. Right-clicking in the table area enables you to select the Properties option. The Properties dialog box (see Figure 14-4) enables you to select options, including encryption, grouping, distinct row, and output settings.

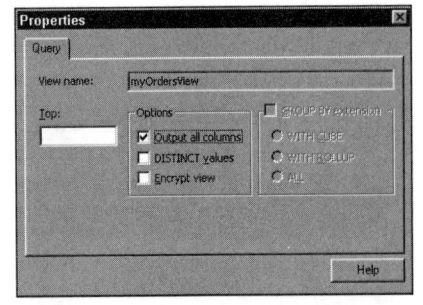

Figure 14-4: The Properties dialog box enables you to change the settings of the view itself.

One of the available options enables you to turn on the encryption on the view. Remember that after you have encrypted a view, it cannot be de-encrypted, and therefore no design changes can be made after encryption has been set.

Modifying a View

The `Alter View` command enables you to modify the current view. The primary reason to alter a view rather than re-create it from scratch is that the security permissions already assigned to that view will be retained when the view is modified. If the view is dropped and reconstructed, the security settings have to be reapplied.

When a command modifies an existing column — and even changes the name of that column — the security privileges for that column remain intact.

The simplified syntax for using the `Alter View` command looks like this:

```
Alter View viewname [ column1, column2, etc.]
   As [ Select statement ]
```

To modify the view customerView that you created earlier to now display all rows with fax columns that do contain null values, follow these steps:

1. Open Microsoft Query or the SQL Query Analyzer, with which you can execute a SQL statement.

2. Enter the following code:

   ```
   ALTER VIEW customerView AS
   SELECT customerid, companyname, fax
   FROM customers
   WHERE fax Is null
   ```

3. Execute the code against the MSDE server.

With these changes, if you query the view, the data returned will be all the rows that have null values in the fax column. For the customers table, the returned recordset should contain 22 rows.

Encrypting a View

From Microsoft Access, you can encrypt a view on the database server. This is helpful when you want to eliminate the possibility of accessing the underlying tables and logic that define a view. Although the encrypted view can be addressed as a data source, the view schema can no longer can be viewed or edited.

To encrypt a view through SQL code, you can alter a view like this:

```
Alter View customerView With Encryption
As SELECT customerid, companyname, fax
FROM customers
WHERE fax Is null
```

Earlier, you were shown the encryption option from within Access that enables you to change the view properties. Alternately, in the Enterprise Manager, you can right-click the View item in the database and select the Properties option. Check the Encrypt View option and click the OK button. The next time you open the view, it will be encrypted.

> **CAUTION:** After a view has been encrypted, it cannot be de-encrypted. Because an encrypted view can't be edited, be sure to have a backup of the `Create View` statement used to generate the view, before you make this permanent setting.

Using Server Functions in a View

All the examples of views have used traditional queries to supply the data that is returned in a view. A view can also use server variables that can be returned as column values for presentation. The server variables can provide information on the current state of the system, login, query, and other factors.

Some of the available server functions and variables can return the following information:

- **Current row count:** The returned set may include a column displaying the number of rows included in the results set through the `@@rowcount` variable.

- **Current date and time:** The `GetDate()` and `Current_Timestamp` functions return the date and time set on the database server. Therefore, the values of the recordset will contain the time the query is being executed.

- **Current language:** The current operating language of the MSDE server can be determined using the ←nguage variable.

- **Current user name and information:** Information about the user, such as the current user name, session user name, and system user name, may be retrieved from system functions.

- **Transaction count:** Data on how many transactions are open on the current connection is available through the `@@TranCount` variable.

To create a view that uses the `rowcount` variable, simply add the system function to the column list of the `Select` statement, like this:

```
Create View customerView As Select @@rowcount As [Row Count],
GETDATE() AS CurrentDate, customerid, companyname
    From customers
```

When executed, this view returns a data set similar to the following:

Row Count	CurrentDate	customerid	companyname
91	2000-01-10 13:14:52.107	ALFKI	Alfreds Futterkiste
91	2000-01-10 13:14:52.107	ANATR	Ana Trujillo Emparedados y
91	2000-01-10 13:14:52.107	ANTON	Antonio Moreno Taquerka
91	2000-01-10 13:14:52.107	AROUT	Around the Horn

By using system functions within your views, execution and calculation can be combined to be processed by the view. That enables the query of the view to retrieve preformatted or calculated column values without any special knowledge of the MSDE functionality.

Using Variables to Customize a View

Views can be useful for isolating specific data for examination by users. Wouldn't it be even more useful if the view could automatically customize itself to show information based on the user login ID? Using that method, a single view could be created that displays only the data that the user is meant to see.

This custom view can be created using the system variable `system_user`, which supplies the login ID of the current user. Then, you can create a table that stores a list of system user names that can be referenced to determine what type of view to display.

If you want to display what the system user login name is currently, simply enter this code for a query:

```
Select system_user
```

A view can be customized to show data based on a user ID of the currently active user. To demonstrate this capability, you can construct a view on the Northwind database that will show only the orders of the currently logged-in employee. A table will be used to translate the logged user name into an employee ID for reference to the Orders table.

Creating the userReference Table

You need a table that contains the reference values to convert the user name of the currently logged-in user to the proper employee ID.

Part II: Using MSDE

To create the necessary table and enter sample data into that table, follow these steps:

1. Execute Microsoft Access.
2. Open the NorthwindCS database. You will be adding a new table and a new view to this database on the MSDE server.
3. Click the Tables item in the Objects tab.
4. Click the New button to create a new table.
5. When prompted for a table name, enter userReference.
6. Enter these two column types:

Col. Name	Type	Length	Precision	Allow Nulls	Primary Key Field
user name	Char	30	0	Yes	No
employeeID	Int	4	10	No	Yes

7. Close the window and save any changes.
8. Click the Open button to edit the contents of the userReference table.
9. Enter the following data into two rows of the table:

user name	EmployeeID
sa	5
gomer	4

10. Close the userReference data entry window.

You entered the data for two potential user names: *sa* and *gomer*. Although you probably don't currently have a user named gomer in your database login, you can change this user name to a different value to match an actual user, or add gomer to your users.

The extra user was merely added to demonstrate how each user name will be placed in this table for reference and automatic lookup in the view. Now that the reference table is created, you can create the view.

Creating the View

With the reference table created, you need only create the custom view with a simple query to customize the presentation of the view. Once again, use Microsoft Access to simplify the view construction:

1. Click the Views item in the Objects section of the NorthwindCS database.

2. Click the New button to create a new view.

3. For the new View window, turn on the SQL entry pane and turn off both the Table and Column Grid panes. This can be done under the View → Show Panes submenu or by using the icons on the toolbar that toggle the various window panes.

4. In the SQL pane, type the following SQL code for the view:

```
SELECT *
FROM Orders
WHERE (EmployeeID IN
      (SELECT EmployeeID
       FROM userReference
       WHERE user_name = SYSTEM_USER))
```

5. Execute the view with the Run toolbar icon (the exclamation point).

6. When prompted for a name to save the new view, set the name to myOrdersView.

The view should display only the orders of the currently logged-on user. If you're logged in to the system as the sa user, your view should appear similar to the one shown in Figure 14-5. If you were to log in under the user with the name gomer, only orders for employee #4 would be displayed.

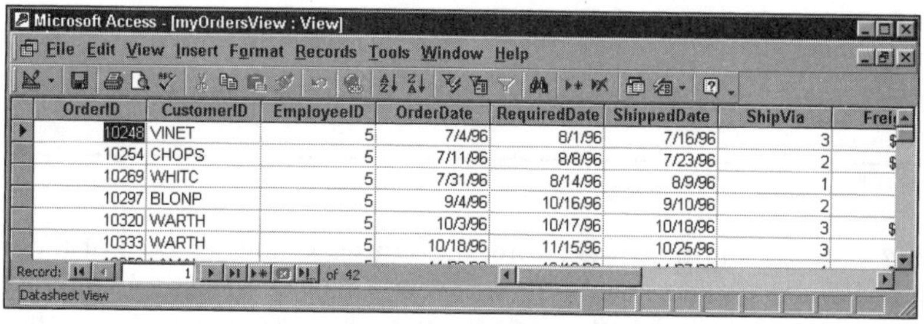

Figure 14-5: Only the orders sold by employee #5 are displayed in the view.

> **NOTE:** This method, although very useful, does require the use of an additional lookup table. It must be noted that the extra table lookup will slow the return of the view recordset. Make sure that the userid column of your lookup table has an index set so that the ID retrieval is fast.

You can use an autocustomizing view to display information for more than a single user. In the query for the view, the In keyword was used to search the subquery instead of a equivalence (=) operator, which would have worked just as well. The In keyword was used to demonstrate the potential of using multiple rows in the userReference table to specify category types in a more general database.

For example, imagine the userReference table contains these two columns and values:

user name	DepartmentName
Sa	Sales
Sa	Management
Gomer	Management

The sa user has access to data for both the management and sales departments, while the gomer user has access only to one. In the same database, you may have a table that contains expenses like this:

Date	ExpenseDesc	Amount	Department
1/12/00	Whiteboard	257.98	Management
1/14/00	Slides	34.39	Sales

By creating a view using the In keyword, the sa user would see both of these entries, whereas gomer would see only the first row. This example should provide you with a better idea of how the customized query can be used to make a view that adapts to the current user.

Obtaining Information about the View

MSDE includes several ways of obtaining information about each view in a database. The information that can be accessed about each of the views is available through a series of system-generated views. Views are used because all the information is stored in system tables of the master database. The view definitions simply create virtual tables to display this information in a way that data related to the currently selected database is presented.

The following two views provide information related to the other views contained in a database:

- **View_Table_Usage:** Contains a row for each table of the views.
- **View_Column_Usage:** Contains a row for each column that is used in all the view definitions for the current database.

To see all the view definitions for the current database, enter this command:

```
Select * From Information_Schema.Views
```

It will return a formatted document of each owner, database, table, view definition, and view settings. Information returned uses the general formatting not associated with traditional recordset queries. Therefore, although the information can be viewed with any SQL execution tool (such as Microsoft Query), the SQL Query Analyzer tool is the best utility to execute this view. When you execute it from the Query Analyzer, the results will look similar to those shown in Figure 14-6.

In contrast, the same query results displayed in the Microsoft Access data grid are much less readable (see Figure 14-7). The formatting for the information is contained within the columns, but cannot be interpreted for output in a standard row-and-column grid.

When you examine the returned data closely, you will find that complete information is included in the entries on each of the views associated with the current database. In the `Information_Schema` returned for the Northwind database, the entry for the customerView that you created earlier looks like this:

```
TABLE CATALOG
NorthwindSQL
create view INFORMATION_SCHEMA.VIEW_COLUMN_USAGE
  as
select
      db_name() as VIEW_CATALOG
      ,user_name(v_obj.uid) as VIEW_SCHEMA
      ,v_obj.name as VIEW_NAME
```

Part II: Using MSDE

```
         ,db NONE NO
\TABLE SCHEMA
INFORMATION_SCHEMA
TABLE NAME
REFERENTIAL_CONSTRAINTS
VIEW DEFINITION
Create View customerView As Select customerid, companyname, fax
    From customers Where fax Is Not null


CHECK OPTION
-

IS UPDATABLE
```

You might notice that in this entry, where the database is indicated, the column is titled Table Catalog. The SQL-92 standard uses slightly different terminology than you are accustomed to using so far in this book. Table 14-1 shows a list of the terms used with MSDE and what they are called in the SQL-92 standard. In the information schema views, the SQL-92 terminology is used.

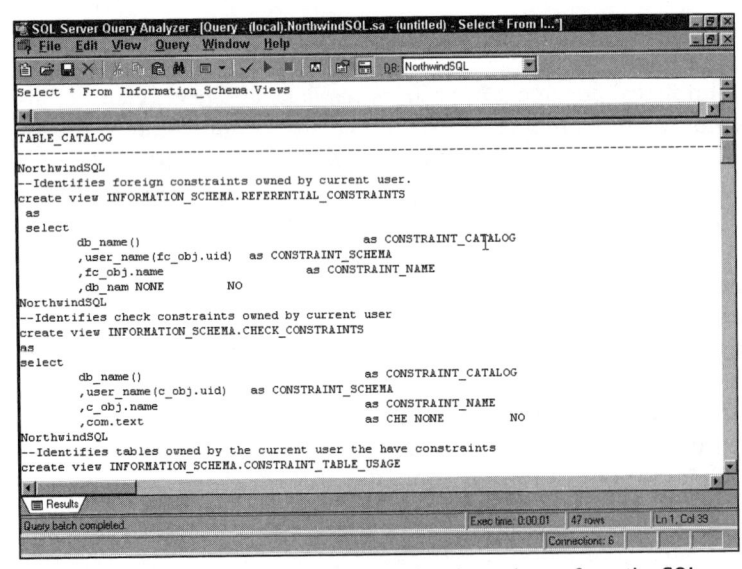

Figure 14-6: The results from examining the view schema from the SQL Query Analyzer.

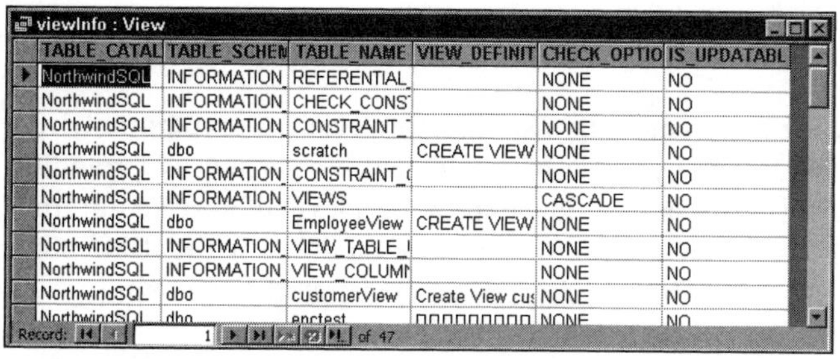
viewInfo : View

TABLE_CATAL	TABLE_SCHEI	TABLE_NAME	VIEW_DEFINIT	CHECK_OPTIO	IS_UPDATABL
NorthwindSQL	INFORMATION	REFERENTIAL_		NONE	NO
NorthwindSQL	INFORMATION	CHECK_CONS		NONE	NO
NorthwindSQL	INFORMATION	CONSTRAINT_		NONE	NO
NorthwindSQL	dbo	scratch	CREATE VIEW	NONE	NO
NorthwindSQL	INFORMATION	CONSTRAINT_(		NONE	NO
NorthwindSQL	INFORMATION	VIEWS		CASCADE	NO
NorthwindSQL	dbo	EmployeeView	CREATE VIEW	NONE	NO
NorthwindSQL	INFORMATION	VIEW_TABLE_I		NONE	NO
NorthwindSQL	INFORMATION	VIEW_COLUMI		NONE	NO
NorthwindSQL	dbo	customerView	Create View cus	NONE	NO
NorthwindSQL	dbo	enctest	▯▯▯▯▯▯▯▯▯▯	NONE	NO

Record: 1 of 47

Figure 14-7: The results from examining the view schema from Microsoft Access.

TABLE 14-1 TERMINOLOGY OF THE MSDE VERSUS THE SQL-92 STANDARD

MSDE Term	SQL-92 Term
Database	Catalog
Owner	Schema
Object	Object
User-defined types (UDTs)	Domain

For views that have been encrypted, the view itself will be listed in the information schema. However, instead of displaying the definition that makes up the view, a series of questions marks (??????) will appear instead.

Accessing Views from Object Models

With ADO, a view is accessed as any other table. However, through the object model for MSDE (known as *SQL-DMO*) that will be covered in Chapter 16, you can address and make changes to each view structure. In the SQL-DMO framework, you must use the View object to access each view.

The View objects are contained within the Views collection. From the View object, you can create new views, modify existing views, query a view, export data from a view, generate view construction SQL code from an existing view, set view security privileges, and delete a current view from the server. After you learn to use the SQL-DMO framework, you will be able to manage views from VBA code.

Summary

Using views can simplify the deployment of a solution, especially for commonly referenced multitable queries. Views can also act as a security barrier, by providing only selected columns of the entire table, and can provide a level of abstraction from the table itself so that the underlying structures can be modified without affecting the queries that address each view. In this chapter, you covered the following:

- **Views:** A view is a virtual presentation of one or more columns from one or more tables. To a user, the view looks like another table, but it is actually a presentation derived from other tables, because a view holds no data of its own.

- **Encryption:** If a view is encrypted with the Encrypt View option, the definition query of the view will no longer be available.

- **Modifying a view:** Using the `Alter View` command, a view may be modified instead of the destroy and re-create view process. Views are altered with this command in order to preserve existing security settings.

- **Customizing a view:** Using server variables, a view may be customized to reflect the settings of a specific user who is addressing it. With a lookup table that contains the settings for various `system_user` logins, the view can be altered to display the appropriate data.

Chapter 15

Replicating Data

IN THIS CHAPTER

- Examining the replication system
- Creating and configuring a replication process
- Examining system stored procedures
- Using replication across other data sources
- Implementing replication security
- Using the Access Replication Manager
- Understanding the SQL distribution and Merge ActiveX controls

ONE OF THE MOST powerful features to be added within the last decade to most database systems is the capability to replicate data. Replication is the operation of synchronizing separate copies of data across multiple data sources that are not continually connected. Each copy may be updated separately.

This capability of disconnecting data sources and resynchronizing them makes it possible to have:

- **Road warriors:** People on the road can have copies of the database on a portable machine. When they have access to an Internet or LAN connection to address the central data store, the replication engine can synchronize the data on the portable with the master database.

- **Internet synchronization:** If a database is very large, replicated copies of it can be modified at separate geographic locations and then the copies can be synchronized at nonpeak hours.

- **Periodic backup:** An automated replication cycle can provide a periodic backup or mirror of a database. Because the database is a replica and not a backup file, the replicated system can "go live" if the primary database fails.

- **Automated information distribution:** Read-only copies of the data can be sent on a regular schedule to almost any type of data source, ranging from a text file to an Oracle server. The process can be activated at scheduled times or concurrent with other events.

Replication functionality is used in such diverse applications as portable point-of-sale systems to Microsoft's new Active Directory, which is included in Windows 2000. In fact, replication is the cornerstone of the Active Directory system that allows the security control for an entire organization to be managed from a single domain controller.

The MSDE server embraces replication with its variety of features. An MSDE server can replicate data across one or more MSDE or SQL Server machines. It can also replicate data to various other data sources such as Microsoft Access databases, OLE DB data sources, and any compatible data source that is addressable through the ODBC interface.

Replication Overview

The implementation of replication on database servers grew out of the explosion of client/server systems and the ascendancy of desktop computers. When mainframe computers dominated the computing landscape, most of the data for an organization was held on a single computer system. For geographically dispersed sites, remote access took place primarily through dial-in or wide area network (WAN) methods, so the data was still centralized on a single machine.

As desktop machines grew in power, desktop servers emerged that were available to the desktop computers over the local area network. In this new paradigm, the processing power of an application was split between the desktop machine and the server. User interface operations were handled by the desktop PC, and the centralized processing (such as database operations) could be active on the server. As the number of these PC-based servers grew, so did the need to enable them to share information.

Additionally, portable computers created a new deployment environment where data could be collected in the field for sales, data acquisition, and other needs. The capability to integrate the data located on these portable machines and a central server became increasingly important. A portable computer, if the data collected with it can be synchronized with a central data source, provides a way to minimize errors because data can be entered immediately regardless of the location instead of requiring later manual transcription.

Replication fills the needs of integrating multiple servers and synchronization of portable or remote data. It enables machines to hold a duplicate set of a centralized data set. Depending on the configuration, this duplicate set may be read-only or changes can be made to it. When reconnected to the centralized data, each data set is synchronized with the other. Although Microsoft Access provides a primitive form of replication, MSDE includes a full-featured system that can handle a majority of the situations where replication is needed.

> Replication on Microsoft Access is not compatible with the replication engine in MSDE or SQL Server. Although MSDE can include Access data sources within a replication set created on the database server, Access cannot include MSDE in an Access-based replication set.

The MSDE Replication System

The MSDE replication system is the relation between a publisher that supplies the data and the subscriber that receives the data. A publisher defines all of the tables, columns, and database structures that will be distributed. It then publishes this information to a distribution database. The distribution database may not contain an actual copy of the data but simply a reference to the publication data sources.

Once the data is available on the distribution database, it can be synchronized with the subscriber's data copy (see Figure 15-1). Rather than downloading the entire data set each time into the subscriber, the replication system uses time, date, and uniqueid codes to send only the data that has been altered.

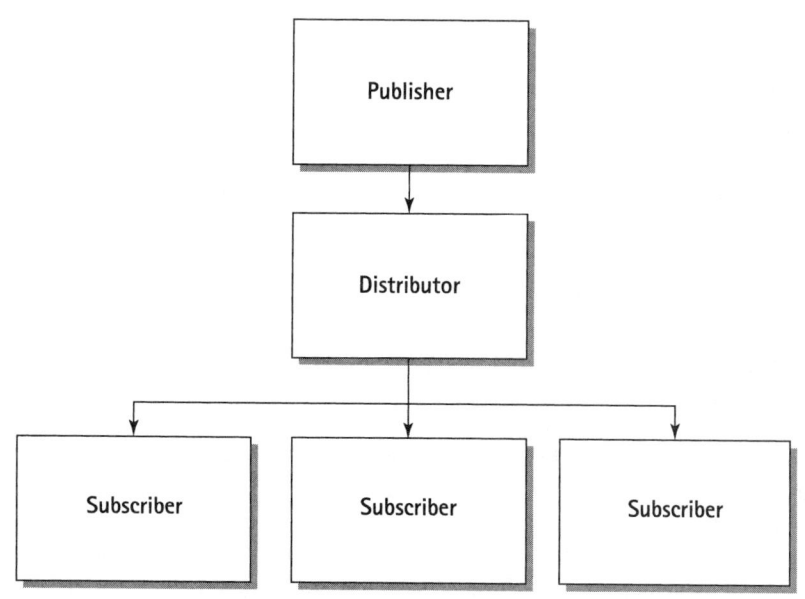

Figure 15-1: The replication system for MSDE contains publishers, subscribers, and distributors.

Although the publisher may be the centralized MSDE server or SQL server, the same machine that publishes the data need not be the server that distributes it. In fact, a single distributor may distribute the data of many publishers (see Figure 15-2). This feature allows a dedicated machine, if necessary, to be optimized to handle all of the transactions.

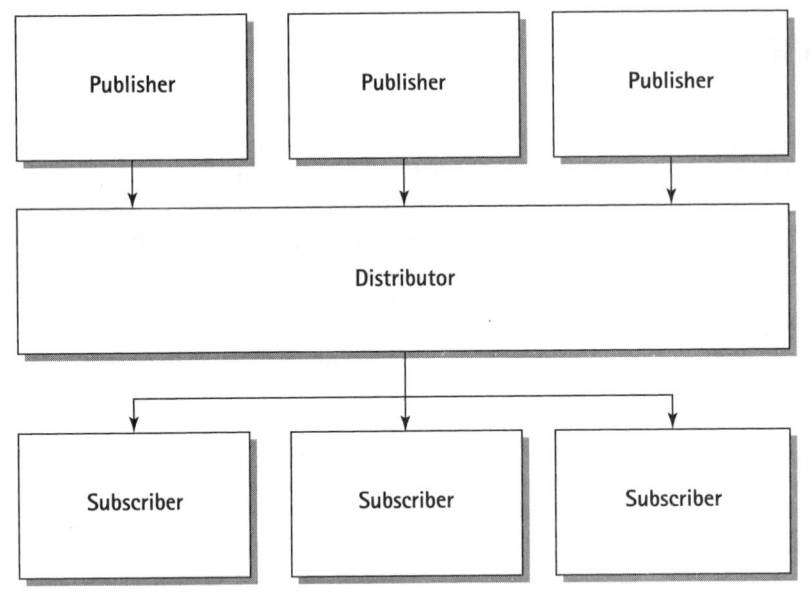

Figure 15-2: A single distributor may accept the data of several publishers for access by many subscribers.

Configuring the MSDE System

Configuring the MSDE system is based on specifying a publisher of data and then configuring various subscribers to accept that data. As changes are made to the data on the publisher, at periodic intervals specified by the replication administrator, the new data is uploaded to the distributor for dissemination to the subscribers.

In more complex replication, the subscribers can also make changes to the data they have received and upload those changes to the publisher for merging into the primary data set. In most deployment scenarios available for MSDE replication, however, read-only subscriptions are favored. Any changes that occur to the data set are done on the publication server. These changes are then provided to the various subscribers.

Because most MSDE replication deployments will have MSDE on both the publishing and the subscribing machines, other replication options are also available. Each table can act as both a publisher and a subscriber. Therefore, a system can be created where secondary copies of the data can be updated on the client and that subscription can update the primary database. Replication is excellent for both data dissemination and roll-up.

Replication may occur with MSDE from a variety of data sources, including an Access database. Therefore, an application may be created to primarily address an Access database that is later synchronized with a primary MSDE database. This type of application is most popular for portable machine solutions that may not have the necessary execution power and system resources to handle execution of a complete MSDE server.

Replication must be configured through the SQL Enterprise Manager, through the object interface of the MSDE server (known as SQL-DMO), and partially through Transact-SQL. The Enterprise Manager is included with SQL Server and provides a graphical user interface for database server configuration. The SQL-DMO interface requires custom programming in VBA to create and modify structures on the server. The Transact-SQL commands are mostly for configuring the distribution server that is used to supply data to the subscribers.

> **Note:** For traditional Access MDB database, the Jet Replication Objects (JRO) can be used to control the replication through VBA. For MSDE, object control occurs through the SQL-DMO objects that are described in Chapter 16.

Because replication can be as complicated as it is powerful, you will often be running a full install of SQL Server for your central replicated data source. The true advantage of MSDE is its capability to integrate with a SQL Server system without any of the licensing costs. That enables you to set up your satellite replication sites on MSDE for free.

> **Note:** Although data is replicated in a replica set, changes to the schema of the database are not. Because schema changes and system tables cannot be backed up by the native MSDE replication, only the data can be transported, meaning replication cannot be used for a complete database failover system. Also, any changes to the underlying structure of your database can break the replication set and make future synchronization with subscribers impossible. Therefore, never make a change to the schema unless you are ready to redefine the publisher and subscriber relationships.

A publisher makes data available for replication. Each replication set has only a single publisher. A subscriber connects for receipt of data from a publisher. A subscriber can become a publisher for another replica set.

The actual process of executing the replication occurs automatically through the SQL Server Agents. The agents are scheduled events that execute on the server to execute a particular operation. The Snapshot and Merge agents handle Merge replication.

> **NOTE:** All replication agents are scheduled through the SQL Server Agent available through the Enterprise Manager. Replication will not execute unless the SQL Server Agent is running.

A set of copies or replicas can be created. Within each set, priorities may be assigned to individual replicas. Moving a hub replica for local and anonymous replication will cause that replica set to be broken. By using the Move Replica command in the Replication Manager application, a hub replica may be relocated.

Choosing a Replication Type

For Microsoft Access, only one method is used to provide replication capabilities. Because a database server is used in more varied and robust applications, the demands on the server make it useful to have various types of replication. Each has its strengths and weaknesses in terms of speed, flexibility, bandwidth requirements, and configuration complexity.

The three types of replication are: snapshot replication, transactional replication, and merge replication. Snapshot replication the simplest form as it makes a read-only copy of published data to send to the subscribers each time. Transactional replication will send the SQL commands that were used for modifications to the publisher's data source to the subscribers for updates.

Merge replication allows updates on the subscriber to be merged into the publisher data source. Access-based replication is most like the Merge replication form found on MSDE. However, even though they have some similarities, they are not compatible.

MAKING A DETERMINATION

Within this complex number of choices, you will have to choose which type of replication best suits your needs. To aid you in this decision, I have created a small decision table (see Table 15-1) that can be used to examine the advantages and disadvantages of each type.

The following table provides a general summary of some of the features, advantages, and disadvantages of the three types of replication. By evaluating these factors, you can most easily determine what replication type would be best for the application that you have in mind.

TABLE 15-1 REPLICATION TYPE COMPARISON TABLE

Description	Snapshot	Transactional	Merge
Complete copy sent each synchronization	Yes	No	No
Power to modify subscription data	No	No	Yes
Power to modify data on the publisher	Yes	Yes	Yes
Bandwidth requirements	High	Low	Medium
Data integrity	Highest	High	Medium
Possible update conflicts	No	Yes	No
Replication with MSDE/SQL Server	Yes	Yes	Yes
Replication with compatible ODBC source	Yes	Yes	Limited
Data types text and image replicated	Yes	Only w/full update	Only w/full update

SNAPSHOT REPLICATION

The snapshot is the simplest form of replication in that it takes a snapshot of the complete data set each time replication occurs. From the publishers, the entire data set in the distribution database is sent every time. The subscribers receiving the new data set copy and replace their current set with the new information.

Snapshot replication is best for small tables and infrequent updates. Because it sends the entire data set, a large amount of data would use a great deal of bandwidth and time for each subscriber. One of the advantages of a snapshot is the integrity of the data. Because a new copy is sent each time, any corruption of the data that occurs on the subscriber is eliminated with the next synchronization.

> **NOTE:** For Snapshot and Transactional replication types, the only way a subscriber can make updates to the data set is through the Immediate Updating Subscribers option. This option requires that the subscriber be connected to the publisher at the time any changes are made. The change is then attempted simultaneously to the publisher and subscriber data sets. If either update fails, the operation is aborted.

TRANSACTIONAL REPLICATION

Transactional replication monitors all transaction updates to the database and sends the individual transactions to the subscribers. That means that Insert, Update, and Delete operations are duplicated through the transaction logs and sent to update the databases of the subscribers.

Only committed transactions are sent to the subscribers. This replication type requires that only a single publisher can make changes to the data set that are transferred to the subscribers. The transaction changes can be sent to subscribers in real time.

Real-time transmission of the database changes allows a transactional replication to be used for maintaining a partial failover system (failover for the data, but not for any schema changes). However, transactional replication does not support replication of text or image data types. A complete table refresh to subscribers is required to update the information in these column types.

> **NOTE:** MSDE does not allow the creation of a Transactional publication. This limitation is based on the license agreement for MSDE.

MERGE REPLICATION

The most complicated form of replication is the Merge type in that updates can occur on either the publisher or any of the subscribers. For merge replication, any database modifications are tracked on both the publishers and the subscribers and any changes are synchronized when the replication connection occurs.

Merge replication is used most often in solutions that require autonomy and periodic synchronization. These requirements describe most mobile applications where the portable subscriber will be out of contact with the central data source for a given period of time but needs to make data modifications such as by taking a sales order or changing an inventory figure.

When tables are published for Merge replication, the underlying structure of each table is modified to allow individual rows to be properly synchronized. The modifications include adding a column called ROWGUIDCOL that is used to maintain a unique identification of each row.

Structuring Replication

To understand replication, you will have to understand the replication structures that are used by the server to perform the data publishing and synchronization. Although some of the terminology used in a replication may be new to you, the terms themselves are fairly self-explanatory as you learn about their place in the system.

The primary structures used in replication are publishers, subscribers, publications, subscriptions, articles, and distributors. You will learn how all of these work together in the following sections. Each part of the replication system must be properly configured for the whole system to work together. As with a chain, any weak link in the replication sequence can make the whole replication process fail.

PUBLISHERS AND PUBLICATIONS

A *publication* is a grouping of data to be published. Each publication can contain one or more *articles*. An article acts much like a SQL view in that it may contain an entire table for publication or certain columns of the table. Publications usually contain multiple articles.

A publication can exist on only a single server and is limited to articles contained in a single database. A single distribution server can handle distribution from several publishers. This distribution server can then be addressed by all of the subscribers for the different publications.

SUBSCRIBERS AND SUBSCRIPTIONS

For every publisher, there are many subscribers. A subscriber may be either a SQL Server–based data source or an ODBC or OLE DB data provider. The subscriber receives data that can be queried or sorted on the client. A subscription may be either a push subscription where the publisher sends the updates on a particular schedule or a pull subscription that makes the subscriber request individual updates.

DISTRIBUTORS

The distributor is the server that actually supplies the data to the subscribers. A single distributor may accept multiple publications from many publishers. It can distribute these publications to any number of subscribers.

The *Distributor,* also known as the Distribution server, contains the distribution database. Publishers can transfer data to the Distributor, which means that the Distributor can be located on a different server than the publisher. This allows the entire replication system to scale well.

Creating and Configuring a Replication Process

Creating and configuring a replication process will aid your understanding of how the replication works. In this example, replication on the Northwind database will be generated so that subscribers can get a snapshot of the current Northwind data. Snapshot replication is used for this example because it is the simplest and most straightforward form of replication.

For this example, you will need two MSDE servers or one MSDE and one SQL server. On one server, the publication from the Northwind database will be created and published. On the second server, a subscription to this publication will be enacted.

> **NOTE:** Although this example uses the SQL Server Enterprise manager for creation, all of the necessary operations may be done by execution through Transact-SQL statements. Later in this chapter, example code is provided to create a subscription and a publication through system stored procedures. If you don't have a SQL Server installation and therefore no copy of Enterprise Manager, you can use this code to create the same objects. See Chapter 24 for the stored procedures required to create a new user account through Transact-SQL code.

Creating an Account for the SQL Server Agent

The default account configured for the SQL Server Agent is a system account. Because a system account cannot be used for a replication system, you must create a special account for the agent to use. It should be configured as a standard domain account.

1. Execute the Enterprise Manager.
2. Expand the server list until you see the server that will be used to publish the current replication. Because security is configured for each database server (unless you are running a fully implemented Windows 2000 site), the new account will be placed on the database server where you create the account.
3. Expand the Security folder.
4. Right-click the Logins item and select the New Login option. This option will display the Login configuration dialog box.
5. Set the name of the new user to ReplicationAgent.
6. Select the SQL Server authentication combo box. The Windows 95/98 system does not support the trusted account setting for an account running on the system, so selecting the SQL Server authentication option will allow this configuration procedure to be used on any Windows platform.

7. Enter a password such as **tomsawyer** for the ReplicationAgent to use. You will need to remember this name and password for entry later in the dialog box for publication access.

8. Select the NorthwindSQL database in the default database combo box.

9. Click the Database Access tab to show the available permissions for this user.

10. Check the Permit column to the left of the Northwind database to provide permissions to access this database.

11. Click OK to accept this new user. You will be asked to confirm the design.

With this account created, the publisher will be able to address the data source so that the replication process can be enacted. You will need to enter this user name and password at the login screen of the Publication Wizard.

> **Note:** If you are running MSDE on the Windows 95/98 platform, when you configure MSDE for the system account login, you must select the Use SQL Server Authentication option to allow secure access to the database server.

Configuring the Publisher

To begin setting up a replication system, you need to configure the publisher to provide the data to the subscriber. Fortunately, the Enterprise Manager includes a number of wizards that automate the setup process and guide you through creating a replication set. The following instructions will lead you through one of these wizards in order to publish the Northwind database for replication.

To create a publication, follow these steps:

1. Execute the Enterprise Manager if it is not already open.

2. Expand the tree of servers and select the MSDE server that will be used as the publisher. Replication is configured on the server itself rather than for a specific database within the server. This allows a single replication process to include one or more databases.

3. Under the Tools menu, select the Replication → Create and Manage Publications option (see Figure 15-3). The management window for the databases that are available for replication will be displayed. You will notice that none of the system databases are displayed in the list because any databases managed by the system cannot be replicated.

Part II: Using MSDE

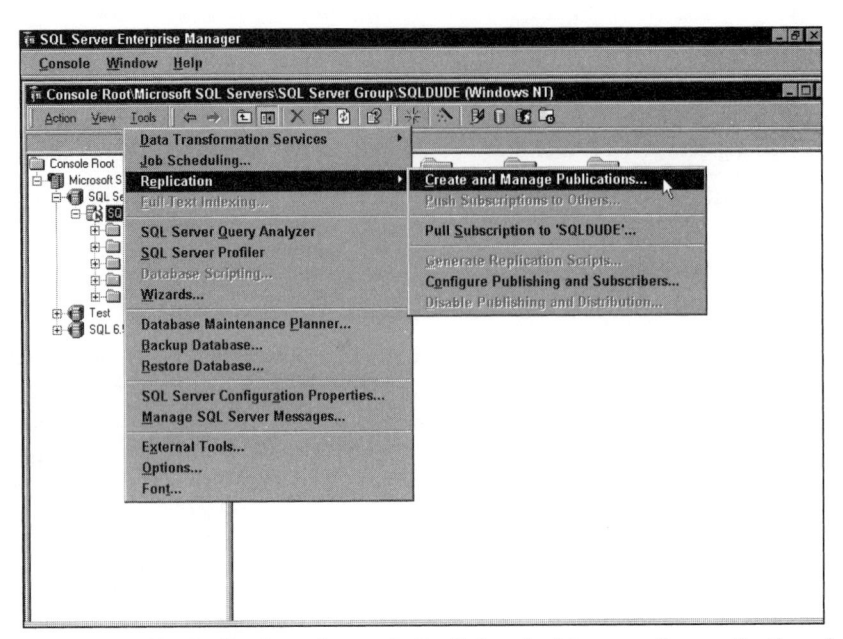

Figure 15-3: The Replication submenu in the Enterprise Manager allows activation of the configuration wizards.

4. Select the NorthwindSQL database (see Figure 15-4) and click Create Publication to execute the Publication Wizard. The first screen of the wizard will display the bullet items of the possible tasks that the wizard will perform. You'll notice that the Northwind database is cited in this bullet text to let you know what database will be used.

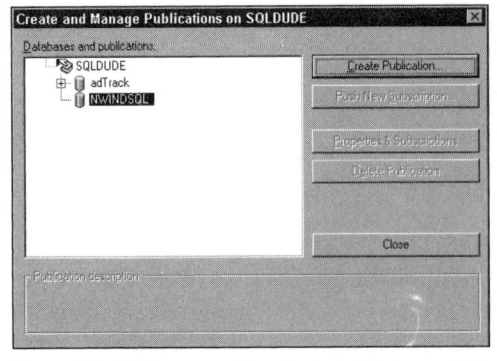

Figure 15-4: The currently selected database will become the basis for the new publication.

5. Click Next to advanced to the Distribution selection screen. Because the Distribution server does not have to be the same as the Publication server, this screen allows you to choose which server will be used for distribution. Unless you have a Distribution server available for development testing, leave the default option to use the current MSDE server as the distribution server.

> At this point, if you received an error about using `sp_addserver` to fix the `@@SERVERNAME` setting, you will have to correct it. Although the MSDE setup program configures the server name to match the computer name during installation, any changes to the computer name will require the `@@SERVERNAME` to be synchronized with it. Simply execute the stored procedure `sp_addserver` with the new name (i.e. `sp_addserver 'myNewName'`) and then stop and restart the MSDE/SQL Server. After the problem is fixed, you will need to reexecute the wizard and redo the steps up to this point.

6. Click Next to advance to the next screen. You may be confronted with an error message box that notifies you that the SQL Server Agent uses a system account. Because using such an account will cause replication between servers to fail, you will need to set another account for the agent to use. If you have already configured the SQL Server Agent to use another account and no error was generated, you can skip to step 9.

7. Click OK to dismiss the system account error dialog. The SQL Server Agent properties window will automatically be displayed (see Figure 15-5).

8. Enter the name and password of the user account (ReplicationAgent) that you created in the last section and click OK. The wizard will check the newly selected account and verify that it is configured for the agent. After the account is configured, you will be returned to the Publication Wizard.

9. Leave the Snapshot publication type selected and click Next to continue in the wizard. In this example, snapshot replication will be used to make a replica of the Northwind database.

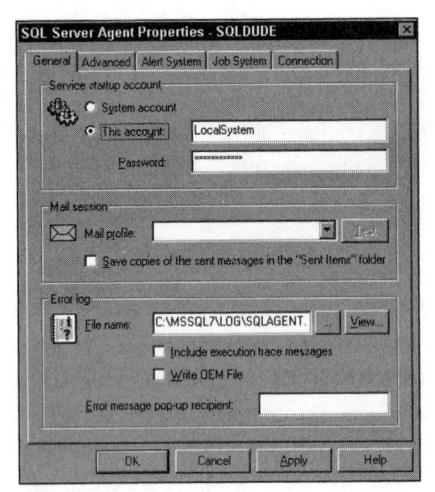

Figure 15-5: The SQL Server Agent Properties window is displayed to allow setting the Service startup account.

10. Select the Yes option on the Immediate Update screen and click Next. Providing Immediate-Updating will allow changes to be made to the subscription snapshot while it is connected to the publisher. The changes are not really made to the subscription directly but are instead sent to the publisher for primary update. If both the publisher and the subscriber can be changed, they are committed at the same time through a two-phase commit using the Microsoft Distributed Transaction Controller (MS DTC).

> **NOTE:** To access the current configuration of the MS DTC, select the Settings → Control Panel option on the Start menu. You will find the MS DTC item in this folder that allows the default DTC and the current DTC protocols to be altered.

11. Click Next to accept the default subscriber type setting that specifies that all of the subscribers will be executing SQL Server. Because this example is made to be used with two MSDE servers or one SQL server and one MSDE server, the ability to access other types is unnecessary. The next wizard screen will allow you to select exactly which tables in the Northwind database should be included in the publication.

12. Click Publish All to place a check in the boxes to the left of each table (see Figure 15-6). From this screen, you can see that both tables and stored procedures can be replicated. For the Northwind database, only the tables will be used in this example.

Chapter 15: Replicating Data 297

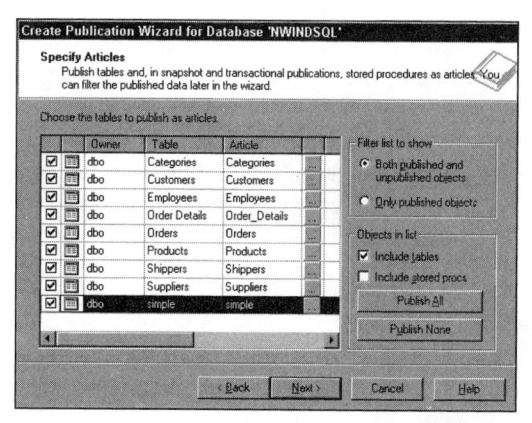

Figure 15-6: Clicking Publish All will select all of the current tables for placement in the publication.

13. Click Next to advance to the publication naming screen. You may encounter a dialog that displays a number of tables that do not have timestamp columns as required for immediate-update capabilities. Click OK to accept that these columns will be added by the replication wizard.

14. Set the Name of the publication to NWindSQLpub (see Figure 15-7) and click Next. A description for the publication that is shown in this window will be automatically created for you. You can alter it if you wish to include additional information before advancing to the next screen.

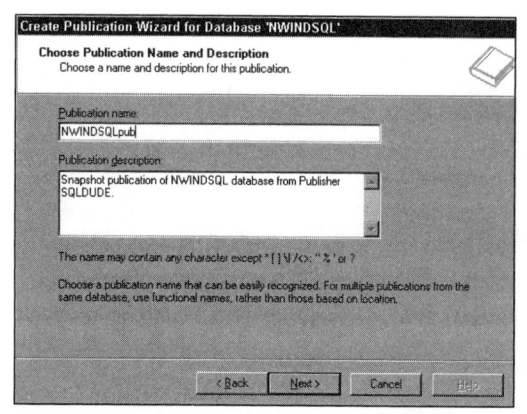

Figure 15-7: This wizard screen is used to set the name and the description for the publication.

15. Click Next to accept that no filters will be created for the publication. In the summary box, you can examine all of the settings that you've made through the wizard.

16. Click Finish to create the publication.
17. When you are prompted whether the SQL Server Agent should be started automatically on boot, click Yes.

When the MSDE or SQL server finishes creating the publication, the publication management window should display it under the Northwind database item (see Figure 15-8).

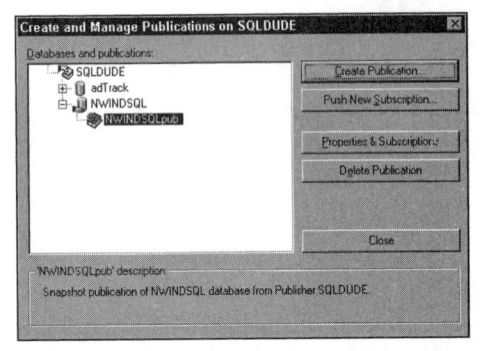

Figure 15-8: The newly created publication will appear in the Northwind database tree.

Don't close this management window yet, because it will be used to create the subscription on the other server. If you want to examine the properties of either the subscription or the publisher, you can click on the Properties & Subscriptions button and the publisher properties window will be displayed (see Figure 15-9).

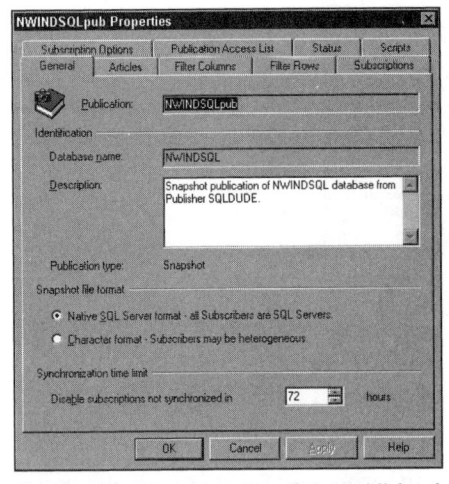

Figure 15-9: The properties of the publisher include all the subscriptions, filters, scripts, security, and so on.

Configuring a Subscriber

Once the publisher has been configured, the subscriber must be created. A single copy of Enterprise Manager can be used to configure many different SQL Server-based servers. Therefore, you may register the subscription server in the same Enterprise Manager that was used to configure the publisher. If you don't want to address it with a single copy, you will need to have an installation of the management program on the subscription server.

In this example, the subscriber will be configured to accept a push subscription where synchronization will occur manually. That way, for testing, you can modify the publication any time and execute a new synchronization to see the data received by the subscription into the subscribed database. The subscriber can be created from the same publication/distribution machine.

To create a subscription, follow these steps:

1. Execute the Enterprise Manager that can address the server that will hold the subscription.

2. Expand the tree of available servers.

3. Expand the item showing the server that will hold the subscription.

4. Right-click the Databases folder and select the New Database option.

5. In the New Database dialog box, enter the name NorthwindReplica and click OK. This will create a new database into which the replication data can be placed without disturbing a copy of the Northwind database that may already exist on the server.

6. Back at the tree of available servers, select the server where the publication has been created.

7. Select Push Subscription to Others under the Tools → Replication menu. The new push subscription will place the snapshot replication on the subscription server.

8. Click Next to progress beyond the wizard introduction screen that describes the features of the wizard.

9. In the Choose Subscribers screen, select the server that will receive the Northwind subscription.

10. Click Next to show the screen that allows you to set up the destination database. Because this server may already contain the Northwind database, you will want to select the NorthwindReplica that you created earlier.

11. Select the NorthwindReplica option either by typing the database name or by clicking Browse Database (see Figure 15-10).

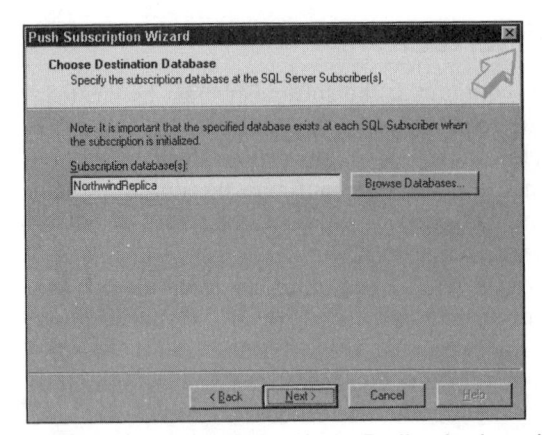

Figure 15-10: Select the NorthwindReplica database that will be used to accept the pushed data from the publication.

12. Click Next.

13. On the Immediate-Updating subscription screen, select the Yes option to make the subscription immediately updating and click Next.

14. Leave the distribution agent scheduling option and click Next.

15. Check the Start the Snapshot Agent check box and click Next. On the displayed screen, you will see a list of the services that need to be executing for the subscription to complete properly. The list will show a status for each service, and you will need to start any services that are currently turned off before you begin the subscription activation.

16. Click Next to accept the snapshot defaults.

17. Click Next.

18. Click Next to approve of all of the subscription options listed.

19. Click Finish to create the initial instance of the push subscription. The subscription will begin executing and create the new instance of the whole database schema in the NorthwindReplica destination before it performs the first data transfer.

Once the subscription has been synchronized, a duplicate of the data set of the Northwind database that was placed in the publication is now available on the subscribed machine.

With this configuration complete, you are ready to examine the activated replication system. The initial copy of the snapshot has been placed on the subscription server. The subsequent updates to the snapshot can either be done manually or automatically scheduled for a particular time.

Partitioning

In the Quick-Start example, all of the columns of all of the tables for the Northwind database were transferred. There is a database technique, known as *partitioning*, that selects only particular columns of a table source to be made available for subscription. Partitioning is done to increase the performance of queries because less data needs to be accessed to return a result set. Partitioning can also be used to provide some data normalization for the replicated sets that is not present in the original tables.

HORIZONTAL AND VERTICAL PARTITIONING

Partitioning does not make any physical changes to the database structure on the publication. On the subscription, however, the tables will be constructed as defined within the partition specification. Two types of partitions are used for replication: vertical partitioning and horizontal partitioning. In *horizontal partitioning*, a subset of rows is present in each table. For *vertical partitioning*, a subset of columns is present in each table (see Figure 15-11).

ID	LastName	FirstName	Middle	Age
1	Smith	John	A	24
2	Jones	Mary	F	21
3	Seeker	Phil	S	39
4	Johnson	Angel	E	62

Horizontal Partitioning

ID	LastName	FirstName	Middle	Age
1	Smith	John	A	24
2	Jones	Mary	F	21
3	Seeker	Phil	S	39
4	Johnson	Angel	E	62

Vertical Partitioning

Figure 15-11: Horizontal and vertical partitioning create subset tables from source tables.

When certain rows are made available for subscription, this is known as horizontal partitioning. A large table can be broken down into several tables, each containing some of the rows of the master table. For example, a table that contains sales data for five years could be horizontally partitioned into five tables: one for each year. Partitioning for queries should minimize the number of tables that need to be coordinated for queries. The SQL keyword Union is often used to combine one or more of the horizontal partitions for a result set.

Vertical partitioning occurs when a table's columns are selected. In a vertical partition, the primary key of the table is included in all of the partitions so that the columns of several of the partitions can be reconstituted if necessary.

> **NOTE** Before you construct a partitioning plan for a replication set, it is often useful to create a series of views that mirror the intended partitions. By using the views, you can actively evaluate how the data will appear before committing to a partition configuration for replication.

PARTITIONING LOCATION

A method known as *location partitioning* can locate data on several different sites and, through replication, guarantee transaction consistency. Partitioning seeks to avoid or at least minimize conflicts when data is synchronized. By partitioning, data from each site is strictly segregated from other sites, usually through the use of a geographic division.

Therefore, a sale in the Kansas branch will never conflict with a sale from the Nebraska branch, because the geographic coding for these sales will make a conflict impossible. Because all transactions within a geographic area were accepted by the transaction processing operations, all operations will fulfill the ACID properties. When the data is finally synchronized, the lack of conflicts will ensure that this remains the case.

Replication Agents

The replication system relies on services that execute autonomously that can activate a process based on time event. Software agents provide this independent execution and run in the background to handle most of the tasks associated with replication. In an earlier section of this chapter, you have already activated the SQL Server Agent in order to initiate your first replication system.

The agent also had to be configured with a user name and password to allow the replication system to log on to the database server. Under the general SQL Server Agent, a number of specific agents are used to accomplish replication tasks.

The four agents in MSDE handle the replication process:

- ◆ **Snapshot agent:** Prepares initial replication set of tables and stored procedures. This agent runs on the distributor and connects to the publisher. Each publication has its own Snapshot agent.

- ◆ **Merge agent:** Merges changes to the data on the distribution database and the subscription data sources.

- **Distribution agent:** Transfers data held in the distribution database to the subscribers of each publication.

- **Log reader agent:** For replica sets that include the transaction log, moves the transaction log to the distribution database.

You can see that each replication type has its own dedicated agent. These agents must be installed and configured on every publication and distribution database server. For an MSDE installation, these agents are placed on the MSDE system but not activated. The agents may be activated through the Enterprise Manager, through Transact-SQL calls, or even through the Microsoft Access management tools for replication.

> **TIP:** Agent execution is handled most effectively when proper resources and processor time are allocated. Because the resource handling is managed by the operating system, Windows NT can provide a much better environment to activate agents than the Windows 95/98 system. If you are going to provide automated replication; for security and optimal execution, I recommend that you use the Windows NT OS for deployment.

Planning for Replication

Early planning to decide how replication will occur is critical to effective replication implementation. Planning involves not only deciding who will be publishers and who, subscribers, but also how to handle the data that will be transferred in the articles of a publication. The decision involved will substantially affect how the actual database schema is constructed. Two of the primary issues with this type of planning are the uniqueID issues and the filtering choices.

UNIQUEID ISSUES

In a replicated system where new records will be inserted on the replicas (a merge-based system), generating unique values can be a problem. If all of the identity columns in the tables where to autoincrement by the identity increment on each replica, many of the rows would end up with an identical number for important columns such as the Primary key field. There are several methods for handling this problem. Each of them has its own niche where implementation would be most appropriate.

Consider using the Not For Replication option on Identity columns. Identity columns have problems being duplicated because of their auto-increment functionality. This option allows several different replication sets to maintain the replication seeds for their particular storage of the data set. For example, one data source may have a seed value of 0. A replica of the data source may have an identity seed of

10,000. Within reasonable limits, these two different starting points prevent new record inserts in either replication set from overlapping.

The Not For Replication option prevents the replication from writing one seed value setting onto another column. That way, the two different replica sets can be synchronized and yet continued operation will not result in the data collision that would have occurred if the seed values of the two tables had been synchronized.

Using multiple seed values for the identity actually creates a fairly cumbersome system. It is much better implementation to use the uniqueID data type for a column that needs a unique value (such as the Primary key field) and use the NewID system stored procedure to generate an ID. The NewID routine will return a 128-bit value known as a Global Unique Identifier (GUID) that is virtually guaranteed to be globally unique.

The advantages to using the GUID include:

- **No collision between IDs:** It is virtually guaranteed to be globally unique because it is based on factors such as a random value, the time and date of the ID request, and the network address of the system that requested it.

- **No special replication configuration:** For tables using identity columns, a merged replication system will require special configuration in order to avoid data collision either by creation of a new identity number when the merge takes place (causing potential relational integrity problems) or by addressing the problems in the conflict resolution setting. The GUID has no such complications.

- **Compatibility with other GUID systems:** The GUID is a standard method of unique identification on the Windows platform for everything from Registry entries to registered ActiveX controls. The system is reliable and well established.

The disadvantages of using GUID include:

- **GUID is not very user friendly:** The numbers generated in an identity field are easy to read (such as 1, 57, 62, . . .), whereas a GUID is far more complicated (such as FCBF580-B670-11D3-BF13-B5F85BB5F275). Because the numbers appear random and are primarily only machine-readable, they cannot be easily written down by hand, be remembered, or give any indication of the number of rows in the data set.

- **More storage:** The size of a GUID field is 16 bytes long, compared with the 4 bytes used for a standard integer identity column. Although this size difference is not an issue in most applications, it does mean that more data will have to be searched in order to find references for query operations such as a join.

♦ **External program storage:** The size of GUID field makes it more difficult to store and manage in a custom program written in a language such as Visual Basic. The long byte length of the value makes manipulation and argument passing more difficult.

Despite the disadvantages, the `NewID()` function can be used effectively in a replicated solution as long as the replication includes the stored procedures. The trigger that stores the ID in the new field of the row will have to be included with each replica in order for the automatic ID generation to work properly.

ADDING TO THE IDENTITY

You can make the primary key a complex key by using multiple columns together. Each replica, particularly if replicas are located in different geographic areas or divisions, can be coded in its own column. The data entry application can then either accept the location or division name as part of the login, be configured for the place it is executing, or read from another table that holds the local values.

Using Transact-SQL code, you could create a table with a double column key like this:

```
CREATE TABLE orders
(
    orderID int identity, division char(8),
    Constraint orderKey Primary Key (orderID, division)
)
```

FILTERING

A number of filters can be used to allow for selective replication of data. These filters can be used for automated selection of data. Some of these filters include:

♦ **Horizontal filtering:** Selecting only certain rows for the replica set. Horizontal filtering can be used for horizontal partitioning.

♦ **Vertical filtering:** Limiting the columns available for replication. Vertical filtering can be used for vertical partitioning.

♦ **Join filters:** Using filters that only allow replication of specified rows in the tables that are joined to the primary table. For example, the Orders table might be replicated in its entirety, but the only Order Details that are replicated are the itemized information on orders over $100. This filter type is only available in Merge replication.

♦ **Static filter:** When passed a comparison expression, using this expression to include or exclude data from the replica set.

- **Dynamic filters:** Allowing a function to be executed each time to evaluate the current row for inclusion or exclusion from the replica set. This filter type is only available in Merge replication.
- **Stored procedure filters:** Defining a stored procedure that is created specifically for use by the replication system using the `For Replication` keyword.

Each replication type requires particular planning to succeed. There are local and anonymous replica types. These replica types can only synchronize with the primary or master data source and not with each other.

Normally, the filtering is done by simply configuring which data needs to be replicated either through column selections or through a query. It is also possible to create a stored procedure that handles the filtering. The `For Replication` keyword is used to set up the procedure for use as a filtering routine in a replication system.

Such a filtering procedure might appear like this:

```
Create Procedure myReplicationFilter For Replication
As
If Exists (Select state From authors (NoLock) Where state = 'CA')
    Return 1
Else
    Return 0
```

This sample filter will only approve a row for inclusion in the replication set if the 'state' column value is set to California. Notice the *(No Lock)* command in the `From` clause. This command allows the `Select` statement to perform a read from a record involved in a transaction or a "dirty read." By preventing either a shared lock and reading through an exclusive lock, this function will never receive an error while attempting to examine a record during the filtering process.

A filter can only contain Transact-SQL code for `Select, Declare, Goto,` and conditional flow-of-control statements. These stored procedures also cannot reference text, ntext, or image column data types.

Managing Replication through Access

The Enterprise Manager is not required for replication on the MSDE server. Replication for MSDE can be handled from the replication wizards that are available in an Access Data Project (ADP). The three settings for a replication system through Access are:

- **Push synchronization:** The publisher automatically updates all subscribers according to a specified schedule or immediately as changes take place to the distribution database.

- **Pull synchronization:** The subscriber requests replication updates. Often used for mobile users or when a large number of subscribers exist such as on an Internet replication.

- **Bi-directional synchronization:** Changes in the published source are transferred to the subscriptions and vice versa when synchronization occurs.

Access supports the following synchronization types:

- **Direct synchronization:** Primarily useful for replication that will occur through a LAN or other permanent connection.

- **Indirect synchronization:** This form of synchronization is used for remote synchronization needs such as mobile data sources connecting through Remote Access Services (RAS) or through a virtual private network.

- **Internet synchronization:** Synchronization through the Internet for a data source.

Although Access can be used for the primary configuration of an ADP-managed replication, you can additionally use the Enterprise Manager or system stored procedures to refine the setup that you've created.

Global visibility is the default visibility for Access 95/97. Global can synchronize with any compatible data source, whereas local and anonymous can only synchronize with the Global data source of their replica set. The Global source may also be used for Briefcase synchronization, whereas the other types of visibility may not.

A Global setup serves as hub or master data source in the replication set. The global data source holds the Design Master for the replica set. For a Local setup, only the control of the topology is granted. An Anonymous configuration can control topology and provide anonymous access via the Internet.

Conflict Management

Whenever multiple copies of a database exist and may be individually modified, there is a chance that two users will modify the same record. When synchronization is attempted, a conflict will arise because both modifications exist. Replication features have a number of ways to deal with these situations.

The default setting for the replication agent is to provide column-level conflict resolution. When a replica is being synchronized, multiple changes to the same record are handled by examining the individual column values of the data. If the modifications did not occur to the same column, then the changes are combined into a single row.

There are five primary types of conflicts:

- **Unique key conflict:** When two sources enter a record with the same unique key.

- **Table validation conflict:** When data is inserted that violates one of the table value rules, such as when a string is inserted into a numeric field or a null value is inserted into a column that is unable to accept nulls.

- **Update and insert conflicts:** When updates or inserts are different when two locations have made modifications to the same data.

- **Delete conflicts:** When a record is deleted on one system when it was changed on another.

- **Constraint conflicts:** Also known as a divergent conflict, these types of conflicts are caused when the constraints on one of the systems accept data that cannot pass the constraints on another system.

By default, conflicts are handled on the column level. The replication engine optionally allows row level tracking to be used to resolve conflicts on the row level. Locking conflicts can also occur but are normally resolved by reattempting the operation. If the locking conflict cannot be resolved, it is submitted to the conflict resolution process.

The retention period is a parameter that determines how long records that haven't been synchronized remain stored in the system. If a conflict is not resolved, the record will not synchronize and remains in limbo until the conflict is addressed or the retention period has expired and the changes are discarded.

There are two primary methods of conflict resolution: priority resolution and custom resolution. *Priority-based resolution* works on the simple principle that some data sources have priority over others. Every publication, when created, is assigned a priority number from 0 (lowest priority) to 100 (highest priority). When two updates are attempted to the same row, the update that has the highest priority is used. Priority-based resolution is the default setting for MSDE.

> **NOTE** A replication set that uses Merge replication cannot guarantee transactional integrity. A transaction may be committed to a subscribed data source, and all of the individual operations of the transaction may succeed. However, when the transaction is synchronized with another replicated set, individual record changes may be discarded if they come into conflict with another update that has priority.

Custom resolution means putting in place some type of custom process such as a routine, stored procedure, or COM object to provide outcome rules for updates in conflict. Known as *custom resolvers*, these are routines that are activated by the Merge agent to resolve a conflict.

PREVENT DELETES OPTION

Setting the Prevent Deletes option makes the replicas unable to delete records in the data set. By disabling the delete capability on the replicas, you assure that the only way a record can be eliminated from the system is through the master database. In many cases, using this setting is preferable for portable application options. It can prevent a portable user from mistakenly eliminating a record that would result in deleting the primary record on the central data source.

CONFLICT VIEWER

In the Enterprise Manager, a utility called the Conflict Viewer allows you to view and manually modify conflicts that occurred in a synchronization. After the Merge Agent has executed, any conflicts that are encountered are resolved using the rules or procedures that have been configured. After resolution has occurred, the Conflict Viewer may be used to review any of these conflicts and modify the resolutions if necessary.

The location of the conflict resolution determines where the Viewer can be used to examine them. If centralized conflict management is configured (the Report conflicting data changes at the Publisher option is selected), then all resolutions occur on the publisher and they may be accessed there. With decentralized conflict management, the conflict is stored on the data source that lost the conflict which may be either the publisher or the subscriber.

Under the Publications folder, if you right-click on a publication, you can select the View Conflicts option to display the Conflict Viewer. The Viewer window will be displayed to show all of the conflicts in a current replicated system.

DATA CONSISTENCY

Data consistency in transactions attempts to minimize the data problems that can occur in a replicated environment. Ideally, the replicated sites would all be consistent with each other and reflect exactly the same data as if all were updated instantly from a central publisher. While this ideal is rarely achieved, transaction consistency attempts to most closely create a system that would have the same conditions if replication was not used.

There are three levels of transaction consistency:

- **Immediate guaranteed consistency:** Where all subscription sites are updated at exactly the same time, allowing each subscription to contain identical data. Because of network latency and possible failed connectivity, immediate guaranteed consistency is difficult to achieve in a typical LAN environment. In this type of consistency, all subscriptions receive the data as if the changes occurred on the main publisher. The MS DTC is used to accomplish this guaranteed consistency.

- **Latent guaranteed consistency:** All subscriptions are updated to reflect the same data eventually. All subscriptions receive the data as if the changes occurred on the main publisher.
- **Convergence:** All of the subscriptions are updated for the new values, but not necessary if the update occurred at a single site.

To maintain consistency, a number of complicated scenarios can be created. These scenarios are handled by the conflict resolution system enabled in the MSDE replication process.

CONFLICT FUNCTION

Replication conflicts do not have to be handled individually in the Conflict Viewer. You may automate conflict handling by creating a function to process the instances of the conflict and return a result. The Conflict Function allows a VBA routine to be set that is called with each conflict and can return the instructions on how a conflict can be resolved.

When a conflict occurs, information about that conflict is stored in a table named conflict_*nnn* where *nnn* is the name of the table where the replication conflict occurred. This table is automatically created if it does not already exist. The conflict table mirrors the structure of the table where the conflict exists. The record that was judged as the "loser" in the conflict is stored in this table. Information on insert or update conflicts is stored in the system table sysmergearticles. Delete conflict information is recorded in the system table MSmerge_delete_conflicts.

A resolver may be created to resolve conflicts on the publisher or the subscriber. It may decide the resolution by reference to properties such as the date and time of the updates or the text of the modified columns.

> **NOTE** It is possible to create a conflict resolution procedure in a programming environment outside of the MSDE server. A custom COM conflict resolver can be programmed to use the ICustomerResolver interface. Creating such a resolver would require development in a programming environment such as Visual C++. A number of C++ examples are included with the full install of SQL Server. This sample code is located in the `C:\MSSQL7\DevTools\Samples\SQLRepl` folder in a typical SQL Server installation.

Using the Enterprise Manager Replication Wizards

The Enterprise Manager contains a number of wizards that can be used to configure the replication settings on the server. The wizards can guide you through the setup of operations for replication that are difficult to create by hand because of the number of steps and parameters involved. These wizards include:

- **Publishing and Distribution wizards:** Automate configuration of the publishing and distribution process.
- **Create Publication Wizard:** Creates an initial publication and allows specification of the articles to be included. This wizard will also do the basic configuration to activate the SQL Server Agent to execute the replication process.
- **Push Subscription Wizard:** Creates a push subscription and includes configuration for how the interaction with the subscription server will occur. The subscriber must be able to accept the pushed data when it is scheduled for the publisher.
- **Pull Subscription Wizard:** Starts a new pull subscription that allows the subscriber to control when updates will occur.
- **Replication Conflict Resolver Wizard:** Used to create a custom conflict resolver. A custom resolver is typically necessary only in an advanced replication configuration.

Each of these wizards actually generates a sequence of Transact-SQL commands that are executed on the MSDE server to alter the replication configuration. Most of these wizards allow the generation of the SQL scripts so you can examine and modify the configuration directly in the Transact-SQL code. In the following sections, you will see how Transact-SQL can be used to create replication systems.

Working with the Replication Monitor

The Replication Monitor is included in the Enterprise Manager to allow you to examine the status of current replication setup. Because the Replication Monitor provides you with a real-time view of the operations of the replication system on the current server, you will need to examine it periodically to make sure the system is operating properly.

Through the Replication Monitor, you can:

- View a list of publishers, publications, and subscriptions
- View scheduled replication agents
- Examine status and history of each agent
- Monitor alerts and conflicts related to replication

The monitor application will allow you to view all of this information in real time, providing an excellent status of the current replication actions. By monitoring the activities of the system, you can also detect bottlenecks and see faults on subscriber machines when a update failure is encountered.

System Stored Procedures

A large number of system stored procedures can be used to configure replication on the MSDE server. You can see that the majority of the procedures are used to directly address and manage subscriptions. By executing these procedures, you can activate a replication process without having the Enterprise Manager or other tools installed.

This section will provide an overview of some of the most important procedures for replication setup along with a number of lists of the additional available routines that relate to replication. One of the best methods for learning to use procedures for replication management involves setting up a replication system using the wizards and then examining the various structures the wizard created. The configuration of these database objects will provide a basis from which to work on other systems. Even without this luxury, following the steps of an example setup can help you to see how a real installation could be accomplished.

> **NOTE** Testing replication is one of the excellent uses of MSDE server. Because it can easily be installed on any machine that has a copy of Microsoft Office 2000, you can set up a number of test servers. These servers can act as surrogates for the final deployment to test the various pieces of the replication in an actual distributed environment.

Creating a Publication through Stored Procedures

To aid you in understanding how a publication can be created with only SQL code, it is important to first understand the primary publication routines that will be used to accomplish the task. The publication process is activated primarily by using four replication procedures:

- ♦ **sp_replicationdboption:** Activates the replication option for a specified database.

- ♦ **sp_addpublication:** Creates a new publication and adds it to the replication system.

Chapter 15: Replicating Data 313

- **sp_grant_publication_access:** Enables specified database users to access the publication.
- **sp_addarticle:** Creates a new article based on passed parameters including the replication set name, table name used in the article, partitioning settings, filtering selections, and so on.

Creating a new publication involves the following steps:

1. Set the replication option for the database to turn replication on.
2. Add a publication.
3. Grant access for users.
4. Add articles for each table to be published.

To create the publication that you used the wizard for earlier, you can use code like this:

```
-- Enabling the replication database
use master
GO

exec sp_replicationdboption N'NWINDSQL', N'publish', true
GO

use [NWINDSQL]
GO

-- Adding the transactional publication
exec sp_addpublication @publication = N'NWINDSQLpub', @restricted =
N'false', @sync_method = N'native', @repl_freq = N'snapshot',
@description = N'Snapshot publication of NWINDSQL database from
Publisher SQLDUDE.', @status = N'active', @allow_push = N'true',
@allow_pull = N'true', @allow_anonymous = N'false',
@enabled_for_internet = N'false', @independent_agent = N'false',
@immediate_sync = N'false', @allow_sync_tran = N'false',
@autogen_sync_procs = N'false', @retention = 72
exec sp_addpublication_snapshot @publication =
N'NWINDSQLpub',@frequency_type = 4, @frequency_interval = 1,
@frequency_relative_interval = 0, @frequency_recurrence_factor = 1,
@frequency_subday = 1, @frequency_subday_interval = 0,
```

```
    @active_start_date = 0, @active_end_date = 0,
    @active_start_time_of_day = 233000, @active_end_time_of_day = 0
GO

exec sp_grant_publication_access @publication = N'NWINDSQLpub',
    @login = N'BUILTIN\Administrators'
GO
exec sp_grant_publication_access @publication = N'NWINDSQLpub',
    @login = N'distributor_admin'
GO
exec sp_grant_publication_access @publication = N'NWINDSQLpub',
    @login = N'sa'
GO

-- Adding the transactional articles
exec sp_addarticle @publication = N'NWINDSQLpub', @article =
    N'Categories', @source_owner = N'dbo', @source_object =
    N'Categories', @destination_table = N'Categories', @type =
    N'logbased', @creation_script = null, @description = null,
    @pre_creation_cmd = N'drop', @schema_option = 0x0000000000000071,
    @status = 0, @vertical_partition = N'false', @ins_cmd = N'SQL',
    @del_cmd = N'SQL', @upd_cmd = N'SQL', @filter = null, @sync_object =
    null
GO

exec sp_addarticle @publication = N'NWINDSQLpub', @article =
    N'Customers', @source_owner = N'dbo', @source_object = N'Customers',
    @destination_table = N'Customers', @type = N'logbased',
    @creation_script = null, @description = null, @pre_creation_cmd =
    N'drop', @schema_option = 0x0000000000000071, @status = 0,
    @vertical_partition = N'false', @ins_cmd = N'SQL', @del_cmd =
    N'SQL', @upd_cmd = N'SQL', @filter = null, @sync_object = null
GO

exec sp_addarticle @publication = N'NWINDSQLpub', @article =
    N'Employees', @source_owner = N'dbo', @source_object = N'Employees',
    @destination_table = N'Employees', @type = N'logbased',
    @creation_script = null, @description = null, @pre_creation_cmd =
    N'drop', @schema_option = 0x0000000000000071, @status = 0,
    @vertical_partition = N'false', @ins_cmd = N'SQL', @del_cmd =
    N'SQL', @upd_cmd = N'SQL', @filter = null, @sync_object = null
GO

exec sp_addarticle @publication = N'NWINDSQLpub', @article =
    N'Order_Details', @source_owner = N'dbo', @source_object = N'Order
```

```
Details', @destination_table = N'Order Details', @type =
N'logbased', @creation_script = null, @description = null,
@pre_creation_cmd = N'drop', @schema_option = 0x0000000000000071,
@status = 0, @vertical_partition = N'false', @ins_cmd = N'SQL',
@del_cmd = N'SQL', @upd_cmd = N'SQL', @filter = null, @sync_object =
null
GO

exec sp_addarticle @publication = N'NWINDSQLpub', @article =
N'Orders', @source_owner = N'dbo', @source_object = N'Orders',
@destination_table = N'Orders', @type = N'logbased',
@creation_script = null, @description = null, @pre_creation_cmd =
N'drop', @schema_option = 0x0000000000000071, @status = 0,
@vertical_partition = N'false', @ins_cmd = N'SQL', @del_cmd =
N'SQL', @upd_cmd = N'SQL', @filter = null, @sync_object = null
GO

exec sp_addarticle @publication = N'NWINDSQLpub', @article =
N'Products', @source_owner = N'dbo', @source_object = N'Products',
@destination_table = N'Products', @type = N'logbased',
@creation_script = null, @description = null, @pre_creation_cmd =
N'drop', @schema_option = 0x0000000000000071, @status = 0,
@vertical_partition = N'false', @ins_cmd = N'SQL', @del_cmd =
N'SQL', @upd_cmd = N'SQL', @filter = null, @sync_object = null
GO

exec sp_addarticle @publication = N'NWINDSQLpub', @article =
N'Shippers', @source_owner = N'dbo', @source_object = N'Shippers',
@destination_table = N'Shippers', @type = N'logbased',
@creation_script = null, @description = null, @pre_creation_cmd =
N'drop', @schema_option = 0x0000000000000071, @status = 0,
@vertical_partition = N'false', @ins_cmd = N'SQL', @del_cmd =
N'SQL', @upd_cmd = N'SQL', @filter = null, @sync_object = null
GO

exec sp_addarticle @publication = N'NWINDSQLpub', @article =
N'simple', @source_owner = N'dbo', @source_object = N'simple',
@destination_table = N'simple', @type = N'logbased',
@creation_script = null, @description = null, @pre_creation_cmd =
N'drop', @schema_option = 0x0000000000000071, @status = 0,
@vertical_partition = N'false', @ins_cmd = N'SQL', @del_cmd =
N'SQL', @upd_cmd = N'SQL', @filter = null, @sync_object = null
GO

exec sp_addarticle @publication = N'NWINDSQLpub', @article =
N'Suppliers', @source_owner = N'dbo', @source_object = N'Suppliers',
```

```
@destination_table = N'Suppliers', @type = N'logbased',
@creation_script = null, @description = null, @pre_creation_cmd =
N'drop', @schema_option = 0x0000000000000071, @status = 0,
@vertical_partition = N'false', @ins_cmd = N'SQL', @del_cmd =
N'SQL', @upd_cmd = N'SQL', @filter = null, @sync_object = null
GO
```

When the publication has been added to the server, subscriptions must be added that accept the replicated data. A subscription is added by registering it on the publication server and then creating the actual subscription on the subscriber machine.

Creating a Subscription through Stored Procedures

Using stored procedures, you can also create a new subscription or activate an existing one. Subscriptions must be registered with the publisher in order to be enabled. The subscription database server must also be properly configured to accept pushed content or to reach out and pull content from the publisher.

These procedures are used in the example code to configure the system for subscription:

- **sp_addsubscriber:** Used to designate a subscriber that can accept article publications. This procedure is called to add the subscription reference to the publisher.

- **sp_addsubscription:** Creates a subscription on the designated database server. This procedure is called to add the subscription reference to the publisher.

- **sp_addpullsubscription:** Creates a pull subscription and configures it for execution. This procedure is called to add the subscription reference to the subscriber.

- **sp_addpullsubscription_agent:** The pull subscription agent can be activated with this procedure. This procedure is called to add a pull subscription reference to the agent on the subscriber.

To add a snapshot pull subscription, the following procedure can be used:

1. Add a publication with the allow_pull property set to true. Each type of subscription has an available parameter that must be set when the publication is created to allow specific types of subscriptions.

2. Register a subscriber to the publisher.

3. Add a new subscription at the publisher.

4. Create and activate a pull subscription on the subscriber.

5. Add an agent to pull the published articles down to the subscriber.

This five-step process can be translated into Transact-SQL code to activate a subscription. To create a subscription like the one shown in the previous section that was created with the Enterprise Manager, you can use Transact-SQL code like this:

```
-- Enabling the replication database
use master
GO

exec sp_replicationdboption 'NWINDSQL', 'publish', true
GO

use [NWINDSQL]
GO

-- Adding the transactional publication
exec sp_addpublication @publication = 'NWINDSQLpub'
```

When you've entered and executed this procedure on a server where both the subscription and publication servers are registered, the subscription will be established. It can then be activated to download a new snapshot to the subscriber whenever necessary.

Subscription Procedures

Subscriptions are the most likely area of a replication system to be managed through the execution of various stored procedures. Because you may want to add a subscriber from the machine that will be accepting the subscription content, this can be most easily accomplished by using a tool such as Microsoft Query to execute the most important setup routines on the publication server. The primary routines for adding a subscription are:

- **sp_addsubscriber:** Adds a subscriber to the publication database with settings such as frequency of updates, recurrence factor, commit batch size, and other. This stored procedure needs to make substantial system changes, so only users that are registered to the sysadmin role on the server may execute it.
- **sp_addsubscription:** Adds the subscription to the subscribed database.

The following stored procedures are also available:

sp_addmergepullsubscription	sp_addmergepullsubscription_agent
sp_addmergesubscription	sp_addpullsubscription_agent
sp_addsubscriber_schedule	sp_change_subscription_properties
sp_changemergepullsubscription	sp_changemergesubscription

sp_changesubscriber	sp_changesubscriber_schedule
sp_dropmergepullsubscription	sp_dropmergesubscription
sp_droppullsubscription	sp_dropsubscriber
sp_dropsubscription	sp_enumfullsubscribers
sp_expired_subscription_cleanup	sp_helpmergepullsubscription
sp_helpmergesubscription	sp_helppullsubscription
sp_helpsubscriberinfo	sp_helpsubscription
sp_helpsubscription_properties	sp_mergesubscription_cleanup
sp_refreshsubscriptions	sp_reinitmergepullsubscription
sp_reinitmergesubscription	sp_reinitpullsubscription
sp_reinitsubscription	sp_subscription_cleanup

Publisher Procedures

For publications, the easiest method for definition is through the wizard. The graphical user interface allows selection of databases and tables to be used as well as setup of advanced features including horizontal filtering, scheduling, and so on. However, all of these functions are available through stored procedures. The primary two procedures for initializing a publication are:

- **sp_addpublication:** Creates a new publication and adds it to the replication system.

- **sp_grant_publication_access:** Enables a specified database user to access the publication.

For complete publication management, the following stored procedures are also available:

sp_addmergepublication	sp_addpublication_snapshot
sp_addpublisher70	sp_addpullsubscription
sp_changedistpublisher	sp_changemergepublication
sp_changepublication	sp_dropdistpublisher
sp_dropmergepublication	sp_droppublication
sp_help_publication_access	sp_helpdistpublisher
sp_helpmergepublication	sp_helppublication
sp_link_publication	sp_publication_validation
sp_revoke_publication_access	

Article Procedures

For articles, the primary procedures are used to add data sets and specify the contents of an article for addition to the publication. You can use these primary procedures for article configuration:

- **sp_addarticle:** Creates a new article based on passed parameters including the replication set name, table name used in the article, partitioning settings, filtering selections, and others.
- **sp_articleview:** In filtering for vertical or horizontal partitioning, this procedure creates a view of the synchronization article. It can only be used on an article that does not yet have any subscribers. The view created by this procedure is then used to create the replica partitions.
- **sp_droparticle:** Drops an unsubscribed article from the publication.

The following stored procedures are also available:

sp_addmergearticle	sp_article_validation
sp_articlefilter	sp_articlesynctranprocs
sp_articleview	sp_changearticle
sp_changemergearticle	sp_droparticle
sp_dropmergearticle	sp_helparticle
sp_helparticlecolumns	sp_helpmergearticle
sp_helpmergearticleconflicts	

Distribution Procedures

The distribution server most commonly used for MSDE systems will be the same as the publication server. You can add distribution servers or configure existing ones through the available stored procedures. For distribution settings, the following stored procedures are available:

sp_adddistpublisher	sp_adddistributiondb
sp_adddistributor	sp_changedistributiondb
sp_changedistributor_password	sp_changedistributor_property
sp_dropdistributiondb	sp_dropdistributor
sp_get_distributor	sp_helpdistributiondb
sp_helpdistributor	

These procedures can be used to set up and configure a distribution server for subscriptions to access.

> **Note:** Both the Distribution and Merge agents are available as the ActiveX controls Microsoft SQL Distribution and Microsoft SQL Merge, respectively. These controls can be embedded into any ActiveX container environment (such as VB, VBA, or Delphi) and used to programmatically control replication activities.

Agent Procedures

The SQL Server Agent is the actual program that handles activation of the replication, reaction to messages from the replication system, and automated execution of conflict resolution. You can configure the SQL Server Agent entirely from stored procedures included in MSDE. For agents, the following stored procedures are available:

sp_add_agent_parameter	sp_add_agent_profile
sp_change_agent_parameter	sp_change_agent_profile
sp_drop_agent_parameter	sp_drop_agent_profile
sp_help_agent_default	sp_help_agent_parameter
sp_help_agent_profile	sp_replication_agent_checkup
sp_update_agent_profile	

The agent should be activated after the subscription has been registered on the publication server and the actual subscription has been created on the subscription server. The agent can then automatically synchronize the data sources.

Miscellaneous Procedures

There are many stored procedures for replication that provide functionality you will rarely need to use. For completeness, the following is a list of the additional stored procedures that perform functions related to replication:

sp_addmergefilter	sp_addsynctriggers
sp_addtabletocontents	sp_articlecolumn
sp_browsereplcmds	sp_changemergefilter
sp_changesubstatus	sp_check_for_sync_trigger
sp_deletemergeconflictrow	sp_dropmergefilter

sp_dsninfo	sp_dumpparamcmd
sp_enumcustomresolvers	sp_enumdsn
sp_generatefilters	sp_getmergedeletetype
sp_helpmergeconflictrows	sp_helpmergedeleteconflictrows
sp_helpmergefilter	sp_helpreplicationdboption
sp_mergedummyupdate	sp_removedbreplication
sp_replcmds	sp_replcounters
sp_repldone	sp_replflush
sp_replicationdboption	sp_replsetoriginator
sp_replshowcmds	sp_repltrans
sp_script_synctran_commands	sp_scriptdelproc
sp_scriptinsproc	sp_scriptmappedupdproc
sp_scriptupdproc	sp_table_validation

All of the replication procedures can be executed through Microsoft Query, ADO, and SQL Query Analyzer. You can also encapsulate execute of the procedures within a custom stored procedure that you create in order to automate replication configuration.

Replication across Other Data Sources

MSDE has the capability of supplying replicated data to data sources that are not based on the SQL Server engine. For example, an MSDE database could be replicated to a Microsoft Access database that would be used for mobile users. The changes to the mobile database could then be merged with the primary MSDE data source.

This functionality is known as *heterogenous data source replication*. Replication is possible to any compatible database through an available ODBC or OLE DB driver. SQL Server natively supports subscriber replication to Microsoft Access, Pocket Access, Oracle, and IBM's DB2. All primary publishing must take place on the MSDE or SQL Server database server.

In addition to sending data to a subscriber, in the SQL-DMO framework are objects that allow a complete custom replication engine to be built for any custom data source. This allows you to create a replication interface for your own programs if necessary.

When the `add_subscriber` procedure is activated, the type of data source that will be used for the subscription can be specified as one of four values: SQL Server (0, the default), ODBC (1), Access/JET/MDB database (2), or an OLE DB/ADO data provider (3). Most of the non-SQL data sources will be using either the ODBC or OLE DB selections.

The simplest implementation of replication can be constructed by using a publisher that sends or pushes data one way to a subscriber. Any changes to the primary publisher are sent to the subscriber so that the two data sources remain synchronized. Such a push-based replication can occur through an OLE DB or ODBC link. The subscriber in this scenario would have no ability to provide updates back to the publisher.

Replication Security

Although full MSDE security implementation will not be thoroughly addressed until Chapter 25, the security needs of replication are special and should be briefly described. If security between replicated sites were to be compromised, a regular update of data could be siphoned off, perhaps automatically distributed by your central replication server. To prevent any security problems, the best starting point is general access security.

Because database information is being transferred between two or more machines, effective security planning is critical to ensure the integrity and privacy of your data. Consider these areas when creating your replicated system:

- **Location of the replicas:** Will the replicas be located on secure machines? Who has access to the data on the replica machines? Is important data being replicated to places that don't need it? Can multiple publications for some of the same data be created for a more secure implementation?

- **Publishing rights:** For protection of data integrity, the publishing machines within a replication system are more important than subscribers. Therefore, which machines are allowed to update data? Are there any machines that have write access that should not?

- **Role settings:** The roles for replication must be configured on the MSDE server to allow the proper login and access for the publication activation and subscriber data access. Make sure that the replication roles are part of your overall security methodology and not separately maintained.

Be aware that security on the Windows 95/98 platform is far less robust and strict than the security implementation of Windows NT. Consider converting workstations that will accept secure data to the Windows NT Workstation operating system to provide extra security.

Role Requirements

The definition of the role of the user that is logged into the MSDE or SQL Server system governs the amount and type of access granted to the user. For example, the role of a *database owner* would provide modification as well as read/write access to a user with that role. A user with the *anonymous user* role, however, would have far more restricted abilities.

One of the major security roles is that of *sysadmin*. Only sysadmin can enable a publisher, subscriber, or distributor. The sysadmin is also the only role allowed to configure and monitor replication agents. The sysadmin role is automatically defined on the installation of the MSDE server.

Agent Login Security

Because agents have the task of activating the replication transfers and synchronization, they must have authorization to make connections between the servers. Three primary agent configuration areas should be examined as potential security placement faults: publication access lists, immediate-update subscriptions, and snapshot folders. Check the Publication Access lists and verify the agents that are allowed permission for addressing the publications. If login security is granted to insecure systems, a doorway has been opened for a security breach.

Additionally, you should closely examine the immediate-update subscribers and Snapshot folder security. Both of these areas provide automated access to internal replication structures. They provide potential areas where secure data may be drawn off.

Using the Access Replication Manager

In Microsoft Access, all replication related to an MSDE data source is handled through the Replication Manager. The Replication Manager enables you to create new replicas, manage existing ones, set schedules for synchronization, handle remote synchronization, and resolve synchronization conflicts.

The Replication functionality is identical to the managers available through the Enterprise Manager. In fact, the same windows and options are available that are shown in the primary replication window. Therefore, you can use this manager to configure replication on systems that don't have the Enterprise Manager installed.

> **NOTE** For a server name in a replication system, the (local) or period (.) entries cannot be used for the name. Explicit server name references must be used. In an Access project, if you have selected an implicit naming option, you can change the server name by selecting the Connection option under the File

menu. If the NetBIOS name for the machine is normally accessed as \\THINKPAD when using machine references, enter the name without the dual backslash prefix (that is, THINKPAD). Use the Test Connection button to make sure the server is found properly.

SQL Distribution and Merge ActiveX Controls

Microsoft includes the ActiveX controls called SQL Distribution and SQL Merge to allow the replication process to be used by custom applications. These controls are signed with digital IDs from Microsoft so that they can even be used within Microsoft Internet Explorer browser. They have been marked "safe for scripting," so the security access level for IE browser does not need to be set to low to allow the controls to execute properly.

In the custom controls dialog of a project, the SQL Distribution control will be listed under the name *Microsoft SQL Distribution control*. When added to a project, the library will be titled SQLDISTXLIB. It can be used to add, drop, or interrogate a subscription. You will have to configure the properties for the publisher, subscriber, and distributor to point to the systems providing these capabilities that you wish to address.

The Merge control is listed as *Microsoft SQL Merge control* and will be titled SQLMERGXLIB in a project. The properties and methods of the Merge control mirror the distribution control, except that the primary object is named SQLMerger rather than SQL Distribution.

Summary

Replication provides the capability to create a process of periodic synchronization of multiple data sources. The growing power of networks and the need to distribute data makes replication one of the most important recently added features to database servers. With MSDE's capability to distribute data to numerous data source types (OLE DB, ODBC, text files, and so on), replication can be used for multiplatform data exchange. In this chapter, you covered:

- **Replication:** The process of making several copies of a single data set and having those copies periodically synchronized with a central master data set. Replication allows decentralized use of an identical data set to be spread across several servers or geographic locations.

- **Publisher:** The primary database that becomes the data provider. Handles all of the merging of update data, conflict resolution, and manages the replication interaction. Must be an MSDE or SQL server.

- **Subscriber:** Primarily receives information from the publisher. A subscriber can be almost any compatible data source through the OLE DB or ODBC driver interfaces.

- **Publication:** Holds the data to be published. In a publication, the actual data sources are held as *articles,* which may contain all of the source data tables or only specified columns.

- **Snapshot replication:** Takes a complete snapshot of all of the data to be replicated and sends a complete copy to each subscriber.

- **Transactional replication:** Replicates all of the `Insert`, `Update`, or `Delete` commands to the subscribed data sources. Therefore, any change that is made to the publisher is integrated into the subscriptions when synchronization occurs.

- **Merge replication:** This is the only form of replication where modifications made to subscriber's copies of data can be easily integrated into the publisher data set. Merge replication is also the most complicated form because of the number of conditions and conflicts that may occur in this two-way environment.

Chapter 16

Using SQL-DMO

IN THIS CHAPTER

- Understanding SQL-DMO objects
- Testing the SQL-DMO system
- Examining the SQL-DMO system
- Creating DBDoc
- Making a MakeDB utility
- Implementing SQL-DMO events
- Examining possible SQL-DMO applications

THROUGH THE ADO OBJECT framework, you can address the database objects such as tables and views on a database server to run queries, insert new records, and use other data access functions. What if you want to directly manipulate the objects of the database server itself? Microsoft provides an object model known as SQL Distributed Management Objects (SQL-DMO) that allows direct access to a SQL Server–based server engine. Through these objects, any MSDE or SQL Server available on the network can be addressed.

Understanding SQL-DMO Objects

The objects of the SQL-DMO framework provide database management features such as the ability to create new databases, modify database devices, alter the schema of objects, and more. Almost anything that can be accomplished from a database utility such as the Enterprise Manager can be done through programming the DMO.

Some of the most important capabilities enable SQL-DMO to be used to:

- Create and modify any object on the database server
- Document the objects currently available in MSDE and access object properties
- Register and unregister database servers
- Implement code that reacts to events that occur on the database server

Programming the SQL-DMO can be accomplished through VBA contained in Microsoft Access or any of the other Office applications. The object model for SQL-DMO is shown in Figure 16-1.

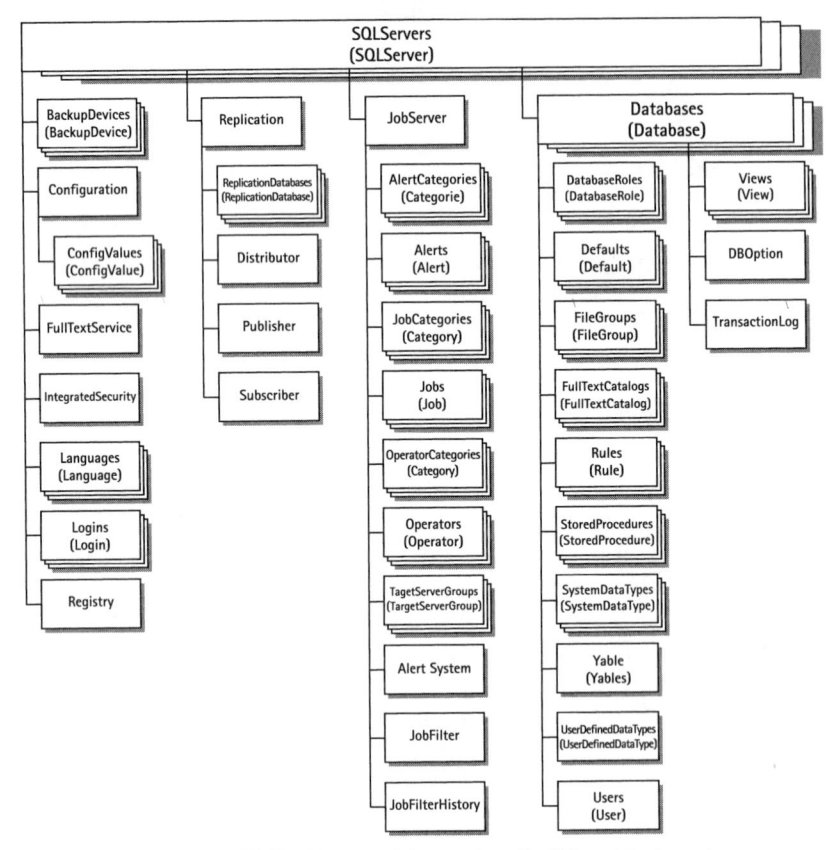

```
SQLServers
(SQLServer)
├── BackupDevices (BackupDevice)
├── Configuration
│   ├── ConfigValues (ConfigValue)
│   ├── FullTextService
│   ├── IntegratedSecurity
│   ├── Languages (Language)
│   ├── Logins (Login)
│   └── Registry
├── Replication
│   ├── ReplicationDatabases (ReplicationDatabase)
│   ├── Distributor
│   ├── Publisher
│   └── Subscriber
├── JobServer
│   ├── AlertCategories (Categorie)
│   ├── Alerts (Alert)
│   ├── JobCategories (Category)
│   ├── Jobs (Job)
│   ├── OperatorCategories (Category)
│   ├── Operators (Operator)
│   ├── TagetServerGroups (TargetServerGroup)
│   ├── Alert System
│   ├── JobFilter
│   └── JobFilterHistory
└── Databases (Database)
    ├── DatabaseRoles (DatabaseRole)
    ├── Defaults (Default)
    ├── FileGroups (FileGroup)
    ├── FullTextCatalogs (FullTextCatalog)
    ├── Rules (Rule)
    ├── StoredProcedures (StoredProcedure)
    ├── SystemDataTypes (SystemDataType)
    ├── Yable (Yables)
    ├── UserDefinedDataTypes (UserDefinedDataType)
    ├── Users (User)
    ├── Views (View)
    ├── DBOption
    └── TransactionLog
```

Figure 16-1: The SQL-DMO object model contains all of the objects and collections needed to fully manage a SQL Server–based server.

The SQL-DMO objects are used by the Enterprise Manager itself to query and manipulate the database objects on the system. In the Enterprise Manager application, you will notice that the tree organization presented in it mimics the organization presented by the hierarchical object model. If you needed to build such an application, you could in fact create a your own custom application that mirrors all of the functionality of the Enterprise Manager.

> **NOTE:** The SQL-DMO object model is automatically installed with the standard MSDE and SQL Server engine installation. If the machine that you wish to install an application that uses the DMO framework does not have MSDE or SQL Server installed, you will need to install and register the `SQLDMO.RLL` file found in the `\MSSQL7\Resources\1033` directory path.

Testing the SQL-DMO System

The SQL-DMO objects can be included by adding the proper class references in a project to the object model. Once the SQL-DMO model is included in the references, a program can create instances of any of the DMO objects. It is also very useful, once these objects are added to the application, to use them directly so that you can observe what the individual methods do and the values of specific properties.

From Microsoft Access, the Immediate execution window can enable you to address the SQL-DMO objects much as a console or command-line interface (such as MS-DOS) can immediately execute commands. That means that the objects of the SQL-DMO framework can be manipulated instantly to test how methods work and what properties are changed given particular operations.

To examine the names of the databases stored on the current MSDE server, follow these steps:

1. Execute Microsoft Access 2000 and open the NorthwindCS project.

2. Under the Tools menu, select the Macro → Visual Basic Editor option. Selecting this option will display the entire VBA development environment that is present in Access. The Immediate window may already be displayed, but if it's not, it will need to be activated.

3. Press Ctrl+G to show the Immediate window.

4. Expand the Immediate window so that more code can be shown (see Figure 16-2). The Immediate window will enable commands to be executed by the VBA system and will display the results of those commands on the lines following each entry.

5. Under the Tools menu, select the References option. The References dialog box will display an alphabetical list of all object models that are installed and registered on the current system. From this dialog box, you can select the object models that will be available to the project.

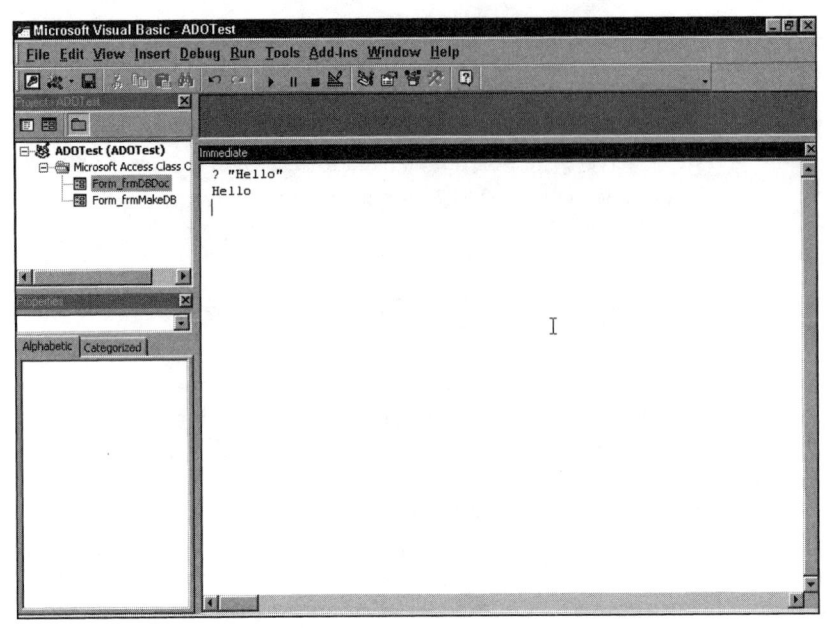

Figure 16-2: Expand the Immediate window so that a greater amount of code can be shown.

6. Find the Microsoft SQLDMO Object Library item in the list, check the box to its left, and click OK to add the SQL-DMO class definitions to the project.

7. The Immediate window executes commands on a line as soon as the Enter key is pressed. The code you see here shows each of the commands that you should type, followed by text with the prefix of a double arrow (>>). This prefix indicates the code that is not typed by you but returned by the machine. Type the following code (just the lines that don't include the double arrow) into the Immediate window:

> **Note:** You will need to replace the name of the server found in the second line with the address of your current server. If the NetBIOS protocol is activated, you can used the machine name such as \\machinename or use a single period (.) character to indicate that DMO should access the server running on the local machine. Otherwise, use the IP address or domain name of the MSDE server.

```
Set myMSDE = CreateObject("SQLDMO.SQLServer")
myMSDE.Connect "MSDEservername","sa",""
? myMSDE.Databases.Count
```

```
>>  6
For i = 1 To 6 : ? myMSDE.databases(i).Name : Next
>>  adTrack
>>  master
>>  model
>>  msdb
>>  NorthwindSQL
>>  tempdb
Set myMSDE = Nothing
```

8. You can examine the SQL-DMO object model and the objects that were just accessed using the Object Browser, which will display all of the current class libraries that are checked in the References dialog box. Click the Object Browser icon on the toolbar or hit F2 to display it.

9. From the top combo box in the window, select the SQLDMO item. That selection will display only the objects related to SQL-DMO. The list box in the left pane of the window labeled Classes displays all of the object classes and enumerated constants of the object model.

10. Click the Databases item. In the right list box, which should be labeled Members of 'Databases', the method `Count` will be listed. This method was used to retrieve the number of registered databases in the Immediate window code.

11. Select the Database item in the Classes list box. The Database item has many properties and methods, among which you will find the Name property that was used to make a list of the databases (see Figure 16-3). Because the specifics (data type, arguments, and so on) of the items listed in the Object Browser are provided, you can use this tool with an object diagram to navigate an object framework.

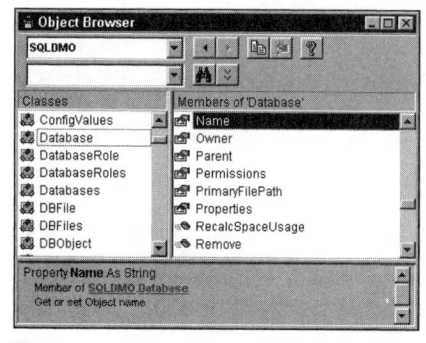

Figure 16-3: The Object Browser enables you to examine all of the objects, collections, events, constants, and properties of the SQL-DMO framework.

Executing the code will display the names of all of the registered databases that are available on the SQL Server engine. The sample entries demonstrate the flexibility of the Immediate window and provide an example of how easily the objects in the DMO can be accessed. For development on any object model, the Object Browser provides an excellent reference to quickly examine the methods and properties of all of the available objects.

SQL-DMO Overview

The structure of the classes contained in SQL-DMO is strictly hierarchical, unlike in ADO. As in ADO, creating some objects will automatically generate other objects lower in the hierarchy. For example, unless you're creating a new database object (such as a table), you will only need to create the SQLServer object. All of the other objects will be instantiated to reflect the current objects on the MSDE server.

Most of the key objects in the framework are stored in collections. A *collection* is much like an array holding references to objects of the same type. In Chapter 9, you saw that the Parameters collection of ADO held an individual Parameter object for each of the parameters that needed to be passed to a stored procedure. In SQL-DMO, most collections allow individual items to be deleted from the collection using the `Remove` method.

When a program makes modifications to the MSDE server (adding a table, configuring a database, or the like), the methods and properties of the SQL-DMO objects are actually converting the changes that are made into Transact-SQL code that is sent to the server. This process occurs transparently, so the programmer can treat the objects from the DMO framework as if changes to these objects were making direct changes to objects on the MSDE server.

The SQLServer Object

As you saw in the Immediate window example, there is an SQLServer object that represents the MSDE server. Each registered server has its own SQLServer object, which is the primary object that enables you to address the databases, devices, logins, and other objects directly related to the individual MSDE server.

From the SQLServer object, you can address all of the current databases as well as add new ones. You can also access:

- **Backup devices:** Any backup devices such as tape drives that are currently registered with the system.

- **Configuration:** Global properties and parameters that are configured for the MSDE server.

- **Full Text Services:** Control of the full text indexing services provided on SQL Server. Note that the full text services are an additional install for SQL Server installations and are not natively included with MSDE.

- **Integrated Security:** Preserved for backward compatibility with SQL Server 6.5 and below when login security was split between Windows NT login and SQL Server security.

- **JobServer:** Allows configuration and control of jobs associates with the SQL Agent.

- **Languages:** For international compatibility, MSDE supports several several languages. All of the currently installed language types may be accessed for error and status information in any of these languages.

- **LinkedServers:** Holds the information about linked servers used for distributed operations such as distributed queries. Contains objects for each server and the logins to the remote machines.

- **Logins:** User login accounts that have access privileges on the MSDE server.

- **Registry:** Contains all of the Registry settings that pertain the MSDE server installation.

- **Remote Servers:** Used to add, remove, or rename remote servers that can currently be addressed by the MSDE server.

- **Replication:** Objects that support replication. These include objects used to manage publishers, subscribers, distributors, and publications.

- **ServerRoles:** For security implementation, roles are defined that may be assigned to users. This collection holds all of the roles present on the server.

There is an individual Database object for each database available on the server. Therefore, the master database object could be referenced like this:

```
Set myMaster = myMSDE.Databases("master")
```

The Databases collection holds references to all of the Database objects. Using the name of the database, an object reference to it can be made.

The Database Object

Each Database object contains all of the information related to the database it represents. Although many of the properties stored in the object can be used to modify the database, some of the attributes will be read-only because they supply summary information on other objects that are contained within the database.

Some of the properties in the Database object include:

- Disk space and file location information on the database
- Table definition references

- Stored procedure references
- Index references
- Security settings for this database

Through the Database object, all of the items held within a database such as tables and stored procedures can be addressed.

Other DMO Objects

The SQLServer and Database objects are the two most important objects for many of the SQL-DMO projects that you will construct. Several other objects are contained in the framework that you may also need to use.

SERVERGROUP OBJECT

The ServerGroups collection holds all of the ServerGroup objects registered on a particular SQL system. For most MSDE setups, the collection will only contain a single object, because only a single group needs to be managed. The ServerGroup object can be used to:

- Add or remove a SQL Server to the current directory registration
- Add or remove a category where registered servers will be placed

REPLICATION OBJECTS

The Replication object allows an application to interface with a current replication setup or manage a replication process. Through the Replication object, an application may directly address the replication system, allowing a custom interface to be created. Publishers, subscribers, publications, subscriptions, and articles can be created and configured with the same breadth that is possible from the replication stored procedures.

The Subscriber object provides a single method, `Script`, which enables a stored procedure to be executed. The Replication object also supports two events: `PercentComplete` and `StatusMessage`. These events can be programmed to execute code when they are called by the SQL-DMO system.

For SQL-DMO, you can control the replication process through several objects. These objects include:

- **Replication object:** Primary object of the replication system that holds all of the collections and objects for the distribution, publication, and subscription to this MSDE server.
- **Distributor object:** The Distributor object is used to control the configuration of the distribution server and the distribution of the publications.

- **DistributionDatabase object:** Allows access to the information and structure of the database that is used by the Distributor for replication. This object is held in the Distributor object.

- **DistributionPublisher object:** Contains all of the properties of the publisher that is maintained by the Distribution object. This object is held in the Distributor object.

- **DistributionPublication object:** The object that represents the properties and settings of the publication itself. This object is used with all three types of replication (merge, transactional, and snapshot).

- **DistributionSubscription object:** Contains all of the properties of the subscription to a publication that is maintained by the Distribution object.

- **DistributionArticle object:** The article that may consist of a database or specific tables within a database that are published for replication. This object represents the image used by the Distributor of each article.

- **RegisteredSubscriber object:** Current data source to which the current publication is sent.

Some of the objects are automatically created by the server, whereas other objects can be created to instantiate additional objects. For replication, all of the system-created objects are available for management. In the last chapter, you covered these objects that are expressed in the SQL-DMO for programmatic control.

> The DistributionPublication is read-only unless the object is being used to create a distribution publication. When the object references an existing publication, the properties are read-only.

Creating DBDoc

In this section, you will create an application in Microsoft Access called DBDoc. It will access the MSDE server through the SQL-DMO framework and store all of the information about the database in an MSDE table. The code for writing the data into the new tables will be the objects of ADO inserting the actual data. SQL-DMO can modify the structure of a database, but ADO is still required to reach the data stored within that structure.

The information about the database object properties will be stored in three tables: one for the database information, one to hold table information, and a final one for stored procedures. Both the tables named *table* and *storedprocedures* will reference back to the databases table to indicate for each row to which database that row belongs.

> **NOTE:** Although this application will be written in an ADP project to store the information on the MSDE server, it could just as easily be placed in a standard Access MDB file. This example demonstrates how easily a properly designed database (providing no stored procedures are involved) can be moved between the two database formats.

Creating the Access Database

Because you are accustomed to working with Microsoft Access already, it can be useful to place the information that is retrieved from the MSDE server directly into a database. From there, you can create Access reports or query the information as you see fit. First, you will need to create a few tables into which the information can be placed.

The names of the three tables needed are: Databases, Tables, and StoredProcs. Each will contain information for a different object type addressed through the SQL-DMO framework. The tables will also be connected by primary and foreign keys to allow, for example, determination of which tables and stored procedures are located in each database.

Databases Table

First, a table needs to be created that will hold all of the information related to each database. Properties such as the database name, the creation date, the current amount of disk space used for data and indexes, and the file path of the storage file will be stored in this table.

1. Open Microsoft Access 2000.
2. Create a new data project database and name it **DBDoc.adp**. This project will hold the forms that enable the user to select which databases will be documented.
3. Follow the steps of the SQL Server Database Wizard allowing the new database to be called DBDocSQL. You will have a new database stored on the MSDE server where the information relating to the database will be stored.
4. Click the Tables item in the Objects column. You will need to create the Databases table for this project.
5. Click New to begin a new table in the Design view.
6. Set the name of the table to Databases.

7. Enter the following columns and their data types:

Column Name	Type	Size	Nulls?	Identity?
DatabaseID	int	4	No	Yes
Name	varchar	50	Yes	No
CreateDate	datetime	8	Yes	No
IndexSpaceUsage	float	8	Yes	No
DataSpaceUsage	float	8	Yes	No
PrimaryFilePath	varchar	50	Yes	No
Username	varchar	50	Yes	No
NumUserDefinedTypes	int	4	Yes	No

8. Select the DatabaseID field and click the Primary Key icon on the toolbar to set this to the primary key.

9. Close the database design window and save the table changes.

> **NOTE:** For the databases, tables, and stored procedures in this application, only a small number of properties are actually recorded in the rows of each documenting table. Numerous other properties could also be retrieved and stored if this information was required. If additional information for each database object is needed, consult the Object Browser on the SQL-DMO classes to determine what other properties are available

With the primary table that stores the database information completed, you will need to construct two other tables that are used to store the table and stored procedure information from each database.

Tables Table

Tables will store all of the column names, types, sizes, and other characteristics related to each table in each database. It will be linked by a foreign key to an entry in the Databases table for referencing queries.

Follow the same procedure in steps 5 through 9 that you used to create the Databases table. This time, name the table as **Tables** and enter the following columns:

Column Name	Type	Size	Nulls?	Identity?
TableID	int	4	No	Yes
Name	varchar	50	Yes	No
DatabaseID	int	4	No	No
CreateDate	datetime	8	Yes	No
HasClusteredIndex	bit	1	No	No
HasIndex	bit	1	No	No
PrimaryKeyName	varchar	50	Yes	No

Set the TableID column in this table to be the Primary Key. When you've completed the column definitions, save this new table under the name Tables.

StoredProcs Table

The StoredProcs table will hold information such as the name, text, type, and startup values of all of the stored procedures in a database. Like the Tables table, it will hold a foreign key reference in each table for a link to the database in which the procedure is located.

Follow the same procedure in steps 5 through 9 that you used to create the Databases table. This time, enter the following columns:

Column Name	Type	Size	Nulls?	Identity?
SPID	int	4	No	Yes
Name	varchar	50	Yes	No
DatabaseID	int	4	No	No
CreateDate	datetime	8	Yes	No
SPText	text	16	Yes	No
Type	int	4	Yes	No
Startup	bit	1	No	No

Set the SPID column in this table to be the Primary Key. When you've completed the column definitions, save this new table under the name StoredProcs. With three tables finished, you will need to create the relationships between the tables so that referential integrity between them is preserved.

Create the Relationships between the Tables

Once all of the tables are created, for proper design you should include the relations between the tables to promote referential integrity. With this set of tables, the Tables and StoredProcs tables need to be linked to records in the Databases table.

Creating these relationships will be done through a database diagram that can be created within Access.

1. Click the Database Diagram item in the Objects column of the main database window (see Figure 16-4). Because there are currently no diagrams in this database, the detail window will be empty except for the "Create database diagram in designer" item that will enable you to create a new diagram.

Figure 16-4: To show the current diagrams for this database stored on the MSDE server, select the Database Diagrams item.

2. Click New to begin a new diagram.
3. Right-click the empty space of the diagram and select the Show Table option.
4. Drag and drop all three tables onto the diagram.
5. Click the DatabaseID column in the Databases table and drag the cursor to the DatabaseID column on the Tables table.

6. Click OK to accept the relation to be created.

7. Use the same drag-and-drop procedure to connect the Databases table to the StoredProcs table. When the diagram is complete, your diagram should show all of the tables and two connections between the Databases table and the two others (see Figure 16-5).

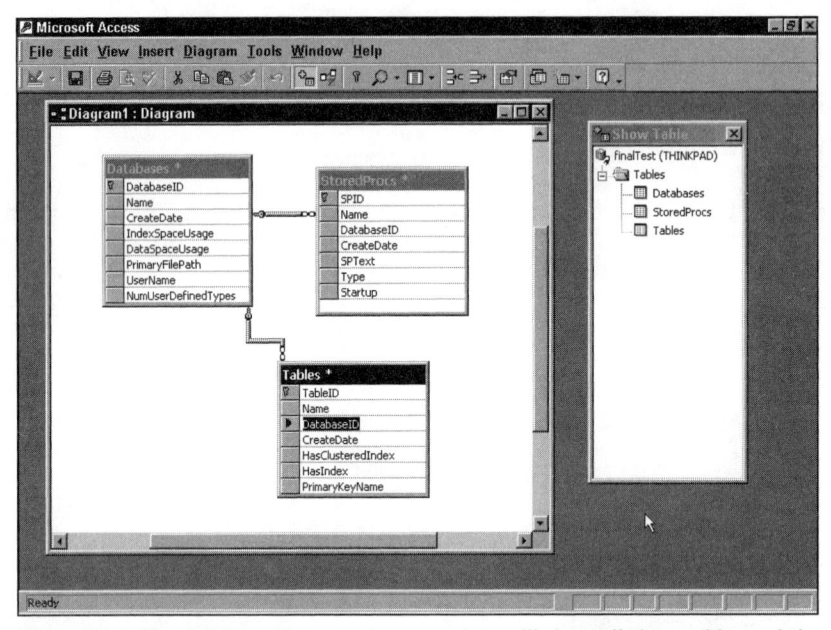

Figure 16-5: The database diagram when complete will show all three tables and the links between them.

8. Close the diagram window and save the diagram with the name **DocDiagram**.

With the database complete, some forms must be created to address the SQL-DMO framework and fill the tables with data. A form that will be used to select which of the databases a user wishes to document and then place that data in each table.

Making the Object Selection Form

An MSDE server can hold a great number of databases, and you may not want to document all of them. Therefore, it is a good idea to create a user interface in the Access form environment from which the databases to be documented can be selected from a list.

To address the SQL-DMO objects and collections from the Access project, you need to include the object model in the current project. That is done by adding a reference to the model in the References dialog. The References dialog is accessible only from the VBA environment, so you will need to create the form that will be used before you include the class library in the project.

1. In the main database window, click the Forms item in the Objects column.

2. Click New on the database window toolbar to create a new form.

3. When prompted for how the form will be constructed, select the Design view option and click OK.

4. Click a blank part of the form to select the form itself for available properties.

5. In the Properties window under the Event tab, click the On Click event button to display the VBA project environment.

6. When the Choose Builder window is displayed, select the Code Builder option and click OK. This option will activate the VBA environment so that the class library references may be set.

7. Select the References option from the Tools menu. All of the classes currently available to the project will be displayed. You will need to add the SQL-DMO classes to most effectively use them.

8. Check the item named Microsoft SQLDMO Object Library in the list and click OK. This selection will make the necessary DMO objects available so that you can begin adding the code and controls for the project.

9. Under the File menu, select the Close and Return to Microsoft Access option to return to the form design environment. Alternatively, you can use Alt+Tab to reenter the Access form environment.

10. Show the control toolbox palette by selecting the Toolbox option from the View menu.

11. From the control toolbox palette, add four command buttons and two list boxes to the form. As you draw each object on the form, the dialog box will be presented to create presets for the buttons and list boxes. Simply click Cancel when each dialog is displayed; this project requires custom coding. The general layout of these controls should match the organization shown in Figure 16-6.

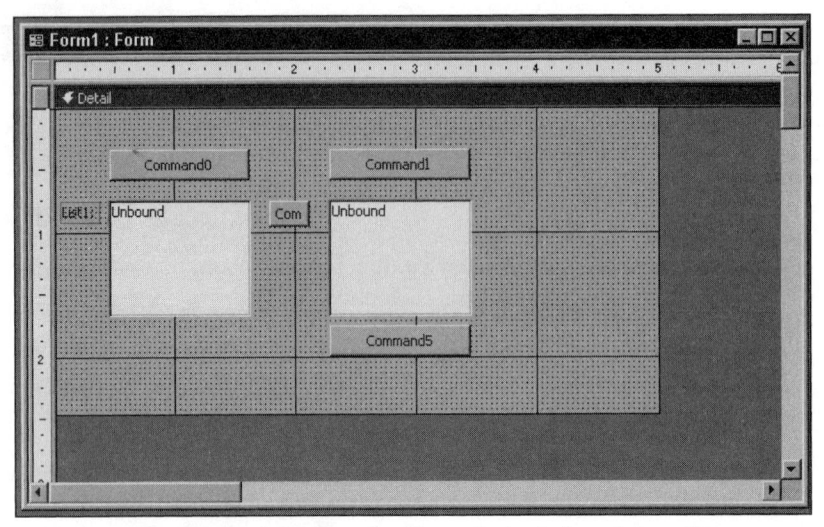

Figure 16-6: The layout of the form should match the design of these three command buttons and two list boxes.

12. On the Data tab of each list box, set the Row Source Type property to **Value List.**

13. On the command button located between the two list boxes, set the Name property to **cmdTransfer** and set the Caption property to **>**.

14. For the command button that appears over the first list box, set the Name property to **cmdGetDBs** and set the Caption property to **Get Databases.**

15. On the command button under the second list box, set the Name property to **cmdDocDBs** and set the Caption property to **Document Databases.**

16. On the command button over the second list box, set the Name property to **cmdClear** and set the Caption property to **Clear.**

17. Set the Name property of the first list box to **lstDatabases.**

18. Set the Name property of the second list box to **lstDocDB**. When the form is complete, it should match the one shown in Figure 16-7.

The reference to the object model is necessary if you want to define objects by their actual names. It is not required, however, because the general data type of Object could be used. For example, in SQL-DMO a database would be normally defined in this manner:

```
Dim myDB As SQLDMO.Database
```

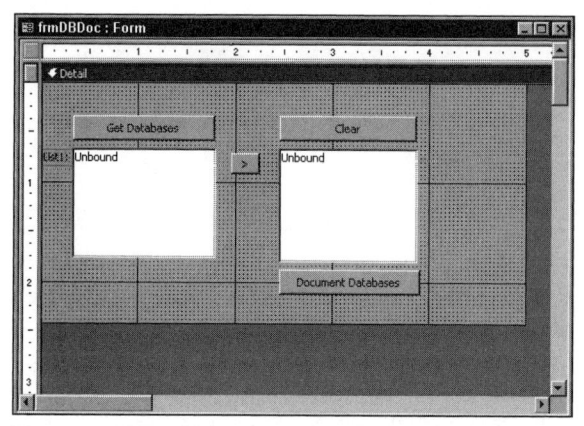

Figure 16-7: The DBDoc application will have four command buttons and two list boxes when it is complete.

Without references to the class library in the References dialog, you would need to define this item as a general object:

```
Dim myDB As Object
```

In the VBA environment, the autocomplete functions would not be enabled if the general objects are used. Also, the syntax checking for the properties and methods used with the objects that appear in your code would not be enabled.

Coding SQL-DMO and ADO Routines

With the object selection form complete, you can create some simple code to populate the databases list box with all of the databases on the system. The code will provide a quick introduction to how a SQL-DMO collection can be used to obtain important database information about the MSDE server.

The code for ADO will take the information garnered from the SQL-DMO objects and write that information into the DBDocSQL database that you created.

To add the object access code, follow these steps:

1. Right-click the Get Databases command button and choose the Properties option.

2. From the Properties window, select the Events tab.

3. Select the row for the Click event and click the small button to the right of the Click box. This selection will display the code window that enables you to enter VBA code for the button.

4. Enter the following code in the Click event routine:

```
Private Sub cmdGetDBs_Click()
    Dim myMSDE As SQLDMO.SQLServer
    Dim myDB As SQLDMO.Database
    Dim myServerName As String, myUsername As String
    Dim myPwd As String
    Dim dbList As String

    myServerName = "." 'change to your server name
    myUsername = "sa": myPwd = ""
    On Error GoTo ProblemGDB

    Set myMSDE = CreateObject("SQLDMO.SQLServer")
    myMSDE.Connect myServerName, myUsername, myPwd
    For Each myDB In myMSDE.Databases
        dbList = dbList + myDB.Name + ";"
    Next
    lstDatabases.RowSource = dbList
    lstDocDB.RowSource = ""
    Exit Sub

ProblemGDB:
        MsgBox "MSDE Error: " & Err.Description, _
        vbExclamation, "MSDE Error"
End Sub
```

5. Click on the View button on the toolbar to switch from Design to Execution mode.

6. Click Get Databases.

The list box should become populated with all of the available databases that exist on your MSDE server. If an error is generated, the error handler will display the error that was returned. The error may be as simple as entering the wrong name and password. If the error says that the server was not found, make sure you have your MSDE server started, as the default option for MSDE is that the service is not started on boot.

With this simple test complete, you can progress to adding the code necessary for the application to retrieve the database information and store it in the Access tables that you've generated.

Retrieving Schema Information

The rest of the application uses the Databases objects that are added to the Document list box to retrieve all of the tables and stored procedures information. The supplied instructions are presented in a step-by-step format to make everything very clear. If you have extensive VBA experience, you will automatically understand where code will be placed. However, if you are less experienced in the VBA environment, the sequential instructions will instruct you as to exactly how the application will be constructed.

> **NOTE:** In the DocDBs button code, the process to eliminate all of the records uses the SQL code: Delete From myTable. For this application you could use the Truncate Table command for faster execution. The truncate command has the disadvantage in most production applications of not recording any of the deletions in the log files. By ignoring the log, the process executes faster but in the event of a server fault, this table could be partially corrupted. Therefore, only use the Truncate Table command in situations where the data is not important.

Before you begin placing new code in the application, you will need to modify the database display code you entered. The only required modification is to move the Dim statements used to define the two variables into the global scope of the form where they can be addressed by any routine executing on the form.

1. Switch back to Design mode by clicking the View icon on the toolbar.

2. Open the code window to display the Click event as you did in the last section.

3. Select the first two lines of code in the Click event that contain the Dim statements and, using the Edit → Cut option, place them on the clipboard. The combo boxes at the top of the code window show the current procedure location that is being displayed in the window itself. In this case, the left combo box (showing the currently selected object) should read cmdGetDBs. The right combo box should display the current procedure selected for the object, the Click event. To place the variable definitions that have just been cut to the clipboard, you will need to move to the form's General Declarations section.

4. From the left combo box, select the (General) item at the top of the drop-down list. When you make this change, the right combo box should automatically change to read (Declarations). In the code window, the cursor should be in a blank space or have a simple Option statement (such as Option Compare or Option Explicit).

5. Position the insertion point on the empty line under the Option Compare statement.

6. Select Edit → Paste to enter the code in this location. These two variables are now available to any routine located on the form. For this project, a few more variables are needed.

7. The General Declarations code should now look like this:

```
Option Compare Database
Dim myMSDE As SQLDMO.SQLServer
Dim myDB As SQLDMO.Database
```

8. Select the cmdTransfer button from the left combo box. The project needs the code to move the databases selected by the user into the list box that will be used for all of those items that will be documented.

9. Enter the following code for the cmdTransfer button:

```
Private Sub cmdTransfer_Click()
    If lstDatabases.ListIndex <> -1 Then
        lstDocDB.RowSource = lstDocDB.RowSource + _
        lstDatabases.ItemData(lstDatabases.ListIndex) + ";"
    End If
End Sub
```

10. Enter the following code for the cmdClear button:

```
Private Sub cmdClear_Click()
    lstDocDB.RowSource = ""
End Sub
```

11. Enter the following code for the cmdDocDBs button:

```
Private Sub cmdDocDBs_Click()
    Dim myConn As New ADODB.Connection
    Dim myRS As New ADODB.Recordset
    Dim myTableRS As New ADODB.Recordset
    Dim mySPRS As New ADODB.Recordset
    Dim myIdentity As New ADODB.Recordset
    Dim dbStr As String
    Dim myTable As SQLDMO.Table
    Dim mySP As SQLDMO.StoredProcedure
    Dim dbName As String
    Dim I,dbID As Integer

    ' Check to make sure MSDE object is active
    If Not myMSDE Is Nothing Then
        ' Set up a connection to write the schema info
        ' that is retrieved
        myConn.ConnectionString = "driver={SQL Server};" & _
            "server=thinkpad;uid=sa;pwd=;database=DBDocSQL"
        ' Locate the cursor on the server
```

```
myConn.CursorLocation = adUseServer
myConn.Open

' Delete all of the data currently contained
' in the tables from previous executions of the
' database documenter
myConn.Execute "Delete From Tables"
myConn.Execute "Delete From StoredProcs"
' This delete statement must come after the other two
' delete statements because of the referential
' integrity created in the database diagram.
' Otherwise records could exist that reference a
' record in this table that would no longer exist.
myConn.Execute "Delete From Databases"

' Set up primary recordset used with the
' Databases table
myRS.CursorLocation = adUseServer
myRS.CursorType = adOpenDynamic
myRS.LockType = adLockOptimistic
Set myRS.ActiveConnection = myConn
myRS.Open "Select * from Databases"

' Set up the recordset used with the
' Tables table
myTableRS.CursorLocation = adUseServer
myTableRS.CursorType = adOpenDynamic
myTableRS.LockType = adLockOptimistic
Set myTableRS.ActiveConnection = myConn
myTableRS.Open "Select * from Tables"

' Set up the recordset used with the
' StoredProces table
mySPRS.CursorLocation = adUseServer
mySPRS.CursorType = adOpenDynamic
mySPRS.LockType = adLockOptimistic
Set mySPRS.ActiveConnection = myConn
mySPRS.Open "Select * from StoredProcs"

' Start documenting each database
For i = 1 To myMSDE.Databases.Count
    ' Get the name of the current database
    dbName = myMSDE.Databases(i).Name

    ' Add a new record to the Databases table to
```

```vb
                        ' store the info about this database.
                        myRS.AddNew
                        myRS.Fields("Name").Value = _
                            myMSDE.Databases(dbName).Name

                        ' Use the IsDate function to determine if date
                        ' is valid and use the Left() function
                        ' to eliminate error caused by SQL Server
                        ' long date/time format with evaluation.
                        If IsDate(Left _
                          (myMSDE.Databases(dbName).CreateDate, 11)) Then
                              myRS.Fields("CreateDate").Value = Left _
                                (myMSDE.Databases(dbName).CreateDate, 11)
                        End If
                        ' Enter other db columns
                        myRS.Fields("PrimaryFilePath").Value = "" _
                            & myMSDE.Databases(dbName).PrimaryFilePath
                        myRS.Fields("IndexSpaceUsage") = _
                            myMSDE.Databases(dbName).IndexSpaceUsage
                        myRS.Fields("DataSpaceUsage") = _
                            myMSDE.Databases(dbName).DataSpaceUsage
                        myRS.Fields("UserName") = _
                            myMSDE.Databases(dbName).UserName

                        ' If UDT collection is valid, count how many
                        ' are present in current database
                        If Not myMSDE.Databases(dbName).UserDefinedDatatypes _
                            Is Nothing Then
                              myRS.Fields("NumUserDefinedTypes") = _
                        myMSDE.Databases(dbName).UserDefinedDatatypes.Count
                        End If
                        ' Write changes into database
                        myRS.Update

                        ' Get identity number of the record that was just
                        ' updated so that number can be written into the
                        ' foreign key fields of the Tables and
                        ' StoredProcs tables.
                        Set myIdentity = myConn.Execute( _
                            "SELECT @@IDENTITY AS 'Identity'")
                        dbID = myIdentity.Fields("Identity").Value

                        ' Write all of the tables associated with this db
                        For Each myTable In _
                            myMSDE.Databases(dbName).Tables
```

```
            myTableRS.AddNew
            myTableRS.Fields("DatabaseID").Value = dbID
            myTableRS.Fields("Name").Value = myTable.Name
            myTableRS.Fields("HasIndex").Value = _
               myTable.HasIndex
           myTableRS.Fields("HasClusteredIndex").Value = _
               myTable.HasClusteredIndex
            If IsDate(Left(myTable.CreateDate, 11)) Then
                myTableRS.Fields("CreateDate").Value = _
                Left(myTable.CreateDate, 11)
            End If
        If Not myTable.PrimaryKey Is Nothing Then
            myTableRS.Fields("PrimaryKeyName").Value = _
                "" & myTable.PrimaryKey.Name
        End If
           myTableRS.Update
        Next

        ' Write all of the stored proc info associated
        ' with this db
        For Each mySP In _
              myMSDE.Databases(dbName).StoredProcedures
            mySPRS.AddNew
            mySPRS.Fields("DatabaseID").Value = dbID
            mySPRS.Fields("Name").Value = mySP.Name
            If IsDate(Left(mySP.CreateDate, 11)) Then
                mySPRS.Fields("CreateDate").Value = _
                   Left(mySP.CreateDate, 11)
            End If
            mySPRS.Fields("Startup").Value = mySP.Startup
            mySPRS.Fields("Type").Value = mySP.Type
            mySPRS.Fields("SPText").Value = mySP.Text

            mySPRS.Update
        Next
    Next
    ' Close all of the recordsets
    myRS.Close
    myTableRS.Close
    mySPRS.Close
    ' Close the connection
    myConn.Close
    ' Clean up the objects in memory
    Set myTableRS = Nothing
    Set mySPRS = Nothing
```

```
              Set myRS = Nothing
              Set myConn = Nothing
              MsgBox "Completed documenting the databases", _
                  vbInformation, "Completed."
       End If
    End Sub
```

12. Enter the following code for the double-click event for the lstDatabases list box to make it transfer items like the transfer button:

```
Private Sub lstDatabases_DblClick(Cancel As Integer)
    lstDocDB.RowSource = lstDocDB.RowSource + _
        lstDatabases.ItemData(lstDatabases.ListIndex) + ";"
End Sub
```

13. Click the View button on the toolbar to change to execution mode.

14. Click Get Databases to begin the session. Once the connection to the database server has been made and the database list has been loaded, move some of the database items into the Document list box with the right arrow. When you've selected the ones you want (see Figure 16-8), click the document button. The application will process the database through the SQL-DMO and place the information in the intended tables.

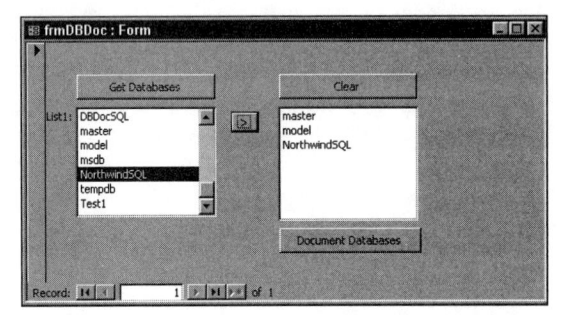

Figure 16-8: Move some of the databases to the Document Databases list box for examination.

15. Close the form and save the most recent changes. If you haven't saved the form previously, you will be asked for a form name. Set the name of the form to **frmDBDoc**.

16. Click the Tables item in the Access navigator window under the Objects column.

17. Double-click the Tables item to browse that table. You will see a table of values for each of the databases that you selected.

Because of the quantity of data that might be generated if many databases were selected, the application uses the `Delete` command that is available in SQL to eliminate all of the existing records in the three tables before the process begins. Be sure that you don't need to save any of the information from a past execution before you begin.

Making a MakeDB Utility

The previous example showed how the SQL-DMO could be used to document existing databases stored on the database server. Because you will most likely want to create objects using the object model in the future, it is useful to construct a simple application that can create a new database or modify an existing one. That way, you can control creation and modification of an MSDE database using any of four methods: through SQL code, with the Access Database Wizard, using the Enterprise Manager, or through SQL-DMO.

This application will enable you to create a new database with any name that is entered into a text box. Once the database is created, a table can be added, a column can be added to that table, and finally an index can be set on one of the columns.

To create the MakeDB application, follow these steps:

1. Insert a new form into the current Access file. You can create this form as part of a new database file if you'd like. Just be sure to add the SQL-DMO selection to the References dialog box of the project. Because this form doesn't write into any native tables like DBdoc, it can even be created in an ADP project.

> **NOTE** For this application, you will need a combo box to display the name of the new or existing database as well as text boxes to accept the parameter settings.

2. Add a text box and four command buttons to the window.

3. Modify the following properties on these controls to match these values. When you've completed adding all of the buttons and modifying them to meet the listed properties, the form should appear like this one in Figure 16-9.

Control	Property	Setting
Command0	Name	cmdCreateDB
Command0	Caption	Create Database
Command1	Name	cmdAddTable
Command1	Caption	Add Table
Command2	Name	cmdAddColumn
Command2	Caption	Add Column
Command3	Name	cmdAddIndex
Command3	Caption	Add Index
Text1	Name	txtDBName

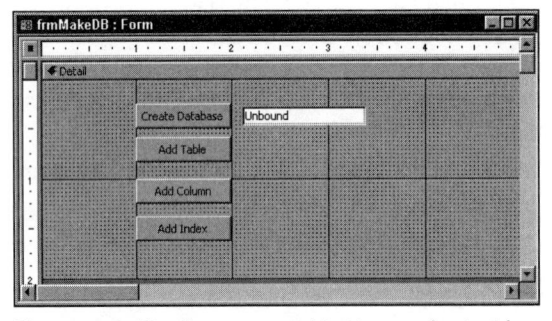

Figure 16-9: The four command buttons and a text box should appear on the form.

4. Add the following code to the General Declarations section of the form:

```
Option Compare Database
Dim myMSDE As SQLDMO.SQLServer
Dim myDB As SQLDMO.Database
Dim dbName As String, tableName As String
Dim tableVisitors As SQLDMO.Table
```

5. Add the following code to the cmdCreateDB command button:

```
Private Sub cmdCreateDB_Click()
    Dim myDBFileData As New SQLDMO.DBFile
    Dim myLogFile As New SQLDMO.LogFile
    Dim myServerName, myUserName, myPwd As String
```

```
    On Error GoTo Problem

    ' Set up server address and login
    myServerName = "."
    myUsername = "sa": myPwd = ""
    ' Create the primary object reference
    Set myMSDE = CreateObject("SQLDMO.SQLServer")
    ' Connect to the server
    myMSDE.Connect myServerName, myUsername, myPwd

    ' Set the focus so Access can retrieve the db name
    txtDBName.SetFocus
    dbName = txtDBName.Text
    ' Check to make certain a name was entered
    If Len(dbName) > 0 Then
        ' Create a new database object instance
        Set myDB = New SQLDMO.Database
        myDB.Name = dbName

        ' Set up the data file
        myDBFileData.Name = dbName + "Data"
        myDBFileData.PhysicalName = "c:\mssql7\data\" _
            + dbName + ".mdf"
        myDBFileData.PrimaryFile = True
        myDBFileData.FileGrowthType = SQLDMOGrowth_MB
        myDBFileData.FileGrowth = 1

        ' Set up the log file
        myDB.FileGroups("PRIMARY").DBFiles.Add myDBFileData
        myLogFile.Name = dbName + "Log1"
        myLogFile.PhysicalName = "c:\mssql7\data\" _
            + dbName + ".ldf"

        ' Add the log file to the LogFiles collection
        myDB.TransactionLog.LogFiles.Add myLogFile
        ' Add the database to the collection
        ' This creates the database on the MSDE server
        myMSDE.Databases.Add myDB
        MsgBox "Database creation successful!", _
            vbInformation, "Database Created"
    End If
    Exit Sub

Problem:
    MsgBox "The following error occurred addressing" & _
        "the MSDE server: " & Err.Description, _
```

```
            vbExclamation, "MSDE Error"
    End Sub
```

6. Click the View button to enter Run mode.

7. Enter the name of a database and click Create Database.

So far, you can enter the name of a new database and create it on the database server. You can see the database that you just created by reexecuting the DBDoc and simply clicking Get Databases. You will see your new database in the list. If you were to document it, only the system-generated objects would be returned.

To make the database more robust, additional SQL-DMO is required to create a new table. The Create Table button will use some of the objects when the database was created including the MSDE object and database name.

Creating a New Table

You can use the Table object to add to the collection for tables that is held by each Database object. The column objects are added first so that they may be created in the table.

1. Return to Design mode by clicking the View button on the toolbar.

2. Add the following code to the `cmdAddTable` command button:

```
Private Sub cmdAddTable_Click()
    Dim colID As New SQLDMO.Column
    Dim colName As New SQLDMO.Column
    Dim col2 As New SQLDMO.Column
    Dim col3 As New SQLDMO.Column

    On Error GoTo ProblemNT

    ' Create three columns for adding to the table
    ' RowID column holds a unique ID for each row in the
    ' table.
    colID.Name = "RowID"
    colID.DataType = "int"
    colID.Identity = True
    colID.IdentityIncrement = 1
    colID.IdentitySeed = 1
    colID.AllowNulls = False

    ' colName is a column to hold a name that is set to
    ' be a varchar data type that is 15 characters long
    colName.Name = "Name"
    colName.DataType = "varchar"
```

```
            colName.Length = 15
            colName.AllowNulls = True

            ' Column2 is a text data type to hold a complete
            ' description of the row
            col2.Name = "Description"
            col2.DataType = "text"
            col2.AllowNulls = True

            ' Configure the table object that will contain
            ' the columns
            Set tableVisitors = New SQLDMO.Table
            tableVisitors.Name = "Visitors"
            tableVisitors.FileGroup = "PRIMARY"

            ' Add the columns to the table object
            tableVisitors.Columns.Add colID
            tableVisitors.Columns.Add colName
            tableVisitors.Columns.Add col2

            ' Add the table to the database that was created
            ' with the Create Database button
            myMSDE.Databases(dbName).Tables.Add tableVisitors
            MsgBox "Table creation successful!", vbInformation, _
                "Table Created"
            Exit Sub

ProblemNT:
            MsgBox "The following error occurred addressing" & _
                "the MSDE server: " & Err.Description, _
                vbExclamation, "MSDE Error"
End Sub
```

When you execute this code, it will create the table with the name entered in the text box and add all of the columns to that table. Even after the table is created, DMO can be used to add additional columns to the table definition.

Adding a Column to an Existing Table

Adding a column to an existing table is done with much the same method as adding them to a new one. The following code modifies that table that was created with the SQL-DMO code from the last section.

1. Return to Design mode by clicking the View button on the toolbar.

2. Add the following code to the `Add Column` command button:

```
Private Sub cmdAddCol_Click()
    Dim colNew As New SQLDMO.Column

    On Error GoTo ProblemAT

    colNew.Name = "LastVisit"
    colNew.DataType = "datetime"
    colNew.AllowNulls = False
    colNew.DRIDefault.Text = "'4/1/2000'"
    tableVisitors.BeginAlter
    tableVisitors.Columns.Add colNew
    tableVisitors.DoAlter

    MsgBox "Column creation successful!", vbInformation, _
        "Column Created"
    Exit Sub

ProblemAT:
    MsgBox "The following error occurred addressing" & _
        "the MSDE server: " & Err.Description, _
        vbExclamation, "MSDE Error"
End Sub
```

The column added can also be removed with the `Remove` method. With the table constructed, indexes can be added to the columns of the table.

Creating an Index

The DMO classes enable you to create an index for the table. The following code adds an index to the table that was created with the SQL-DMO code.

To add the code for index creation, follow these steps:

1. Return to Design mode by clicking the View button on the toolbar.

2. Add the following code to the `Add Index` command button:

```
Private Sub cmdAddIndex_Click()
    ' Create a new index object
    Dim idxName As New SQLDMO.Index

    ' Set the index name
    idxName.Name = "idx_Name"
    idxName.FileGroup = "PRIMARY"
    ' Define the index type
    idxName.Type = SQLDMOIndex_Unique
```

```
        ' Indicate the column of the index
        idxName.IndexedColumns = "[Name]"
        ' Construct the index on the server and
        ' add it to the specified table
        tableVisitors.Indexes.Add idxName
        MsgBox "Index creation successful!", vbInformation, _
            "Index Created"
    End Sub
```

Depending on the number of rows in an existing database, adding the index may take some time. Once the index has been added, the queries that you would make on the DBDoc tables would be significantly faster because both of the joins between the Databases table and the other two tables use the DatabaseID for coordination.

SQL-DMO Events

The object model also allows code to execute in response to events that occur on the database server. There are 14 events that can be programmed to react with your own code. The following events are supported for the DMO objects:

- **BatchImported (msg As String):** The activation of a bulk copy procedure causes this event to occur. This event is evoked only when the BulkCopy object is passed as a parameter to the `ImportData` method of the table object.

- **CommandSent (SQL As String):** This event is activated when any SQL command is sent to the MSDE server. The SQL string contains the command that was sent to the database server.

- **ConnectionBroken (msg As String) As Boolean:** Activates when the connection to the server is broken only when the AutoReconnect property is set to False.

- **Complete (msg As String):** Activates when a backup or restored operation is complete.

- **NextMedia (msg As String):** When a backup or restore operation exhausts the current medium (such as a backup tape) and requires a switch to the next medium in a backup series, this event code is evoked.

- **PercentComplete (msg As String, percent As Long):** A progress event that is activated at intervals during a backup, restore, or replication. The percent parameter passed to the event code contains the completed percentage as a whole number (i.e. 15 = 15%).

- **PercentCompleteAtStep (msg As String, percent As Long):** A progress event that is activated at intervals during a schema or data copy operation. The percent parameter passed to the event code contains the completed percentage as a whole number (such as 15 = 15%).

- **QueryTimeout:** When execution of a query times out, the code for this event will be activated.

- **RemoteLoginFailed:** For the automatic connection service between MSDE and another SQL Server–based engine, if the login to the remote server fails, this event is activated.

- **RowsCopied (msg As String, rows As Long):** The completion of a bulk copy operation will activate this event if the UseServerSideBCP property on the BulkCopy object is set to False. The rows parameter returns the number of rows copied in the bulk operation.

- **ScriptTransferPercentComplete (msg As String, percent As Long):** A progress event that is activated at intervals during an execution of a command batch for one of the SQL Server components. The percent parameter passed to the event code contains the completed percentage as a whole number.

- **ServerMessage:** Messages either generated by the Transact-SQL `Print` command or minor errors that didn't prevent the completion of the operation are returned through this event.

- **StatusMessage (msg As String):** This event activates periodically during various operations such as transfer and replication so that the current status can be reported to the user or stored in some type of log.

- **TransferPercentComplete (msg As String, percent As Long):** When an operation involving a component referenced by the Transfer object is complete, this event is activated.

To code for events, you can simply add the event routines with the properly named subroutines. You can use code like this:

```
Sub myobject_Complete (msg As String)
    ' Place my code here
End Sub
```

Coding for event routines enables your application to be more responsive by including information such as the current status of several processes.

Possible SQL-DMO Applications

With the completion of your second DMO project, you should have a fair grasp of how the objects may be used for both examination and modification. Because the MSDE object model may be used from several different environments, you could use it for any number of applications such as:

- **Outlook application:** Create a VBA or VB Script document the current server status and e-mail it to database administrators or post it to a public folder for historical tracking.

- **Excel application:** Survey all of the SQL Server engine database servers on the network and record the statistics in a workbook. Summary information could be generated as well as pivot tables for drill-down examination of aspects of the enterprise database implementation.

- **Word application:** A complete formatted report could show the code text of the stored procedures available on each MSDE server to provide documentation of a code library of existing routines and sample code to create new ones.

- **PowerPoint presentation:** Slides could be generated to show each existing database and the indexes used on each. The presentation could be distributed to ascertain from project developers if these are the same columns that will be used for projects in development or if optimization will be required.

- **Visual Basic application:** Duplicating the functionality of the Enterprise Manager, you could create a database management utility customized to the needs of your organization. Using Visual Basic, the application could be compiled into a utility.

These few examples hopefully will help you generate application ideas of your own that you can put to use in your organization. Because SQL-DMO enables you full control over the database server, you will probably find yourself building small utility over time to minimize the operations you find yourself needing again and again.

Summary

By using the SQL-DMO framework, your program can completely control the MSDE server. From procedural programming code (such as VBA or Visual Basic), you can manipulate all of the functions that are available for manual configuration within the Enterprise Manager. In this chapter, you covered:

- **SQL Distributed Management Objects (DMO):** The object model available to read and modify any SQL Server–based database server available on the network. SQL-DMO can be used to create or modify databases, logs, devices, stored procedures, or any database object that is located on the server.

- **Replication objects:** The replication process can be initiated or controlled using the SQL-DMO process.

- **Programming DMO:** From VBA included in Access, Excel, or any other office application, you can use DMO to query and manage every aspect of the MSDE server.

- **DBDoc application:** The DBDoc application uses the DMO framework to retrieve information about selected databases and stores them in a local Access MDB database.

- **MakeDB application:** The MakeDB application will create a new database or a new table, or else modify an existing one to add additional columns and indexes.

- **DMO events:** VBA code can be used to create procedures that are activated when events concerning the current instantiation of the DMO objects occur. Events such as process completion, periodic status updates, timeouts, and connection failures can be handled by event code.

Chapter 17

Creating User-Defined Data Types

IN THIS CHAPTER

- Understanding UDTs
- Creating a new type in Transact-SQL
- Using the new type
- Building a default to a UDT
- Binding a rule to a UDT

MICROSOFT ACCESS HAS A limited number of data types (such as integer, date/time, and so forth) available for column definition. MSDE, on the other hand, allows new types to be defined using existing data types as building blocks. Each data type definition can aid you in ensuring the integrity of tables that use them by restricting null values and setting the size, precision, and scale in the actual type definition. You can also set the name of the new data type to allow a more descriptive name for table definitions.

Understanding UDTs

A simple example of using a user-defined type (UDT) is the creation of a zip code type. When database tables that accept addresses are created, a great deal of variation often exists in the column type used. If the ZIP code field only needs to store a five-digit number of a ZIP code in the U.S., an integer field might be used. However, defining the ZIP code as a number eliminates the possibility of storing a ZIP+4 value.

Additionally, the postal codes for international shipping often include alphabetic characters, which cannot be used in a numeric field type.

By creating a UDT for a zipcode data type, all tables can use this data type for their ZIP code columns. Thereafter, all of the tables would have a uniform standardized column definition for that ZIP code type.

Besides standardization, one of the most important aspects of a UDT is the capability to bind a rule or a default to a defined type. This capability is not available for system data types. UDTs are created from preexisting system data types. For example, an integer could be defined as a new type with the name inventorycount and be used for tables that track inventory.

Only the timestamp data type cannot be used as a system type from which to create a new type (see Chapter 6 for a complete description of each system data type). The system itself includes one UDT called sysname. It is used in the system tables to hold a Unicode variable character column type with 128 or fewer characters. Creating this type enabled the MSDE designers to ensure that all the names of database objects would have a standard length and type.

You can create new UDTs to be used in a database through direct Transact-SQL code, the Enterprise Manager, or available SQL-DMO objects. Which of these three methods you find easiest for defining UDTs typically depends on the environment you're most comfortable using. Because both the Enterprise Manager and the SQL-DMO definition capabilities simply mirror those of the Transact-SQL definition, SQL code will be used in the next section to demonstrate the creation of a sample user type.

Creating a New Type in Transact-SQL

When creating a new type in Transact-SQL, you need to use the stored procedure `sp_addtype`. This procedure adds the new type to the current database on the MSDE server. Whichever database is currently selected when this procedure is executed will store the data type.

Unless the type is defined in the model database, it will be available for definition only to the tables stored in the database in which it was created. The UDT is added to the systypes table in the current database. Adding the UDT to the model database makes it available for use by all the databases you create on the MSDE server.

Also, you cannot alter the length, precision, or scale for a UDT when defining a column with a UDT. To modify these factors, you have to change the actual UDT definition in the database. Modification to the UDT definition can occur only after you remove the UDT from any columns, rules, or defaults that use it.

The name of a UDT must be unique within each database. If located in the model database, it must be unique to the database system. A UDT may be defined from any of these existing system database types, which include the following: 'binary(n)', image, smalldatetime, bit, int, smallint, 'char(n)', 'nchar(n)', text, datetime, ntext, tinyint, decimal, numeric, uniqueidentifier, 'decimal[(p[, s])]', 'numeric[(p[, s])]', 'varbinary(n)', float, 'nvarchar(n)', 'varchar(n)', 'float(n)', or real.

A user-defined type is created using three parameters: the type name, the system data type that it will be based on, and whether a column of that type can accept null values. The general syntax for the `sp_addtype` procedure looks like this:

```
sp_addtype [@typename =] type,
   [@phystype =] system_data_type
   [, [@nulltype =] 'null_type']
```

The `@typename` stores the name that the new value will be stored under. The `@phytype` indicates the type that the new UDT will be based upon. Finally, the `@nulltype` is an option parameter that indicates whether or not the new data type can accept a null.

You must encapsulate within a string any data type that requires a length value that must be supplied using parentheses. Like the null value in the last definition, that means that the apostrophe is used to delimit the string.

To create a new data type for inventory, follow these steps:

1. Execute Microsoft Query.

2. Select the Execute SQL statements option from the File menu.

3. Click the Data Sources button to select a data source to use for the execution.

4. Select the dsnNorthwindSQL data source that you created initially in Chapter 1.

5. Make sure the default database is set to the NorthwindSQL database.

6. Enter the following code in the SQL statement text box:

   ```
   Execute sp_addtype inventoryNum, int, 'NOT NULL'
   ```

7. Click the Execute button to create the new data type. You will see a dialog box that notifies you that the type has been created.

After you create the type, it can be used for any future table definition within the database in which it was created.

> **NOTE** User-defined data types can be used in an Access ADP project and will be listed in the available data types combo box when defining a new column. However, UDTs may not be used by name when connecting through an attached table or ODBC data source. In these cases, the column values have to be treated the same as the system data types from which they derive their definition.

Using the New Type

After you create the type, it can be used in the database in which its definition exists. With the `Create Table` command in SQL, the inventoryNum data type you created in the last section can be used as follows:

```
create table bulkitems
   ( productid int identity,
     productName varchar(30),
     description varchar(120),
     qtyInStock inventoryNum,
     qtyBackOrdered int )
```

The inventoryNum type was created so that columns set to that type don't allow null values. This setting ensures that all of the inventory counts must have some number, even if that number is zero.

> **NOTE:** Use the limitation of nulls judiciously. By eliminating nulls, you can minimize the amount of potential client errors that can be generated when attempting to use a value from a column in which it is not allowed (such as when using the + string-concatenation operator). However, eliminating nulls may increase the storage requirements of the database.

To examine which UDTs exist on the current database, you can use the `sp_datatype_info` procedure to return information on all of the data types. It returns a recordset with rows describing each data type. The columns contain the properties of each type.

Binding a Default to a UDT

You can bind a user-defined type to a default object. When a default value is set in the defined type, columns use this value when a new record is first created, unless a value is entered for that column. Be aware that when you are creating a new table in the Enterprise Manager or Microsoft Access, a column defined with a UDT bound to a default will not automatically display the default value in the Database Designer. Nonetheless, the bound default value will be enabled for that column.

You can create a new default object that can hold a value of almost any available data type (except the timestamp, cursor, text, and image data types). Code to create a numeric default value for the inventoryNum data type looks like this:

```
Create Default defInvNum As 0
```

To bind the newly created default to the inventoryNum data type that was defined earlier, you can use the `sp_bindefault` command, as follows:

```
Execute sp_bindefault 'defInvNum', 'inventoryNum'
```

> **Note:** The single letter *D* in the `sp_bindefault` command (instead of `sp_binddefault`) is not a spelling error in this book. The system stored procedure is defined with this name.

From Enterprise Manager, you can add a default and bind it to a UDT. Simply expand the database in which you want the rule added and right-click the Default item. Select the New Default option from the context menu. You can then enter the name and text of the default to be created. Clicking the Bind UDTs button enables you to select the type of UDT in which the default will be bound.

Binding a Rule to a UDT

A rule can be bound to a new type to allow automated formatting or data checking to be performed before a value is accepted into a column defined with that type. Only one rule may be bound to a UDT, but the same rule can be bound to multiple UDTs or columns.

> **Note:** Under most conditions, Microsoft recommends defining check constraints with the `Create Table` command, instead of creating a rule. Although only a single rule may be placed on a column or UDT, multiple check constraints can be used. However, a check constraint cannot be bound to a UDT and must be set with each table. Therefore, rules must be used for limitations on a new type.

A rule is activated every time either the `Insert` or `Update` SQL command is called and the data that is entered into a column is checked against the most recently bound rule. A rule is created with the `Create Rule` statement in the T-SQL language. After the rule has been created, it can be bound using the `sp_bindrule` routine, which enables a rule to be bound to either a UDT or a column within a table. Information relating to the binding will be stored in the syscolumns and systypes tables in the master database.

The code for a rule can be any logic that could be used in the `Where` clause of a `Select` statement that does not reference database objects (columns, other tables, and so on). To add a rule to the inventoryNum type, the rule must first be created with code like this:

```
Create Rule minRangeRule
As
@value > 0
```

This rule contains a simple mathematical evaluation to ensure that the value bound to the rule is greater than zero. The value that is entered for a column that is bound to this rule is passed to the rule through the `@value` variable. This example creates a rule that can be used with the inventoryNum UDT that you created. Because the inventoryNum UDT is used for inventory quantities, a column of this type can never have less than zero items stored in it. If a sale needs to be made on an item not in stock, that value can be placed in the qtyBackOrdered column of the table.

> **Note:** Data existing before the binding occurs is not processed by the rule. Therefore, a table may contain data that does not conform to the rule if the binding occurred after the data was entered. Only if the rule was present when the table was created can you be assured that all data was checked by the rule.

In a rule, you can use arithmetic operators (+, -, /, *, and so on), relational operators (=, !=, and so on), Boolean operators (`And`, `Or`, `Not`, and so on), and predicates (`In`, `Between`, `Like`, and so on). All of these operators for a rule must be compatible with the data type that the UDT represents. For an improper data comparison, an error will occur during the `Insert` or `Update` operation, not when the rule is being defined, because until the rule is bound, it is unknown to the MSDE engine. A rule cannot be defined for a data type that would be a text, image, or timestamp column type.

The `sp_bindrule` system stored procedure is used to bind the rule to a column or a user-defined data type. The general syntax for this procedure appears as follows:

```
sp_bindrule [@rulename =] 'rule',
    [@objname =] 'object_name'
    [, [@futureonly =] 'futureonly_flag']
```

To bind the minRangeRule to the inventoryNum data type, you can execute this code:

```
Execute sp_bindrule 'minRangeRule', 'inventoryNum'
```

Chapter 17: Creating User-Defined Data Types

A rule can be eliminated by using the `Drop Rule` command. Because the name of each rule must be unique, you must drop a rule before it may be redefined. If already bound, the definition also has to be unbound before the drop process can be initiated.

You can also bind a rule in the Enterprise Manager. Simply expand the database to which you want the rule added and right-click the Rule item. Select the New Rule option from the context menu. You can then enter the name and text of the rule to be created. Clicking the Bind UDTs button enables you to select the type of UDT to which the rule will be bound.

To display the code contained in a rule, execute the `sp_helptext` function followed by the name of the rule. When examining the results of an execution on an existing rule, the text will be returned as a number of rows (one for each line defined by a carriage return) stored in a column named *text*. To obtain the text of the minRangeRule, you can execute the following code:

```
Execute sp_helptext minRangeRule
```

The `sp_unbindrule` will unbind the rule from the current data type or column. The syntax for this stored procedure appears like this:

```
sp_unbindrule [@objname =] 'object_name'
   [, [@futureonly =] 'futureonly_flag']
```

In the preceding code, the `@objname` parameter specifies which object the rule will unbind. In this case, that would be the name of the UDT that is currently bound to a rule. The `@futureonly` leaves all the existing tables containing the UDT bound to the rule, but eliminates the binding from occurring on future table creation with the user type.

After the rule is bound, it cannot be dropped until it is unbound, as follows:

```
Execute sp_unbindrule 'inventoryNum', 'futureonly'
```

Binding a new rule to a column or UDT overrides the previously bound rule. A rule bound directly to a column takes precedence over a rule that is bound to a UDT used to create that column.

> **TIP** Although defining new types can be useful in many circumstances, try to limit the number of new type definitions for a database. Too many definitions of custom types makes code difficult to read, often requiring references back to the type definition to determine what values will be accepted by the type.

If a default value is bound to a UDT, the value must comply with the rule. When the default value violates the rule, an error will be generated each time an attempt is made to add a new row to the table.

With the In keyword, the value inserted can be checked against a list of values to determine whether it is valid. You can use a rule coded like this:

```
CREATE RULE list_rule
AS
@list IN ('1389', '0736', '0877')
```

For phone numbers or ZIP codes that need to be stored in a particular format, you can use a rule similar to the following:

```
CREATE RULE pattern_rule
AS
@value LIKE '_ _-%[0-9]'
```

Although multiple rules cannot be assigned to a single column, you can create a rule that takes into account several different checks, by using Boolean checks.

```
CREATE RULE Boolean_rule
AS
@value > 0 And @value < 100
```

Using rules can greatly increase the integrity of a database by making certain that incorrect values are never entered. By adding this logic on the server rather than in the client code, the entire application protects this integrity.

Summary

A user-defined type can be defined on an individual database, or placed in the model database for availability to all databases. Each new type may be used to enforce constraints, standardization, and clarification of table definitions. In this chapter, you covered the following:

♦ **User-defined data types (UDTs):** A UDT is a new data type made from one of the existing system data types. A UDT may be used effectively to enforce data-format or structure rules on data to be entered into a table that has columns defined with the new data type. A UDT can provide standardization of a column type throughout the database.

- **Limitations of UDTs:** Although a UDT can mirror most data types, the timestamp type cannot be used for a UDT definition. Additionally, each newly defined type is stored in the database in which it was created and is available only within that database unless it is stored in the model database. In the model database, it can be used in any table on the database server.

- **sp_addtype:** This stored procedure adds the type to the database with three parameters: the name of the new type, the system data type on which it will be based, and whether nulls will be accepted in a column defined as the type.

- **Binding to a rule:** A UDT may be bound to a rule to enforce some form of data checking. The rule can execute any expression that could be used as a Where clause of a Select statement as long as no database objects (other tables, databases, and so forth) are addressed by the code.

- **Binding to a default:** Default values may be bound to a UDT to supply a value to a column when a new row is created. If a rule is bound to the UDT, the default value must comply with the rule; otherwise, an error will be generated each time a new row is inserted.

Part III

Advanced MSDE

CHAPTER 18
Monitoring MSDE

CHAPTER 19
Working with SQL Server Agent

CHAPTER 20
Accessing the Web with Remote Data Services

CHAPTER 21
Tuning for Optimum Performance

CHAPTER 22
Working with MSDE Logs

CHAPTER 23
Moving Data Into and Out of MSDE

CHAPTER 24
Using Stored Procedures in MSDE

CHAPTER 25
Implementing Security

Chapter 18

Monitoring MSDE

IN THIS CHAPTER

- Monitoring with Transact-SQL
- Monitoring with SQL-DMO and VBA
- Using the Current Activity window in Enterprise Manager
- Working with Windows NT Performance Monitor
- Monitoring replication
- Monitoring through the log files
- Using SQL Server Profiler

AN MSDE SERVER IS VERY different from a database engine such as Access because the execution of the engine itself can be fine-tuned to streamline performance. Everything from cache sizes to transaction log maintenance can be adjusted so that the highest average throughput is achieved. To properly set the configuration properties, however, you first need to be able to determine the processing that takes place.

Examining the database server activity under deployment conditions is critical to successfully understanding what is actually occurring on the server and what resources can be optimized for best performance. Many real-time methods of monitoring activity on an MSDE server are available. You can use Transact-SQL, SQL-DMO, Enterprise Manager, Performance Monitor, Replication Monitor, and log files to view different aspects of the server performance.

Monitoring with Transact-SQL

For MSDE deployment, perhaps the easiest way to check the server operation is through Transact-SQL statements. Several stored procedures address the current state of the MSDE server. The following are some of the key system stored procedures for MSDE server status:

- **sp_monitor:** The most commonly used procedure, it display statistics such as reading, writing, and processor usage.
- **sp_lock:** Displays current locks that are active on the MSDE server.

- **sp_who:** Displays the current users logged in to the database server and the operations they are requesting to be performed.
- **sp_spaceused:** Displays the size of database objects.

Through the use of these four procedures, you can look at the activity statistics of the MSDE server for current locks, users, command batch, size of databases and tables, size of the transaction log, current and last active transactions, and performance information for memory or network throughput.

Monitoring General Performance: sp_monitor

The `sp_monitor` procedure is the central system stored procedure used to examine MSDE statistics. The procedure returns a table of current server process values with information for each parameter stored in an individual column.

When the `sp_monitor` routine is executed, it returns results such as the following:

```
last_run                    current_run                 seconds
-------------------------   -------------------------   -------
2000-02-10 12:06:18.570     2000-02-10 12:07:25.350     67

cpu_busy                    io_busy                     idle
-------------------------   -------------------------   -----------
0(0)-0%                     0(0)-0%                     0(0)-0%

packets_received            packets_sent                packet_errors
-------------------------   -------------------------   -------------
31(19)                      30(19)                      0(0)

total_read          total_write         total_errors        connections
------------------  ------------------  ------------------  -----------
500(6)              137(4)              0(0)                14(2)
```

From this example data, you can see that many of the columns contain two numbers — one contained within parentheses and another outside of them. The number outside the parentheses indicates the value since the database server was last started (or rebooted). Inside the parentheses, the numbers show the values since the last time `sp_monitor` was executed. Some of the columns (cpu_busy, io_busy, and idle) also contain the percentage of the total processor time.

This returned information uses formatting commands, so when examining the result set in Microsoft Query, only the first three columns (last_run, current_run, and seconds) are displayed in the data grid. To see the complete data set, you need to use either a tool that accepts and displays the formatting, such as the SQL Query Analyzer, or you need to access the row entries directly through the ADO Recordset or Command objects.

Table 18-1 lists and describes the columns returned by the `sp_monitor` execution.

Chapter 18: Monitoring MSDE

TABLE 18-1 COLUMNS RETURNED BY EXECUTION OF SP_MONITOR

Column	Identifies
last_run	Time of last execution of the `sp_monitor` procedure
current_run	Time of current execution of `sp_monitor`
seconds	Number of seconds between the last_run and the current_run
cpu_busy	Amount of CPU time, in seconds, currently dedicated to MSDE server processing
io_busy	Amount of input and output that occurs on the MSDE server
idle	Number of seconds that MSDE is idle
packets_received	Number of packets received by the MSDE server
packets_sent	Number of packets sent by the MSDE server
packet_errors	Number of errors generated by packet transmission
total_read	Total number of reads on the MSDE server
total_write	Total number of writes on the MSDE server
total_errors	Total errors generated by the reads and writes
connections	Current number of connections open to the MSDE server

The returned information can be filtered so that none of the idle events are displayed, to maximize the amount of useful data returned (increase the signal-to-noise ratio). In addition to the stored procedures that return information concerning the MSDE processes, some system variables also contain data related to current conditions. Several variables provide individual access to the statistical information displayed using the `sp_monitor` procedure. The `@@CPU_BUSY` variable holds the amount of processor time being used by the database server.

The following are the variables holding system-related information:

@@CPU_BUSY

@@PACKET_ERRORS

@@IDLE

@@TIMETICKS

@@IO_BUSY

@@TOTAL_ERRORS

@@PACK_RECEIVED

@@TOTAL_READ

@@PACK_SENT

@@TOTAL_WRITE

All of these variables contain values for activity since the database server was last started. They do not provide the same data as the sp_monitor routine, which returns values of activity only since the procedure was last executed. These variables can therefore provide a better overview of general system performance.

Another variable, @@Fetch_Status, holds a value indicating the status of the last database fetch that was executed against a cursor on the currently open database. The returned values indicate success (0), failure (-1), or failure because the requested rows were missing (-2). The returned status is global to the current command execution, so this status must be checked immediately after the fetch operation to ensure that it is related to the desired operation. If other parts of the program make calls, including stored procedure calls, the status may reflect the results of the calls instead of the intended operation. The server-side cursors and the Fetch statements related to them often occur implicitly, because most applications let a framework such as ADO handle the cursor management and manipulation.

The variables available for each of the system statistics can be returned through a simple Select statement like this:

```
Select @@cpu_busy
```

Executing this statement returns a set that contains a single column with the statistic's value:

```
@@cpu_busy
10
```

Using sp_who for User Information

The sp_who procedure returns information on users who are currently using the database server or servers currently logged (as replication communication). With Transact-SQL, the sp_who procedure can return information about users and processes that are executing on the server.

The sp_who procedure is used, from the master database, like this:

```
sp_who
```

This returns a data set like this:

```
spid       status   loginame   hostname   blk   dbname              cmd
   1     sleeping         sa   THINKPAD     0   master   SIGNAL HANDLER
   2   background         sa   THINKPAD     0   master     LOCK MONITOR
```

To enter a filter for this procedure, use the `Active` keyword as a login name:

```
sp_who 'active'
```

You can use this procedure to look at traffic for a particular user by passing the name of that user, as follows:

```
sp_who 'myusername'
```

Instead of a username, a process ID can be passed:

```
sp_who '10'
```

> **Note:** Numeric values, such as a process ID, need to be passed as a string. Therefore, make sure that they are encapsulated within the apostrophe (') prefix and suffix.

Monitoring with SQL-DMO and VBA

Through the DMO objects, most of the activity that occurs on the MSDE server can be watched. In fact, monitoring the performance of the database through the DMO framework is more flexible than Transact-SQL access, because it can be handled in real time. Using the Database objects of the model, the database server may enumerate many of the ongoing database processes that occur, including user logins, locks, groups, files, and so forth.

The following are the routines available to retrieve for enumerated values from the Database object:

- **EnumCandidateKeys:** Provides the tables of a database and the constraints to those tables that define primary keys.

- **EnumDependencies:** Contains the database user objects and the dependencies of those objects. The dependencies include rules, declarative referential integrity settings, and other structures.

- **EnumFileGroups:** Returns all the file groups defined in the MSDE server.

Part III: Advanced MSDE

- **EnumFiles:** Enumerates the available files that the current database uses for data storage.
- **EnumLocks:** Contains the resource locks for the current MSDE server.
- **EnumLoginMappings:** Lists the logins and the database users who are related to those mappings.
- **EnumNTGroups:** Lists the available NT groups that are currently transferred from the OS to the database in an integrated or mixed mode of security.
- **EnumUsers:** Lists the available users who are currently available to the database.

To create an application to examine the users on the MSDE server, follow these steps:

1. Execute Microsoft Access 2000.
2. Create a new MDB database named **MSDEmonitor.MDB**.
3. Add a form to this project.
4. Under the Tools menu, select the References option, check the Microsoft SQLDMO library item, and click the OK button. This selection adds to this project the SQL-DMO object model needed by the program.
5. On the form, add a command button and set the name of the button to **cmdGetLocks**.
6. Open the Click event for the cmdGetLocks button and enter the following code:

```
Private Sub cmdGetLocks_Click()
    Dim myMSDE As SQLDMO.SQLServer
    Dim myDB As SQLDMO.Database
    Dim myServerName As String, myUsername As String
    Dim myPwd As String
    Dim dbList As String
    Dim myResults As QueryResults
    Dim tablefields As String
    Dim i, j As Integer

    myServerName = "."
    myUsername = "sa": myPwd = ""
    On Error GoTo ProblemGDB

    Set myMSDE = CreateObject("SQLDMO.SQLServer")
    myMSDE.Connect myServerName, myUsername, myPwd
```

```
' Create a reference to the NorthwindSQL database
Set myDB = myMSDE.Databases("NorthwindSQL")
' Clear the string that will hold the field values
tablefields = ""
' Cycle through all of the locks for the myDB
For i = 1 To myDB.EnumLocks.Rows
    tablefields = tablefields & i & ") "
    ' Step through the columns
    For j = 1 To myDB.EnumLocks.Columns
        Select Case myDB.EnumLocks.ColumnType(j)
            ' Add the various data types to the strings
            Case SQLDMO_DTypeUVarchar
                tablefields = tablefields & _
                myDB.EnumLocks.ColumnName(j) & ":" & _
                myDB.EnumLocks.GetColumnString(i, j) & ", "
            Case SQLDMO_DTypeInt1
                tablefields = tablefields & _
                myDB.EnumLocks.ColumnName(j) & ":" & _
                myDB.EnumLocks.GetColumnLong(i, j) & ", "
            Case SQLDMO_DTypeInt4
                tablefields = tablefields & _
                myDB.EnumLocks.ColumnName(j) & ":" & _
                myDB.EnumLocks.GetColumnLong(i, j) & ", "
        End Select
    Next
    ' Introduce a carriage return for display
    tablefields = tablefields & Chr(13)
Next
' Display all of the available locks
MsgBox "Lock status of " & myDB.Name & ": " & Chr(13) & _
    tablefields, vbInformation, "Current Northwind locks"
Exit Sub

ProblemGDB:
    MsgBox "MSDE Error: " & Err.Description, _
    vbExclamation, "MSDE Error"

End Sub
```

7. Save the form as **MSDEMonitor**, enter the execution mode, and click the button.

After the application is complete, you may run it to examine the current locks for the MSDE server. This skeleton of code can be augmented to display the other enumerated types available through the database object.

Using the Current Activity Window in Enterprise Manager

The Enterprise Manager is an advanced graphical tool for monitoring operations that are occurring on the MSDE server. From the Activity window in the Enterprise Manager, you can watch current users, processes, and locks that are executing on the server. Enterprise Manager has three different status reports you can watch: Process Info, Locks per Process ID, and Locks per Object.

Management of the MSDE server occurs through the Microsoft Management Console (MMC), so you need to execute this console to examine the monitors.

1. Execute the Enterprise Manager.

2. Expand the MSDE server item and the Management folder inside.

3. Within the Management folder, expand the Current Activity folder, which shows the three different status monitors that are available.

4. Click the Process Info icon (see Figure 18-1). All the processes currently active on the MSDE server are individually listed.

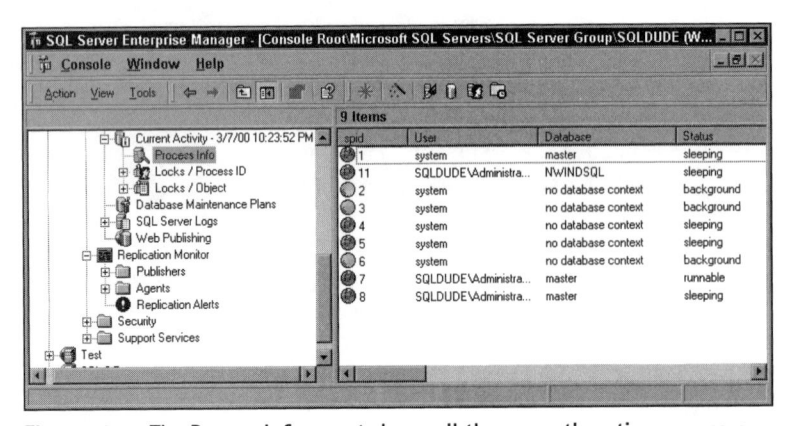

Figure 18-1: The Process Info report shows all the currently active processes.

5. Click the Locks/Process ID icon (see Figure 18-2), which displays all the current locks that are sorted by process ID.

6. Click the Locks/Object icon, which displays all the current locks that are sorted by the objects that own each lock. In Figure 18-3, the master object is selected and the details pane is displaying all the locks related to it.

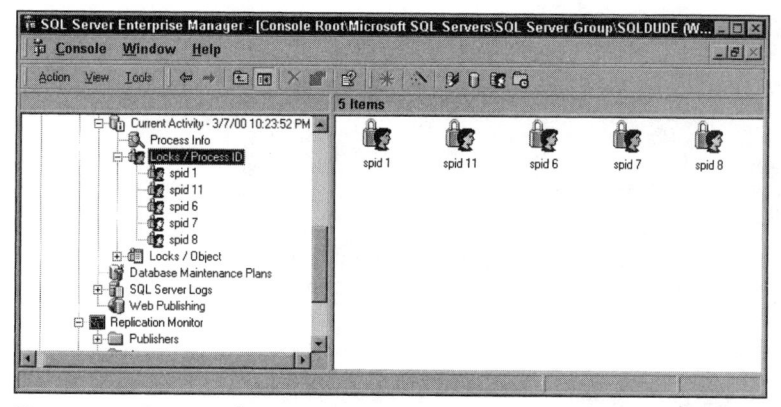

Figure 18-2: The Locks/Process ID report shows all the currently active locks.

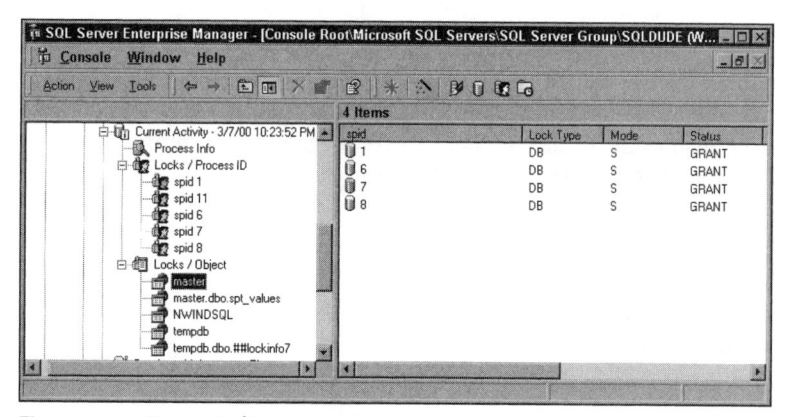

Figure 18-3: The Locks/Object report also shows all the currently active locks.

The current activity for each of these three areas is not updated automatically. You must select the Refresh option from the context menu for the update.

Working with Windows NT Performance Monitor

If you are running the MSDE server on a Windows NT installation, you can set up various activities to monitor from within the Performance Monitor utility. The Performance Monitor can examine activity on the machine it is currently executing upon, or on any other trusted NT machine on the LAN (see Figure 18-4).

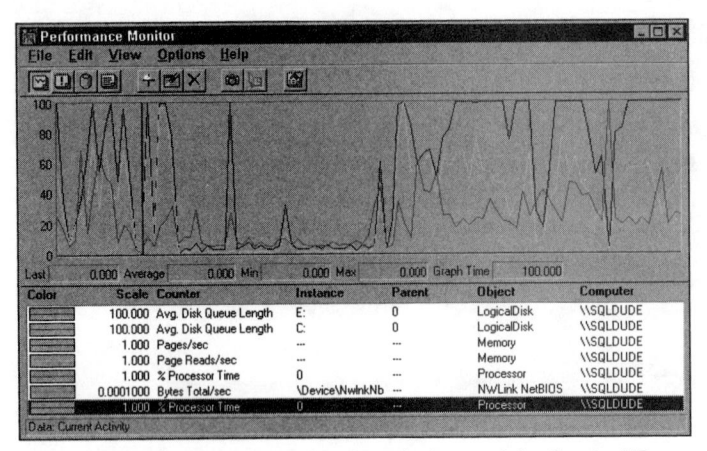

Figure 18-4: The Performance Monitor displays activity for the NT server.

The Performance Monitor provides numerous important statistics to determine how the server that MSDE is executing on is actually performing. Vital information, such as network statistics, memory access, virtual memory paging, and process execution, can be displayed on a real-time graphical chart. The information can also be saved to a disk log for later examination and analysis.

> **Note:** Windows 98 includes the System Monitor program, which can be used to monitor network traffic in much the same way that the Performance Monitor allows. The System Monitor can be found in the Start menu under the Programs → Accessories → System Tools menu.

The indicators of the Performance Monitor that are important to effective MSDE execution are divided into these categories:

- **Cache:** Displays statistics for reads and writes from the cache. When the cache needs to be flushed to disk, performance is impeded. Indicators enable cache information to be displayed, including synchronous and asynchronous reads and writes, copy reads and writes, and lazy writes.

- **Logical Disk:** Shows the logical drive allocations made on the server that have read and write capabilities, including hard drives, partitions, and so forth. These drives will each have a letter allocation, such as C:, D:, Z:, and so on.

- **Memory:** Indicates processes related to memory, usage, paging to the hard drive, and page faults.

- **Paging File:** Indicates the activity of the file on a designated drive that provides virtual memory paging. The more often paging is used, the worse the performance of the server.

- **Physical Disk:** Displays any physical drives configured for use by the system.

- **Process:** Shows any processes currently running on the machine. For MSDE server, processes available include `SQLMangr` and `SQLServr`.

- **Processor:** Indicates factors that are related to the processor, such as percentage in use, interrupts per second, user time. Also any interrupt errors caused by either deferred procedure calls (DPC) or asynchronous procedure calls (APC) can be displayed.

- **Server:** Shows activity related to server operations. Most of these properties denote operations that NT is handling as a print, file, or application server and are not directly related to MSDE operation. However, server activity can be judged in relation to database server performance if the server is not strictly dedicated to database handling.

- **System:** Displays performance information of the system itself, including processor times, active user time, registry access values, file control, interrupts, and other related activities.

- **Thread:** Displays statistics for individual thread activity. The name of each instance of a thread is preceded with the process from which the thread was spawned. Each thread will be sequentially named: `SQLMangr ==> 0`, `SQLMangr ==> 1`, and so on.

To examine server activity, follow these steps:

1. Execute the Performance Monitor from the Start menu under the Administrative Tools → Performance Monitor option.

2. Click the Add Counter button on the toolbar or select the Add To Chart option under the Edit menu to add an activity to monitor. From this window, multiple indicators may be added to the current chart before it is closed. The various categories available for monitoring are listed in the Object drop-down list box (see Figure 18-5).

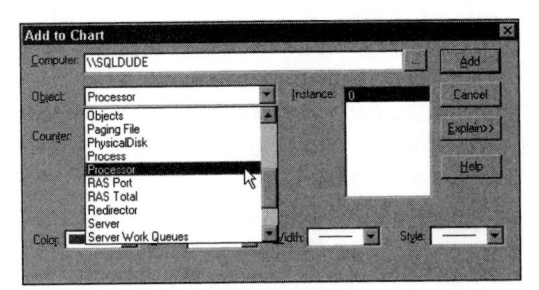

Figure 18-5: Categories of indicators are listed in the Object drop-down list box.

The indicators that you decide to add for monitoring will depend on what parts of the system you believe need to be examined most closely. Generally, the two most important areas that should be examined for MSDE performance are disk access statistics and process execution.

Monitoring Disk Access

The Windows NT operating system uses a queue for disk access requests when more requests occur than can be handled immediately by the OS. Whenever queuing occurs, performance is lost, particularly when running a database server environment such as MSDE. You can monitor the number of queuing requests that occur on the system and determine whether disk access needs to be altered.

To enable disk checking, you must first activate the disk counter functions to give the monitoring tools access to a statistic to report. Activation is done at the command line using this command:

```
diskperf -y
```

After the command has been executed, you need to reboot your NT system for the disk performance reporting to take effect. After you reboot your NT system, the Performance Monitor includes several options to examine the values created by the counter. These selections include:

- ◆ **Current disk queue:** The current level of disk queuing occurring on the system.

- ◆ **Average disk queue:** A more useful statistic, because it averages all disk queues since it was added to the Performance Monitor. The longer you leave this statistic running, the better idea you will have of the actual amount of queuing that occurs in a situation.

These options will be listed under headings for both logical and physical drives. Logical drives denote the operating system designations (such as C:, D:, and so forth) for physical drives, partitions, and RAID allocations. The physical drives information relates directly to the actual physical drives that can be seen in the Disk Administrator utility in the Administrative Tools menu. If the RAID drives are created with hardware interfaces, the disk counter values have to be divided by the number of drives in the RAID to determine the actual physical queuing number.

After you complete all monitoring, make sure you execute the command to turn off this counter:

```
diskperf -n
```

The Disk Bytes/Sec and Disk Transfers/Sec indicators provide overall disk performance readings. These can provide valuable information to indicate whether you need faster drive performance, more memory, or additional processor power.

Processor Queue Length

The Processor queue length indicator indicates when the microprocessor of the server system is receiving more requests than it can handle and therefore must queue these requests. Most well-performing single-processor systems have some queue level length, because even a very powerful processor cannot handle all requests instantaneously.

A good average queue length is around 2 requests. If the queue is substantially longer than 2 requests waiting, either a bottleneck exists somewhere in the server system or a faster processor is required. On many smaller servers, you will find that the primary bottleneck for processing is simply a lack of server RAM that makes virtual memory paging occur often. This problem strains both server and disk resources.

The following are three of the indicators available through the Performance Monitor of virtual memory paging:

- **Memory: Pages/Sec:** Displays information about the extra memory which is being requested that is not available in physical RAM. Watching this value provides an indication of how often virtual memory is needed. For best performance, this value should be close to zero.

- **Memory: Page Faults/Sec:** Shows the requests for pages of memory that is located in physical RAM, but must be swapped into a useable area. Page faults of this type are most likely caused by the MSDE server, if it is not running on a dedicated machine.

- **Process: Page Faults/Sec (for SQLSERVR process):** Shows the page faults caused by the MSDE server.

After observing these indicators, you will be able to accurately judge whether augmenting the memory resources of the server will increase performance. In my personal experience with MSDE and SQL Server, I have found that, in many situations, extra memory can speed database processing far more than increased processor or drive speed can. Increasing the amount of memory may mean that common data can be cached, making responses lightning-fast.

If many page faults are occurring in the SQLSERVR process, the working memory set should be configured to be exactly the same as the memory allocated to the MSDE server. This can be accomplished with the following Transact-SQL command:

```
sp_configure 'set working set size', 1
```

Monitoring Replication

From the Replication Monitor utility available in the Enterprise Manager, you can examine the publishers, agents, and replication alerts. For monitoring agents, the Agent History window displays information related to the activity of replication. Preset monitoring includes: All Sessions, Sessions in the last 24 hours, Sessions in the last 2 days, Sessions in the last seven days, and Sessions with errors. The information for these presets is presented in several columns in the Agent History window.

Some of the monitoring factors include: Status; # of actions; Action Message; Start Time; End Time; Duration; Delivery rate; Latency, # Trans; # Cmds; Publisher inserts, updates, deletes, & conflicts; and Subscriber inserts, updates, deletes, & conflicts.

In the Enterprise Manager, you can monitor replication events such as the following:

- Alerts created by replication events
- Replication agent scheduling, history, and execution
- Distributor lists of publishers, publications, subscribers, and subscriptions

These monitoring features are available only to the machine that has distribution capabilities by a user who is a member of the sysadmin group (or role). Replication monitoring is usually a standard management practice that has less tuning to accomplish and more general system process activity inspection.

Monitoring Through the Log Files

The MSDE server keeps several logs that can help you to examine the system and optimize performance. In the Log directory of the MSSQL7 folder, all of the log entries kept by the SQL Server engine are stored in files with the name ErrorLog. The SQL Server Agent stores its own log information in files named SqlAgent. The logs can be examined to monitor events in non-real time.

Additional logs exist for long-running queries and ODBC connections. Detailed information on all of these log files is included in Chapter 22, in addition to an extensive description of the structure and features of the transaction log.

Using SQL Server Profiler

Included in the complete SQL Server installation is a tool known as the SQL Server Profiler that provides real-time tracing of various aspects of SQL database execution. You can access the SQL Server Profiler from the Tools menu of the Enterprise Manager. The Profiler is a separate tool and executes outside the MMC in which the Enterprise Manager exists.

To create a new trace in SQL Server Profiler, follow these steps:

1. Execute the Enterprise Manager.

2. Under the Tools menu, select the SQL Server Profiler option to display SQL Server Profiler.

3. Select the New Trace option under the File menu. You will see the Trace Properties dialog box (see Figure 18-6) for the primary trace properties.

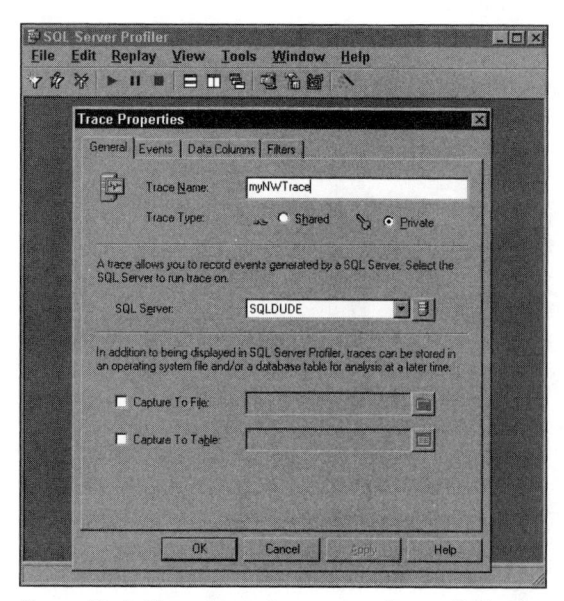

Figure 18-6: The primary trace properties available through SQL Server Profiler

4. Select the Events tab (see Figure 18-7) and expand the Cursors item.

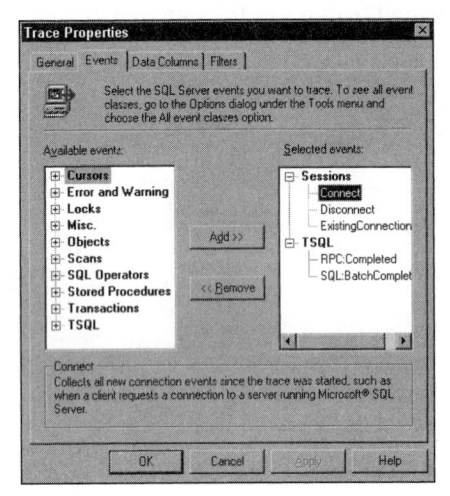

Figure 18-7: The Events tab of the current trace

5. Select the Data Columns tab (see Figure 18-8). All the available data types will be shown to select data types.

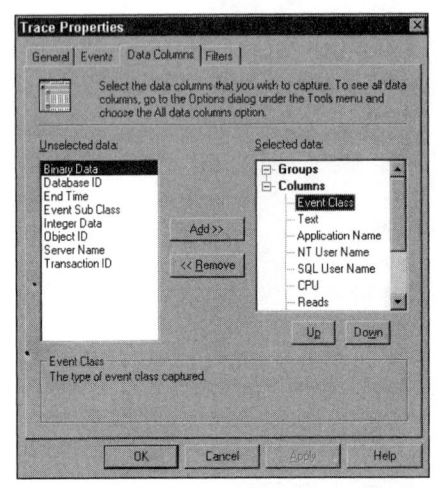

Figure 18-8: The Data Columns tab displays the columns and types for trace.

6. Select the Filters tab (see Figure 18-9) and expand the Cursors item under the proper database entry.

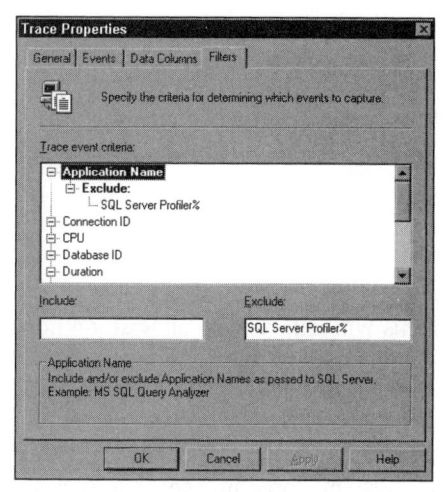

Figure 18-9: The filters to refine the data returned by the trace

7. Click the OK button to begin the trace execution. You will see all the events that occur for the trace in the Private Trace window (see Figure 18-10).

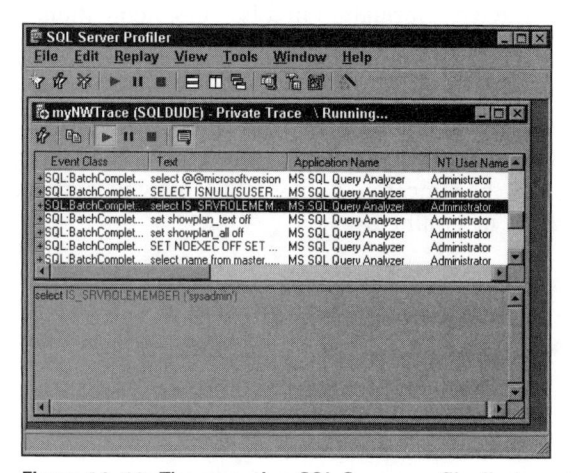

Figure 18-10: The executing SQL Server profile displays all the events monitored by the trace.

The SQL Server Profiler can be used to watch everything from client access to index execution. This information can be recorded into a trace file for examination. Because this tool can monitor all of these variables in real time, it can be used effectively on a deployment server to watch the actual events that are occurring. Especially during peak MSDE access, this information can help you to determine the parts of your system (databases, indexes, and so forth) that can most benefit from tuning.

Summary

By monitoring the operations taking place on your MSDE server, you can see the actual functioning of the server, and this will help you to understand how to optimize performance. In this chapter, you covered the following:

- **Transact-SQL monitoring:** Through various stored procedures, you can retrieve information on the current execution status of processes on the MSDE server. The `sp_monitor` system stored procedure provides valuable statistical information on MSDE processes.

- **Enterprise Manager:** Provides a graphical method of examining Transact-SQL activity. Factors such as processes locks can be viewed in real time from the Current Activity window.

- **SQL Server Profiler:** The tool included with SQL Server enables you to profile and trace events and processes on the MSDE server. It can record all the selected and filtered information in a log for examination.

- **Performance Monitor:** The Performance Monitor utility included with the Windows NT operating system enables you to add various indicators for charting. These indicators relate to memory, processors, processes, instances, and other resources affected on the server. By examining the live data displayed by the indicators during MSDE activity, bottlenecks to performance can be determined.

Chapter 19

Working with SQL Server Agent

IN THIS CHAPTER

- Understanding how the SQL Server agent works
- Programming the agent
- Using the Enterprise Manager
- Examining the agent log
- Grouping objects in categories
- Scheduling

IN MICROSOFT ACCESS, CREATING an application that automatically performs tasks according to a time schedule is very difficult. If the application is closed at the time the task is to occur, it won't be executed. Because Access is entirely processed on the client side, it is difficult to coordinate automated tasks for many different processes.

On an MSDE server, there is no problem creating time-based automated tasks that execute. Because the server is always running, you can schedule any tasks to be activated either in sync with events that occur or according to a day/date/time schedule. On the MSDE server, a technology called the SQL Server Agent can act autonomously to execute operations. For scheduled tasks, you can assign an agent to perform it.

How SQL Server Agent Works

In Chapter 13, you briefly used the SQL Server Agent to execute the steps of a package created with the Data Transformation Services (DTS). The agent can be used for much more than DTS operations. Nearly any operation related to the MSDE server can be activated using a set of operational tasks defined in the agent.

Some of the tasks that may be used with the agent include:

- **Executing package operations:** Any package located on the MSDE server can be executed either wholly or in part by an agent.

- **Monitoring processes of the MSDE server:** Because agents are always executing, an agent can be created to monitor the operations on the database server.
- **Firing alerts:** In response to an event or the results of executing job steps, the agent can fire an alert, issue an e-mail message, call a pager, store a message in a log, or otherwise signal special events.

The Enterprise Manager contains an Agents folder that holds all of the agents currently installed on the system and their current execution status. The SQL Server Agent is a service that executes separately from the MSDE server. Therefore, if it is not already installed to start up on system boot, then you will have to activate it before it can be used.

Starting the SQL Server Agent

There are several methods for starting the SQL Server Agent, much as there are for starting the MSDE server. The four primary methods for activating the agent are:

- **Service Manager:** The Service Manager, in addition to allowing Start, Pause, and Stop commands to be issued for the MSDE server, can do the same for the SQL Server Agent. By selecting the agent under the Services combo box in the application, you can use the control buttons for command.
- **Enterprise Manager:** The Enterprise Manager can be used to configure and activate the agent through properties and wizards.
- **sqlagent executable:** From the command line, the sqlagent utility may execute the agent, primarily for debugging purposes.
- **Command line through the net send command:** On the Windows NT platform, a `net send` command can begin agent execution.

Using the Service Manager is the most common method of starting the server, although the other methods have some advantages such as context (if you're already in the Enterprise Manager) or batch execution (for the command line forms).

USING THE SERVICE MANAGER FOR STARTUP

For the MSDE server, you can use the Service Manager to activate the agent. To begin the SQL Server Agent, follow these steps:

1. Under the Start menu, execute the Service Manager under the Programs → MSDE menu.
2. Select the SQLServerAgent option (see Figure 19-1) from the list so that the status of the agent will be displayed.

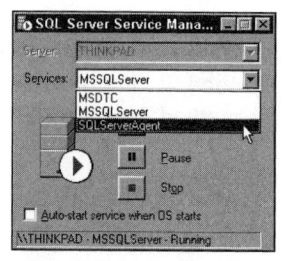

Figure 19-1: The Services combo box can be set to SQLServerAgent to start the agent service.

3. Click the green right-arrow to start the SQLServerAgent service.

You can also access the Service Manager from the system tray by right-clicking the MSDE status icon and selecting the Open SQL Server Service Manager option. From the system tray, you do not even need to show the Service Manager for agent activation. Instead, you can select it directly from the tray menus.

When you right-click the system tray MSDE icon, a context menu will be displayed that contains the Current service on \\MyMachine menu, which allows selection of the SQLServerAgent option. When this option is selected, the context menu and the tray icon will reflect the current settings of the agent. The option on the context menu titled SQLServerAgent – Start will launch the agent.

USING NET SEND FOR STARTUP
To start the agent from the console in Windows NT, you can use this command:

```
net start SQLServerAgent
```

or

```
net start MSsqlserver
```

You can also use the pause, stop, and continue commands (`net pause`, `net stop`, `net continue`) to manage the agent service.

USING THE COMMAND LINE FOR STARTUP
An application called sqlagent can execute the agent for access from the command line. The command-line task window must remain open while this program is executing and cannot be controlled by the Service Manager. Using this method, the agent is started as a program rather than a direct service. It is important to start the agent as a service so that logging of the current user will not shut down the service.

You can use the sqlagent application when debugging by executing this command at the console:

```
sqlagent -c -v
```

The -v switch turns on the verbose mode, which writes the diagnostic information, automatically written to the SQL Server Agent log, into the command prompt window. When the agent is activated through this method, it cannot be controlled through the Service Manager. Therefore, only use this method for starting the agent when you need to use it for debugging.

> **Note:** The MSDE server itself can be started manually using this command: `sqlservr -c`. Note that this command must be executed from the Binn directory of the folder that contains MSDE. Also, this command will run MSDE as a program that can be terminated by a Ctrl+C. Because it takes the command line, it is best not to use this form when running the SQL Agent.

Executing the agent through this method will require the console window to remain open. The agent can be stopped by pressing Ctrl+C, which will halt execution of the sqlagent executable.

Working with Replication Agents

There are several agents specifically available to automate the replication tasks. These agents can be configured at the time a push or pull subscription is created. For each of the replication types, there are agents that handle the subscriptions and the distribution activities.

When a distribution database is first created, agent cleanup, transaction cleanup, and history cleanup tasks are automatically added to the distribution server. It is for these agents that the wizard instructs you to make sure the SQL Server Agent service is active on the server that handles distribution.

How the Snapshot Agent Works

The Snapshot agent creates all of the key pieces of a snapshot of a publication. It creates the initial snapshot of tables and stored procedures. All of the information from the replicated data is selected and placed on the distribution server by this agent. It then stores the current status of the replication data on the distributor. Each publication has an individual agent.

> **Note:** The Snapshot agent locks the published information on the distribution server when the transfer is taking place. Therefore, no replication subscribers will be able to address those articles while the Distributor update occurs. To minimize potential problems, schedule the snapshot to occur when the fewest possible subscriber updates will occur (such as early in the morning).

The agent moves the required data to the snapshot folder. The schema of the replicated objects (tables, stored procedures, and so on) are recreated each time the replication process is executed. It connects the publisher to the distribution database and locks all articles that will be transferred. The article locks will eliminate any possible user access to prevent data integrity errors. After the locks are in place, the schema is created on the distributor. These files are stored in a separate file for each article with the .sch extension. Any indexes or referential integrity files are stored in script files with the .idx extension.

Data is then copied into a file on the distributor. If replication is to SQL Server-based data sources, the data is stored in the native file format of the BCP and Bulk Insert command (see Chapter 23 for more information) with the .bcp extension. If not, the data is stored in traditional text files with the .txt extension.

When this process occurs, two tables are updated:

- **MSRepl_commands:** Holds the file paths to all of the files for the replication set. These include files with .bcp, .txt, .sch, and .idx extensions. This table contains eight columns: publisher_database_id, xact_seqno, type, article_id, originator_id, command_id, partial_command, and command.

- **MSRepl_Transactions:** Holds references to the tasks that are used for replicating this particular replication set. This table contains four columns: publisher_database_id, xact_seqno, xact_seqno, and entry_time. There is one row in this table for each replication sequence.

Locks are released when these table updates are complete. The log history file is marked to reflect the completion of the snapshot replication process. In a push replication environment, the agent will delete the replication set of files once all subscribers have been updated. In a pull environment, the files will remain until each subscriber pulls a new copy of the database or a new replication execution of the replica set occurs.

All of these operations occur through the SQL Server Agent. By having different agents for each of the processes, the system can execute the snapshot operations without intervention from the users.

Using Agent Utilities

Several utilities are available for execution from the MS-DOS prompt (Windows 95/98) or the console (Windows NT) that can configure and activate the replication agents. Four agent utilities are defined: Snapshot Agent, Log Reader Agent, Distribution Agent, and Merge Agent. Each of these utilities can be used for agent execution.

SNAPSHOT AGENT

The snapshot.exe utility handles snapshot replication. The Snapshot Agent:

- Prepares snapshots files for publications

- Stores files on the Distributor
- Records synchronization status

The status is recorded in the distribution database. You can execute the agent this way:

```
C:\MSSql7\Binn\snapshot -PublisherDBmyDB -Publication myPub
```

At the command prompt a listing of all of the available switches for each application is activated by using the `-?` switch. For the distrib.exe utility, you could retrieve help like this:

```
C:\MSSql7\Binn\distrib -?
```

The snapshot agent can be activated from the command line by using the Replication Snapshot Agent Utility (snapshot). The executable for this utility is located in the \binn directory of the MSDE directory (usually located at C:\mssql7). You can obtain help for the available parameters by using the `-?` switch.

DISTRIBUTION AGENT

The Distribution agent runs on the distributor and moves publication data to subscribers. This includes copying data and tables to each subscriber. The agent first connects to the publication data source from the distribution database server.

For push subscriptions, this agent executes on the distribution server. In pull subscriptions, it executes on the subscription machine. Scheduled execution is based on the clock of the machine that executes the agent. Read information from the two replication tables on the distributor (MSRepl_commands and MSRepl_transactions) to determine whether replication is necessary.

The distribution agent can send synchronization data to the subscribers. It can ensure data integrity and execute necessary index scripts. The distribution agent can be activated from the command line by using the Replication Distribution Agent Utility (distrib). The executable for this utility is located in the \binn directory of the MSDE directory (usually located at `C:\mssql7`).

LOG READER AGENT

The Log Reader agent operates on the transaction log to move transactions from the server that holds each publication to the distribution database. Because MSDE does not support transaction replication, this agent is not available through MSDE.

> **Note:** Because the transaction log form of replication is only available on Windows NT, you must be using a machine with the full version of SQL Server installed on that operating system in order to execute the logread utility.

MERGE AGENT

The Merge agent performs a merge synchronization between publishers and subscribers. For transaction and snapshot replication, Merge agents are not used. The Merge agent connects the publisher and the subscriber, and it provides updates on both sides. The merge works in a step-by-step fashion, first uploading the changes from the subscriber to the publisher and then downloading publisher changes to the subscriber.

Configuring the SQL Server Agent

Many settings determine how and when the SQL Agent will execute. Configuring the SQL Server Agent can be done either through the Enterprise Manager or directly through Transact-SQL calls. One of the factors that may be configured is the idle processing settings.

IDLE TIME PROCESSOR EXECUTION

In the Windows NT/2000 operating system, the amount of available processing power at any time is rated as a percentage. For example, if operations are using 17 percent of the total capacity of the microprocessor, 83 percent of the processor is idle. During this idle time, the operating system will execute optional or low priority tasks. The SQL Agent can be set to be one of these tasks so that the agent can execute when server resources are not strained completing other tasks.

Before you specify a particular agent task be executed in idle time, you should try manually executing that task and monitoring the memory and processor resources used by that operation. On Windows NT, this information is available through the Task Manager, which can be accessed by hitting the Ctrl+Alt+Del keys. You can also use the Performance Monitor to monitor other resource usage such as the network traffic generated by the task.

When you understand the resources used by the task you wish to schedule, you can appropriately configure the idle process settings so that there are enough free resources to adequately handle the task you intend for idle time. There are two settings for the idle process: the required free CPU percentage and the length of time it consistently has this free amount before the process is activated.

Changing the default settings for these two factors is done through the Enterprise Manager. Locate the SQL Agent icon in the tree list and display the properties window by right-clicking the agent and selecting the Properties option. In the Properties window, select the Advanced tab. You will see the idle process settings that you can modify for the agent (see Figure 19-2). The percentage setting applies to all of the processors in a symmetrical multiprocessor (SMP) system.

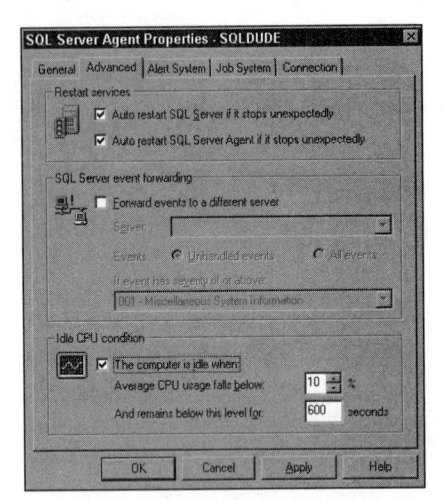

Figure 19-2: In the Enterprise Manager, the Advanced Properties tab will display the idle process settings.

WINDOWS 95/98 LIMITATIONS

If you are not running the MSDE server on Windows NT, you will encounter several limitations when using agents. These include:

- **No autorestart:** When the agent process shuts down or a machine reboot is encountered, the agent process will not automatically restart. You will have to manually start the SQL Server Agent service on each server boot.

- **Non-sysadmins limitations:** If the account is not configured in the sysadmin role, CmdExec and ActiveScripting processes of a job will not execute.

- **Lack of idle execution:** Any job set to execute on an idle condition will not activate. The Windows 95/98 operating system doesn't support SQL Agent execution during idle time.

Defining Operators

Although security accounts are used to specify users, roles, and groups, agents can notify a type of user known as an *operator*. An operator is not defined from an existing user account but is instead defined from scratch. Operators are defined with methods of contact including e-mail, pager, or a `net send` command.

> The `net send` command can only be used on a server running on the Windows NT platform. There is no supported equivalent available on the Windows 95/98 platform.

When a new operator is defined, an object is created that contains the name of the operator, the contact method, and the times when that operator is available. Operator names must be less than 128 characters long.

Of all the operator accounts, there can be an operator designated as the *fail-safe* operator. When none of the other operator notifications can be successful, the fail-safe operator is notified. As a security feature, the fail-safe operator cannot be deleted until the fail-safe designation is transferred to another operator account.

Notification of the fail-safe operator is activated only under two circumstances: when the pager cannot be reached because it is off-duty or the incorrect number is entered, or when the msdb database is not available that contains the other notification operators.

Programming the Agent

Work with the agent processes under the MSDE server is controlled primarily through programming constructs. Numerous system stored procedures are available to Transact-SQL code that can be used to create, manage, and schedule tasks that will be executed by the SQL Server Agent. It is also possible to use the Package object model to manage agent processes.

Creating a job on the Agent

A job can be created from scratch using only Transact-SQL code. In Chapter 13, you used the Import and Export Data Wizards to create a package that contained a series of steps for an export job. The sample that you will create here will be simpler in that it will enact a backup process for the Northwind database rather that the more complex data interaction of transforming one data source to another.

There are three primary procedures that will be used in this program: `sp_add_job`, `sp_add_job_step`, and `sp_add_jobschedule`. Sp_add_job will add the job to the MSDE server, `sp_add_job_step` will create the job steps for the job, and `sp_add_jobschedule` will create a schedule for executing the job.

It will be easiest to make the job creation routine a procedure. That way it can be modified and reused to create other jobs in the future. Execute Microsoft Access 2000 and open the NorthwindCS.adp project file. This procedure can be defined and executed within the Northwind database on the MSDE server. Create a new procedure and enter the following code:

```
Create Procedure makeMyJob
As
Execute Sp_add_job 'NW Backup', @enabled = 1,
    @description = 'Backup NW data',
    @owner_login_name = 'sa', @notify_level_eventlog = 2,
    @notify_level_email = 2, @notify_email_operator_name = 'sa'
Execute sp_add_jobstep 'NW Backup', 'LOCAL', 'BackupJob'
Execute sp_add_jobschedule @job_name = 'NW Backup',
    @name = 'ScheduledBU',
    @freq_type = 8,
    @freq_interval = 8,
    @active_start_time = '2:00:00'
```

In the code, set the date definition to reflect the date of your system so that the backup will execute at the appropriate time. The login user will be sent an error message by e-mail if the job fails.

Transact-SQL Implementation

Several Transact-SQL commands are used to create and manage agents and their jobs. Transact-SQL can be used from Microsoft Query or ADO, so monitoring or configuring agents is extremely convenient for an MSDE server no matter your current location on the LAN or WAN. Normal MSDE/SQL Server security will be used for login.

For these stored procedure definitions the bar/pipe (|) symbol represents an Or condition where one argument or another may be used. For example, the syntax `sp_delete_jobschedule(@job_id | @job_name)` indicates that the parameter in the parentheses can be either a `@job_id` value or a jobname that may be passed for execution. The parentheses should not be included when actually calling this procedure. A jobschedule can be deleted by using code like this:

```
Exec sp_delete_jobschedule 'myJob'
```

or

```
Exec sp_delete_jobschedule 10
```

Chapter 19: Working with SQL Server Agent   401

In the procedure definitions in the following sections, when the number of parameters for a procedure is greater than three, the argument definitions have been omitted. A great number of parameters indicates that the complexity of the procedure prohibits including a simple example of its use.

> **Note:** Several stored procedures were removed from the SQL Server 7 implementation of the database engine that were present in earlier versions. These procedures include: sp_addalert, sp_addnotification, sp_addoperator, sp_addtask, sp_dropalert, sp_dropnotification, sp_dropoperator, sp_droptask, sp_helpalert, sp_helphistory, sp_helpnotification, sp_helpoperator, sp_purgehistory, sp_runtask, sp_stoptask, sp_updatealert, sp_updatenotification, and sp_updateoperator. All of these procedures are available in MSDE and SQL Server 7 and in most cases with only minor name changes (such as changing the word *drop* in the routine name to *delete*). If you encounter any of these procedures in existing code or sample code from old sources such as magazine, simply find the equivalent new routine.

ADDING AGENT OBJECTS

For adding new objects such as categories or jobs to an agent, stored procedures are available for all of the new agent creation routines. Once these various operations have been added to the agent and scheduled as part of a job, the agent will execute them at the proper time. Be sure to attempt a test execution of each job step to ensure that the operation it performs will work properly when used in the job batch.

> **Note:** The sp_add_jobserver procedure can be executed after each added job step to update the actual servers. Jobs are cached by the SQL Server Agent after the sp_add_jobserver call. Therefore, for fastest processing by the server, leave the add jobserver procedure until after the last job step is added.

The following procedures relate to adding objects to the SQL Server Agent:

- **sp_add_category(@class, @type, @name):** Adds a new category to the server for classification of jobs, alerts, and operators. The @class argument is a string that can have one of three values: JOB, ALERT, or OPERATOR. The @type can be one of three values: LOCAL, MULTI-SERVER, or NONE. The @type cannot be set to NONE for the job class.

- **sp_add_job:** Creates a new job on the server for execution. Only the name of the job must be set at creation time. The simplest command to add a new job would appear like this:

  ```
  sp_add_job 'NewJob'
  ```

- **sp_add_jobschedule:** Adds a schedule to a job. In Chapter 13, this procedure was used to schedule the execution of a DTS package.

- **sp_add_jobserver:** Specifies the server where the job will execute. Can be used to create a distributed job with code like this:

  ```
  sp_add_jobserver 'NewJob', 'mySecondMSDEServer'
  ```

- **sp_add_jobstep:** Adds a step to a job task. A step can be defined with the @Command argument as a ActiveX Script such as VB Script or JavaScript (ACTIVESCRIPTING), operating system command (CMDEXEC), Transact-SQL code which is the default (TSQL), or execution of a replication job (DISTRIBUTION, SNAPSHOT, LOGREADER, MERGE).

- **sp_add_notification:** Creates a notification object related to an alert. The notification set through the @notification_method can be an e-mail message (1), a page (2), or a net send command (4). For notification by e-mail, the SQL Server Agent must be configured for e-mail through the Enterprise Manager.

- **sp_add_operator:** Adds an operator user to the MSDE server. Parameters that define an operator include: operator name, e-mail address of user, pager number, category of operator, and times available for operator availability.

- **sp_add_targetservergroup:** Creates a new server group. A group can contain several servers that can be assigned a job. The job will be distributed to the server with the most available resources.

- **sp_add_targetsvrgrp_member:** Adds a server to an existing target server group.

- **sp_manage_jobs_by_login (@action [, @current_owner_login_name] [, @new_owner_login_name]):** Can be used to delete or reassign jobs based on the login names. The @action can hold a command such as DELETE or REASSIGN. Only users in the sysadmin group can execute this procedure.

DOCUMENT AGENT OBJECTS

These procedures are used to display details about the configured aspects of the agent objects on the MSDE agent. Like the various sp_help procedures that are used to display rules, defaults, and the code of stored procedures, these routines retrieve information from the system tables and return it in a recordset.

- **sp_help_jobserver (@job_id | @job_name [,@show_last_run_details]):** Displays all of the information related to the server that is assigned to the specified job. The information displayed includes the server ID, the server name, the enlistment date, and the last poll date. The `@show_last_run_details` argument, if included in the procedure call, requires either a 1 (show the details) or a 0 (don't show details) to include four extra columns displaying the last time, date, duration, and outcome of execution on the job server.

- **sp_help_jobstep (@job_id | @job_name [,@step_id] [,@step_name]):** Returns the information related to a specified job step. If the arguments for `@step_id` or `@step_name` are not specified, all of the steps associated with the specified job are returned. Many columns are returns for each step that includes information for items such as the status of the step, the last time and date it was executed, the database on which it is located, and more.

- **sp_help_operator (@operator_name, @operator_id):** Returns the details of the specified operator. All of the information entered when creating the operator, such as name, e-mail address, pager contact, availability time and dates, and category, is returned in columns of the result set. This procedure must be run from the msdb database.

- **sp_help_targetserver (@servername):** Lists all of the available target servers registered with the specified server. Information returned by the procedure includes server name and ID, time zone adjustments, status, local time, poll interval, and others.

- **sp_help_targetservergroup (@name):** Lists all of the available target servers in a target server group.

DELETING AGENT OBJECTS

Certain procedures can be used to delete an object related to agent processes. Most of these procedures require only a single parameter to indicate which object needs to be deleted.

- **sp_delete_alert:** Removes an alert and all notifications attached to that alert.

- **sp_post_msx_operation (@operation [,@object_type] [,@job_id =] job_id] [,@specific_target_server] [,@value]):** Insert operations into the sysdownloadlist table for download and execution to target servers. If the object type is JOB, then the operations INSERT, UPDATE, DELETE, START, and STOP are available. For a SERVER object type, the operations are RE-ENLIST, DEFECT, SYNC-TIME, and SET-POLL.

- **sp_delete_category (@class, @name):** Eliminates a category on the server. The `@class` argument can be one of three values: JOB, ALERT, and OPERATOR.

- **sp_purge_jobhistory (@job_id | @job_name):** This procedure will purge the contained history stored with a job.

- **sp_delete_job (@job_id | @job_name):** Deletes the specified job from the server.

- **sp_delete_jobschedule (@job_id | @job_name):** Deletes a job schedule.

- **sp_delete_jobserver(@job_id | @job_name, @server_name):** Removes a job server that can be used as a target for processing a specified job.

- **sp_remove_job_from_targets:** Removes the job assignment from a distributed system on a target system.

- **sp_delete_jobstep:** Deletes a job step on the server.

- **sp_delete_notification(@alert_name):** Eliminates a notification using the `@alertName` argument to select the notification to be deleted. The alert itself is not deleted by this command, only the notification associated with it.

- **sp_delete_operator:** Deletes an operator from the MSDE server.

- **sp_delete_targetservergroup:** Deletes the target server group itself. This procedure first removes all of the servers from the group and then eliminates the group itself.

- **sp_delete_targetsvrgrp_member:** Removes a server from a target server group.

- **sp_droptask:** Removes a task from the MSDE server. This procedure is only retained for backward compatibility with older versions of the SQL Server database engine.

MISCELLANEOUS AGENT RELATED PROCEDURES

These procedures relate to various aspects of agent maintenance. The following procedures can be used to manage the SQL Server Agent functions:

- **sp_resync_targetserver (@server_name):** Deletes all of the target server operations in a registered multiserver system group. After the deletion, a new set of operations is posted to the servers. To execute this procedure, the user must belong to the sysadmin group.

- **sp_start_job (@job_id | @job_name [, @server_name] [, @step_name]):** Begin executing job steps that have been defined on target servers immediately. Using the `@step_name` parameter allows the job to be started at any operational step.

- **sp_add_alert:** Creates a new alert on the specified server. Parameters used in new alert definition include alert name, error severity required for activation, notification message, category name, and others.

- **sp_help_jobschedule (@job_id | @job_name):** Returns the job schedule when passed a desired job.

- **sp_msx_enlist:** This procedure allows adds the current server to a multi-server operation. This procedure modifies the Registry, so use it with caution. It will add all of the jobs on the server. It must be executed by a user in the sysadmin group.

- **sp_msx_defect:** This procedure allows a server to defect or remove itself, from a multiserver operations. This procedure modifies the Registry, so use it with caution. It will remove all of the jobs on the server. It must be executed by a user in the sysadmin group.

- **sp_apply_job_to_targets (@job_id | @job_name [, @target_server_groups] [,@target_servers] [,@operation]):** Adds a job to a target server or a target server group. The @operation argument must be either set to APPLY or REMOVE. Must be executed by a user in the sysadmin group.

- **sp_stop_job:** Attempts to halt a currently executing job. If the process in the job being executed is an operating system exec step, the execution will be halted prematurely. Because stopping an OS task can cause system instability, try to use this command only when necessary.

- **sp_delete_targetserver:** Removes the server from the list of registered target servers that can be used for job execution.

- **sp_update_alert:** Modifies an existing alert. Factors such as delays, severity settings, delays, occurrences, and performance condition are changeable. Only a user in the sysadmin group can execute this procedure.

- **sp_update_category (@class, @name, @new_name):** Renames a specified category. The @class argument may contain one of three possible settings: ALERT, JOB, or OPERATOR.

- **sp_update_job:** Modifies the settings of an existing job. Factors such as notification level, start step Id number (@start_step_id), owner login name, delete level, and notification e-mail name.

- **sp_update_jobschedule:** Changes the schedule for an existing job. Factors such as the frequency, type of frequency (@freq_type), frequency interval (@freq_interval), and active start and end date (@active_start_date and @active_end_date). This procedure must be run for the msdb database.

- **sp_help_alert:** List the alerts information available on the system. Returns a row for each alert with columns that indicate settings of the alert such as the severity level to which the alert responds, the enabled status, the last response time, and the last response alert. This procedure must be run on the msdb database by a user in the sysadmin group.

- **sp_update_jobstep:** Modifies a job step for such factors as step name, subsystem, server, and database name where the job is stored. This procedure must be run from the msdb database.

- **sp_help_category ([@class,] [@type,] [@name,] [@suffix]):** Returns the requested information about classes of alerts, jobs, or operators. The @class should be passed as one of three types: JOB, ALERT, or OPERATOR. The @type argument can be one of three types: LOCAL, MULTI-SERVER, or NONE.

- **sp_update_notification (@alert_name, @operator_name, @notification_method):** Changes the procedure used for alert notification. This procedure must be executed from within the msdb database.

- **sp_help_downloadlist (@job_id | @job_name):** Returns all of the rows for a supplied job or all rows if no job is specified. These rows are stored in the master table of sysdownloadlist.

- **sp_update_operator:** Updates the operator settings for alerts and jobs.

- **sp_help_job (@job_id | @job_name):** Returns the job information when passed a desired job.

- **sp_update_targetservergroup (@name, @new_name):** Changes the name of a target server group. This procedure must be execute with the msdb database selected.

- **sp_help_jobhistory (@job_id | @job_name):** Returns the job history when passed a desired job.

Using the SQL-DMO Objects

Through the object model for the SQL-DMO, you can construct an application to monitor the agent processes. The JobServer object (see Figure 19-3) is the primary object that contains all of the access objects to the SQL Server agent. Using the JobServer object, the agent may be started or stopped, jobs and alerts can be configured, and multiserver job assignment may occur. The Job, JobStep, and JobSchedule objects, used for a new job, can be created, or you can schedule an existing one to execute.

```
                    ┌─────────────────┐
                    │   Job Server    │
                    └─────────────────┘
        ┌─────────────────┐   ┌─────────────────┐
        │ AlertCategories │   │   AlertSystem   │
        │ (AlertCategory) │   └─────────────────┘
        └─────────────────┘
        ┌─────────────────┐   ┌─────────────────┐
        │     Alerts      │   │    JobFilter    │
        │     (Alert)     │   └─────────────────┘
        └─────────────────┘
        ┌─────────────────┐   ┌─────────────────┐
        │  JobCategories  │   │ JobHistoryFilter│
        │  (JobCategory)  │   └─────────────────┘
        └─────────────────┘
        ┌─────────────────┐
        │      Jobs       │
        │      (Job)      │
        └─────────────────┘
        ┌─────────────────────┐
        │ OperatorCategories  │
        │ (OperatorCategory)  │
        └─────────────────────┘
        ┌─────────────────┐
        │    Operators    │
        │   (Operator)    │
        └─────────────────┘
        ┌──────────────────────┐
        │  TargetServerGroups  │
        │ (TargetServerGroup)  │
        └──────────────────────┘
        ┌─────────────────┐
        │  TargetServers  │
        │  (TargetServer) │
        └─────────────────┘
```

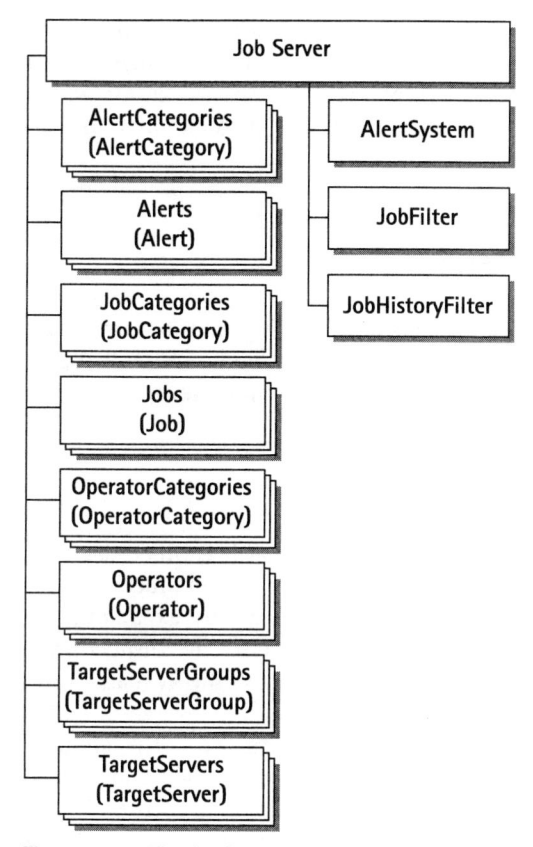

Figure 19-3: The JobServer object in the SQL-DMO framework provides access to the SQL Server Agent.

Many of the methods (such as the `BeginAlter` and `CancelAlter` methods) mirror those available through the DTS Package objects. Because the DTS Package uses the SQL Server Agent, both object sets actually execute the same operations on the MSDE server.

Using the Enterprise Manager

The Enterprise Manager can be used to watch all of the agents through the Microsoft Management Console window. It can be used to most easily configure agents or create new ones. Because all of the Agent objects are displayed in the graphical interface as items and folders, operations such as adding new jobs or executing existing ones are available through the context menus.

In the Enterprise Manager, you can also graphically monitor the execution of the agents. Monitoring the activities of the agents will give you a better understanding of how to optimize their configuration as well as the operating system on which they are executing. You can also use the Enterprise Manager to examine the log files created by the SQL Agent.

Examining the Agent Log

A SQL Server Agent log maintains a list of errors and warnings that occurred during the execution of an agent process. You can examine this log to ensure that previously scheduled jobs executed properly. The log is made up of several different files, commonly stored in this directory:

```
C:\MSSQL7\Log\sqlagent.*
```

The extension of the log file will be .out for the most recent log. Other historical logs will have extensions that are numbers indicating their creation order.

You can view the agent error log in the Enterprise Manager by expanding the Agent tree and right-clicking the SQL Server Agent item. Select the Display Error Log option that will display the error log window. You can use the available filter user interface items to selectively view certain error types.

The log can contain errors, warnings, or progress information. The progress information is turned off by default so that it does not fill up the log and expend unnecessary server resources. In the SQL Server Agent item properties in the Enterprise Manager, you can activate the logging of progress information by checking the "Include execution trace messages" item.

There can be up to nine agent error logs, each with a file extension of the number of that particular log (for instance, myAgentLog.1 through myAgentLog.9). The extensions denote the chronology of the logs such that .1 contains the most recent errors whereas .9 contains the oldest.

The four methods that may activate a job are as follows:

- **Job-scheduling engine:** Activation is based on a time or date event where the job is executed according to the agent schedule.

- **Manual activation:** Through Transact-SQL, the Enterprise Manager, or SQL-DMO, a job may be called for execution.

- **Startup sequence:** When the MSDE or SQL Server is initially started, the server can execute the task.

- **Alert engine:** Depending on events that occur on the database server, such as a shutdown event alert sent by an Uninterruptible Power Supply (UPS), the job may be executed.

Any of these execution methods can run a job on the local server or a remote server provided secure access is available. On the MSDE server, any user may create a job, but execution scheduling must be enabled by a user with the proper owner or sysadmin privileges. Only the owner of the job or one of the sysadmin users may edit an existing job.

The primary properties that must be configured for a job are:

- **Name:** The name (less than 128 characters) is used for the job activation. Each name must be unique.

- **Category:** A job is categorized for ease of grouping and filtering. Fourteen default categories are created when the MSDE system is installed. More categories may be added in order to group jobs by function or department such as creating categories for replication or accounting jobs.

- **Execution steps:** The actual process or steps that occur for the job are held in a collection for each job. These job steps can be a replication task, code in Transact-SQL, operating system console commands, or script in an ActiveX scripting language (such as VB Script or JavaScript).

- **Schedule:** When a job will execute will depend on the schedule. The schedule is only used for time- and date-based events. Manual, alert, and startup activation are configured in other parts of the job.

- **Notification:** Any alerts that should be issued concerning the status of the agent process execution. Notification can occur through e-mail, pager sending, or a `net send` command.

Execution Steps

In the execution steps, or job steps, the operating system console commands are executed through the CmdExec structure. It can run executable (`.exe` or `.com`), batch (`.bat`), and command (`.cmd`) files. The CmdExec requires a full path to the file it will run. After an execution step of this type completes execution, it returns an exit code to indicate the success or failure of the execution.

The execution steps have some limitations including an inability to pass any values between steps. No strings, Boolean values, or numbers may be passed from one step to another. To provide persistent data that one step can create and another step retrieve, you will have to create scratch tables or temporary tables into which data can be written on the completion of a step. A subsequent step that needs this data can then read the information from the table.

TRANSACT-SQL EXECUTION

If Transact-SQL code is used for the step, multiple commands may be included in the code by using the Go command to execute each set of operations in the SQL text. The Go command functions in the same manner as when it is used in the SQL Query

Analyzer. It executes all of the SQL commands to the point in the code that it occurs – since the last Go command or since the beginning, if there is no previous command.

ACTIVEX SCRIPTING

An ActiveX script can be inserted into the agent for execution. This script can be written in any available ActiveX scripting language including the default languages VB Script and JScript (the JavaScript-compatible and ECMA-compatible language) that are included with the scripting engine. Third-party languages, such as Perlscript, are also available that may be plugged-into the scripting engine.

The SQLActiveScriptHost is the primary object for the environment that allows printing into the Agent log and provides a method for creating objects. If you have ever programmed in Active Server Pages (ASP) on Internet Information Server (IIS), you will recognize that the Server object in the ASP object model works in a similar fashion.

The SQLActiveScriptHost has two methods: `PrintObject` and `CreateObject`. The `PrintObject` method will send any text string into the agent log. `CreateObject` is used to instantiate any ActiveX object. The SQLActiveScriptHost is automatically instantiated and available for use by any of the agent scripting code.

> **NOTE:** Because the `CreateObject` keyword is available from the scripting environment, you might be wondering why it would be necessary to use the method that is part of the SQLActiveScriptHost object to accomplish the same task. When you use the method included in SQLActiveScriptHost, the server easily tracks the objects that are created for a particular task. When memory allocation and garbage collection occur, it is easier for the system to manage and dispose of objects directly related to a script execution. Therefore, using the method on the script host object optimizes the performance of the database server.

When an execution step is created to use a script, the language to be used by the script code must be specified. The default language type is the VB Script language.

The Alerts Event System for Agents

The SQL Server Agent continuously monitors the operating system event log and watches for comments, warnings, or errors related to the MSDE execution. By configuring the Alert system in the SQL Server Agent, you can have the agent execute a job that you've defined in response to one or more events that occurred on the system.

If an event related to the MSDE server occurs, the SQL Server agent can perform one of three operations: execute a user-defined job, notify the operator of the MSDE system, or forward the event message to the event log on another server.

In addition to executing a job, the MSDE server can simply notify a user that the event has occurred. Notification can occur through e-mail, pager, or using the `net send` command to alert the user over a LAN. Both the e-mail and the pager require that mail server account information is configured through the SQL Server Agent Properties window. The `net send` command is a console command and does not require explicit settings except those passed by the Alert itself. Note that the `net send` command is not available on Windows 95/98-based systems.

Not all errors that occur in a SQL Server-based system are stored to the system event log for monitoring by the SQL Server Agent. Only events that have a severity level greater than 19, events created using the `raiserror` command using the With Log keywords, events or generated with `xp_logevent` will be placed in the system log for possible agent reaction.

> **Note:** The severity level can be lowered from the default of 19 for logging to the system event log using the system stored procedure called `sp_altermessage`. Through this routine, specific errors can be set to always write to the system log. Beware that if these errors occur frequently, the system event log file may become incredibly large.

An alert is defined to respond to four different event types: a particular error number appearing in the system log, an error of a specific severity occurring, an error generated that applies to a specified database, or text in the error matching a search string. Alerts can be defined that use only one or multiple of these criteria before the SQL Server Agent addresses that event.

When the event is forwarded to the log of another system, you can create a master server to receive all of the events from agents. That master server can then become an Alerts Management Server that handles all of the alerts for centralization and scalability. The processes that must execute when an event occurs will be activated on this central server, thereby minimizing the execution load on the individual database servers.

The `sp_add_notification` procedure can be used in Transact-SQL to create an alert notification to use e-mail, a pager, or the `net send` command to transmit an alert to an intended user. This stored procedure must be executed from the msdb database on the MSDE server, and it can only be executed by a user with sysadmin privileges.

Grouping Objects in Categories

Jobs, alerts, and operators can all be placed within a category, which is used to group these object types. For job categories, filtering may be enacted on the basis of a category. A job is added to a category to make it easier to provide manage groups of jobs. There are 14 default categories, of which 9 are directly related to replication. The default categories are:

- **[Uncategorized (Local)]:** All jobs that are created without an explicitly defined category are assigned to this one.
- **[Database Maintenance]:** Used for rebuilding indexes, reorganization, removing empty database pages, backing up data, and performance of internal consistency checks.
- **[Full-Text]:** For jobs relating to the full-text search capability on SQL Server. Note that the full-text engine is not included with MSDE, hence full-text jobs cannot be executed on it.
- **[Jobs from MSX]:** When a SQL Server–based database server is set to be the master server (MSX), the [Uncategorized (Multi-Server)] category is created. When a job from the master server is downloaded into another database server, the job is placed in this category.
- **[REPL - Alert Response], [REPL - Checkup], [REPL - Distribution], [REPL - Distribution Cleanup], [REPL - History Cleanup], [REPL - LogReader], [REPL - Merge], [REPL - Snapshot]:** Handle the replication-based jobs for which each is named.
- **[REPL - Subscription Cleanup]:** Cleanup and deletion of subscription publications once all of the subscriptions have been updated.
- **[Web Assistant]:** Denotes the jobs that are created from Web database information distribution.

You can rename any user category using the `sp_update_category` procedure by passing it the class of category to change followed by the name and the new name to use. The class of category should be passed as `ALERT`, `JOB`, or `OPERATOR` like this:

```
sp_update_category 'JOB', 'oldjobname', 'newjobname'
```

Don't rename any of the categories that are automatically created by the system. If a system procedure subsequently attempted to activate jobs sorted by a change category, it would not be found and an error would result.

> **Note:** The Jobs from MSX category is used to hold jobs that were received from a distributed job created on a master server. You can create a distributed job and make the current server the master server by executing the Make Master Server Wizard within the Enterprise Manager. It will guide you through setting up security, creating the master operator, selecting the destination (target) servers, and defining the job and how it will be allocated across the various servers.

Scheduling

Scheduling the agent process is the most important part of making sure your job executes properly. It is fairly easy to make a scheduling mistake and not have the process execute when you want it.

The SQL Server Agent Monitor is automatically executed on a Windows NT machine when the agent is started. The monitor routine will remain executing in the background watching the condition of the agent service. If the SQL Server Agent terminates abnormally, you can set the Agent Monitor to automatically restart the service.

After a job has been created, both the job definition and the existing history of the job's execution can be examined. If the job has been executed at least once, the history will contain the time, date, and interval of each execution. If you are the owner or a sysadmin user, almost every aspect of an existing job may be modified including the steps that are used for its execution.

It is also possible to generate complete a Transact-SQL script for the definition of each job. That allows you to easily move the job to another server, archive the job logic, or make precise modifications to the code of the job definition itself. To generate the SQL script for the job definition, expand the SQL Server Agent folder in the Enterprise Manager. If you right-click the Jobs item, the Script All Jobs/Script All option will generate the Transact-SQL code into a named ASCII or Unicode text file.

Summary

The SQL Server Agent provides a method for automating administrative tasks. Agents can execute script code, Transact-SQL code, or an external program in response to events or scheduling. Execution may also be started manually. In this chapter, you covered:

- **Agents:** The agent system provides a framework for autonomous execution of tasks related to the database. An agent can be activated manually, in response to an alert, according to a time and date schedule, or at the time of the database server startup. Agents are used extensively by the database system when executing replication processes.

- **Snapshot agent:** Handles the process of snapshot replication. Can be used to create the initial publications and configure the snapshot process.

- **Distribution agent:** Handles all of the processing of the distribution for replication.

- **Job:** An agent executes a job that has been defined within the particular agent. All jobs have a name, execution or job steps, and a schedule of when the job may be activated.

- **Job categories:** Each jobs is placed in a category for grouping and filtering. There are 14 default categories, and the MSDE administrator can define additional ones where jobs will be stored.
- **Execution/job steps:** A job contains one or more steps that execute when the job is activated. Each step may contain a command, Transact-SQL code, or script code. Multiple steps allow control-of-flow to occur so that execution of the job may alter step execution sequence in response to a result returned by one of the steps.

Chapter 20

Accessing the Web with Remote Data Services

IN THIS CHAPTER

- ◆ Examining RDS
- ◆ Scripting in the browser
- ◆ Connecting to ADO access through RDS
- ◆ Using ADO Recordset classes
- ◆ Establishing secure access through RDS

ALTHOUGH YOU HAVE DONE extensive work so far with MSDE, one of the premier technologies in recent times – the Internet – has been addressed only briefly. Using a SQL Server–based database server with the Web requires knowledge of ActiveX Data Objects (ADO), Internet Information Server (IIS), Active Server Pages (ASP), VB Script, and several other technologies. For this information, you might take a look at one of my other books, *Building Web Database Applications with Visual Studio 6*, for complete Web information.

Remote Data Services (RDS) is a technology that doesn't use Web server code execution, but that can be very useful to an MSDE developer. RDS enables you to access the MSDE database through the Internet Explorer Web browser. By using the RDS technology, you can build the equivalent of a client/server system with the Web browser for execution of the client application.

The objects available in RDS can do the following:

- ◆ Receive information over the Internet for examination and manipulation within the Web browser
- ◆ Store the data retrieved over the Internet into a client-side recordset
- ◆ Enable updates of that information to be sent back to the data source

RDS is a complete database communications system that contains various different parts, including a subset of the entire ADO class framework. RDS also includes the Remote Data control (RDC), a control that is functionally similar to the data control in Visual Basic. The RDC allows interaction with a data source and can be bound to controls for a data interface within the browser. The RDC can use a standard SQL query to connect to a remote source and allow other controls, such as text boxes and option lists, to be bound to it.

An Overview of RDS

The Remote Data Services is a comprehensive Web data access system. It has objects that execute on both the server side (Web server) and the client side (Web browser). The RDS system includes these technologies:

- **Web Server Control:** An object that executes on IIS or the Personal Web Server (PWS) to provide a bridge between the client and the data source through the communications protocols of the Web server.

- **Remote Data control (RDC):** A client-side control that runs in the user's browser to provide navigation and datasource binding. Much of the database interaction is handled automatically by the RDC, rather than requiring custom programming for column value display and editing.

- **ADO Recordset (ADOR):** A subset of ADO that streamlines the entire object model down to a small number of objects that take up far fewer resources than does a complete ADO implementation. The ADOR is available for use within the browser and also available on some versions of the Windows CE operating system (for handheld and palmtop devices).

To create an RDS system, therefore, both the server and the client must be running the proper compatible components. The basic implementation of an RDS system requires a special understanding of Web server technology, because it is so different from traditional Web database connectivity. A Web database solution uses the server-side ASP execution (see Figure 20-1) to retrieve the data with server code and return it to the Web browser as a formatted HTML document. Only during the request of data and the return of the HTML page does a connection exist between the Web server and the browser.

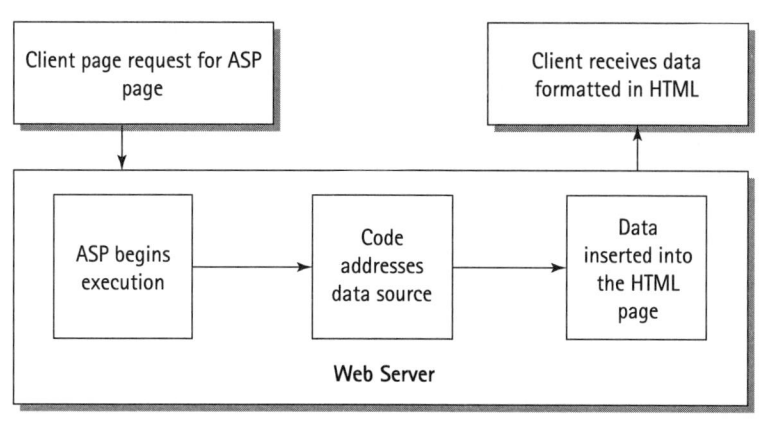

Chapter 20: Accessing the Web with Remote Data Services 417

Figure 20-1: A typical Web database solution executes all database processing on the server and returns a static HTML page.

For an RDS solution (see Figure 20-2), the connection between the data source and the ActiveX control on the Web page can remain active. Controls on the Web page may be bound to the ADO data control, and updates may be made to data that is sent back to the data source.

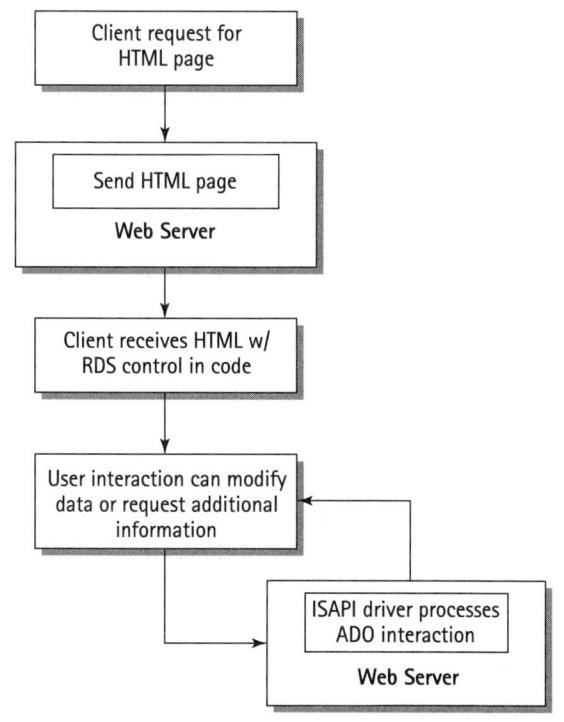

Figure 20-2: An RDS solution retrieves a page from the Web server with the RDS ActiveX control.

Typical non-Web datasource interaction occurs through an established connection or session (see Figure 20-3). After the database user logs in to the database server system, a session begins in which the user has a secure identity established that, as long as the session remains open, does not have to be reestablished. When the session is complete, either a logoff command or a timeout will close the session.

Client access

Active database session

MSDE Server

Figure 20-3: Typical database interaction occurs through a database session.

The Web is not based on a communications protocol designed for sessions. To promote the ease of use that enabled the Web to flourish, no logon procedure exists. This fact enables a Web server to serve hundreds or thousands of different users simultaneously without having to track sessions for each user. It also enables users to click a hyperlink and quickly and conveniently jump to a new site without any laborious logon or logoff procedure.

What may be excellent for general Web serving, however, poses special problems for a designer who wants to implement a Web-based database solution. It is typically left to the developer to simulate a database session in order to allow for login and secure communication between the user's browser and the Web server–based database system. To ease the development requirements for such solutions, Microsoft has developed various technologies that do most of the "heavy lifting" for you on IIS. RDS is one of these technologies.

Through RDS, which functions over the standard Web HTTP protocol, a simulated discontinuous session is created between the client browser and the database server through the Web server (see Figure 20-4). The data retrieved from each RDS request is cached on the client machine for access within the browser. The simulated session does not keep a live connection open with the database server, so little of the overhead associated with traditional sessions is incurred. The only interaction between the browser and the database occurs when another query is requested or an update is sent from the client.

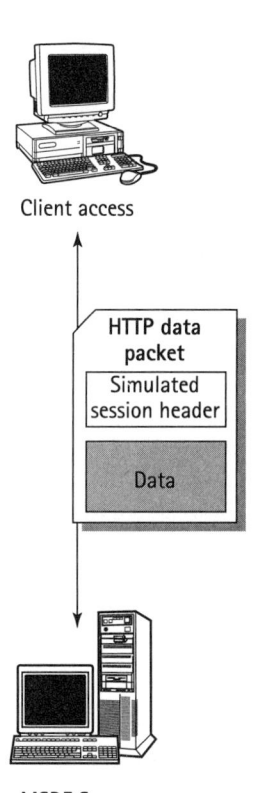

Figure 20-4: RDS provides a simulated session between the browser user and a database on the server.

In addition to configuring the actual RDS components, several other resources must be configured to achieve good performance. Aside from optimization of the Web server, database connection tuning, such as the use of connection pooling, can provide much faster responses. Connection pooling is one of the most effective means of speeding access for high-volume sites.

Pooling entails keeping multiple open connections to a database server. A reference to an object connection is passed to the object requestor (such as a Connection object). After the requestor has finished with the connection, it is simply returned to the pool rather than being eliminated. This process reduces the amount of time required for the creation and destruction of connections. Check the configuration of your ODBC driver to set the proper values for best pooling efficiency.

> **NOTE:** Connection pooling is primarily useful when many simultaneous users are addressing a site consistently. Because a pooled connection is released after a timeout period has elapsed (the default period is 90 seconds), any performance gains are lost if another user does not access the pooled connection in that time. Most MSDE server applications are low-volume (the suggested maximum simultaneous number of users is 5), so connection pooling will be of less interest to MSDE developers until their applications grow to a size that requires a full SQL Server installation.

RDS System Requirements

RDS only executes against particular Web servers. RDS is available for Microsoft Web servers running on Windows 95/98 or Windows NT/2000. The server-side components are supported with a special type of driver, known as an Internet Server Application Programming Interface (*ISAPI*) driver, which is available only with Microsoft products.

The most popular method of running a Web server on the Windows NT/2000 platform is IIS. IIS is available on Windows NT 4 as part of the Windows NT Option Pack. Windows 2000 includes IIS as an option of the standard installation procedure.

Windows 95/98 users can also run the RDS components. Available for free download on the Microsoft Web site, the Personal Web Server can address ISAPI drivers and ASP code. PWS is also included with each copy of Microsoft FrontPage on the CD-ROM.

RDS Execution Process

The RDS system works through a distinct process to enable the client to have database access. When the client object requests a recordset on the server, the RDS server program is invoked. The server program typically consists of an execution process that invokes the ADO model to connect to the database server.

With the server program executing, the query will execute against the data source. The returned recordset will be passed through the server program to the client object that requested it. Often, the client program is using the RDC, which receives the recordset.

RDS Programming

Programming the client side of RDS requires addressing an ActiveX component. The ActiveX component enables you to create and manipulate a client-side recordset. The client-side control can be programmed through scripting with JavaScript and VB Script or any other scripting language available through the ActiveX Scripting component model.

> **TIP** I suggest that you favor JavaScript (or Microsoft's version, known as JScript) on the client, because JavaScript is standard across most browsers, including Netscape Navigator. Although Netscape does not currently support ActiveX controls, it may do so in the future. This possibility was enhanced when Netscape made the source code of Navigator available through the Mozilla project (www.mozilla.org). Using JavaScript (on the client side) today may increase the chances that your Web page will be compatible with all major browser brands in the future.

Scripting in the Browser

In the previous chapters of this book, you have used the VBA language extensively from Microsoft Access. The scripting environment within a browser is a different development situation. Unlike the VBA implementation in the Office program that has a form editor, code windows, debugger, and other included tools, no direct development environment is provided for browser scripting.

> **NOTE** If you plan to do extensive Web programming work, you can purchase tools such as Microsoft Visual InterDev that aid you in scripting development. Visual InterDev is included in the Microsoft Visual Studio suite.

Choosing VB Script over JavaScript

For most client-side scripting, it is recommended that you use JavaScript (or Microsoft's JScript). However, the examples in this chapter use VB Script because of its similarity to the VBA and Visual Basic languages that you already understand. The JavaScript language is quite a bit different from the Visual Basic language. VB Script was created as a subset of the full Visual Basic language implementation.

In contrast, the foundations of JavaScript mirror the syntax and structures of Java and C++. Whereas you will be able to easily understand the VB Script samples (given your Visual Basic experience), teaching you JavaScript is beyond the scope of this book. Because RDS is not available on Netscape yet anyway, the code currently needs to run only on the Internet Explorer browser.

> **TIP** You might want to check out the excellent book on JavaScript available from IDG Books called *JavaScript Bible*, by Danny Goodman. It explains coding JavaScript for both the Netscape and Internet Explorer browsers.

Constants in VB Script

Unlike when you place code within a VBA project, no References dialog box exists on the browser client to determine which class libraries are available to the scripted application. This lack of a reference to object libraries means that the enumerated constant values for object models are not available.

Code that would work in VBA using the names of constants will fail on the browser, because the named constants aren't available. This code sets the ReadyState property to a library constant and will not work properly in VB Script:

```
If ADC1.ReadyState = ReadyStateComplete Then
```

In VB Script, variables can be defined dynamically within a statement. The preceding code example will not find a constant named ReadyStateComplete and will simply create a variable by that name. Because the variable is defined dynamically, the code will seem to execute properly. In reality, a variable named ReadyState Complete is created and filled with a null value, which is subsequently placed in the ReadyState property.

To avoid this problem, you need to either use the actual constant value or define a variable by that name that is set to the proper value. In this example, you could use the actual constant values in your code, such as follows:

```
If ADC1.ReadyState = 4 Then ' ReadyStateComplete
```

Note that the name of the constant has been included in the remark that follows this statement. Although this is not strictly necessary, the remark serves two very important functions:

- It retains the name of the enumerated constant in the code, so if conversion back to VBA is every necessary, the process is simplified.

- It makes the code easier to read and maintain later. By having the name of the constant, it also simplifies looking up the function of that value in the documentation or Object Browser.

> **TIP** In previous chapters, you used the Immediate window in the VBA environment to instantly execute code. If you need to know the values of specific enumerated constants, you can quickly and easily add a reference of the desired object model to a project. Then, you can print the values to the Immediate window (using the ? command) or look them up in the Object Browser.

Object Creation in VB Script

In the browser environment, you don't have the advantage of creating a new object using the class name. For example, to create a Recordset object in VBA, you could use code such as this:

```
Set myRS = New ADO.Recordset
```

Without the ability to select references, you need to use the complete class ID of the object. In your browser code, you would create a data control using the class ID number that uniquely identifies it, like this:

```
<OBJECT CLASSID=
   "clsid:BD96C556-65A3-11D0-983A-00C04FC29E33" ID="ADC1">
```

For important objects, such as the components in RDS, the class ID number is widely available. If you don't have the number in some sample code or reference work, you can use Microsoft FrontPage, a free utility such as Microsoft FrontPad (included as an optional application on the Office 2000 CD-ROM), Visual InterDev, or any other Web development environment to insert the ActiveX control to place the class ID in the code for you.

ADO Access to RDS

RDS, like the data control in Visual Basic, simply provides a user interface layer on top of the ADO programming library. Most of the programming access to RDS comes through a few methods available through ADO. To address the underlying ADO functionality, the RDC first must be created on the Web page.

You can create the RDC object using the <OBJECT> tag in the HTML page. Remember that this object will be created on the client side and will address the other server-side components that have been installed on the Web server. Within the browser, the HTML code to create a data access source for RDS looks like this:

```
<OBJECT CLASSID=
   "clsid:BD96C556-65A3-11D0-983A-00C04FC29E33" ID="ADC1">
   <PARAM NAME="SQL" VALUE="Select * from Products">
   <PARAM NAME="Connect" VALUE="DSN=AdvWorks;">
   <PARAM NAME="Server" VALUE="http://SalesWeb/"></OBJECT>
```

Like other HTML objects (such as Java applets), properties for an object are passed with a <PARAM> tag. In this example, RDS accepts essentially the same parameters that would be passed for connection through ADO, including a SQL query

Part III: Advanced MSDE

string, the `ConnectionString`, and login information. The `Server` parameter is used to indicate the URL of the server that will be used for RDS to provide the bridge to the database server.

> **NOTE** The `CLASSID` for the RDS data control is BD96C556-65A3-11D0-983A-00C04FC29E33. This value is standard on machines that have RDS installed. Therefore, you can use this class number in browser scripts with confidence that it will address the correct control on the client machine.

Like a data control on a VBA or Visual Basic form, more than one RDC may be present on a single Web page. Each data control can represent a different query and different data set. Bound controls on the page need to be linked to a data control, and any of the available RDCs can be used for binding.

The `RDS.DataControl` object is the object reference that is used for bound controls. A single `DataControl` object can be bound to many data-aware controls.

Enter the following code and save it with the filename MSDE_RDS.htm to create a simple RDS application:

```
<HTML>
<BODY>
<H1>RDS example</H1>
<OBJECT CLASSID=
   "clsid:BD96C556-65A3-11D0-983A-00C04FC29E33" ID="ADC1"
WIDTH=1 HEIGHT=1>
    <PARAM NAME="SQL" VALUE="Select * from customers">
    <PARAM NAME="Connect" VALUE="DSN=dsnNorthwindSQL;UID=sa;PWD=;">
    <PARAM NAME="Server" VALUE="http://localServer"></OBJECT>
<H2>Records:</H2>

<FORM NAME="myForm">
Company name: <INPUT NAME="myCompany" VALUE="" MAXLENGTH=50 SIZE=50>
<P>
Contact name: <INPUT NAME="myContact" VALUE="" MAXLENGTH=50 SIZE=50>
<P>
<INPUT TYPE="BUTTON" Value="Next Record in set" Name="cmdGo">
</FORM>

<Script Language="VBScript">

Sub displayRecords()
      ' Set the values of the form controls to the values
      ' supplied by the fields of the recordset
```

```
      myForm.myCompany.Value = myRS.Fields("contactName").Value
      myForm.myContact.Value = myRS.Fields("company").Value
End Sub

Sub cmdGo_OnClick()
   ' Check to make sure there are additional records to display
   If myRS.EOF Then
      MsgBox "No more records to display",16,"End-of-set"
   Else
      myRS.MoveNext
      displayRecords
   End If
End Sub

' Activate the connection when the page is first addressed
ADC1.Refresh
Set myRS = ADC1.Recordset
displayRecords

</SCRIPT>
</BODY>
</HTML>
```

After you save the code, you need to create an ODBC data source on the client machine and name the data source as **dsnNorthwind**. Point this data source at your MSDE server and select the default database as the Northwind database. The data source is needed to enable the RDC to address the database server. In the HTML file, set the username and password to values that allow access to MSDE. The preceding example includes the username *sa* with an empty password.

When this page is loaded into the browser, it will attempt to make a connection to the data source specified in the RDC. It will then display the contact name and company name of the first record in the set. Each click of the Next button will display the next record in the set. In order for this page to execute properly, the Web server specified by the `Server` parameter must have the server-side RDS components installed. These components are included with IIS in version 4 and above.

Server Activation

On the Web server, a service called the DataFactory is the default program included for RDS execution of ADO queries. The RDSServer.DataFactory is a program that is called a *business object,* because it encapsulates business functionality to provide an additional tier in the application structure. This component is automatically activated by the RDS data control through the IIS execution engine (using the ADS ISAPI handling driver).

Client Activation

Data Access Components (DAC) is a set of components provided by Microsoft that supplies client-side data access. The set of DAC objects contains all the client-side components used by RDS. On the client, the following two objects are used to manage the data and recordsets:

- ◆ **RDS.DataSpace:** Provides a programming interface for the data access to the server-side data factory.
- ◆ **RDS.DataControl:** Provides a graphical interface for the data access to the server-side data factory.

The DataControl actually uses the Dataspace object to communicate with the DataFactory on the server side. The DataControl has several methods for navigation and record editing. These functions are parallel in nature to similar ones used in ADO, but their names may be slightly different (such as `SubmitChanges` instead of `Update` for record changes).

> **Note:** In the past, updates to the DAC set has caused working applications to stop functioning properly. Because installing updates is often beyond the control even of system administrators (DAC updates occur with installation of Internet Explorer), it is difficult to manage what version the client is using. When you create an application using DAC, try to include text to indicate the version that is compatible with your application. If problems occur, the version can be checked.

You need to configure the data source for the client interaction. Disconnecting the recordset from a data source allows the connection to be broken while the data that has been retrieved can still be accessed, sorted, and manipulated. Instead of making a connection and then disconnecting, a recordset can also be created from scratch and then used.

ADO Recordset Classes

Under the References dialog box, you might notice that two ADO classes exist: Microsoft ADO Library and Microsoft ADO Recordset. The Recordset classes are the slim version of ADO for client access. Recordset classes are missing the following capabilities that are available in the complete ADO installation:

- **Connection object:** The `Connection` object is implicit in the ADOR framework. When a recordset is connected to a data source, the connection is stored in the `ActiveConnection` property, but a `Connection` object cannot be created independently.

- **Command object:** Because the ADOR was built for querying and examining data, it has no `Command` object. Stored procedures are accessed by passing them to a Recordset object to execute as the requested query.

- **Events:** The event structure is not supported with ADOR, so you cannot create code to be activated by the objects when a database event occurs.

- **Asynchronous queries:** The events structure of the ADO model in the Recordset classes is eliminated, so no infrastructure exists to support asynchronous queries.

- **Hierarchical recordsets:** The drill-down recordset capabilities present in ADO are not included in the subset of ADOR.

For most client-side applications, these advanced features are unnecessary, particularly for browser-based applications in which scripting code is not meant to take the place of a complete compiled application, because of speed and user interface issues.

The Recordset classes are also available on the Windows CE devices for portable data access. Amazingly, a small handheld device that weighs under half a pound can be used to execute full database queries against an MSDE server and manage the returned data.

ADO on Windows CE can be programmed in Visual C++ or, more conveniently, in Visual Basic 6. The Windows CE environment can be simulated on a desktop machine that is running Windows NT. The application is then compiled down to the executable that is specific to the processor used on the Windows CE device. Popular CE processors include Hitachi and MIPS brands.

ADO is only present on Windows CE machines that have CE 2.0 or later. Any recently purchased device that is not a palmtop will most likely have support. Most of the Windows CE palmtop devices have a smaller, more limited version of the CE operating system. Be sure to check your intended device before you begin planning implementation, to make certain the data access features are available.

> **NOTE:** The Windows CE operating system is updated frequently, and with the number of new devices that are released for the OS, you will want to check device compatibility before you begin creating a CE solution. You can check out the Windows CE developer site (`www.microsoft.com/windowsce/developer`) on Microsoft's Web site for more information.

Secure Access Through RDS

The primary method of addressing data through the RDS system is to use anonymous access. Like any other Web page, any user that can access a specific URL where the RDS solution is located can view it. Security can be handled through the simple Web server folder access security protocols. If the user cannot access a directory, then that user cannot receive the RDS client code and execute that application. Several other methods can also be used with the RDS system.

Making certain that the security safeguards are in place is very important with RDS systems, because many of these applications are made to use the Internet, which is far less secure than a typical LAN. See Chapter 25 for information on securing your database and connectivity to it.

Summary

Remote Data Services (RDS) provides datasource access through a Web server to enable you to create complete database applications within a Web solution. The client component of RDS allows client-side access to recordsets and data. The server-side components enable IIS to become a bridge between an OLE DB source and the Internet through the HTTP protocol. In this chapter, you covered the following:

- **Remote Data Services (RDS):** Enables an application executing in the Internet Explorer browser to query a data source on a Web server and use a client-side recordset to manipulate the data. The client-side recordset remains disconnected from the data source unless a new query, a requery, or an update is required.

- **Data Access Components (DAC):** The set of components that provides client-side data access, including disconnected recordsets and client-side cursors. The Remote data control acts like a traditional VB data control. It enables controls (such as text boxes, check boxes, and so forth) to be bound to the data control. The Data Space object provides the actual connection to the data source.

- **ADO Recordset (ADOR):** A subset of the entire ADO objects, ADOR provides client recordset access but lacks some of the advanced features of the complete ADO implementation, such as independent Connection objects, Command objects, events, and so forth. ADOR is available for use on the IE browser and Windows CE devices.

Chapter 21

Tuning for Optimum Performance

IN THIS CHAPTER

- Streamlining MSDE solutions
- Comparing actual performance versus perceived performance
- Organizing a database
- Optimizing clients, stored procedures, indexes, queries, and database servers
- Working with tempdb space

ALTHOUGH MANY OF THE database organization tasks should be performed early in a project (such as normalization planning, security policy definition, and so forth), performance tuning should be left until as late in the project as possible. Every good developer enforces some type of baseline performance that must be met during the development cycle before the next milestone is accepted. However, adjusting the structure of the database or choosing the type of index for tuning considerations is usually best left until the application is approaching polished form. Careful planning at the start should take care of most of the speed concerns that are generated during the process of development, whereas tuning at the end of the project will streamline the final application.

By its very nature, performance tuning eliminates implementation choices and specializes the code and database structures to perform the exact required tasks in the minimum amount of time with the fewest resources. Eliminating choices also limits flexibility. Therefore, tuning that is enacted too early in the process can straightjacket the developer in the number of options available to make necessary or desired shifts in development direction. A significant amount of optimization that is performed before the final stages of the project are reached can be useless at best. At worst, such optimization can be counterproductive when other changes are made to a system that is not feature-complete.

MSDE Solution Optimization

A database project developed with the MSDE database server has many different aspects. Unlike a database solution created with a client engine such as Microsoft Access, an MSDE application can be optimized for performance on both the client and the server. Even changing the balance of processing between the client and the server can change the dynamic of final application performance. Some of the ways that database applications can be tuned include optimizing the following:

- The client application
- Database organization (such as column location)
- Indexes
- Stored procedures
- The database server itself
- Connectivity settings (record caching, cursor configuration, and so forth)

The most important aspect of performance tuning lies in choosing the right area in which to spend a majority of your time. Some areas quickly reach a point of diminishing returns, and a team can expend their limited time optimizing a feature that doesn't significantly affect users.

A common example of this wasted effort is to focus too much on administrative reports. Because a report usually involves one or more large queries, development teams can spend a tremendous amount of time optimizing these reports, often cutting the query times down by a factor of four. Despite this seemingly effective use of time, the administrative reports upon which so much effort is expended to optimize may be run once a month or performed on overnight execution, so the query times mean very little.

In the same application, however, a common dialog box that is accessed by every user a dozen times a day may have a combo box list that takes half a minute to fill. Optimizing this small query could mean significantly more to the organization with only a fraction of the effort that was required on the report queries.

Actual Performance Versus Perceived Performance

Before you begin optimizing your application, it is important to recognize that the actual performance examined by developers can be much different from the perceived performance of that program by the users. Speed problems that frustrate developers often go unnoticed by users of the system, and vice versa. What may seem like a critical speed defect in the execution of the application may be seen by the user as a normal, or at least acceptable, speed. Meanwhile, a complicated process such as a nested query may seem blazing fast to the developer (especially in light of the complexity that is understood to be involved), but may make the program appear as slow as molasses to the end user.

The point is that the end user should be the yardstick by which the performance is judged. Therefore, the most crucial optimization that may need to take place may be in areas that you haven't examined because, as the developer, you find the speed adequate. In client applications, small additions to the user interface, such as a progress bar, may actually make a process seem much faster than the same process running without an indicator or showing the simple hourglass.

Therefore, part of your optimization plan should be to look at how the perceived performance can be increased. Some effective ways to achieve perceived performance increases on a database application include the following:

- **Asynchronous queries:** The ADO framework allows a query to be executed asynchronously, which means control returns to the calling application. An event will be activated when the query has completed. This enables the program to return control to the user so that the user can continue using the program while waiting for the request to be answered.

- **Local recordsets:** Data can be cached on the client application, and fast operations, such as simple drill-down or sorting, can be handled on the client machine.

- **Batch updates:** For large data updates, a batch can be created so that all the changes are sent to the server simultaneously. When a substantial number of operations is required, a batch can dramatically decrease the total update time. More importantly for perceived performance, however, is the fact that individual operations will seem instantaneous to the user.

- **Stored procedure execution:** Moving logic from the client to the server enables the user to continue using the client machine without the need of an asynchronous system to be put in place. If the database server is a high-performance machine, the logic itself will likely execute much more quickly.

Understanding the perception of the solution by the users who must run it can help you to determine which areas should be chosen as the focus of the bulk of effort for tuning. The best place to begin general performance optimization is to reevaluate the organization of the database itself, before actual deployment begins.

Database Organization

Within an MSDE server, a database is almost a self-contained unit. All the tables, stored procedures, rules, constraints, and user-defined types that are related to a particular application are generally stored within a single database. Techniques such as denormalization can help you to organize that database most effectively for use. For the database server itself, you may encounter a situation in which the master database becomes cluttered or corrupted, causing system performance problems. The master database can be rebuilt to eliminate such problems.

Denormalization

When you studied normalization in Chapter 4, you saw how well proper normalization can increase the readability of the data. For optimization, however, a developer must sometimes head in the opposite direction to achieve the performance that is needed for the application.

Moving columns among tables or duplicating information should be done only when a clear benefit is visible. Going against basic normalization should clearly be the exception and not the rule. If you are unsure whether making a "dirty" change will positively affect your application, don't do it.

Usually, the best method of development is to define your tables as part of a normalized system at the beginning of the project. At the end of the project, parts of the database can be selectively denormalized.

Rebuilding the Master Database

Corruption of the master database can cause your entire MSDE server system to fail. The MSDE system includes a utility called the *Rebuild Master Utility (rebuildm)* that rebuilds from scratch the master database on the server. A rebuild may be necessary if the master database is corrupted. Also, changes to the sort order, character set, or Unicode settings can be made without requiring reinstallation of the database server.

> **CAUTION:** You should rebuild a database only in the most dire circumstances, because all database objects are deleted with the rebuild. Any data currently stored in the database will be lost, so be sure you have a complete backup.

The rebuildm utility is located in the \BINN folder of the MSDE installation and can be executed from the command line or console. You will be asked to locate the directory in which the master database is held. After you select the directory and accept or alter the default options, the master database will be reconstructed.

> **NOTE:** Earlier versions of SQL Server allowed the master database to be rebuilt from within the Enterprise Manager. This option is no longer available. You must use the rebuildm utility for reconstruction on MSDE and SQL Server 7 and above.

Client Optimization

Often overlooked by database developers is the optimization that can take place on the client application itself. Developers often focus on interactivity optimization issues and don't look closely at database communication processes that enable the client to complete operations against the server. Access developers are accustomed to the client application and the database being inseparable, whereas in an MSDE system, the client and the server execute independently.

Factors such as the communications protocol, batch optimization, and communication-overhead analysis all can be taken into account when addressing performance issues.

ADO Versus ODBC

ADO is the default object framework that is used when addressing the MSDE source. Because the SQL Server Data Provider is optimized to allow access to all of the functionality of the MSDE server through Command, Connection, and Recordset objects, almost all new solutions are developed with it.

However, ODBC is often much faster than ADO for simple data retrieval. Although ADO is the cornerstone of Microsoft's current data access plans, ODBC can be used very reliably, especially when accessing MSDE. The ODBCDirect object model and the Visual Basic Remote Data Objects (RDO) create only a very thin layer of interface over the direct ODBC calls and can initiate calls to a data source with far less overhead than ADO.

If your application sends a large number of individual commands to the MSDE server, you might gain performance advantages from ODBC. As a very broad example, suppose your application might send thousands of Update statements per hour to the MSDE server. In this scenario, the application would be much faster under the ODBC interface. However, if your application sends a single SQL command that updates a thousand records, any optimization would be so small as to be unnoticeable.

Using SQL Batch Statements

Most of the common programming that addresses data sets on the client makes individual row requests of the data source. For example, a common ADO request might be to delete a record. If the desired solution needs to delete all records of potential customers who never placed an order, for example, one ADO solution would be to select these records and delete them sequentially. This method is actually one I personally have seen used in many applications.

Bringing these records all the way to the client and then deleting them is useless if a command on the server would achieve the task more elegantly, more quickly, and with less overhead. So, using a single Delete command in SQL with the appropriate Where clause could eliminate all the desired records with all of the central processing occurring on the server. When hundreds of records are involved, the batch command can be orders of magnitude faster.

Therefore, whenever you see a process on the client that uses some type of For...Next loop to advantage through records, consider whether an available SQL command could do the job more effectively.

Using the Application Performance Explorer (APE)

If you own Microsoft Visual Studio (a suite of development tools that includes VB, Visual C++, Visual InterDev, and more), you have an excellent tool that can perform general transaction modeling for your applications. Application Performance Explorer (APE) is a utility that enables you to create a simulation model of your client/server applications. It can then perform time tests on the execution environment and provide an idea of the overhead that you will be facing when numerous users are working over the network.

APE (see Figure 21-1) enables you to set up a model of your current or projected system. By entering the number of communications between one machine and another, RPC calls, COM instance interactions, and other factors, the program will execute a sample model. It can then provide estimates, such as per-transaction performance, so that you can better understand your system.

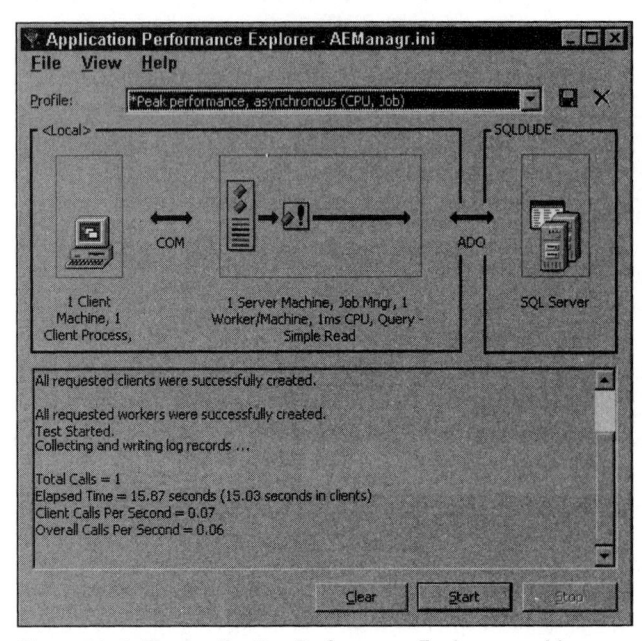

Figure 21-1: The Application Performance Explorer provides communication modeling.

Stored Procedure Optimization

Stored procedures may be optimized not only in their code, similar to a traditional procedural language, but also in their operating environment. Because a stored procedure can execute a query or execute some other form of processing, procedures often execute more quickly with any enhancement to the operating environment.

Query Caching

Stored procedures, when executed on the database server, are cached for similar query execution. For example, if one query requests all of the customers from the state of California, the server will cache this query, the execution plan of the query, and the memory structures used to complete it. If a similar query is issued shortly after the initial request, all of the cache execution structures are reactivated and used by the new query.

This means that a similar query will execute in far less time than the initial one of that type. However, if the query appears nearly the same (uses the same columns and so forth) but is very different in the data that must be sorted or the amount of data to be returned, significant performance penalties will occur. The old structures will be used by default, making the query much slower than it might have been when issued to a fresh server.

The best method of avoiding this problem is to recognize whether your application will issue many queries that, on the surface, seem very similar yet generate greatly different results. In that case, the stored procedure can flush the structures after every query. This means that your solution will forgo the performance gains that occur when the queries are similar, but you will also avoid trying to fit a square peg of a query into a round hole.

Setting up the view or stored procedure to avoid these restrictions is done using the With Recompile command when creating the database objects. This setting forces the execution model to recompile the stored procedure with each new execution.

Using the Show Plan Feature to Examine a Query Process

One way to optimize a stored procedure is to examine how the procedure actually executes. The execution plan is available by executing the SET SHOWPLAN_ALL and SET SHOWPLAN_TEXT stored procedures. The "Query Optimization" section later in this chapter provides information on using these settings to examine the plan used for a query. These commands also display the plan for execution of a stored procedure and all the processes that are invoked when the stored procedure is activated.

Index Optimization

Optimizing the indexes is certainly one of the most critical tasks you can perform to decrease the time it takes to generate desired query results. Index optimization is almost as much an art as it is a science, because greater experience in the field makes it much more apparent where indexes need to be placed for best performance.

Indexes are optimized in several ways:

- **Changing the indexed columns:** When the solution is deployed, queries expected to be used frequently are actually seldom referenced. Relocating an index to another column can positively impact your application.

- **Using complex or compound indexes:** Indexing by multiple columns may help speed searches. If the search for a customer record always uses the state and ZIP code together in a query, creating a complex index that includes both of these columns can make the query return results much faster.

- **Removing unneeded indexes:** Each index that is included in the table imposes a performance burden for both the server processor and disk storage. When a new record is added, an old one deleted, or a value changed, each index that references the key fields involved in these modified tables must be recalculated.

In Microsoft Access, you may be accustomed to simply adding an index to a particular table and having it associated with the appropriate field. On the MSDE server, each index has its own name so that it may be referenced individually. Naming the indexes also enables you to manually optimize your solution by explicitly indicating a particular index for use during a procedure.

Complex or Compound Indexes

When multiple columns are referenced in a single index, the index is known as a *complex* or *compound* index. For example, a single index can provide sorting capabilities for the last name, first name, and middle initial column values in a table so that any queries can quickly check all three of these fields with little loss in performance.

> **TIP** Be careful not to include too many columns in a single index. If the index does not match the criteria specified in the `Select` statement, it will not be used. This consequence, added to the fact that each additional column slows down inserts, deletes, and modifications, makes it attractive for minimizing the number of complex indexes in a database.

Clustering Indexes

A clustered index is used to actually sort the rows in a table, instead of simply providing a reference list. In contrast to a standard index that contains a reference list of the pointers to rows in a table, a clustered index actually defines the physical order in which the data for the table will be stored. Therefore, the logical and physical orders of the records for this type of index are the same.

Clustered indexes have the following advantages over standard indexes:

- **Primary key sorting:** A clustered index defined on the primary key of the table will provide the fastest available retrieval of a row by a specified ID. The primary key is automatically used as the clustered index value when the table is created unless this option is disabled or another column is defined as the clustered index at the time of table creation.

- **Most common value searching:** A frequently searched value type will have a performance advantage when defined as the clustered index for the table.

- **Subsequent record retrieval:** Because the records are stored in the physical order of the index, after the first value is found that matches the search criteria, the records that also match the criteria are located physically directly after the first record.

- **Minimized sorting:** Common queries that use the ORDER BY statement to arrange the sort order of the result sets will be accelerated if the rows are physically stored in the same order as the sort.

A clustered index can be defined to store the data sorting by multiple columns, such as last name and then first name. Because this index determines the physical storage format, only a single clustered index may be used per table.

> **NOTE:** When a clustered index contains many columns for the sort order, the nonclustered indexes can become very large. Each nonclustered index entry contains the key of the clustered index, so nonclustered index size reflects the clustered index definition. Try to minimize the number of clustered sort columns, to maximize performance of the database.

Adding a clustered index to a table actually copies the data from the table into a duplicate with the proper sorting setup and then deletes the original table.

Try to avoid placing a clustered index on a column whose values frequently change. Every time a new record is inserted or the value of the defined columns in the clustered sort order changes, the MSDE server must rearrange the data to physically accommodate the column changes. For a high-volume database that frequently alters the sort column values of individual rows, performance may be severely degraded. That is one of the reasons why most clustered indexes are defined on the primary key for records — this value seldom, if ever, changes.

To minimize the amount of hard drive activity created by the insertion of new records, MSDE includes a variable known as the FillFactor, which is a percentage value from 0 to 100 that defines how much of a data page should be left empty to allow for new insert placement. By leaving extra space on each data page, the frequency with which the existing pages must be reordered is minimized. The greater amount of extra space kept for insertions, however, increases the drive space required for the database. Therefore, it is a tradeoff of space for performance.

When the value of the FillFactor is set to 100, 100 percent of each page will be used before another page is added for new data. If it's set to 60, only 60 percent will be used before a new page is added. Therefore, additional room exists for the rows to grow within the page, minimizing the amount of processor-intensive reorganization of the table.

Therefore, when many changes will be made to the table, a lower setting for the FillFactor will enhance performance. On a read-only table, the FillFactor could be set to 100, because no insertions will occur that require a repagination of the table.

The default FillFactor for the MSDE server can be set through the sp_configure procedure. To set the FillFactor to 70 percent for the entire server, you can use a command like this:

```
Execute sp_configure 'fill factor', 70
Go
Reconfigure
Go
```

Any sp_configure execution requires the Reconfigure command to be executed before the new setting will take effect. For a table, the FillFactor is specified with the creation of each index. The syntax for the Create Index procedure appears as follows:

```
CREATE [UNIQUE] [CLUSTERED | NONCLUSTERED]
    INDEX index_name ON table (column [,...n])
[WITH
        [PAD_INDEX]
        [[,] FILLFACTOR = fillfactor]
        [[,] IGNORE_DUP_KEY]
        [[,] DROP_EXISTING]
        [[,] STATISTICS_NORECOMPUTE]
]
[ON filegroup]
```

You can create a new sample table by using this code:

```
CREATE TABLE myOrders
(
    orderID int identity, division char(8),
    Constraint orderKey Primary Key (orderID, division)
)
```

From this sample table, add a clustered index as follows:

```
Create Clustered Index clstr_myOrders On myOrders
    With FILLFACTOR = 20
```

This example code demonstrates creating a clustered index that has a fill factor of 20 percent, in consideration that many new rows will be inserted into the table.

> **NOTE** For those seeking a deeper level of understanding of the index, it is stored in *b-tree* format. The b-tree is a method of quickly sorting and storing data in a hierarchical format. With a root node at the top, each leaf node in the b-tree represents a page of data on the database server. Each leaf is part of a double-linked list that contains a reference to the previous leaf on the list at that level, and the next leaf at that level.

Nonclustered indexes use the same basic organization of clustered indexes, except within the hierarchical b-tree used for sorting, the physical data isn't stored in each leaf of the tree. Instead, a reference to the data is stored in the leaf, meaning that while searching and retrieval is slightly slower, many nonclustered indexes can be created and performance isn't hurt significantly by frequent changes to the column values by which the index is sorted. If no clustered index is defined for a table, the nonclustered index simply uses a pointer to each row, rather than using the sort keys provided by the clustered index to reference rows.

Index Tuning Wizard

In the Enterprise Manager, the Index Tuning Wizard can examine a query and return suggestions on what indexes might be created to optimize the query. It can even implement many of the recommendations that are made. The substantial benefits of the wizard are realized when a workload is analyzed over a period of time with the Profiling tool. With this information, the Index Tuning Wizard can make the best suggestions for optimization under actual work conditions.

To use the Index Tuning Wizard, follow these steps:

1. Execute the Enterprise Server.

2. Select the SQL Server Query Analyzer under the Tools menu to display the Query Analyzer. Before an index can be optimized, a sample query is required that will be used to test the performance of the current indexes.

3. In the DB combo box in the upper-right corner of the window, select the NorthwindSQL database.

4. Enter the following SQL code into the query window:

```
SELECT Orders.CustomerID, Orders.OrderID,
Customers.CompanyName,
    Customers.ContactName, [Order Details].ProductID,
Products.ProductName,
    [Order Details].Quantity, [Order Details].UnitPrice,
[Order Details].Discount
FROM Products
INNER JOIN
    (Customers INNER JOIN
        (Orders INNER JOIN [Order Details] ON Orders.OrderID =
[Order Details].OrderID)
        ON Customers.CustomerID = Orders.CustomerID)
        ON Products.ProductID = [Order Details].ProductID;
```

5. Under the File menu, select the Save As option and name the file **OrdersQuery.sql** and store it in a location in which you can find it in a minute.

6. Reactivate the Enterprise Manager and click the MSDE database server in the list of available servers.

7. Select the Wizards option under the Tools menu.

8. Expand the Management item to show the available wizards that are held in that category and select the Index Tuning Wizard item (see Figure 21-2).

9. Click the OK button to execute the wizard.

10. Click the Next button to advance to the server selection page.

11. Select the NorthwindSQL database from the Database drop-down list box. Leave the Keep all existing indexes option checked so that the current indexes will be saved.

Chapter 21: Tuning for Optimum Performance 441

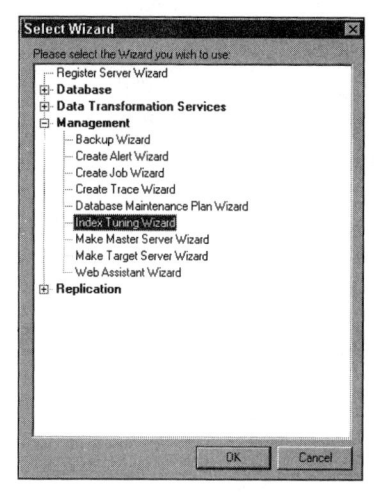

Figure 21-2: The Index Tuning Wizard is located in the Management list of available wizards.

12. Click the Perform thorough analysis option to check it (see Figure 21-3).

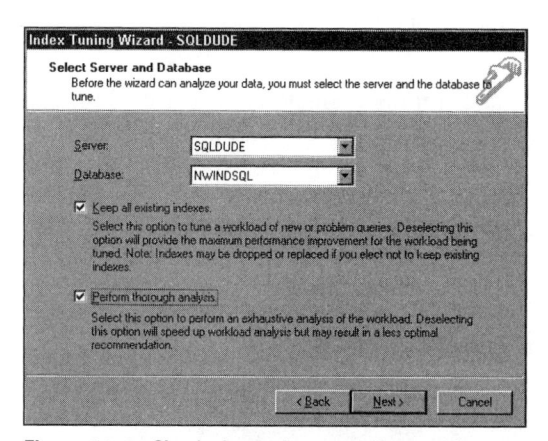

Figure 21-3: Check the option to perform a thorough analysis on the indexes of the database tables.

13. Click the Next button to advance to the Identity Workload screen.

14. Leave the I have saved workload file option selected and click the Next button.

15. Select the MyWorkload file option, and a File dialog box will be displayed.

16. Select the OrdersQuery.sql file you created earlier in the Query Analyzer, and click the OK button.

17. Click the Next button to advance to the table selection screen (see Figure 21-4), which enables you to select all of the tables that should be examined by the Index Tuning Wizard. You should see all of the tables in the currently available database. Because this example will tune all of the Northwind tables, you can leave all of them in the Tables to tune list box.

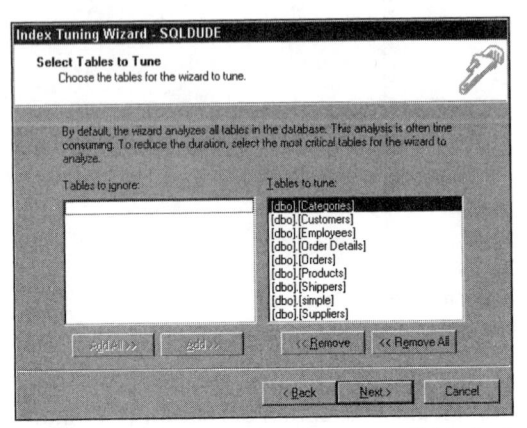

Figure 21-4: All of the tables that are available for index optimization will be listed in the Tables to tune list box.

18. Click the Next button to begin the evaluation. A progress box should be displayed that indicates the process that is taking place. The wizard will examine each table, make a list of recommended indexes, and indicate whether the indexes already exist (see Figure 21-5). If you scroll down the list, you will see that many of the necessary indexes are currently present in the database.

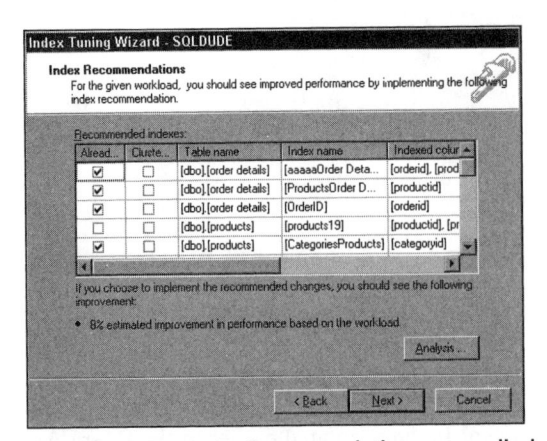

Figure 21-5: The Index Recommendations screen displays the new potential indexes and estimates the performance increase.

19. Click the Analysis button to display the reports of the analysis performed. Several reports are available, including these: Index Usage (current and recommended), Table Analysis, Query Cost, Workload Analysis, and Tuning Summary. All of these reports may be examined in the grid shown in the window or saved to a text file for later examination.
20. Click the Close button to dismiss the Analysis window.
21. Click the Next button to progress to the update indexes page.
22. Click the Save script file option. A Save dialog box is automatically presented, enabling you to store to a file the Transact-SQL code for the index creation.
23. Enter the filename **OrdersQueryIndexes.sql** and click the Save button. This file will contain all of the Transact-SQL code needed for the index creation.
24. Click the Next button to advance to the final confirmation screen.
25. Click the Finish button to save the script to the specified file. You will be alerted that the Index Tuning Wizard was successful. If you dismiss this window, you will be returned to the Enterprise Manager.

By saving the recommended index creation to a file, you can examine what changes would be made to the database, and modify them where appropriate. This file can also be used to update servers that cannot run the wizard, such as MSDE deployment servers, because they do not have an Enterprise Manager installation.

Query Optimization

The optimization of your SQL query can be critical to getting the best performance out of your server. Having an understanding of how the MSDE server will actually execute the query process will help you design queries that can be most easily used with the database engine.

Several items that you might use in the query itself make it difficult for the database server to process the query in the shortest amount of time. Usually, the items that cause the slowdown problems come from code that forces the query functions to ignore the indexes available for a particular column and examine the data longhand.

One example of this problem is the use of the `IsNull` function on a column value. Criteria in the `Where` clause that used the `IsNull` function disable the index for that column to use for searching.

Also causing indexes to be ignored are the commands `DISTINCT` and `GROUP BY`. When these appear in a query, the indexes for the tables are disabled.

Checking the Execution Plan

The execution plan used by a query or stored procedure can be valuable for analysis to determine what changes must be made to make the plan more effective. For example, if a large part of the query executes without index references, an index can be added to increase throughput. The plan will reveal exactly which objects are used by a query or stored procedure.

DISPLAYING THE EXECUTION PLAN

Two settings, SET SHOWPLAN_ALL and SET SHOWPLAN_TEXT, display the plan when execution takes place. The query will not be performed while these settings are on; the plan will be displayed instead. These commands must be directly executed on the server and cannot be included within a stored procedure.

A simple query on the Northwind database with the SHOWPLAN_ALL setting activated could look like this:

```
Set SHOWPLAN_ALL ON
Go
select * from customers where CustomerID = 'ALFKI'
Go
```

When the SET SHOWPLAN_ALL command is executed with the ON switch, a more complex recordset (refer to the Query Analyzer) is returned:

StmtText
select * from customers where customerid = 'ALFKI'
  |--Clustered Index
     Seek(OBJECT:([Northwind].[dbo].[Customers].[PK_Customers]),
     SEEK:([Customers].[CustomerID]=Convert([@1])) ORDERED)

StmtId	NodeId	Parent	PhysicalOp	LogicalOp
3	1	0	NULL	NULL
3	3	1	Clustered Index Seek	Clustered Index Seek

Argument
NULL
CT:([Northwind].[dbo].[Customers].[PK_Customers]),
   SEEK:([CustomerID]=Convert([@1])) ORDERED

DefinedValues
NULL
[Customers].[CustomerID], [Customers].[CompanyName], [Customers].[ContactName],
   [Customers].[ContactTitle], [Customers].[Address], [Customers].[City],

[Customers].[Region], [Customers].[PostalCode], [Customers].[Country],
[Customers].[Phone]...

EstimateRows	EstimateIO	EstimateCPU	AvgRowSize	TotalSubtreeCost
NULL	NULL	NULL	NULL	NULL
1.0	6.3284999E-3	7.9600002E-5	303	0.0064081

OutputList
NULL
[Customers].[CustomerID], [Customers].[CompanyName], [Customers].[ContactName],
[Customers].[ContactTitle], [Customers].[Address], [Customers].[City],
[Customers].[Region], [Customers].[PostalCode], [Customers].[Country],
[Customers].[Phone]...

Warnings	Type	Parallel	EstimateExecutions
NULL	SELECT	0	NULL
NULL	PLAN_ROW	0	1.0

(2 row(s) affected)

After the SHOWPLAN_TEXT setting has been activated, information on the execution of the query will be displayed. When a query such as select * from customers where CustomerID = 'ALFKI' is executed with the Show Plan option on, the results appear like this:

```
StmtText
select * from customers where CustomerID = 'ALFKI'
(1 row affected)
 StmtText
   |--Bookmark
Lookup(BOOKMARK:([Bmk1000]),OBJECT:([NorthwindSQL].[dbo].[Customers]))
       |--Index Seek(OBJECT:([NorthwindSQL].[dbo].[Customers].[aaaaaCustomers_P
       K]), SEEK:([Customers].[CustomerID]=Convert([@1])) ORDERED)
(2 rows affected)
```

This returned text is broken down by categories. The StmtText contains the text of the query to be executed.

From the returned information, you can see that the index used for the search is displayed. Any statement executed with the plan setting on will attempt to display the plan. Commands that don't return result sets, such as the Create Table command, will return an error when executed. Executing the OFF switch will turn off the Show Plan option:

SET SHOWPLAN_TEXT OFF

> **Note:** The information returned by the `SHOWPLAN_TEXT` setting is not the same as `SHOWPLAN_ALL`. The `ALL` information is returned as a recordset, whereas the `TEXT` setting is formatted with text commands. Therefore, a tool such as osql or isql should be used to examine the plans with the `SHOWPLAN_TEXT` option.

GRAPHICAL DISPLAY THROUGH SQL SERVER QUERY ANALYZER

The SQL Server Query Analyzer, included with SQL Server, enables a developer to examine how a query is actually executed. Early in this book, you read how different programming is in SQL (a results language) from programming in a language such as Visual Basic (a procedural language). In SQL, you request the final results that you desire, and the SQL engine determines the best way to return those results.

The Query Analyzer tool enables you to examine specifically how the query is executed, which makes it possible to modify the query or tune the database server to best execute important query requests.

The SQL Query Analyzer takes the information that is returned as a recordset by the `SHOWPLAN_ALL` and `SHOWPLAN_TEXT` options and converts it to a graphical display (see Figure 21-6). The diagram in Figure 21-6 shows that placing the cursor over any step in the process will display a pop-up box that contains all of the statistical information related to that step.

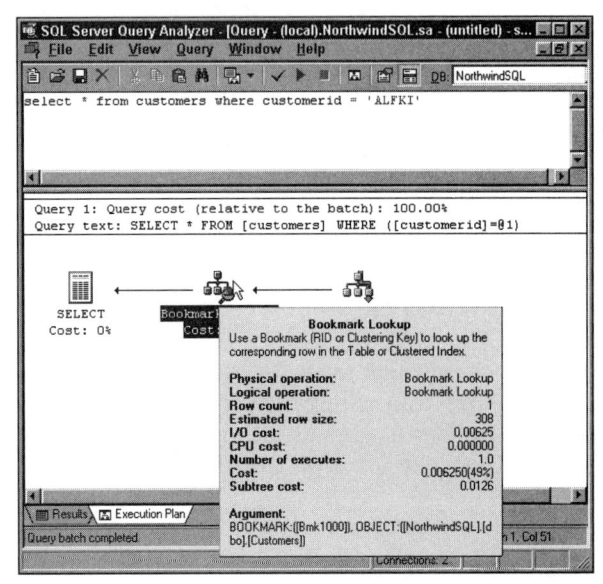

Figure 21-6: The SQL Server Query Analyzer provides a graphic display of the information returned by the `SHOWPLAN` settings.

Flattening Nested Queries

Chapter 6 introduced you to nested queries and demonstrated how powerful a nested query actually can be. Chapter 6 also warned about the potential overhead of using these query types, because they tend to exponentially raise the query times involved in returning results.

Nested queries probably should be your most optimized type of query in the application, because a small performance increase on the subquery can provide enormous performance gains for the overall query. The fewer nested queries (or flatter) that you can make a query, the faster your query will tend to execute.

For certain types of joins, such as those in which one of the join tables is much smaller than another, a *nested loop join* can be used effectively. Also known as an *iterative join,* a source table is used as the input for the secondary table in the join.

When small tables are used, nested loop joins can be much faster for joins than the merge or hash techniques. For large table joins, however, performance suffers using the nested loop join.

Merge Joins

The *merge* join compares the values between two tables based on a number of columns that are held in common. If the values in the comparison column of each row are equal, the data will be included in the data set; if they are not equal, the row with the lesser value is discarded. When a merge join is activated and no Order By clause is included with the query, it is the fastest available technique for join operations.

Hash Joins

A hashed index is a technique the MSDE server uses to speed the searches of values such as strings. A hash is used to optimize a join by introducing a memory structure that is automatically created to hold summary values that can be searched far more quickly than the actual data.

Database Server Optimization

The MSDE server has a broad range of settings that can be used to make it execute most effectively. Increasing the capabilities of the server or tracing and subsequently eliminating errors generated on the server can help minimize bottlenecks to optimum database performance.

Server Machine

Most of the changes that can be made to increase performance of the server machine are fairly obvious. Examining the currently used RAM resources (through the Task Manager on Windows NT) can tell you how large the page file is that's used to provide for virtual memory. Any use of virtual memory will decrease performance, so increasing the RAM to a larger amount than what is currently used can dramatically speed up processing.

Likewise, if server processor resources are over 80 percent expended, spikes in processing requests will not allow the server to have the adequate capacity to run at full speed. An increase in the processor speed or number of processors in the server machine will optimize the database execution.

Note that the operating system on which the MSDE server is running can also affect performance. The SQL Server engine was written to run most effectively on Windows NT. If multiple processors are available, NT can effectively scale the performance to use those processors. In contrast, Windows 95/98 has been optimized for single-processor use, and MSDE server inherits these capabilities from the operating system.

Using the Tracing Capabilities

Through Transact-SQL code, you can activate various trace flags that can be used to modify the execution of the database server. Some of the trace flags allow the temporary disabling of a particular service (such as checking for interim constraint violations) or the generation and printing of execution-related information such as the estimated and actual cost of doing a sort. By activating these trace functions, you can modify the operations of your MSDE server to observe potential conditions or to retrieve statistical information on some of the operations that execute on the server.

The trace functions can also be activated from the console (or MS-DOS prompt) by executing the sqlservr program. To disable line-number information on syntax errors (code 106), you could enter code like this at the prompt:

```
sqlservr /dC:\MSSQL7\data\master.dat /T106
```

When you execute this statement, you will be notified that the trace has been enabled. The command must be executed when the MSDE service is stopped.

Working with tempdb Space

The temporary database (tempdb) is used by the MSDE server for writing scratch information, such as when a query contains the SQL statement ORDER BY. If the tempdb runs low on disk space, serious performance degradation can occur. When tempdb actually runs out of space, the operation that is being attempted will fault.

By default, this database is set for unlimited growth, which means that if the current operation needs extra space, tempdb can expand to consume all of the available drive space. This growth can be controlled by setting a maximum-size parameter on the database. Likewise, you can reset the tempdb to automatically expand as much as needed.

The tempdb file may also be moved to place it on a drive that may have more space for its expansion. A change to the location of the tempdb file will not take place until the MSDE server has been stopped and restarted. After the tempdb file has been moved to a new location, the old file will still exist and must be deleted manually.

When more space is needed, a parameter is available that specifies the growth increment of the database that is used. For example, tempdb may currently be 2MB in size, and the growth increment is set to 5MB (the default). An executing query may need more space, and the size of the database will be bumped to 7MB. You may want to set this parameter to a new value if expansion is often required.

All the parameters of the tempdb may be adjusted either through the Enterprise Manager or with Transact-SQL code. Using the Transact-SQL commands enables you to make the modification from any machine on the network without having the Enterprise Manager installed.

Using Transact-SQL Commands

It is also possible to reset the size of the tempdb through Transact-SQL code. You can use the `Alter Database` procedure to change the size to provide the breathing room for best performance. Use the `Alter Database` command with the `MODIFY FILE` section types. Within this section, several parameters are available to determine the modification. The `MAXSIZE` argument adjusts the size that the tempdb file can reach. The `FILEGROWTH` parameter in the `MODIFY FILE` parameters sets the increment by which the file will be increased as additional space is needed.

To change the location of tempdb, you can use Transact-SQL code like this:

```
ALTER DATABASE tempdb
MODIFY FILE
(
 NAME = tempdb,
 FILENAME = 'c:\mssql7\data\tempdb.mdf',
 SIZE = 5MB,
 MAXSIZE = 100MB,
 FILEGROWTH = 5MB
)
GO
```

The `SIZE` parameter must be at least as large as the current tempdb file. The larger size of tempdb will often increase the speed of a system on which many users do simultaneous queries that require sorted data sets.

Using the Enterprise Manager

Although the changes can be made through Transact-SQL, you may favor the graphical interface of the Enterprise Manager. It can also remotely modify a SQL Server-based database server if the server is registered in one of the Enterprise

Manager's groups. The Enterprise Manager can be used to modify the tempdb settings through the Properties window. In the Enterprise Manager, follow these steps to expand the tempdb size:

1. Execute the Enterprise Manager in the MMC.

2. Expand the database server and the Database folder item to display the tempdb database item.

3. Right-click the tempdb item and select the Properties option.

4. From the Properties window, click the General tab (see Figure 21-7). You can see that both the location of the database and the automatic file-growth settings may be altered.

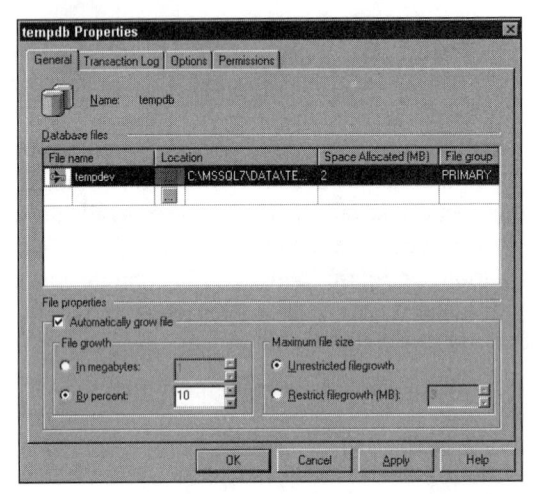

Figure 21-7: The Properties window provides settings for the tempdb database.

5. Alter any desired setting, such as moving the tempdb file to a drive that has more space if the place it is located is in danger of low disk space.

6. Click the OK button to accept any changes that were made.

Of course, both the Enterprise Manager and the Transact-SQL code modify the same objects, so any changes in one place will be reflected in the other. Additionally, maintenance of the MSDE server performed through the SQL-DMO object model provides another method of addressing these same objects.

Summary

Optimizing your database solution can truly enhance both its execution and the user's perception of execution. Optimization is a necessary final step for any project and thus time should be allocated for tuning before the deployment. Although the best performance should be pursued during development, the final optimization can use near-deployment conditions and sample workloads to determine exactly where the bottlenecks are most likely to occur. After this information is gained, the solution can be adjusted before users must rely on it. In this chapter, you covered the following:

- **Client optimization:** The client may be one key point where the perceived performance of the application may be enhanced. The use of asynchronous queries or status information may increase the perception of speed. In certain cases, modeling and changing the underlying data communication between the client and the server will increase performance.

- **Index optimization:** By altering the indexes, the key queries of your application can increase the responsiveness and speed that the user experiences. By examining the execution plan and using tools such as the Index Tuning Wizard, you can optimize the most commonly used queries.

- **Database tuning:** Settings for everything from the cursor defaults to the timeout values can be adjusted to maximize available database server resources.

- **With Recompile:** This command sets a stored procedure to recompile each time, eliminating any caches or other memory structures that have been built to optimize performance, but may impede performance under certain conditions.

- **Trace features:** A number of trace flags may be switched on to temporarily enable tracking of server conditions or disable other functions, such as constraint checking.

Chapter 22

Working with MSDE Logs

IN THIS CHAPTER

- Examining the MSDE activity logs
- Understanding the function of transaction logs
- Activating Long Running Query logs

THE MSDE DATABASE SERVER can accept many simultaneous users and execute numerous complex processes. Monitoring the activity of the server is done primarily through summary information, because of the large amount of data generated. Writing non-real-time status information into a log file is an established method of storing data on events that occur on the system. Examining and properly maintaining these files can be critical to effectively managing your MSDE server.

In addition to the status logs kept for a wide variety of execution processes (including replication, agents, DTS events, and so forth), logs are kept of the transactions that occur on the server. The transaction logs maximize the potential for accurate database recovery in case a problem occurs. Microsoft Access users will find that managing a transaction log does not have a direct parallel to any operations in an Access database. Implementation of the transaction log is one of the key technological features that distinguishes a complete database server such as MSDE from a database engine such as Access.

MSDE Activity Logs

MSDE writes a substantial amount of information into log files. Actual errors are usually a small percentage of the actual entries contained in these logs. The bulk of entries are made up of informational logs that indicate conditions such as the server initialization, transaction handling, changes to properties of the server, and so forth.

The following are the two primary logs maintained under MSDE server execution:

- **Error log:** Contains all of the general information relating to the MSDE server itself.

◆ **Agent log:** Contains status and error entries that occur in relation to agent execution. If the SQL Server Agent is not executing on your database server, the agent log will not appear on the server drive.

Error Logs

The error log kept by the MSDE server contains errors and information related to the processes executed on the server such as database startup activity, connection information, DLL access, file opening, transactional status, and so on. These logs are stored in the *Log* directory within the main server directory.

The error log file containing the most current information has the name *Errorlog* without an extension. Historical files of Errorlog have a numbered extension (Errorlog.1, Errorlog.2, and so on). You can view the log files with a standard text editor such as Notepad, or they are available through the Enterprise Manager in the Management Folder stored in the SQL Server Error Logs item.

Entries for the database log appear like this:

```
2000-02-28 21:50:13.10 spid1    Loading SQL Server's character set.
2000-02-28 21:50:13.35 spid1    3 transactions rolled forward in database
   'master' (1).
2000-02-28 21:50:13.41 spid1    0 transactions rolled back in database
   'master' (1).
```

These particular entries display the time and type of events that have occurred, such as the roll forward (recovery of transactions) and roll back (revocation of transactions) operations of the MSDE database.

> **NOTE** You might see an error in the error log like this: Failed to obtain TransactionDispenserInterface: XACT_E_TMNOTAVAILABLE. This error indicates that the Distributed Transaction Coordinator (MS DTC, located in Control Panel → Settings) is not functioning properly. If this error occurs, be sure to check your DTC configuration to determine the cause of the problem.

Some of the most important messages contained in the log are warnings issued that indicate whether memory problems are occurring. Cursor and cache overload are two common memory problems that may be indicated. Any resource shortage that is indicated by log entries should be immediately remedied for best performance of the server.

The log file may also contain information or errors generated by a user-defined program. Through code in a stored procedure or directly through SQL execution, you can write text into the MSDE error log. The `xp_logevent` procedure will write any error you need to create into the log. In addition to the text description of the error, the entry can include an error number and a severity number.

> **NOTE:** If MSDE is executing on Windows NT, the operating system itself will maintain a log called the Application Log for errors, information, and warnings that relate to OS processes. When an error reaches a certain level of severity, it will be placed not only in the MSDE error log, but also in the Application Log. You may effectively reference the Application Log when an MSDE error occurs to gain an understanding of the context of the error. Often, other warnings in the Application Log (such as low drive space) will generate the problems encountered by the MSDE server.

To write to the MSDE error log, you can use the `xp_logevent` procedure with code like this:

```
xp_logevent 60000, 'My error message'
```

This code writes an error with a specified error code of 60,000 (safe range for a user-defined error) with a simple text message. The severity level of the error entry can be included as an optional parameter. To set the severity of the error to 2 (user-defined error), you can use code like this:

```
xp_logevent 60000, 'My error message', 2
```

Setting the severity level of the error determines how the error-processing system will react to that error (by ignoring the error, issuing alerts, writing into the NT Application Log, or some other similar response) The error severity levels describe the type of error. Table 22-1 provides a list of the severity types and their descriptions. High severity levels with numbers 17 and higher are reported in the NT Application Log when the MSDE server is executing on the Windows NT OS. Error levels are basically divided into three groups: levels 1-10 are status errors, levels 11-16 are correctable errors, and levels 17-25 are hardware errors.

TABLE 22-1 SEVERITY NUMBERS AND THEIR SPECIFIC ERROR TYPES

Severity Number	Description
1–9	*Information Error* – Error occurred that did not effect execution.
10	*Status Information* – Returned when you have passed incorrect information to the database server.

Continued

TABLE 22-1 SEVERITY NUMBERS AND THEIR SPECIFIC ERROR TYPES *(Continued)*

Severity Number	Description
11–16	*Correctable User Errors* – A fault that prompts the user for correction of the error, such as an input message box.
17	*Insufficient Resources* – Resources might include disk space, memory errors, locks, or encroachment on limits set by the system administrator.
18	*Non-fatal Internal Error Detected* – An internal error, such as within a query optimization, has occurred. However, the error was nonfatal and the process continued despite its occurrence.
19	*SQL Server Error in Resource* – An internal limitation was exceeded and the current batch process was aborted.
20	*SQL Server Fatal Error in Current Process* – The current process faulted. Because of the multithreaded implementation of the MSDE server, this error may indicate that a process failed, but the server itself is still likely to be executing.
21	*SQL Server Fatal Error in Database (dbid) Processes* – This fault indicates all the current processes have faulted, but the server itself is still likely to be executing.
22	*SQL Server Fatal Error Table Integrity Suspect* – The table or index has faulted and the database objects may be damaged. Restarting the MSDE server may correct the problem. If not, the individual objects may have to be deleted and then restored from a backup.
23	*SQL Server Fatal Error: Database Integrity Suspect* – The database has faulted and the database objects may be damaged. Restarting the MSDE server may correct the problem.
24–25	*Hardware Error* – Media failure.

The error log files, unlike the database and transaction log files, are not kept open the entire time an MSDE server is executing. Only when a new entry is appended to the log is the file unavailable to other programs.

Agent Logs

The SQL Server Agent writes information related to agent execution into a log file. The current log file is stored as Sqlagent.out, and the historical files have the Sqlagent name but contain a numeric extension.

Entries for the agent log appear as follows:

```
2/15/00 1:13:08 PM - + [396] An idle CPU condition has not been defined - OnIdle
   job schedules will have no effect
2/15/00 11:30:38 PM - + [162] Internal request (from SetJobNextRunDate [reason:
   schedule will not run again]) to deactivate schedule 5
```

For more information on the execution of agents and monitoring the agent process, see the information on agents in Chapter 19.

Transaction Logs

The entire operation of the MSDE server is built around the ability to maintain accurate logs of changes to data so that data integrity is ensured and the database system is recoverable in the case of a fault or catastrophic failure. For the most part, the transaction log operates on its own, and as a developer, you have to consider little beyond opening and closing transactions from within your applications.

However, you can tailor the logging system to your needs to maintain optimum performance. It is often useful to understand the implicit workings of the system to aid you in system recovery in case a crash ever occurs.

For each database used by MSDE, two different files are kept: the Log file (with the extension `*.ldf`) and the Data file (with the extension `*.mdf`). The Data file contains all the data that has been committed by transactions and written into the database. Modifications to the database are stored in the Log file, which contains a log of transactions that have occurred. The Log file is used by the database to return the database to the most stable state after a catastrophic failure has occurred. Using this architecture, MSDE can ensure that the database retains its integrity far better than a single-file database, such as Microsoft Access.

Transaction logs contain the following:

- **Logical Sequence Number (LSN):** Each transaction in the log contains an LSN number that uniquely identifies the transaction and its sequence in the activity chain.

- **Transaction start:** Each transaction, when opened, stores a start marker within the log.

- **Modifications to rows:** Any change to row data of existing records is noted in the log, including row deletions.

- **New row insertions:** The data for a newly added record is recorded.

- **Modification to database objects:** SQL operations, such as the creation of a new index, do not store the actual change but instead store the command. Only command storage is necessary, because operations such as index creation are reversible by invalidating the command.

◆ **Transaction completion or rollback:** Any commit that records the modifications or any rollback that revokes them is stored in the log.

By containing all of this information, a log can be used to reconstruct database structure by a specified time. At a checkpoint, the MSDE server will record all of the modifications in the log to the actual database file, and if the truncate option is set, these recorded operations will be eliminated from the logs. After a failure, recovery of the database begins from the place in the log where the last checkpoint was reached and successfully completed.

> **Note:** When the server is paused, restarted, or rebooted while users are still connected, all of the committed transactions may not be written into the database. Each time the MSDE server is started, it checks for outstanding transactions that have been committed and writes into the actual database those that haven't been stored. Therefore, be aware that even if the MSDE server is shut down, under these conditions, the transaction log may contain transactions that have yet to be written into the core database. You can also manually execute the Transact-SQL command Restore to write all transactions into the database.

ACID Properties of a Transaction

The entire database industry has evolved technology around transactions and has developed terminology to go with that technology. Understanding the features encapsulated in the Atomicity Consistency Isolation Durability (ACID) properties of each transaction is one of the keys to understanding how databases ensure transactional integrity. Each of these ACID properties helps to define the type of transaction that has the most integrity:

◆ **Atomicity:** The transaction is self-contained, whereby either all the operations it contains are executed or they all are revoked.

◆ **Consistency:** After the transaction is complete, all data is consistent according to constraints, relational integrity, and so forth.

◆ **Isolation:** Concurrent modifications are isolated from other concurrent modifications.

◆ **Durability:** Changes made by a transaction are permanent and can be recovered even in the event of a database failure.

Often, a system will support most but not all of these four properties for a transaction. For example, a Microsoft Access database (MDB) has the key atomicity and consistency functions, but lacks a complete transaction log for durability functions. Under normal transactional interaction with the MSDE database server, all the ACID properties are supported for a transaction.

One of the potential problems in a replicated system is a threat to the durability of transactions that occur on the replica subscriptions. In a replicated environment, a transaction may make changes to several different rows within a transaction. These changes may be successful on the subscription, but when synchronized at the publisher, one of the row changes may experience a conflict. If that row is discarded, the other transactional changes may succeed, breaking the durability of the system.

With a system in which referential integrity is critical (such as a system for financial transactions), the replication type should be set to Transactional replication. Because this option is not available when the publisher is an MSDE server, you have to use a complete SQL Server installation when durability is required in a replicated system.

Truncating the Log

Transaction logs grow as more operations occur on the MSDE server. A transaction log can become large in size and very unwieldy. You can select the option Truncate Log On Checkpoint (in the database properties in the Enterprise Manager), which will eliminate old transactions that have already been written into the database. Truncation will occur every time a checkpoint is reached. A checkpoint is defined as the length of time between updates when recovery information is physically written into the database. The truncation setting should not be turned on for a production database, because the log is valuable for recovering from a data fault. For a staging or development server, however, truncation makes managing the database much easier.

Data in the MSDE server is stored in a series of data "pages." When changes are made to information on the server, these changes are made to the pages, and the pages will be marked as "dirty." The process of writing dirty pages to the database occurs at various times, but each checkpoint writes all current dirty pages to the database.

To reduce the amount of space required for the transaction log of a database, you can set MSDE to truncate all the entered transactions at each checkpoint. For a particular database, the truncate option may be activated by the following code:

```
Execute sp_dboption 'NorthwindSQL', 'trunc. log on chkpt.', 'TRUE'
```

This procedure execution must be run from the master database, which holds the primary database information. After execution has completed, the MSDE server will return an acknowledgement that states that the setting for the checkpoint has been changed.

A checkpoint is executed after a period of minutes set as the *recovery interval*. The default recovery interval on an MSDE server install is 0 minutes. To set the value of the checkpoint time to 5 minutes, you can execute code like this from the master database:

```
Execute sp_configure 'recovery interval', '5'
```

To execute the truncation process manually, you can execute the `Checkpoint` command, as shown in the following code:

```
Checkpoint
```

> **NOTE** The `Checkpoint` command is not a stored procedure, so preceding the command with the `Execute` statement will generate an error.

All of these settings may also be made via the Enterprise Manager application, if available. You can set the Truncate Log On Checkpoint option by following these steps:

1. Execute the Enterprise Manager.
2. Right-click the database that you want to configure (such as the NorthwindSQL database), and select the Properties option. This option displays the Properties window for the database.
3. Check the box that reads Truncate Log On Checkpoint.
4. Click the OK button to accept the changes to the database properties.

The recovery interval is actually a global parameter for the MSDE server (whereas checkpoint truncation is set for individual databases). The length of time between checkpoints can be set as follows:

1. Execute the Enterprise Manager.
2. Right-click the database server that you want to configure, and select the Properties option.
3. Select the Database Settings tab in the window (see Figure 22-1).
4. Set the Recovery interval to 3 minutes.
5. Click the OK button to accept this new setting.

With this global setting adjusted, the checkpoint will be activated every three minutes for maintenance of the transaction log. On a deployment or production server, you would disable the checkpoint option and, instead, back up the transaction log. When a backup is created, the log is truncated to the current transaction level.

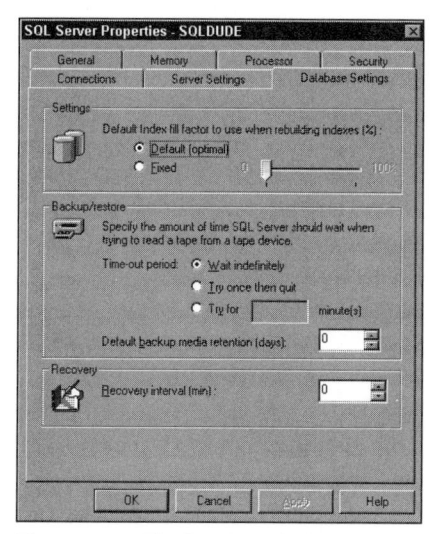

[Figure: SQL Server Properties - SOLDUDE dialog showing Database Settings tab]

Figure 22-1: The Database Settings tab for the MSDE server contains the recovery interval settings.

Managing Transaction Logs

Transaction logs are normally managed automatically by the MSDE system, but you can manually configure them. By default, when a new database is created, a single log file is also generated to store transactions for that database. This log file is generally placed in the same drive location or directory that holds the database itself.

You can move the transaction log file to a different location or even add additional files across several drives to hold transactions for a single database. When multiple transaction files are used, transactions are filled sequentially, so a file added to the log list may not be used until the previous file has completed filling.

After a new file has been added to the list of transaction logs, it cannot be deleted unless it is empty of all transactions. The Truncate Log On Checkpoint option that is available for the database may be used to empty old transactions. Also, a backup of the transactions in the log file will empty completed transactions and free up the log file.

> **NOTE:** MSDE transaction logs should not be placed on any compressed drives. Windows 95 and 98 include the DriveSpace compression capabilities (available through the Programs → Accessories → System Tools → DriveSpace item on the Start menu). Be sure that this compression method or other compression methods are not active on a log file drive.

Adding a log file is accomplished using the Transact-SQL command `Alter Database`. When executing this command, the `Add File` parameter may specify an additional log file.

Your data source should select the master database, after which you can execute Transact-SQL code such as this:

```
ALTER DATABASE myDB
ADD LOG FILE
( NAME = extraLog,
  FILENAME = 'c:\mssql7\data\extraLog.ldf',
  SIZE = 10MB,
  MAXSIZE = 100MB,
  FILEGROWTH = 5MB)
```

To remove the transaction log file, you can use this command:

```
ALTER DATABASE myDB
REMOVE FILE extraLog
```

The log file will allow removal only if no transactions are stored in it. If transactions currently are in the file, an error will be returned.

You can use the `sp_spaceused` stored procedure to determine the size of the current log file:

```
sp_spaceused extraLog
```

When no truncation setting is enabled, the transaction log must be backed up before early transactions can be cleared. This backup can be accomplished through the `Backup Log` command in Transact-SQL. The syntax for the `Backup Log` command is used:

```
BACKUP LOG {database_name | @database_name_var}
{
    [WITH
        { NO_LOG | TRUNCATE_ONLY }]
}
|
{
    TO <backup_device> [,...n]
    [WITH
        [BLOCKSIZE = {blocksize | @blocksize_variable}]
        [[,] DESCRIPTION = {text | @text_variable}]
        [[,] EXPIREDATE = {date | @date_var}
```

```
            | RETAINDAYS = {days | @days_var}]
        [[,] FORMAT | NOFORMAT]
        [[,] {INIT | NOINIT}]
        [[,] MEDIADESCRIPTION = {text | @text_variable}]
        [[,] MEDIANAME = {media_name | @media_name_variable}]
        [[,] [NAME = {backup_set_name | @backup_set_name_var}]
        [[,] NO_TRUNCATE]
        [[,] {NOSKIP | SKIP}]
        [[,] {NOUNLOAD | UNLOAD}]
        [[,] [RESTART]
        [[,] STATS [= percentage]]
    ]
}
```

First, you need to create a backup device to which the log may be stored, using the `sp_addDumpDevice` command like this:

```
EXEC sp_addumpdevice 'disk', 'MyTransLog',
    'c:\mssql7\backup\MyTransLog.dat'
```

You can back up a log file using the `Backup Log` command like this:

```
BACKUP LOG MyDB
    TO MyTransLog
```

> **NOTE:** You should not execute a transaction log backup if the Truncate Log On Checkpoint option is currently activated. Note that transaction log backup is different from the standard MSDE database backup that can be executed on a database with the truncate option set.

SQL-DMO Transaction Log Access

SQL-DMO allows access to the properties of the transaction log file. Although none of the individual entries of the log may be accessed through the available objects, properties such as file-growth increments, maximum size, name, location, and connection to the parent database can all be addressed.

The `TransactionLog` object is available to each `Database` object on the server (see Figure 22-2). All the log files used for the transaction log are individually stored as `LogFile` objects in the `LogFiles` collection. In most cases, a single `LogFile` object will be associated with a given database.

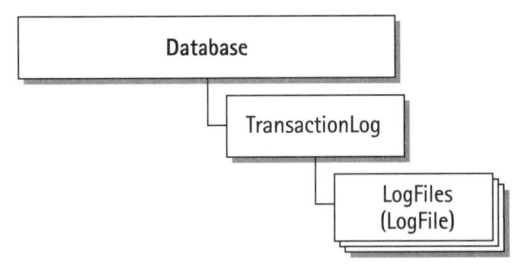

Figure 22-2: Each Database object contains a TransactionLog object that contains references to all of the log files used by it.

Long-Running Query Logs

For queries that take a long time to execute, a method is available of recording information for all queries that exceed a particular time limit. This log is an excellent way to determine which queries are critically in need of optimization.

The long-running query log can be activated from the ODBC data source that is designated for accessing a particular database. To modify an ODBC data source to log operation errors, follow these steps:

1. Under the Start menu, select the Settings → Control Panel option.

2. From the Control Panels folder, double-click the ODBC item.

3. Select the data source to which you want to add long-running query logging capabilities.

4. Click the Configure button at the bottom of the window.

5. Click the Next button until the log file settings page is displayed (see Figure 22-3).

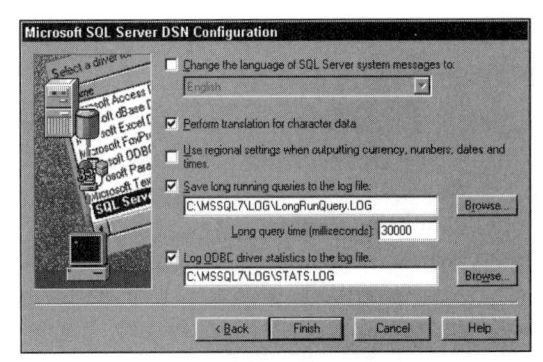

Figure 22-3: For the ODBC data source, long-running queries and driver information may be logged.

6. Click the Save long running queries to the log file option and set the path of the long-running queries.

7. Click the Log ODBC driver statistics to the log file option and set the path for the driver statistics log.

8. Click the OK button to save these changes.

You can examine these logs after the MSDE server has been executing, and determine how the ODBC driver is handling interaction with the database server.

Summary

Effectively managing error and transaction logs is a critical skill needed to promote high database performance and ensure data integrity. Properly configuring and managing the logs enables you to optimize an MSDE server. In this chapter, you covered the following:

- **Error and agent logs:** The MSDE server stores information in error logs, whereas the agent logs store any information related to SQL Server Agent processes. Both files are stored in text file format in the Log directory of the database server folder.

- **Transaction logs:** The transaction log of an MSDE server holds all the information for changes to the database created by the Insert, Update, or Delete SQL commands. Because all transactions are stored to the log, a system fault such as a power failure can be recovered from up to a specified point in time. The log ensures data integrity on the database server.

- **Truncate at checkpoints:** To minimize the size of the transaction log, you can set the Truncate Log On Checkpoint option to eliminate older transactions when a checkpoint is reached. Checkpoints are activated at specific intervals (in minutes) that may be configured on the MSDE server.

- **Configuring through Transact-SQL:** The SQLSetConnectAttr function can be used to configure the file that is used to store certain log entries, as well as to pass commands to the log system to perform operations.

Chapter 23

Moving Data Into and Out of MSDE

IN THIS CHAPTER

- Choosing an approach
- Using the Import and Export Data Wizard
- Copying in bulk
- Using the Data Transformation Services (DTS)
- Using the NT mirroring capabilities
- Reviewing replication
- Losing information

MOST ORGANIZATIONS ALREADY have a large number of existing data stores, which often means that the process of beginning a database from scratch is secondary to adapting, upsizing, reworking, or incorporating existing data into a project. You've seen how this can be done through the Upsizing Wizard to move data (the Northwind database) previously stored in one format (Access MDB file) to the MSDE server.

MSDE includes several robust methods for transferring data to and from the database server. Each of these methods is best suited to a particular situation and environment, such as the need to move data from Transact-SQL or the operating system command line. By examining the different methods, you can determine the most appropriate method to use for the conditions you face.

Choosing an Approach

Selecting a method for data transfer can be effected by numerous factors, from datatype conversion to the merging or parsing of several columns. If necessary, you could even write a program to do the transfer yourself through a middleware solution such as ADO or ODBC. However, this is rarely necessary because of the breadth of automated approaches included with the database server. The primary methods of transfer include:

- **Import and Export Data Wizard:** Uses the Data Transformation Services to import and export data (demonstrated in Chapter 13). With a graphical user interface, it can immediately transfer and transform data, and even create a package of the transformation that you can later modify.
- **Bulk Copy Program (BCP):** Command-line utility that can transfer data into and out of the MSDE server. Several command-line switches determine the actions of a BCP execution. BCP is one of the most commonly used workhorse applications when constructing and modifying a SQL Server-based solution.
- **Bulk Insert SQL command:** Does the same operations available through BCP, but can be executed within the server or within another stored procedure.
- **Data Transformation Services:** The central method of automated transfer and transformation between MSDE and the outside world. (The DTS system is described in depth in Chapter 13.)
- **Replication system:** Can be used to move data primarily out of the MSDE system, although updates are possible in special configurations. (The replication system is described in Chapter 15.)

By using one of these methods or a combination of them, you can transform data into almost any format on the MSDE server or store it in an external source. Typically, the first pressing need when adding a new database solution such as MSDE is to transfer data into a format that can be used by the server. MSDE includes an excellent program called the Import and Export Data Wizard to aid you in this transfer.

Using the Import and Export Data Wizard

The only graphic utility included with MSDE is the Import and Export Data Wizard that is used to transfer data between MSDE and other data sources. This wizard can be used for most of your simple data transfers. Chapter 13 demonstrated this wizard sending a complex query to retrieve data for placement in an Access database. However, the import and export can be a much simpler task, such as taking a single table and exporting it to a text file. This text file containing the table information can then be imported into a fresh new database and table.

Exporting the Northwind Database

To test the Import and Export Data Wizard, a table from the Northwind database can be easily transferred to a comma-delimited text file on the hard drive. This file can then be examined in a text editor such as Notepad or imported into any program that accepts comma-delimited data files.

To export the Customers table to a text file, follow these steps:

1. Execute the Import and Export Data program under the MSDE menu. This wizard is actually a standalone program created from the combination of the Import and Export DTS Wizards available through the Enterprise Manager.

2. Click the Next button to advance to the first options screen. To execute any type of data transfer, you must select source and destination data sources. This first screen enables you to specify what the source will be. For this example, the default Source entry of the Microsoft OLE DB Provider for SQL Server is fine. The selection for the server as (local) should also be fine if you are transferring the data on the machine that the MSDE server is executing. If not, select the source server from the combo box.

3. Enter the user name and password (see Figure 23-1). If you haven't changed the default for MSDE, you can enter **sa** for the user name and leave the password blank. With the user name and password entered, the wizard can now address the source server to retrieve all of the databases that are available on it.

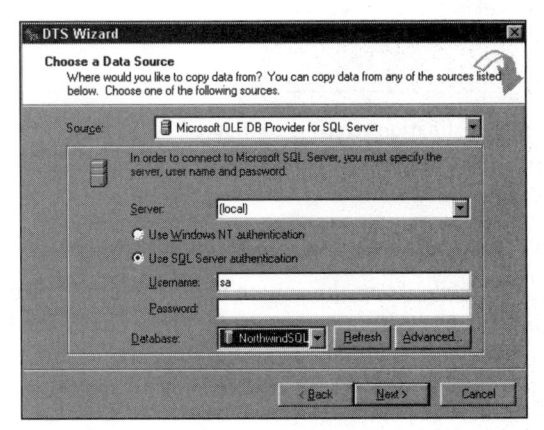

Figure 23-1: The Choose a Data Source screen of the wizard enables you to select the source MSDE server.

4. Click the Refresh button to load the available database names. Where the combo box was previously filled only with a single option, the default database, now a list appears of all of the databases available on the selected server.

5. Select the NorthwindSQL database from the Database combo box.

6. Click the Next button to advance to the Choose a Destination screen, which you configure in the same manner as the Choose a Data Source screen.

7. For the destination, select the Text File option from the Destination combo box.

8. Enter the filename as **C:\NorthwindDump.txt** (see Figure 23-2). Set the path to any filename and location that you want to use. Clicking the button with the three dots (...), to the right of the File name box, will show a traditional Save File dialog box in which to enter the path.

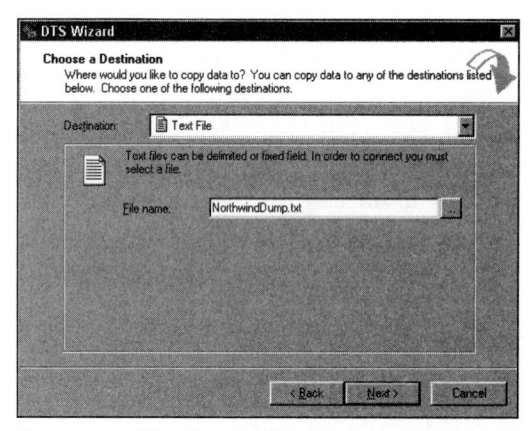

Figure 23-2: The Choose a Destination screen is configured to save the data to a text file titled NorthwindDump.txt.

9. Click the Next button to advance to the transfer method screen.

10. Select the option Copy table(s) from the source database (see Figure 23-3) and click the Next button. The alternate option for the transfer method enables a SQL query to select specific parts of the data. When the Copy table(s) option is selected, the next screen enables you to specify the destination format.

11. Select the Source Table as [NorthwindSQL].[dbo].[Customers]. This will move all of the records from the Customers table into the text file.

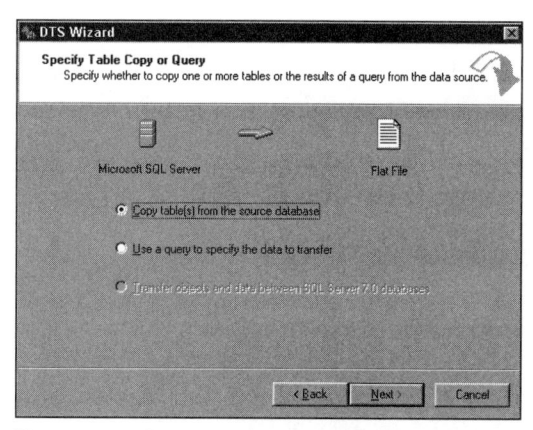

Figure 23-3: Setting the transfer method to simply copy the source table directly to the output source

12. Click the First row has column names checkbox to check the option (see Figure 23-4). The text file will then contain the column names at the top of the exported data. Any options set on this screen (such as setting the Column delimiter to a tab character) will affect the format of the output file. Note that this screen would be different if the destination data source had not been set as a text file.

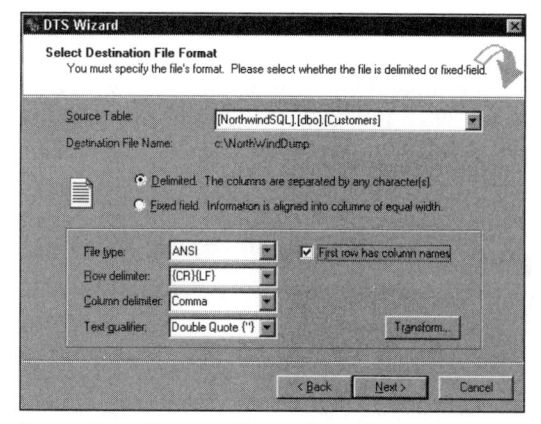

Figure 23-4: The text file configuration screen enables you to set options such as the file type, row and column delimiters, and storage type.

13. Click the Next button to advance to the screen that enables you to schedule when the export will occur. You have two sets of options for configuration: When and Save. The When options enable you to schedule whether the process executes immediately or is scheduled for later execution.

472 Part III: Advanced MSDE

The Save options enable you to store the package so that you can examine or modify it for later execution.

14. To run the process immediately (see Figure 23-5), leave the default options and click the Next button. You have now completed the wizard configuration options.

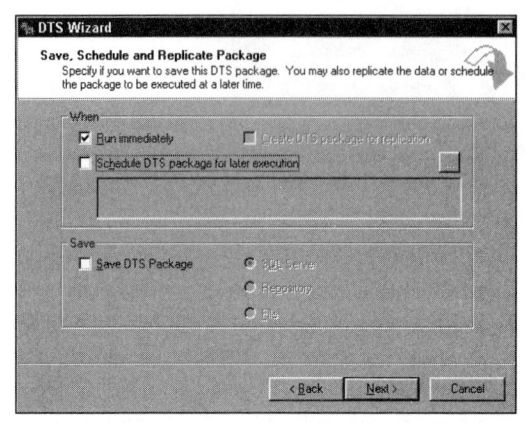

Figure 23-5: To schedule the process to run immediately, only the Run immediately option needs to be checked.

15. If all the listed options are correct, click the Finish button to begin the process.

16. The transformation will occur, and you will be presented with a status box as the export occurs. When finished, a success dialog box (see Figure 23-6) is displayed to indicate that 1 table was transferred to a flat file database (the text file).

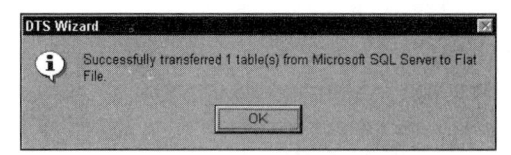

Figure 23-6: When the process succeeds, the dialog box for success is displayed.

You can examine the file that was created on the C drive in the Notepad application. All 91 records of the Customers table will be present in the file as well as an additional row for the column names.

Now that you have a preformatted data source outside of the MSDE server, the Import and Export Data program can be used to load this same data into a new database.

Importing the Customers Table

The following process of importing through this wizard mirrors the export process, but it has a few additional steps, such as creating a database to accept the information and naming the table to be used:

1. Execute the Import and Export Data program under the MSDE menu.
2. Click the Next button to advance beyond the primary screen.
3. In the Source combo box, select the Text File option to allow an import from the text file.
4. Click the Browse button to the right of the File Name text box to display a File Open dialog box.
5. Select the file that was exported in the last section.
6. Click the Next button to advance to the destination screen.
7. In the Select File Format step, click the First row has column names option to properly import the formatted file.
8. Click the Next button to advance to the Specify Column Delimiter screen. A list box will be displayed showing the data from the text file formatted with the proper columns and column headings. If the file was originally exported properly, the screen should look like the one shown in Figure 23-7.

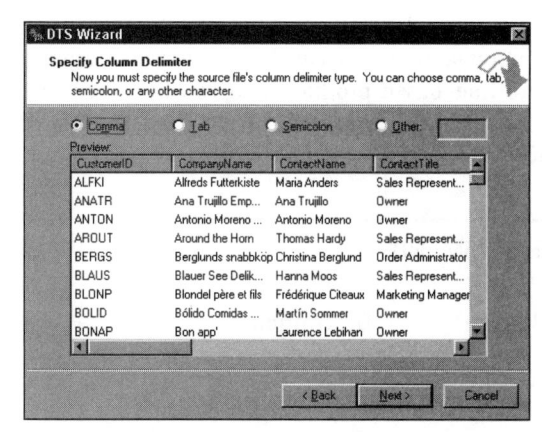

Figure 23-7: The Preview grid should properly display the column headings and column values from the text file.

9. Click the Next button to advance to the destination screen.
10. Select the MSDE server, enter the proper user name and password, set the Database to NorthwindSQL, and click the Next button.

11. In the Destination Table column, set the name of the table to **CustomersImport**.
12. Click the Next button.
13. To run the process immediately, leave the set options and click the Next button.
14. Click the Finish button to begin the import process.

You can now use Microsoft Query, Microsoft Access, or another tool to examine the data. If you enter the Design View on the new table in Access, you will see that the CustomersImport table does not have a primary key setting. Examining it in contrast to the original Customers table will demonstrate some of the information that is lost when data is transferred to a text file.

Copying in Bulk

Methods for transferring bulk amounts of data exist both inside and outside of the SQL Server–based MSDE server. The `Bulk Insert` command can be executed within the SQL code or through a SQL execution statement. The BCP command-line utility allows data to be copied in and out of the database server from outside the server.

BCP Program Utility

The key utility over the years for most developers addressing the SQL Server engine is BCP. BCP provides bulk import and export capabilities for the database server. The BCP utility is a command line–based program that can be executed from the MS-DOS prompt (Windows 95/98) or the Console prompt (Windows NT). The commands available from the BCP utility are shown in Table 23-1.

TABLE 23-1 THE BCP SWITCH COMMANDS

Command	Command Name	Description
-S	Server name	Indicates the name of the SQL Server or MSDE server to be addressed.
-U	Username	Identifies the login user name to the server that will be used for the bulk transfer.
-P	Password	Identifies the login password to the server that will be used for the bulk transfer.
-i	Input file	Specifies the path and filename of the input source.

Chapter 23: Moving Data Into and Out of MSDE

Command	Command Name	Description
-o	Outfile	Specifies the path and filename of the output file.
-f	Format file	Determines the format of the input or output file if either side doesn't match the schema or structure of the other. The columns may be in different order, have a different number, or use a different delimiting character, and the formatting file can adjust for these differences during the bulk operation.
-m	Max errors	Specifies the maximum number of errors that may occur before the operation is aborted. The default number of errors is set to 10.
-F	First row	Specifies the first row to copy by number in the bulk operation. The default value of 1 is used if this parameter is unspecified.
-L	Last row	Specifies the last row to copy in the bulk process. If the number 0 (the default) is passed, the last row is set to the end.
-n	Native type copy	Instructs BCP to use the native data types for the copy operation.
-N	Native type copy with Unicode character data	Instructs BCP to use the native data types for the copy operation and Unicode for character data.
-C	Code page specifier	Specifies one of three values (ACP, OEM, or RAW), or a specific code page is used for setting the internal code page use.
-T	Trusted connection	Specifies that BCP communication occurs over a trusted connection and the user name and password parameters need not be supplied.
-k	Keep null values	During the transfer process, columns that have null values are automatically filled with the default value of the column if one is specified. This switch makes BCP keep the null values on records even if a default value is available.

Continued

TABLE 23-1 THE BCP SWITCH COMMANDS *(Continued)*

Command	Command Name	Description
-h	"Load hints"	Specifies that join hints, query hints, and table hints should be loaded for the bulk process. Using TABLOCK (table lock) hints whenever possible is recommended.
-c	Character type	Configures the transfer to use the character data type.
-6	SQL Server 6.x file format	Configures the bulk operation to store the information in the previous version's file format (MSDE uses the format of SQL Server 7).
-t	Field termination	Specifies the character used for field termination in char or widechar text data files. The default value is the tab (ASCII value 7) character.
-v	Version	Makes the BCP utility return the name, version, and copyright header of the BCP program.
-E	Keep identity values	With this option set, the values in columns that are selected as identities retain the values contained in the data file. By default, identity column values are ignored and new unique numbers are assigned when each row is inserted. Keeping the values can cause errors if existing records already have used the unique values of the importing data. On the other hand, related tables must keep the same values, in order to keep referential integrity intact. Therefore, carefully consider your application before using this switch.
-e	Error file	Specifies the path and filename of the error file.
-b	Batch size	Each batch of rows copied is encapsulated in a transaction, so the larger the batch size, the less transaction overhead that's incurred during the transfer. The default value copies all records in a single batch.

Command	Command Name	Description
-w	Wide character type	Specifies that BCP should use the Unicode character set (2 bytes for every character) as opposed to ASCII (1 byte per character).
-q	Quoted identifier	Instructs BCP to expect quotes to surround items such as table or view names that contain non-ASCII characters.
-r	Row terminator	Identifies the character used to terminate a row in an ASCII or Unicode file. By default, the character for row termination is the newline character.
-a	Packetsize	Sets the number of bytes per packet that is used for BCP communication to and from the server. This entry overrides the setting made in the Enterprise Manager or with the `sp_configure` command.
-R	Regional enable	For dates, time, and currency data, this switch uses the regional information for data import instead of ignoring it, which is the default.

You might have noticed that the commands sent to BCP are case-sensitive. Be sure to use the proper capitalization or when requesting the first row (with the -F), you may activate the pattern formatting (-f) command!

To use BCP to copy data from the NorthwindSQL database, you can use a command like this:

```
bcp "NorthwindSQL..Customers" out customers.txt -c -q -Sthinkpad -U"sa" -P""
```

The customers.txt file will be created and will contain all of the customer records. The BCP utility will return information about the process, such as the number of rows that are copied, the total number of seconds required for the process, and the average number of rows per second that were stored in the file.

To copy data from a file back into a database (although you probably don't want to execute this command now), you can use this command:

```
bcp "NorthwindSQL..Customers" in customers.txt -c -q -Sthinkpad -U"sa" -P""
```

BCP commands may also include a query to select specific records. Enter the following code at the console or command line on a single line:

```
bcp "SELECT * FROM NorthwindSQL..Customers Where CompanyName like
'C%'"
   queryout Query.txt -c -Sthinkpad -Usa -P
```

When you are doing data transfers, you must pay extra attention to tables that contain identity fields. The `-E` command may be used to copy identity column values from the data file. This command temporarily suspends the MSDE server's assignment of identity values and uses the values from the importing data. If this switch is not used, identities contained in a data file are ignored during the import and new unique values are generated for each row.

The native format of the BCP utility uses native database types stored in a binary file for use with BCP or the `Bulk Insert` command and cannot be loaded by another program. Native format files are typically stored in files with the extension of .bcp. The `-n` switch activates native mode. Native mode is most useful when transferring a data file from one MSDE or SQL Server to another, or when BCP is used for data backup.

The native format stores characters using ASCII character format (a single byte per character). A Unicode native format also is available, which is used for Snapshot replication when the data is transferred to the distributor. All of the character column values are stored in Unicode, while other data is stored in binary format. This mode is activated using the `-N` switch when executing the utility. The `-N` command is only available to copies of BCP that are included with SQL Server 7, MSDE, or later versions of the database server.

By using the `-t` and `-r` switches in the BCP command, you can specify the field and row terminators. These switches can be followed by an actual character (such as A, C, and so forth) or a character signifier (such as \n for newline or \t for tab). The default settings use commas between columns and a carriage return and newline between rows. These switches can be used for output, to generate the type of file you want, as well as for input, to specify the formatting type that is in place.

You can use a formatting file (with the .fmt extension) to allow a predefined format to be used for the output. This file may be saved from a previous bulk copy process that was activated with the `-f` flag, which creates a file called bcp.fmt, unless a specific filename is set instead. Creative use of this formatting file can even enable you to use the BCP utility for HTML formatting, because opening and closing tags can be inserted.

Bulk Insert SQL Command

The `Bulk Insert` command is a SQL command used to load a quantity of raw data into a database. The `Bulk Insert` stored procedure actually activates the BCP utility to do a bulk copy. `Bulk Insert` provides a way in SQL code that allows the bulk copy routine to be executed manually or included within the definition of a stored procedure.

The general syntax of the `Bulk Insert` command appears as follows:

```
BULK INSERT [['dbname'.]['owner'].]{'tablename' FROM data_file}
[WITH
(
[ BATCHSIZE [= batch_size]]
[[,] CHECK_CONSTRAINTS]
[[,] CODEPAGE [= 'ACP' | 'OEM' | 'RAW' | 'code_page']]
[[,] DATAFILETYPE [=
{'char' | 'native'| 'widechar' | 'widenative'}]]
[[,] FIELDTERMINATOR [= 'field_terminator']]
[[,] FIRSTROW [= first_row]]
[[,] FORMATFILE [= 'format_file_path']]
[[,] KEEPIDENTITY]
[[,] KEEPNULLS]
[[,] KILOBYTES_PER_BATCH [= kilobytes_per_batch]]
[[,] LASTROW [= last_row]]
[[,] MAXERRORS [= max_errors]]
[[,] ORDER ({column [ASC | DESC]} [,...n])]
[[,] ROWS_PER_BATCH [= rows_per_batch]]
[[,] ROWTERMINATOR [= 'row_terminator']]
[[,] TABLOCK]
)
]
```

All the settings for this command mirror the options available to the BCP command-line utility. Most of the commands used by the `Bulk Insert` statement provide a more explicit name for each flag than BCP does, such as the `KEEPIDENTITY` switch versus the BCP command of -E for the same function.

You can execute a simple copy of the Customers table, similar to the one shown with the BCP utility, with a command such as this:

```
BULK INSERT NorthwindSQL..Customers FROM 'c:\Customers.txt'
    WITH (DATAFILETYPE = 'char')
```

In the `Bulk Insert` example, the `DATAFILETYPE` was set to a value of `'char'`. Within the `Bulk Insert` command, you can specify how the data will be stored in the file by using the `DATAFILETYPE` argument. The data file type can be specified as one of these four types:

- **char**: Character data will be addressed in standard ASCII format.
- **native**: All data will be stored using the native database types, so the file will be available for use only with the `Bulk Insert` command or BCP.

- **widechar:** Each character will be stored in Unicode format.
- **widenative:** Like the native data file type, except the columns that are of data types char, varchar, or text are converted to Unicode.

If the file is stored in native format, you can use either `Bulk Insert` or BCP to specify both an input and output file to copy the data from this format, if necessary. Using this capability enables you to export the data stored in the native format without having to copy it into an MSDE database and back out for traditional data file access.

The `FormatFile` property specifies the file path of the destination file of the bulk insert. It uses the same FMT file that BCP interprets when a format for the process is required.

With the `Bulk Insert` command, you can achieve all the functions available from the BCP command within the SQL environment. Because they use the same data transfer system, native files created with `Bulk Insert` can be addressed from BCP, and vice versa.

Using the Data Transformation Services (DTS)

The Data Transformation Services (DTS) are available to automate the transfer of information from MSDE to various datasource types. DTS can use ODBC, OLE DB, or standard text files to transform data from one format or structure to another. In Chapter 13, you used the DTS capabilities extensively through packages that you created. Through VBA, you can create, manage, and control these packages by using program code.

Figure 23-8 shows the DTS object diagram and the primary Package object. Package objects are located in the Microsoft DTSPackage Object Library. Within each package are objects for tasks, connections, and steps, as well as the `Global Variables` object that contains properties that affect all the other objects contained within a package.

In VBA, you can add the DTS objects to a project by selecting the Microsoft DTSPackage Object Library item in the References dialog box. Using the Object Browser, you can examine the objects in the DTS system.

Creating a DTS Package in VBA

After you add the DTS classes to a project, the objects can be easily created in VBA code. Any interaction with DTS requires the creation of a Package object. In this example, you can use the Package object to create a new package, create two connections, and add a task to pump data from one connection to another.

Chapter 23: Moving Data Into and Out of MSDE

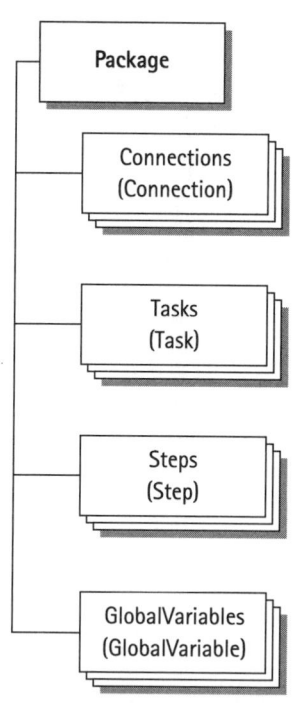

Figure 23-8: The DTS object diagram shows the four collections held by each Package object.

The task will take data from the Northwind database and pump it to a text file named NorthwindDump.txt. After the creation of the package is complete, the dtsrun utility will be used to demonstrate how this package can be executed from the command line.

To create a project that constructs a new DTS package, follow these steps:

1. Execute Microsoft Access 2000.

2. Open a project, such as the ADOTest.mdb project that you created in Chapter 9. Any Access project (including an ADP project) may be used, because you will simply be adding a new form that allows for transformation code that will create a new DTS process.

3. Using the toolbox palette, draw a command button on the form, set the caption to **Create Transform**, and set the name to **cmdPkgExport**.

4. Through the Properties window, display the `Click` event of the command button.

5. Select the Code Builder to open the VBA environment.

6. Under the Tools menu, select the References option.

7. Locate the Microsoft DTSPackage Object Library item in the list of classes (see Figure 23-9), check the item to add it to the project, and click the OK button to dismiss the References dialog. This option adds the DTS objects to the project and allows access to the Package object.

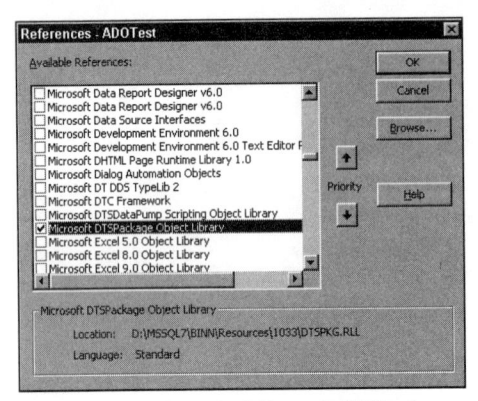

Figure 23-9: Select the Microsoft DTSPackage Object Library option to be included in the project.

8. Select the command button in the code window (left combo box) and the Click event (right combo box) for the button.

9. Enter the following code into the code window:

```
Private Sub cmdPkgExport_Click()
    Dim myPkg As DTS.Package
    Dim myConn As DTS.Connection
    Dim myTask As DTS.Task
    Dim myStep As DTS.Step
    Dim myTransform As DTS.Transformation
    Dim myPumpTask As DTS.DataPumpTask

    ' Create a new package
    Set myPkg = CreateObject("DTS.Package")
    myPkg.Name = "pkgVBAExport"
    myPkg.Description = "Export package created with VBA"

    Set myConn = Nothing
    Set myConn = myPkg.Connections.New
    ' Source
    myConn.ID = 1
    myConn.DataSource = _
        "Provider=sqloledb;Server=thinkpad;Database=Northwind"
```

```
    myConn.UserID = "sa"
    myConn.Password = ""
    myPkg.Connections.Add myConn

    Set myConn = Nothing
    Set myConn = myPkg.Connections.New
    ' Destination
    myConn.ID = 2
    myConn.DataSource = "c:\NorthwindDump.txt"
    myPkg.Connections.Add myConn

    ' Create a new task in the package
    Set myTask = myPkg.Tasks.New("DTSDataPumpTask")
    myTask.Name = "PumpTask"
    ' Create as a custom task from data source 1 to 2
    Set myPumpTask = myTask.CustomTask
    myPumpTask.SourceConnectionID = 1
    myPumpTask.SourceSQLStatement = _
        "Select * from NorthwindSQL..Customers"
    myPumpTask.DestinationConnectionID = 2
    myPumpTask.DestinationObjectName = "CustomersOut"

    ' Add task to a new transformation
    Set myTransform = myPumpTask.Transformations.New _
        ("DTS.DataPumpTransformCopy")
    myTransform.Name = "Transform"
    myTransform.TransformFlags = 512 _
        ' DTSTransformFlag_AllowLosslessConversion
    myPumpTask.Transformations.Add myTransform
    myPkg.Tasks.Add myTask
    Set myTask = Nothing
    Set myStep = myPkg.Steps.New
    myStep.Name = "Step1"
    myStep.TaskName = "PumpTask"
    myPkg.Steps.Add myStep
    ' Store on the MSDE server
    myPkg.SaveToSQLServer "thinkpad", "sa", ""

    ' Clear object variables
    Set myStep = Nothing
    Set myTransform = Nothing
    Set myPumpTask = Nothing
    Set myPkg = Nothing
End Sub
```

10. Click the View Microsoft Access button on the toolbar to return to the Access environment.

11. Click the Design button to switch to execution mode.

When you execute this application and click the Create Transform button, a new package will be constructed through the DTS objects. This package will provide a simple export of the Customers table to an ASCII text file. You can use the dtsrun utility from the command line to execute the package, like this:

```
Dtsrun /Sthinkpad /Usa /P /NpkgVBAExport
```

This code can be used as a foundation for other package applications, because it sets up the addressing of the database server. After the connection is made to the MSDE server, you can create a Package object that references any of the package items available on the database server. You could add another button to the form and add this code to create a reference to the package just created:

```
Private Sub cmdPkgList_Click()
    Dim myPkg As DTS.Package

    Set myPkg = CreateObject("DTS.Package")
    ' Load the pkgVBAExport package from the server
    myPkg.LoadFromSQLServer "thinkpad", "sa", "", , , , ,
"pkgVBAExport"
    MsgBox myPkg.Name
End Sub
```

Handling DTS Package Events in VBA

Two basic types of events can occur in a DTS system: error/status events and connection point events. Error and status events are activated if a particular error occurs or for periodic execution while an operation is occurring.

ERROR AND STATUS EVENTS

Error messages are supported through the standard `Err` object, which may be queried for the error number and description of the error itself. From VBA, you can use the `On Error` structure to capture the error. To display the error for a package, you could use code similar to this:

```
Private Sub myPackage_OnError(ByVal EventSource As String, _
    ByVal ErrorCode As Long, ByVal Source As String, _
    ByVal Description As String, ByVal HelpFile As String, _
    ByVal HelpContext As Long, ByVal IDofInterfaceWithError As _
    String, pbCancel As Boolean)
    MsgBox Description
```

```
    pbCancel = True
End Sub
```

CONNECTION POINT EVENTS

For VBA, connection point events are handled using the `WithEvents` keyword. This keyword is used while an object variable is being dimensioned. For example, to create a Package object using the `WithEvents` keyword, the code would appear like this:

```
Dim WithEvents myPackage As DTS.Package
```

When using the `WithEvents` keyword, you cannot use the `New` keyword to immediately create a new object. The `Set` command must be used for new object creation, either using the `CreateObject` command or through code such as this:

```
Dim WithEvents myPackage As DTS.Package
Set myPackage = New DTS.Package
```

When the `WithEvents` command is used, you must define subroutines to handle every available event, to prevent an error from occurring. The subroutines can be empty as long as they exist in the project.

The following events can be created for a package called `myPackage`:

```
Private Sub myPackage_OnFinish(ByVal EventSource As String)
    MsgBox "Package complete: " & EventSource
End Sub

Private Sub myPackage_OnProgress(ByVal EventSource As String, _
ByVal ProgressDescription As String, ByVal PercentComplete As Long,_
ByVal ProgressCountLow As Long, ByVal ProgressCountHigh As Long)
    MsgBox "Percent complete: " & PercentComplete
End Sub

Private Sub myPackage_OnQueryCancel(ByVal EventSource As String, _
   pbCancel As Boolean)
    MsgBox "Cancel Query: " & EventSource
End Sub

Private Sub myPackage_OnStart(ByVal EventSource As String)
    MsgBox "Start Package: " & EventSource
End Sub
```

With the packages that have been constructed through programming, you can customize the transfer of data based on the selections made in the application.

Using the NT Mirroring Capabilities

If you are using Windows NT, the features of hard disk mirroring enable you to link a drive to duplicate all information on a primary drive. Using the mirroring capabilities can be an effective method of creating a complete duplicate of a database system for failover capabilities.

Mirrors are created using the Disk Manager application, available under the Administrative Tools submenu of the Start menu. It displays all mounted drives and their current partition settings. After the mirror has been enacted and the data has been stored on the secondary drive, you can break the mirror and remove the drive to load the data onto another system.

Replication

In Chapter 15, you studied replication, which is really just a specialized form of importing and exporting data. As you learned in that chapter, replication can be used to create a one-way send path to regularly commit an automated transfer of information to any ODBC- or OLE DB–compliant data source.

Replication can be used for limited failover systems. The limitation of the replication features lies primarily in the fact that system tables and schema changes are not replicated. If you construct the schema on the backup system, however, the replication system provides an effective means of scheduled data duplication for a failover system.

Although the replication system is complex, it can provide the ideal method of importing and exporting data if a high level of automation and data flow control is required. Because replication has all of the systems necessary to handle data-integration conflicts, it may be more adaptable to a particular custom solution than is the common DTS system.

Losing Information

In most of the methods described in this chapter (except the direct backup), information contained in the data might be lost during an export. It is important to consider and address what data will be lost and to determine whether this information is important to your solution.

Here are some examples of the types of loss of data and associated information encountered with a simple data transfer from MSDE to a secondary data source:

- ♦ Microsoft Access allows comments to be placed in the description field of each column in design mode. When upsizing an Access database, the MSDE table structure has no provision for accepting these comments, so they are not present in the new MSDE table.

- Text file exports lose all data typing.

- Most export formats do not retain constraints or rules.

- Relations between tables that are used for referential integrity are most often eliminated.

- Identity columns, particularly the seed values, are lost. Because a column with the identity setting turned on automatically advances the value with each additional row added, this information is not carried over to an export. Often, when data is re-imported, even for a column previously set for identity values, the identity setting is not re-created.

Much of the lost information is specific to the datasource type (such as constraints, rules, and stored procedures) and cannot be effectively transported among types. Therefore, much of the data loss is inevitable.

Summary

Numerous methods are available for moving data into and out of the MSDE server. In addition to building custom programs, several technologies are included with MSDE that can aid in automating this process. In this chapter, you covered the following:

- **Import and Export Data program:** Included with a standard MSDE installation, this program allows data to be transformed for import into MSDE or export to nearly any datasource type.

- **Data Transformation Services (DTS):** DTS allows packages to be created that can transform data and transfer it among data sources. Data can be modified by scripts or specific data selected with a query for export or import. The DTS system lies at the heart of the Import and Export Data program.

- **BCP:** Using the BCP utility is one of the simplest and most effective methods of moving data into and out of the MSDE server. Because the BCP utility can be executed from the command line, a developer can access it easily from the OS, allowing BAT files to be created to repeat command tasks or schedule execution using an OS Task Scheduler.

- **Bulk Insert:** The `Bulk Insert` SQL command can be used to insert a large amount of data into a table. It uses the same method of transfer as BCP, so the options available mirror the BCP utility.

- **Replication:** Replication can be used to move data on a specific schedule to any ODBC-compatible data sources. Like the DTS system, replication can be used to transform data to allow export that modifies the data during the process.

- **NT mirroring:** If you are using Windows NT, the mirroring capabilities can be used to transfer the entire MSDE server, as well as all the data files, to a secondary hard drive.

Chapter 24

Using Stored Procedures in MSDE

IN THIS CHAPTER

- Using the SP configure routine
- Executing the replication stored procedures
- Sending mail
- Using the agent stored procedures
- Executing security procedures
- Creating distributed queries procedures
- Examining various useful stored procedures
- Using the SQL-DMO model

THIS CHAPTER PROVIDES a reference summary of most of the stored procedures that are included with the MSDE server. Almost all of the procedures listed have an equivalent method in the SQL-DMO object model. Wherever possible, I have included the object or collection that is related to the category of stored procedures so that you can look at the proper class library.

For most of the global properties of the MSDE server, you can use the `sp_configure` stored procedure to modify the current values. This alteration for a majority of these properties will not be activated until after the database server is restarted.

The SP Configure Routine

One of the system stored procedures with the largest number of available parameters is the `sp_configure` routine. This procedure accepts a string value that determines which property will be set by the routine execution.

The syntax for the `sp_configure` procedure appears like this:

```
sp_configure [@configname =] 'name' [,[@configvalue =] 'value']
```

The procedure can be used like this:

```
sp_configure 'set working set size', 1
```

Available configuration options include: 'set working set size' (0), 'fill factor' (0), 'show advanced option' (0), and 'recovery interval' (0). Other options include: affinity mask, allow updates, cost threshold for parallelism, cursor threshold, default language, default sortorder ID, extended memory size, index create memory, language in cache, language neutral full-text, lightweight pooling, locks, max async I/O, max degree of parallelism, and max server memory. Note that the number that appears in parentheses following the parameter name is the default value used by the MSDE server.

Some of the less familiar settings include: max text repl size (65536), max worker threads (255), media retention (0), min memory per query (1024), min server memory (0), nested triggers (1), network packet size (4096), open objects (500), priority boost (0), query governor cost limit (0), query wait (600), recovery interval (0), remote access (1), remote login timeout (5), remote proc trans (0), remote query timeout (0), resource timeout (10), scan for startup procs (0), show advanced options (1), spin counter (10000), time slice (100), two digit year cutoff (2049), Unicode comparison style (196609), Unicode locale ID (1033), user connections (0), user options (0)

Most of these parameters are also available for examination and modification through various Property windows in the Enterprise Server.

Replication Stored Procedures

In Chapter 15, most of the primary stored procedures for managing a replicated system were covered. There are a great number of these procedures that will aid you in refining the setup of the system and the interaction between the distributors, subscribers, and publishers.

These procedures are used in the example code to configure the system for subscription:

- ◆ sp_addsubscriber(@subscriber [,@type] [,@login] [,@password] [,@commit_batch_size] [,@status_batch_size] [,@flush_frequency] [,@frequency_type] [,@frequency_interval] [,@frequency_relative_interval] [,@frequency_recurrence_factor] [,@frequency_subday] [,@frequency_subday_interval] [,@active_start_time_of_day] [,@active_end_time_of_day] [,@active_start_date] [,@active_end_date] [,@description] [,[@security_mode] [,@encrypted_password]): Use to designate a subscriber that can accept article publications. This procedure includes settings such as frequency of updates, recurrence factor, commit batch size, and other. This stored procedure needs to make substantial system changes, so only users that are registered to the sysadmin role on the server may execute it.

- **sp_addsubscription(@publication [,@article] [,@subscriber] [,@destination_db, @sync_type] [,@status] [@subscription_type] [,@update_mode] [,@loopback_detection] [,@frequency_type] [,@frequency_interval] [,@frequency_relative_interval] [,@frequency_recurrence_factor] [,@frequency_subday] [,@frequency_subday_interval] [,@active_start_time_of_day] [,@active_end_time_of_day] [,@active_start_date] [,@active_end_date] [,@optional_command_line] [,@reserved] [,@enabled_for_syncmgr]):** Creates a subscription on the designated database server. This procedure is called to add the subscription reference to the publisher. Adds the subscription to the subscribed database.

- **sp_addpullsubscription:** Creates a pull subscription and configures it for execution. This procedure is called to add the subscription reference to the subscriber.

- **sp_addpullsubscription_agent:** The pull subscription agent can be activated with this procedure. This procedure is called to add a pull subscription reference to the agent on the subscriber.

The following stored procedures related to subscriptions are also available:

```
sp_addmergepullsubscription
sp_addmergepullsubscription_agent
sp_addmergesubscription
sp_addpullsubscription_agent
sp_addsubscriber_schedule
sp_change_subscription_properties
sp_changemergepullsubscription
sp_changemergesubscription
sp_changesubscriber
sp_changesubscriber_schedule
sp_dropmergepullsubscription
sp_dropmergesubscription
sp_droppullsubscription
sp_dropsubscriber
sp_dropsubscription
```

```
sp_enumfullsubscribers
sp_expired_subscription_cleanup
sp_helpmergepullsubscription
sp_helpmergesubscription
sp_helppullsubscription
sp_helpsubscriberinfo
sp_helpsubscription
sp_helpsubscription_properties
sp_mergesubscription_cleanup
sp_refreshsubscriptions
sp_reinitmergepullsubscription
sp_reinitmergesubscription
sp_reinitpullsubscription
sp_reinitsubscription
sp_subscription_cleanup
```

For administering publications, there are a number of stored procedures that are available to manage a publication. These include:

- **sp_addpublication:** Creates a new publication and adds it to the replication system.
- **sp_grant_publication_access:** Enables specified database user to access the publication.

The following stored procedures related to publications are also available:

sp_addmergepublication	sp_droppublication
sp_addpublication_snapshot	sp_help_publication_access
sp_addpublisher70	sp_helpdistpublisher
sp_addpullsubscription	sp_helpmergepublication
sp_changedistpublisher	sp_helppublication
sp_changemergepublication	sp_link_publication
sp_changepublication	sp_publication_validation
sp_dropdistpublisher	sp_revoke_publication_access
sp_dropmergepublication	

For articles, the primary procedures are used to add data sets and specify the contents of an article for addition to the publication. You can use these primary procedures for article configuration:

- **sp_addarticle:** Creates a new article based on passed parameters including the replication set name, table name used in the article, partitioning settings, filtering selections, and so on.
- **sp_articleview:** In filtering for vertical or horizontal partitioning, this procedure creates a view of the synchronization article. It can only be used on an article that does not yet have any subscribers. The view created by this procedure is then used for the creation of the replica partitions.
- **sp_droparticle:** Drops an unsubscribed article from the publication.

For distribution settings, the following stored procedures are available:

sp_adddistpublisher	sp_changedistributiondb
sp_adddistributiondb	sp_changedistributor_password
sp_adddistributor	sp_changedistributor_property

sp_dropdistributiondb   sp_helpdistributiondb

sp_dropdistributor   sp_helpdistributor

sp_get_distributor

These procedures can be used to set up and configure a distribution server for subscriptions to access.

For agents, the following stored procedures are available:

sp_add_agent_parameter   sp_help_agent_default

sp_add_agent_profile   sp_help_agent_parameter

sp_change_agent_parameter   sp_help_agent_profile

sp_change_agent_profile   sp_replication_agent_checkup

sp_drop_agent_parameter   sp_update_agent_profile

sp_drop_agent_profile

The agent should be activated after the subscription had been registered on the publication server and the actual subscription created on the subscription server. The agent can then automatically synchronize the data sources.

- **sp_replicationdboption**: Activates the replication option for a specified database.

- **sp_addpublication**: Creates a new publication and adds it to the replication system.

- **sp_grant_publication_access**: Enables specified database user to access the publication.

- **sp_changedistributor_password**: Changes the password of a distributor. To successfully complete this function, the username and password that is passed for execution must identify a user that is in the sysadmin group. If not, an error will be returned.

- **sp_changedistributiondb**: Alters the database that is used to store a distribution database.

- **sp_dsninfo(@dsn [,@info_type] [,@login] [,@password] [@dso_type])**: Provides information on a data source used to connect to a server. The @dsn parameter should contain the name of an ODBC or OLE DB connection that is currently actively addressing the MSDE server. The @dso_type can be used to direct whether information on an ODBC source (1, the default) is being requested or an OLE DB (3) name is being passed. The returned recordset will contain information on the source version, database being addressed, and replication capabilities.

- **sp_dumpparamcmd (@originator_id [,@publisher_database_id] [,@article_id] [,@xact_seqno]):** Returns information about a parameterized command stored on the distributor.

- **sp_enumcustomresolvers([@distributor]):** For replication resolvers, this command returns a list of all custom resolvers available.

- **sp_enumdsn():** Will return all of the connections available for the current account.

- **sp_generatefilters(@publication):** Generates filters on foreign key tables when the specified publication is replicated. Only users in the system administrator role or the owner of the publication can execute this procedure.

- **sp_addtabletocontents (@table_name [,@ownername]):** For the merge tracking tables, references to rows in the source tables not available in the tracking table are inserted. The new rows are referenced using the column values from the rowguidcol column.

Sending Mail

Sending mail through the SQL Mail connector is possible if the SQL Server is configured to use the connector. It can also process mail manually that was sent to the configured mail server.

Enterprise Manager is required to configure the SQL Mail connector. Be aware that the SMTP server used for the mail connector is not included with MSDE; the service is therefore unavailable, without additional installation. If an SMTP server is installed and configured for use on the machine, the following procedure can be used in MSDE Transact-SQL code to send mail:

- **xp_deletemail:** Deletes mail stored on the mail server.
- **xp_startmail:** Opens a connection to the configured mail server.
- **xp_readmail:** Processes received mail individually.
- **xp_stopmail:** Stops the mail server.
- **xp_sendmail:** Sends a current mail message.
- **xp_findnextmsg:** Finds the next mail for processing.
- **xp_processmail:** This procedure uses the other three mail processing routines (`xp_readmail`, `xp_findnextmsg`, and `xp_deletemail`) to process the incoming mail that is stored in the folders on the mail server.

Agent Stored Procedures

The SQL Server Agent has many key procedures for autonomous scheduled execution. These include:

- **sp_add_category(@class, @type, @name)**: Adds a new category to the server for classification of jobs, alerts, and operators. The `@class` argument is a string that can have one of three values: `JOB`, `ALERT`, or `OPERATOR`. The `@type` can be one of three values: `LOCAL`, `MULTI-SERVER`, or `NONE`. The `@type` cannot be set to `NONE` for the job class.

- **sp_add_job**: Creates a new job on the server for execution. Only the name of the job must be set at creation time. The simplest command to add a new job would appear like this: `sp_add_job 'NewJob'`

- **sp_add_jobschedule**: Adds a schedule to a job. In Chapter 13, this procedure was used to schedule the execution of a DTS package.

- **sp_add_jobserver**: Specifies the server where the job will execute. Can be used to create a distributed job with code like this: `sp_add_jobserver 'NewJob', 'mySecondMSDEServer'`

- **sp_add_jobstep**: Adds a step to a job task. A step can be defined with the `@Command` argument as a ActiveX Script such as VB Script or JavaScript (`ACTIVESCRIPTING`), operating system command (`CMDEXEC`), Transact-SQL code which is the default (`TSQL`), or execution of a replication job (`DISTRIBUTION`, `SNAPSHOT`, `LOGREADER`, `MERGE`).

- **sp_add_notification**: Creates a notification object related to an alert. The notification set through the `@notification_method` can be an e-mail message (1), a page (2), or a `net send` command (4). For notification by e-mail, the SQL Server Agent must be configured for e-mail through the Enterprise Manager.

- **sp_add_operator**: Adds an operator user to the MSDE server. Parameters that define an operator include: operator name, e-mail address of user, pager number, category of operator, and times available for operator availability.

- **sp_add_targetservergroup**: Creates a new server group. A group can contain a number of servers that can be assigned a job. The job will be distributed to the server with the most available resources.

- **sp_add_targetsvrgrp_member**: Adds a server to an existing target server group.

- **sp_manage_jobs_by_login (@action [, @current_owner_login_name] [, @new_owner_login_name])**: Can be used to delete or reassign jobs based on the login names. The `@action` can hold a command such as `DELETE` or `REASSIGN`. Only users in the sysadmin group can execute this procedure.

- **sp_addtask**: Adds a new task to the MSDE server.

- **sp_help_jobserver (@job_id | @job_name [,@show_last_run_details])**: Displays all of the information related to the server that is assigned to the specified job. The information displayed includes the server ID, server name, enlistment date, and last poll date. The @show_last_run_details argument, if included in the procedure call, requires either a 1 (show the details) or a 0 (don't show details) to include four extra columns displaying the last time, date, duration, and outcome of execution on the job server.

- **sp_help_jobstep (@job_id | @job_name [,@step_id] [,@step_name])**: Returns the information related to a specified job step. If the arguments for @step_id or @step_name are not specified, all of the steps associated with the specified job are returned. Many columns are returns for each step that includes information for items such as the status of the step, the last time and date it was executed, the database on which it is located, and more.

- **sp_help_operator (@operator_name, @operator_id)**: Returns the details of the specified operator. All of the information entered when creating the operator, such as name, e-mail address, pager contact, availability time and dates, and category, is returned in columns of the result set. This procedure must be run from the msdb database.

- **sp_help_targetserver (@servername)**: Lists all of the available target servers registered with the specified server. Information returned by the procedure includes server name and ID, time zone adjustments, status, local time, poll interval, and others.

- **sp_help_targetservergroup (@name)**: Lists all of the available target servers in a target server group.

- **sp_delete_alert**: Removes an alert and all notifications attached to that alert.

- **sp_post_msx_operation (@operation [,@object_type] [,@job_id =] job_id] [,@specific_target_server] [,@value])**: Insert operations into the sysdownloadlist table for download and execution to target servers. If the object type is JOB, then the operations INSERT, UPDATE, DELETE, START, and STOP are available. For a SERVER object type, the operations RE-ENLIST, DEFECT, SYNC-TIME, and SET-POLL commands.

- **sp_delete_category (@class, @name)**: Eliminates a category on the server. The @class argument can be one of three values: JOB, ALERT, and OPERATOR.

- **sp_purge_jobhistory (@job_id | @job_name)**: This procedure will purge the contained history stored with a job.

Chapter 24: Using Stored Procedures in MSDE

- **sp_delete_job (@job_id | @job_name):** Deletes the specified job from the server.

- **sp_delete_jobschedule (@job_id | @job_name):** Deletes a job schedule.

- **sp_delete_jobserver(@job_id | @job_name, @server_name):** Removes a job server that can be used as a target for processing a specified job.

- **sp_remove_job_from_targets:** Removes the job assignment from a distributed system on a target system.

- **sp_delete_jobstep:** Deletes a job step on the server.

- **sp_delete_notification(@alert_name):** Eliminates a notification using the @alertName argument to select the notification to be deleted. The alert itself is not deleted by this command, only the notification associated with it.

- **sp_delete_operator:** Deletes an operator from the MSDE server.

- **sp_delete_targetservergroup:** Deletes the target server group itself. This procedure first removes all of the servers from the group and then eliminates the group itself.

- **sp_delete_targetsvrgrp_member:** Removes a server from a target server group.

- **sp_droptask:** Removes a task from the MSDE server. This procedure is only retained for backward compatibility with older versions of the SQL Server database engine.

- **sp_resync_targetserver (@server_name):** Deletes all of the target server operations in a registered multiserver system group. After the deletion, a new set of operations is posted to the servers. To execute this procedure, the user must belong to the sysadmin group.

- **sp_start_job (@job_id | @job_name [, @server_name] [, @step_name]):** Begins executing job steps that have been defined on target servers immediately. Using the @step_name parameter allows the job to be started at any operational step.

- **sp_add_alert:** Creates a new alert on the specified server. Parameters used in new alert definition include alert name, error severity required for activation, notification message, category name, and others.

- **sp_help_jobschedule (@job_id | @job_name):** Returns the job schedule when passed a desired job.

- **sp_msx_enlist:** This procedure allows adds the current server to a multiserver operation. This procedure modifies the Registry, so use it with caution. It will add all of the jobs on the server. It must be executed by a user in the sysadmin group.

- **sp_msx_defect:** This procedure allows a server to defect or remove itself from a multiserver operation. This procedure modifies the Registry, so use it with caution. It will remove all of the jobs on the server. It must be executed by a user in the sysadmin group.

- **sp_apply_job_to_targets (@job_id | @job_name [, @target_server_groups] [,@target_servers] [,@operation]):** Adds a job to a target server or a target server group. The `@operation` argument must be either set to `APPLY` or `REMOVE`. Must be executed by a user in the sysadmin group.

- **sp_stop_job:** Attempts to halt a currently executing job. If the process in the job being executed is an operating system exec step, the execution will be halted prematurely. Because stopping an OS task can cause system instability, try to use this command only when necessary.

- **sp_delete_targetserver:** Removes the server from the list of registered target servers that can be used for job execution.

- **sp_update_alert:** Modifies an existing alert. Factors such as delays, severity settings, occurrences, and performance conditions are changeable. Only a user in the sysadmin group can execute this procedure.

- **sp_update_category (@class, @name, @new_name):** Renames a specified category. The `@class` argument may contain one of three possible settings: `ALERT`, `JOB`, or `OPERATOR`.

- **sp_update_job:** Modifies the settings of an existing job. Covers factors such as notification level, start step ID number (`@start_step_id`), owner login name, delete level, and notification e-mail name.

- **sp_update_jobschedule:** Changes the schedule for an existing job. Factors such as the frequency, type of frequency (`@freq_type`), frequency interval (`@freq_interval`), and active start and end date (`@active_start_date` and `@active_end_date`). This procedure must be run for the msdb database.

- **sp_help_alert:** List the alerts information available on the system. Returns a row for each alert with columns that indicate settings of the alert, such as the severity level to which the alert responds, the enabled status, the last response time, and the last response alert. This procedure must be run on the msdb database by a user in the sysadmin group.

- **sp_update_jobstep:** Modifies a job step for such factors as step name, subsystem, server, and database name where the job is stored. This procedure must be run from the msdb database.

- **sp_help_category ([@class,] [@type,] [@name,] [@suffix]):** Returns the requested information about classes of alerts, jobs, or operators. The `@class` should be passed as one of three types: `JOB`, `ALERT`, or `OPERATOR`. The `@type` argument can be one of three types: `LOCAL`, `MULTI-SERVER`, or `NONE`.

- **sp_update_notification (@alert_name, @operator_name, @notification_method):** Changes the procedure used for alert notification. This procedure must be executed from within the msdb database.

- **sp_help_downloadlist (@job_id | @job_name):** Returns all of the rows for a supplied job or all rows if no job is specified. These rows are stored in the master table of sysdownloadlist.

- **sp_update_operator:** Updates the operator settings for alerts and jobs.

- **sp_help_job (@job_id | @job_name):** Returns the job information when passed a desired job.

- **sp_update_targetservergroup (@name, @new_name):** Changes the name of a target server group. This procedure must be execute with the msdb database selected.

- **sp_help_jobhistory (@job_id | @job_name):** Returns the job history when passed a desired job.

Security Procedures

Every security function available through the Enterprise Server or SQL-DMO can also be set and modified with the appropriate stored procedure.

User Commands

To modify aspects of the individual login names, there are a number of procedures that apply to this management. The SQL commands for security that apply to individual user accounts include:

- **sp_addlogin(@loginame [,@passwd] [,@defdb] [,@deflanguage] [,@sid] [,@encryptopt]):** Adds a new login that allows connection through standard MSDE security. If no password is specified, the login will allow connection with the database server without a password.

- **sp_grantdbaccess (@loginname [,@name_in_db] [Output]):** Adds a new user to the MSDE security (such as `MyGroup\MyName`). The `@loginname` must be less than 129 characters. The `@name_in_db` parameter is simply for a more descriptive user name such that `@loginname` may be `'gsmith'` whereas `@name_in_db` may be set to `'George Smith'`.

- **sp_grantlogin (@loginName):** Creates a login account but must be passed as a user and group (i.e., `'MyGroup\MyName'`). This procedure will provide access, whereas the `sp_denylogin` routine will revoke the granted permission.

- **sp_denylogin (@loginName):** Revokes a login created with the `sp_grantlogin` procedure.

- **sp_revokelogin (@loginName):** Revokes a login created with the `sp_grantlogin` procedure or NT account integration. This procedure differs from `sp_denylogin` in that it has been created specifically to revoke a login created through NT security integration.

- **sp_revokedbaccess (@name_in_db):** Removes database access for a specified account name. The name for revocation may be an entire group/role or an individual user (i.e., `'MyGroup\MyName'`).

- **sp_changeobjectowner (@objname, @newowner):** Changes the owner of a database object to the user account specified by `@newowner`. Only users that own the specified object or members of the sysadmin role can execute this procedure.

- **sp_validatelogins():** For integrated security, checks the users and groups of the Windows NT security model against the users and roles available on the MSDE server. All of the users and groups on the MSDE server that no longer have a valid account in the NT system are reported here.

Role and Group Commands

For roles or groups, other commands are used because of the number of different situations that grouping logins comprises. The SQL commands for security that apply to roles or groups include:

- **sp_addrole(@rolename [,@ownername]):** Adds a new role to the current database. This procedure cannot be used within a user-defined transaction. Once a role has been added to the system, the `sp_helpuser` procedure can be used to view which members have been added to a role.

- **sp_addrolemember(@rolename, @membername):** Adds a new role member to an existing role in the current database.

- **sp_addapprole(@rolename [,@password]):** Creates a special role type for applications. An application role does not contain members; instead the user connection is added to the group when the application associated with the role is executed.

- **sp_approlepassword(@rolename [,@newpwd]):** Installs a new password for the specified application role. Only the owner of the application role or a member of the sysadmin role can execute this routine for an application role.

- **sp_addsrvrolemember(@loginname [,@rolename]):** Adds the specified loginname to the fixed server role. Fixed roles include sysadmin, securityadmin, serveradmin, setupadmin, processadmin, diskadmin, or dbcreator. Only a current member of the specified fixed server role can execute this routine to add another login name.

- **sp_droprole(@rolename, @membername):** Drops a specified role in the selected database on the MSDE server.

- **sp_droprolemember(@rolename, @membername):** Drops a current role member in the selected database on the MSDE server.

- **sp_dropapprole (@rolename):** Drops a specified application role in the selected database on the MSDE server.

- **sp_dropsrvrolemember(@srvrolename):** Displays the permissions that are currently set for a fixed server role. Roles include: sysadmin, securityadmin, serveradmin, setupadmin, processadmin, diskadmin, and dbcreator.

- **sp_setapprole(@rolename, @password [,@encrypt]):** Activates the security permissions for the specified application role. The `@password` parameter can be encrypted. If `@password` is encrypted, the method of encryption is specified in the `@encrypt` variable which can be set to either *none* or *odbc*. The encryption is handled by the ODBC interface activated by the `Encrypt` function when directly addressing the driver.

- **sp_helpsrvrolemember(@loginname, @rolename):** Removes a SQL Server login or group that was added through the NT integrated security. The available role names include: sysadmin, securityadmin, serveradmin, setupadmin, processadmin, diskadmin, and dbcreator.

- **sp_revokedbaccess(@name_in_db):** Removes the specified login account, the aliases, and all permissions for the account. This routine revokes accounts that are created with `sp_grantdbaccess`.

- **sp_addlinkedsrvlogin (@rmtsrvname [,@useself] [,@locallogin] [,@rmtuser] [,@rmtpassword]:** Creates or updates a remote server listing on the local machine. The information supplied to this routine is used to allow the local machine to log in to the remote machine for execution of a distributed operation. This routine is used particularly when Windows NT trusted security is not used in a system (perhaps because one of the servers is running on the Windows 95/98 platform), so specific account login is required.

- **sp_droplinkedsrvlogin(@rmtsrvname, @locallogin):** Deletes a login mapping in place between a local and remote server used for a linked system. Only members of the sysadmin or securityadmin roles may execute this routine.

- **sp_helprole([@rolename]):** Information of the specified role is returned. If no role is passed as an argument, properties for all of the roles is displayed.

- **sp_helprolemember:** Returns information on the specified role member.

- **sp_helpsrvrole**: Returns the fixed server roles available on the current system.

- **sp_helpdbfixedrole([@rolename])**: Returns the fixed database roles available on the current system. If no rolename is passed to the routine, all of the fixed roles are included.

- **sp_helpntgroup**: Displays information on the groups that are mapped to MSDE roles.

- **sp_dbfixedrolepermission([@rolename])**: Returns the permissions of a system fixed database role. Roles include: db_owner, db_accessadmin, db_securityadmin, db_ddladmin, db_backupoperator, db_datareader, db_datawriter, db_denydatareader, and db_denydatawriter. If no @rolename parameter is passed to the routine, information on all of the fixed role permissions is returned.

- **sp_srvrolepermission(@srvrolename)**: Displays information related to the specified server role. The available role names include: sysadmin, securityadmin, serveradmin, setupadmin, processadmin, diskadmin, and dbcreator.

Distributed Queries Procedures

Distributed updates and modifications that exist across multiple servers are generally automatically taken care of by the Microsoft Distributed Transaction Controller. For distributed queries, however, a linked list of servers is used. The following procedures are used to configure and manage the linked servers that are used in the distributed operations:

- **sp_addlinkedserver(@server [, @srvproduct] [, @provider] [, @datasrc] [,@location] [, @provstr] [, @catalog]**: Adds a server to the list of linked servers to allow for remote execution of distributed operations. A linked server does not have to be an SQL Server or MSDE server but can be any data source available through a compatible OLE DB driver (including Oracle, ODBC sources, Excel spreadsheets, etc.).

- **sp_indexes(@table_server [,@table_name] [,@table_schema] [,@table_catalog] [,@index_name] [,@is_unique]**: Returns index information for a table located on a remote server.

- **sp_addlinkedsrvlogin([@rmtsrvname [,@useself] [,@locallogin] [,@rmtuser] [,@rmtpassword])**: Either creates a new linked login or updates the existing one for login parameters for the remote server.

Miscellaneous Useful Stored Procedures

The following are a number of general-purpose routines that allow activation of recompiles, system monitoring, and source code examination. Each procedure provides a management function that may be helpful when maintaining your MSDE server remotely because simple SQL execute can activate them.

- **sp_recompile(@objname):** You can explicitly recompiled a stored procedure by using the `sp_recompile` function. The procedure will be set for recompiling and will not actually recompile until it is next called. This routine can also be used for recompiling triggers, and it allows you to specify an object, such as a table, where all local stored procedures dependent on that object will be recompiled on the next execution.

- **sp_helptext(@objname):** You can use the `sp_helptext` function to display the source code of a procedure as long as that procedure has not been encrypted. Information supplied by this function includes: objects used by the procedure, owner, creation date, parameters, and the names of other procedures that it addresses.

- **sp_monitor():** A useful procedure that displays statistics such as reading, writing, and processor usage. All of these statistics are returned as columns in the result set. Most of them are displayed as values because this procedure was last executed and values since the server was started.

- **sp_lock([@spid1] [,@spid2]):** Displays current locks that are active on the MSDE server. The `@spid1` and `@spid2` parameters denote system process identification numbers that may be obtained from the `sp_who` routine.

- **sp_who([@login_name]):** Displays current users logged into the database server and the operations they are requesting to be performed

- **sp_spaceused(@objname [,@updateusage]):** Returns the size of database objects. For a database table, the number of rows, reserved disk space, and used disk space are all returned. The `@updateusage` parameter may be passed the string 'TRUE' or 'FALSE' to recalculate the space numbers. The default `@updateusage` setting is 'FALSE'.

The SQL-DMO Model

Remember that you can easily examine all of the properties, methods, and events that are present in the DMO framework by adding the class library (listed as Microsoft SQLDMO Object Library) to the project references and then opening the

Object Browser (see Figure 24-1). The Visual Basic and VBA development environments will display the Object Browser from an icon on the toolbar or when you press F2.

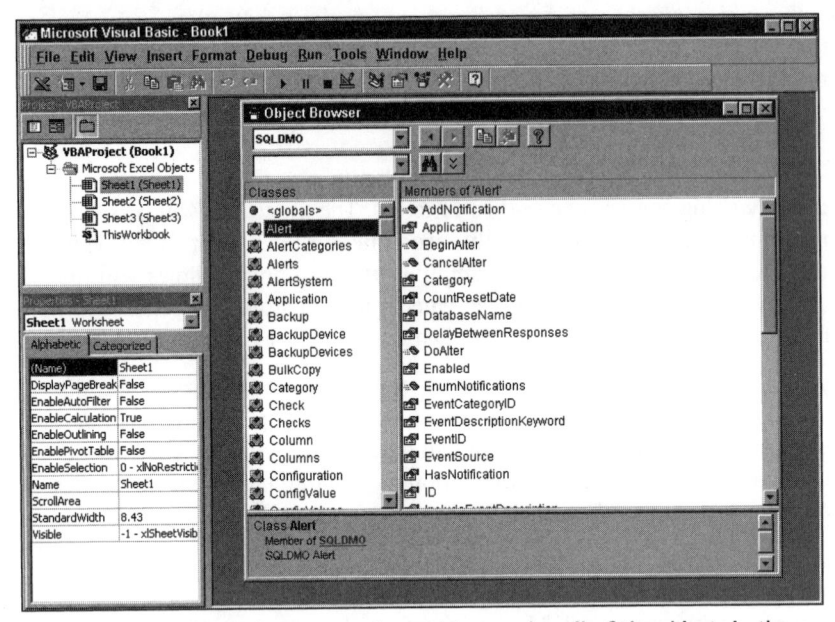

Figure 24-1: The Object Browser can be used to examine all of the objects in the SQL-DMO class library.

Summary

Effectively using available system stored procedures is the cornerstone of proper MSDE management. By using system procedures for everything from security configuration to agent process execution, your database server can be addressed from any machine on the LAN. In this chapter you covered:

- **sp_configure:** The `sp_configure` routine is used to set global settings for the MSDE server.
- **Security stored procedures:** Add users or roles as well as set specific permissions for any available database objects.
- **Agent stored procedures:** The SQL Server Agent processes can be modified or executed through the available routines.

- **Distributed query procedures:** For distributed queries, the server network for processing the query can be monitored or configured through a number of system routines.

- **SQL-DMO model:** All of the configuration that is available through stored procedures can also be addressed through the properties and methods of the SQL-DMO framework.

Chapter 25

Implementing Security

IN THIS CHAPTER

- ◆ Planning general and MSDE specific security
- ◆ Implementing database roles
- ◆ Performing security management through SQL code
- ◆ Configuring security for linked MSDE servers
- ◆ Executing security code
- ◆ Implementing Replication and Package security
- ◆ Using Active Directory and Windows 2000
- ◆ Implementing general tips for security planning

AN MSDE SERVER CAN efficiently provide data to applications across a LAN or even the breadth of the Internet. The critical role that information plays in today's organization makes ensuring security for the data a critical part of setting up any database system. By properly planning and implementing security controls, you can minimize unauthorized access and unintended modification. Unauthorized access may cause intentional or unintentional data corruption. If your security is compromised, the information that you retrieve from the data source may not be reliable.

The difficulty of configuring MSDE for your security needs is not caused by a poorly designed security interface from Microsoft. Instead, the power and flexibility of the MSDE server means that numerous different pieces of the system must be adequately protected. Security settings are available for everything from basic login to table access to package execution to replication server distribution.

Proper configuration of security begins by planning how best to protect your data both for privacy reasons and data integrity. Carefully planning not only how a security system will be initially deployed, but also how it will be maintained, is critical to effective implementation of any database solution.

Security Planning

Planning security requires a fair amount of thought and foresight into problems that may crop up. Considerations are far broader than simply keeping a hacker out of your database system. Important privacy issues are often involved with database access. A database may contain anything from corporate finances to salary figures to technical data that require access restricted to only those authorized to address it.

The primary areas involved in planning include:

- **OS integration:** The security capabilities of the operating system can either help or impede deployment. Investigating what operating systems will need to be addressed is important to proper planning. If a Web-based client is being used, password security is another issue.

- **Defining users, groups, and roles:** Setting up the proper users, groups, and roles (MSDE's version of groups) along with the appropriate permissions provides the foundation upon which the secure system is built. As the system is maintained and new users are added, if the initial planning of the available groups was done properly, the new accounts can simply be added to existing groups without any redefinition or special settings required.

- **Access pathways:** Wiring, communication protocols, routing, and firewalls are all aspects of the pathways that will be used to pass information between the client and the server. These aspects of security are traditionally handled by the network administrator and fall outside the responsibility of the database administrator.

- **Login access:** Providing users with a method of setting passwords, logging into the system, and protecting password access can be one of the most demanding jobs of creating a new system. A simple mistake such as storing a password for the data source in ASP Web page code may provide a gateway for unauthorized access.

- **Database structures:** How you partition the databases and tables as well as the geographic placement of the data is of primary concern to security. If one site is completely secure but the important data is replicated to an insecure site, the potential for a breach is greatly increased.

To create a plan for how security will be implemented, it is usually best to create a list of all of the objects that will need to be secured. This object list includes databases, tables, columns, and the servers themselves that are used for data access, replication, and export.

Once you have compiled this list, a second list should be made of all of the users and groups that will need to access these objects. In Table 25-1, you can see a sample of how a table could be created from these two lists.

The left column of the table specifies the object that is being addressed. The top row indicates all of the groups where individual users can be placed. Keep in mind that a single user can be placed in multiple groups, and therefore, permissions may overlap.

Table 25-1 The Users and Groups Access List

Object/User	Sysadmin	Developer	Group Leader	Sales Manager	Salespeople
DB-Northwind	All	SR,SW,R,W,D	R,W	R,W	R,W
Tbl-Orders	All	SR,SW,R,W,D	R,W,D	R,W,D	R,W
Tbl-Order Details	All	SR,SW,R,W,D	R,W,D	R,W,D	R,W
Tbl-Customers	All	SR,SW,R,W,D	R,W,D	R,W	R,W
Tbl-Employees	All	SR,SW,R,W,D	R,W,D	R	-

The intersection of the rows and the columns indicates the permissions given to that specific group for a particular object. For this form of table, the key may appear like this:

```
SR = Schema read        W = Write
SW = Schema write       D = Delete
R  = Read
```

Creating this type of documentation may seem tedious. However, if stored with the solution, it can provide a critical guide for later updates to the system. A designer who needs to make an update such as a table or group addition to the system can quickly see how existing objects are treated and can make the augmentation accordingly.

This permissions table will provide a foundation to plan all the other aspects of the system. You will be able to see the major categories of users and the objects that will need to be secured. When the individual objects are listed in the table (to any level of granularity), it is much easier to see the level of secure data that will be transported by the replication and export systems.

> **Note:** Although proper planning is critical, even the best planning cannot prevent security holes that are discovered in the products themselves. Because the MSDE server is based on the seventh generation of SQL Server, all of the obvious problems have been addressed. Nonetheless, make sure you include an upgrade schedule in your security plan to apply new versions of critical applications, hot fixes, and other patches to remedy newly discovered security holes. You can check a general listing of security concerns on the Microsoft site (www.microsoft.com) or check L0PHT (that's L-Zero-P-H-T) which is available on the Web at www.10pht.com.

MSDE Security

Although a plan will tell you which objects are to be secured and the categories of users that will address them, the system of security deployment will determine exactly how the application you are creating will interface with the secure system. By examining the capabilities of MSDE, you will be able to decide how security can be implemented.

The security available through MSDE depends on the needs of your deployment. If you are deploying MSDE on Windows NT server, which is Microsoft's premier secure platform, you have a variety of choices to make. In a Windows 95/98 environment or mixed-platform deployment, the solution must use the standard SQL Server security.

MSDE has three primary security configurations when run on Windows NT: standard security, NT security, and integrated security. The standard SQL Server security allows all of the users, groups, and roles to be defined within the MSDE server. For NT security, the users and groups are inherited from the Windows NT users and groups that are defined at the operating system level. For integrated security, login accounts from both sources are available for connection to the MSDE server.

All of the logins are stored as individual objects available through the SQL-DMO model. Directly under the main SQL Server object (see Figure 25-1), each login is stored as an independent object in the Logins collection.

```
┌─────────────────┐
│   SQLServer     │
└─────────────────┘
         │
         ┌─────────────┐
         │   Logins    │
         │   (Login)   │
         └─────────────┘
```

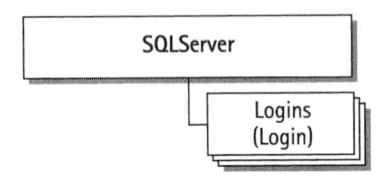

Figure 25-1: The Logins collection in the SQL-DMO object holds all of the login accounts for the MSDE server.

> **NOTE:** All of the login security modes provide the login security protocol. Once the identity of the user has been established, communication with the data source can occur through a trusted connection regardless of the login mode.

Configuring the Security Authentication Mode

You can set any of these login modes for the MSDE server during the installation process or through system stored procedures or the Enterprise Manager after the MSDE server has been installed.

To set the current mode through the Enterprise Manager, follow these steps:

1. Execute the Enterprise Manager.
2. Expand the folders and select the MSDE server you wish to configure.
3. Right-click the server and select the Properties option.
4. Click the Security tab to see the available options. Through the properties window, you can set the authentication mode to either mixed mode or integrated security (see Figure 25-2).

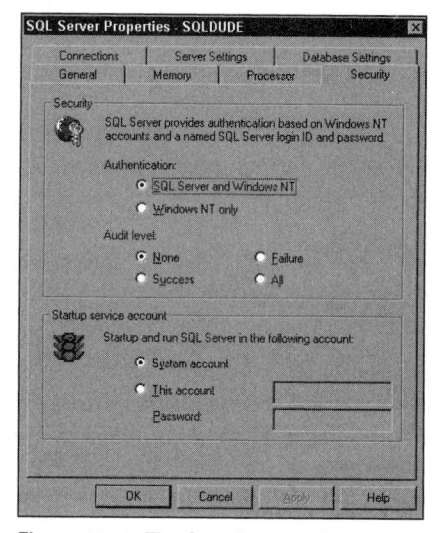

Figure 25-2: The Security tab of the database properties window provides the setting for the MSDE security mode.

You can also set up such parameters as the audit level for secured access and the startup account to run the MSDE server process under. Auditing can be set to four different modes: None, Success, Failure, or All. The Success setting will log all successful login attempts, whereas Failure will log those that are unsuccessful. All will log both. None will log neither. This auditing is helpful in determining individual usage of the server and also in tracking failed attempts such as those that might mark a hacker's attack.

Standard SQL Server Security

The MSDE/SQL Server engine has its own native security for login and access. The engine keeps all listings of the users and groups/roles in an internal database. Each login is stored as an entry in the syslogins table of the master database.

In Figure 25-3, you can see the Enterprise Server displaying the default fixed roles available for MSDE. The Server Roles item that is selected in the figure is one of four security areas available in the Security folder for each server registered in the manager. Every user or database role can be granted privileges to database objects, or those privileges can be revoked.

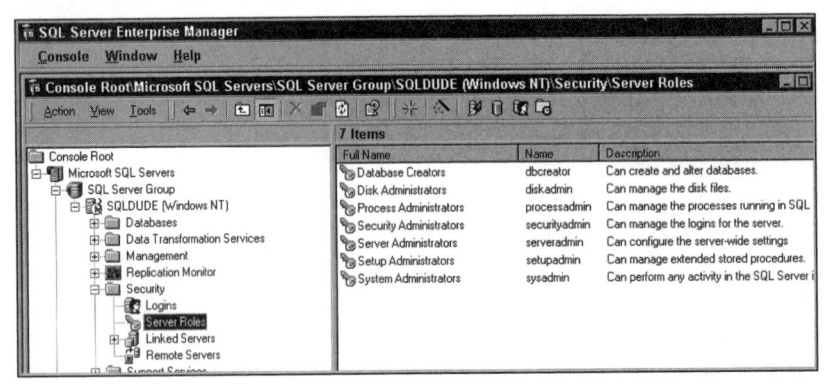

Figure 25-3: The Enterprise Manager will display all the accounts and roles available.

By right-clicking a database object and selecting the Properties option, you can examine the Permissions tab to see the security settings.

Under each database, security settings can be refined. Expanding a database will reveal items for Users and Roles. If you examine the Properties of any of the users or roles defined for the database, you will see a Permissions button. Clicking Permissions will open the Security window for any of the database objects (like the one shown in Figure 25-4), and permissions may be given for read access, write access, delete access, insert, and referential integrity settings.

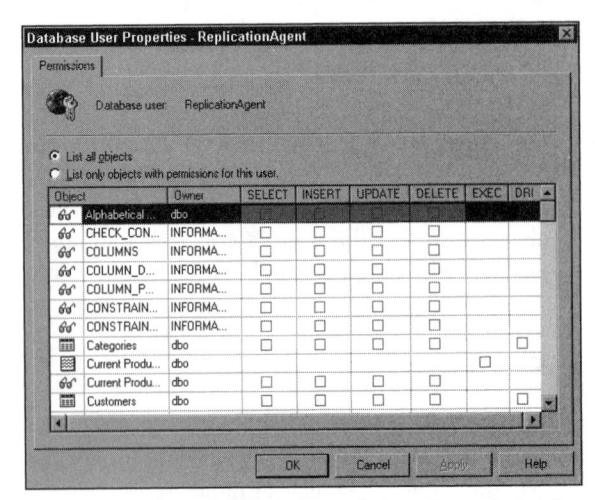

Figure 25-4: Several different permissions for each database object may be granted to each user or group.

If you expand any of the databases, you can also see that Users and Roles items are contained in these folders (see Figure 25-5). Each database contains the logins that are available to access objects within that database.

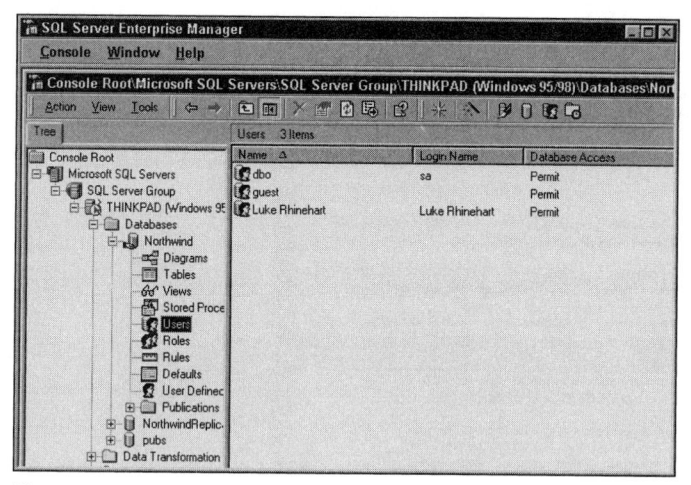

Figure 25-5: Each database contains the user logins and roles that are specific to it.

> **Note:** The new security services of Windows 2000 allow duplicate user names as long as they are located hierarchically in different organizations. This structure allows more than one jsmith user name to be contained within an organization managed by the same server.

The actual security settings on the MSDE server (for database, tables, and so on) are wholly maintained by the database server itself. Whenever remote access occurs over the Internet or another access method based on the TCP/IP protocol, the security setting for that protocol on the operating system level is used.

Windows NT Trusted Security

The Windows NT operating system is Microsoft's enterprise operating system for organizations. One of the advantages that it provides is the robust security model that secures the entire server machine on which it runs because the security features were included in the foundation code of the OS. Windows NT security has become the customary way to define user logins for MSDE and SQL Server. Rather than maintaining two separate sets of user logins, the user accounts may be maintained as part of the NT Administrator's tasks.

With trusted security, only the trusted connections will be allowed and all other login attempts will be denied. All users and groups are created in the User Manager for Domains (see Figure 25-6) utility of the operating system itself. Once the login accounts are created at the OS level, individual permissions for the database objects are set within the MSDE server.

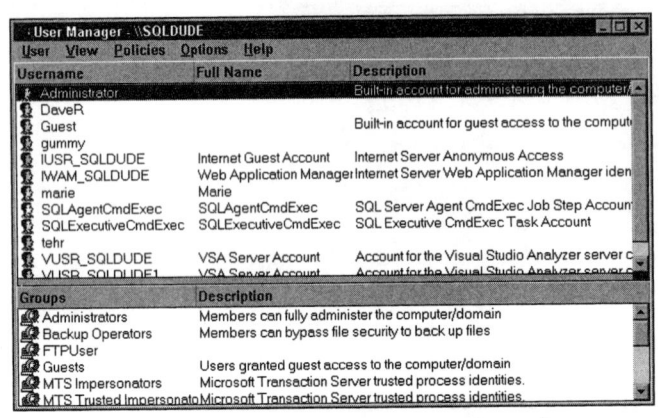

Figure 25-6: The User Manager for Domains can be used to configure users and groups for integrated or mixed security.

Trusted connections make a connection between Windows NT-based machines. User names and passwords may not contain any backslash (\) characters and may not be set to a null string. Each user name must be unique; a name cannot match another user name on the server or in the current domain.

Once the user has logged into the NT system, when MSDE access is attempted, the database server simply checks the NT security profile and determines whether the current user is logged into the system. If verified, the MSDE server allows any database access set for that login name. The xp_grantlogin and xp_revokelogin system stored procedures can be used to provide permissions for the accounts created under this security model.

To have integrated security with MSDE, the database server must be specifically configured for the NT security settings into the SQL Server-based environment. This includes adding local or global groups and how they relate to SQL roles. A Windows NT user or group can log in without explicitly giving permission on SQL Server.

The guest user is a default account on the SQL Server-based database server. A guest can log in to the database without any special permissions to database access except those granted explicitly to all users. The guest account can be granted or denied access to any database, although it must always be granted on the master and tempdb databases (to allow database use).

Mixed Security Model

With mixed security, MSDE obtains user name and login information from both NT and standard SQL Server security. Users and groups may be added via standard SQL Server security that are exclusive to the database server and will not be available for login to NT. At the same time, all of the users and groups assigned via NT security will be available for access within the database server, if they have been added as logins on the server. For NT users, this means that a single login name and password can be used for both NT and MSDE login.

Mixed security is an effective way of managing both the database server and the primary file or application server at the same time. If you work with a system administrator who manages the server that MSDE will be deployed on, this option may be the most appropriate way for you to work together to manage a system.

> **NOTE:** You can actually examine the Registry entry for the security mode setting with the RegEdit.exe application located in the \Windows\System directory of your system. The path HKEY_LOCAL_MACHINE\SOFTWARE\Microsoft\MSSQLServer\ MSSQLServer holds a number that indicates the current mode. The value 0 indicates standard security, whereas values of 1 or 2 are used for integrated and mixed mode, respectively. Although you can change this setting manually, it is recommended that you use the available administrative tools instead.

Default Login

MSDE includes a default login setting that is not contained with the normal login accounts. Under Windows NT, you can use the `xp_loginconfig` to determine the current default login settings. Executing this system stored procedure will display the current settings for the MSDE server.

When you have executed this system stored procedure, the following result set will be returned:

```
name              config_value
login mode        mixed
default login     guest
default domain    REDMOND
audit level       none
set hostname      false
map _             domain separator
map $             space
map #             -
```

Windows 95/98 Security

The MSDE server can be run on Windows 95/98 as well as Windows NT. Unfortunately, the security on Windows 95/98 is fairly simple, and this system is therefore not a recommended platform for solutions requiring all but the most basic precautionary security measures.

When you are deploying to client machines that use the 95/98 operating system, you will need to use MSDE standard security for the login. Integrated security will still work for allowing the login name and password to be used even if the trusted security isn't used.

OS and Browser Integration

The operating systems that will provide access to the application vary greatly in their secure capabilities. Deciding whether Windows NT or Windows 95/98 will be used is the tip of the iceberg. With the dramatic growth of Web-based solutions, the operating system itself is supplanted by the Web browser.

The Internet Explorer browser can provide Windows NT authentication. That means that the password sent to log in the user or address a database is encrypted so that access even over the Internet is secure. The Internet Explorer browser is made to explicitly support this security protocol, as is the Netscape Navigator browser. Although the Netscape browser will display the login window, it will not properly pass the login information to the server.

There are two stages of security validation: authentication and permission validation. Authentication verifies that the user exists and can connect to the server. Permissions validation occurs when the user attempts to address objects on the server and the permissions granted to the user or the groups that the user belongs are determined. Although authentication uses one of the three modes of login, regular communication and exchange of data occur over one of the available network protocols that must be separately configured.

Network Protocol Options

Four protocols are available for use with the MSDE server: Named Pipes (or NetBIOS), TCP/IP, IPX/SPX (Novell's protocol), and multiprotocol. Named Pipes is the default protocol for file interaction over the network for the Windows operating system. When you use a machine and volume name address such as \\myMachine\myFolder for mounting a remote drive, you are using the Named Pipes protocol. Often, MSDE will communicate with client machines using this as the default protocol. However, Named Pipes has limited routing capabilities and is therefore very difficult to use beyond a LAN. For geographically disparate sites, Named Pipes is a poor choice for database communication.

The TCP/IP protocol is the one that will be used for most of your MSDE deployment. It is the fastest protocol with the lowest amount of network overhead. TCP/IP is the standard protocol used by the Internet, so accessibility of a data source is easy whether on a LAN or located anywhere in the world and accessible through the Internet or other WAN. To address the server through this protocol, you can use either the IP number of the MSDE machine (for instance, 127.100.100.100) or its domain name (for instance, myMSDE.myCorp.com). Microsoft has announced that from Windows 2000 onward, future operating systems will embrace TCP/IP as their standard protocol.

IPX/SPX is used for older installations that use a Novell server as the primary network server. This protocol is then used for server name resolution. Multiprotocol settings allow one or several of these protocols to be used. Protocol resolution and other operations make multiprotocol operation execute more slowly than selecting a single protocol option.

The protocol used by the MSDE server can be set during the installation process or after the MSDE server has been installed through the Server Network Utility (see Figure 25-7) application available under the MSDE menu. This is the protocol that the server is "listening" on. If a client is configured to communicate with a different protocol (through the client configuration utility), then that client will be unable to connect.

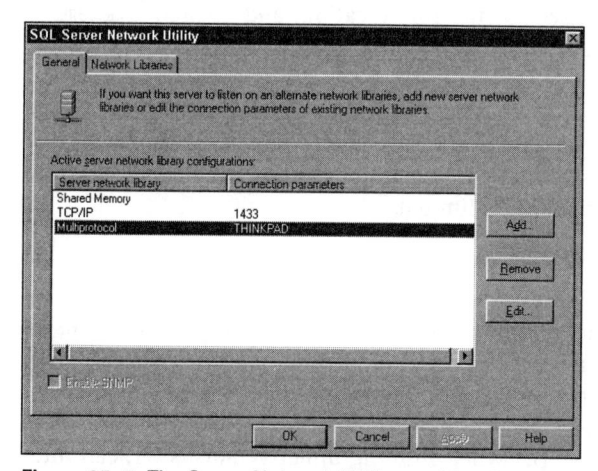

Figure 25-7: The Server Network Utility enables the addition or removal of protocols for server use.

Database Roles

In addition to the standard security definition of groups and users, MSDE allows the definition of *roles*. Roles allow an additional level of differentiation by setting the security according to a user's activities. For example, the database may include be a role for the users that maintain the data warehouse sources for reporting. Therefore, a role might be created called ReportSourceAdmin. Unlike a group, a role is defined specifically within a single database and cannot be used for security settings across several databases.

It may seem as though roles provide many of the same features as security groups. Although similar, groups and roles are very different in implementation. Roles have the following advantages:

- **Roles are defined with a database:** Roles can be provided in a database that don't grant permissions anywhere else, avoiding unintended access permission.

- **Multiple roles may be active:** A logged-on user may be part of several database roles at the same time.

- **The owner of a role has admin control:** Unlike the process of defining users and groups that requires administrator permissions for altering, the creator of the role has the ability to add or remove users from the current role.

Creating a role on the MSDE server can be accomplished through the Enterprise Manager, Transact-SQL, or the SQL-DMO framework. For Transact-SQL, the `sp_addrole` procedure can be used for the role creation, and `sp_addrolemember` routine can be used to add a user to the role. The `sp_droprole` system procedure will remove a current row from the system.

Because a given role only applies to a specific database, roles can often be given with greater latitude than groups without the subsequent risk of a security breach. Use the role settings for a database task rather than defining a database group to ensure that the breadth of permissions is limited.

Roles versus Groups

In standard NT security and most other systems, security is defined in terms of users and groups. For MSDE and SQL Server 7, groups have been replaced by the concept of a *role*. Even the stored procedures that retain the word "group" in their names actually address the role system.

The security model used by MSDE, when running under Windows NT, can integrate with NT server (see Figure 25-8). The integrated model can then accept logins that are defined in either the database security model or the operating system security model.

When mixed-mode or NT security is used, NT groups are treated as MSDE roles when security is addressed. A user may have more than one role within a single database. Database roles may or may not have owners. If the role has an owner, the owner of the role and the sysadmins are the only ones that can add or remove users to or from the role.

The roles to which a user is admitted can be viewed by examining the properties of a user within the Enterprise Manager (see Figure 25-9). Adding additional checks will insert the user into those roles if the security permissions of the configuring user have that security power.

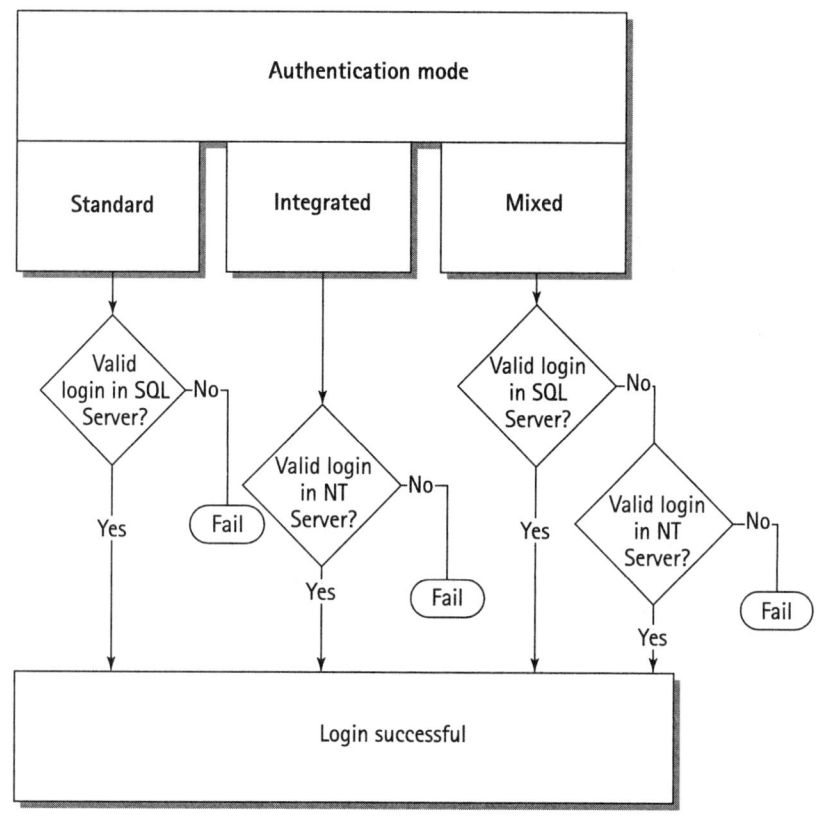

Figure 25-8: The authentication process can use both NT security and mixed-mode security.

Figure 25-9: The roles to which a user belongs are shown in the properties window of a particular user.

An additional type of role different from the standard is called an *application role*. An application role is a role that users cannot be added to. Instead, when a user executes an application associated with the application role, the connection of that user is implicitly added to the role.

Guest Account

In the MSDE server, a default account known as the *guest* account is created. The guest account has default read access to the master and tempdb databases to allow object access. New databases, by default, do not include permissions for the guest account. Instead, they must be added.

To grant access for the guest account in a new database, you can select the database and then execute this command:

```
Execute sp_grantaccess guest, guest
```

Database Owners

When new objects are created, the creator of that object is known as the *owner*. The owner has special rights for modification and deletion of the owned items. The term *dbo* stands for database owner and used in most references to indicate the owner.

Many stored procedures can be accessed only by owner. To allow the sysadmin role to address these objects, any users in the sysadmin role are automatically set to be, in a manner, universal dbo users. When any system administrator creates an object, the owner recorded for that object is stored as dbo.

Security Management through SQL Code

Most aspects of security for the MSDE server can be configured through simple SQL commands instead of using a tool such as the Enterprise Manager. The strength of using the SQL commands for security management lies in the ability to change MSDE security settings from any machine that can address the database server, without requiring the installation of Enterprise Manager on these client machines.

Two roles, db_securityadmin and db_owner, are used for security administration. As a member of one of these two roles, you may control the modifications and security settings for each database.

Primary Security Commands

The Transact-SQL keywords for security include Grant, Deny, and Revoke. These commands are used to provide permissions to various database objects. The data modification attributes of logins will take effect as soon as the command is successfully executed. When a new user is first created, the user account is not added to any roles/groups and has no default permissions granted.

GRANT COMMAND

The Grant command will allow any column, table, view, stored procedure, or SQL statement to be accessible to a user, role, or everyone. The Grant command is used in two different ways: to provide access to SQL commands and to provide access to SQL objects. SQL statement permissions are allocated for creating tables and rules, and for activating backups. For existing database objects, the Grant command can provide specifications down to the column level.

For statement permissions, the syntax for Grant appears like this:

```
GRANT {ALL | statement[,...n]}
TO security_account[,...n]
```

With this form of the Grant command, assignment of access to the following SQL statements is possible: Create Database, Create Default, Create Procedure, Create Rule, Create Table, Create View, Backup Database, and Backup Log. You can use the command like this:

```
Grant Create Database To myUser
```

For object permissions, the syntax appears like this:

```
GRANT
    {ALL [PRIVILEGES] | permission[,...n]}
    {
        [(column[,...n])] ON {table | view}
        | ON {table | view}[(column[,...n])]
        | ON {stored_procedure | extended_procedure}
    }
TO security_account[,...n]
[WITH GRANT OPTION]
[AS {group | role}]
```

As you can see from the syntax, permissions can be specified for tables, views, columns within the views or tables, and stored or extended stored procedures.

To grant the ability to activate a Select query in the NorthwindSQL database, you can use a command like this:

```
Grant Select On NorthwindSQL To myUser
```

You can also grant modification to specific objects with code such as this:

```
Grant Insert, Update, Delete On NorthwindSQL To salesRole
```

DENY COMMAND

The Deny command will explicitly specify a resource to which a user or role will not have access. Like the Grant command, Deny can be set for any column, table, view, stored procedure, or SQL statement to be denied to a user, role, or everyone.

For statement permissions, the syntax for the Deny command appears like this:

```
DENY{ALL | statement[,...n]}
TO security_account[,...n]
```

For object permissions, the syntax appears like this:

```
DENY
    {ALL [PRIVILEGES] | permission[,...n]}
    {
        [(column[,...n])] ON {table | view}
        | ON {table | view}[(column[,...n])]
        | ON {stored_procedure | extended_procedure}
    }
TO security_account[,...n]
[CASCADE]
```

The Deny command is executed in the same manner as the Grant command, as in this example denying a user select permissions to the NorthwindSQL database:

```
Deny Select On NorthwindSQL To myUser
```

REVOKE COMMAND

The Revoke command is used to remove access to a resource that was previously allowed with the Grant command. Like the Deny command, it follows the same command form used by the Grant command.

For statement permissions, the syntax for the Revoke command appears like this:

```
REVOKE {ALL | statement[,...n]}
FROM security_account[,...n]
```

For object permissions, the syntax appears like this:

```
REVOKE [GRANT OPTION FOR]
    {ALL [PRIVILEGES] | permission[,...n]}
    {
        [(column[,...n])] ON {table | view}
        | ON {table | view}[(column[,...n])]
        | {stored_procedure | extended_procedure}
    }
```

```
{TO | FROM}
    security_account[,...n]
[CASCADE]
[AS {group | role}]
```

System Stored Procedures

Although the primary routines to grant, deny, or revoke access to database objects exist as SQL commands, most refined security administration occurs through system stored procedures. The three SQL commands provide a baseline compatibility with the SQL standard, whereas the stored procedures are customized to the MSDE server system and its features.

USER COMMANDS

Several procedures are used to modify aspects of individual login names. The SQL commands for security that apply to individual user accounts include:

- **sp_addlogin(@loginame [,@passwd] [,@defdb] [,@deflanguage] [,@sid] [,@encryptopt]):** Adds a new login that allows connection through standard MSDE security. If no password is specified, the login will allow connection with the database server without a password.

- **sp_grantdbaccess (@loginname [,@name_in_db] [Output]):** Adds a new user to the MSDE security (in the form 'MyGroup\MyName'). The @loginname must be less than 129 characters. The @name_in_db parameter is simply for a more descriptive user name such that @loginname may be 'gsmith', while @name_in_db may be set to 'George Smith'.

- **sp_grantlogin (@loginName):** Creates a login account but must be passed as a user and group (in the form 'MyGroup\MyName'). This procedure will provide access, whereas the sp_denylogin routine will revoke the granted permission.

- **sp_denylogin (@loginName):** Revokes a login created with the sp_grantlogin procedure.

- **sp_revokelogin (@loginName):** Revokes a login created with the sp_grantlogin procedure or NT account integration. This procedure differs from sp_denylogin in that it has been created specifically to revoke a login created through NT security integration.

- **sp_revokedbaccess (@name_in_db):** Removes database access for a specified account name. The name for revocation may be an entire group/role or an individual user (i.e. 'MyGroup\MyName').

- **sp_changeobjectowner (@objname, @newowner):** Changes the owner of a database object to the user account specified by @newowner. Only users that own the specified object or members of the sysadmin role can execute this procedure.

- **sp_validatelogins()**: For integrated security, checks the users and groups of the Windows NT security model against the users and roles available on the MSDE server. All of the users and groups on the MSDE server that no longer have a valid account in the NT system are reported here.

ROLE AND GROUP COMMANDS

For roles or groups, other commands are used because of the number of different situations that grouping logins comprises. The SQL commands for security that apply to roles or groups include:

- **sp_addrole(@rolename [,@ownername])**: Adds a new role to the current database. This procedure cannot be used within a user-defined transaction. Once a role has been added to the system, the sp_helpuser procedure can be used to view which members have been added to a role.

- **sp_addrolemember(@rolename, @membername)**: Adds a new role member to an existing role in the current database.

- **sp_addapprole(@rolename [,@password])**: Creates a special role type for applications. An application role does not contain members; instead, the user is added to the group when executing the application associated with the role.

- **sp_approlepassword(@rolename [,@newpwd])**: Installs a new password for the specified application role. Only the owner of the application role or a member of the sysadmin role can execute this routine for an application role.

- **sp_addsrvrolemember(@loginname [,@rolename])**: Add the specified login name to the fixed server role. Fixed roles include sysadmin, securityadmin, serveradmin, setupadmin, processadmin, diskadmin, or dbcreator. Only a current member of the specified fixed server role can execute this routine to add another login name.

- **sp_droprole(@rolename, @membername)**: Drops a specified role in the selected database on the MSDE server.

- **sp_droprolemember(@rolename, @membername)**: Drops a current role member in the selected database on the MSDE server.

- **sp_dropapprole (@rolename)**: Drops a specified application role in the selected database on the MSDE server.

- **sp_dropsrvrolemember(@srvrolename)**: Displays the permissions that are currently set for a fixed server role. Roles include: sysadmin, securityadmin, serveradmin, setupadmin, processadmin, diskadmin, and dbcreator.

- **sp_setapprole(@rolename, @password [,@encrypt])**: Activates the security permissions for the specified application role. The @password parameter can be encrypted. If the @password is encrypted, the method of encryption is specified in the @encrypt variable, which can be set to either none or odbc. The encryption is handled by the ODBC interface activated by the Encrypt function when directly addressing the driver.

- **sp_helpsrvrolemember(@loginname, @rolename):** Removes a SQL Server login or group that was added through the NT integrated security. The available role names include: sysadmin, securityadmin, serveradmin, setupadmin, processadmin, diskadmin, and dbcreator.

- **sp_revokedbaccess(@name_in_db):** Removes the specified login account, the aliases, and all permissions for the account. This routine revokes accounts that are created with sp_grantdbaccess.

- **sp_addlinkedsrvlogin (@rmtsrvname [,@useself] [,@locallogin] [,@rmtuser] [,@rmtpassword]:** Creates or updates a remote server listing on the local machine. The information supplied to this routine is used to allow the local machine to log in to the remote machine for execution of a distributed operation. This routine is used particularly when Windows NT trusted security is not used in a system (perhaps one of the servers is running on the Windows 95/98 platform), so specific account login is required.

- **sp_droplinkedsrvlogin(@rmtsrvname, @locallogin):** Deletes a login mapping in place between a local server and a remote server used for a linked system. Only members of the sysadmin or securityadmin roles may execute this routine.

- **sp_helprole([@rolename]):** Information of the specified role is returned. If no role is passed as an argument, properties for all of the roles is displayed.

- **sp_helprolemember:** Returns information on the specified role member.

- **sp_helpsrvrole:** Returns the fixed server roles available on the current system.

- **sp_helpdbfixedrole([@rolename]):** Returns the fixed database roles available on the current system. If no rolename is passed to the routine, all of the fixed roles are included.

- **sp_helpntgroup:** Displays information on the groups that are mapped to MSDE roles.

- **sp_dbfixedrolepermission([@rolename]):** Returns the permissions of a system fixed database role. Roles include: db_owner, db_accessadmin, db_securityadmin, db_ddladmin, db_backupoperator, db_datareader, db_datawriter, db_denydatareader, and db_denydatawriter. If no @rolename parameter is passed to the routine, information on all of the fixed role permissions is returned.

- **sp_srvrolepermission(@srvrolename):** Displays information related to the specified server role. The available role names include: sysadmin, securityadmin, serveradmin, setupadmin, processadmin, diskadmin, and dbcreator.

Security for Linked MSDE Servers

Multiple database servers can be linked together for distributed processing of a query. To accomplish this operation distribution, the proper security must be in place to enable more than one server to securely communicate. This distribution can be used for queries, updates, modifications, and transactions.

The structured linked servers are chained together to allow distributed processing of intensive operations. Distributed operations are created by breaking down the request into several rowsets. Once the linked server set has been created, each server in the linked list is referred to using its four-part server name (such as mylinksrv.northwind.dbo.customers). Under this name scheme, a single SQL command can address resources on several different servers.

Distributed queries can be very effective for data located in several different geographic locations. Each server can query its own set of information and merely return the data the meets the specified criteria. All of the various rows are then combined and returned to the query requestor as a single recordset.

The linked system can be created through Transact-SQL code, the Enterprise Manager, or the SQL-DMO objects. The two procedures sp_addlinkedsrvlogin and sp_droplinkedsrvlogin are used to manage the remote login from one server to another. The sp_addlinkedsrvlogin procedure specifies an account to be used for the linking process. It does not actually add a new account but instead activates an existing account for use with the linked systems.

When you execute the procedure to add a linked server, the default will take the existing login and make the connection to the remote server with the current account. This process uses Windows NT authentication, so if either of the servers is running Windows 95/98, a login and password will need to be specified.

The sp_linkedservers procedure displays as a seven-column recordset servers that have been set up as linked servers. Statistics returned about each linked server include: the server name, the name of the OLE DB provider that is supplying access, the product name of the server, the data source property, the providerstring property, the location, and the OLE DB catalog that contains the server. The sp_serveroption procedure can be used to set options for a remote or linked server such as the capability to handle a distributed query or the character set settings of the linked list. The sp_addlinkedserver procedure is also used for adding an additional server into the list.

If the sp_dropserver is used to remove the server from the list of available servers for remote access, the server will automatically be removed from within any linked configurations where it exists. Therefore, be careful that the server you dropped is not expected for use by the other servers to which it is linked.

> **Note:** Because linked systems must use some type of middleware (such as ODBC or OLE DB) to provide communication among the servers, any limitations placed on the communications channels will limit the capabilities of the link. Therefore, if communication between two servers is set as read-only in the ODBC data source, the linked system will encounter errors when attempting to execute information.

Within each reference of a distributed query, you will need to use a four-part qualifying name so that the command will know which server contains the specified object. The syntax for setting the location for a four-part reference appears like this:

```
Servername.database.dbo.tablename
```

A query would look like this:

```
MSDE1.NorthwindSQL.dbo.Orders
```

> **Note:** Distributed queries can execute across multiple heterogeneous servers. Therefore, all of the linked servers do not need to be SQL Server or MSDE servers. Any source available through the ODBC or OLE DB provider middleware can be used in a linked server list.

Executing Some Security Code

To provide an example of how these features might be used, the steps that follow will create a new role and then a new user to add to that role. Then the role can be given read-only permission to the Northwind database. To perform this security setting creation process, follow these steps:

1. Execute MS Query. All of the security setting commands can be executed from this query utility included with Office 2000.
2. Select the Execute SQL statement from the File menu.
3. Select the dsnNorthwindSQL data source to address the NorthwindSQL database.
4. Enter the following code into the SQL statement text box:

   ```
   sp_addlogin 'LukeR', 'dice', 'Northwind'
   ```

5. Click Execute to submit it to the MSDE server. You should receive a message after a moment that the operation completed successfully. This code will add a new login account to the standard security of the MSDE server. At this point, however, the login does not have permission to use any database capabilities.

6. Enter the following code into the SQL statement text box:

```
sp_grantdbaccess 'LukeR'
```

7. Click Execute to submit it to the MSDE server. You should receive a message after a moment that the operation completed successfully. This statement brings the login account under standard security so that permissions can now be granted to it for database objects.

8. Setting up the actual object security occurs through the Grant keyword of the SQL language. To set permissions for the new account to allow everything (querying, updating, deleting, and so on) to the Northwind database, enter the following code in the SQL statement box:

```
Grant All TO LukeR
```

9. Click Execute to create the security settings.

Once execution of the code has completed, the new user will have been established in the NorthwindSQL database. If you access the Northwind database through Microsoft Query, you can now log in to the database using this user name and password.

Replication Security

In Chapter 15, security for replication was briefly discussed. Now that you more clearly understand the general security involved with the MSDE server, the roles used by the replication engine will need to be properly configured in order to allow secure access and execution of the replication process.

Secure server-to-server replication requires integrated security. With security integrated in the Windows NT operating system, a pull subscription can call the distributor through a Remote Procedure Call (RPC) process to activate the data download. The same is true when a distributor needs to push data to subscribers.

Although normal users can access publication or subscription information, typically only a user in the sysadmin role or with the proper permissions can initiate a replication process. Most replication processes after initially being set up by a sysadmin will automatically execute on the machine with a specified trusted account.

Replication capabilities include the capability to designate a *restricted publication*. This publication is restricted to a list of specified servers, which are the only data sources that may subscribe to it. Unrestricted publications is the default setting for new publications.

Package Security

In the DTS system, each package can be assigned a separate password. This prevents secure data from being bulk-transferred to a potentially insecure medium. The package security options follow many of the conventions available to the replication systems. Packages are only available for modification to the owner or the system admins.

For a DTS package, there are actually two different levels of security: the owner level and the user level. The owner level provides the ability to execute the package as well as modify it. The user level can only execute the package.

When an owner password is entered for the package, the next saving of that package will encrypt it in the MSDE system. All of its methods and properties will be encrypted to unauthorized users except the following five properties: Name, Description, ID, VersionID, and CreationDate. Accessing the package with either the user or owner password will allow access to the other properties and the package methods.

Active Directory and Windows 2000

The new security model included with Windows 2000 further integrates the security between MSDE, SQL Server, and Windows NT. Active Directory is the new global domain security system. In one replicated directory structure, all of the resources of a domain can be contained. Configuring Active Directory for use with the MSDE system provides an integration of the users and groups with the database users and roles definitions. It also allows machine name resolution to occur either through the standard NetBIOS machine names (\\myServer) or through the newer dynamically allocated domain names (myServer.myOrg.com).

The Active Directory system centralizes all management of the security settings for the network in a single interface with various security plug-ins. Complete MSDE configuration of logins is only available if the entire domain is using a Windows 2000 domain controller and MSDE is being executed on the various server systems.

When the Active Directory system is in place, security tasks may be delegated to specific users. For example, the salesmanager role can be given administrative access to the security settings for all of the databases or tables related directly to sales. That will allow that manager to create and modify users for permission access to the sales-related database objects.

General Tips for Security Planning

When installing security on a system, several general rules of thumb can help you most effectively complete the setup. These general guidelines include:

- **Give permissions to roles, not individuals:** Roles can be easily maintained and modified, whereas individual user permissions are far more difficult to track because of their sheer numbers. This guideline is one of the most important to consider when implementing a security setup. If individuals are granted permissions, changes to the status of the user or changes to the database itself may leave privileges that are unintended or fail to grant the proper new ones.

- **Favor vertical partitioning over providing columns with specific security settings:** Placing columns in separate related tables allows the entire table to be locked off for security permissions so that no mistakes are made if a new role or user is created to address that table.

- **Document the security intentions:** Keep documentation of the security assumptions that were made when the permissions system are defined. It is very easy to forget what understandings were made when the system is originally created. Further, the person that may be maintaining the system may not be the same as the initial creator of it.

- **Document deployment operating systems and machines:** Assumptions made around a specific system used by the solution (such as choosing DCOM for Windows 95) can limit the choices that are available for implementation on the server.

Security on MSDE allows definition of permissions down to the column level. Windows 2000 uses integrated NT security for SQL Server for global domain login. You may have noticed that MSDE security is dramatically different from traditional Access security. There is no method of integrating Access security that is stored in the Access MDW file with an MSDE data source.

Summary

Proper security is one of the cornerstones of any multiuser system because a security breach can mean a loss of privacy, data, and confidence in the system. By configuring MSDE for security in the areas of database, table, column, replication, and package access, you can control the groups, individuals, and machines that may address the data on the server. In this chapter, you covered:

- **Defining users and roles:** Roles should always be defined with privileges assigned to each group. Users are subsequently added to the groups and therefore inherit the permissions of the roles.

- **Security granularity:** The granularity of security available to any given system determines the levels of authorization that can be granted. MSDE allows security settings to be determined down to the column level on tables.

- **Replication security:** The role-based security of replication uses the SQL Server roles to define what users and machines can gain access to the replication system. Poorly configured replication can be a serious security breach because internal data is being copied to an external source.

- **Integrated NT security:** The Windows NT login security can be integrated with the users on the MSDE server. Through this integration process, the replication functions can be more easily accessed for publications from one server to another.

- **Active Directory:** A central part of Windows 2000, Active Directory allows global enterprise security management. For MSDE, that allows a user authorized to access the MSDE server to connect to it from any domain in the enterprise.

- **Access security versus MSDE security:** Access security is integrated directly with the Access system, whereas MSDE is much more integrated with the security features of the operating system. For this reason, MSDE runs more securely on a Windows NT deployment than under Windows 95/98.

Appendix

What's on the CD-ROM

IN THIS APPENDIX

- ◆ MSDE Developer's Guide
- ◆ Rapid SQL
- ◆ DB Artisan
- ◆ ER/Studio
- ◆ UltraEdit
- ◆ COM-Gen 2000

ON THE CD-ROM that is included with this book, all of the source code and sample projects are included. Also on the disc are several excellent applications for database construction. These applications are included in their trial versions, most of them time limited. To clarify what you will find on the CD-ROM and the locations of each item, following are descriptions of the various folders and tools that are included.

MSDE Developer's Guide

On the CD-ROM included with this book, you will find the MSDEDev folder that contains all of the source code, example projects, and data used in the text. The only exception to the database items used in this book is the Northwind database. This database is owned by Microsoft and is included with Microsoft Access, Visual Studio (and all of its applications such as VB, VC++, and so forth), and numerous other Microsoft packages. In the first few chapters, you will find instructions on locating this database and upsizing it onto the MSDE server for use.

The individual items are listed in Table A-1. You will find a listing of the types of items that are located in each folder. There are a total of seven item types: text files, backup databases, Visual Interdev project files (VIP), Access MDB files, ADP project files, ASP files, and SQL files. The files with the .SQL extension are simply text files that contain executable SQL code and queries. They may be loaded into a text editor such as Notepad or UltraEdit (included on the CD-ROM) for editing.

TABLE A-1 MSDEDEV FOLDER SOURCE CODE, EXAMPLES, AND DATA

Chapter	Folder Name	Contents
1	MSDEDEV\01_Concepts	SQL
2	MSDEDEV\02_AccVsMSDEDEV	MDB, SQL
3	MSDEDEV\03_AccWiz	ADP, MDB
4	MSDEDEV\04_Architecture	SQL
5	MSDEDEV\05_SQL	SQL
6	MSDEDEV\06_AdvSQL	SQL
7	MSDEDEV\07_StoredProc	SQL, MDB
8	MSDEDEV\08_ADP	ADP
9	MSDEDEV\09_ADO	MDB
10	MSDEDEV\10_VBA	MDB
11	MSDEDEV\11_EntManager	SQL
12	MSDEDEV\12_DBDesigner	VIP, SQL, ASP
13	MSDEDEV\13_Packages	SQL, SQL
14	MSDEDEV\14_Views	SQL
15	MSDEDEV\15_Replication	SQL
16	MSDEDEV\16_SQLDMO	SQL, MDB
17	MSDEDEV\17_UDT	SQL
18	MSDEDEV\18_Monitoring	SQL
19	MSDEDEV\19_SQLAgent	SQL
20	MSDEDEV\20_RDS	SQL, MDB, ASP
21	MSDEDEV\21_Tuning	SQL
22	MSDEDEV\22_Logs	SQL, LOG
23	MSDEDEV\23_MoveData	SQL
24	MSDEDEV\24_SysSPs	SQL
25	MSDEDEV\25_Security	SQL, MDB

Rapid SQL

For general database application development, Microsoft Access provides an excellent all-in-one tool for generating the tables, scripts, queries, and other aspects of the project in an MDB file. Although the ADP project type of Access supplies these features to an MSDE project, the client/server nature of an MSDE application makes the traditional Access features only a partial solution. An MSDE database application may tap data sources on many different servers, have different front-end access options (including Access, ASP, and Java), and may need substantial integration between server-side and client-side code.

The application Rapid SQL from Embarcadero Technologies (www.embarcadero.com) provides many of the features necessary for effective MSDE development. It can be used to create SQL scripts (see Figure A-1), version server-side code, and edit HTML, ASP, and Java code. It can be used to address a SQL data source directly so that you can edit code on the server itself.

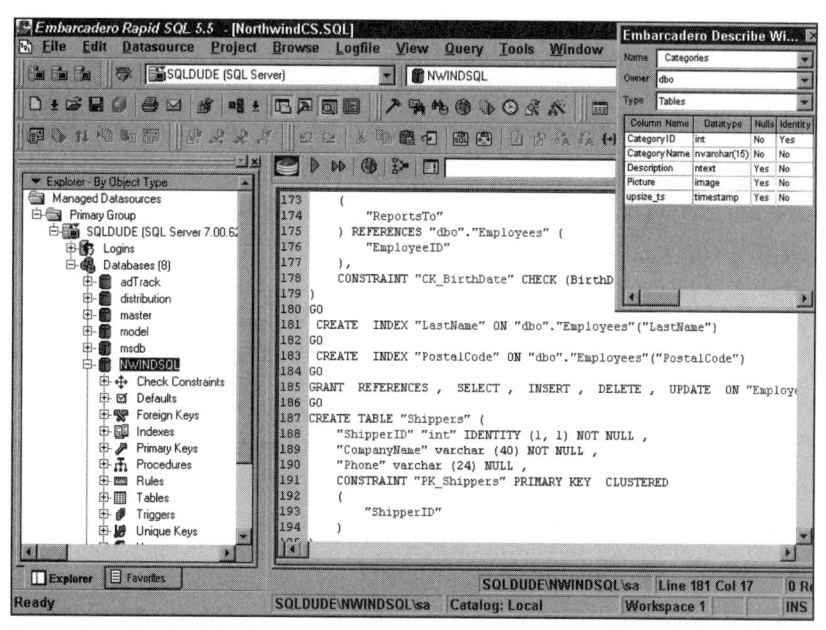

Figure A-1: The Rapid SQL application can edit SQL source code from files or from the data source itself.

Features of Rapid SQL include the following:

- Multiple environments for simultaneous connections to data sources that are supported so editing across many database servers is possible
- Parallel multithread queries for simultaneous query execution testing

- Color syntax highlighting and syntax help for SQL commands
- Integration with Java compiler for automated executable and applet generation
- Organization of items into logical projects for easy development and maintenance
- Version control for scripts and source files that can be integrated with the version control supported by Visual SourceSafe (including in Visual Studio)

Generating SQL server-side code and even client queries can be a lengthy process. Using a tool, such as Rapid SQL, simplifies single designer initial development, but its real strength lies with team/group development and later maintenance.

DB Artisan

The DB Artisan product from Embarcadero Technologies (www.embarcadero.com) is an excellent database administration tool. Although you are already familiar with the SQL Enterprise Manager, DB Artisan provides even more robust features. In addition to managing multiple SQL Server and MSDE servers from a single console, databases in Oracle, Sybase, and DB2 can be managed as well.

Features of DB Artisan include the following:

- Creation, duplication, and modification of database objects including databases, tables, columns, relationships, index, and so forth
- Scheduled execution and script creation
- User, role, group, and password administration for login and privileges
- Database and index size and integrity management
- Backup and restore capabilities
- Process monitoring and optimization

All of these features are available for any of the supported databases. DB Artisan also enables you to transport database schema information from one database server platform to another (such as Oracle to MSDE server).

ER/Studio

In Microsoft Access and the Database Designer, diagramming tools are included to build database tables and set proper relationships between them. These tools provide only the basic features for database construction. For professional level design, investing in a tool such as Platinum ERWin from Computer Associates (www.cai.com) or ER/Studio from Embarcadero Technologies (www.embarcadero.com) can save large amounts of time and money by streamlining how you design and maintain database objects. These tools also provide a complete prototyping environment for thorough planning.

ER/Studio (a trial edition is included on the CD-ROM) is a visual data modeling application that enables you to create all of the databases, tables, and relationships of a data solution. A database structure created in ER/Studio does not have to be placed only on MSDE or other SQL Server-based database server because it can export the data model to popular databases such as Oracle, DB2, and other complete database servers.

One of the key strengths to using such a modeling tool is the ability to create logical models of the data structure. Although a physical model actually resides on the database server, a logical model can be created as a prototype or a what-if structure of an existing database. This feature can be extremely useful for presenting a normalized design for a denormalized database or for modeling how a database might be normalized in the future.

Round-trip design, featured in ER/Studio (also in Visual Studio's Visual Modeler), enables a designer to create a logical model, render it to a physical model, alter the physical model, and reload the altered design for further modification. In the case of round-trip design for databases, you could use ER/Studio to create a logical model of a database. Once satisfied with the implementation, you could export it to the MSDE server. In the life of the database, you may have to make some alterations to the schema such as removing a column with the Enterprise Manager. The new design could be re-imported into the ER/Studio application for further work.

ER/Studio can generate reports detailing the design of the database. The application includes the ability to document the entire design process with notes, definitions, and automatically generated verbal descriptions of relations between tables. It also has the ability to create macros in a VBA-like language for the automation of repetitive tasks.

UltraEdit

An excellent developer's editor is a program called UltraEdit. UltraEdit is a text and binary file editor that can be used for your Web database applications. It provides several useful features including colored text for keywords in HTML, ASP, C++, and more (see Figure A-2). Because UltraEdit also provides built-in FTP retrieval and storage for documents, it can be used to maintain a Web site through FTP access.

Perhaps the most useful feature for Web developers is the ability to create a project file that contains all of the individual files of an application. Opening the project file will load all of the ASP, HTML, and text files that are included in the project.

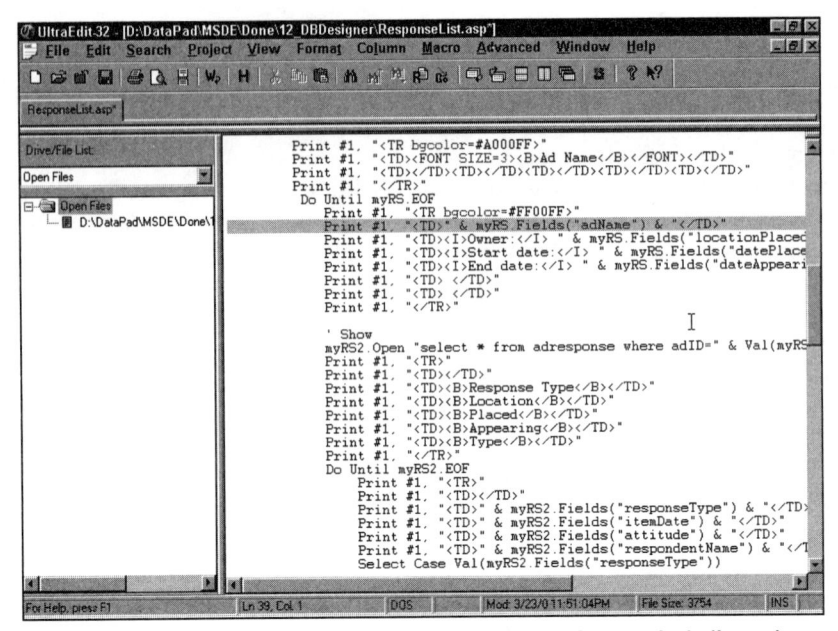

Figure A-2: The UltraEdit text editor provides a wealth of features including color highlighting and project grouping.

The UltraEdit application has the following features:

- Color highlighting of HTML, Basic, and VB Scripting keywords and tags
- Unicode support
- Automatic file backup
- Convenient multidocument navigation with document tabs
- Hexadecimal mode to allow editing of binary files
- Recording and playback of macros
- Formatting, such as linefeed modifications, word wraps, spaces to tabs, text file type conversions (Unix to MS-DOS, MS-DOS to Macintosh), and so forth
- Loading and saving capabilities to FTP sites
- Multifile search and replace
- Column editing mode

Although this editor does not have any type of direct database editing features like Rapid SQL, its excellent quality, low price, and HTML support make it perfect for developing ASP or HTML Web solutions.

COM-Gen 2000

If you are developing your MSDE solution in Visual Basic, the COM-Gen 2000 utility is one of the most useful and inexpensive tools you can buy. This utility will take a data source and create classes for access to existing database schema structures. Each class has the proper routines for adding new records, modifying column values, deleting records, and record navigation.

By generating these classes, you can isolate the database structure from your project access to it. In fact, the classes generated by COM-Gen can be independently compiled into an ActiveX component to create multiple tier projects.

Index

SYMBOLS

@@Error function, 129
@@NestLevel system function, 130
@@Rowcount variable, 134
@@Total_Error function, 129
@@TranCount system function, 133

A

Access
    linking tables, 59-61
    replicating data, 306-307
Access Data Project (ADP)
    compatibility with early SQL server versions, 142
    connection properties, 149-150
    creating files, 56-58
    creating projects, 143
    data communication with MSDE data source, 142
    data storage, 141-142
    database diagrams, 147-149
    generally, 141
    MDB files *vs.*, 141-142
    New dialog box, 143-144
    ODBC and, 142
    stored procedures, 147
    tables, 145-146
    Upsizing Wizard, 144
    views, 146
Access Jet engine. *See* Jet engine (Access)
accessing transaction logs using SQL-DMO, 463-464

ACID (Atomicity Consistency Isolation Durability) transaction properties, 458
action queries (ADO), 160
Active Server Pages (ASP), 153, 221-231
ActiveX controls (replicating data), 324
ActiveX Data Objects (ADO). *See also* Advanced ADO
    access to RDS, 423-427
    action queries, 160
    asynchronous background execution, 166-167
    asynchronous queries, 166-167
    Command object, 154, 167-171
    connection events, 160
    Connection object, 154, 157-161, 166-167
    Error object, 160-161
    executing, 155-157
    Field object, 164-165
    generally, 151-155
    hierarchical Recordsets, 165
    interface, 153
    MSDE and, 153
    object model, 154-155
    OLE DB interface layer, 152
    Parameter object, 170-171
    Property object, 171
    Recordset classes, 426-427
    Recordset object, 154, 161-167
    starting, 155-157

ActiveX scripting and SQL Server Agents, 410
activity logs (MSDE), 453-457
adapting data between formats. *See* upsizing data
adding comments to SQL code, 112-113
adding to identity (replicating data), 305
ADO. *See* ActiveX Data Objects (ADO)
ADO Recordset (ADOR), 416
ADP. *See* Access Data Project (ADP)
Advanced ADO
 asynchronous queries, 174-175
 hierarchical aggregates, 179
 hierarchical queries, 175-177
 hierarchical Recordsets, 177-179
agent error log (SQL Server Agents), 408-411
agent login security, 323
agent logs (MSDE), 456-457
agents (replicating data), 302-303, 320
aggregate functions (advanced SQL), 99-105
alerts event system (SQL Server Agents), 410-411
All operator, 109
Alter Procedure command, 118, 131
altering
 stored procedures, 131
 views, 273
Any modifier, 109
Application Performance Explorer (APE), 434

articles (replicating data), 319
As keyword, 85
ASP (Active Server Pages), 153, 221-231
asynchronous background execution (ADO), 166-167
asynchronous queries (ADO), 166-167
asynchronous queries (Advanced ADO), 174-175
Atomicity Consistency Isolation Durability (ACID) transaction properties, 458
autocustomizing views, 278
automated tasks on MSDE servers. *See* SQL Server Agent
Avg aggregate function (SQL), 100

B

backup
 folder (Enterprise Manager), 197
 MSDE *vs.* Access, 30-31
BatchImported event (SQL-DMO), 357
BCP utility for upsizing data, 474-478
Begin Distributed Transaction, 132
Begin Transaction, 132
Between keyword, 88
bi-directional synchronization (replicating data), 307
binary column type, 65, 67
bit column type, 66
bit field type, 67
Boolean operators, 88-89
browser integration and security, 516
b-tree format of index, 439
Building Web Database Applications with Visual Studio 6, 415

Index 543

Bulk Insert command, 478–480
business object (ADO for RDS), 425

C

caching queries, 435
CAL (client access license), 33
Cartesian product, 84
cascading deletes, 46
cascading updates, 46
Cast function (Transact-SQL), 181
catalog (full-text indexing), 205
changing
    stored procedures, 131
    views, 273
Char column type, 65
check constraints when creating tables, 365
checkpoint when truncating MSDE transaction logs, 459–460
class references and SQL-DMO, 329
CLASSID for RDS data control, 424
cleaning data, 69–71
client access license (CAL), 33
client activation (ADO for RDS), 426
client-based databases, 26–28
closing Service Manager utility, 12
clustered indexes (MSDE), 437–439
coding (Transact-SQL), MSDE *vs.* Access, 32–33
coding (VBA), MSDE *vs.* Access, 32–33
Column Grid pane (View Designer), 270–271
Column Mappings and Transformations dialog box, 249

columns
    adding to existing tables (SQL-DMO), 355–356
    data types, 65–67
    defining, 64
    inserting into indexes, 436
Command object (ADO), 154, 167–171
CommandBroken As Boolean event (SQL-DMO), 357
command-line
    errors (MSDE), 36–37
    installer (MSDE), 35–37
    switches (MSDE), 35–36
commands. *See individual names*
CommandSent event (SQL-DMO), 357
commenting SQL code, 112–113
Commit Transaction, 132
Commit [Work], 132
compacting databases, 61
comparison operators, 87–88, 109
comparison subqueries, 109
compatibility with Windows CE (RDS), 427
Complete event (SQL-DMO), 357
complex indexes (MSDE), 436
composite index, 5
compound indexes (MSDE), 436
compression and MSDE transaction logs, 461
Compute By clause, 103–104
Compute clause, 103–104
conflict function (replicating data), 310
conflict viewer (replicating data), 309
connection
    ADP file properties, 149–150
        Continued

544 Index

connection *(continued)*
   events (ADO), 160
   object (ADO), 154, 157–161, 166–167
   objects (DTS), 240–241, 242
   point events (DTS package), 485
   pooling (RDS), 420
ConnectionBroken event (SQL-DMO), 357
consistency (transaction property), 458
constraint conflicts (replicating data), 308
control-of-flow structure in stored procedures, 126
`Convert` function (Transact-SQL), 181–182
converting image data types, 183
correlated subqueries, 109–110
`Count` function, 99–100
`Create Default` command, 364–365
Create New Data Source dialog box, 16, 81, 211
`Create Proc` command, 120
`Create Procedure` command, 117, 133, 167–169
Create Publication Wizard (replicating data), 311
Create Relationship dialog box (Database Designer), 219
`Create Rule` command, 366
`create table` command (MSDE), 65–67
`Create View` command, 265–266
creating
   ADP files, 56–58

   ADP projects, 143–144
   indexes using SQL-DMO, 356–357
   jobs on SQL Server Agents, 399–400
   multiple copies of databases *(See* replicating data)
   multiple procedures with same name, 125
   publications (replicating data), 312–316
   relationships between tables using SQL-DMO (sample application), 339–340
   subscriptions (replicating data), 316–317
   tables using SQL-DMO, 336–340, 354–355
   UDTs, 362–363
   userReference Table (views), 275–276
   views, 264–266, 268–271
creating databases
   using Access, 56–58
   basic design concepts, 63–72
   columns, 64–68
   displaying data, 18–20
   entering data, 17–18
   null values, 14–15
   querying data, 18–20
   sample exercise, 13–14
   using SQL create database command, 13–16
   SQL create table command, 14, 17
   tables, 17
current activity folder (Enterprise Manager), 197

Current Activity window (Enterprise Manager), 380–381
cursor column type, 66
cursor output, 125
custom conflict resolutions (replicating data), 308–310
custom task (DTS), 242–243
customizing views, 275–278

D

data
 cleaning, 69–71
 communication between ADP files and MSDE data source, 142
 consistency conflict resolver (replicating data), 309–310
 constant values and conversion returns (from VBA to Transact-SQL), 182
 shaping, 176–177
 storage for ADP files, 141–142
Data Access Components (DAC), 426
Data Access Objects (DAO), 151–152
Data Link Properties window, 149
data pump interfaces (DTS), 257
Data Transformation Services (DTS)
 custom tasks (Enterprise Manager), 196
 Designer, 257–259
 dtsrun utility, 259–260
 executing, 243–252, 252–254
 folder (Enterprise Manager), 194–196
 generally, 237–240, 480–485
 programming, 254–257
 scheduling execution, 252–254
 starting, 243–252
 wizards, 245
data types
 column, 65–67
 system, 65–67
 user-defined, 67
Data View window, 213–214
database
 activity monitoring routines, 377–378
 creators, 69
 maintenance plans (Enterprise Manager), 198
 modeling, 232–234
 owners, 69, 520
 performance (See performance, database)
 schema, 9
Database Designer
 altering databases, 213–215
 ASP reporting pages, 221–231
 changing databases, 213–215
 creating database diagrams, 218–221
 creating databases, generally, 208–209
 creating Visual InterDev projects, 209–213
 entering data in tables, 215–218
 filling tables with data, 215–218
 modifying databases, 213–215
 new response submissions, 228–231
 visual modeling, 232–234
database diagrams
 ADP files, 147–149
 generally, 9, 92
 Visual InterDev projects, 218–221

Database object (SQL-DMO), 333-334
database server
    activities, monitoring (*See*
        monitoring database server
        activity)
    generally, 26-28
    query, 28
databases folder (Enterprise Manager),
    191-194
dates, scheduling (DTS), 252-254
datetime column type, 66
decimal column type, 66
Declared Referential Integrity (DRI)
    relationships, 45-46
de-encrypting views, 274
default definitions, 45
default login and security, 515
default values, 45, 68-69, 123
deferred name resolution, 130-131
defining
    columns, 64
    variables (stored procedures),
        121-122
Delete command, 93-94
delete conflicts (replicating data),
    308
deleting
    records from databases, 61
    stored procedures, 130, 131
denormalization, 76, 432
deny command (MSDE security),
    522
deployment server, 13
Diagram pane (View Designer), 270
dialog boxes. *See individual names*
direct synchronization (replicating
    data), 307

disk access monitoring (Windows NT),
    384-385
distributed queries
    generally, 527
    stored procedures, 502
Distributed Queries Procedures (DQP),
    185
Distributed Transaction Controller
    (DTC), 132
distributed transaction coordinator
    (DTC) (Enterprise Manager),
    203-204
Distribution Agent (SQL Server), 396
distribution (replicating data)
    agent, 303
    procedures, 319-320
Distribution Wizard (replicating data),
    311
distributor (replicating data), 285-288,
    291, 394
downloading MSDE engine, 10
DQP (Distributed Queries Procedures),
    185
DRI (Declared Referential Integrity)
    relationships, 45-46
Drop command, 125
Drop Procedure command, 131
Drop Rule command, 367
DTC (Distributed Transaction
    Controller), 132
DTC (distributed transaction
    coordinator) (Enterprise
    Manager), 203-204
DTS. *See* Data Transformation
    Services (DTS)
dtsrun utility (DTS), 259-260
duplicate user names, 513

durability (transaction property), 458
dynamic filters (replicating data), 306

E

e-mail
  SQL Mail connection, 494
  SQL Server, 185–186
embedded VBA code, 180
encryption
  generally, 124
  views, 273–274
ENCRYPTION keyword, 136
Enterprise Manager
  accessing, 189–190
  Current Activity window, 380–381
  databases folder, 191–194
  DTS Designer and, 257
  DTS folder, 194–196
  generally, 190
  management folder, 196–201
  monitoring database server activity, 380–381
  rebuilding master databases, 432
  replicating data (*See* replicating data)
  Replication Monitor and, 311–312
  replication wizards and, 310–311
  security folder, 201–203
  server registration, 190–191
  SQL Mail connection, 494
  SQL Server Agents and, 392
  SQL-DMO and, 328
  support services folder, 203–204
  tempdb space, 449–450
  tools menu, 204–205

enumerated constants (RDS), 422
error and status events (DTS package), 484–485
error codes (MSDE command-line installer), 36–37
error logs (MSDE), 454–456
Error object (ADO), 160–161
errors
  Invalid use of NULL, 51
  key entry, 70
events
  DTS package, 484–485
  SQL-DMO, 357–358
exclusive locks, 72
Execute keyword, 120–121
Execute SQL dialog box, 15, 18
executing
  ADO, 155–157
  DTS, 243–252
  MS Query, 13
  MSDE engine, 11
  RDS, 420
  Service Manager utility, 11
  SQL Server Agent, 392–394
execution plan and optimizing query performance, 444–446
Exists keyword, 109–110
Export Data Wizard (Enterprise Manager), 195
extended stored procedures, 137

F

Field object (ADO), 164–165
fields
  foreign key, 7
  generally, 3–4
  primary key, 6

file-based
    database engines, 26-28
    query, 28
filtering (replicating data), 305-306
first normal form, 74
FlexGrid control, 176
Float column type, 65
foreign key fields, 7, 337, 338
form (HTML), 228-231
From clause, 93
From keyword, 83
full-text indexing (Enterprise
    Manager), 204-205

G

Generate SQL Scripts option
    (Enterprise Manager), 193-194
global temporary procedures, 135
Global Unique Identifier (GUID), 304
Go command, 138
Goto command, 128
grant command (MSDE security),
    521
Group By commands, 101-103
group commands (MSDE security),
    500-502, 524-526
Grouping (SQL aggregate function),
    100
groups (database) *vs.* roles, 518-520
guest accounts, 520
GUID (Global Unique Identifier), 304

H

hash joins, 112, 447
Having clause, 103
heterogeneous data source replication,
    321

hierarchical
    aggregates (Advanced ADO), 179
    queries (Advanced ADO), 175-177
    Recordsets (ADO), 165
    Recordsets (Advanced ADO),
        177-179
Hierarchical FlexGrid control, 176
high-access data, 76
horizontal filtering (replicating data),
    305
horizontal partitioning, 301-302

I

ICustomerResolver interface
    (replicating data), 310
identify setting on columns, 68
idle time processor (SQL Server
    Agents), 397-398
if...then...else structure, 126-127
illegal
    default values, 68-69
    null values, 68-69
image
    column type, 66, 67
    data type conversion, 183
Immediate execution window
    (Access), 329-332
Import and Export Data Wizard,
    468-474
Import Data Wizard (Enterprise
    Manager), 192-193, 195
In keyword, 104-105, 108, 278
incorporating existing data into
    projects. *See* upsizing data
Index Tuning Wizard, 439-443
indexes
    b-tree format, 439

clustered (MSDE), 437–439
columns, inserting into, 436
complex (MSDE), 436
compound (MSDE), 436
creating, using SQL-DMO, 356–357
full-text (Enterprise Manager), 204–205
generally, 4–5
Index Tuning Wizard, 439–443
nonclustered, 439
optimizing, 436–443
indirect synchronization (replicating data), 307
inner joins, 7
inner queries, 107–111
insert conflicts (replicating data), 308
`Insert Into` command, 92
installing MS Query, 12
installing MSDE
    using command line, 35–37
    engine, 9–12
    help files, 37
    standard databases, 37–38
installing SQL Server
    over MSDE, 38
    sample databases, 38
int column type, 65
Internet Explorer Web browser and databases. *See* Remote Data Services (RDS)
Internet Information Server (IIS) and Database Designer, 208
Internet synchronization (replicating data), 307
`is` keyword, 93
isolation (transaction property), 458

iteration control in stored procedures, 127–128
iterative joins (MSDE), 447

J

JavaScript and RDS, 421
JavaScript Bible, 421
Jet engine (Access)
    moving databases to MSDE, 42–43
    MSDE *vs.,* 23–35
Jet Replication Objects (JRO), 287
join filters (replicating data), 305
joining two or more related tables, 7–9
joins
    advanced, 111–112
    generally, 7–9
    hash, 447
    iterative, 447
    merge, 447
    more than four, 76
    nested loop, 447
JRO (Jet Replication Objects), 287

K

key entry errors, 70
key fields, 6–7

L

labels, 128
left joins, 8–9
Like operators, 89–91
Link Tables dialog box, 60
linked
    MSDE servers and security, 526–527
    servers folder (Enterprise Manager), 203

Index

linking tables in Access, 59–61
location partitioning, 302
locking modes, 72
log files for monitoring database server activity, 386–387
log reader agent (replicating data), 303
Log Reader Agent (SQL Server), 396–397
logical sequence number (LSN) (MSDE transaction logs), 457
login security modes, 510
logread utility and SQL Server Agents, 396
logs (MSDE). *See individual types*
long-running query logs (MSDE), 464–465
lost information when upsizing data, 486–487
low-access data, 76
LSN (logical sequence number) (MSDE transaction logs), 457

M

Make Master Server Wizard, 412
management folder (Enterprise Manager), 196–201
Management Plan option (Enterprise Manager), 193
manipulating objects on database servers directly. *See* SQL Distributed Management Objects (SQL-DMO)
master databases, 37
mathematical operators, 85–87
Max aggregate function (SQL), 100
MDB files *vs.* ADP files, 141–142

merge
  joins, 112, 447
  replication, 289, 290, 302
Merge Agent (SQL Server), 397
Microsoft Transaction Server (MTS), 195
migrating data
  from Access to MSDE (*See* Upsizing Wizard)
  from MSDE to SQL Server, 38–39
Min aggregate function (SQL), 100
minimizing data duplication (normalization), 72–76
model databases, 37, 232–234
modifying
  stored procedures, 131
  views, 273
modulo, 86
money column type, 66
monitoring database server activity
  using Enterprise Manager, 380–381
  generally, 373
  using log files, 386–387
  Replication Monitor, 386
  using SQL Server Profiler, 387–390
  using SQL-DMO, 377–379
  using Transact-SQL, 373–377
  using VBA, 377–379
  using Windows NT, 381–386
monitoring disk access (Windows NT), 384–385
MS Query
  executing, 13
  installing, 12
msdb databases, 38

Index

multiple-user situations
  access, 71–72
  locking modes, 72
multiquery select statements, 107–111

N

native-mode access, 57
nchar column type, 66
nested
  loop joins, 112, 447
  queries, 107–111, 447
  stored procedures, 130
`net send` command (Windows NT), 399
network access, MSDE *vs.* Access, 28
network protocol options and security, 516–517
New dialog box, 143–144
NextMedia event (SQL-DMO), 357
`NextRecordset` method (ADO), 161
nonclustered indexes, 439
noncorrelated subquery, 110
normalization, 72–76
Northwind sample database, upsizing to MSDE, 41–44, 49–56
ntext column type, 67
null values, 14–15, 68–69, 86, 364
numeric column type, 66
nvarchar column type, 67

O

Object Browser (Access), 241, 331, 337, 504
object model for ActiveX Data Objects (ADO), 154–155
object selection form (SQL-DMO), 340–343
object transfer (DTS), 257
ODBC middleware, 58–59
OLE DB interface layer (ADO), 152
`Open` command, 121
opening ADO connections, 158–159
operators (SQL Server Agents), 398–399
order by clause, 91
`Order By` command, 107
outer joins, 8–9
outer queries, 107–111
`Output` keyword, 124
`Output` parameter, 123–124

P

package objects (DTS), 238, 240–243
package security, 529
Parameter object (ADO), 170–171
partitioning, 301–302
passwords (Enterprise Manager), 202
PercentComplete event (SQL-DMO), 357
PercentCompleteAtStep event (SQL-DMO), 358
performance, database
  actual *vs.* perceived, 430–431
  ADO *vs.* ODBC, 433
  APE, 434
  clients, optimizing, 433–434
  denormalization, 432
  execution plan, 444–446
  generally, 429–430
  index, optimizing, 436–443
  Index Tuning Wizard, 439–443
  ODBC *vs.* ADO, 433
  optimizing clients, 433–434

Continued

performance, database *(continued)*
  optimizing indexes, 436–443
  optimizing servers, 447–448
  optimizing stored procedures, 435
  organization, 431–432
  query caching, 435
  querying databases, 443–447
  rebuilding master databases, 432
  servers, optimizing, 447–448
  show plan feature, 435
  SQL Batch Statements, 433–434
  stored procedures, optimizing, 435
  trace flags, 448
Performance Monitor (Windows NT), 381–386
Personal Web Server (PWS) and Database Designer, 208
population (full-text indexing), 205
precedence in MSDE for mathematical operators, 86
preexisting data and rules, 366
prevent deletes option conflict resolver (replicating data), 309
primary key fields, 6, 338, 339
primary queries, 107–111
Print command, 134
priority-based conflict resolutions (replicating data), 308
private temporary procedures, 135
processor queue length monitoring (Windows NT), 385–386
production server, 13
programming ADO Connection objects, 159–160
Project Explorer window, 211

Properties dialog box (View Designer), 272
Property object (ADO), 171
Publication Wizard, 294–215
publications (replicating data)
  creating, 312–316
  generally, 291
  procedures, 318–319
publisher (replicating data), 285–288, 291, 293–298
publishing rights (replicating data), 322
Publishing Wizard (replicating data), 311
Pull Subscription Wizard (replicating data), 311
pull synchronization (replicating data), 307
Push Subscription Wizard (replicating data), 311
push synchronization (replicating data), 306

Q

query
  caching, 435
  grid, 119
  nested, 447
Query Wizard, 19–20, 81–83
querying databases
  after upsizing, 55–56
  asynchronous queries, 166–167
  database server, 28
  denormalization and, 76
  distributed procedures, 185
  file-based, 28
  mathematical operators, 85–87

using MS Query, 80–83
optimizing performance, 443–447
order by clause, 91
using Recordset objects (ADO), 161–167
`Select` clause, 83–85
`Where` clause, 87–91
QueryTimeout event (SQL-DMO), 358
quickstarting. *See* starting

R

`RaiseError` function, 129
Rational Rose modeling tool, 233
RDC (remote data control), 416
real column type, 66
rebuildm utility, 432
receiving variables (stored procedures), 122–123
records, 3–4
Recordset object (ADO), 154, 161–167
recovery interval (truncating MSDE transaction logs), 459
recursive function, 130
References dialog box (Access), 331, 341, 343
References dialog box (RDS), 426
registered servers and SQLServer object, 332
relational
   database system, 5–6
   tables, 6–9
Relationships window (Access). *See* Declared Referential Integrity (DRI) relationships
remote data control (RDC), 416
Remote Data Services (RDS)
   ADO access, 423–427

ADO Recordset classes, 426–427
executing, 420
generally, 415–420
programming, 420
scripting in browser, 421–423
secure access, 428
system requirements, 420
Remote Procedure Call (RPC), 528
RemoteLoginFailed (SQL-DMO event), 358
renaming stored procedures, 131
repeating subquery, 110
replicating data
   Access Replication Manager, 323–324
   ACID transaction properties, 459
   across other data sources, 321–322
   ActiveX controls, 324
   agents, 302–303
   choosing replication type, 288–291
   compatibility between Access and MSDE or SQL Server, 285
   configuring MSDE system, 286–288, 293
   configuring publisher, 293–298
   configuring subscriber, 299–300
   conflicts, 307–310
   creating accounts for SQL Server Agent, 292–293
   Enterprise Manager, 204, 292
   generally, 283–285, 486
   managing, through Access, 306–307
   merge replication, 289, 290
   monitoring database server activity, 386

Continued

replicating data *(continued)*
   MSDE system, 285-288, 293
   partitioning, 301-302
   planning, 303-306
   publisher, configuring, 293-298
   restricted publication, 528-529
   security, 322-323, 528-529
   selecting replication type, 288-291
   snapshot replication, 289-290
   SQL Distribution control, 324
   SQL Merge control, 324
   SQL Server Agents, 288, 292-293, 394
   SQL-DMO and, 334-335
   stored procedures, 490-494
   structures, 291
   subscriber, configuring, 299-300
   system stored procedures, 312-321
   transactional replication, 289, 290
   wizards, 294-298, 310-311
Replication Conflict Resolver Wizard (replicating data), 311
Replication Manager (Access), 323-324
Replication Monitor, 311-312
Replication objects (SQL-DMO), 334-335
reports by Upsizing Wizard, 54-55
required field flags, 45
retrieving enumerated values from database objects, 377-378
`Return` command, 123
`Return` keyword (stored procedures), 123-124
returning arguments (stored procedures), 123-124

revoke command (MSDE security), 522-523
reworking data between formats. *See* upsizing data
right joins, 8-9
role commands (MSDE security), 500-502, 524-526
roles (database)
   groups *vs.*, 518-520
   security and, 517-520
Rollback Transaction, 132
Rollback [Work], 132
`RowCount(num)` command, 134
RowsCopied (SQL-DMO event), 358
RPC (Remote Procedure Call), 528

S

Save Transaction, 132
scalability, MSDE *vs.* Access, 31-32
scheduling
   DTS execution, 252-254
   SQL Server Agents, 413, 495-499
scripts in DTS processes, 254-255
ScriptTransferPercentComplete event (SQL-DMO), 358
second normal form, 75
security
   active directory, 529
   authentication mode, 510-511
   commands, 520-526
   database owners, 520
   database roles, 517-520
   default login, 515
   executing code, 527-528
   folder (Enterprise Manager), 201-203
   guest accounts, 520

Index 555

linked MSDE servers, 526–527
managing using SQL code, 520–526
mixed model, 515
MSDE, 510–517
network protocol options, 516–517
OS and browser integration, 516
packages, 529
planning, 507–509, 530
RDS, 428
replicating data, 322–323, 528–529
restricted publication, 528–529
SQL Server, 511–513
stored procedures, 499–502
Windows 95/98, 516
Windows 2000, 529
Windows NT trusted, 513–514
security level (Alerts Events System), 411
Select Case command, 127
Select clause, 106–107
Select Into command, 111
Select keyword, 83
Select statements, multiquery, 107–111
server activation (ADO for RDS), 425
server roles (Enterprise Manager), 203
Server.CreateObject() method, 153
Servergroup object (SQL-DMO), 334
ServerMessage event (SQL-DMO), 358
Service Accounts screen, 10–11
Service Manager utility, 12
Set ArithAbort command, 129
Set ArithIgnore command, 129
Set ShowPlan On command, 134
Set StatisticsTime On command, 134
setting identify on columns, 68
Shape command, 177–179
shape language, 176–177
shared locks, 72
show plan feature (MSDE) and optimizing database performance, 435
shrinking databases, 61
smalldatetime column type, 66
smallint column type, 65
smallmoney column type, 66
Snapshot Agent (SQL Server), 394–396
snapshot replication, 289–290, 302
sorted order, 91
sorting information. *See* indexes
sp_addextendedproc routing, 137
sp_add_jobserver procedure, 401
sp_bindefault command, 365
sp_configure routine (MSDE), 489–490
sp_executesql function, 136
sp_helptext function, 134, 136
sp_monitor procedure (Transact-SQL), 374–376
sp_procoption procedure, 135
sp_recompile function, 134
sp_rename function, 131
sp_unbindrule command, 367
sp_who procedure (Transact-SQL), 374–376
SQL Batch Statements and database performance, 433–434

556 Index

SQL code and managing security, 520–526
SQL Distributed Management Objects (SQL-DMO)
    accessing transaction logs, 463–464
    changing tables, 355–356
    class references, 329, 332
    coding ADO routines (sample application), 343–344
    coding routines (sample application), 343–344
    creating databases, 351–354
    creating databases (sample application), 335–336
    creating indexes, 356–357
    creating tables, 354–355
    creating tables (sample application), 336–340
    events, 357–358
    generally, 327–329, 332, 359
    modifying tables, 355–356
    monitoring database server activity, 377–379
    object selection form (sample application), 340–343
    object types, 332–335
    retrieving schema information (sample application), 343–344
    stored procedures, 503–504
    testing, 329–332
    transaction log access, 463–464
SQL Distribution control (replicating data), 324
SQL Mail connection (MSDE), 494
SQL mail (Enterprise Manager), 204
SQL Merge control (replicating data), 324
SQL pane (View Designer), 271
SQL `Select` statement, 80. *See also* querying databases
SQL Server
    agent (Enterprise Manager), 196–197
    compatibility, MSDE *vs.* Access, 31–32
    e-mail, 185–186
    evolution of development, 24
    logs folder (Enterprise Manager), 198
    security, 511–513
    version 7 installation and MSDE, 9–10
SQL Server Agent
    agent error log, 408–411
    Alerts Event System, 410–411
    categorizing objects, 411–412
    configuring, 397–398
    creating jobs, 399–400
    defining operators, 398–399
    Deleting Agent objects (Transact-SQL), 403–404
    Distribution, 396
    Document Agent objects (Transact-SQL), 402–403
    Enterprise Manager and, 407–408
    executing, 392–394
    generally, 391–392
    grouping objects in categories, 411–412
    idle time processor, 397–398
    implementing Transact-SQL, 400–406

Index

Log Reader, 396–397
Merge, 397
miscellaneous procedures (Transact-SQL), 404–406
objects, 401–402, 406–407, 411–412
procedures, 400–406
programming, 399–407
replicating data, 288, 292–293, 394
scheduling, 413
Snapshot, 394–396
starting, 392–394
stored procedures, 495–499
Windows 95/98 limitations, 398
SQL Server Login dialog box, 19
SQL Server Profiler, 205, 387–390
SQL Server Query Analyzer, 168, 446
SQL (structured query language), 79
SQL-92 terminology *vs.* MSDE, 281
SQLActiveScriptHost (ActiveX script), 410
SQLServer object, 332–333
staging server, 13
starting
    ADO, 155–157
    DTS, 243–252
    MS Query, 13
    MSDE engine, 11
    RDS, 420
    Service Manager utility, 11
    SQL Server Agents, 392–394
static filter (replicating data), 305
StatusMessage (SQL-DMO event), 358
STDev (SQL aggregate function), 100
STDevP (SQL aggregate function), 100
Step objects (DTS), 241, 243

storage capabilities, MSDE *vs.* Access, 29
stored procedures
    Access Data Project (ADP) files, 147
    agent, 495–499
    agent (replicating data), 320
    altering, 131
    using arguments and variables, 121–125
    article (replicating data), 319
    control-of-flow commands, 126
    creating, 117–120
    deferred name resolution, 130–131
    deleting, 131
    distributed queries, 502
    distribution (replicating data), 319–320
    e-mail, 494
    e-mailing with SQL Server, 185–186
    executing, 120–121
    extended, 137
    filters (replicating data), 306
    generally, 116–117
    Go command, 138
    Goto command, 128
    if...then...else structures, 126–127
    iteration control, 127–128
    labels, 128
    miscellaneous, 320–321, 503
    nesting, 130
    older versions, 401
    optimizing, 435
    publications (replicating data), 312–316, 318–319

Continued

stored procedures *(continued)*
  querying databases, 136
  renaming, 131
  replication, 490-494
  security, 499-502
  subscriptions (replicating data), 316-318
  system, 312-321
  temporary, 135-136
  transaction control, 132-133
  triggers, 183-185
  troubleshooting, 128-129
  user-defined system, 135
  WaitFor command, 137-138
structured query language (SQL), 79
subquery queries, 107-111
subscriber (replicating data), 285-288, 291, 299-300, 394
subscriptions (replicating data)
  creating, 316-317
  generally, 291
  procedures, 317-318
Sum aggregate function (SQL), 100
support services folder (Enterprise Manager), 203-204
Sybase, 24
system data types, 65-67

T

Table Designer window, 145
table triggers, 145-146
table validation conflict (replicating data), 308
tables
  ADP files, 145-146
  creating using SQL-DMO, 336-340, 354-355
  linking in Access, 59-61
  relational, 6-9
Task objects (DTS), 240-241, 242-243
tempdb databases, 38, 136, 448-450
temporary stored procedures, 135-136
text column type, 66, 67
third normal form, 75
time, scheduling (DTS), 252-254
time constant values and conversion returns (from VBA to Transact-SQL), 182
timestamp columns, 47, 66
tinyint column type, 65
tools menu (Enterprise Manager), 204-205
trace flags and optimizing database performance, 448
transaction control (stored procedures), 132
transaction logs
  access using SQL-DMO, 463-464
  compression, 461
  generally, 457-459
  managing, 461-463
  MSDE *vs.* Access, 29-30
  truncating, 459-461
transactional replication, 289, 290
transactions
  MSDE *vs.* Access, 29-30
  naming, 133
Transact-SQL
  control-of-flow in stored procedures, 126
  converting from VBA, 180-183
  generally, 115-116
  Goto command, 128

Index

if...then...else structure, 126–127
iteration control, 127–128
labels, 128
managing security, 520–526
monitoring database server
activity, 373–377
MSDE *vs.* Access, 32–33
SQL Server Agents and, 400–406, 409–410
tempdb space, 449
troubleshooting, 128–129
TransferPercentComplete event (SQL-DMO), 358
transferring files from Access to MSDE. *See* Upsizing Wizard
transporting data from MSDE to SQL Server, 38–39
triggers
Transact-SQL, 183–185
in upsizing, 44–45
troubleshooting
conflicts when replicating data, 307–310
data errors, 69–71
illegal default and null values, 68–69
replication conflicts, 307–310
`sp_addserver` error, 295
stored procedures, 128–129
Transact-SQL, 128–129
upsizing, 47–48
Truncate Log option (Enterprise Manager), 194
`Truncate Table` command, 345
truncating transaction logs, 459–461

trusted security (Windows NT), 513–514
tuning databases for optimum performance. *See* performance, database

U

UDT. *See* user-defined types (UDTs)
Unicode format, 194
`Union` keyword, 105–107
unique key conflict (replicating data), 307
uniqueid issues (replicating data), 303–305
uniqueidentifier column type, 66
`Update` command, 92–93, 94
update conflicts (replicating data), 308
update locks, 72
upsizing data. *See also* Upsizing Wizard
BCP utility, 474–478
`Bulk Insert` command, 478–480
copying in bulk, 474–480
Data Transformation Services (DTS), 480–485
generally, 467–468
Import and Export Data Wizard, 468–474
importing tables, 473–474
lost information, 486–487
replication, 486
switch commands for BCP utility, 474–477
Windows NT mirroring capabilities, 486

Upsizing Wizard
   Access Data Project (ADP) files
      and, 144
   generally, 42–48
   reports, 54–55
   sample move, 49–56
usage information on views, 279
user commands (MSDE security),
      499–500, 523–524
user-defined system stored
      procedures, 135
user-defined types (UDTs)
   Access ADP project and, 363
   binding a rule to, 365–368
   binding default value to, 364–365
   check constraints when creating
      tables, 365
   creating, 362–363
   default values, 364–365
   generally, 67, 361–362, 364
   null values, 364
   rules, 365–368
userReference Table (views), 275–276

V

validation rules, 45
Var (SQL aggregate function), 101
varbinary column type, 66, 67
varchar column type, 65
variables in views, 275–278
VarP (SQL aggregate function), 101
VB script (RDS)
   constants, 422
   creating objects, 423
   JavaScript *vs.*, 421
VBA coding
   common functions, 180–183

   converting to Transact-SQL,
      180–183
   DTS package, 480–485
   monitoring database server
      activity, 377–379
   MSDE *vs.* Access, 32–33
   programming from DTS, 255–257
   SQL-DMO and, 328
vertical filtering (replicating data),
      305
vertical partitioning, 301–302
View Designer (Access), 268–271
views
   accessing, from object models,
      281
   ADP files, 146
   altering, 273
   autocustomizing, 278
   changing, 273
   creating, generally, 264–265
   creating, in Access, 268–271
   creating, in SQL, 265–266
   creating userReference Table,
      275–276
   customizing, 275–278
   encrypting, 273–274
   generally, 263–264
   limitations, 266–268
   modifying, 273
   obtaining information about,
      279–280
   properties, 272–273
   server functions, 274–275
   storing, 272
   usage information, 279–280
   variables, 275–278
virtual private network (VPN), 28

Visual InterDev
    ASP reporting pages, 221–231
    creating database diagrams, 218–221
    creating projects, 209–213
    entering data in tables, 215–218
    extension Web programming and, 421
    filling tables with data, 215–218
    modifying databases, 213–215
Visual Modeler, 233–234
VPN (virtual private network), 28

W

`WaitFor` command, 137–138
Web Assistant Wizard (Enterprise Manager), 199–201
Web Project Wizard, 210
Web publishing (Enterprise Manager), 198–201
Web server control (RDS), 416
`Where` keyword, 83, 84
wildcard characters, 90–91
Windows 95/98, security with, 516
Windows 2000, security with, 529
Windows NT
    mirroring capabilities, 486
    monitoring database activity, 381–386
    trusted security, 513–514
`With Recompile` procedure, 121
wizards. *See individual names*
World Wide Web databases. *See* Remote Data Services (RDS)

Notes

Notes

Notes

Notes

Notes

Notes

Notes

Notes

Notes

Notes

IDG Books Worldwide, Inc. End-User License Agreement

READ THIS. You should carefully read these terms and conditions before opening the software packet(s) included with this book ("Book"). This is a license agreement ("Agreement") between you and IDG Books Worldwide, Inc. ("IDGB"). By opening the accompanying software packet(s), you acknowledge that you have read and accept the following terms and conditions. If you do not agree and do not want to be bound by such terms and conditions, promptly return the Book and the unopened software packet(s) to the place you obtained them for a full refund.

1. **License Grant**. IDGB grants to you (either an individual or entity) a nonexclusive license to use one copy of the enclosed software program(s) (collectively, the "Software") solely for your own personal or business purposes on a single computer (whether a standard computer or a workstation component of a multiuser network). The Software is in use on a computer when it is loaded into temporary memory (RAM) or installed into permanent memory (hard disk, CD-ROM, or other storage device). IDGB reserves all rights not expressly granted herein.

2. **Ownership**. IDGB is the owner of all right, title, and interest, including copyright, in and to the compilation of the Software recorded on the disk(s) or CD-ROM ("Software Media"). Copyright to the individual programs recorded on the Software Media is owned by the author or other authorized copyright owner of each program. Ownership of the Software and all proprietary rights relating thereto remain with IDGB and its licensers.

3. **Restrictions On Use and Transfer**.

    (a) You may only (i) make one copy of the Software for backup or archival purposes, or (ii) transfer the Software to a single hard disk, provided that you keep the original for backup or archival purposes. You may not (i) rent or lease the Software, (ii) copy or reproduce the Software through a LAN or other network system or through any computer subscriber system or bulletin-board system, or (iii) modify, adapt, or create derivative works based on the Software.

    (b) You may not reverse engineer, decompile, or disassemble the Software. You may transfer the Software and user documentation on a permanent basis, provided that the transferee agrees to accept the terms and conditions of this Agreement and you retain no copies. If the Software is an update or has been updated, any transfer must include the most recent update and all prior versions.

4. <u>Restrictions on Use of Individual Programs</u>. You must follow the individual requirements and restrictions detailed for each individual program in Appendix A of this Book. These limitations are also contained in the individual license agreements recorded on the Software Media. These limitations may include a requirement that after using the program for a specified period of time, the user must pay a registration fee or discontinue use. By opening the Software packet(s), you will be agreeing to abide by the licenses and restrictions for these individual programs that are detailed in Appendix A and on the Software Media. None of the material on this Software Media or listed in this Book may ever be redistributed, in original or modified form, for commercial purposes.

5. <u>Limited Warranty</u>.

   (a) IDGB warrants that the Software and Software Media are free from defects in materials and workmanship under normal use for a period of sixty (60) days from the date of purchase of this Book. If IDGB receives notification within the warranty period of defects in materials or workmanship, IDGB will replace the defective Software Media.

   (b) IDGB AND THE AUTHOR OF THE BOOK DISCLAIM ALL OTHER WARRANTIES, EXPRESS OR IMPLIED, INCLUDING WITHOUT LIMITATION IMPLIED WARRANTIES OF MERCHANTABILITY AND FITNESS FOR A PARTICULAR PURPOSE, WITH RESPECT TO THE SOFTWARE, THE PROGRAMS, THE SOURCE CODE CONTAINED THEREIN, AND/OR THE TECHNIQUES DESCRIBED IN THIS BOOK. IDGB DOES NOT WARRANT THAT THE FUNCTIONS CONTAINED IN THE SOFTWARE WILL MEET YOUR REQUIREMENTS OR THAT THE OPERATION OF THE SOFTWARE WILL BE ERROR FREE.

   (c) This limited warranty gives you specific legal rights, and you may have other rights that vary from jurisdiction to jurisdiction.

6. <u>Remedies</u>.

   (a) IDGB's entire liability and your exclusive remedy for defects in materials and workmanship shall be limited to replacement of the Software Media, which may be returned to IDGB with a copy of your receipt at the following address: Software Media Fulfillment Department, Attn.: *MSDE Developer's Guide*, IDG Books Worldwide, Inc., 10475 Crosspoint Blvd., Indianapolis, IN 46256, or call 1-800-762-2974. Please allow three to four weeks for delivery. This Limited Warranty is void if failure of the Software Media has resulted from accident, abuse, or misapplication. Any replacement Software Media will be warranted for the remainder of the original warranty period or thirty (30) days, whichever is longer.

   (b) In no event shall IDGB or the author be liable for any damages whatsoever (including without limitation damages for loss of business profits, business interruption, loss of business information, or any other pecuniary loss) arising from the use of or inability to use the Book or the Software, even if IDGB has been advised of the possibility of such damages.

(c) Because some jurisdictions do not allow the exclusion or limitation of liability for consequential or incidental damages, the above limitation or exclusion may not apply to you.

7. **U.S. Government Restricted Rights**. Use, duplication, or disclosure of the Software by the U.S. Government is subject to restrictions stated in paragraph (c)(1)(ii) of the Rights in Technical Data and Computer Software clause of DFARS 252.227-7013, and in subparagraphs (a) through (d) of the Commercial Computer – Restricted Rights clause at FAR 52.227-19, and in similar clauses in the NASA FAR supplement, when applicable.

8. **General**. This Agreement constitutes the entire understanding of the parties and revokes and supersedes all prior agreements, oral or written, between them and may not be modified or amended except in a writing signed by both parties hereto that specifically refers to this Agreement. This Agreement shall take precedence over any other documents that may be in conflict herewith. If any one or more provisions contained in this Agreement are held by any court or tribunal to be invalid, illegal, or otherwise unenforceable, each and every other provision shall remain in full force and effect.

my2cents.idgbooks.com

Register This Book — And Win!

Visit **http://my2cents.idgbooks.com** to register this book and we'll automatically enter you in our fantastic monthly prize giveaway. It's also your opportunity to give us feedback: let us know what you thought of this book and how you would like to see other topics covered.

Discover IDG Books Online!

The IDG Books Online Web site is your online resource for tackling technology — at home and at the office. Frequently updated, the IDG Books Online Web site features exclusive software, insider information, online books, and live events!

10 Productive & Career-Enhancing Things You Can Do at www.idgbooks.com

- Nab source code for your own programming projects.
- Download software.
- Read Web exclusives: special articles and book excerpts by IDG Books Worldwide authors.
- Take advantage of resources to help you advance your career as a Novell or Microsoft professional.
- Buy IDG Books Worldwide titles or find a convenient bookstore that carries them.
- Register your book and win a prize.
- Chat live online with authors.
- Sign up for regular e-mail updates about our latest books.
- Suggest a book you'd like to read or write.
- Give us your 2¢ about our books and about our Web site.

You say you're not on the Web yet? It's easy to get started with IDG Books' *Discover the Internet,* available at local retailers everywhere.

CD-ROM Installation Instructions

Each software item on the *MSDE Developer's Guide* CD-ROM is located in its own folder. To install a particular piece of software, open its folder, and locate the executable (.exe) file named Setup.exe or Install.exe. Run the executable file to begin installing the software.

The CD-ROM also contains sample files that are designed to be used with MSDE. More details about these files can be found in the Appendix.